WORKING ATOMIC WEIGHTS*

Name	Symbol	Atomic Number	Atomic Weight	Name	Symbol	Atomic Number	Atomic Weight
Actinium	Ac	89	(227)†	Mercury	Hg	80	200.6
Aluminum	Al	13	27.0	Molybdenum	Mo	42	95.9
Americium	Am	95	(243)	Neodymium	Nd	60	144.2
Antimony	Sb	51	121.8	Neon	Ne	10	20.2
Argon	Ar	18	39.9	Neptunium	Np	93	(237)
Arsenic	As	33	74.9	Nickel	Ni	28	58.7
Astatine	At	85	(210)	Niobium	Nb	41	92.9
Barium	Ba	56	137.3	Nitrogen	N	7	14.01
Berkelium	Bk	97	(247)	Nobelium	No	102	(259)
Beryllium	Be	4	9.01	Osmium	Os	76	190.2
Bismuth	Bi	83	209.0	Oxygen	O	8	16.00
Boron	B	5	10.8	Palladium	Pd	46	106.4
Bromine	Br	35	79.9	Phosphorus	P	15	31.0
Cadmium	Cd	48	112.4	Platinum	Pt	78	195.1
Calcium	Ca	20	40.1	Plutonium	Pu	94	(244)
Californium	Cf	98	(251)	Polonium	Po	84	(209)
Carbon	C	6	12.01	Potassium	K	19	39.1
Cerium	Ce	58	140.1	Praseodymium	Pr	59	140.9
Cesium	Cs	55	132.9	Promethium	Pm	61	(145)
Chlorine	Cl	17	35.5	Protactinium	Pa	91	(231)
Chromium	Cr	24	52.0	Radium	Ra	88	(226)
Cobalt	Co	27	58.9	Radon	Rn	86	(222)
Copper	Cu	29	63.5	Rhenium	Re	75	186.2
Curium	Cm	96	(247)	Rhodium	Rh	45	102.9
Dysprosium	Dy	66	162.5	Rubidium	Rb	37	85.5
Einsteinium	Es	99	(254)	Ruthenium	Ru	44	101.1
Erbium	Er	68	167.3	Samarium	Sm	62	150.4
Europium	Eu	63	152.0	Scandium	Sc	21	45.0
Fermium	Fm	100	(257)	Selenium	Se	34	79.0
Fluorine	F	9	19.0	Silicon	Si	14	28.1
Francium	Fr	87	(223)	Silver	Ag	47	107.9
Gadolinium	Gd	64	157.2	Sodium	Na	11	23.0
Gallium	Ga	31	69.7	Strontium	Sr	38	87.6
Germanium	Ge	32	72.6	Sulfur	S	16	32.1
Gold	Au	79	197.0	Tantalum	Ta	73	180.9
Hafnium	Hf	72	178.5	Technetium	Tc	43	(97)
Helium	He	2	4.00	Tellurium	Te	52	127.6
Holmium	Ho	67	164.9	Terbium	Tb	65	158.9
Hydrogen	H	1	1.008	Thallium	Tl	81	204.4
Indium	In	49	114.8	Thorium	Th	90	232.0
Iodine	I	53	126.9	Thulium	Tm	69	168.9
Iridium	Ir	77	192.2	Tin	Sn	50	118.7
Iron	Fe	26	55.8	Titanium	Ti	22	47.9
Krypton	Kr	36	83.8	Tungsten	W	74	183.8
Lanthanum	La	57	138.9	Uranium	U	92	238.0
Lawrencium	Lr	103	(260)	Vanadium	V	23	50.9
Lead	Pb	82	207.2	Xenon	Xe	54	131.3
Lithium	Li	3	6.94	Ytterbium	Yb	70	173.0
Lutetium	Lu	71	175.0	Yttrium	Y	39	88.9
Magnesium	Mg	12	24.3	Zinc	Zn	30	65.4
Manganese	Mn	25	54.9	Zirconium	Zr	40	91.2
Mendelevium	Md	101	(258)	—	—	104‡	(261)
				—	—	105	(262)

*More precise values of the atomic weights based on the latest IUPAC reports are given in Table 3-1.

†For those elements all of whose isotopes are radioactive, the parentheses indicate the isotope with the longest half-life. (For a definition of *half-life*, see Section 7-4.2.)

‡The names and symbols of elements 104 and 105 have not yet been determined.

CHEMISTRY
EXPERIMENTAL
FOUNDATIONS

PRENTICE-HALL, INC., ENGLEWOOD CLIFFS, NEW JERSEY

Second Edition

*Mama's appoint
March 15 3:15*

ROBERT W. PARRY

Professor of Chemistry
University of Utah

PHYLLIS M. DIETZ

Chemistry Teacher
Fountain Valley High School
Fountain Valley, California

ROBERT L. TELLEFSEN

Chemistry Teacher
Vintage High School
Napa, California

LUKE E. STEINER

Professor of Chemistry Emeritus
Oberlin College

CHEMISTRY

EXPERIMENTAL FOUNDATIONS

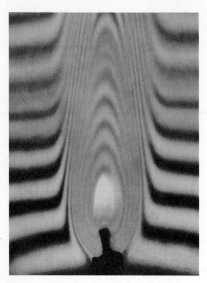

The cover photograph depicts a lighted candle silhouetted against the multicolored interference pattern produced by a Michelson interferometer using white light. The brilliant light of the interferometer has washed out nearly all the light of the flame, but the hot gases from the flame have sharply deformed the interference pattern and produced a large discontinuity on the edge of the flame. This unique view of the candle symbolizes our revision, which takes a new look at chemistry as a dynamic and distinctly contemporary science.

Photographed expressly for *Chemistry: Experimental Foundations* by Drs. Cagnet, Françon, and Mallick of the Laboratoire d'Optique of the Faculté des Sciences de Paris in France.

CHEMISTRY: Experimental Foundations, Second Edition
Robert W. Parry, Phyllis M. Dietz,
Robert L. Tellefsen, and Luke E. Steiner

Supplementary Materials:

Laboratory Manual

Laboratory Notebook

Achievement Tests

Teachers Guide

Transparencies

10 9 8 7 6 5 4 3

Illustrations and drawings by John Walter and Associates, and George Bakacs

Prentice-Hall International, Inc., *London*
Prentice-Hall of Australia, Pty. Ltd., *Sydney*
Prentice-Hall of Canada, Ltd., *Toronto*
Prentice-Hall of India Private Ltd., *New Delhi*
Prentice-Hall of Japan, Inc., *Tokyo*

CHEMISTRY: EXPERIMENTAL FOUNDATIONS is an authorized revision of the original CHEM Study textbook. As in the original book, experimentation is the vehicle for presenting chemistry as it is today. Unifying principles are developed from experimental observation. Through the use of such principles, one can avoid seemingly endless memorization. Chemistry emerges as a science rather than as a mass of information. The cornerstone of modern science—the development of principle from observation—is the cornerstone of this revision.

This is a chemistry book, not a book *about* chemistry. It asks you to participate in scientific activity and to share the excitement of discovery. At the end of the course you will *not* know all about chemistry, but you should know something of the way in which a chemist works and of the power and limitations of scientific methods. We hope, further, that you will have formed the habit of questioning, and that you will seek true understanding rather than being satisfied with dogmatic assertions. In this hope lie many of the most important, yet hidden, benefits of a study of science.

We live in a scientific age, one in which science and its product, technology, dominate. Successful technology demands very careful application of fundamental scientific principles. But before technology can succeed, science must advance. We hope this book can contribute to that advancement.

Some change in the development of fundamental material has been made relative to the First Edition. The most significant changes involve an attempt to simplify the presentation of oxidation-reduction and electrochemistry, and the replacement of the chapter on astrochemistry with a chapter describing the elements of the nitrogen family and their influence on the environment. The authors believe that while astrochemistry is interesting, terrestrial chemistry is crucial to our future. Additional material on subjects such as mass spectroscopy and electric cars is presented in the Appendices for the interested reader. Because chemistry is a living discipline, all biographies included are of living chemists.

In preparing this revision the authors have been assisted by many people. As was the case with the First Edition of this book, our debt to the Prentice-Hall staff is unusually large. The First Edition of this book was literally made possible by the efforts of science editors Marion Cahill McDanield and Kelvin L. Kean, and by the administrative skills of Edgar P. Thomas and James M. Guiher. Similarly, this Second Edition has been made possible by the superb editorial skills, personal diplomacy, and unusually fine judgment of N. Sue Barnes and Kelvin L. Kean. Other members of the Prentice-Hall staff who merit special thanks include Anthony Caruso and the other members of the production staff who have worked so hard in producing this book. The authors are sincerely grateful to all.

Many outstanding high school and college teachers contributed in valuable ways to the preparation of the First Edition of this book. We express our continuing appreciation particularly to Harold Pratt, Jefferson County Public Schools, Lakewood, Colorado; Kermit Waln, Thomas Jefferson High School, Denver, Colorado; Raymond T. Byrne, Batavia High School, Batavia, New York; and Charles Tier, St. Joseph's High School, Metuchen, New Jersey.

A new and distinguished group of reviewers gave generously of their time to review all or part of the manuscript for the Second Edition. The authors are particularly appreciative of the constructive criticisms and encouraging comments rendered by Dr. Richard J. Merrill, Mt. Diablo Unified School District, Concord, California; Richard F. Ebeling, West High School, Aurora, Illinois; Lloyd S. Nikkel, Glenlawn Collegiate Institute, St. Vital, Manitoba, Canada; Dr. Jack G. Calvert, Ohio State University; Dr. Calvin Giddings, University of Utah; and Dr. Noel DeNevers, University of Utah. Their valuable advice and sound judgment added significantly to the value and accuracy of the text.

We also wish to thank Darlene Walker for her assistance in preparing parts of the manuscript.

Finally, to the many teachers and students who used the First Edition and guided us in this revision we extend our deepest appreciation for their continuing help.

RWP
PMD
RLT
LES

CONTENTS

21

22

. . . I wish you not only the joy of great discovery; I wish for you a world of confidence in . . . *humanity,* a world of confidence in *reason,* so that as you work you may be inspired by the hope that what you find *will make men freer and better* . . . .

J. ROBERT OPPENHEIMER (1904–1967)

THE OBSERVATIONAL BASIS OF CHEMISTRY

1

Which image is real and which is a reflection? Only careful observation will tell.

WHAT DO SCIENTISTS REALLY DO? WHAT DOES IT MEAN TO BE A chemist? How does a chemist spend his or her time? Are the TV commercials honest when they show someone in a white coat frowning through horn-rimmed glasses at dramatically bubbling concoctions which may be tooth paste or infernal machines? How can you tell which you've discovered so they will know what to award you the Nobel prize for?

We don't promise to answer *all* of these questions in one easy chapter, but at least we'll clue you in on SOME OF THE SUCCESS SECRETS OF THE PEOPLE IN THE INDEPENDENT TESTING LABORATORIES.

1-1 WHAT IS CHEMISTRY?

What does the word *chemistry* suggest to you? To many people chemistry means miracle fibers such as nylon and Dacron, medicines from aspirin to antibiotics, polymers from floor tiles to bread wrappers, fuels from heating oil to high-test gasoline, and thousands of other products which make our surroundings more comfortable and attractive. This is the chemistry that shows above the surface and which benefits us all in a very material way. But chemistry to a chemist is more like an iceberg: most of its activity is not visible on casual inspection. What then is chemistry?

As we all know, a dictionary definition of baseball does not carry with it the emotional thrill of a ball driven out of the park or of a close decision at home plate. To a baseball player or a baseball fan, baseball is not easily defined. You have to play the game! Certainly no dictionary definition of music can describe the wild excitement or the dreamy, romantic mood which it can generate. Chemistry, like baseball and music, is not defined with any ease. It is a living subject, requiring mental and physical activity. Like baseball, you have to participate in the activity to understand it properly. Let us put the chemical ball into play by taking a brief look at the activities of science.

1-2 THE ACTIVITIES OF SCIENCE

Have you ever noticed earthworms on top of the ground after a heavy rain? Hungry birds are quick to spot these worms and eat them. On days when it does not rain, the birds frequently gather around the lawn sprinkler. Our feathered friends, primitive scientists that they are, seem to make a generalization: water in the ground means worms on top. The life of the bird is better because of this simple generalization.

People are different in degree but not in kind. They observe and study their surroundings more carefully than do any other creatures. They organize the information they have gathered. Then they examine the organized information for regularities; like the birds, people also note that water in the ground means worms on top. Many fishermen have profited from this generalization.

Unlike birds, people are not content just to find and use the simple regularity. They wonder why the regularity exists. Does the water in the ground prevent the worm from getting air? This is a reasonable

Fig. 1-1 Water in the ground means worms on top.

hypothesis and suggests that earthworms will drown if we place them in a glass of water. "Wondering why" has suggested a possible characteristic of earthworms. More sophisticated questions are possible. We might ask: how much water is needed in the ground to drive the worms to the surface? Why does the worm need air? How does the worm use it? People differ from birds because they wonder about these things.

People differ in another very important way. Communication between birds is primitive and inefficient. People, on the other hand, have developed an effective communication system which permits them to pass their observations and thoughts on to others throughout the world. Communication lies at the heart of *all* intellectual activity. The observations and thoughts of thousands of men and women in all areas are available to us. Birds do not have a public library.

In summary, we can now list the basic activities of science:

(1) to accumulate information through observation;
(2) to organize this information and to seek regularities in it;
(3) to wonder why the regularities exist; and
(4) to communicate the findings and their probable explanations to others.

There is no fixed order in which these activities must be carried out; no rigid "scientific method" requires that the steps be done in the order given above; in fact, "wondering why" usually suggests the need for more carefully controlled observations. A carefully controlled sequence of observations is frequently called an **experiment.** Conditions for experiments in chemistry are often controlled most easily in a laboratory, but the study of nature should not be confined to a single room. Science is all around us!

1-3   OBSERVATION AND DESCRIPTION

The power of observation is in no way peculiar to science. The ingenious detective who astounds everyone with his ability to draw conclusions from what he sees has fascinated mystery story readers from the days of Sherlock Holmes to the days of James Bond, Agent 007. Many of you know of James Bond's amazing skills in many areas, but the uncanny powers of observation possessed by Sherlock Holmes are less familiar. If you do not know Mr. Holmes, an introduction is in order; if you do know him, you will probably enjoy seeing him in action again.

THE POWER OF OBSERVATION

Dr. Watson is describing an encounter between the great detective, Sherlock Holmes, his client, Mr. Wilson, and himself. (From Sir Arthur Conan Doyle, "The Red-Headed League.")

The portly client puffed out his chest with an appearance of some little pride and pulled a dirty and wrinkled newspaper from the inside pocket of his greatcoat. As he glanced down the advertisement column, with his head thrust forward and the paper flattened out upon his knee, I took a good look at the man and endeavoured, after the fashion of my companion, to read the indications which might be presented by his dress or appearance.

I did not gain very much, however, by my inspection. Our visitor bore every mark of being an average commonplace British tradesman, obese, pompous, and slow. He wore rather baggy gray shepherd's check trousers, a not over-clean black frock-coat, unbuttoned in the front, and a drab waistcoat with a heavy brassy Albert chain, and a square pierced bit of metal dangling down as an ornament. A frayed top-hat and a faded brown overcoat with a wrinkled velvet collar lay upon a chair beside him. Altogether, look as I would, there was nothing remarkable about the man save his blazing red head and the expression of extreme chagrin and discontent upon his features.

Sherlock Holmes's quick eye took in my occupation, and he shook his head with a smile as he noticed my questioning glances. "Beyond the obvious facts that he has at some time done manual labour, that he takes snuff, that he is a Freemason, that he has been in China, and that he has done a considerable amount of writing lately, I can deduce nothing else."

Mr. Jabez Wilson started up in his chair, with his forefinger upon the paper, but his eyes upon my companion.

"How, in the name of good-fortune, did you know all that, Mr. Holmes?" he asked. "How did you know, for example, that I did manual labour? It's as true as gospel, for I began as a ship's carpenter."

"Your hands, my dear sir. Your right hand is quite a size larger than your left. You have worked with it, and the muscles are more developed."

"Well, the snuff, then, and the Freemasonry?"

"I won't insult your intelligence by telling you how I read that, especially as, rather against the strict rules of your order, you use an arc-and-compass breastpin."

"Ah, of course, I forgot that. But the writing?"

"What else can be indicated by that right cuff so very shiny for five inches, and the left one with the smooth patch near the elbow where you rest it upon the desk?"

"Well, but China?"

"The fish which you have tattooed immediately above your right wrist could only have been done in China. I have made a small study of tattoo marks and have even contributed to the literature of the subject. That trick of staining the fishes' scales of a delicate pink is quite peculiar to China. When, in addition, I see a Chinese coin hanging from your watch-chain, the matter becomes even more simple."

Mr. Jabez Wilson laughed heavily. "Well, I never!" said he. "I thought at first that you had done something clever, but I see that there was nothing in it, after all." *

Scientists particularly appreciate Mr. Wilson's last comment. Much of science seems routine and easy after the answer is known, but the problem usually looks different at the start. Every activity has Monday-morning quarterbacks like Wilson. Mr. Holmes was continually disturbed by Dr. Watson's poor powers of observation. He once told him ("A Scandal in Bohemia"): "You *see*, but you do *not observe*." Good scientists, like good detectives, cannot afford the luxury of *seeing without observing*. Science and clever detective work have much in common. Subtle clues lead to an explanation if one *observes*. If one only *sees*, the answer may pass by unnoticed.

*Reprinted by Permission of the Estate of Sir Arthur Conan Doyle.

Fig. 1-2 Good observation requires concentration, alertness to detail, patience, and practice.

Good observation takes concentration, alertness to detail, patience, and practice. We must identify and control the important variables governing a process. Consider an example from your own experience—the burning candle. How do we sort out the conditions which need to be controlled? Be ready for surprises here; conditions which seem important at first may have little effect on the process, whereas conditions that do not seem important may be crucial. For example, the nature of the torch or match used to light the candle is of no real significance once the process is underway, but the location of the candle in the room may be crucial in determining its burning characteristics. Why is the location important? Because a candle is strongly influenced by air currents or "drafts" and the air currents vary in different parts of the room. One must *observe* and not just *see* to be a Sherlock Holmes or a good experimentalist.

Review your own description of a burning candle and compare it with the one in Appendix 1. How many of your observations are listed there? How many observations have you made which are not listed in Appendix 1? (A count of four means you are as good as Sherlock Holmes.)

1-4 THE SEARCH FOR REGULARITIES

Observation always leads to questions. One of the first questions to concern us is: what regularities appear? The discovery of regularities permits a simplification of the observations. In our earlier discussion the regularity "water in the ground means worms on top" summarized thousands of separate observations by both birds and people. Instead of each observation standing alone, many are classed together and can be considered more effectively.

The search for regularities is usually fun, but it is not always easy. In any process of exploration, wrong turns may lead to blind alleys. Not every step is an advance, and yet there is no way to advance other than by taking steps. Some move us ahead; some move us back. We hope that more lead us ahead than take us back. How the search proceeds can be seen in the following fable from science fiction.

Fig. 1-3 Martians in a new environment.

1-4.1 Martin the Martian

Martin the Martian brought his spacecraft down in a clearing surrounded by a cold, earthly woods. Martin was an unusually brilliant being, even for a Martian, but he was operating in a new environment: Mars has no oxygen and therefore no fire as we know it. It was cold as Martin stepped into the dark night. He looked around quickly and saw in the distance some creatures, making strange sounds, who were huddled around a glowing pile of cylindrical objects. Martin approached the group as closely as he dared. He found to his surprise that a great deal of heat was coming from the glowing pile of cylinders. If only Martin could get his own pile of hot cylinders, life would be much more comfortable for him. How to do it? That was the problem. Surely if these backward creatures on Earth could make a heat source, any Martian could do as well.

TABLE 1-1 "BURNABILITY" OF OBJECTS

English Designation of Object	Observation
Tree limb	Burns fairly well if not soaked in water.
Fence post	Burns well.
Rubber hose	Burns, but causes air pollution. Can't stand this!
Dynamite cap	Catastrophe! Wise to avoid these in future! Scattered hot cylinders.
Large rock	Didn't burn.
Large glass marble	Didn't burn; seemed to crack open.
Wooden pole	Burns well; get lots of these.

His first step was to wait until the Earthlings disappeared into their tents. Then Martin quietly approached the pile of cylinders, pulled out several cylinders (logs) by their cool ends, and carried the glowing pieces over to a spot near his spaceship. Soon he, too, had a pile of glowing cylinders. He warmed himself and felt pleased with the high level of Martian science.

His happiness was short-lived. His cylinders began to disappear as the evening wore on. The Earthlings had piled all kinds of materials on their fire and the flames had leaped higher. What should Martin put on his fire? He went into the woods as he had seen the Earthlings do, but found no logs. His Martian science courses had not taught him what else to bring back.

Experimentation was the only answer. He collected all kinds of materials and piled each object on his fire. In each case, he wrote down what he saw. After a few trips the information shown in Table 1-1 appeared as a page in his notebook. (We have translated his entries for you, since few schools offer Martian I.)

As Martin surveyed the limited data in his notebook, his mathematically trained soul was stirred. He suddenly noticed that everything which burned was cylindrical. He had run into problems with the dynamite cap and the rubber hose, but he thought he could recognize these objects in the future. They were special cases of burning. He put forth a *hypothesis:*

cylindrical objects burn

In the future he would only collect cylindrical objects.

Using his hypothesis as a guide, Martin brought to his campsite an old cane, a baseball bat, and more tree limbs. All burned brightly and Martin was proud of his rapid mastery of the Earthly environment. He noted with pride that he had passed up a large wooden door, a large box of newspapers, and a piece of chain. Clearly, only cylindrical objects burn!

Are you laughing at our Martian visitor? Clearly, his generalization is untrue; he is being misled. But wait: the generalization states a regularity discovered among all of the observations available to him—namely, the items on *his* list. *A generalization is reliable only within the bounds of the experiments that lead to the rule.*

On his next trip to gather fuel, Martin staggered into camp dragging three pieces of iron pipe, two ginger ale bottles, and the axle

Fig. 1-4 Clearly, all cylindrical objects do *not* burn.

from an old car. He passed up the wooden door, a long wooden 4″ × 4″, and a sack of wooden tent stakes. His fire dwindled and died. Martin was astonished!

During the long cold night that followed, Martin the Martian became Martin the Miserable Martian. His hypothesis was in trouble. He had to draw some new and disturbing conclusions, and he was *very cold*. His new conclusions were

(1) all cylindrical objects do *not* burn;
(2) tree limbs, fence posts, and other cylindrical objects listed in the table still burn;
(3) the list is still useful.

In the bright, warm sun of the next day, Martin looked at his list and at the objects which burned. Stimulated by the warm sunshine and the appearance of the things which did burn, he proposed a new hypothesis:

wooden objects burn

Martin is on the right track. His miserable nights are behind him.

If at this point you are inclined to wonder about the low state of Martian science, be careful. Martin has used good scientific practice. All of us, beginning students and experienced scientists alike, make observations, organize them, and seek regularities to help us in the effective use of our knowledge. Preliminary regularities are frequently stated as hypotheses; good hypotheses grow into theories as confidence in the generalization grows. A theory is retained as long as it is consistent with the known facts of nature or as long as it is an aid in systematizing knowledge.

Recent scientific history reads much like our Martian fable. In 1960, chemists around the world were teaching students in high schools and colleges that gases with eight electrons in the outer shell form no compounds. Such gases were said to be inert. But in 1962, Professor Neil Bartlett, a scientist working in Canada, made the "inert" gas xenon combine with a new compound made of the elements platinum and fluorine. Professor Bartlett had figuratively thrown the iron pipe into the fire. Just as all cylindrical objects do not burn, some atoms with eight electrons in the outer shell *do* form compounds. Most of our ideas on "inert" gases were changed seriously as a result of Professor Bartlett's work. An old and accepted generalization was destroyed by clever observations that created a whole new field of chemistry. (See Section 8-3.2.)

Science has its limitations and scientists make mistakes, but such mistakes are unavoidable if we are to make progress.

1-4.2 Regularities in the Melting of Solids

Like Martin the Martian, we too have been accumulating information. Some information on the melting of solids has been gathered in the laboratory, and we are now in a position to propose a generalization.

Hypothesis: a solid melts to a liquid when the temperature is raised sufficiently. *The temperature at which a solid melts is characteristic of that solid.* When the warm liquid is recooled, it solidifies at this same temperature.

Further experiments will show that this hypothesis is true for thousands and thousands of solids, but some further restriction is needed. (Even the generalization, "all wooden objects burn," needs some further restriction, since ebony burns poorly.) This need for further restriction for some substances can be turned to our advantage in trying to classify materials. For example, people have found or prepared hundreds of thousands of substances which will melt at a sharp and characteristic temperature when the solid is heated, and which will freeze at this same temperature when the liquid is cooled. Other materials will soften without sharp melting or may even give irregular behavior, as did the dynamite cap in the Martian's fire. A few materials like carbon will melt only at extreme temperatures under very high pressures. Some characterization of materials on the basis of melting behavior would appear to be reasonable. Indeed, chemists have found that the *melting temperature and melting behavior are useful pieces of information in the identification of a substance.* One of the characteristic properties recorded for use in identifying a new pure material is its **melting point.** Ice melts at 0.00 °C in water exposed to air. We take advantage of this fact when we fill our soft drink cooler with ice in the summertime.

A special set of words has been found useful in dealing with processes such as melting and freezing. We say that ice is the **solid phase** of water and that water is the **liquid phase.** Ice and water are different **phases** of the same substance. The change that occurs when a solid melts or a liquid freezes is called a **phase change.** In later chapters we shall consider other phase changes, such as the change of a liquid to a gas or a gas to a liquid.

Fig. 1-5 The temperature at which ice melts is characteristic and never changes.

EXERCISE 1-1

You are given a liquid which may be any *one* of three pure substances—benzene, toluene, or xylene. How could you tell which one of these three liquids had been given to you? Use the following characteristics:

Substance	Formula	Melting Point (°C)	Boiling Point (°C)	Color	Density (g/ml)
Benzene	C_6H_6	5.5	80.10	colorless	0.879
Toluene	C_7H_8	−95	110.63	colorless	0.867
Xylene	C_8H_{10}	−29	144.41	colorless	0.880

1-5 WONDERING WHY

We have already experienced some of the activities of science. First comes careful observation under controlled conditions, then organization of the information and the search for regularities of behavior. There is one more activity that, like dessert, fittingly comes last. This activity may be called "wondering why," and it arises from an irresistible urge to know more than merely "what happens?" We must also seek the answer to "*why* does it happen?" This activity is probably the most creative and the most rewarding part of a science. It differentiates our science from that of the bird's "observation." What does it mean to answer a question beginning "why?"

1-5.1 Explanations: A Model for Gases

Let us see what it means to search for an explanation to a familiar problem. What happens, for example, when someone blows up a balloon? As a person forces breath (a gas) into the balloon, the balloon grows larger, the rubber is stretched more tightly, and the balloon becomes harder. Can we "explain" *what we see?* Can our "explanation" suggest new experiments? The answer to these questions begins with "wondering why." Why does the balloon grow larger? Why does it become harder?

There are two ways to proceed in trying to answer these questions. We have already examined one of these ways—to look more closely at the balloon, to record carefully what we see, and to seek regularities in what we observe. The second is to look *away* from the balloon and to seek similar behavior in another situation that we understand better. Sometimes the well-understood situation or **model** is very useful in helping us to understand the problem at hand. If we have few data, many different models will "explain" what is known; on the other hand, as we learn more and more about a problem, the number of models which will fit the facts becomes smaller and smaller. Let us try to formulate a model to represent the gas in the balloon by using a system which is familiar to all of us.

Most of us have seen small balls made of "super-rubber." When such balls are dropped to the floor, they rebound upward, rising *almost* to the height from which they were dropped. When thrown directly against the wall in a small room, the ball bounces back and forth between the walls many times before gradually slowing down and stopping. Could there be a connection between the motion of the rubber balls and the air in the balloon?

A collection of bouncing balls is a *relatively simple system* for experimental study and can be described in quantitative terms. As such, it might be a good model system for representing the gas in the balloon. Suppose we picture air, or any other gas, as a collection of miniature balls bouncing around and colliding with the walls of the container. When a ball strikes the container, it pushes against it. But the wall pushes back with an equal force, and the ball leaves the wall going in a different direction. If there were an enormous number of particles, there would be many such collisions per second. Such a model could account for the "*push*" of the gas on the balloon wall. The "push"

acting on a given area of wall surface (say, a square this big: ☐)

is called the **gas pressure.** We could say that the collisions of the balls with the balloon wall account for the observed **pressure** of the gas. If more gas is added to the balloon, there will be more particles, hence more wall collisions per second. This means more "push" per unit of wall area, hence higher pressure. As the pressure (*push per unit of area*) on the balloon wall increases, the rubber walls will stretch outward exposing *more wall area*. This process continues until the push per unit of area is only slightly larger than it was before. In short, the balloon grows bigger if more gas is added and the pressure of gas in the balloon increases only slightly.

Our model, based on bouncing rubber balls, has passed its first test: it reproduces several of the observations made when we blew up the balloon. In this sense it is a good model and deserves more careful examination. It leads to many predictions which will be explored more carefully in Chapter 4.

EXERCISE 1-2

Suppose that we add gas to an empty steel tank with a pressure gauge attached. The gauge will read 1 atmosphere when we have a given quantity of gas present. What would the pressure be if we doubled the amount of gas in the tank?

1-5.2 Differences Between Model and System

The model for gas behavior describes the observations we have made so far. Unfortunately, this success can often lead to trouble. When a model is a very good one, we may start to think that the model *is* the system; then confusion results. Let us see how such a problem can arise.

Fig. 1-6.1 "Super-rubber" balls in motion.

Fig. 1-6.2 Air particles in motion in an enclosed space.

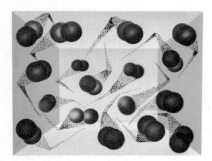

When our "super-rubber" ball was dropped from a given height above the floor, it rebounded to a level *almost* as high as that from which it fell originally (Figure 1-6.1). *Note that it did not bounce up quite as high as its original position.* If the ball, after being dropped, had bounced up exactly to its original position, we would have said that it was **perfectly elastic.** *A perfectly elastic ball would bounce forever once it got started.* On the other hand, collisions of the "super-rubber" ball with the walls or floor are *not* perfectly elastic; we know the ball will slow down a little after each collision and finally stop—no matter how hard we throw it originally (Figure 1-7.1). How would we expect the gas to behave if we assumed that the little particles in our gas were exactly like "super-rubber" balls?

Let us consider the following experiment. A sample of argon gas is sealed into a heavy steel tank containing a gauge to tell us the pressure of the gas inside the tank. (Remember that pressure is a measure of the push of the gas particles against a given area of the tank's surface.) We read and record the pressure shown on the pressure gauge and then let the tank stand in the room at a constant temperature for five years. The model now permits us to make a prediction. If each small particle of gas were *exactly* like a "super-rubber" ball, it would slow up a little after each collision with the wall. After five years, the particles of gas would have stopped bouncing and would have fallen to the bottom of the tank (Figure 1-7.2). The pressure in the tank (due to the push exerted by gas particles when they hit the walls) should gradually fall to zero and should be zero after a five-year interval.

The model has made a prediction which can be tested experimentally. Repeated observation will show that, as long as the tank is stored in a room of reasonably constant temperature, the pressure will *not* drop if the tank does not leak. The observation is in direct conflict with our prediction. Clearly, the small particles of the gas in the steel tank do *not* slow down after each collision as the "super-rubber" balls do. We must then conclude that if the moving-particle model for a gas is to be correct, *the collisions of the argon particles with the walls and with each other must be perfectly elastic.* The particles do not quit bouncing as time passes.

We see now that the model system ("super-rubber" balls) cannot be *exactly* like the gas in the balloon—but the resemblance is fairly close. Further, we know where at least one of the differences between a real gas and a model of a gas lies: on the average, gas particles must undergo *perfectly elastic* collisions; they must be *more elastic* than the "super-rubber" balls.

EXERCISE 1-3

A balloon filled with gas gradually shrinks on standing for some time. Suggest a model to explain this simple observation.

This is the characteristic pattern of an explanation. It begins with a "why?" question that asks about a process that is *not* well understood (why does a balloon expand as we blow into it?). An answer is suggested in terms of a process that is better understood ("super-rubber" balls bouncing off the walls). The model may suggest new experiments or observations which can be performed. The results may show that our unknown system is very much like the model system or differs from it in certain ways (inelastic versus elastic collisions). If differences are extreme, we may abandon the model system and search for a new one. If differences are not extreme, the model will be retained or modified while we remember that the model and the system are not exactly the same. Since it is difficult to visualize the particles that make up the air, we attempt to explain the properties of the gas (air) in terms of the behavior of "super-rubber" balls, which are easy to see, to handle, to measure, and to study. Their behavior is well understood.

The search for explanation is, then, the search for likenesses that connect the system under study with a model system already studied. The explanation is considered to be "good" when

(1) the model system is well understood—that is, when the regularities in the behavior of the model system have been thoroughly explored; and
(2) there are close similarities between the system being studied and the model system.

Our "super-rubber" ball model constitutes a good explanation because

(1) how a "super-rubber" ball rebounds is well understood—we can calculate in mathematical detail just how much push the ball exerts on the wall at each bounce; and
(2) there seems to be a close similarity between the random motion of "super-rubber" balls and the motion of gas particles—exactly the same mathematics describes the pressure behavior if the gas is pictured as a collection of many small particles, endlessly in motion, bouncing elastically against the walls of the container.

The particle explanation of the gas phase is therefore a good one. Now, perhaps, you can see that answering the question "why?" is merely a highly sophisticated form of seeking regularities. It is indeed a regularity of nature that gases and "super-rubber" balls have properties in common. The special creativity shown in the discovery of this regularity is that the likeness is not readily apparent; only with considerable thought can it be established. Fittingly, there is a special reward for the discovery of such hidden likenesses. The discoverer can bring to bear on the system being studied all the experience and knowledge accumulated from the well-understood system.

1-6 CONCLUSIONS AND THE ACCURACY OF OBSERVATIONS

Let us put some of our earlier generalizations to work in solving a practical problem. Assume that you are mixing chemicals and that a reaction takes place. One of the products which you separate from the reaction mixture is a white crystalline solid. Chemical theory (which

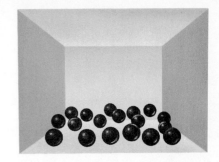

Fig. 1-7.1 "Super-rubber" balls after many collisions.

Fig. 1-7.2 If each small particle of gas were exactly like a "super-rubber" ball, it would slow up a little after each collision with the wall.

TABLE 1-2

Material	Melting Point (°C)	Boiling Point (°C)
A	32.0	212
B	10.1	110
C	27.5	78
D	26.0	150
E	12.0	93
F	18.0	298
G	25.2	95
H	40.0	321
I	0.0	120
J	−25.0	55

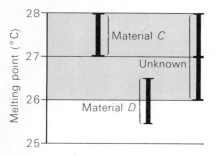

Fig. 1-8 Within the limits defined by uncertainty the unknown could be either material C or material D.

we shall talk about later) tells us that the product is probably *one* of the ten materials listed in Table 1-2. Can the product be identified using a few experiments and the numbers in the table? The answer is: it depends! Let us see how.

Procedures first considered in Exercise 1-1 suggest that it would be helpful to measure the melting point of the solid product. We do so and find a value of 27 °C, which is then recorded as the melting point of the unknown solid. Armed with this information about our material, we now look at the list of possible compounds. We find a value of 27.5 °C listed as the melting point of material C. This seems to be the value closest to the value of 27 °C recorded for our unknown, so we tentatively identify the unknown solid as material C.

But wait! Are we sure that material D, with a melting point of 26 °C is ruled out? It depends on how accurately the value of 27 °C is known and how accurately the values in the table are known. Suppose the values *in the table* could be off as much as 0.5 °C either way. Then it is possible that the value recorded for material C (27.5 °C) should really have been as high as 27.5 + 0.5 °C = 28.0 °C, or as low as 27.5 − 0.5 °C = 27.0 °C. It would be convenient for us to record this value as 27.5 ± 0.5 °C. Both the high and low possibilities are indicated easily this way.

What about our own observation? If it were off as much as one degree in either direction, allowed values for the melting point of the unknown solid could be 28 °C, 27 °C, or 26 °C. This sequence might be conveniently recorded as 27 ± 1 °C.

Let us now look at the values for material D in the table. Using the uncertainty of ±0.5 °C for D, values ranging from 26.5 °C to 25.5 °C are acceptable.

It is now clear that the lowest of the possibilities for our measured value (26 °C) falls well within the range of possible values for material D (26.5 °C to 25.5 °C). That is, material D could melt at a temperature as high as 26.5 °C, while the unknown could have a melting point as low as 26 °C. We see now that the unknown can be either C or D if the limits of error used above are valid (Figure 1-8).

EXERCISE 1-4

Suppose our laboratory measurement of the melting point could be in error by as much as 2 °C either way. What possibilities for the unknown solid now exist? Can you suggest other experiments which might help you decide between the possibilities for the unknown solid?

1-6.1 Uncertainty in Science

As we have just seen, the ability to use melting points to identify substances depends upon how precisely the melting points are known. One might say: why did we not do our work properly in the first place? Why did we not determine the melting points of everything exactly? Then we would not have these annoying questions of uncertainty to bother us.

Unfortunately, the very nature of scientific observation is such that *we have some uncertainty in every measurement we make.* Suppose, as an example, that in determining a melting point we must read the thermometer shown in expanded form in Figure 1-9. It is clear on even casual inspection that the temperature is *about* 31 °C. Yet a report of 31 °C might be considered unsatisfactory for many uses, since it does not convey *all* the available information. More careful inspection of the figure shows that a value of 30.9 °C can easily be read. Probably all observers would agree that the value is 30.9 and not 30.8 or 31.0. We feel reasonably certain about the three numerals—three, zero, and nine.

Are we then in a position to read the value more closely than 30.9? Very careful examination of the figure shows that the top of the mercury column is a little above 30.9. Is it 30.92? Can we be sure it is not 30.91 or 30.95? In all honesty, we cannot say! The fourth numeral is quite uncertain, but an *estimate* of its value tells us that the reading is a little *above* 30.9. Certainly, a report of 30.92251 would be misleading at best, and might even be dishonest in a sense, since it implies information we do not have. Other people reading the same instrument could perhaps read 30.91 °C or 30.94 °C; but any objective observer would have to conclude that we really did not read the last three numerals in 30.92251. Instead we manufactured them without any observational basis.

What, then, would be a meaningful way to record what we see? Since we all agree on the value 30.9 °C, these numerals (which *are* certain) should be recorded. Since the next uncertain numeral adds a little extra information, we can justify recording this as well. We could thus make a case for writing down four numerals, say 30.92, all of which are *significant!* The numerals 251 in 30.92251 are *not* significant; they convey no meaningful information and are not recorded. Scientists have formalized this notation somewhat. They say that the number 30.92 has four **significant figures.** *All of the certain numerals plus the next uncertain one are classed as significant figures.* This is a convenient and simple way to indicate something about the **reproducibility** or **precision** of the measurement. It tells us that all observers would agree on the value 30.9 but that the last numeral might vary from one observer to another. We shall use the method of significant figures frequently to indicate the precision of our measurements.

One other point about significant figures is worth mentioning. Suppose we have a number which is read as 200, but may actually be as high as 300 or as low as 100. How many significant figures do we have? Clearly, even the first number is uncertain, so we cannot have more than *one* significant figure. The zeros recorded are useful in locating the decimal point, but they certainly *do not* tell us anything about the reproducibility of the measurement. We can then state that *the number of significant figures has nothing to do with the location of the decimal point. Zeros that merely indicate the location of the decimal point are not significant.*

For example, each of the numbers 36.09, 3.609, 0.003609, and 360.9 has *four* significant figures. The number 36.090 has *five* significant figures. The numeral in the thousandths place was read and has the value zero; otherwise we would have written 36.09 to indicate that

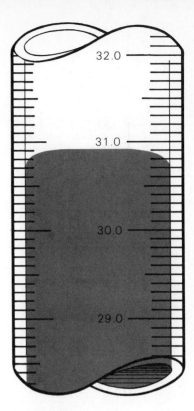

Fig. 1-9

we did not read beyond the hundredths place. But what about the number 36090? In this case, the last 0 may be significant, or it may merely mark the decimal place. How do we indicate significance? To make it clear that the last numeral is significant, the number should be written with five significant figures as 3.6090×10^4. If the last numeral is not significant, 3.609×10^4 should be used.

There is one very serious limitation in using significant figures alone to indicate uncertainty. While we know that the last numeral is uncertain when we write four significant figures, we do not know *how* uncertain. The number with *four significant figures,* 30.92, could be 30.92 ± 0.03 or it could be 30.92 ± 0.01. Clearly, 30.92 ± 0.03 conveys more information than just 30.92. The method of indicating uncertainty by plus-or-minus values has much to recommend it if the size of the uncertainty in the last place is known. Another useful way to indicate uncertainty is to indicate the percentage of uncertainty in the number. For example, 30.92 ± 0.03 could also be written $30.92 \pm 0.1\%$. The method selected to indicate uncertainty will frequently depend on the system studied. For the problem involving the melting point of solids, the ± 0.5 °C or ± 1.0 °C was very useful in arriving at our decision. Significant figures alone would not have been as helpful.

1-6.2 Accuracy and Precision

So far, this treatment of uncertainty seems to center on the question: how closely can different observers read the same instrument? Answers to this question tell us something about the *precision of the measurement.* A measurement of melting point by a given thermometer may be extremely reproducible, giving the same result to about ± 0.03 °C each time. Such a result is **precise,** but it does not necessarily mean that we know the melting point with great **accuracy!** You say why not? Different observers can use *this* thermometer and get the same result each time. Why is the result not *accurate?*

The answer to this question may lie in the nature of the measuring instruments used. Let us illustrate the point by answering the question, "what time is it?" Suppose that your classroom has a large clock in the front of the room. At a given instant all members of the class are asked to read the time as precisely as possible. Some of the readings are 10:25.0, 10:27.0, 10:26.5, 10:26.0, and 10:25.5. The readings seem to be precise within about ± 1 minute, but it would be foolish for us to believe that we know the *exact time* to within ± 1 minute. Why? Because the clock in the front of the room may be slow or fast. Suppose it were 4 minutes slow and the time for the region, as given by the astronomical observatory, were 10:30.0. The readings as determined by the class would be *accurate* to within no better than ± 4 min. A cheap watch, properly set, would give a more *accurate* reading than the wall clock which had not been properly maintained. In short, *accuracy represents how closely the measurement approaches to a true or accepted value. Precision describes the reproducibility of the measurement using a given measuring instrument or experimental set-up.*

Any measurement has some uncertainty resulting from limitations in the measuring device and in the experimenter's ability to use the

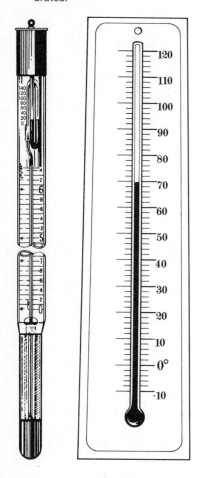

Fig. 1-10 Left: Beckmann differential thermometers certified by the National Bureau of Standards are both precise and accurate. Each is calibrated against an NBS standard. (Courtesy of Lux Scientific Instrument Corporation.) Right: Household thermometers are rarely precise or accurate. They can be read within one or two degrees and are never calibrated.

device. Estimation of the uncertainty associated with the use of each different piece of your laboratory apparatus is given in the Laboratory Manual. It will be helpful in determining the degree of confidence you can have in a laboratory measurement taken with any given instrument.

It is important to indicate the uncertainty in a measurement. This is done most easily by using the proper number of significant figures. It is, however, more meaningful to indicate plus-or-minus values after the result. Uncertainty in measurement influences quantities calculated from these measurements. How the value of a calculated result depends upon uncertainties in the measurements will be explored in your laboratory work. (See Appendix 4 of the Laboratory Manual.)

1-7 COMMUNICATING SCIENTIFIC INFORMATION

One of the most important reasons for human progress is the ability to communicate information to others. It is not necessary for each of us to invent the atomic description of matter. That was done for us by others and passed on to us by means of lectures, books, and papers. The *way* in which ideas are communicated to others is of extreme importance. In fact, one can almost say that *a scientific advance is important only if it is told to others in a manner which they can understand.* This statement is beautifully illustrated by the following episode from the early history of the atomic theory:

In 1789 William Higgins, then in Britain, published a book entitled *A Comparative View of the Phlogiston and Antiphlogiston Theories.* In this book many of the arguments which were to form the basis for the atomic theory were introduced; however, Higgins's presentation was difficult to follow and his views were not widely read or accepted. Some nineteen years later John Dalton, a Manchester schoolteacher, published independently a book entitled *A New System of Chemical Philosophy.* Dalton, though a man of limited scholarly attainment and background, made a masterful presentation of his ideas. He used pictures and symbols to make the concept of atoms into a working hypothesis for all chemists of the era. Dalton's book attracted much attention and led ultimately to the acceptance of the atomic theory.

In 1814 Higgins formally claimed that his book, published in 1789, had contained a description of the atomic theory. Indeed, Higgins's claim to priority was supported by Humphry Davy, who had written in 1811: "It is not a little curious that the first views of the Atomic Chemistry, which has been so expanded by Dalton, are to be found in a work published in 1789 by William Higgins." Many historians of science have since examined Higgins's book and few have recognized the atomic theory in its pages. For this reason, Dalton is usually given sole credit for the atomic theory; Higgins is seldom mentioned. This latter fact is unfortunate since it does appear that Higgins did indeed anticipate some of the concepts of the atomic theory. But because his presentation failed to communicate his ideas in a manner which could be understood and applied by most scientists of the day, his contribution attracted little attention and was not considered to be of great value.

Fig. 1-11 A scientific advance is important only if it is told to others in a manner which they can understand.

We repeat: a scientific advance is important *only* if it is told to others *in a manner which they can understand.* As we go along, we will encounter many different ways to present an idea. In the end, it is the *reader,* not the *author,* who decides which method is best.

Today ideas in science come at us from all directions. We have books, review and research journals, direct laboratory observation, and television. Review journals carry articles written by competent scientists to summarize all the available information in a field. Such articles go out of date very rapidly. The American Chemical Society publishes a review journal with the name *Chemical Reviews.* Research journals record the results of original experiments and describe new and developing ideas in science. The American Chemical Society also publishes such research journals as the *Journal of the American Chemical Society, Journal of Organic Chemistry, Journal of Physical Chemistry, Inorganic Chemistry,* and *Biochemistry.* The National Research Council of Canada publishes the *Canadian Journal of Chemistry;* the Chemical Institute of Canada publishes *Chemistry in Canada,* and so it goes. Chemical societies throughout the world publish journals recording ideas and experiments on the frontiers of science.

Fig. 1-12

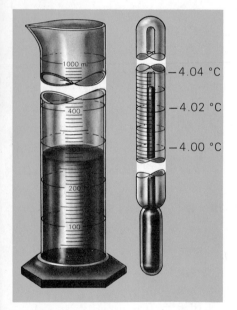

1-8 HIGHLIGHTS

The study of our surroundings involves a number of activities such as:

(1) *Accumulating information through observation.*
(2) *Organizing information and seeking regularities.*
(3) *Wondering why these regularities exist.* In giving an explanation it may be necessary to "build" or formulate a scientific model. A good model will lead to new information and to new insight into the system.
(4) *Communicating information.*

There is no fixed order for these activities. But, when properly done, they lead to scientific advances such as the theory of relativity, a vaccine for polio, rockets capable of traveling to other planets, and the synthesis of a virus (life?) in the laboratory (see Chapter 21). Where we go from here is anyone's guess—and your responsibility!

QUESTIONS and PROBLEMS

1 A student makes the following statements about a beaker of liquid which is heated from room temperature to vigorous boiling. (i) The beaker contains about 200 ml of a colorless liquid. (ii) When the burner is lighted beneath the beaker, water vapor appears on the outside of the beaker, near the bottom. (iii) As the liquid warms, streaming currents appear in it. (iv) With continued heating, small bubbles appear at the bottom and sides of the beaker and stay attached to the glass. (v) After several minutes, the small bubbles move to the top of the liquid and break. (vi) As the liquid starts to boil, many more of the air bubbles move to the top and break. (vii) A thermometer placed in the boiling liquid reads 99.6 ± 0.2 °C. (viii) The water contains polio virus.

(a) Which of the above statements are only observation and which include interpretation? (b) Which of the statements are quantitative observations? (c) Which of the above statements are not justified by the evidence accumulated solely in the boiling process?

2 A detective investigating a crime reported the following "observations" in his preliminary report. (i) The body was discovered at 4:17 P.M. (according to the neighbor's watch). (ii) The body was 5'8" long, clothed in blue coveralls and a necktie. (iii) The man's wife was standing next to the body. (iv) The cause of death was a $4\frac{1}{2}''$ switchblade knife inserted in the ribs. (v) The murder victim had a gun in his right hand. (vi) The door was locked. (vii) There were no signs of forcible entry through the window.

(a) Which of the above include interpretations? (b) Which of the above are quantitative descriptions?

3 Given the following list of melting and boiling points of various substances, list as many regularities as you can for these data.

Substance	Melting Point (°C)	Boiling Point (°C)
1. copper metal	1083	2583
2. silver metal	961	2193
3. iron metal	1535	2800
4. moth balls*	53	175
5. sugar	112	—
6. water	0	100
7. wax	53–55	282

*Substances 4–7 are all nonmetals.

4 How would the regularities from question 3 be affected if the list were to include the following substances as well?

| mercury metal | −39 | 357 |
| salt (a nonmetal) | 800 | 1413 |

5 Another model for a gas is that of bees flying around in a closed jar. (a) In what ways is this model similar to our "super-rubber" ball model for a gas? (b) In what ways is the bee model inadequate for describing a gas?

6 Let us assume that the "super-rubber" ball model for a gas is an accurate one. What would happen to the *pressure* if the balls moved more rapidly in a metal tank of fixed volume?

7 Using Figure 1-12, what volume does the graduated cylinder show, and what temperature is indicated? Read each as precisely as possible and record the uncertainty which *you* feel is present in each measurement.

8 A dieter weighed himself one week and found his weight to be 175 pounds. Two weeks later his weight was 170 pounds. Assume that his scale has an uncertainty of ± 1 pound. (a) What is the maximum possible weight loss? (b) What is the minimum possible weight loss? (c) Express the weight loss using the $\pm$ notation.

9 The mass of a piece of metal may be as much as 264 g (grams), or as little as 260 g. How many significant figures are used to express the mass of the metal? How would the mass be given using the plus-or-minus designation? What is the percentage uncertainty in the measurement?

10 The piece of metal used in question 9 is cut in two. One piece has a mass of 230 ± 2 g. What is the *largest* mass that the other piece could have? What is the *smallest* mass that the other piece could have? Express the mass of the other piece using a plus-or-minus estimate to indicate the uncertainty in your measurement.

11 A student measured the melting temperature of an unknown substance as 68.2 ± 0.2 °C. Handbook values for the melting points of various substances are as follows: Substance A, 67 ± 1.0 °C; substance B, 67.5 ± 0.5 °C; substance C, 67.6 ± 1.0 °C; substance D, 68 ± 1.0 °C; substance E, 70 ± 1.0 °C. Which of the substances might the student's unknown be?

12 The burning of a candle is a relatively complex process which raises many questions. We have listed seven questions here which are worthy of answers, but we are *not* in a position to answer them yet. We shall, however, keep them in mind as we progress. (a) Why did the candle not burn while it was stored in the drawer? (b) Why is energy liberated in the burning of a candle? (c) What was the role of the match used to light the candle? (d) Why is the flame longer than it is wide? (e) Why does a flame emit colored light? (f) What is the role of the wick of the candle? (g) Why does the wick only glow at its tip?

Can you add questions to this list based on your own work with the candle? There are surely many more questions about a phenomenon as complex as the burning of a candle!

. . . hypotheses ought to be fitted merely to explain the properties of things and not attempt to predetermine them except insofar as they can be an aid to experiments . . . .

SIR ISAAC NEWTON (1642–1727)

OUR MODEL GROWS: MOLECULES, 2 MOLES, AND MOLECULAR WEIGHTS

When hydrogen chloride and ammonia mix, a white smoke appears. Can this tell us anything about numbers of molecules reacting?

IN CHAPTER 1 WE FOUND THAT THE BEHAVIOR OF GASES BECAME LESS mysterious when we related it to the model of "super-rubber" balls in constant motion. Building on this model, it should be possible to count the particles and to find out the mass of each kind.

But such knowledge doesn't help us much in the laboratory, since the particles are much too small to be counted or weighed individually. But never fear, chemists have a solution. You never count out sugar by the individual particle—it would be tedious and ridiculous. You buy sugar by the kilogram (30.8 million particles) or the pound (14 million particles). In the kitchen you measure it by the gram (30,800 particles) or by the cup (7 million particles). A heaping teaspoon of sugar contains about 110,000 particles. Chemists, too, use similar devices.

In this chapter you will discover that a mole isn't necessarily the small furry animal you always thought it was.

One of the activities of science is the search for regularities. Valid regularities permit us to make reasonable predictions about the results of future experiments. If the apparent regularity is false (for example, "all cylindrical objects burn"), it soon runs into conflict with experiment. Then it is either forgotten or modified so it becomes true. If the apparent regularity is true (for example, "all wooden objects burn"), it will predict with reasonable accuracy the results of many experiments and can be used to replace long lists of data. A good regularity saves lots of wear and tear on the memory.

As more and more of the predictions of a regularity are verified, our faith in its value grows; finally, we dignify the regularity by calling it a **law.** *A regularity that directly correlates experimental results is generally called a* **rule** *or* **law.** As we shall see, a law is most useful if it is a quantitative statement. We shall often use a law as the starting point when we "wonder why." In seeking an explanation for a regularity, it is customary to reason by analogy and to attempt to explain the law in terms of things which are better understood. For example, in Chapter 1 it was suggested that a gas is made up of little particles which are like constantly moving "super-rubber" balls. In using the analogy, we constructed a mental **model** for the gas. *The explanation of the behavior of the gas in terms of the motion of these particles is called a* **theory** *or* **principle.**

As you can see, rules, laws, models, theories, and principles all have a common aim. They systematize our experimental knowledge. They all state regularities among known facts. The words *model* and *theory* are even used interchangeably at times. They attempt to summarize the regularity.

When seeking an explanation, we sometimes find more than one acceptable model. If this happens, the model or theory which is most useful is usually preferred. A useful model points to new directions of thought, suggests new experiments, and can be expanded or modified to account for the results of many new studies. A useful model is the heart of scientific thought.

2-1 GROWTH OF A MODEL

In order to watch a theory grow, let us examine in more detail the model which was used to describe a gas confined in a balloon. The gas was pictured as a collection of small, rapidly moving particles which rebounded from the walls of the balloon in a series of perfectly elastic collisions. As the particles rebounded from the balloon wall, they pushed on it and pressure resulted. This description of the system reminded us of a collection of rapidly moving "super-rubber" balls confined in a box. Although the analogy was close, there was at least one obvious and significant point of difference. We know that "super-rubber" balls in a box would gradually slow down and stop as the box was allowed to stand. Collisions between "super-rubber" balls and the walls (and with each other) are *not* perfectly elastic. As a result of imperfect elasticity, each ball slows down slightly after every collision and finally stops. On the other hand, collisions of air particles with the walls of the balloon must be regarded as being perfectly elastic on the average or we run into a serious conflict with experiment. If the particles of a gas were to slow down slightly after every collision, the pressure in a closed steel tank would gradually diminish as the tank stood in a classroom, held at a constant temperature. *Experience tells us that this does not happen.* Despite this known and understandable difference in the behavior of gas particles and "super-rubber" balls, the "super-rubber" ball model for gases is a very good one. Its development is worthwhile.

Correlations in science are most useful when they are quantitative, when they answer the question "how much?" as well as "what happens?" *A numerical relationship between the pressure applied to a gas and the volume it occupies would be called a* **quantitative** *correlation.* Let us try some simple, but significant experiments in an effort to establish a *quantitative relationship* between pressure and volume.

2-1.1 Pressure-Volume Measurements for Air

The equipment for this study is simple. We need (1) a plastic syringe, sealed at the end, similar to the one used in the laboratory in Experiment 4; (2) a thin piece of wire; (3) a wooden block into which the syringe fits; and (4) seven or eight ordinary building bricks.

To do the experiment, the syringe is filled with air. The wire is inserted beside the plunger to let air escape as the plunger is adjusted to 35.0 ml. The wire is then removed and a brick is balanced on top of the plunger (see Figure 2-1.1). The volume of air trapped in the syringe under the load of one brick is then read and recorded in Table 2-1. We record the pressure as "one brick," a convenient temporary unit. Two bricks are added and the volume is read again. The apparatus and steps in the experiment are shown in Figure 2-1.2. Actual values obtained by the authors for air in five trials are shown in Table 2-1. Values of this type were easily obtained in your own laboratory work for Experiment 4.

2-1.2 Pressure Due to the Atmosphere—Total Pressure

The numbers in Table 2-1 show that as the pressure (number of bricks) increases, the volume decreases; a simple **qualitative** relationship is

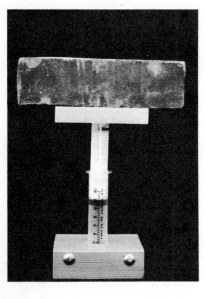

Fig. 2-1.1 Apparatus for studying change in volume as pressure on a gas is increased.

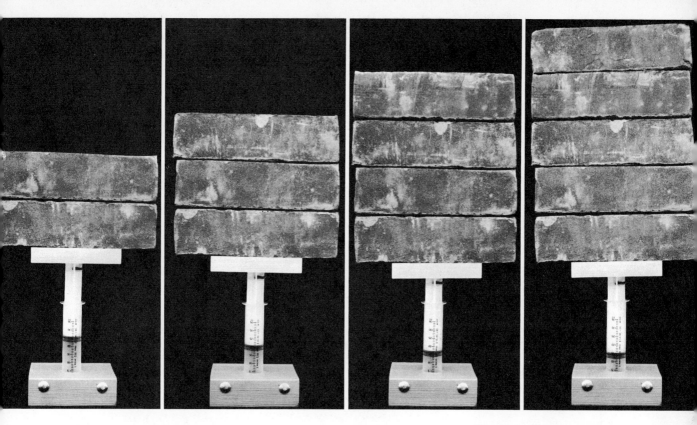

Fig. 2-1.2 Pressure × volume = a constant. As pressure increases, volume decreases.

TABLE **2-1** PRELIMINARY PRESSURE-VOLUME

MEASUREMENTS FOR AIR

Pressure* (bricks)	Volume (ml)†					Average Volume (ml)	$\frac{1}{\text{Volume}}$ (1/ml)
	Trial 1	Trial 2	Trial 3	Trial 4	Trial 5		
1.0	27.0	29.0	28.0	28.0	29.5	28.5	3.50×10^{-2}
2.0	23.0	22.0	23.0	22.0	22.0	22.5	4.45×10^{-2}
3.0	18.0	17.0	17.0	17.5	18.0	17.5	5.70×10^{-2}
4.0	14.0	14.5	13.5	14.0	13.5	14.0	7.15×10^{-2}
5.0	12.0	12.0	12.0	12.5	11.5	12.0	8.30×10^{-2}
6.0	10.5	11.0	9.5	10.0	10.5	10.0	1.0×10^{-1}
7.0	9.0	9.5	9.5	8.5	9.0	9.0	1.1×10^{-1}
8.0	8.5	8.0	8.8	8.5	8.0	8.0	1.2×10^{-1}

*Only whole bricks were used. †Read to closest 0.5.

clear. Before we try to obtain a *quantitative relationship* between pressure and volume, we must know what the *total pressure* on the gas really is.

What is pushing down on the plunger? Several bricks are exerting pressure. In addition, an invisible column of air extends from the top of the plunger up into space. (See Figure 2-2, page 24.) This air has weight, too, and must be considered in determining the total weight on the plunger. In Experiment 4, you determined this value graphically and added it to each pressure reading in books. We can also

PRESSURE DUE to

the ATMOSPHERE

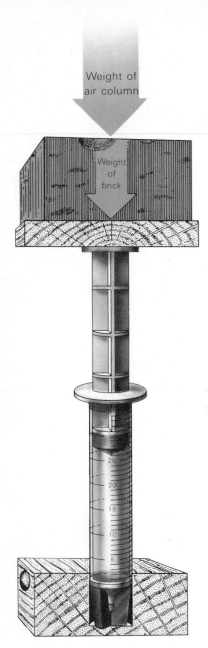

Weight of air column

Weight of brick

Fig. 2-2 An invisible column of air also pushes down (increases pressure) and confines the gas (decreases volume) in the cylinder.

show that the air column has a weight equivalent to that of about 1.7* of our bricks by applying relatively simple algebra to the numbers of Table 2-1. Let us add the weight of the atmosphere to each pressure reading of Table 2-1. The result is seen in the third column of Table 2-2. The total pressure is the pressure due to the weight of the bricks plus the pressure due to the weight of the atmosphere. Table 2-2 now contains two columns (3 and 4) which tell us *quantitatively* how *volume* of a gas changes with the *total pressure* applied to that gas.

TABLE 2-2 CORRECTED PRESSURE-VOLUME MEASUREMENTS FOR AIR

(1) Pressure Due to Bricks	(2) Pressure Due to Air (bricks)	(3) Total Pressure (bricks) (1) + (2)	(4) Average Volume (ml)	(5) Pressure × Volume (bricks × ml)
1	1.7	2.7	28.5	77
2	1.7	3.7	22.5	83
3	1.7	4.7	17.5	82
4	1.7	5.7	14.0	80
5	1.7	6.7	12.0	80
6	1.7	7.7	10.0	77
7	1.7	8.7	9.0	78
8	1.7	9.7	8.0	78

2-1.3 Presentation of Data

We now have numbers in a table. What is the best way to present these numbers so that we can obtain a maximum amount of new information? What more can the values of Table 2-2 tell us? To answer this question, let us present our data in pictorial form.

In Figure 2-3 we have plotted pressure versus volume and a curve is obtained—a short section of a hyperbola. In Figure 2-4 we have plotted pressure versus 1/volume and a straight line is obtained. This is a particularly significant and useful relationship because it shows simply that pressure is directly proportional to 1 divided by the volume (1/V). The statement suggests a simple mathematical relationship:

$$P \text{ is proportional to } \frac{1}{V}$$

or

$$P = \text{proportionality constant} \times (1/V)$$

If both sides of this equation are multiplied by V, we obtain the mathematical expression

$$PV = \text{a constant}$$

*We can also calculate this value independently if we know the weight of the brick, the pressure of the air in grams per square centimetre, and the size of the piston in the cylinder. The value of 1.7 is again obtained.

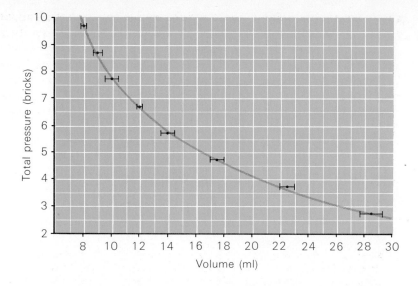

Fig. 2-3 Pressure versus volume of a gas.

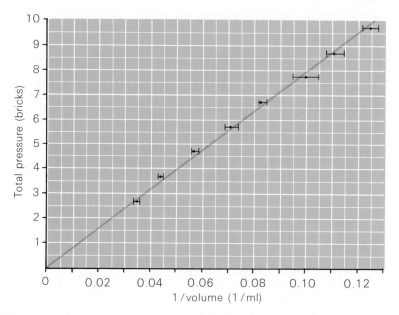

Fig. 2-4 Pressure versus 1/volume of a gas.

This expression leads us to multiply pressure by volume in Table 2-2. The result is shown in the last column of Table 2-2. It indicates that pressure × volume *is* a constant. The $P \times V$ values shown in Table 2-2 are as constant as one could expect from our relatively crude measurements. More precise measurements demonstrate clearly that for a gas such as air, $P \times V$ is indeed a constant under the conditions used here.

In summary, we have presented our data on pressure and volume of a gas sample in four ways:

(1) in a *qualitative* statement which asserts that volume decreases as pressure increases;
(2) in a table which summarizes *quantitatively* the values of volume as the pressure increases;

(3) in two graphs, the first showing *pressure* versus *volume* and giving a curve, and the second showing *pressure* versus *1 divided by volume* and giving a straight line; and

(4) in the form of a mathematical statement, $P \times V =$ a constant, which was suggested by the plot of P versus $1/V$.

EXERCISE 2-1

Look at the numbers in Table 2-2. Suppose the value of 14.0 ml shown as the volume under a pressure of four bricks were really 14.5 millilitres. What would the value of pressure $(P) \times$ volume (V) be? Suppose it were 13.5 ml, what would the value of $P \times V$ be? What range in values of $P \times V$ is indicated just by the precision with which the volume was read? Repeat for the volume value at two bricks.

2-1.4 Quantitative Pressure-Volume Data and the Growth of the Model

We have summarized significant information about the relationship between pressure and volume for air. How does the particle model correlate with the data which have been accumulated? We picture the small particles which make up air as rebounding back and forth between the container walls. In such a model the pressure is determined by

(1) the size of the push each colliding particle gives to the walls of the container; and

(2) the number of collisions made with a unit area of the wall in any one second.

If the volume were cut to half its former value and the number of particles held constant, we would expect *twice* as many particles per unit of volume (*i.e.*, per millilitre). With twice as many particles per unit of volume, we would expect twice as many collisions with a unit area of the wall in any one second (the frequency of collisions is doubled). The model suggests that doubling the number of collisions made with the wall should double the "push" per unit area, hence double the total pressure. Experiment and model agree. We have seen that when the amount of gas and the temperature are held constant and the total pressure is doubled, the volume is cut to half its original value. (Compare the volume for 2.7 bricks and for 5.7 bricks in Table 2-2.) The model is supported by the quantitative data.

2-1.5 Pressure-Volume Measurements for Other Gases

All observations made up until now on air agree with the "super-rubber" ball model. Do gases other than air behave in the same way? Many gases with sharply contrasting properties are available for our study. Tanks labeled oxygen, hydrogen, carbon dioxide, carbon tetra-fluoride, ammonia, hydrogen chloride, or hydrogen bromide can be purchased and their gases tested. Each of these pure gases can be put

TABLE 2-3 PRESSURE-VOLUME MEASUREMENTS FOR SELECTED GASES AT ROOM TEMPERATURE (25 °C)

| **Carbon Dioxide** | | | | | **Nitrogen (Trial 1)** | | | |
Pressure Due to Bricks	Total Pressure (bricks)	Volume (ml)	Pressure × Volume (bricks × ml)		Pressure Due to Bricks	Total Pressure (bricks)	Volume (ml)	Pressure × Volume (bricks × ml)
1	2.7	29.2	79		1	2.7	29.2	79
2	3.7	21.5	80		2	3.7	22.8	84
3	4.7	17.0	80		3	4.7	17.8	84
4	5.7	13.5	77		4	5.7	15.0	85
5	6.7	11.7	78		5	6.7	12.5	84

| **Ammonia** | | | | | **Nitrogen (Trial 2)** | | | |
Pressure Due to Bricks	Total Pressure (bricks)	Volume (ml)	Pressure × Volume (bricks × ml)		Pressure Due to Bricks	Total Pressure (bricks)	Volume (ml)	Pressure × Volume (bricks × ml)
1	2.7	27.0	73		1	2.7	29.2	79
2	3.7	22.1	82		2	3.7	22.5	83
3	4.7	18.0	84		3	4.7	18.0	85
4	5.7	13.6	78		4	5.7	14.7	84
5	6.7	12.0	80		5	6.7	12.1	81

| **Hydrogen Bromide** | | | |
Pressure Due to Bricks	Total Pressure (bricks)	Volume (ml)	Pressure × Volume (bricks × ml)
1	2.7	29.2	79
2	3.7	21.6	80
3	4.7	17.0	80
4	5.7	13.8	79
5	6.7	11.9	80

into the pressure-volume syringe and studied. The results of several of these studies are shown in Table 2-3. We were careful to start with the same volume of each gas at the atmospheric pressure in the room. In each case, the syringe was filled to the same volume with a given gas; then bricks were added one by one to increase the pressure. The volume was recorded for each pressure reading. Since all observations were made in the same room over a short period of time, the temperature was very nearly constant for all observations. The data in Table 2-3 indicate an amazing and fortunate fact. *Not only does the relationship "P × V = a constant" seem to apply to all gases studied, but, within the precision of our measurements, the numerical constant is the same for the four new gases as well as for air.*

Why should this be? What property or properties of gases are implied by this observation? For one thing this observation says that each gas exhibits behavior consistent with the particle model we used successfully for air. Each gas behaves like air. Perhaps, then, *all gases are made up of particles?* Furthermore, the fact that all gases show the

PRESSURE-VOLUME MEASUREMENTS
for OTHER GASES

same value for pressure × volume suggests that, if all gases *are* made up of particles, the bombardment by particles must produce about the same pressure regardless of the kind of gas used. Perhaps all gas particles are the same and we have equal numbers of particles of similar type in the syringe each time.

2-1.6 Properties of Gases

If all gas particles were the same, all gases would have the same properties. Experience tells us that this cannot be true. Because of ammonia's unforgettably obnoxious odor, no one could possibly confuse it with nitrogen. Experiments show that the gases we worked with show striking differences outside the syringe. Hydrogen bromide gas and ammonia gas dissolve readily in water, while nitrogen does not. Carbon dioxide gas dissolves only to a limited extent.

Gas particles, then, are *not* the same. Different gases must be made up of *different* kinds of particles. If this were not so, the differences between gases would be very difficult to understand. A name for these particles of gases would be helpful. *The particles of gases are called* **molecules.** Molecules of different gases differ. But we are still left with the question: why do different gases give the same value of pressure × volume in our syringe experiments? To find the answer we need more experimental information.

MIXTURES OF GASES

What happens when gases are mixed? We have already established that when more gas molecules are forced into a given volume, the pressure due to the gas rises. Thus, if the volume occupied by a given quantity of gas at constant temperature is cut in half, the pressure doubles. Forcing one gas into another should bring about an increase in the number of molecules per unit volume, hence an increase in pressure.

To test this hypothesis, a syringeful of nitrogen is forced into a syringeful of hydrogen bromide. We find that the pressure *must be doubled* if the combined gas mixture is to be retained in one syringe. In a similar way a syringeful of nitrogen is forced into a syringeful of ammonia. Again, the pressure must be doubled if all the gas is to be retained in one syringe. The behavior of these gas mixtures is in agreement with the particle model.

Let us now check the result by forcing a syringeful of ammonia into a syringeful of hydrogen bromide. Our initial observation surprises us. A white smoke and powder appear in the hydrogen bromide syringe and the plungers in both syringes move to the bottom. *A solid of trivial volume is formed from the two syringefuls of gas:*

$$1 \left\{ \begin{matrix} \text{syringeful of} \\ \text{hydrogen} \\ \text{bromide} \end{matrix} \right\} \text{plus } 1 \left\{ \begin{matrix} \text{syringeful} \\ \text{of} \\ \text{ammonia} \end{matrix} \right\} \text{gives} \left\{ \begin{matrix} \text{white solid} \\ \text{of trivial volume} \\ \text{compared to gases} \end{matrix} \right\}$$

What happens if we take one syringeful of ammonia and *half* a syringeful of hydrogen bromide? Experiment shows that white powder and smoke again appear, but the volume does not drop to zero. Instead, half a syringeful of gas remains. This remaining gas has the properties of ammonia. Our experiments show that only *half the ammonia is used!*

$$\tfrac{1}{2}\left\{\begin{array}{l}\text{syringeful}\\\text{of}\\\text{hydrogen}\\\text{bromide}\end{array}\right\} \text{ plus } 1\left\{\begin{array}{l}\text{syringeful}\\\text{of}\\\text{ammonia}\end{array}\right\} \text{ gives } \left\{\begin{array}{l}\text{white}\\\text{solid}\end{array}\right\} \text{ plus } \tfrac{1}{2}\left\{\begin{array}{l}\text{syringeful}\\\text{of}\\\text{ammonia}\end{array}\right\}$$

or

$$\tfrac{1}{2}\left\{\begin{array}{l}\text{syringeful of}\\\text{hydrogen bromide}\end{array}\right\} \text{ plus } \tfrac{1}{2}\left\{\begin{array}{l}\text{syringeful of}\\\text{ammonia}\end{array}\right\} \text{ gives } \left\{\begin{array}{l}\text{white}\\\text{solid}\end{array}\right\}$$

If we repeat the experiment using one syringeful of hydrogen bromide but only half a syringeful of ammonia, the white solid again appears, but only *half* the hydrogen bromide is used.

$$1\left\{\begin{array}{l}\text{syringeful}\\\text{of}\\\text{hydrogen}\\\text{bromide}\end{array}\right\} \text{ plus } \tfrac{1}{2}\left\{\begin{array}{l}\text{syringeful}\\\text{of}\\\text{ammonia}\end{array}\right\} \text{ gives } \left\{\begin{array}{l}\text{white}\\\text{solid}\end{array}\right\} \text{ plus } \tfrac{1}{2}\left\{\begin{array}{l}\text{syringeful}\\\text{of}\\\text{hydrogen}\\\text{bromide}\end{array}\right\}$$

The result of these three experiments can be summarized by the statement

$$1\left\{\begin{array}{l}\text{volume of}\\\text{hydrogen bromide}\end{array}\right\} \text{ plus } 1\left\{\begin{array}{l}\text{volume of}\\\text{ammonia}\end{array}\right\} \text{ gives } \left\{\begin{array}{l}\text{white solid of}\\\text{trivial volume}\end{array}\right\}$$

How does this result fit in with the particle model for gases? The simplest interpretation is that one molecule of hydrogen bromide combines with one molecule of ammonia to give a particle which helps to form the white solid.

$$1\left\{\begin{array}{l}\text{molecule of}\\\text{hydrogen bromide}\end{array}\right\} \text{ plus } 1\left\{\begin{array}{l}\text{molecule of}\\\text{ammonia}\end{array}\right\} \text{ gives } \left\{\begin{array}{l}\text{particle which}\\\text{makes up the}\\\text{white solid}\end{array}\right\}$$

Such a hypothesis would be consistent with our observations if one syringeful of hydrogen bromide gas contained the same number of hydrogen bromide molecules as ammonia molecules in one syringeful of ammonia gas. Remember that one *volume* of ammonia reacts with one *volume* of hydrogen bromide. This is a bold suggestion. It could explain the pressure-volume constant if one molecule of ammonia were as effective as one molecule of hydrogen bromide in generating pressure.

2-1.7 Avogadro's Hypothesis

The simplicity of the equation relating volume and pressure suggested to the French physicist André Ampère (1775–1836) around 1810 that equal volumes of gases at the same temperature and pressure contain an equal number of molecules. This thought was little more than speculation until the Italian chemist Amedeo Avogadro (1776–1856), working independently, combined the information on combining volumes of gases with the pressure-volume data. He proposed what is usually called **Avogadro's hypothesis:** *equal volumes of gases, measured at the same temperature and pressure, contain an equal number of molecules.*

You may object, saying that the evidence which we presented is consistent with Avogadro's hypothesis, but it certainly does not prove the hypothesis. There may be many other explanations which would offer equally good interpretations of the facts. Your position would be perfectly reasonable and justifiable. In fact, you would be in rather distinguished company. John Dalton (founder of the atomic theory) and J. J. Berzelius (one of the great chemists of all time) took this position and for almost 50 years Avogadro's hypothesis was not accepted. *No single experiment or series of experiments ever established the validity of Avogadro's hypothesis.* Rather, the slow accumulation of facts, all of which could be explained simply and directly by Avogadro's hypothesis, finally brought about its general acceptance. It stands today as one of the cornerstones of modern science. The controversy over Avogadro's views and the vigorous interplay of personalities during the period 1800 to 1860 make that part of the history of science fascinating reading.*

We shall tentatively accept Avogadro's hypothesis and see how it can explain the many observations we shall make throughout this course. This, in fact, is precisely how the hypothesis was accepted into the structure of modern chemistry.

2-2 MOLECULAR WEIGHTS, THE MOLE, AND THE MOLAR VOLUME

Avogadro's hypothesis, like the statement "all wooden objects burn," has far-reaching consequences. We already know that gases differ from one another. Properties of gases vary widely. It is logical to assume that molecules of different gases have different masses. One way in which we might determine *relative* masses of some gas molecules would be to weigh† 1 litre‡ of each of several different gases, just as you weighed one plastic bagful of different gases in Experiment 5. If, then, Avogadro's hypothesis is true and molecules of two different gases have different masses, the 1-litre samples of each gas (measured at the same temperature and pressure) will have different masses. The ratio of the mass of 1 *litre* of gas *A* to 1 *litre* of gas *B* should be the same as the ratio of the mass of *one molecule* of gas *A* to *one molecule* of gas *B*. This follows because we are assuming that equal volumes of gases at the same temperature and pressure have the same number of mole-

---

*See, for example, E. Farber, *The Evolution of Chemistry,* Chapter 11, The Ronald Press, New York, 1969.

†In actual fact we determine the mass, not the weight, with a chemical balance, but the word "weigh" is so common in the language that it is retained here.

‡A litre is one of the units of volume used in science; it is equal to 1,000 ml or 1.06 quarts.

cules. Let us investigate the masses of equal volumes of gases measured at the same temperature and pressure.

2-2.1 The Relative Masses of Gases

We are going to fill a 1-litre bulb with gas (see Figure 2-5), weigh the bulb plus gas, then pump out the gas, and weigh the empty bulb. The difference between these two values will give us the mass of the gas in the bulb. By selecting a pressure to confine the gas which is equal to the average pressure of the earth's atmosphere at sea level (a pressure of 1.7 bricks), and by selecting a cold temperature of -5 °C (degrees Celsius*) at which to measure the gas volume, the masses will be close to whole numbers. This will simplify the arithmetic involved in obtaining mass ratios. For that reason alone, we shall work under these cold and unusual conditions for our initial experiments.

One litre of *carbon dioxide* has a mass of 2.0 grams† (g) at -5 °C and 1 atmosphere (atm) pressure. One litre of *carbon tetrafluoride* has a mass of 4.0 g under these same conditions. If 1 litre of carbon dioxide contains the same number of molecules as does 1 litre of carbon tetrafluoride, then *one molecule* of carbon tetrafluoride must be 4.0 g/2.0 g or twice as heavy as *one molecule* of carbon dioxide. If the *relative mass* of a carbon dioxide molecule were 1.0, then the relative mass of a carbon tetrafluoride molecule would be 2.0. If we knew the mass of a carbon dioxide molecule, we could determine the mass of a carbon tetrafluoride molecule.

This procedure for obtaining the *relative* masses of gas particles using carbon dioxide as a standard can be applied to many gases. As an example, let us weigh hydrogen molecules. One litre of hydrogen at 1 atm pressure and -5 °C has a mass of 0.092 g. If the relative mass of the carbon dioxide molecule is taken as 1.0, then the relative mass of the hydrogen molecule is

$$\frac{\text{mass of hydrogen sample}}{\text{mass of carbon dioxide sample}} = \frac{0.092 \text{ g}}{2.0 \text{ g}} = 0.046 = \frac{1}{22}$$

$$\frac{\text{mass of hydrogen molecule}}{\text{mass of carbon dioxide molecule}} = \frac{\frac{1}{22}}{1} = \frac{1}{22}$$

If the carbon dioxide molecule is 1.0, the hydrogen molecule is $\frac{1}{22}$. But *fractional* numbers for particle masses are inconvenient. Since we can use any particle as a reference standard and can arbitrarily assign any mass to it, we could call the relative mass of hydrogen particles 1.0; then a carbon dioxide particle would have a *relative* mass of 22 and a carbon tetrafluoride particle would have a relative mass of 44 $\left(\frac{4.0 \text{ g}}{0.092 \text{ g}} = 44 \right)$. This standard is fine if we do not find a gas lighter than hydrogen. If we do,

Fig. 2-5 One-litre bulb for weighing a gas.

---

*Temperatures in chemistry are measured in degrees Celsius. The scale is defined more precisely in Chapter 4.
†The kilogram is the basic unit of mass in science. One gram equals $\frac{1}{1000}$ kg. The world standard for mass is a kilogram platinum cylinder in Paris.

we shall be back to fractional masses. Fortunately, no gas available to us in the laboratory in weighable amounts is lighter than hydrogen. It is convenient, therefore, to adopt hydrogen as our *temporary* standard. Then all other gases will have relative masses greater than the standard.

Since we are concerned only with *relative* masses, the actual number assigned to our temporary standard is arbitrary. It is most convenient to assign gaseous hydrogen molecules a relative mass of 2.0. As you may know, each hydrogen molecule is composed of two separate units called **atoms.** By assigning a value of 2.0 to a hydrogen *molecule,* a value of 1.0 can be assigned to the lightest atom, the hydrogen *atom.* Arbitrarily, then, a hydrogen molecule is assigned a relative *mass* of 2.0. On this scale a carbon dioxide molecule will have a relative mass of 2.0×22 or 44 and a carbon tetrafluoride molecule a relative mass of 2.0×44 or 88.

EXERCISE 2-2

One litre of the gas methane (a component of household natural gas) has a mass of 0.736 g at $-5\ °C$ and 1 atm pressure. What is the relative mass of a methane molecule if hydrogen molecules are taken as 2.0? One litre of hydrogen at 1 atm and $-5\ °C$ has a mass of 0.092 g.

2-2.2 Molecular Weights

We have just used Avogadro's hypothesis to calculate the relative masses of molecules of different gases. It is appropriate to call these relative masses **molecular weights.*** As you will recall from the preceding section, any gas can be selected as a standard (first we used carbon dioxide, then hydrogen) and any value can be assigned to the standard. (We assigned a value of 1.0 to carbon dioxide, then found it more convenient to assign a value of 2.0 to hydrogen.)

If the relative mass of an oxygen molecule is determined using hydrogen with a value of 2.0 as a standard, we find that the molecular weight of oxygen is 32. Early chemists could obtain oxygen in pure form simply by heating an orange powder called mercuric oxide. Furthermore, when oxygen was assigned the molecular weight of 32.00, molecular weights of a large number of other gases turned out to be whole numbers. These two facts made oxygen a very convenient primary standard for early chemists. To this day, when we determine the molecular weight of gases by weighing a sample of the gas and a sample of a standard, oxygen is usually selected as the experimental standard and a value of 32.00 is *assigned* to it.†

***Mass** and **weight** are frequently used as equivalent terms; however, they do have different meanings. Weight refers to the gravitational attraction between an object and the earth. Mass refers to the actual *quantity* of material present. We shall frequently use the more scientifically precise term mass instead of weight, but we are still saddled with the archaic terms molecular weight and atomic weight. The International Union of Pure and Applied Chemistry (IUPAC) still recognizes the terms atomic weight and molecular weight.

†More precise methods for determining molecular weight utilize the mass spectrometer and use carbon = 12.0000 as the primary standard. See Appendix 3 for details.

Let us now briefly summarize the procedure we can use to obtain molecular weights of gaseous substances:

(1) We weigh a given volume of a standard gas (usually oxygen) at a given temperature and pressure.
(2) We *assign* a molecular weight to the standard. Chemists use oxygen and assign it a value of 32.00.
(3) We weigh an equal volume of the unknown gas using the same temperature and pressure as we used for the standard gas.
(4) We calculate the molecular weight of the unknown gas by means of the relationship

$$\frac{\text{molecular weight of unknown}}{\text{molecular weight of standard}} = \frac{\text{mass of unknown gas sample}}{\text{mass of standard gas sample}}$$

If oxygen is the standard, the value for the molecular weight of the standard is 32.00. If another gas is used as a standard, its molecular weight must be known at least as accurately as we desire the molecular weight of the unknown. Finally, neither the temperature nor pressure need be known as long as the unknown and the standard are weighed under the same conditions.

EXERCISE 2-3

A sample of the gas named diborane is weighed in a bulb. The gas is found to have a mass of 0.600 g. The diborane is removed from the bulb and replaced with an equal volume of oxygen gas measured under the same conditions of temperature and pressure. The sample of oxygen has a mass of 0.696 g. What is the molecular weight of the diborane?

2-2.3   The Mole

An experimental procedure for determining molecular weights (the relative masses of molecules) has been outlined. Notice that in using this procedure, we made two arbitrary choices. First, oxygen was selected as the standard gas; and second, a molecular weight of 32.00 was assigned to it. After we made these choices, we could determine the molecular weight of any other gas.

An interesting question now arises: what unit should be assigned to molecular weight values? In choosing a unit, it is convenient to select a unit appropriate to the usual dimensions of the item being weighed. For example, we use grams to measure out laboratory reagents, tons to express the weight of ocean liners, and pounds to buy hamburger meat. Because an individual molecule is so small, we need a very small, new unit to express the mass of a single molecule. We unknowingly defined this new unit when we selected the oxygen molecule as a standard and assigned it a value of 32.00. This new unit, the **unified atomic mass unit (u)**,* is so small that 32.00 u are present in the mass of a *single* oxygen molecule.

---

*By international agreement, the unified atomic mass unit, u, is defined in terms of a specific carbon atom. It is equal to 1.66053×10^{-27} kg. The abbreviation used formerly was **amu**.

By definition, then, the oxygen molecule has a mass of 32 u. One hydrogen molecule has a mass of 2 u; one carbon dioxide molecule, a mass of 44 u; and one carbon tetrafluoride molecule, a mass of 88 u. Note that these are *relative* masses which are based on our earlier experiments. Each value gives the relative mass of a molecule as compared to the standard oxygen molecule.

While the unified atomic mass unit is convenient for expressing the mass of a single molecule, it is not convenient in laboratory operations. For example, it is impossible to weigh out 32 unified atomic mass units of oxygen. But it is very easy to weigh out 32 *grams* (g) of oxygen. We need two mass scales then—one for individual molecules (u) and one for weighing reagents in laboratory operations (g).

You will remember that we assigned molecular weights to gases by weighing equal volumes of different gases and applying a convenient scale to the relative masses which we obtained from our laboratory work. Our approach was based on Avogadro's hypothesis, which tells us that if we are weighing equal volumes of two different gases at the same temperature and pressure, we are weighing equal numbers of molecules of the two gases. One molecular weight (in grams) of any gas, then, must contain the same number of molecules as one molecular weight of any other gas. By using methods which are a little beyond us right now, it can be shown that one molecular weight in grams of oxygen (32.0 grams) contains 6.02×10^{23} individual oxygen molecules. This number of particles is called a **mole.** *One molecular weight (in grams) of any substance contains one mole of molecules—6.02×10^{23} molecules.* This value, 6.02×10^{23}, is known as **Avogadro's Number.**

The mole is to the chemist as the dozen is to the grocer. The chemist handles chemicals in moles (6.02×10^{23} units) just as the grocer handles eggs in dozens (12 units). *One mole of any gas contains 6.02×10^{23} molecules and has a mass in grams which is equal to the molecular weight of that gas.* For example, one mole of hydrogen has a mass of 2.02 g; one mole of ammonia has a mass of 17.0 g; and one mole of carbon dioxide has a mass of 44.0 g.

2-2.4 Determining the Number of Moles from Laboratory Quantities

You will remember from Section 2-1.6 that we interpreted the data from combining volumes of hydrogen bromide gas and ammonia gas to mean that one *molecule* of hydrogen bromide gas combines with one *molecule* of ammonia gas to form the white solid. It is the individual molecules of substances which combine in chemical reactions. Yet individual molecules are difficult to count and impossible to weigh in the laboratory. Using the chemist's "dozen," the mole, we can say that

1 *mole* of hydrogen bromide gas combines
with 1 *mole* of ammonia gas

or

1 *molecular weight in grams* of hydrogen bromide gas combines
with 1 *molecular weight in grams* of ammonia gas

Now we have a means of converting quantities which we can weigh in the laboratory into numbers of individual molecules or numbers of moles of the molecules which do the reacting.

Though the term *mole* may look strange at first, you can learn to use it just as easily as you now use the word *dozen*. Let us run some parallel calculations using both moles and dozens. To begin, we shall work with dozens.

Example (1a) How many dozens of eggs are contained in 48 eggs?

You know that there are 12 eggs per dozen. This is written 12 eggs/doz. We then divide 48 eggs by 12 eggs/doz:

$$\frac{48 \text{ eggs}}{12\dfrac{\text{eggs}}{\text{doz eggs}}} \tag{1}$$

The units can be handled just like numbers here. The unit "eggs/doz eggs" is really just like a numerical fraction. Reducing the fraction to lowest terms, we have

$$48 \text{ eggs} \times \frac{1 \text{ doz eggs}}{12 \text{ eggs}} = 4.0 \text{ doz eggs} \tag{2}$$

The unit "eggs" in numerator and denominator reduces to 1, giving 4.0 as the proper number and "doz eggs" as the proper unit.

Working with units in this way is called **simple unit analysis.** It is most helpful in providing a check on calculations. If the units of the answer are incorrect, a mistake has been made somewhere in the procedure.

Example (1b) How many moles of carbon dioxide (CO_2) will be found in 18.06×10^{23} molecules of carbon dioxide?

If we remember that there are 6.02×10^{23} particles per mole, the problem can be written as a straightforward division process:

$$\frac{18.06 \times 10^{23} \text{ molecules } CO_2}{6.02 \times 10^{23}\dfrac{\text{molecules } CO_2}{\text{mole } CO_2}}$$

$$= 18.06 \times 10^{23} \text{ molecules } CO_2 \times \frac{1 \text{ mole } CO_2}{6.02 \times 10^{23} \text{ molecules } CO_2}$$

$$= 3.00 \text{ moles } CO_2 \tag{3}$$

Note that 6.02×10^{23} units per mole is used just like 12 eggs per dozen. The unit "molecules CO_2" reduces to 1 and the unit "mole CO_2" remains after we divide.

We can pursue the analogy further. Let us assume that a dozen hen eggs weighs 1.5 pounds. Then we ask:

Example (2a) How many dozens of hen eggs will be found in a crate containing 60 pounds of eggs?

The answer is obtained by a straightforward division process:

$$\frac{60 \ \text{lb eggs}}{1.5 \ \frac{\text{lb eggs}}{\text{doz eggs}}} = 40 \ \text{doz eggs} \qquad (4)$$

Note that unit analysis again indicates the correct units for the answer.

EXERCISE 2-4

Invert the fraction

$$\frac{\text{lb eggs}}{\frac{\text{lb eggs}}{\text{doz eggs}}}$$

and multiply to show that the final unit is doz eggs.

The mass relationships involving moles are identical. Only the units differ.

Example (2b) How many *moles* of hydrogen gas will be found in a tank containing 40 g of hydrogen?

We know that each *mole* of hydrogen gas has a mass of 2.0 g (compare with 1.5 lb per doz eggs). We then write

$$\frac{40 \ \text{g hydrogen}}{2.0 \ \frac{\text{g hydrogen}}{\text{mole hydrogen}}} = 20 \ \text{moles hydrogen} \qquad (5)$$

Example (3a) If a dozen eggs weighs 1.5 pounds, what will be the weight of 6 dozen eggs?

$$6 \ \text{dozen eggs} \times \frac{1.5 \ \text{pounds eggs}}{\text{dozen eggs}} = 9 \ \text{pounds of eggs} \qquad (6)$$

Example (3b) If one mole of oxygen gas has a mass of 32.0 grams, what will be the mass of 6 moles of oxygen gas?

$$6 \ \text{moles of oxygen gas} \times \frac{32.0 \ \text{g oxygen gas}}{\text{mole of oxygen gas}}$$
$$= 2 \times 10^2 \ \text{g of oxygen gas} \qquad (7)$$

These illustrations indicate the relationship between moles of molecules, individual molecules, and molecular weight. To summarize:

$$\text{number of moles} = \frac{\text{mass of substance (g)}}{\text{mass of 1 mole (g/mole)}} \qquad (8)$$

number of grams of a substance

$$= \text{number of moles} \times \text{mass of 1 mole (g/mole)} \quad (9)$$

number of molecules

$$= \text{number of moles} \times \left(6.02 \times 10^{23} \frac{\text{molecules}}{\text{mole}}\right) \quad (10)$$

These turn out to be exceedingly useful relationships.

EXERCISE 2-5

How many moles of carbon dioxide are in a tank containing 88 g of carbon dioxide? (Remember that the molecular weight of carbon dioxide is 44.0.)

EXERCISE 2-6

How many moles of oxygen molecules are contained in a 16.0-gram sample of oxygen? How many individual molecules of oxygen are contained in the sample?

EXERCISE 2-7

How many grams of hydrogen gas are contained in a 5.0-mole sample of hydrogen? (Remember that the molecular weight of hydrogen is 2.0.)

EXERCISE 2-8

How many grams of carbon tetrafluoride gas are contained in a 0.10-mole sample of that gas? (The molecular weight of carbon tetrafluoride gas is 88.0.) How many individual molecules of gas are contained in the sample?

2-2.5 The Volume Occupied by One Mole of a Gas— The Molar Volume

Another way of determining the number of moles present in a sample of gas is by measuring the volume of gas under well defined conditions. If we know what volume 1 mole of a gas occupies under a given set of conditions, we can calculate the number of moles present in our sample. Let us work through some examples and see what conditions must be specified.

What volume does 1 mole of a gas such as oxygen occupy? Our previous study of pressure-volume relationships (Section 2-1.1) showed that the volume of a gas is dependent upon the pressure on the gas. If we want to determine the volume occupied by 1 mole of gas, we must specify the pressure. Let us adopt the average pressure of the air at sea level as our standard of pressure for this measurement and call it 1 atmosphere (atm). Similarly, we must specify a temperature. A convenient and easily reproduced temperature is that of ice melting slowly under 1 atm of pressure. This temperature, defined as zero degrees Celsius (0 °C), is the standard which we shall use. These temperature and pressure conditions are so useful that they are called **standard temperature and pressure,** abbreviated **STP.** STP means a temperature of 0 °C* and 1 atmosphere† pressure (760 mm of Hg).

Under these STP conditions (1 atm and 0 °C) 1 mole of oxygen (32.00 g) has a volume of 22.4 litres and 1 mole of nitrogen (28.00 g) has a volume of 22.4 litres. Values for two other gases are shown in Table 2-4. Notice that these values are also close to 22.4 litres per mole. Similar measurements made on many other gases show that 1 mole of a gas occupies approximately 22.4 litres at 0 °C and 1 atm of pressure.

TABLE 2-4 LABORATORY DATA FOR DETERMINING THE VOLUME OCCUPIED BY 1 MOLE* OF A GAS AT 0 °C AND 1 ATM PRESSURE

Gas	(1) Mass of Flask (1.00 Litre) Empty (g)	(2) Mass of Flask Plus Gas (g)	(3) Mass of 1.00 Litre of Gas (g/litre)	(4) Mass of 1 Mole of Gas (g/mole)	(5) Molar† Volume (litres/mole) (4)/(3) = (5)
Oxygen	157.35	158.78	1.43	32.0	22.4
Nitrogen	157.35	158.60	1.25	28.0	22.4
Carbon monoxide	157.35	158.59	1.24	28.0	22.5
Carbon dioxide	157.35	159.32	1.97	44.0	22.3

*Remember that the mole is the quantity equivalent to one molecular weight in grams.
†The value for the volume of 1 mole of a gas can be obtained from laboratory data by dividing the mass of 1 mole of gas by the mass of 1 litre of the gas, measured in the laboratory at 0 °C and 1 atm pressure. We shall use this relationship later. A unit check shows

$$\frac{g/mole}{g/litre} = \frac{litres}{mole}$$

We have seen in Section 2-1.3 that for a given quantity of gas held at constant temperature, the pressure multiplied by the volume is a constant. *If we take 1 mole of a gas at 0 °C and 1 atm pressure,* we can write

$$volume = \frac{22.4 \text{ litres}}{mole}$$

Standard temperature is 0.00 °C. It is the temperature of an ice-water slush standing in an insulated container such as a Thermos bottle. It is easily established in the laboratory.
†Air pressure fluctuates from day to day and from place to place and decreases as the altitude increases, so it is not possible to describe accurately a "standard atmospheric pressure." Instead, an *arbitrary* standard pressure has been chosen which is relatively close to an average pressure at sea level. *A standard pressure, 1.00 standard atmosphere, is that pressure which will support a pure mercury column 760.00 mm high, measured at 0.00 °C.* This pressure is frequently referred to as 1.00 atmosphere (1 atm).

The quantity 22.4 litres, found in Table 2-4, is the approximate *molar volume* of any gas at STP. If we know the total volume of gas and the volume of 1 mole of gas, the number of moles is easily calculated. Suppose we have 44.8 litres of gas at STP and we know that 1 mole of gas occupies 22.4 litres. Common sense tells us that we have 2 moles of gas. This relationship can be given in more general terms by the expression:

number of moles of gas

$$= \frac{\text{number of litres of gas at STP}}{\text{number of litres 1 mole of gas occupies at STP}}$$

or

$$\text{number of moles of gas} = \frac{\text{number of litres of gas at STP}}{22.4 \dfrac{\text{litres of gas at STP}}{\text{mole of gas}}}$$

Simple arithmetic then shows that

number of litres of gas at STP

$$= \left(\begin{array}{c} \text{number of} \\ \text{moles of gas} \end{array} \right) \left(22.4 \dfrac{\text{litres at STP}}{\text{mole of gas}} \right)$$

EXERCISE 2-9

How many moles of hydrogen gas are contained in 2.24 litres of hydrogen gas measured at STP?

EXERCISE 2-10

How many moles of carbon dioxide gas are contained in 10.0 litres of carbon dioxide at STP? (*Answer:* 0.446 moles carbon dioxide.)

EXERCISE 2-11

What volume will 3.0 moles of oxygen occupy at 0 °C and 1 atm pressure?

2-3   HIGHLIGHTS

The model advanced in Chapter 1 to explain the behavior of a gas in a balloon has grown rapidly. Quantitative pressure-volume measurements for many gases showed that

pressure × volume = a constant

as long as we started with the same initial volume of gas measured at the same temperature and pressure. This fact was combined with information on combining volumes of gases to provide initial evidence for **Avogadro's hypothesis:** equal volumes of gases at the same temperature and pressure contain the same number of molecules.

Using Avogadro's hypothesis as a starting point, we obtained **relative masses** of gaseous molecules. A standard gas was needed to establish a **molecular weight** scale. Oxygen was selected as the standard gas and assigned a value of 32.00 for its molecular weight. The relative mass of any other gas on this scale is the molecular weight of the gas. A 32.00-g sample of oxygen is a **mole** of oxygen. A mole is 6.02×10^{23} units. One mole of oxygen gas (or of any substance) contains $\mathbf{6.02 \times 10^{23}}$ **molecules.** The mole is to the chemist as the dozen is to the baker. One mole of a *gas* occupies 22.4 litres if the gas is measured at 0 °C and 1 atm pressure (STP).* The number of moles of a substance can be obtained from the mass of the substance if we divide the mass by the molecular weight. The number of moles of a gas can also be obtained from the volume of the gas at STP if we divide the measured volume by the volume occupied by one mole of gas under the conditions used.

It is now possible to convert laboratory quantities to numbers of moles and numbers of moles to laboratory quantities. The foundation for quantitative relationships in chemistry has been laid. Powerful tools have been developed.

*Deviations from this statement are considered in Chapter 5.

QUESTIONS and PROBLEMS

1 A beaker of water at room temperature is heated, with temperature readings taken each minute. All readings are ±0.2 °C. They are as follows: 26.0; 32.4; 39.4; 46.0; 52.2; 58.8; 65.6; 72.2; 80.0; 85.6; and 91.8. (a) Make a qualitative statement about the observed data. (b) Express the results quantitatively, in a table. (c) Express the results graphically. (d) Develop a mathematical relationship between the time of heating, t, and the temperature, T.

2 A sample of gas measured under 10.0 atmospheres pressure is found to occupy a volume of 1.6 litres. What volume would it occupy under a pressure of 1.0 atmosphere? (The temperature remains constant throughout.)

3 What volume of oxygen gas, measured at 1.00 atmosphere pressure, would it take to fill a standard 100-litre tank in which the pressure is 108 atmospheres?

4 How many 1-litre plastic bags could you expect to fill (at room pressure) from a ½-litre cylinder of gas under 110 atmospheres pressure? (Remember, the last ½ litre of gas will not come out of the tank into the bag.)

5 A syringeful of air occupies 50.0 ml at 1.0 atmosphere pressure. A strong student, pushing with all his might, is able to compress this air to a volume of 5.0 ml. (a) What is the total pressure on the 5.0 ml of air? (b) How much pressure, in atmospheres, has the student exerted?

6 In an experiment similar to Experiment 5, the air is pumped out of a glass container. The evacuated flask has a mass of 126.44 ± 0.01 g. When filled with oxygen at room temperature and pressure, the flask now has a mass of 127.79 ± 0.01 g. The flask is then emptied and refilled with an unknown gas, again at room temperature and pressure. The flask now has a mass of 127.15 ± 0.01 g. (a) What is the ratio:

$$\frac{\text{mass of unknown gas contained in the flask}}{\text{mass of oxygen contained in the flask}}$$

(b) What is the ratio:

$$\frac{\text{mass of one molecule of unknown gas}}{\text{mass of one molecule of oxygen}}$$

(c) What is the ratio:

$$\frac{\text{molecular weight of unknown gas}}{\text{molecular weight of oxygen}}$$

(d) Since the molecular weight of oxygen has been established at 32.00, what is the molecular weight of the unknown gas?

7 The flask used in question 6, when emptied and filled with helium, had a mass of 126.60 ± 0.01 g. (a) What is the ratio:

$$\frac{\text{mass of helium contained in the flask}}{\text{mass of oxygen contained in the flask}}$$

(b) What is the ratio:

$$\frac{\text{mass of one molecule of helium}}{\text{mass of one molecule of oxygen}}$$

(c) What is the ratio:

$$\frac{\text{molecular weight of helium}}{\text{molecular weight of oxygen}}$$

(d) Since the molecular weight of oxygen has been chosen as 32.00, what is the molecular weight of helium? (e) If the molecular weight of oxygen had been chosen as 1.00, what would the molecular weight of helium have been? (f) Considering your answer to (e), why do you suppose that the molecular weight of oxygen was established at 32.00 rather than 1.00? (g) Why do you suppose that we obtained a value of 3.8 in (d) when the accepted value is 4.0? Would a better balance help? Explain by considering significant figures.

8 How many carbon dioxide molecules are there in (a) $\frac{1}{2}$ mole of carbon dioxide? (b) $\frac{1}{10}$ mole of carbon dioxide?

9 If the molecular weight of nitrogen is 28, what would be the mass of (a) $\frac{1}{2}$ mole of nitrogen gas? (b) $\frac{1}{10}$ mole of nitrogen gas?

10 The U.S. Government is currently spending about 200 billion dollars per year (2×10^{11} dollars/year). If spending continues at this rate, how long would it take for the government to spend one mole of dollars?

11 How many grams of each substance are represented by the following: (a) 2.0 moles of magnesium oxide (molecular weight = 40.3)? (b) 0.50 mole of sodium chloride (molecular weight = 58.5)? (c) 0.10 mole of copper (molecular weight = 63.5)? (d) 0.02 mole of silver nitrate (molecular weight = 170)?

12 How many moles of each substance are present in the following: (a) 22 grams of carbon dioxide (molecular weight = 44)? (b) 85.0 grams of ammonia (molecular weight = 17.0)? (c) 0.64 gram of copper (molecular weight = 63.5)?

13 Calculate the mass in grams of: (a) 5.00 moles of carbon (molecular weight = 12.0) (b) 10.0 moles of oxygen molecules (c) 7.00 moles of iodine (molecular weight = 254) (d) 5.00 moles of zinc oxide (molecular weight = 81.4) (e) 0.200 mole of aluminum oxide (molecular weight = 102).

14 (a) How many particles are there in 1 mole of carbon dioxide gas? (b) What volume will this gas occupy at 0 °C and 1 atmosphere (STP)? (c) What volume would $\frac{1}{2}$ mole of carbon dioxide occupy at STP? (d) What volume for $\frac{1}{10}$ mole?

15 A tank of nitrogen gas (molecular weight = 28) contains 980 grams of that gas. (a) How many moles of gas is this? (b) How many molecules of gas is this? (c) What volume would this gas occupy at 0 °C and 1.00 atm pressure (STP)? (d) If the volume of the tank is 6.0 litres, what is the pressure of the gas at 0 °C?

16 A tank of helium gas (molecular weight = 4.00) contains 144 grams of that gas. (a) How many moles of helium is this? (b) How many molecules of helium is this? (c) What volume would this gas occupy at STP? (d) If the volume of the tank is 6.0 litres, what is the pressure of the gas at 0 °C?

17 (a) What volume would you expect 1 mole of helium (molecular weight = 4.00) to occupy at STP? (b) 4.00 g of helium? (c) 2.00 g of helium? (d) 1.00 g of helium? (e) 8.00 g of helium?

Because of its practical use, and for its own intrinsic interest, the principle of the conservation of energy may be regarded as one of the great achievements of the human mind.

SIR WILLIAM CECIL DAMPIER (1867–1952)

THE ATOMIC THEORY: ONE OF OUR BEST SCIENTIFIC MODELS

3

Only a few chemical reactions involve as great an energy change as this, but all involve some energy change.

OUR KNOWLEDGE, ACQUIRED IN CHAPTER 2, THAT MOLECULES OF different gases have different masses, leads us to "wonder why." Perhaps molecules themselves are composed of still smaller particles which cause the differences in mass and other characteristics of different gases.

We find that the kind and arrangement of these smaller particles, called *atoms*, determine what kind of substance we're talking about. In all chemical reactions, from the burning of a candle to the explosion of TNT, collections of atoms break apart and new collections form. Our elastic "super-rubber" ball model apparently can be stretched and stretched. We even develop a shorthand for naming chemical particles and describing the changes which happen to them.

In the previous chapter we saw that molecules of different substances have different masses, but one gas molecule is just as effective as another in generating pressure on the walls of a container. Molecules have some similarities and some differences. Let us focus attention on the differences between collections of molecules in gases and possible explanations for these differences.

3-1   ATOMS

The gas molecule seems to be the unit particle in our "super-rubber" ball model for gases; still it would be logical to ask: can molecules be broken into simpler particles? Most of us already know the answer to this question. *Molecules can be broken into atoms.* The word *atom* is a firmly established part of our culture. We speak of the Atomic Energy Commission, an atomic power plant, the atomic bomb, the atomic age, and even of the atomic theory. What is the scientific background for our belief in atoms? Let us look again at some experiments.

3-1.1   The Combining Volumes of Gases— Chemical Change

In a darkened room we mix 1 litre of gaseous hydrogen and 1 litre of gaseous chlorine in a bulb. If we then shine an ultraviolet sunlamp on the bulb, we see a flash and hear a resounding bang. A sizable amount of energy has been released. Further, if we examine the contents of the bulb after the explosion, we find no remaining hydrogen and no chlorine. A new material called hydrogen chloride is present in the bulb. Its properties are completely different from those of the hydrogen and chlorine we used in the beginning. Chlorine, for example, is a green gas, but hydrogen chloride is colorless; these two gases can be easily distinguished by color. Both hydrogen and hydrogen chloride are colorless; but their behavior with water is strikingly different. When hydrogen is fed into an inverted bottle filled with water, hydrogen bubbles collect above the water surface. When hydrogen chloride is similarly fed into water, most of the gas disappears into the water—we say that most of the hydrogen chloride dissolves and only a small portion of the gas appears above the water surface. Many other differences could be mentioned. The new substance, hydrogen chloride, is completely different from the mixture of hydrogen and chlorine with which we started.

We say that a change resulting from a reaction such as that of hydrogen gas with chlorine gas is a **chemical change.** *In a chemical change the products are very different from the reactants and an energy change is usually observed.* The flash, bang, and heat indicate energy released.

EXERCISE 3-1

> When a spark is passed through a mixture of gaseous hydrogen and gaseous oxygen, water is produced. Is this a chemical change? Defend your answer by comparing reactants and products as to their melting points, role in combustion, and role in supporting life.

What are the molecular implications of this chemical reaction? It would be helpful to compare volumes so we could apply Avogadro's hypothesis and count molecules. Experiment shows that

$$1 \left\{ \begin{array}{l} \text{litre of} \\ \text{hydrogen} \end{array} \right\} \text{plus } 1 \left\{ \begin{array}{l} \text{litre of} \\ \text{chlorine} \end{array} \right\} \text{gives } 2 \left\{ \begin{array}{l} \text{litres of} \\ \text{hydrogen chloride} \end{array} \right\}$$

All gas volumes are measured at the same temperature and pressure. It is not important for us to know exactly how many molecules are present in 1 litre of hydrogen; we can arbitrarily represent this number as n. Avogadro's hypothesis tells us that we must also have n *molecules* of chlorine and $2n$ *molecules* of hydrogen chloride, since equal volumes of gases at the same temperature and pressure contain equal numbers of molecules. We can now write

$$n \left\{ \begin{array}{l} \text{molecules of} \\ \text{hydrogen} \end{array} \right\} + n \left\{ \begin{array}{l} \text{molecules of} \\ \text{chlorine} \end{array} \right\} \longrightarrow 2n \left\{ \begin{array}{l} \text{molecules of} \\ \text{hydrogen chloride} \end{array} \right\}$$

The symbol + now replaces "plus" and the arrow replaces "gives" in the earlier expression. If we were to let n equal 1 (a sample too small to work with), we could write

$$1 \left\{ \begin{array}{l} \text{molecule of} \\ \text{hydrogen} \end{array} \right\} + 1 \left\{ \begin{array}{l} \text{molecule of} \\ \text{chlorine} \end{array} \right\} \longrightarrow 2 \left\{ \begin{array}{l} \text{molecules of} \\ \text{hydrogen chloride} \end{array} \right\}$$

We can now make a most significant observation: each simple *molecule* of hydrogen chloride was formed from *half a molecule of hydrogen* plus *half a molecule of chlorine.* Clearly, each single molecule of hydrogen was broken into two identical pieces in the reaction. Each piece was then used to make a molecule of hydrogen chloride. Similarly, each chlorine molecule had to be broken into two identical parts in the reaction. This conclusion is not altered if we let n, the number of molecules, equal 2, 20, 3,137, or 3,721,256,372, because the value of n can be eliminated by dividing both sides of the equation by n. The number of hydrogen chloride molecules is always twice the number of molecules of hydrogen or chlorine regardless of the value of n.

Since the hydrogen molecule must be broken into two pieces in this reaction, it is convenient to identify the pieces. These smaller fragments or building blocks for molecules are the **atoms.** Experiments of the type just described provide some of the evidence for belief in the existence of atoms of hydrogen and chlorine. It is apparent that each hydrogen molecule must contain at least two atoms, since each molecule is broken into two identical parts in the formation of hydrogen chloride. The observations could also be explained if each hydrogen molecule contained four, six, eight, ten, or any even number of atoms. The observations would not be consistent with the existence of one, three, five, seven, or any odd number of hydrogen atoms in the hydrogen molecule, since a molecule containing an odd number of atoms could not be broken into two equal parts without splitting at least one atom into two pieces. According to the definitions and models we are using, an atom *cannot* be split in a *normal chemical process*. We conclude that a molecule of hydrogen must contain an even number of atoms. We can apply the same argument to the chlorine molecule. Each chlorine molecule must contain an even number of atoms. A similar study of the reaction between nitric oxide and oxygen shows that each oxygen molecule also must contain an even number of atoms:

$$2n \begin{Bmatrix} \text{molecules} \\ \text{nitric oxide} \end{Bmatrix} + n \begin{Bmatrix} \text{molecules} \\ \text{oxygen} \end{Bmatrix} \longrightarrow 2n \begin{Bmatrix} \text{molecules} \\ \text{nitrogen dioxide} \end{Bmatrix}$$

Scientists always seek the simplest explanation of the known facts. The simplest interpretation is that each molecule of hydrogen contains *two* atoms; each molecule of chlorine contains *two* atoms; and each molecule of oxygen contains *two* atoms. All experiments performed up to the present time are consistent with the simplest assumption. We conclude, then, that each molecule of hydrogen contains two hydrogen atoms, each molecule of chlorine contains two chlorine atoms, and each molecule of oxygen contains two oxygen atoms. Such molecules are said to be **diatomic.** They contain two atoms. In addition to hydrogen, chlorine, and oxygen, the elements nitrogen, fluorine, bromine, and iodine also exist as diatomic molecules. These substances occur so frequently in chemical reactions that the list is worth remembering.

Some molecules contain many more than two atoms. For example, the following volume relationships describe the formation of the gas ammonia from nitrogen and hydrogen:

$$1 \begin{Bmatrix} \text{litre} \\ \text{nitrogen} \end{Bmatrix} + 3 \begin{Bmatrix} \text{litres} \\ \text{hydrogen} \end{Bmatrix} \longrightarrow 2 \begin{Bmatrix} \text{litres} \\ \text{ammonia} \end{Bmatrix}$$

Diatomic Molecules
Bromine
Chlorine
Fluorine
Hydrogen
Iodine
Nitrogen
Oxygen

The COMBINING

VOLUMES of GASES

If we divide both sides of the equation by 2, we see that each ammonia molecule must contain half of a nitrogen molecule and three halves of a hydrogen molecule:

$$\frac{1}{2}\begin{Bmatrix}\text{litre}\\\text{nitrogen}\end{Bmatrix} + \frac{3}{2}\begin{Bmatrix}\text{litres}\\\text{hydrogen}\end{Bmatrix} \longrightarrow 1\begin{Bmatrix}\text{litre}\\\text{ammonia}\end{Bmatrix}$$

$$\frac{1}{2}\begin{Bmatrix}\text{molecule}\\\text{nitrogen}\end{Bmatrix} + \frac{3}{2}\begin{Bmatrix}\text{molecules}\\\text{hydrogen}\end{Bmatrix} \longrightarrow 1\begin{Bmatrix}\text{molecule}\\\text{ammonia}\end{Bmatrix}$$

Since half of a nitrogen molecule is one nitrogen atom and half of a hydrogen molecule is one hydrogen atom, the gas ammonia must contain one nitrogen atom and three hydrogen atoms. The ammonia molecule, then, contains four atoms.

While we needed the concept of molecules to understand or "explain" the *pressure-volume* relationship of gases, we need the concept of atoms to help us understand the *chemical changes* gases undergo.

3-1.2 Formulas and Equations

In trying to *describe* the chemical changes which occur when hydrogen gas and chlorine gas explode, we wrote

$$n\begin{Bmatrix}\text{molecules}\\\text{hydrogen}\end{Bmatrix} + n\begin{Bmatrix}\text{molecules}\\\text{chlorine}\end{Bmatrix} \longrightarrow 2n\begin{Bmatrix}\text{molecules}\\\text{hydrogen chloride}\end{Bmatrix}$$

While this statement as written is accurate and contains much information, it can be condensed. A form of scientific shorthand is desirable and available.

Suppose we represent one hydrogen atom by the symbol H. Since a hydrogen molecule contains two hydrogen atoms, the hydrogen can be represented as H—H where the line between the H's suggests some kind of bond holding the two atoms together. If a chlorine atom is represented as Cl, a chlorine molecule would be Cl—Cl, and a hydrogen chloride molecule would be H—Cl. The chemical process can now be summarized by writing a **chemical equation:**

$$\text{H—H} + \text{Cl—Cl} \longrightarrow 2\ \text{H—Cl} \tag{1}$$

In this notation it is clear that one molecule of hydrogen, containing two hydrogen atoms, combines with one molecule of chlorine, containing two chlorine atoms, to give two molecules of hydrogen chloride, each containing one hydrogen atom and one chlorine atom. Further, bonds between the hydrogen atoms in the hydrogen molecule are broken during reaction. Bonds between the chlorine atoms in the chlorine molecule are also broken during reaction. (As you will learn later, the ultraviolet light used to start the reaction breaks the bonds between the chlorine atoms. That is what initiates the explosion.) Finally, new bonds between hydrogen and chlorine must be formed to give hydrogen chloride. This breaking of bonds and formation of new bonds is one of the important characteristics of a chemical process.

EXERCISE 3-2

(1) Write an *equation* using the notation H—H for hydrogen, and so on, to represent the reaction of nitrogen and hydrogen to give ammonia (see page 45).

(2) *Two* litres of hydrogen gas combine with *1* litre of oxygen gas to give *2* litres of water vapor. Write an equation using the notation above to represent the process.

While we have simplified the notation tremendously by using H—H in place of the words "molecule of hydrogen," we can simplify the notation even further. A hydrogen molecule can be written as H_2. The subscript 2 indicates that we have two hydrogen atoms in each molecule. Similarly, the chlorine molecule can be written as Cl_2. Since the hydrogen chloride molecule contains one hydrogen atom and one chlorine atom, it is written as HCl and the bond between atoms is implied. The **chemical equation** which represents the process observed is then

$$H_2 + Cl_2 \longrightarrow 2\ HCl \tag{2}$$

The equation is simply a representation, in an abbreviated form, of laboratory observations. The notations H_2 and HCl are called the **formulas** of the molecules they represent.

EXERCISE 3-3

Use the following symbols: carbon = C, hydrogen = H, oxygen = O, nitrogen = N, and chlorine = Cl.

(1) Two litres of carbon monoxide combine with 1 litre of oxygen to give 2 litres of carbon dioxide. (All volumes are measured at the same temperature and pressure.) If carbon monoxide has the formula CO, what is the formula for carbon dioxide? Write the equation for the burning of CO to give carbon dioxide. Burning is the process in which CO combines with molecular oxygen.

(2) Two litres of nitric oxide decompose to form 1 litre of nitrogen and 1 litre of oxygen. (All volumes are measured at the same temperature and pressure.) Write the word equation for the process. Write the symbols for the *products* formed, indicating the relative numbers of molecules of each product. Now write the formula for nitric oxide.

3-1.3 Chemical Implications of Atoms

The concept of atoms brings many other benefits. By assuming the existence of atoms we can answer the question: why do molecules differ? We can explain differences between various molecules in terms of the kinds and arrangement of atoms in each molecule. For example, water is different from hydrogen chloride or ammonia because it contains a different combination of atoms arranged in a different way.

Throughout the course we shall investigate properties of substances found in nature or prepared in the laboratory; we shall seek explanations in terms of the numbers, types, and arrangements of the atoms present. Frequently, the detailed arrangement of atoms in a molecule is extremely important in defining the properties of that molecule. Many illustrations will appear as we progress.

3-1.4 Structural Formulas and Molecular Models

You have just been told that the way in which atoms are bonded is very important in determining the properties of a substance. It would be helpful to represent the *arrangement* of atoms in the molecule as well as the number and kinds of atoms present. For this purpose **structural formulas** and **models** are used. Thus, the structural formula for water is

$$\begin{array}{c} \text{O} \\ \diagup \; \diagdown \\ \text{H} \qquad \text{H} \end{array}$$

As in the case of the H—H and H—Cl molecules, the dashes indicate the chemical bonds or the connections between atoms. The angular arrangement indicates that the two hydrogen atoms and the oxygen atom do not lie in a straight line but make an H—OH angle of about 104 degrees.* Sometimes, for more complicated molecules, structural details such as bond angles cannot be represented easily on a piece of paper. A structural formula is a representation on a piece of paper of the three-dimensional molecule. For example, the molecule methane (CH_4) is represented by the planar structural formula

$$\begin{array}{c} \text{H} \\ | \\ \text{H} \!-\! \text{C} \!-\! \text{H} \\ | \\ \text{H} \end{array}$$

even though the actual molecule has four hydrogens arranged around carbon at the corners of a regular tetrahedron (see Figure 3-1).

The structural formula for methane and the actual molecular model (see Figure 3-1) illustrate that no written formula is quite as effective as a molecular model in helping to visualize molecular shapes. Since molecular shape is so important in establishing properties of substances, a number of physical models can be used to represent molecules. Some of the more commonly used models are seen in Figure 3-2. Selection of the particular kind depends upon what must be emphasized. The **ball-and-stick model** and **ball-and-spring model** indicate bond orientations. Ball-and-spring models are useful to indicate molecular flexibility and molecular vibration. The **space-filling model** provides a more realistic view of the spatial relationships and the crowding among *nonbonded atoms* and molecules. (See Figure 3-3.)

3-1.5 Atoms and Molecules in Liquids and Solids

So far, we have accumulated evidence to indicate that gases are made up of molecules and gas molecules are made up of atoms. We have

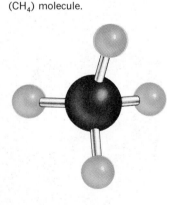

Fig. 3-1 Model of a methane (CH_4) molecule.

*Details of molecular geometry are obtained using experiments of the type described at the end of Chapter 17.

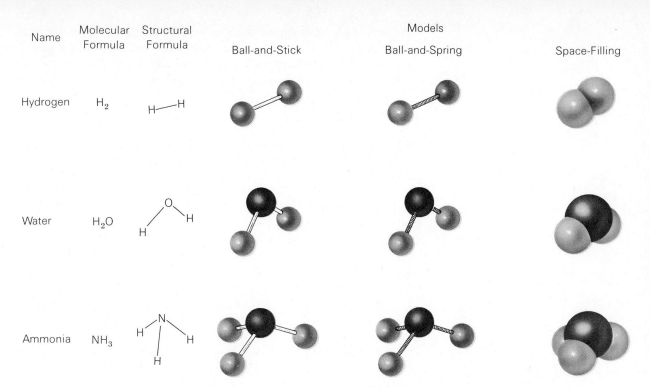

Name	Molecular Formula	Structural Formula	Models		
			Ball-and-Stick	Ball-and-Spring	Space-Filling
Hydrogen	H_2	H—H			
Water	H_2O				
Ammonia	NH_3				

also observed the burning of a candle in the laboratory. Gases such as carbon dioxide and water vapor (steam) were recognized as products of the burning of the candle.

We might now raise the question: what is the candle made of? Since a candle burns to produce gases, collections of molecules containing atoms, the simplest assumption that we can make is that the *candle itself contains molecules made up of atoms.* These "candle molecules" would then combine with the *diatomic* oxygen molecules (remember: diatomic means two atoms per molecule) to give gaseous products. This simple assumption, that *liquids and solids contain atoms and that such atoms are combined to give molecules of the liquid or solid,* is consistent with all we know about both liquids and solids. **All matter is made up of atoms.** This is the fundamental postulate of the atomic theory. The atomic theory is amazingly powerful and can well be considered the cornerstone of all modern science.

Fig. 3-2 Different representations of hydrogen (H_2), water (H_2O), and ammonia (NH_3) molecules.

Fig. 3-3 A model showing the crowding of nonbonded atoms.

3-2 ELEMENTS AND COMPOUNDS

In giving the pictorial equation for the reaction between gaseous chlorine and hydrogen we wrote

$$H—H + Cl—Cl \longrightarrow 2 \ H—Cl \qquad (1)$$

If we look at this equation, we immediately see two distinct classes of molecules. In the first class *identical atoms* are bound together to make the molecules; we see H—H and Cl—Cl. A substance made up of one kind of atom is called an **element.** The second class of molecule observed in our equation is hydrogen chloride. Pure hydrogen chloride has *identical molecules,* each of which contains one hydrogen *atom* and one chlorine *atom* in chemical combination. Hydrogen chloride, *a substance which contains more than one kind of atom in chemical combination, is a* **compound.**

3-2.1 The Elements

We repeat, *an element is a substance that contains only one kind of atom.* A few of the elements such as gold, silver, and iron were known to the ancient Greeks and Romans. At the beginning of the nineteenth century only about 26 elements were known. One hundred years later 81 elements were known. Figure 3-4 shows the number of known elements as a function of time. This graph shows that the rate of discovery of new elements is declining; further, it shows that we have about 105 known elements today. An important fact not shown by the graph is that all new elements today are made by nuclear reactions (Chapter 7); they are not discovered in nature. An extrapolation of the graph (an extension beyond the last known point) suggests that there may be a limit to the number of elements which can exist. However, many distinguished nuclear scientists now question this limit. They suggest that relatively stable elements of much higher mass may well be made in the future. If such is the case, the curve would bend sharply upward.

3-2.2 Atomic Weights and Molecular Weights

If each mole of oxygen contains 6.02×10^{23} molecules, and if each molecule of oxygen contains two atoms, then 1 *mole* of oxygen *molecules* contains 12.04×10^{23} atoms. We may ask the question: what is the mass of 1 mole (6.02×10^{23}) of oxygen *atoms?* Clearly it will be half the mass of 1 mole of oxygen *molecules,* or 16.00 g. We can then state that 1 mole of oxygen *atoms* (6.02×10^{23} atoms) will have a mass of 16.00 g. The molecular weight of a substance was defined earlier as the *relative mass* of a molecule of the substance expressed on a scale in which the oxygen molecule is assigned a value of 32.00 u. It is reasonable to define an **atomic weight** as *the mass of an atom on this same scale.* The oxygen atom has an *atomic weight* of 16.00, since the *diatomic* oxygen molecule is assigned a molecular weight of 32.00. *The*

Fig. 3-4.1 (Left) The discovery of the elements: total number of known elements as a function of time.

Fig. 3-4.2 (Right) The discovery of the elements: number of elements discovered in each half-century since 1700.

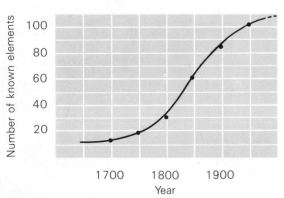

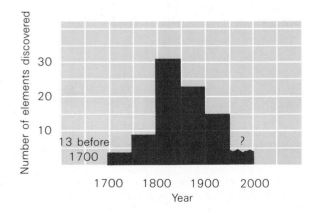

atomic weight of an atom is the relative mass of that atom expressed on a scale in which an oxygen atom is assigned a value of 16.00. One mole of atoms of an element is 6.02×10^{23} atoms. This mole of atoms has a mass equal to the atomic weight of the element expressed in grams. For oxygen the atomic weight is 16.00. One mole of oxygen *atoms* has a mass of 16.00 g. For hydrogen the atomic weight is 1.008; 1 mole of hydrogen *atoms* has a mass of 1.008 g. For carbon the atomic weight is 12.01, and 1 mole of carbon *atoms* has a mass of 12.01 g. Atomic weight values are used frequently. A table of working values is given inside the front cover. Table 3-1 on page 52 lists precise atomic weights.

Common sense tells us that the mass of an object should be equal to the sum of the masses of its parts. If we want to know the *molecular weight* of HCl, we simply add the atomic weight of one hydrogen atom and the atomic weight of one chlorine atom:

$$\text{mol wt HCl} = \text{at. wt H} + \text{at. wt Cl} = 1.0 + 35.5 = 36.5$$

EXERCISE 3-4

(1) Show that the mass of 1 mole of CO_2 is 44.0 g.
(2) Show that the mass of 1 mole of SO_2 is 64.1 g.
(3) Calculate the mass in grams of 6.02×10^{23} molecules of CO. Calculate the mass in grams of 3.01×10^{23} molecules of fluorine (F_2).

EXERCISE 3-5

What is the molecular weight of hydrogen cyanide (HCN)? (Use the table of atomic weights inside the front cover.) How many moles of HCN are present in a 2.7-g sample? (*Answer:* mol wt of HCN = 27.0; 0.10 mole HCN.)

EXERCISE 3-6

What is the molecular weight of carbon tetrachloride (CCl_4)? How many moles are contained in a 7.7-g sample of CCl_4? (*Answer:* mol wt of CCl_4 = 154; 0.050 mole CCl_4.)

EXERCISE 3-7

What is the mass, in grams, of 0.10 mole of HCl? (Use atomic weights.)

EDWARD WICHERS
(1892–   )

Edward Wichers is an American chemist who spent most of his professional life with the United States Bureau of Standards in Washington, D.C. Although a distinguished chemist in his own right, Dr. Wichers is given special recognition here for his role as a scientific statesman. As a result of his leadership, professional competence, and dedication, separate atomic weight scales used by chemists and physicists were abandoned in 1961 and replaced by a new scale. Carbon-12 was selected as the new atomic weight standard and assigned a value of 12.000000. This careful choice resulted in a minimum number of changes for chemists and physicists. Dr. Wichers' resolution of one of the more difficult organizational problems of science has simplified life for future generations of scientists.

Edward Wichers played a key role in the International Union of Pure and Applied Chemistry for many years, serving as its vice-president from 1952–1959. He retired as Associate Director of the Bureau of Standards in 1962.

*Actually, atomic weight is now based on a *specific* carbon atom as a standard. This standard is difficult to describe in terms of experiments at this time. The change from oxygen to a specific carbon atom is unimportant in most chemistry. It is only −0.0045 percent change. The difference may be important in nuclear processes. A table of precise atomic weights is given in Table 3-1.

ATOMIC WEIGHTS and

MOLECULAR WEIGHTS

TABLE **3-1** ATOMIC WEIGHTS ACCEPTED BY THE INTERNATIONAL
UNION OF PURE AND APPLIED CHEMISTRY

Name	Symbol	Atomic Number	Atomic Weight	Name	Symbol	Atomic Number	Atomic Weight
Actinium	Ac	89	(227)*	Molybdenum	Mo	42	95.94
Aluminum	Al	13	26.9815	Neodymium	Nd	60	144.24
Americium	Am	95	(243)	Neon	Ne	10	20.179
Antimony	Sb	51	121.75	Neptunium	Np	93	(237)
Argon	Ar	18	39.948	Nickel	Ni	28	58.70
Arsenic	As	33	74.9216	Niobium	Nb	41	92.906
Astatine	At	85	(210)	Nitrogen	N	7	14.0067
Barium	Ba	56	137.34	Nobelium	No	102	(259)
Berkelium	Bk	97	(247)	Osmium	Os	76	190.2
Beryllium	Be	4	9.0122	Oxygen	O	8	15.9994
Bismuth	Bi	83	208.980	Palladium	Pd	46	106.4
Boron	B	5	10.811	Phosphorus	P	15	30.9738
Bromine	Br	35	79.904	Platinum	Pt	78	195.09
Cadmium	Cd	48	112.40	Plutonium	Pu	94	(244)
Calcium	Ca	20	40.08	Polonium	Po	84	(209)
Californium	Cf	98	(251)	Potassium	K	19	39.098
Carbon	C	6	12.01115	Praseodymium	Pr	59	140.908
Cerium	Ce	58	140.12	Promethium	Pm	61	(145)
Cesium	Cs	55	132.905	Protactinium	Pa	91	(231)
Chlorine	Cl	17	35.453	Radium	Ra	88	(226)
Chromium	Cr	24	51.996	Radon	Rn	86	(222)
Cobalt	Co	27	58.9332	Rhenium	Re	75	186.2
Copper	Cu	29	63.546	Rhodium	Rh	45	102.906
Curium	Cm	96	(247)	Rubidium	Rb	37	85.47
Dysprosium	Dy	66	162.50	Ruthenium	Ru	44	101.07
Einsteinium	Es	99	(254)	Samarium	Sm	62	150.35
Erbium	Er	68	167.26	Scandium	Sc	21	44.956
Europium	Eu	63	151.96	Selenium	Se	34	78.96
Fermium	Fm	100	(257)	Silicon	Si	14	28.086
Fluorine	F	9	18.9984	Silver	Ag	47	107.868
Francium	Fr	87	(223)	Sodium	Na	11	22.9898
Gadolinium	Gd	64	157.25	Strontium	Sr	38	87.62
Gallium	Ga	31	69.72	Sulfur	S	16	32.064
Germanium	Ge	32	72.59	Tantalum	Ta	73	180.948
Gold	Au	79	196.967	Technetium	Tc	43	(97)
Hafnium	Hf	72	178.49	Tellurium	Te	52	127.60
Helium	He	2	4.0026	Terbium	Tb	65	158.925
Holmium	Ho	67	164.930	Thallium	Tl	81	204.37
Hydrogen	H	1	1.00797	Thorium	Th	90	232.038
Indium	In	49	114.82	Thulium	Tm	69	168.934
Iodine	I	53	126.9045	Tin	Sn	50	118.69
Iridium	Ir	77	192.2	Titanium	Ti	22	47.90
Iron	Fe	26	55.847	Tungsten	W	74	183.85
Krypton	Kr	36	83.80	Uranium	U	92	238.03
Lanthanum	La	57	138.91	Vanadium	V	23	50.941
Lawrencium	Lr	103	(260)	Xenon	Xe	54	131.30
Lead	Pb	82	207.2	Ytterbium	Yb	70	173.04
Lithium	Li	3	6.941	Yttrium	Y	39	88.906
Lutetium	Lu	71	174.97	Zinc	Zn	30	65.38
Magnesium	Mg	12	24.305	Zirconium	Zr	40	91.22
Manganese	Mn	25	54.9380	—	—	104†	(261)
Mendelevium	Md	101	(258)	—	—	105	(262)
Mercury	Hg	80	200.59				

* For those elements all of whose isotopes are radioactive, the parentheses indicate the isotope with the longest half-life. (For a definition of *half-life*, see Section 7-3.2.)
† The names and symbols of elements 104 and 105 have not yet been determined.

3-2.3 More on Symbols, Formulas, and Names

SYMBOLS OF THE ELEMENTS

In Section 3-1.2 we explored ways for effectively representing chemical processes. Word equations and equations using symbols were given. The obvious choice of the symbol to represent an element was the first letter of the name of the element. We chose O for oxygen, H for hydrogen, N for nitrogen, and C for carbon. Eight other elements* are named by this simple and obvious convention.

Since there are 105 elements to name but only 26 letters to use, it is obvious that a second letter must be used to identify some elements. What choices for the second letter are most reasonable? Since chemistry is an international subject, international agreement on symbols is desirable. Although difficult to get, such agreement has been obtained. The symbols listed in Table 3-1 have been adopted by the International Union of Pure and Applied Chemistry, an international organization of chemists. After using just the first letter of the name for a symbol, the most obvious choice is the first *two* letters of the name. Many elements are named by this convention: helium is He, lithium is Li, beryllium is Be, neon is Ne, aluminum is Al, silicon is Si, argon is Ar, calcium is Ca, and titanium is Ti. Some additional elements have been named using this convention. How many of the group of 34 can you identify? (See Table 3-1.)

In a few cases it is convenient to use the first letter followed by a letter *other than* the second letter of the name. Frequently the choice of the second letter is obvious from the sound of the name. For example, magnesium is Mg, chlorine is Cl, chromium is Cr, manganese is Mn, and zinc is Zn. Many additional elements have been named in this way.

Finally, ten rather common elements have symbols derived from the Latin name of the element rather than the English name. Indeed, many elements in this group are easily obtained from their ores and were therefore known to the alchemists, hence the Latin name. For example, gold is Au from the Latin *aurum* and silver is Ag from the Latin *argentum*. Because the elements in this group are rather common and their symbols are frequently needed, these are collected in Table 3-2 (page 54). You are urged to look over these eleven symbols.

FORMULAS AND NAMES

We indicated earlier that the symbols for the elements can be used in writing formulas for molecules. The hydrogen molecule is H_2, hydrogen chloride is HCl, and water is H_2O. We repeat: the symbols have a *quantitative* significance. In the formula of a molecule containing hydrogen, H stands for *one* atom. A molecule of ordinary table sugar has the formula $C_{12}H_{22}O_{11}$ because the sugar molecule contains 12 carbon atoms, 22 hydrogen atoms, and 11 oxygen atoms. Note that the hydrogen and oxygen are present in a 2 to 1 ratio, just as they are in water. This formula suggested to earlier chemists that sugar was

---

*These elements are boron, fluorine, sulfur, phosphorus, iodine, vanadium, uranium, and yttrium.

Common Name	Symbol	Symbol Source*
Antimony	Sb	stibnum
Copper	Cu	cuprum
Gold	Au	aurum
Iron	Fe	ferrum
Lead	Pb	plumbum
Mercury	Hg	hydrargyrum
Potassium	K	kalium
Silver	Ag	argentum
Sodium	Na	natrium
Tin	Sn	stannum
Tungsten	W	wolfram

*All entries in this column are Latin, except for *wolfram*, which is German.

made from carbon and water, hence was a **hydrate** of carbon. Traces of the ancient idea are still found in our listing of sugar as a carbo*hydrate* (carbon-hydrate).

NOMENCLATURE

We have indicated both names and symbols for many *elements*. What about the names of *compounds?* Is there logic to the system naming them? The answer is a qualified "yes." There are some rules, but they—like the rules of grammar—are not always obeyed in practice.

The simplest kind of compound is one containing only two *kinds* of atoms. This is called a **binary compound.** The name of a binary compound is formed by taking the name of the element most like a metal, joining it to the stem of the name of the element least like a metal, and adding *-ide*. Let us see how this works. Common table salt is NaCl; the name is sodium chloride. *Chlor-* is the stem of chlorine. We add *-ide* for the second part of the name of the substance. Similarly, the compound $CaCl_2$ is named calcium chloride. It is used on the roads in the summer to keep down dust. We have already called the compound HCl hydrogen chloride. The gas H_2S is hydrogen sulfide.

EXERCISE 3-8

Name: Na_2S, CaF_2, MgO, Al_2O_3, and $ScCl_3$. The stem of oxygen is *ox-*, of fluorine *fluor-*, of sulfur *sulf-*.

At times *more than one kind of molecule containing the same two kinds of atoms* can be formed. For example, carbon forms at least two compounds with oxygen, CO and CO_2. If we apply the rule for naming binary compounds, we would say there are two carbon *ox*ides. In order to differentiate these oxides, one is called carbon *mon*oxide and the other is called carbon *di*oxide. The prefix *mono-* means one; *di-* means two. Other prefixes are listed in Table 3-3. Thus, carbon monoxide is an oxide containing one carbon atom and one oxygen atom. (When the number of carbon atoms is not specified, one atom is assumed.) Carbon dioxide contains one carbon atom and two oxygen atoms. Sulfur trioxide is SO_3. Carbon tetrafluoride is CF_4. Nitrogen trifluoride is NF_3, while N_2F_2 is dinitrogen difluoride.

3-3 BALANCED CHEMICAL EQUATIONS— SYMBOLS TO SHOW THE CONSERVATION OF MASS

Some of the advantages of the atomic theory and its symbols are obvious, but some very important ones remain hidden. For example, by using the atomic theory we can tell how much of a given product will be obtained from known amounts of reactants. Let us examine these numerical or quantitative relationships using the mole as the measuring unit.

3-3.1 The Conservation of Mass

As a consequence of our discussion in Section 3-1.1 we find that if a chemical equation is properly written, it must ultimately show that *the total number of atoms of each kind does not change as a result of the reaction.* This idea was one of the basic postulates of John Dalton when he proposed the atomic theory. He wrote: "We might as well attempt to introduce a new planet into the solar system, or to annihilate one already in existence, as to create or destroy a particle of hydrogen." We observed this principle when we wrote equations based on combining volume relationships. For example, when hydrogen burns, our observations can be summarized by writing

$$2 \begin{Bmatrix} \text{volumes} \\ \text{hydrogen} \\ \text{gas} \end{Bmatrix} \text{ plus } 1 \begin{Bmatrix} \text{volume} \\ \text{oxygen} \\ \text{gas} \end{Bmatrix} \text{ gives } 2 \begin{Bmatrix} \text{volumes} \\ \text{water} \\ \text{vapor} \end{Bmatrix} \text{ plus } \begin{Bmatrix} \text{energy} \\ \text{as heat} \end{Bmatrix} \quad (3)$$

Remembering that an *equation is simply a special shorthand notation for laboratory observations,* we can reduce this description to the following equation:

$$2 \text{ H}_2 + \text{O}_2 \longrightarrow 2 \text{ H}_2\text{O} + \text{energy as heat} \quad (4)$$

There are four hydrogen atoms on the left and four hydrogen atoms on the right. Similarly, there are two oxygen atoms on both the left and the right. In chemical reactions atoms are *conserved*. In other words, *atoms are neither created nor destroyed in chemical reactions.* Since we often measure a quantity in terms of its mass, we say that *mass is conserved.* This fact, summarized as the **Law of Conservation of Mass,** is true within our ability to weigh on laboratory balances. The conservation of mass is fundamental to our use of arithmetic in chemical equations. A chemical equation is **balanced** when it shows conservation of numbers of atoms and, consequently, conservation of mass.

The CONSERVATION of MASS

3-3.2 Writing Balanced Equations for Reactions

How can we write a balanced equation for a reaction? We must:

(1) Know what reactants are consumed and what products are formed. (This information is obtained in the laboratory.)
(2) Know the correct formula of each reactant and each product. (This information is calculated from laboratory observations and will be discussed in detail in Chapter 19.)
(3) Satisfy the Law of Conservation of Atoms.

These steps were applied one at a time when we wrote the balanced equation for the burning of hydrogen gas in oxygen to give water vapor or the burning of hydrogen gas in chlorine to give hydrogen chloride. These steps can be applied equally well to reactions involving both solids and gases. For example, metallic magnesium burns in air to give magnesium oxide, heat, and a dazzling white light. Careful experiments have shown that gaseous oxygen from the air is used in this burning operation. Further experiments show that the product formed (magnesium oxide) has the formula MgO. Let us now carry out steps (1) and (2) by writing down the correct formulas for all reactants and products.

$$Mg + O_2 \longrightarrow MgO + \text{energy as heat and light} \qquad (5)$$

This expression does not yet conserve atoms. To conserve atoms we must place appropriate numbers before each formula so that the same numbers of atoms of each element appear on both the left- and right-hand sides of the equation. *We must not change the formulas in this process since they came from separate laboratory studies.*

Let us start the balancing operation by arbitrarily considering one molecule of oxygen. Since one molecule of oxygen contains *two atoms* of oxygen, it will form *two* molecules of MgO.* (Each molecule of MgO contains *one* atom of oxygen, as the absence of a subscript tells us.) We then write

$$? \, Mg + 1 \, O_2 \longrightarrow 2 \, MgO + \text{energy} \qquad (6)$$

The question mark reminds us that the number of atoms of Mg has not been decided yet. Clearly, two Mg atoms are now needed on the left-hand side of the equation; hence we write

$$2 \, Mg + 1 \, O_2 \longrightarrow 2 \, MgO + \text{energy} \qquad (7)$$

The equation (7) is now balanced: we have the same number of magnesium and oxygen atoms on both the left- and right-hand sides of the equation.

*As you will see later, solid MgO does not contain distinct molecules of MgO, but the idea of an MgO molecule to define the mole is convenient and acceptable.

3-3.3 Balanced Equations and the Mole

Suppose we were to start with *two* oxygen molecules instead of one. We would then have four oxygen atoms, which would produce four units of MgO. Clearly, four Mg atoms would be required. We could then write

$$(2 \times 2\ Mg) + (2 \times 1\ O_2) \longrightarrow (2 \times 2\ MgO) + (2 \times energy) \quad (8)$$

The original numbers in front of each substance on both the left- and right-hand sides of the balanced equation (7) can be multiplied by 2 *or any other number,* just as long as every coefficient is multiplied by the same number. We can write for the general case

$$(n \times 2\ Mg) + (n \times 1\ O_2) \longrightarrow (n \times 2\ MgO) + (n \times energy) \quad (9)$$

EXERCISE 3-9

Show that atoms are conserved when $n = 8$ and when $n = 44$ in equation (9).

EXERCISE 3-10

Suppose ten hydrogen molecules and ten oxygen molecules are mixed. How many molecules of water could be formed? What would be left over? (*Answer:* ten water molecules formed; five oxygen molecules left over.)

EXERCISE 3-11

One million oxygen molecules react with sufficient hydrogen molecules to form water molecules. How many water molecules are formed? How many hydrogen molecules are consumed?

If n were 6.02×10^{23}, we could write

$$(6.02 \times 10^{23} \times 2\ Mg) + (6.02 \times 10^{23} \times 1\ O_2) \longrightarrow$$
$$(6.02 \times 10^{23} \times 2\ MgO) + (6.02 \times 10^{23}\ energy) \quad (10)$$

or

2 moles magnesium atoms + 1 mole oxygen gas $\longrightarrow$
$$\text{2 moles magnesium oxide} + \text{much more energy} \quad (10a)$$

Numbers of atoms are conserved as before; the equation is balanced. *The balanced equation can be interpreted in terms of moles as well as individual atoms and molecules.* We can always multiply the coefficients by a common factor or divide by a common factor and obtain equally valid equations. In all equations the coefficient 1 may be dropped, but it is never wrong to retain it.

3-3.4 Balanced Equations and Mass Balance

As in the burning of hydrogen, our balanced equation shows the conservation of mass. Two moles of magnesium metal have a mass of 48.6 g. (See the table on page 52.) One mole of oxygen has a mass of 32.0 g. These combine to give $48.6 + 32.0 = 80.6$ g of MgO. Let us summarize the information given to us by a balanced equation.

$$2\,Mg + O_2 \longrightarrow 2\,MgO + energy \tag{11}$$

$$2\begin{Bmatrix}\text{magnesium} \\ \text{atoms}\end{Bmatrix} + 1\begin{Bmatrix}\text{oxygen} \\ \text{molecule}\end{Bmatrix} \longrightarrow$$
$$2\begin{Bmatrix}\text{magnesium} \\ \text{oxide} \\ \text{molecules}\end{Bmatrix} + \{energy\} \tag{11a}$$

$$2\begin{Bmatrix}\text{moles} \\ \text{magnesium} \\ \text{atoms}\end{Bmatrix} + 1\begin{Bmatrix}\text{mole} \\ \text{oxygen} \\ \text{molecules}\end{Bmatrix} \longrightarrow$$
$$2\begin{Bmatrix}\text{moles magnesium} \\ \text{oxide molecules}\end{Bmatrix} + \{energy\} \tag{11b}$$

$$48.6\begin{Bmatrix}\text{grams} \\ \text{magnesium} \\ \text{metal}\end{Bmatrix} + 32.0\begin{Bmatrix}\text{grams} \\ \text{oxygen} \\ \text{gas}\end{Bmatrix} \longrightarrow$$
$$80.6\begin{Bmatrix}\text{grams} \\ \text{magnesium} \\ \text{oxide solid}\end{Bmatrix} + \{energy\} \tag{11c}$$

If equation (11) can imply moles [equation (11b) above], we can just as well begin by choosing 1 mole of magnesium metal (24.3 g). This will form 1 mole of magnesium oxide. One mole of magnesium oxide contains 1 mole of oxygen atoms. This is the number of oxygen atoms contained in $\frac{1}{2}$ mole of oxygen molecules. Thus, we can write

$$1\,Mg + \tfrac{1}{2}\,O_2 \longrightarrow 1\,MgO + energy \tag{12}$$

This is also a balanced equation. It is just as correct as the original balanced equation involving whole numbers and can be converted to the original if we multiply both sides of the equation by 2.

3-3.5 Other Examples

Let us examine a somewhat more complex equation associated with the burning of natural gas. Natural gas is largely methane, which has the formula CH_4. When methane burns, it produces carbon dioxide (CO_2) and water (H_2O). Oxygen from the air is also used. Whenever fuels containing carbon and hydrogen are burned completely, oxygen is a reactant and carbon dioxide and water are products. The equation summarizing these experimental facts is

$$?\,CH_4 + ?\,O_2 \longrightarrow ?\,CO_2 + ?\,H_2O + energy \tag{13}$$

Let us arbitrarily select 1 mole of methane as our starting quantity. Since 1 mole of methane contains 1 mole of carbon atoms, *1 mole of* CO_2 will be generated. We now can write

$$1 \ CH_4 + ? \ O_2 \longrightarrow 1 \ CO_2 + ? \ H_2O + energy \qquad (13a)$$

As before, the question marks remind us that we have not yet determined the numbers for oxygen and water. Since 1 mole of methane (CH_4) contains 4 moles of hydrogen atoms, 2 moles of water (H_2O) will be generated:

$$1 \ CH_4 + ? \ O_2 \longrightarrow 1 \ CO_2 + 2 \ H_2O + energy \qquad (13b)$$

The products now contain 2 moles of oxygen atoms in 1 mole of CO_2 (1×2) and 2 moles of oxygen atoms in 2 moles of H_2O (2×1). A total of 4 *moles of oxygen atoms*—or 2 moles of oxygen molecules (O_2)—is required:

$$1 \ CH_4 + 2 \ O_2 \longrightarrow 1 \ CO_2 + 2 \ H_2O + energy \qquad (14)$$

Check the atoms on both sides of the equation to be sure that everything balances.

EXERCISE 3-12

Balance the equation for the combustion of CH_4 starting with 1 mole of O_2 rather than 1 mole of CH_4; then show that the equation is balanced.

EXERCISE 3-13

Ammonia gas (NH_3) can be burned with oxygen gas (O_2) to give nitrogen gas (N_2) and water (H_2O). See if you can follow the logic of the following steps in balancing this reaction.

$$NH_3 + O_2 \longrightarrow N_2 + H_2O$$
$$NH_3 + O_2 \longrightarrow 1 \ N_2 + H_2O$$
$$2 \ NH_3 + O_2 \longrightarrow 1 \ N_2 + H_2O$$
$$2 \ NH_3 + O_2 \longrightarrow 1 \ N_2 + 3 \ H_2O$$
$$2 \ NH_3 + \tfrac{3}{2} O_2 \longrightarrow 1 \ N_2 + 3 \ H_2O$$

State briefly what was done in each step.

The same logic is used in writing a balanced equation for the burning of candle wax or paraffin. Paraffin (candle wax) is made up of molecules of several sizes. We shall use the molecular formula $C_{25}H_{52}$ as representative of its molecules. Since the numbers are larger, the system appears to be more complex, but the technique is just the same. One mole of candle wax contains the Avogadro number (6.02×10^{23}) of these molecules ($C_{25}H_{52}$). The starting expression is then

$$C_{25}H_{52} + O_2 \longrightarrow CO_2 + H_2O \qquad (15)$$

Let us start with 1 mole of paraffin since this formula contains the largest number of atoms in the above equation. Since there are 25 moles of carbon atoms in 1 mole of paraffin, we must form 25 moles of CO_2.

$$1 \ C_{25}H_{52} + ? \ O_2 \longrightarrow 25 \ CO_2 + ? \ H_2O \qquad (15a)$$

Since there are 52 moles of hydrogen atoms in 1 mole of paraffin, we must form 52/2 or 26 moles of H_2O.

$$1 \ C_{25}H_{52} + ? \ O_2 \longrightarrow 25 \ CO_2 + 26 \ H_2O \qquad (15b)$$

Again a question mark is used for numbers which are not yet established. Note that we need 25 moles of oxygen molecules to form the CO_2 and 26/2 or 13 moles of oxygen molecules to form the 26 moles of H_2O. Then, $25 + 13 = 38$ moles of oxygen molecules. We can now write the balanced equation

$$1 \ C_{25}H_{52} + 38 \ O_2 \longrightarrow 25 \ CO_2 + 26 \ H_2O \qquad (16)$$

EXERCISE 3-14

Check the number of atoms on each side of the equation for the burning of paraffin to show that it is balanced.

EXERCISE 3-15

Balance the equation for the burning (combustion) of sugar ($C_{12}H_{22}O_{11}$) in O_2 to give CO_2 and H_2O.

3-4 CALCULATIONS BASED UPON BALANCED CHEMICAL EQUATIONS

In Section 2-2 we learned to convert grams of a pure substance to moles of substance and litres of gas to moles of gas. In Section 3-3 we learned to balance chemical equations. These two skills can now be combined to help us determine the quantities of reactants and products involved in a chemical process. Let us see how this works.

A balanced chemical equation tells us that a definite number of *moles* of reactants will give a definite number of *moles* of products. The mole is the unit involved in the chemical equation. On the other hand, a laboratory chemist measures materials in units such as grams or litres. If laboratory observations are to be used in chemical equations, masses or volumes must be converted to moles. When this has been done, the balanced equation can be used to determine how many moles of product are produced from the reactants used. Once the number of moles of products has been established, it is an easy matter to convert this quantity back to appropriate laboratory units such as grams or litres. We shall start with a simple example to illustrate a general procedure which is applicable to many chemical problems.

Example (1)   What mass of magnesium oxide would be produced by burning 7.29 grams of magnesium atoms?

The balanced equation is

$$2 \text{ Mg} + O_2 \longrightarrow 2 \text{ MgO} + \text{energy} \qquad (11)$$

(a)   Our first step is to change 7.29 grams of magnesium atoms to moles of magnesium (review Section 2-2.4):

$$\frac{7.29 \text{ g Mg}}{24.3 \text{ g Mg/mole Mg}} = 0.300 \text{ mole Mg} \qquad (17)$$

(b)   The balanced equation shows that for every 2 moles of magnesium burned, 2 moles of magnesium oxide are formed. For 0.300 mole of magnesium atoms, 0.300 mole of MgO would be formed:

$$0.300 \text{ mole Mg} \times \frac{2 \text{ moles MgO}}{2 \text{ moles Mg}} = 0.300 \text{ mole MgO} \quad (18)$$

FROM PROBLEM   FROM EQUATION

(c)   The third step is to convert the 0.300 mole of MgO into the desired laboratory units (grams).

$$0.300 \text{ mole MgO} \times \frac{40.3 \text{ grams MgO}}{1 \text{ mole MgO}} = 12.1 \text{ grams MgO} \quad (19)$$

Example (2)   The relationships used in Example (1) could equally well be used to answer another question: how many litres of oxygen gas (at STP) are necessary to burn 7.29 grams of magnesium?

The balanced equation is

$$2 \text{ Mg} + O_2 \longrightarrow 2 \text{ MgO} + \text{energy} \qquad (11)$$

(a)   This step remains the same:

$$\frac{7.29 \text{ g Mg}}{24.3 \text{ g Mg/mole Mg}} = 0.300 \text{ mole Mg} \qquad (17)$$

(b)   From the balanced equation, we see that for every *two* moles of magnesium burned, *one* mole of O_2 is needed. For 0.300 mole of Mg, we need $\frac{1}{2} \times 0.300$ or 0.150 mole of O_2:

$$0.300 \text{ mole Mg} \times \frac{1 \text{ mole } O_2}{2 \text{ moles Mg}} = 0.150 \text{ mole } O_2 \quad (20)$$

FROM PROBLEM   FROM EQUATION

(c)   The third step is to find the volume which 0.150 mole of O_2

occupies at STP. Remember that 1 mole of O_2 at STP occupies 22.4 litres; then we can write

$$0.150 \text{ \st{mole } \st{O_2}} \times \frac{22.4 \text{ litres } O_2 \text{ (at STP)}}{1 \text{ \st{mole } \st{O_2}}}$$

$$= 3.36 \text{ litres } O_2 \text{ at STP} \quad (21)$$

3-4.1 Steps in the Procedure

Our procedure as outlined above consists of three clearly recognizable steps.

Step I. Convert "laboratory units" of the problem to moles. (See Sections 2-2.4 and 2-2.5.) Grams can be converted to moles by using the relationship

$$\text{number of moles} = \frac{\text{number of grams}}{\text{molecular weight}}$$

The volume of a gas can be converted to moles by the relationship

number of moles

$$= \frac{\text{volume of gas under defined conditions}}{\text{molar volume of gas under those defined conditions}}$$

Step II. Use the balanced equation to determine the ratio of moles of what is asked for in the problem to moles of what is "given" in the problem. Using this ratio and the number of moles of "given," calculate the number of moles of unknown. That is, if 0.300 mole of Mg is given in the problem, the ratio of moles Mg to moles MgO, being 1:1, tells us that 0.300 mole of MgO will be produced.

Step III. Convert the number of moles obtained in Step II to the desired laboratory units. This is the reverse of Step I. Moles can be converted into grams by using the relationship:

$$\text{number of grams} = \text{number of moles} \times \text{molecular weight}$$

Moles of gas can be converted into litres of gas by the relationship:

$$\{\text{number of litres}\} = \left\{ \begin{array}{l} \text{number of} \\ \text{moles gas} \end{array} \right\} \times \left\{ \begin{array}{l} \text{molar volume of} \\ \text{gas at the conditions} \\ \text{specified in the} \\ \text{problem} \end{array} \right.$$

3-4.2 Other Examples of Calculations

In Section 3-3.5 we balanced the equation for the burning of methane:

$$CH_4 + 2\,O_2 \longrightarrow CO_2 + 2\,H_2O + \text{energy} \quad (14)$$

Example (3) How many grams of water vapor will result from the burning of 24.0 grams of methane?

(a)
$$\frac{24.0 \text{ g } CH_4}{16.0 \text{ g } CH_4/\text{mole } CH_4} = 1.50 \text{ moles } CH_4 \qquad (22)$$

(b)
$$1.50 \text{ moles } CH_4 \times \frac{2 \text{ moles } H_2O}{1 \text{ mole } CH_4} = 3.00 \text{ moles } H_2O \qquad (23)$$

(c)
$$3.00 \text{ moles } H_2O \times \frac{18.0 \text{ g } H_2O}{1 \text{ mole } H_2O} = 54.0 \text{ g } H_2O \qquad (24)$$

Example (4) What volume of CO_2, measured at STP, will result from the burning of 24.0 grams of methane?

(a) From Example (3),
$$24.0 \text{ grams } CH_4 = 1.50 \text{ moles } CH_4 \qquad (25)$$

(b)
$$1.50 \text{ moles } CH_4 \times \frac{1 \text{ mole } CO_2}{1 \text{ mole } CH_4} = 1.50 \text{ moles } CO_2 \qquad (26)$$

(c)
$$1.50 \text{ moles } CO_2 \times \frac{22.4 \text{ litres } CO_2 \text{ (at STP)}}{1 \text{ mole } CO_2} = 33.6 \text{ litres } CO_2 \quad (27)$$

Example (5) Ammonia gas can be burned under appropriate conditions to give water and nitric oxide. The balanced equation is

$$4 \text{ NH}_3 + 5 \text{ O}_2 \longrightarrow 4 \text{ NO} + 6 \text{ H}_2O \qquad (28)$$

(a) How many moles of oxygen are required to burn 68 g of ammonia?

First we might ask: how many moles of ammonia are found in 68 g of NH_3? Using the information from Section 2-2, we can write

$$\frac{68 \text{ g } NH_3}{17 \text{ g } NH_3/\text{mole } NH_3} = \frac{68}{17} \text{ moles } NH_3 = 4.0 \text{ moles } NH_3 \quad (29)$$

Then

$$4.0 \text{ moles } NH_3 \times \underbrace{\frac{5 \text{ moles } O_2}{4 \text{ moles } NH_3}}_{\substack{\text{FROM BALANCED} \\ \text{EQUATION}}}$$

$$= 5.0 \text{ moles } O_2 \text{ to burn 68 g } NH_3 \quad (30)$$

(b) How many grams of nitric oxide will be produced?

The balanced equation tells us that 4.0 moles of NH_3 will yield 4.0 moles of NO:

$$4.0 \text{ moles } NH_3 \times \frac{4.0 \text{ moles } NO}{4.0 \text{ moles } NH_3} = 4.0 \text{ moles } NO \qquad (31)$$

If 1 mole of NO has a mass of 30 g (14 + 16 = 30), then 4.0 moles have a mass of

$$4.0 \text{ moles NO} \times \frac{30 \text{ g NO}}{\text{mole NO}} = 120 \text{ g NO} \qquad (32)$$

(c) What mass of water will be produced if we burn 10 g of NH_3?

The first step involves conversion of grams of ammonia to moles of NH_3 using the methods of Section 2-2. We write

$$\frac{10 \text{ g NH}_3}{17 \text{ g NH}_3/\text{mole NH}_3} = 0.59 \text{ mole NH}_3 \qquad (33)$$

The second step involves determining the number of moles of H_2O produced by 0.59 mole of NH_3.

$$0.59 \text{ mole NH}_3 \times \frac{6 \text{ moles H}_2\text{O}}{4 \text{ moles NH}_3} = 0.88 \text{ mole H}_2\text{O} \qquad (34)$$

The third and final step involves converting moles of water to grams of water. Simple multiplication is required:

$$0.88 \text{ mole H}_2\text{O} \times \frac{18 \text{ g H}_2\text{O}}{\text{mole H}_2\text{O}} = 16 \text{ g H}_2\text{O} \qquad (35)$$

In actual practice it is not necessary to work out the arithmetic of each step before proceeding to the next step. The entire problem can be formulated as follows:

$$10 \text{ g NH}_3 \times \frac{1 \text{ mole NH}_3}{17 \text{ g NH}_3} \times \frac{6 \text{ moles H}_2\text{O}}{4 \text{ moles NH}_3} \times \frac{18 \text{ g H}_2\text{O}}{\text{mole H}_2\text{O}}$$
$$= 16 \text{ g H}_2\text{O} \quad (36)$$

Note that units reduce until only grams of H_2O remain.

EXERCISE 3-16

Show that 3.80 moles of oxygen are needed to burn 35.2 g of paraffin by the reaction considered in Exercise 3-14.

EXERCISE 3-17

How many moles of oxygen (O_2) are required to produce 242 g of magnesium oxide (MgO) by the equation

$$2 \text{ Mg} + 1 \text{ O}_2 \longrightarrow 2 \text{ MgO}$$

(1) Write the equation for the reaction which took place in Experiment 8.

(2) In Experiment 8 you determined the number of moles of copper which reacted with the silver nitrate solution. How many moles of copper were in the wire assembly at the start?

(3) Why do you not use the value obtained in (2) to help you find the coefficients in the equation for (1)?

3-5 ENERGY CHANGE IN CHEMICAL REACTIONS: THE CONSERVATION OF ENERGY

Up to the present time, we have been careful to identify the number of moles of each reactant and the number of moles of each product involved in a given chemical equation; but we have been content to simply write "energy" for the energy produced. On the other hand, Experiment 9 has shown that the burning of a given mass of candle gives a definite and identifiable quantity of heat energy. The **calorie** is the unit which we used to measure heat energy. It is the quantity of energy required to raise the temperature of 1 g of water 1 °C. In measuring large amounts of heat, we frequently use the kilocalorie. One kilocalorie = 1,000 calories.

If we burn twice as much candle, twice as much heat will be generated. Our equation should show this fact. A similar relationship is established in burning magnesium to give magnesium oxide. If we allow 1 mole of magnesium atoms to react with $\frac{1}{2}$ mole of gaseous oxygen molecules, forming 1 mole of magnesium oxide, 146,000 calories of energy (heat) will be evolved.* This fact can be expressed by adding a quantitative energy term to our balanced equation:

$$Mg(solid) + \tfrac{1}{2} O_2(gas) \longrightarrow MgO(solid) + 146{,}000 \text{ cal}$$

or

$$Mg(solid) + \tfrac{1}{2} O_2(gas) \longrightarrow MgO(solid) + 146 \text{ kcal} \qquad (37)$$

The quantity of energy liberated when 1 mole of magnesium is burned to give 1 mole of magnesium oxide is called the **molar heat of combustion** of magnesium.

Obviously, if 2 moles of magnesium are burned to give 2 moles of magnesium oxide, 1 mole of gaseous molecular oxygen will be needed and 2 × 146 kcal of energy will be liberated. Similarly, if only 0.025 mole of magnesium is burned to give 0.025 mole of magnesium oxide, 0.025 × 146 kcal of heat or about 3.7 kcal will be released.

---

*It is assumed in this measurement that reactants were originally at 25 °C and products were cooled to 25 °C before final measurement of the heat evolved.

A comparable set of relationships can be used to describe the burning of hydrogen gas to give water. The molar heat of combustion of gaseous H_2 to give liquid H_2O at 25 °C is 68 kcal:

$$H_2 + \tfrac{1}{2} O_2 \longrightarrow H_2O + 68 \text{ kcal} \tag{38}$$

$$2 H_2 + O_2 \longrightarrow 2 H_2O + 136 \text{ kcal} \tag{38a}$$

$$0.025 H_2 + \frac{0.025}{2} O_2 \longrightarrow 0.025 H_2O + 3.7 \text{ kcal} \tag{38b}$$

Energy can be treated as a regular product of these chemical reactions. A reaction in which energy appears as a product is called an **exothermic reaction** (heat is released).

EXERCISE 3-19

(1) How much heat is released when 2.00 moles of hydrogen burn to form water? when 0.50 mole burns to form water?
(2) How much heat energy is released when 36.45 g of magnesium metal are burned in air to give solid MgO? [*Answer to (2):* 219 kcal.]

3-5.1   The Source of Energy in Chemical Processes

Where does the energy in the burning of hydrogen come from? This is an appropriate "wondering why" question. For the answer, let us see what might be happening to the molecules in the burning process:

$$H—H + H—H + O—O \longrightarrow H—O^{H} + H—O^{H} \tag{39}$$

For hydrogen molecules to react with oxygen to form water molecules, the bonds between hydrogen atoms in each molecule must be broken at some point in the process. This requires energy. Similarly, the bond between the two oxygen atoms in the oxygen molecule must be broken at some point in the process. This also uses up energy.

The steps considered so far have absorbed energy, not released it! Where then does the energy which is released come from? The only possible source of energy left to be considered is the formation of bonds between two hydrogen atoms and an oxygen atom to give a water molecule. A large amount of energy must be released when H—O bonds are formed, since this process supplies all of the energy needed to (1) break the H—H bonds in hydrogen molecules; (2) break the O—O bonds in oxygen molecules; and (3) release all of the heat observed as a product of the reaction. This breaking of chemical bonds and formation of new bonds is the *defining characteristic* of a chemical process.

Because breaking and forming bonds generally involves relatively large amounts of energy, chemical processes are usually accompanied by sizable energy changes. Let us review our laboratory observations to see how this works.

When we melted wax, the solid wax could be recovered merely by cooling. No chemical bonds were broken. On the other hand, when

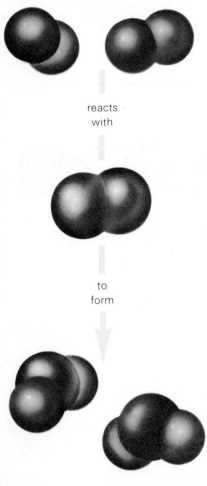

Fig. 3-5 Formation of water molecules from hydrogen molecules and oxygen molecules.

reacts
with

to
form

we burned the candle, the products of combustion could not be converted back into wax or a shiny new candle by cooling! Instead, carbon dioxide (CO_2) and liquid water (H_2O) were identified as products: *in the burning of the wax, new products were created—chemical bonds were broken, and new bonds were formed.* It is not surprising then that the energy released in the combustion of wax was well over two hundred times greater than the energy released when the same amount of wax freezes to a solid. Sizable amounts of energy are usually associated with processes involving the breaking of bonds and formation of bonds.

3-5.2 The Conservation of Energy

The balancing of chemical equations is based on the **Law of Conservation of Mass.** Mass can be neither created nor destroyed. Energy has also been handled in our chemical equations and treated like a product of the reaction. We can then write: *energy* can be neither created nor destroyed. A very large collection of experimental evidence indicates that this statement is true for all chemical processes. Like the Law of Conservation of Mass, the **Law of Conservation of Energy** provides one of the cornerstones of modern science.

3-5.3 The Decomposition of Water

We have just observed that when 1 mole of gaseous H_2 and $\frac{1}{2}$ mole of gaseous O_2 combine to give 1 mole of liquid water, 68 kcal of energy are released. According to the Law of Conservation of Energy, 68 kcal must be added to convert 1 mole of water back to 1 mole of H_2 and $\frac{1}{2}$ mole of O_2.

Let us examine the experiments to test this prediction. If we place water with a few drops of sulfuric acid in the electrolysis apparatus shown in Figure 3-7, and pass a direct electric current through the

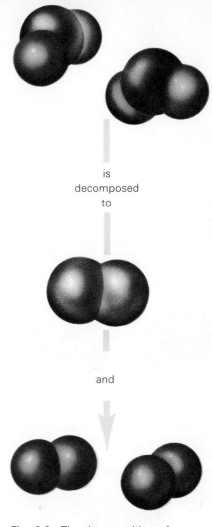

is
decomposed
to

and

Fig. 3-6 The decomposition of water shown with molecular models.

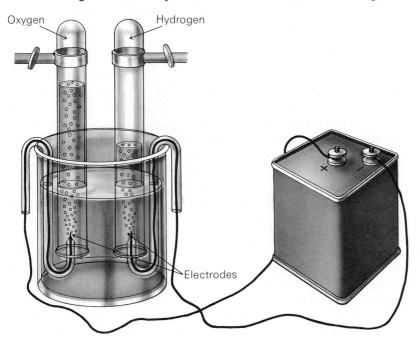

Oxygen — Hydrogen

Electrodes

Fig. 3-7 The apparatus for electrolytic decomposition of water.

solution, water will be decomposed. In the apparatus shown, two electrical conductors (called electrodes) are immersed in the liquid. When the electrodes are connected to a source of electrical energy, hydrogen gas appears at one electrode and oxygen gas appears at the other. If we operate the apparatus until 1 mole of water has decomposed (18 g of H_2O), 1 mole of hydrogen gas and $\frac{1}{2}$ mole of oxygen gas will be produced. We observe also that electrical energy equivalent to 68 kcal of heat will be used. The equation for this process is

$$68 \text{ kcal} + H_2O \longrightarrow \tfrac{1}{2} O_2 + H_2 \qquad (40)$$

The equation is just the reverse of the equation written for the combustion of 1 mole of hydrogen gas. Such a process in which energy is a reactant is called an **endothermic reaction.**

3-6 HIGHLIGHTS

When some gases were combined, new molecules formed. A **chemical change** had occurred. In order to explain chemical change without abandoning Avogadro's hypothesis, it was necessary to break molecules into smaller units called **atoms.** Atoms are present in all matter.

If all the atoms making up the molecule are the same, the molecule is that of an **element.** If more than one kind of atom is present in the molecule, it is that of a **compound.** The three-dimensional geometrical arrangement of atoms in an element or compound can be represented by a structural **model. A structural formula** is a two-dimensional representation of known structural information about that compound.

Atomic weights give relative masses of *atoms,* just as molecular weights give relative masses of molecules. Molecular weights of molecules can be obtained by adding up the atomic weights of the atoms which make up the molecule.

Thus, a model (theory) grows and becomes more quantitative. The model, supported by careful experimentation, led to the **Law of Conservation of Mass:** mass can be neither created nor destroyed. Because of this law *equations must balance.* Through use of this law we can determine quantities of products or reactants involved in chemical changes.

Another conservation law, the **Law of Conservation of Energy,** was suggested by the appearance of balanced equations involving energy terms. This law—energy can be neither created nor destroyed—is supported by a large body of human experience. Processes in which energy appears as a product are called **exothermic reactions.** Processes in which energy appears as a reactant are called **endothermic reactions.**

The atomic theory, as now developed to correlate chemical behavior, is much more complicated than is needed to explain the simple gas behavior first mentioned in Chapter 1. Nevertheless, correlations developed between "super-rubber" balls and the air in a balloon have provided us with a substantial start in understanding chemistry.

QUESTIONS and PROBLEMS

1 Two litres of hydrogen gas combine completely with 1 litre of oxygen gas to form 2 litres of water vapor. All gases are measured at the same temperature and pressure. (a) What gases would you expect if 2 litres of hydrogen gas were allowed to react with only $\frac{1}{2}$ litre of oxygen gas? (b) What gases would you expect if 1 litre of hydrogen gas were allowed to react as completely as possible with 1 litre of oxygen gas?

2 One litre of hydrogen gas combines completely with 1 litre of chlorine gas to form 2 litres of hydrogen chloride gas. All gases are measured at the same temperature and pressure. If any ratio other than 1:1 of hydrogen to chlorine is used, the gas which is in excess remains after the reaction has occurred. (a) Explain these facts using Avogadro's hypothesis. (b) How can these data be used to show that both hydrogen and chlorine must consist of diatomic molecules?

3 Write chemical equations to represent each of the following: (a) Two volumes of hydrogen gas combine with one volume of oxygen gas to form two volumes of water vapor (H_2O). (b) One volume of hydrogen gas combines with one volume of bromine gas to form two volumes of hydrogen bromide gas.

4 Two volumes of hydrogen fluoride gas combine with one volume of the gas dinitrogen difluoride to form two volumes of a gas G. (a) Assume that Avogadro's hypothesis is valid. Then write the equation for the process described. (b) How many molecules of G are produced from one molecule of dinitrogen difluoride? (c) Write the formula for G. (d) In view of the data given above, could dinitrogen difluoride have a formula of NF? Explain.

5 Given 58 grams of butane (C_4H_{10}) molecules: (a) What is the molecular weight of butane? (b) How many *moles of molecules* of C_4H_{10} are present? (c) How many *molecules* of C_4H_{10} are present? (d) What is the *total* number of *atoms in each molecule* of C_4H_{10}? (e) What is the total number of *moles of atoms* in each *mole of C_4H_{10} molecules*? (f) What is the total number of *moles of atoms* in the sample? (g) What is the total number of *atoms* in the sample?

6 (a) Determine the mass, in grams, of one gold atom. One mole of gold atoms has a mass of 197 grams. (b) A person has a filling that contains 0.296 gram of gold. Goldwise, how many moles in his molars? (c) How many *atoms* of gold are in the person's tooth?

7 The mass of 1.00 litre of a certain gas at STP is 6.88 ± 0.01 g. (a) What is the mass of 22.4 litres of the gas? (b) How many molecules of gas are present in this volume? (c) What is the molecular weight of the gas? (d) Which, if any, of the following gases could it be? Cl_2, SO_3, CCl_4, UF_6.

8 5.00 litres of a gas have a mass of 9.80 ± 0.01 g at STP. (a) What is the molecular weight of the gas? (b) Which, if any, of the following could it be? N_2, O_2, Cl_2, CO_2, SO_2.

9 If the molecular weight of sulfur is 256.8, and its atomic weight is 32.1, what is the formula of the sulfur molecule?

10 When an orange powder is heated strongly in a Bunsen burner flame, a colorless gas is given off and a silvery deposit appears on the sides of the test tube. (a) Is the orange substance an element or a compound? Give evidence for your answer. (b) Can you tell if the colorless gas and silvery deposit are elements or compounds? If not, what further tests would you make?

11 When an electric current is passed through molten table salt, a greenish, poisonous gas and a highly reactive, soft metal result. Is table salt an element or a compound? Explain the basis of your choice.

12 When a shiny black solid is heated gently, a violet gas evolves. When cooled, the violet gas condenses into a shiny black solid having the same physical characteristics as the original. Can you classify the shiny solid as an element or a compound? Explain.

13 From Table 3-1 write the chemical symbols for the following elements: (a) hydrogen (b) helium (c) lithium (d) beryllium (e) boron (f) carbon (g) nitrogen (h) oxygen.

14 Write the chemical symbols for the following elements: (a) phosphorus (b) potassium (c) magnesium (d) manganese (e) sulfur (f) sodium (g) copper (h) silicon (i) silver.

15 The following elements naturally occur as *diatomic* molecules. Write the formula for one molecule of each: (a) hydrogen (b) nitrogen (c) oxygen (d) fluorine (e) chlorine (f) bromine (g) iodine.

16 Write chemical formulas for the following compounds: (a) carbon monoxide (b) carbon dioxide (c) sulfur dioxide (d) sulfur trioxide (e) sodium chloride (f) copper oxide (g) nitrogen dioxide (h) silicon dioxide (i) carbon tetrachloride (j) hydrogen chloride.

17 Name the following compounds: (a) Na_2S (b) CF_4 (c) CO_2 (d) Cu_2O (e) N_2O_3 (f) MnO_2 (g) MgO (h) CS_2.

18 For each of the following chemical substances (i) list the kinds of atoms present; (ii) state how many atoms of each kind are present; (iii) indicate which formulas represent elements and which compounds; (iv) find the atomic or molecular weight of each substance. (a) CO_2 (b) H_2O (c) $AgNO_3$ (d) Cu (e) $K_2Cr_2O_7$ (f) $Pb(NO_3)_2$ (g) C_2H_5OH (h) C (i) $CaH_4(PO_4)_2$.

19 Consider the following data:

Element	Atomic Weight
A	12.01
B	35.5

A and *B* combine to form a new substance, *X*. Four moles of *B* atoms combine with 1 mole of *A* atoms to give 1 mole of *X* molecules. Write the equation for the process. What is the mass of 1 mole of *X*? (a) 47.5 g, (b) 74.0 g, (c) 83.0 g, (d) 154.0 g, or (e) 166.0 g.

20 A 112-litre container is filled with neon gas at STP. (a) How many moles of neon are in the container? (b) How many molecules of neon are in the container? (c) What is the mass of this amount of neon?

21 How many moles are present in each of the following: (a) 36.0 grams of water (H_2O) (b) 8.5 grams of ammonia (NH_3) (c) 6.35 grams of copper (d) 2.16 grams of silver (e) 0.85 gram of silver nitrate ($AgNO_3$) (f) 7.10 grams of chlorine gas.

22 What is the mass, in grams, of each of the following? (a) 1.00 mole of sulfur dioxide (b) 2.5 moles of carbon monoxide (c) 0.10 mole of hydrogen fluoride (d) 0.50 mole of oxygen gas (e) 0.50 mole of aluminum (f) 0.040 mole of trisodium phosphate (Na_3PO_4).

23 Balance the following chemical equations. Start with one mole of the underlined substance.

(a) $\underline{C} + O_2 \longrightarrow CO_2$
(b) $\underline{H_2} + O_2 \longrightarrow H_2O$
(c) $\underline{Na} + Cl_2 \longrightarrow NaCl$
(d) $\underline{CH_4} + \overline{O_2} \longrightarrow CO_2 + H_2O$

(e) $CH_3OH + O_2 \longrightarrow CO_2 + H_2O$
(f) $\underline{C_3H_8} + O_2 \longrightarrow CO_2 + H_2O$
(g) $\underline{N_2} + H_2 \longrightarrow NH_3$
(h) $\underline{KClO_3} \longrightarrow KCl + O_2$
(i) $\overline{NaOH} + \underline{CO_2} \longrightarrow Na_2CO_3 + H_2O$

24 Write balanced chemical equations for the following: (a) water is decomposed into its elements (b) potassium chloride is synthesized (made) from its elements (c) sulfur trioxide is made from sulfur dioxide and oxygen (d) the burning of acetylene (C_2H_2) in air (e) the burning of butane (C_4H_{10}) in air (f) ammonia gas (NH_3) reacts with hydrogen chloride gas to produce the white solid NH_4Cl (g) ammonia gas burns to produce nitrogen dioxide and water (h) nitrogen monoxide + oxygen gas gives nitrogen dioxide (i) diiron trioxide + aluminum gives dialuminum trioxide + iron (j) diiodine pentoxide + carbon monoxide gives iodine + carbon dioxide.

25 When sodium metal is dropped into water, a vigorous reaction occurs. Hydrogen gas is evolved and a solution of sodium hydroxide (NaOH) is formed. (a) Write the balanced equation for this reaction. (b) If 2.3 g of sodium are put into water, how many moles of hydrogen will be produced? (c) What volume will this hydrogen occupy at STP? (d) What will be the mass of this hydrogen?

26 When mercuric oxide (HgO) is heated strongly, it decomposes into its elements. (a) Write the balanced equation for this reaction. (b) How many moles of HgO are necessary to produce 11.2 litres of oxygen at STP? (c) What is the mass of the quantity of HgO in (b)? (d) How many grams of mercury will be produced by the reaction?

27 Calcium metal can be produced by passing an electric current through molten $CaCl_2$. Chlorine gas is the other product of this reaction. (a) Write the balanced equation for this reaction. (b) How many grams of calcium would be obtained from the electrolysis of 1.00 kg (1 kg = 1000 g) of $CaCl_2$? (c) What volume of chlorine, measured at STP, would be produced?

28 When copper oxide is heated in the presence of hydrogen gas, the products are copper metal and water vapor. (a) Write the balanced equation for this reaction. (b) How many grams of copper metal will be obtained from the heating of 4.0 g of copper oxide with an excess of hydrogen gas?

29 When charcoal (assumed to be carbon) burns under proper conditions, carbon dioxide is the only product. (a) Write the balanced equation for this reaction. (b) If a charcoal briquet has a mass of 24.0 grams, how many moles of oxygen gas are necessary for this reaction to go to completion? (c) What volume would this oxygen occupy at STP? (d) Since air is only about $\frac{1}{5}$ oxygen, what volume of *air* (at STP) is necessary for the reaction? (e) What volume of air (at STP) is necessary for a 20-briquet charcoal fire to burn completely? (f) Since, when inadequate oxygen is available, carbon burns to form carbon *mon*oxide, why is it inadvisable to operate a charcoal barbecue in an enclosed space?

30 One gallon of gasoline can be considered as about 25 moles of octane (C_8H_{18}). (a) Write the equation for the complete combustion of 1 mole of C_8H_{18}. (Assume that the only products are carbon dioxide and water.) (b) How many moles of oxygen are required for the burning of 1 mole of octane? One gallon of octane? (c) How many grams of oxygen are used in the burning of 1 gallon of gasoline? (d) How many grams of carbon dioxide are formed in the burning of 1 gallon of gasoline? (e) One acre of open grassland produces about 2,500 lb of oxygen per year, or about 3,000 grams per day. How many acres of grassland are necessary to replace the oxygen used by your car if you burn 1 gallon of gasoline each day? (You might ponder the thought that 1 gallon of gasoline carries one car only 12-25 miles, and that an acre is an area of about 100×500 ft, or about 4,000 metres^2. How large is *your* lawn compared to the oxygen needs of your car?) (f) An acre of deciduous forest produces about 1 million kg of oxygen per year, or about 1,000 times the amount of oxygen produced by one acre of grassland. In view of your answer to (e), what is the practical reason for considering forested "greenbelts" within and surrounding cities as an environmental necessity?

31 An average human being uses about 500 kg (1 kg = 1000 g) of oxygen per year in an extremely complex series of reactions, one of which is

$$C_6H_{12}O_6 + O_2 \longrightarrow CO_2 + H_2O$$

(a) Balance the above equation. (b) How many moles of oxygen are contained in 500 kg of oxygen? (c) If an acre of grassland produces 1,000 kg of oxygen per year, how many people (considering oxygen requirements alone) can one acre of grassland support?

32 When a mole of aluminum metal is burned to Al_2O_3, 200 kcal of heat are given off. (a) Write the balanced equation for this reaction,

including the energy term as part of the equation. (b) Is this reaction exothermic or endothermic?

33 Metallic sodium is obtained chiefly by the electrolysis of molten sodium chloride (NaCl). For each mole of sodium produced, 98 kilocalories of electrical energy are needed. (a) Write the balanced equation for this reaction, including the energy term as part of the equation. (b) Is this reaction exothermic or endothermic? (c) Write the balanced equation for the reaction of sodium with chlorine gas. Include the energy term as part of the equation and indicate whether the reaction is exothermic or endothermic. (d) How much energy would be produced by the reaction of 11.5 grams of sodium with an excess of chlorine gas?

34 (a) Balance the equations for the decomposition (to elements) of ammonia (NH_3), nitrogen trifluoride (NF_3), and nitrogen trichloride (NCl_3). Base each equation upon the production of one mole of N_2.

$$NH_3 \longrightarrow 1\ N_2 + H_2$$
$$NF_3 \longrightarrow 1\ N_2 + F_2$$
$$NCl_3 \longrightarrow 1\ N_2 + Cl_2$$

(b) Rewrite the equations to include the information that the decomposition of ammonia is *endothermic*, absorbing 22.1 kilocalories/mole of N_2 formed; that the decomposition of NF_3 is *endothermic*, absorbing 54.4 kcal/mole of N_2; and that the decomposition of NCl_3 is *exothermic*, releasing 109.4 kcal/mole of N_2. (c) One of the three compounds NH_3, NF_3, and NCl_3 is dangerously explosive. Which would you expect to be the explosive substance? Why?

35 Methane, the main constituent of natural gas, has the formula CH_4 and a molar heat of combustion of 18,000 calories. (a) Write the balanced equation for the burning of 1 mole of methane, including the energy term as part of the equation. (b) How many grams of methane would have to be burned to warm 100 grams of water from $10\,°C$ to $100\,°C$?

36 Liquid hydrogen was used as a fuel in the Saturn rockets which carried our astronauts to the moon. Hydrogen has a molar heat of combustion of 68.3 kcal. (a) Write the balanced equation for the combustion of 1 mole of hydrogen, including the energy term as part of the equation. (b) How many kilocalories of heat will be given off by the burning of 1.00 kg of hydrogen?

I am never content until I have constructed a mechanical model of the object that I am studying. If I succeed in making one, I understand; otherwise, I do not.

WILLIAM THOMSON, LORD KELVIN (1824–1907)

MORE ABOUT GASES: 4
THE KINETIC THEORY

Inflating a balloon is a simple demonstration of kinetic theory.

THIS CHAPTER COULD WELL BE TITLED "MUCH ADO ABOUT ALMOST Nothing," since gases are mostly empty space. It is the empty space which permits a gas to be easily compressed. It is the endless, rapid motion of the particles banging against one another and the walls of the container which causes a gas to fill space and exert pressure. Heating of gas particles causes them to move more rapidly and bang more vigorously against the walls of the container. Either the pressure or the volume, or both, must get larger if the temperature is raised.

In order to describe an amount of gas, then, we must specify not only the volume it occupies, but the temperature and pressure at which it was measured. In this chapter we learn of these measurements and the inter-relationships among them.

The model suggested in Chapter 1 to explain the behavior of air in a balloon has grown rapidly. In Chapter 2 we made observations on the way in which the volume of a given quantity of gas changes as pressure on the gas is increased. The model explained these observations in both a qualitative and a quantitative way. Next we *assumed* that Avogadro's hypothesis was true. We used this hypothesis, together with our model for gases and some chemical observations to develop the concepts of molecules and molecular weights. In Chapter 3 it was necessary to break molecules into atoms in order to understand some chemical reactions. Atoms have mass (weight); we found a table of atomic weights helpful. These concepts then provided a quantitative procedure for examining masses of chemically reacting materials; they gave us a substantial basis for further development of the atomic theory. The study of gases, therefore, is fundamental to our understanding of chemical concepts.

The gaseous state is the simplest form of matter; yet because most gases are difficult or impossible to see directly, their study requires a good imagination. We found in Chapter 2 that the mathematical statement, "pressure × volume = a constant," is true for gases in general. This simple regularity, along with other regularities found in this chapter, leads to the *kinetic theory* and an understanding of temperature on the molecular level.

4-1 MOLAR VOLUMES AND THE DISTANCE BETWEEN PARTICLES IN THE GAS PHASE

Our model of a gas proposed the existence of particles (molecules) which have a rapid, random motion and which collide with one another and with the walls of the container. One of the interesting questions which we have not yet answered is: how far apart are these particles? Is the distance between molecules much larger than the size (diameter) of the molecules themselves?

The answer can be found by comparing the volumes occupied by 1 mole (6.02×10^{23} molecules) of a substance when it exists as a solid, a liquid, and a gas. In Chapter 2 we calculated the volume of 1 mole of a *gas* at standard temperature and pressure (STP). Recall that STP is 0 °C (melting ice temperature) and 1 atmosphere pressure (the pressure exerted by air at sea level). This quantity of gas was called the **molar volume** of the gas. We found that all gases have a molar volume which is fairly close to the value 22.4 litres at 0 °C and 1 atm pressure (STP).

One mole of a pure material in the solid state has a definite and reproducible volume, too, if we specify the temperature and pressure. In contrast to gases, however, volumes for different solids are *not* the same, even at the same temperature and pressure. Similarly, 1 mole of a pure material in the liquid state has a definite volume at a given temperature and pressure, but different liquids have different molar volumes. Let us examine molar volumes for a relatively simple material and see what this study tells us about the distance between molecules in the gas phase.

4-1.1 The Molar Volume of Nitrogen and Intermolecular Distances in Gases

In Chapter 3 we learned that gaseous nitrogen is composed of nitrogen molecules having the formula N_2. One mole of nitrogen has a mass of 28.0 grams (molecular weight $= 2 \times 14.0$) and occupies a volume of 22.4 litres or 22,400 millilitres at 0 °C and 1 atm pressure.

Let us now investigate nitrogen in its solid and liquid states. When a sample of gaseous nitrogen is cooled somewhat below -210 °C, a white solid forms. If we measure the volume occupied by a 28.0-g sample of the white solid, a value very close to 27.2 millilitres is obtained.* Above -210 °C the solid melts to give liquid nitrogen. The volume occupied by 28.0 g of this liquid at a temperature slightly above -210 °C is 34.6 ml.

These significant numbers on nitrogen are easily summarized:

$$\text{molar volume gaseous } N_2 = 22{,}400 \quad \text{ml}$$
$$\text{molar volume liquid } N_2 \quad = \quad\;\; 34.6 \;\; \text{ml}$$
$$\text{molar volume solid } N_2 \quad = \quad\;\; 27.2 \;\; \text{ml}$$

Note that the volume occupied by 1 mole of gas is 650 times larger than the volume occupied by 1 mole of liquid nitrogen (22,400 ml/34.6 ml) and 825 times larger than the volume occupied by 1 mole of solid nitrogen (22,400 ml/27.2 ml). *If we assume that the size of a molecule itself does not change significantly in going from liquid to gas, then we must conclude that the molecules have become separated from each other in the gas phase.* The free space between gaseous molecules must be about 650 times larger than the space occupied by liquid molecules. Experiments with other materials lead to similar conclusions about the gaseous state. *The actual volume of the molecules in a gas is trivial in comparison to the volume occupied by the gas itself.*

---

*The molar volume of the solid is obtained from its density by dividing 28.0 g/mole by the density 1.03 g/ml.

$$\text{molar volume solid } N_2 = \frac{28.0 \text{ g/mole}}{1.03 \text{ g/ml}} = 27.2 \text{ ml/mole}$$

Gases are compressed relatively easily because it is not difficult to force more molecules into the empty space between molecules. On the other hand, liquids and solids are compressed with great difficulty because there is very little space between molecules.

EXERCISE 4-1

How many molecules of nitrogen are present in 1.00 litre of gas at 0 °C and 1 atm pressure? (*Answer:* 2.69×10^{22} molecules.)

EXERCISE 4-2

Calculate the volume (in ml) occupied by one nitrogen molecule in the solid phase. (*Answer:* 4.52×10^{-23} ml/molecule.)

4-1.2   The Effect of a Change in Temperature on the Molar Volume of a Gas

One of the very significant relationships of Chapter 2 is contained in the statement: *one mole* of gas occupies 22.4 litres at 0 °C and 1 atm pressure. This statement is true for all of the gases which we have considered. If we do not want to hold the pressure at 1 atm, the volume can be calculated from the relationship

$$P \times V = 22.4 \left(\frac{\text{litres} \times \text{atm}}{\text{mole}} \right) \qquad (1)$$

provided that the temperature is held constant at 0 °C. For example, if the pressure is raised to 2 atm, the volume for 1 mole can be calculated from the relationship

$$2 \text{ atm} \times V = 22.4 \left(\frac{\text{litres} \times \text{atm}}{\text{mole}} \right) \qquad (2)$$

or

$$V = 11.2 \text{ litres/mole at 2 atm and 0 °C}$$

EXERCISE 4-3

(1) What volume would 1.0 mole of gas occupy at 4.0 atm pressure and 0 °C?
(2) What volume would 2.00 moles of gas occupy at 4.00 atm pressure and 0 °C?

It is relatively easy to calculate a new gas volume after the pressure is changed *if we hold both the quantity of gas and the temperature constant;* but what happens to the gas volume if we change the temperature? An experiment provides the answer.

Table 4-1 shows the results of some crude pressure-volume measurements made on 1 mole of ammonia gas at 25 °C (at approximately room temperature). Within experimental uncertainty, the pressure-

TABLE 4-1 PRESSURE AND VOLUME OF 1 MOLE OF AMMONIA GAS (NH_3) AT 25 °C

Pressure (atm)	Volume (litres)	$P \times V$ (atm $\times$ litres)
0.200	123	24.6
0.400	60.0	24.0
0.600	43.0	25.8
0.800	29.3	23.4
1.00	25.7	25.7
1.50	15.9	23.9
2.00	12.1	24.2
		Average $\overline{24.5 \pm 0.7}$

EFFECT of TEMPERATURE CHANGE
on MOLAR VOLUME of a GAS

Pressure (atm)	Volume (litres)	$P \times V$ (atm × litres)
0.1000	244.5	24.45
0.2000	122.2	24.44
0.4000	61.02	24.41
0.8000	30.44	24.35
2.000	12.17	24.34
		Average 24.40

Fig. 4-1 A gas bulb used to weigh and handle gases in the laboratory. By cooling the tube below the bulb with liquid nitrogen (temperature = −196 °C), most materials can be condensed or frozen inside the tube. This makes it possible to move materials into the flask from other points in a closed system. This way the flask can be filled.

volume product for 1 mole of ammonia at 25 °C is 24.5 ± 0.7 as long as the pressure is between 0.2 and 2.0 atmospheres. This value is significantly larger than the value 22.4 ± 0.7 found at 0 °C for ammonia in measurements of similar accuracy.

If we examine the precision of the measurements which gave us the values 22.4 and 24.5, it is apparent that even though the values are uncertain to ± 0.7, the difference between the two numbers is real and not a result of poor laboratory measurements or crude instrumentation. A more accurate study of the ammonia system at 25 °C confirms our earlier conclusion. The data are in Table 4-2. We note that the average value is 24.40 ± 0.06. On the other hand, we see that the individual values are not randomly distributed around 24.40. Instead, there is a steady decline from 24.45 at 0.1 atm to 24.34 at 2.0 atm. This is significant and will be examined more carefully in Chapter 5.

Our observations on 1 mole of ammonia can now be summarized by two expressions:

$$P \times V = 22.4 \text{ litres} \times \text{atm } at \ 0 °C \qquad (3)$$

$$P \times V = 24.4 \text{ litres} \times \text{atm } at \ 25 °C \qquad (4)$$

This result does not surprise us since most of us know from earlier experience that a gas expands when heated at constant pressure.

We were pleased earlier to note that the expression

$$P \times V = 22.4 \text{ litres} \times \text{atm at } 0 °C \qquad (3)$$

applies to 1-mole samples of many gases, not just to O_2, NH_3, or N_2. We now wonder how general is the relationship

$$P \times V = 24.4 \text{ litres} \times \text{atm at } 25 °C \qquad (4)$$

for a 1-mole sample. Consider the following experiment. The air is pumped out of the litre flask shown in Figure 4-1. The flask is weighed empty (without air). It is then weighed again after it has been filled with a new gas at 1 atm pressure and 25 °C. The difference in mass is the mass of 1 litre of the new gas that was added. From this information and the molecular weight of the gas, we can calculate the volume of 1 mole of that gas at 25 °C and 1 atm. Table 4-3 shows the results. We find that all gases have about the same molar volume at 25 °C and 1 atm. More precise measurements show that whether the gas is O_2, N_2, CO, or CO_2, the same volume—24.4 ± 0.2 litres—contains 6.02×10^{23} molecules at 25 °C and 1 atm.

4-2 MEASUREMENTS ON GASES

Our model for gases requires increasingly precise measurements of gas properties. It is therefore appropriate to pause and consider in more detail just how measurements on gases are made. Let us first examine the logic and the physics behind the measurement of gas pressure.

TABLE **4-3** THE VOLUME OF 1 MOLE OF GAS AT 25 °C AND
1 ATM PRESSURE

Gas	Mass of Flask Empty M_1 (g)	Mass of Flask + Gas M_2 (g)	Mass of 1 Litre of Gas $M_2 - M_1$ (g/litre)	Mass of 1 Mole M_3 (g/mole)	Volume $M_3/(M_2 - M_1)$ (litre/mole)
Oxygen (O$_2$)	157.35	158.66	1.31	32.0	24.5
Nitrogen (N$_2$)	157.35	158.50	1.15	28.0	24.3
Carbon monoxide (CO)	157.35	158.50	1.15	28.0	24.4
Carbon dioxide (CO$_2$)	157.35	159.16	1.81	44.0	24.3

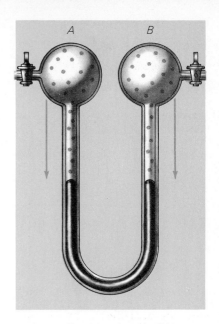

Fig. 4-2.1 Pressure of gas in side A equals pressure of gas in side B.

4-2.1 Measuring the Pressure on a Gas

We have been using the word *pressure* for some time. The original definition referred to pressure as the "push" on a unit area of the wall of the containing vessel. Our model for gases attributed this "push" to collisions between rapidly moving molecules and the walls of the container. This model was attractive because it could explain a very important observation about pressure: *a gas exerts pressure equally on all the walls of its container.* This fact is important in the operation of all pressure-measuring devices.

Consider the device shown in Figure 4-2.1. Two bulbs, each of the same volume and containing the same amount of a given gas, are connected by a U-tube half filled with liquid mercury. Molecules in the bulbs strike all walls of the container randomly, including the surface of the mercury in the U-tube. Since each bulb has the same volume and each contains the same number of molecules of a given gas, an equal number of collisions, generating comparable force, should be expected on each square centimetre of mercury surface in bulbs A and B. In short, the "push" per unit area on the two surfaces of mercury should be the same and the surfaces should stand at the same height. We recall that **pressure** *is defined as* **force** *or* "*push*" **per unit area of surface.**

Now add a sizable quantity of gas to the bulb on the right (bulb B) in Figure 4-2.2. The number of collisions with a unit area of the mercury surface on the right side (B) should now be larger than the number of collisions with the same area of mercury surface on the left side (A). More collisions mean that the push per unit area (or pressure) will be higher on side B. The mercury column then moves until the force per unit area due to the weight of the mercury column (height h) just balances the extra force per unit area produced by additional molecular collisions on side B. Our model suggests that the height of the mercury column (h) might be a good measure of the difference in pressure (or push on the surfaces) in bulbs A and B.

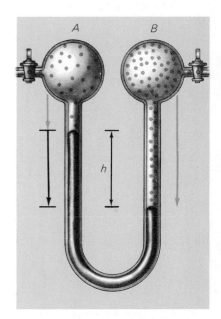

Fig. 4-2.2 Pressure of gas in A plus pressure due to weight of mercury column of height h equals pressure of gas in B.

MEASURING the PRESSURE

on a GAS

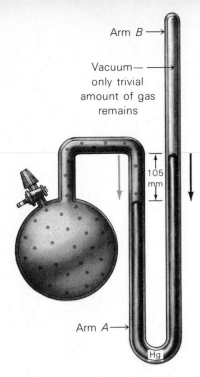

Fig. 4-3.1 Closed-end manometer. Gas pressure in arm *A* equals pressure due to weight of mercury column in arm *B*. (Pressure of gas = 105 mm.)

Fig. 4-3.2 Open-end manometer. Gas pressure (105 mm) equals atmospheric pressure (760 mm) minus pressure of mercury column (655 mm).

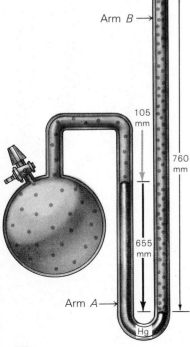

Such a U-tube, known as a **manometer,** permits us to measure the *difference* in pressure exerted on the surfaces of the two arms of the manometer. Two types of manometers are shown in Figure 4-3. Figure 4-3.1 shows a closed-end manometer. Here all the gas above the mercury surface (except for a trivial amount of mercury vapor) has been removed from arm *B*. Thus, the pressure in the bulb is balanced by the force or "push" per unit area resulting from the weight of the mercury column; the gas pressure is given as 105 millimetres of mercury (expressed as 105 mm Hg).

The apparatus shown in Figure 4-3.2 differs in that the right-hand tube is open. In this type of manometer, *atmospheric pressure* is exerted on the right-hand mercury column. Hence the pressure of the gas in the flask plus the pressure exerted by the mercury column equals atmospheric pressure.

$$\begin{Bmatrix} \text{atmospheric} \\ \text{pressure} \end{Bmatrix} = \begin{Bmatrix} \text{pressure} \\ \text{in flask} \end{Bmatrix} + \begin{Bmatrix} \text{pressure exerted} \\ \text{by mercury column} \end{Bmatrix} \quad (5)$$

$$(760 \text{ mm Hg}) = (105 \text{ mm Hg}) + (655 \text{ mm Hg})$$

The pressure indicated by our open-end manometer can now be calculated as 760 mm − 655 mm = 105 mm. The value indicated for the pressure in the flask is the same as that indicated by the closed-end manometer. This open-end manometer has the disadvantage that an absolute measurement of pressure in the flask *cannot* be made until the atmospheric pressure is known. It is, however, easier to build than is the closed-end manometer.

The atmospheric pressure is usually measured by means of a **barometer** (see Figure 4-4). A barometer can be made by filling a long tube (closed at one end) with mercury and then placing the open end under the surface of a pool of mercury in a dish. If the tube is long enough, mercury will flow from the tube until the column of mercury exerts a downward pressure which is exactly balanced by the pressure of the air. In Figure 4-4 the pressure of the air is 760 mm. The air pressure pushes down on the surface of the mercury in the dish, thus holding up mercury in the tube.

EXERCISE 4-4

A flask of gas is attached to an open-end manometer. For the following three cases decide whether the gas pressure is equal to, greater than, or less than atmospheric pressure.

(1) The mercury level on the flask side is 20 mm lower than the level on the atmosphere side.
(2) The mercury levels are equal.
(3) The mercury level on the flask side is 20 mm higher than the level on the atmosphere side.

Explain your reasoning.

EXERCISE 4-5

If the atmospheric pressure is 748 mm, what is the pressure of the gas sample for the three cases in Exercise 4-4?

4-2.2 Temperature and Its Measurement

What is temperature? What does the word mean to you? First, it tells you that if the thermometer outside your window reads −20 °F, you will be cold if you go out to sunbathe. It also tells you that if the thermometer outside reads 110 °F, you will be very hot, particularly if you are foolish enough to go for a walk in the sun. Temperature tells you something about your personal comfort; it does this because temperature is a number which tells you which way thermal energy or heat will flow. If the temperature is significantly lower than the temperature of your body, thermal energy (heat) will pass from your body to the surroundings. If your body cannot replace this energy (heat) fast enough, you feel cold. On the other hand, if energy (heat) is flowing into your body from its surroundings at a rate which is greater than the rate at which energy is removed, you feel hot!

Let us consider another example. If a piece of hot metal is dropped into a glass of water at room temperature, the temperature of the water rises (the water becomes hotter) and the temperature of the metal falls (the metal becomes colder). Ultimately, the metal and water will reach a point where standardized thermometers will show identical readings for each (Figure 4-5). No net exchange of energy can be observed between water and metal. The water and metal are in **thermal equilibrium.** We say that the water and the metal have the same temperature. In an experimental sense, *temperature can be considered as a number which tells us which way thermal energy (or heat) flows between two bodies.*

So far we have been concerned only with temperatures of liquids and solids; yet gas temperatures are far easier to understand on a molecular level. Let us examine the temperature of gases.

To measure the temperature of a gas, we immerse a thermometer in it. We now know that if the thermometer is colder than the system, thermal energy flows into the thermometer until the gas and the thermometer are at the same temperature. If the thermometer is hotter

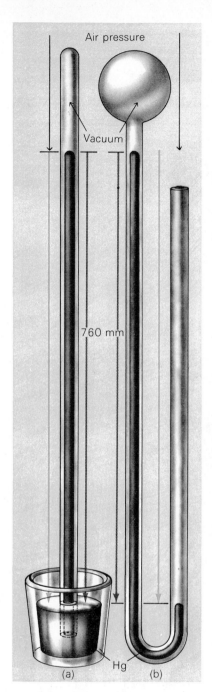

Fig. 4-4 (a) Barometer and (b) open-end manometer. A barometer is really an open-end manometer with a vacuum in the closed end above the mercury column. Compare with Figure 4-3.2.

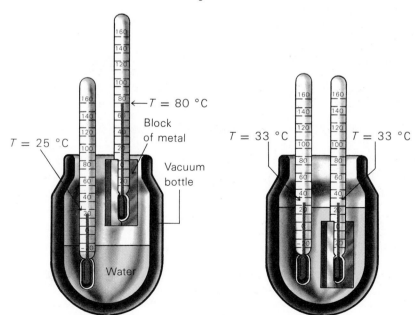

Fig. 4-5 The meaning of temperature. When two objects at different temperatures are brought together, they will reach thermal equilibrium; both will have the same temperature.

than the gas, thermal energy flows from the thermometer to the gas. When thermal equilibrium is reached, the gas and the thermometer have the same temperature. We then read the temperature of the gas as indicated by the thermometer.

There are many kinds of thermometers. Any material can be fashioned into a thermometer if it has a readily measured property that changes with temperature. Almost all solids and liquids change volume when the temperature is changed. We use this property of mercury and glass to construct the ordinary mercury thermometer. Both the glass bulb and glass stem of the thermometer expand *slightly* as the thermometer becomes hotter. On the other hand, the mercury contained inside the bulb and the glass stem expands much more with a given change in temperature than does the glass which holds it. As the mercury occupies more volume, its level rises in the stem and we read a number which indicates this new and higher volume and thus a new and higher temperature.

Gases can also be used to indicate changes in temperature. A gas held at constant volume will exert a higher pressure as the temperature is increased. One can then convert the higher pressure reading into its corresponding temperature reading by means of a table or mathematical relationship.

The way in which we express temperature—the definition of the temperature scale (or degree)—is rather arbitrary. In general we need two fixed points; for the Celsius (or centigrade) scale these points are the freezing point of water (which is called zero, 0.00) and the boiling point of water under a pressure of 760.000 mm (which is called 100.00). If the property (such as expansion of mercury up the stem) changes regularly between these two fixed points, we just mark the fixed points, label them, and divide the measured difference between them (*i.e.*, distance between boiling and freezing marks) into 100 equal parts called degrees. The most troublesome point arises if the property does not change regularly with temperature; then more involved methods of standardization must be used. This detail will not concern us here, but it is important in making very accurate thermometers.

EXERCISE 4-6

Express the pressures in Figure 4-3 in atmospheres rather than millimetres of mercury.

4-2.3 A Commentary on Avogadro's Hypothesis

One of the most important relationships in all of our former arguments is Avogadro's hypothesis: *equal volumes of gases measured at the same temperature and pressure contain equal numbers of molecules.* This relationship permits us to determine the relative masses of gaseous molecules and places molecular and atomic weights on a sound experimental footing. Its truth was established not by a single experiment but by many separate observations such as those we have been considering. Since we are investigating questions of measurement, some commentary on the reliability of Avogadro's hypothesis seems appropriate. Avogadro's hypothesis is important not because it is exact, but because it applies to all gases regardless of whether their molecules are large or small. The molecules of different gases actually have different sizes and slightly different attractions for each other. As a result, different gases do *not* have *exactly* the same number of molecules in a given volume. Such variations are, however, usually small and generally can be reduced to less than 1 percent by controlling experimental conditions. These deviations do not necessarily impair the usefulness of Avogadro's hypothesis in determining the molecular weight of a gas and in "counting" molecules. This is a very fortunate fact of nature!

Examination of Table 4-3 (see page 77) substantiates this fact. Molecular weights of gases can be determined independently and very accurately by an instrument known as a mass spectrometer (to be discussed in Appendix 3). If the molecular weights of gases, determined in a mass spectrometer, are used as a basis for weighing out 1 mole of each of several gases, we can make a direct measurement of the molar volumes for these gases. Data for oxygen, nitrogen, carbon monoxide, and carbon dioxide are shown in Table 4-3. We see that these gases follow Avogadro's hypothesis to three significant figures.

4-3 THE KINETIC THEORY

The model of a gas as a collection of particles in endless motion requires that each particle possess *energy of motion,* called **kinetic energy.** We should not be surprised to learn, then, that the model for gases is called the **kinetic theory of gases.** An application of the quantitative mathematical concepts of the kinetic theory permits us to be a little more specific in our description of molecular motion.

Considerable evidence, direct and indirect, indicates that gas molecules travel in straight lines until they meet other gas molecules or the walls of the container. Then they bounce off; some hit head-on and some at an angle; the net result is a helter-skelter movement of molecules in all directions and at all speeds. Since an individual molecule will change both speed and direction of motion even in a single second to give a zig-zag path, it is pointless to speak of the velocity of a given molecule. We can, however, speak of the *average speed* of a collection of molecules at any instant. The average speed of a collection of gas molecules does not change with time unless the temperature is changed. It is a measurable and reproducible quantity. At room temperature the average speed of a nitrogen molecule is determined to be about 400 metres per second or about 900 miles per hour. Although the average distance between molecules is small in an absolute sense, it is large in comparison to the size of the molecules themselves (Section 4-1.1). This means that molecules can travel relatively long distances without colliding. On the average, at room temperature and 1 atm pressure a molecule will travel about 15 times the average distance between molecules before colliding with another molecule.

The molecules making up solids and liquids are also in motion but such motion is harder to describe because the particles are closer together, and they bump into each other constantly.

4-3.1 Pressure Changes Resulting from a Change in the Number of Molecules

Earlier we noted that gas pressure is a result of collisions between molecules and the container walls. Also, we noted that twice as many molecules in the same volume will give twice as many collisions per unit of time and area, hence twice as much force per unit area. (Review Section 2-1.4, page 26.) The pressure will be twice the original value. In brief, the number of collisions per unit area per second is proportional to the number of molecules per unit of volume (temperature assumed constant). Experimentally this means: *if volume and temperature remain constant, the pressure is directly proportional to the number of moles of gas per unit volume.*

EXERCISE 4-7

What happens when an air hose is fastened to an automobile tire in the service station? Can you think of any case where the pressure of the tire could go down rather than up?

EXERCISE 4-8

A container of fixed volume contains 2 moles of gas at room temperature. The pressure in the container is 4 atm. Three moles of gas are added to the container at the same temperature. Use the result just stated to show that the pressure is now 10 atm.

4-3.2 Partial Pressures

We have talked about the pressure in vessels filled with pure gases such as O_2, N_2, and NH_3. Is the description of gases changed seriously if we work with a gas mixture? This question can be answered by using the kinetic model for a gas to interpret a rather simple set of experiments.

Consider the box illustrated in Figure 4-6. This box has a total volume of 5 litres. It is divided into two sections by a breakable wall or diaphragm. One section has a volume of 4 litres; the other has a volume of one. The 4-litre section is filled with N_2 at *1 atm pressure* and the 1-litre section is filled with O_2 at *1 atm pressure*. The entire box is held at 25 °C or room temperature. Note that each section of the box contains gas at 1 atm.

Let us now pull the handle and break the diaphragm. The N_2 and O_2 molecules mix. We observe the two manometers carefully after the diaphragm is broken; we find that the pressure is *the same* as it was before the diaphragm was broken.

Can we rationalize this observation in terms of the kinetic theory? In Section 4-1.2 we found that the pressure-volume relationship for gases can be expressed as

$$P \times V = \text{a constant at } 25 \text{ °C} \qquad (6)$$

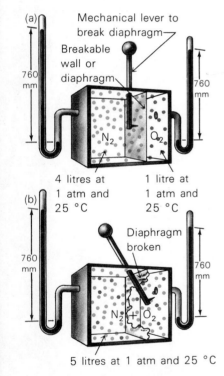

(a)

Mechanical lever to break diaphragm

Breakable wall or diaphragm

760 mm

760 mm

N_2 O_2

4 litres at 1 atm and 25 °C

1 litre at 1 atm and 25 °C

(b)

Diaphragm broken

760 mm

760 mm

$N_2 + O_2$

5 litres at 1 atm and 25 °C

Fig. 4-6 Partial pressure. Manometers read the same (a) before and (b) after the diaphragm is broken.

Thus we can write for N_2 before the diaphragm is broken

$$1 \text{ atm} \times 4 \text{ litres} = 4 \text{ litres} \times \text{atm at } 25 \text{ °C}$$

(The value of the constant here is 4, not 24.4, because we have taken only 4 litres, not 1 mole or 24.4 litres, at 25 °C.) After the diaphragm is broken, the volume through which N_2 molecules can roam is 5 litres. Qualitatively, we can see that the pressure due to N_2 must fall. How much does it fall? Since we know $P \times V = 4$ for our sample of N_2 at 25 °C, we can calculate the value of P when the volume goes to 5 rather than 4 litres.

$$P \times 5 \text{ litres} = 4 \text{ litres} \times \text{atm}$$
$$P = \tfrac{4}{5} \text{ atm} \tag{7}$$

We find that N_2 in the total container exerts a pressure of $\tfrac{4}{5}$ atm.

Similar calculations can be made for oxygen. The original pressure is 1 atm and the original volume is 1 litre; therefore,

$$P \times V = 1 \text{ litre} \times 1 \text{ atm} = 1 \text{ (litre} \times \text{atm)}$$

for O_2 at 25 °C. (Note that the constant here is 1, not 24.4, because we took only 1 litre, *not* 1 mole or 24.4 litres, of O_2 at 25 °C.) If the volume available to O_2 molecules is expanded to 5 litres, we get

$$P \times 5 \text{ litres} = 1 \text{ litre} \times \text{atm}$$
$$P = \tfrac{1}{5} \text{ atm} \tag{8}$$

The oxygen in the container after the diaphragm is broken exerts a pressure of $\tfrac{1}{5}$ atm.

We can then write

$$
\begin{aligned}
P \text{ due to } N_2 &= \tfrac{4}{5} \text{ atm} \\
\underline{P \text{ due to } O_2 = \tfrac{1}{5} \text{ atm}} \\
\text{total } P \quad\;\; = 1 \text{ atm}
\end{aligned}
$$

One atmosphere of total pressure was observed in our experiment after the diaphragm was broken. *The model agrees with the experimental observation.*

We call the pressure due to nitrogen the *partial pressure of nitrogen.* This is sometimes indicated as $P_{N_2} = \tfrac{4}{5}$ atm. We call the pressure due to oxygen the *partial pressure of oxygen,* or $P_{O_2} = \tfrac{1}{5}$ atm. The pressure exerted by each of the gases in a gas mixture is called the **partial pressure** of that gas. The partial pressure is the pressure that the gas would exert if it were alone in the container. The **total pressure** is the sum of the partial pressures.

$$P_{\text{Total}} = P_{N_2} + P_{O_2} = \tfrac{4}{5} \text{ atm} + \tfrac{1}{5} \text{ atm} = 1 \text{ atm} \tag{9}$$

The above simple additive relationship is a result of the makeup of a gaseous phase. *There is so much space between the molecules that each molecule behaves almost independently.* Each molecule contributes

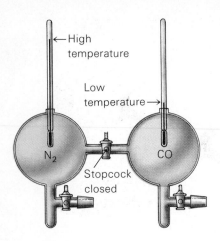

Fig. 4-7.1 When two gases at different temperatures are kept in separate containers, they will stay at different temperatures.

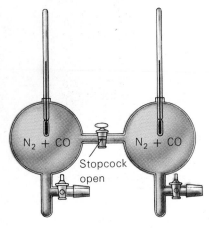

Fig. 4-7.2 When mixed the two gases will exchange energy and reach thermal equilibrium.

its share to the total pressure through its occasional collisions with the container walls. The total pressure is simply the *sum* of these individual molecular collisions.

EXERCISE 4-9

If 21.0 percent of the molecules in the air are oxygen molecules, what is the partial pressure of oxygen gas in the air when the barometer reads 740 mm Hg?

4-3.3 Temperature and the Kinetic Theory

What does temperature imply on a molecular scale, particularly as it applies to gases? We have agreed that the pressure exerted by gas molecules *at a given temperature* will be dependent upon the number of molecules hitting a unit of surface in a given time. But the masses of the molecules and their velocities will also be important. For example, a baseball exerts more force than a tennis ball thrown with the same velocity. A baseball exerts more push if it is a "fast ball" than if it is a "slow ball." To understand how the kinetic theory deals with these factors we must consider temperature.

We defined temperature as a number that tells us which way thermal energy (heat) will flow when two systems are brought into close contact with each other. Suppose we have two gases, nitrogen (N_2) and carbon monoxide (CO), in separate containers. The nitrogen is at a much higher temperature originally than is the carbon monoxide (see Figure 4-7.1). According to our definition of temperature, if N_2 is mixed with CO (Figure 4-7.2), some of the energy of the nitrogen must be transferred to the carbon monoxide because energy flows from the body at higher temperature (N_2) to the body at lower temperature (CO).

The energy of the nitrogen is stored in the energy of motion of its molecules. Thus the molecules of N_2 originally had more energy of motion (kinetic energy) on the average than did the molecules of CO. The kinetic energy of a molecule is determined both by its mass and its velocity:

$$\text{kinetic energy} = \tfrac{1}{2}\ \text{mass} \times (\text{velocity})^2$$

or

$$KE = \tfrac{1}{2}\ mv^2 \tag{10}$$

Since molecules of CO and N_2 both have the same molecular weight (28), the hotter nitrogen molecules must have a higher average speed than the cooler CO molecules. Collisions of the rapidly moving molecules of N_2 with the somewhat more slowly moving molecules of CO slow down the N_2 molecules *on the average* and speed up the carbon monoxide molecules *on the average*. In this way kinetic energy is transferred from N_2 molecules to CO molecules until the average speed of the CO molecules equals the average speed of the N_2 molecules. The gases then have equal kinetic energy; no further net transfer of energy from N_2 to CO is expected. When kinetic energy is no longer transferred from N_2 to CO, the gases are in thermal equilibrium: *the two gases are at the same temperature.*

This example illustrates a more general and basic postulate of the kinetic theory. *When gases are at the same temperature, the molecules of the gases have the same average kinetic energy.* In this example, CO and N_2 were deliberately chosen because they have the same molecular weight. What if we choose gases with different molecular weights, such as CH_4 (mol wt = 16) and SO_2 (mol wt = 64)?

If samples of CH_4 and SO_2 are at the same temperature, their molecules must have the same average kinetic energy, *i.e.*,

$$KE_{CH_4} = KE_{SO_2} \qquad (11)$$

where KE_{CH_4} is the average kinetic energy of 1 mole of CH_4 and KE_{SO_2} is the average kinetic energy for 1 mole of SO_2. For any object, $KE = \frac{1}{2}mv^2$, where m is the mass and v is its velocity. Thus, we see that the lighter CH_4 molecules must be moving faster, on the average, than the heavier SO_2 molecules in order for their kinetic energies to be equal.

4-3.4 Absolute Temperature and the Dependence of Volume and Pressure on Temperature

The quantitative relationships between gas temperature and gas pressure or gas volume were first studied by Jacques Charles in 1787. The relationships he developed are referred to frequently as **Charles' law.** A few simple experiments will show what is involved.

In a small-bore glass tube, $\frac{1}{4}$ metre in length and closed at one end, we place a drop of mercury. This mercury falls and finally traps a sample of air in the bottom of the tube (see Figure 4-8). Since the tube has a uniform bore, we can use the length of the air sample as a measure of its volume. The mercury plug moves up or down and maintains a constant pressure.

We may place the tube in ice water (0 °C) and measure the relative volume of the air sample. If the tube is immersed in boiling water (100 °C), the relative volume has a higher value. From these observations and from similar measurements at other temperatures, we collect data such as those in Table 4-4.

When we plot these results with relative volumes on the vertical axis (ordinate) and temperatures on the horizontal axis (abscissa), we obtain the graph in Figure 4-9 (page 86). The straight line passes through the experimental points. When extended upward, it shows that the volume at 273 °C is double that at 0 °C. Extrapolated, or extended downward, the line shows that the volume would become zero at −273 °C. The *volume change* per degree Celsius is $\frac{1}{273}$ of the volume at 0 °C.

If gases are heated or cooled at constant volume, the *pressure change* per degree Celsius is also $\frac{1}{273}$ of its value at 0 °C. Thus the pressure of a gas should become zero at −273 °C. Actually, all gases liquefy before their temperature reaches −273 °C. In terms of the

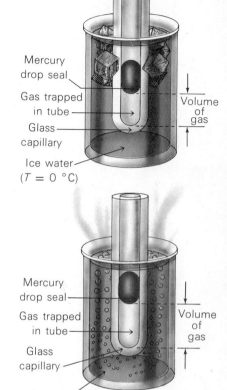

Mercury
drop seal

Gas trapped
in tube

Glass
capillary

Ice water
($T = 0$ °C)

Volume
of
gas

Mercury
drop seal

Gas trapped
in tube

Glass
capillary

Boiling water ($T = 100$ °C)

Volume
of
gas

Fig. 4-8 The volume of a given quantity of gas will increase when the gas is heated.

TABLE 4-4 CHANGE OF VOLUME OF A GAS WITH CHANGE IN TEMPERATURE

Temperature (°C)	Relative Volume As Measured by Length of Sample
0	1.00
50	1.18
100	1.37
200	1.73

ABSOLUTE TEMPERATURE

kinetic theory, the motion of the molecules would cease at this temperature.* The kinetic energy would become zero. The liquid state appears before the kinetic energy becomes zero.

There are great advantages to an *absolute* temperature scale that has its zero point at −273 °C. As noted earlier, the "zero" of temperature in the Celsius scale is fixed at an arbitrary temperature selected because it is easily measured. In contrast, the zero point of the absolute scale has a definite meaning in the kinetic theory. Furthermore, we find that *the volume of a fixed amount of gas (at constant pressure) varies directly with temperature expressed on an absolute temperature scale.† The pressure of a fixed amount of gas (at constant volume) varies directly with temperature.* According to the kinetic theory, the average kinetic energy of the molecules varies directly with the absolute temperature. For these reasons, in dealing with gas relations, we shall usually express temperature on an absolute temperature scale.

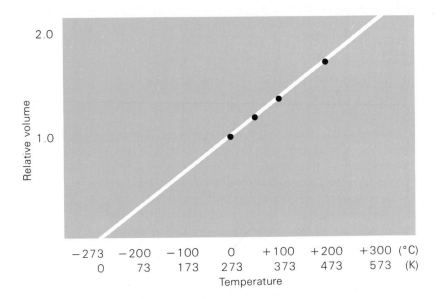

Fig. 4-9 A plot of temperature versus volume for gases.

This temperature scale, with the same size degree as the Celsius scale, is called the kelvin scale and values on this scale are expressed in kelvins (K).‡ Both kelvin and Celsius temperatures are shown in Figure 4-9. Notice that all numerical values on the kelvin scale are 273 degrees higher than the corresponding temperatures on the Celsius scale (more precisely, 273.1 degrees higher).

*The motion referred to here is the motion of the molecules with respect to the container, not the vibrations and rotations of the atoms in the molecule.
†This direct relation between volume and temperature (at constant pressure) is called Charles' law.

$$V = k \cdot T$$

‡By international agreement, the degree sign (°) is omitted when referring to absolute temperatures. The word kelvin is not capitalized because it is one of the internationally defined base units of science.

EXERCISE 4-10

(1) Express the following temperatures in kelvins:

Boiling point of water	100 °C
Freezing point of mercury	−38.9 °C
Boiling point of liquid nitrogen	−196 °C

(2) Express the following temperatures in degrees Celsius:

Melting point of lead	600 K
A normal room temperature	298 K
Boiling point of liquid helium	4 K

EXERCISE 4-11

In the laboratory a student obtained the following result: 2.00×10^{-3} mole of magnesium, reacting with dilute hydrochloric acid, produces a volume of hydrogen that occupies 49.0 ml at 25 °C and 1.00 atm pressure.

(1) If 1 mole of magnesium produces 1 mole of hydrogen, use these data to calculate the volume of 1 mole of hydrogen.
(2) Calculate the volume 1 mole of hydrogen will occupy at 0 °C (273 K) and 1.00 atm.

We have remarked that at a temperature of zero on the absolute temperature scale there would be no motion of molecules relative to the container. The kinetic energy of translation (motion with respect to the container) would become zero. Very interesting phenomena occur at temperatures near 0 K. (The superconductivity* of many metals and the superfluidity of liquid helium are two examples.) Hence, scientists are extremely interested in methods of reaching temperatures as close to absolute zero as possible. Two low-temperature coolants commonly used are liquid hydrogen (which boils at 20 K) and liquid helium (which boils at 4 K). Helium, under reduced pressure, boils at even lower temperatures and provides a means of reaching temperatures near 1 K. More unusual techniques have been developed to produce still lower temperatures (as low as 0.001 K), but even measuring these temperatures becomes a severe problem.

4-4 A GENERAL GAS EQUATION

In considering gases we have identified four general variables which are interrelated. These variables—pressure, volume, temperature, and number of moles of gas—have been considered in pairs until now. We have held two variables constant and then studied variations in the remaining two. For example, in our very first investigation of the relationship between pressure and volume, we considered a fixed

---

*If a metal is a superconductor its resistance to passage of the electric current drops to very near zero. Such conductors would be great for power transmission.

TABLE **4-5** PRESSURE-VOLUME
PRODUCT FOR GASES AT 0 °C
AND 1 ATM

Number of Molecules ($\times 10^{23}$)	Volume (litres)	$P \times V$ (atm $\times$ litres)
0.268	1.00	1.00
0.536	2.00	2.00
1.07	4.00	4.00
3.01	11.2	11.2
6.02	22.4	22.4
12.0	44.8	44.8
18.1	67.2	67.2

TABLE **4-6** PRESSURE-VOLUME
PRODUCT FOR GASES AT 25 °C
AND 1 ATM

Number of Molecules ($\times 10^{23}$)	Volume (litres)	$P \times V$ (atm $\times$ litres)
0.268	1.09	1.09
0.536	2.18	2.18
1.07	4.37	4.37
3.01	12.2	12.2
6.02	24.4	24.4
12.0	48.8	48.8
18.1	73.2	73.2

quantity or number of moles of gas at constant temperature. Number of moles and temperature were therefore held constant while pressure and volume were varied. In studying the relationship of temperature and volume in Section 4-3.4, the number of moles of gas and the pressure were held constant while volume and temperature were varied. Is this pattern always necessary or desirable? Let us see if a more general equation can be developed.

4-4.1 Development of a General Gas Equation

In studying the general relationship between pressure and volume we found that pressure $\times$ volume = a constant. Values for $P \times V$ for different amounts of gas and at two temperatures are given in Tables 4-5 and 4-6. An examination of the data shows that the size of the constant depends on (1) the quantity of gas and (2) the temperature. It is convenient to measure the quantity of gas in moles. We remember that for 1 mole of gas at 0 °C and 1 atmosphere, $V = 22.4$ litres. Then for 1 mole of gas,

$$P \times V = 1 \text{ atm} \times 22.4 \frac{\text{litres}}{\text{mole}} \tag{12}$$

Since the constant is twice as large for 2 moles and three times as large for 3 moles, we can write (for 0 °C)

$$P \times V = \underbrace{1 \text{ atm}}_{P} \times \underbrace{n \times 22.4 \frac{\text{litres}}{\text{mole}}}_{\text{VOLUME AT 273 K}} \tag{13}$$

where n is the number of moles of gas taken.

We now have the three variables P, V, and n related through a single expression, but the equation is only good at 0 °C. How can the effects of temperature be included? We remember from Section 4-3.4 that an increase in temperature increases the volume of the gas. For example, at 25 °C and 1 atmosphere the volume of 1 mole of gas is 24.4 litres. The general expression showing how the volume of 1 mole of gas at 1 atmosphere varies with temperature is

$$V = 22.4 \frac{\text{litres}}{\text{mole}} \times \frac{T}{273 \text{ K}} \tag{14}$$

where T is the temperature on the kelvin scale. Placing this expression in for the volume of 1 mole of gas, we obtain the expression:

$$P \times V = \underbrace{1 \text{ atm}}_{P} \times \underbrace{n \times 22.4 \frac{\text{litres}}{\text{mole}} \times \frac{T}{273 \text{ K}}}_{\text{VOLUME OF } n \text{ MOLES AT } T} \tag{15}$$

or

$$P \cdot V = nT \left[\frac{22.4}{273} \frac{\text{litres} \times \text{atm}}{\text{mole} \times \text{K}} \right] \tag{16}$$

The numerical quantity in the brackets does not change as we change P, V, n, or T. It simply reflects our earlier arbitrary choices for molar volume, standard temperature, and standard pressure. Since this number does not change, it is worthwhile doing the division needed to evaluate the constant.

$$\frac{22.4 \times 1}{1 \times 273} \frac{\text{litres} \times \text{atmospheres}}{\text{number moles} \times \text{K}} = 0.0821 \frac{\text{litres} \times \text{atm}}{\text{mole} \times \text{K}} \quad (17)$$

The unit "mole" must be included in the denominator because the volume of 22.4 litres is for *1 mole* of gas at 1 atmosphere and 273 K.

This quantity is of great importance in physical chemistry. It is assigned the symbol R and is known as the **ideal gas constant.** The general gas equation can then be written as

$$PV = nRT \quad (18)$$

If P is given in mm Hg and V is given in ml, R has a different numerical value, but the same overall significance.

$$\frac{22,400 \text{ ml} \times 760 \text{ mm Hg}}{\text{mole} \times 273 \text{ K}} = \frac{62,400 \text{ ml} \times \text{mm Hg}}{\text{mole} \times \text{K}}$$

The expression $PV = nRT$ is known as the **ideal gas law.** Chemists find it a most convenient and powerful equation. The numerical value selected for R depends on the units which are being used in the problem. This fact is summarized in Table 4-7.

TABLE 4-7 VALUES OF THE IDEAL GAS CONSTANT

Pressure in:	Volume in:	Value of R is:
atm	litres	$0.0821\left(\dfrac{\text{litres} \times \text{atm}}{\text{mole} \times \text{K}}\right)$
mm Hg	litres	$62.4\left(\dfrac{\text{litres} \times \text{mm Hg}}{\text{mole} \times \text{K}}\right)$
mm Hg	ml	$62,400\left(\dfrac{\text{ml} \times \text{mm Hg}}{\text{mole} \times \text{K}}\right)$
atm	ml	$82.1\left(\dfrac{\text{ml} \times \text{atm}}{\text{mole} \times \text{K}}\right)$

4-4.2 Some Examples of Gas Law Calculations

Some sample problems are included here to indicate how gas law calculations can be made.

Example (1) A 1.00-litre gas sample at 0 °C and 1 atm pressure has a mass of 0.715 ± 0.005 g. Which one of the following gases could be indicated: CO_2, CO, N_2, O_2, CH_4, NH_3, HCl?

The information given permits the calculation of the mass of 22.4 litres of gas measured at STP. This is the molecular weight of the gas. We then can write

$$\text{molar mass gas} = \frac{(0.715 \pm 0.005)\ \text{g}}{\text{litre}} \times \frac{22.4\ \text{litres}}{\text{mole}} = \frac{16.0\ \text{g}}{\text{mole}}$$

molecular weight gas $= 16.0$

To decide which of the gases is indicated, we must calculate the molecular weight for each of the gases shown. For CO_2 the value is equal to the atomic weight of carbon plus two times the atomic weight of oxygen or $12.0 + (2 \times 16.0) = 44.0$. Similar calculations for all other gases give these molecular weights: $CO = 28, N_2 = 28, O_2 = 32,$ $CH_4 = 16, NH_3 = 17,$ and $HCl = 36.5$. The answer appears to be CH_4, which has a molecular weight of 16.

Example (2) What pressure would be required to compress a 2.00-mole sample of gas into 10.0 litres at 0 °C?

We start with the knowledge that *1 mole* of gas at STP (0 °C and 1 atm) occupies 22.4 litres. Two moles of gas will then occupy 44.8 litres. We can write for 2 moles of gas:

$$P \times V = 44.8\ \text{litres} \times \text{atm}$$

If $V = 10.0$ litres (given), then

$$P \times 10.0\ \text{litres} = 44.8\ \text{litres} \times \text{atm}$$

or

$$P = 4.48\ \text{atm}$$

Example (3) Barometer A (a barometer is used to measure atmospheric pressure) has some gas on top of the column. It reads 742 mm Hg. A new barometer, B, from the storeroom reads 757 mm Hg. What is the gas pressure above the mercury in barometer A? (See Figure 4-10.)

Barometer A is now serving as a manometer which measures the *difference* between the pressure above the mercury column and the pressure of the atmosphere outside. Pressure reading by barometer A = atmospheric pressure − pressure inside. Hence,

742 mm Hg = 757 mm Hg − pressure inside
pressure inside = 15 mm Hg

Example (4a) What is the partial pressure of each gas in a mixture containing by volume: 20 percent He, 30 percent CO, 10 percent H_2, and 40 percent CH_4 if the total pressure is 800 mm Hg?

Fig. 4-10

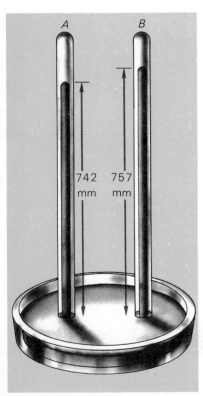

A   B

742 mm 757 mm

Twenty percent He by volume means that 20 percent of the molecules in the container are He. Thus,

$$
\begin{aligned}
800 \text{ mm Hg} \times 0.20 &= 160 \text{ mm He} \\
800 \text{ mm Hg} \times 0.30 &= 240 \text{ mm CO} \\
800 \text{ mm Hg} \times 0.10 &= 80 \text{ mm H}_2 \\
800 \text{ mm Hg} \times 0.40 &= \underline{320 \text{ mm CH}_4} \\
& \ 800 \text{ mm total}
\end{aligned}
$$

Example (4b) What would be the *total pressure* if water vapor at a pressure of 18 mm were added to the dry gases with no change in total volume?

$$\text{total pressure} = 800 + 18 = 818 \text{ mm Hg}$$

Example (5) (Use of the ideal gas law.) What volume would be occupied by 3 moles of nitrogen under a pressure of 120 atm and a temperature of 50 °C?

Given: $PV = nRT$

$$
\begin{aligned}
P &= 120 \text{ atm} \\
V &= \text{volume (litres)} \\
T &= 50 \text{ °C} + 273 = 323 \text{ K} \\
n &= 3 \text{ moles}
\end{aligned}
$$

Since P is given in atm and V in litres, we shall use R in these units:

$$R = 0.082 \left(\frac{\text{litres} \times \text{atm}}{\text{mole} \times \text{K}} \right)$$

$$120 \text{ atm} \times V = 3 \text{ moles} \times 0.082 \left(\frac{\text{litres} \times \text{atm}}{\text{mole} \times \text{K}} \right) \times 323 \text{ K}$$

$$V = \frac{3 \times 0.082 \times 323}{120} \text{ litres} = 0.66 \text{ litre}$$

EXERCISE 4-12

How many moles of a gas will occupy 900 ml at a pressure of 4,500 mm Hg and a temperature of −73 °C? (Use the ideal gas law.) (*Answer:* 0.32 mole.)

4-5 THE POWER OF THEORY

Avogadro's hypothesis was described first in Section 2-1.7. In Section 4-4.1 separate observations on gas behavior were combined algebraically to obtain the ideal gas law, $PV = nRT$. One of the triumphs of the kinetic theory is its ability to come up with both Avogadro's hypothesis and the ideal gas law from a mathematical analysis of the motion of gas particles. Such an analysis is not particularly hard to follow. Ask your teacher if you are interested. The ability of the kinetic theory to duplicate several sets of independent observations gives us confidence in the theoretical model upon which the kinetic theory rests.

4-6 HIGHLIGHTS

Gases are mostly empty space; in contrast, liquids and solids represent more closely packed molecules. Many of the peculiar general properties of gases such as their common molar volume (22.4 litres at STP) result from the fact that the molecules are separated by relatively large distances and have very little attraction for each other.

We have explored the meaning of temperature. According to the **kinetic theory,** when two gases are at the same temperature, the molecules of the two gases have the same average kinetic energies. Changing the temperature of a sample of gas at constant pressure reveals that the volume is directly proportional to the temperature if the temperature is expressed in terms of a new, absolute scale. The melting point of ice (0 °C) on this new scale, the **kelvin scale,** is 273 K. The boiling point of water at 1 atm (100 °C) is 373 K. The zero temperature on the kelvin scale corresponds to the hypothetical loss of all molecular motion.

By combining our observations on temperature-volume, pressure-volume, temperature-pressure, and volume-number-of-moles relationships, we obtained an extremely useful relationship—the **ideal gas law,** $PV = nRT$, a relationship which also follows from the kinetic theory.

This progress substantiates our confidence in the usefulness of the atomic theory and it encourages us to develop the model further. We shall see that the concepts we have developed in our consideration of gases are also useful in considering the behavior of condensed phases—liquids and solids.

QUESTIONS and PROBLEMS

1 Hydrogen gas (H_2) liquefies at -252.5 °C under a pressure of 1 atm. The liquid has a density of 0.0700 g/ml. The molar volume of gaseous hydrogen is approximately 22.4 litres at STP. (a) Calculate the molar volume of liquid hydrogen. (b) At STP, what is the ratio:

$$\frac{\text{molar volume of gaseous hydrogen}}{\text{molar volume of liquid hydrogen}}$$

(c) How is it possible for the same number of molecules to occupy two such different volumes? (d) Why was liquid, rather than gaseous, hydrogen used as fuel in our Saturn rockets?

2 For each of the following, calculate (i) the number of moles of gas present in the sample, and (ii) the molecular weight of the gas. (a) 11.0 g of a gas occupy 5.60 litres at STP. (b) 0.80 g of a gas occupies 4.88 litres at 25 °C and 1 atm. (c) 21.0 g of a gas occupy 18.3 litres at 25 °C and 1 atm. (d) 0.96 g of a gas occupies 672 ml at STP.

3 For each of the following, calculate (i) the number of moles of gas present in the sample, and (ii) the molecular weight of the gas. (a) A gas, 6.5 g of which occupy 5.6 litres at STP. (b) A gas, 5.68 g of which occupy 1.792 litres at STP. (c) A gas, 1.20 g of which occupy 6.10×10^2 ml at 25 °C and 1 atm. (d) A gas, 3.74 g of which occupy 2.464 litres at 25 °C and 1 atm. (e) A gas, 5.55 g of which occupy 6.72 litres at STP.

4 Acetylene (C_2H_2) in acetylene lanterns is generated by the reaction of water on calcium carbide (CaC_2) as follows:

$$CaC_2 + H_2O \longrightarrow Ca(OH)_2 + C_2H_2$$

(a) Balance the equation. (b) Calculate the volume of C_2H_2 (measured at 25 °C and 1 atm) released if 0.450 mole of CaC_2 is used in the above reaction.

5 Metallic silver can be reclaimed from silver chloride by the following reaction:

$$AgCl + H_2 \longrightarrow Ag + HCl$$

(a) Balance the equation. (b) What volume of hydrogen, measured at 25 °C and 1 atm, would be used in changing 28.7 g of AgCl back to metallic silver?

6 When hydrogen is needed in the laboratory, it is commonly made by the reaction of zinc metal with hydrochloric acid (HCl). The products of the reaction are hydrogen gas and zinc dichloride. (a) Write the balanced equation for the reaction. (b) How many moles of zinc must be used to produce 5.0 litres of hydrogen gas measured at room conditions? (c) How many grams of zinc would be necessary to produce the 5.0 litres of hydrogen gas? (d) How many grams of zinc would be necessary to produce enough hydrogen gas for the reaction in question 5(b)?

7 Oxygen is often generated in the laboratory by the reaction between sodium peroxide (Na_2O_2) and water, under appropriate conditions. Sodium hydroxide (NaOH) is the other product. (a) Write the balanced equation for the reaction. (b) How many grams of Na_2O_2 must be used to generate 1.0 litre of oxygen at 25 °C and 1 atm? Assume all Na_2O_2 reacts.

8 Calculate the mass of each of the following: (a) 150 litres of N_2H_4 measured at STP. (b) 150 litres of N_2H_4 measured at 25 °C and 1 atm. (c) 5.60 kilolitres of oxygen measured at STP. (d) 61.0 kl of NH_3 measured at 25 °C and 1 atm.

9 How many *molecules* of gas are present in each of the following samples? (a) 120 g of a gas which occupy 89.6 litres measured at STP. (b) 2.45 g of a gas which occupy 122 litres measured at 25 °C and 1 atm.

10 Given the following unbalanced equation:

$$Cu_2O + H_2 \longrightarrow Cu + H_2O$$

(a) Balance the equation. (b) Calculate the volume of hydrogen, measured at STP, needed to react with 8.30 moles of Cu_2O.

11 (a) Balance the equation:

$$Fe + H_2O \longrightarrow Fe_3O_4 + H_2$$

(b) Calculate the number of moles of iron needed to produce 6.500 litres of hydrogen by the above reaction if the volume of hydrogen is measured at STP.

12 Liquid vegetable oils, such as cottonseed oil, can be converted into solids of the margarine type by the process of hydrogenation. Although cottonseed oil is not a pure chemical substance, but a mixture of esters of fatty acids, the reaction can be typified by the following *unbalanced* equation:

$$\underset{\text{OLEIN}}{(C_{17}H_{33}COO)_3C_3H_5} + H_2 \longrightarrow$$

$$\underset{\text{STEARIN}}{(C_{17}H_{35}COO)_3C_3H_5}$$

(a) Balance the equation. (b) If 3.0×10^3 litres of hydrogen gas (measured at 25 °C and 1 atm) enter into the reaction, how many moles of olein are hydrogenated?

13 Clean, dry air has a molecular composition as follows: nitrogen, 78.1 percent; oxygen, 21.0 percent; argon, 0.9 percent; others, trace amounts. If the air in your laboratory is clean and dry, and the pressure is 0.990 atm, what is the partial pressure of each gas?

14 A flask contains 2.00 moles of oxygen gas and 8.00 moles of nitrogen gas. When the flask is connected to a manometer, the total pressure is found to be 1.80 atm. Calculate the partial pressures of oxygen and nitrogen.

15 A mixture of gases in a flask has the following composition: 0.500 mole of UF_6, 1.200 moles of CO_2, and 0.800 mole of Kr. If the total pressure in the flask is 0.980 atm, what is the partial pressure of each gas?

16 A flask contained enough oxygen molecules to exert a pressure of 0.50 atm. If twice as many nitrogen molecules and three times as many helium molecules are introduced, what will be the total pressure on the flask? (Assume no interaction among the substances.)

17 Analysis of a container of gases gave the following percentages, *by mass,* for each: 3.60 percent helium, 18.2 percent neon, 75.4 percent krypton, and 2.80 percent carbon monoxide. Calculate the partial pressure for each of these gases if the total pressure is 0.750 atm.

18 A mixture of 2.00 g of CH_4 and 15.55 g of Si_2H_6, both gases, is placed in a flask. The total pressure exerted by this mixture is 0.980 atm. Calculate the partial pressure of each gas.

19 A mixture of gases contains 0.60 g of H_2, 4.4 g of CO_2, and 0.80 g of He. The total pressure is 1.3 atm. If the CO_2 is solidified and then removed and the other gases warmed back to their original temperature, (a) what is the **93**

new total pressure of the remaining gases? (b) What is the partial pressure of each remaining gas? (Assume that there is no interaction among the gases.)

20 Nitrogen gas is collected by the displacement of water. (a) If the total pressure is 759.9 mm and the temperature is 23 °C, what is the pressure exerted by the nitrogen? (*Hint:* See Table 10-1 in the Laboratory Manual.) (b) What would the pressure of the nitrogen be if the temperature were 30 °C?

21 Ammonia (NH_3) and sulfur dioxide (SO_2) are both gases with readily distinguishable odors. If a cylinder of each were opened in a draftless room, which odor would you expect to smell first? Why?

22 A sample of dry helium gas in a rigid container is brought to different temperatures by placing it successively in boiling water, an ice-water mixture, a Dry Ice-alcohol mixture, and liquid nitrogen. At each temperature, the pressure is measured. The results are shown below:

	Temperature (°C)	Pressure (atm)
Boiling water	100	1.24
Ice-water mixture	0	0.93
Dry Ice-alcohol	−79	0.67
Liquid nitrogen	−196	0.27

Plot these data on a graph. From the graph find the value of absolute zero in degrees Celsius.

23 The freezing and boiling points in degrees Celsius of some common substances are listed below. Express each of these temperatures in kelvins.

	Freezing Point (°C)	Boiling Point (°C)
Hydrogen	−259	−253
Methane	−182	−161.5
Ethyl alcohol	−117.3	78.5
Water	0.0	100

24 Express the following temperatures in degrees Celsius: (a) 273 K (b) 298 K (c) 373 K (d) 100 K (e) 0 K.

25 (a) In order to decrease the pressure exerted by a gas, how must the volume change if all other conditions remain unchanged? (b) If the volume of a container holding a gas is decreased, what will be the effect on the pressure if all other conditions remain unchanged? (c) If the number of gas molecules is decreased, what will be the effect on the pressure if all other conditions remain unchanged? (d) If the number of gas molecules is decreased, what must happen to the volume if all other conditions are to remain unchanged?

26 A gas occupies 0.300 litre and exerts a pressure of 0.800 atm. What must its volume become in order for the pressure to be 1.20 atm?

27 If a 100-ml sample of gas is heated from 25 °C to 50 °C (pressure and number of molecules remaining constant), what will be the resulting volume?

28 A gas occupies 10.0 litres at a measured pressure of 1.4 atm. Consider each of the following problems independently of each other. (a) If the volume is changed to 25.0 litres, what will be the pressure (assuming no change in the amount of gas or the temperature)? (b) If $\frac{1}{4}$ of the molecules are removed, what will the volume have to be in order that there be no change in pressure or temperature? (c) What must the volume be if the pressure registers 0.800 atm (no change in temperature or amount of gas)? (d) If gas is added so that the number of moles of gas is quadrupled, what will the pressure be if there is no change in volume or temperature?

29 Show how you would calculate R from the following data: (a) pressure = 760 mm, volume = 12.2 litres, temperature = 298 K, and number of moles = 0.50; (b) pressure = 760 mm, molecular weight of gas = 64.1, density of gas = 2.97 g/litre, temperature = 273 K; (c) pressure = 108 cm Hg, volume = 3.36 litres, number of grams in sample = 3.03 g, molecular weight = 2.02, temperature = 38.6 K.

30 A sample of nitrogen gas in a syringe occupies 15.0 ml when under a pressure of 6 bricks. Given the further information that the sample has a mass of 0.040 gram and the temperature is 25 °C, calculate the value of R in the general gas equation. Be sure to express your answer in the proper units.

31 In Experiment 4, a sample of air in a syringe occupied 9.8 ml at 25 °C when under a total pressure of 9 books. If the air in the syringe consisted of 1.43×10^{-3} mole of molecules, calculate the value of R in the general gas equation. Watch units.

32 Suppose standard conditions had been selected as 25 °C and 2.0 atm instead of 0.00 °C and 1.00 atm. What would the new value of R have been?

33 How many moles of gas are present in a volume of 16.4 litres at a pressure of 5.0 atm and a temperature of 250 K?

34 What is the volume, in ml, of 0.080 mole of gas at 400 mm Hg pressure and 800 K?

35 What is the pressure (in atm) of 8.3 moles of a gas which occupy 0.070 litre at a temperature of 427 °C?

36 At what temperature (in K) must 0.75 mole of a gas be in order to fit into a volume of 10.0 litres at a pressure of 1,500 mm Hg?

From a drop of water, a logician could infer the possibility of an Atlantic Ocean or a Niagara Falls without having seen or heard of one or the other.

SIR ARTHUR CONAN DOYLE (1859–1930)

LIQUIDS AND SOLIDS: 5
CONDENSED PHASES OF MATTER

Water in its two condensed phases—at 0 °C water can exist as both a liquid and a solid.

THE "IDEAL GAS" HAS THUS FAR BEEN CONSIDERED AS A COLLECTION of rebounding particles which are so far apart that attraction between particles is negligible. We find that no gas is truly "ideal," that the attraction between particles *is* of consequence, and that there is great variation in the strength of these attractive forces. It is as a result of this attraction between real particles that solids and liquids—the crowded or condensed phases of matter—exist.

As gas particles are found to be less than "perfect" on crowding, their differences become more interesting than their similarities. The magnitude of the attractive forces between particles determines many of the physical properties of any substance—boiling point and freezing point, the amount of energy necessary to produce a phase change, and behavior when mixed with other substances. While solids and liquids are not as "simple" to study as free and unattached gas particles, there is a certain relief in dealing with substances in a form that we can see, feel, measure, and weigh more readily than we can gases.

Our model for gases has moved from a purely qualitative description of gas behavior to a quantitative and mathematical description. (1) Experimentally we found that the expression $PV = $ a constant describes the behavior of a number of gases if a constant quantity of gas at a constant temperature is considered. (2) We were then able to use the "super-rubber" ball model for gases to derive the expression $PV = $ a constant (again, quantity of gas and temperature assumed constant). (3) It was then possible to combine a number of separate experimental observations to obtain the more general expression $PV = nRT$.

So far the successes of our model have been spectacular; but before we become too self-satisfied, let us try a few more experiments. Trouble lies ahead—but trouble which may mean progress! The late Peter Debye, Nobel Laureate in chemistry, once said, "I love to see unexpected experimental results; I am bound to learn something." Here is the experiment; we hope we learn something.

5-1 PHASE CHANGES

5-1.1 The Pressure-Volume Behavior of Ammonia at High Pressure—Non-Ideal Gases

In Table 4-2 of Chapter 4 we summarized results obtained when 1 mole of ammonia gas (NH_3) was compressed at 25 °C. The volume of the gas was carefully measured as the pressure was increased by stages. The relationship $PV = 24.4 \pm 0.1$ was obeyed very well for pressures from 0.1 to 2.0 atm, but we noticed (page 76) even then that the values were not randomly distributed around 24.4. Instead, a gradual decrease of the "constant" from 24.45 at 0.1 atm to 24.34 at 2.0 atm was seen. Why? What happens if we go beyond 2 atm? Is the relationship $PV = 24.4 \pm 0.1$ still true?

TABLE 5-1 ACCURATE PRESSURE-VOLUME MEASUREMENTS FOR 17.00 GRAMS OF AMMONIA GAS AT 25 °C

Pressure (atm)	Volume (litres)	$P \times V$ (atm × litres)
0.1000	244.5	24.45
0.2000	122.2	24.44
0.4000	61.02	24.41
0.8000	30.44	24.35
2.000	12.17	24.34
4.000	5.975	23.90
8.000	2.925	23.40
9.800	2.360	23.10 (condensation beginning)
9.800	0.020	0.20 (no gas left; liquid only)
20.00	0.020	0.40 (only liquid present)
50.00	0.020	1.0 (only liquid present)

The data shown in Table 5-1 indicate that the relationship $PV = $ a constant is not valid at pressures greater than 2 atm. The value of the "constant" (originally 24.4) becomes noticeably smaller above 2.0 atm until, at a pressure of 9.8 atm, liquid droplets begin to appear in the gas container. The value of the product obtained by multiplying pressure and volume drops rapidly from 23.10. As we try to increase the gas pressure above 9.8 atm by pushing a piston into the container, *we find that more gas is converted to liquid and the pressure returns to 9.8 atm.* We are surprised to learn that *the pressure on the ammonia cannot be raised above 9.8 atm at 25 °C until all the gas has been converted to liquid* (Figure 5-1.2). As soon as the last of the gas has disappeared, pressure on the liquid can be increased without any obvious volume change. For a liquid the PV product increases again as pressure increases but without a significant volume change. It is clear that the simple relationship $PV = $ a constant is not a good description of the liquid phase, and our simple gas law fails most rapidly during the change from gas to liquid. These experiments are illustrated in Figure 5-1.

Fig. 5-1.1 Behavior of ammonia as pressure is increased while temperature remains at 25 °C.

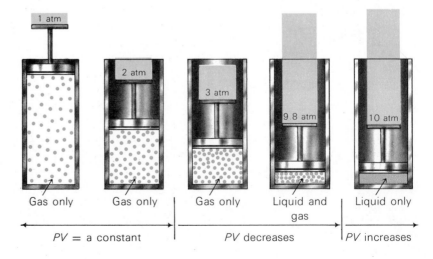

Gas only	Gas only	Gas only	Liquid and gas	Liquid only

$PV = $ a constant | PV decreases | PV increases

Liquid   Only liquid

Fig. 5-1.2 Enlarged view of the liquefaction of ammonia at 25 °C.

These observations give us much to "wonder why" about. For example:

(1) Why did the value of the constant 24.4 begin to get smaller above about 2 atm pressure?
(2) What is so special about a pressure of 9.8 atm for ammonia at 25 °C?
(3) What is the relation between liquid and gaseous phases?
(4) Why does the expression $PV =$ a constant not apply to liquids as well as gases?
(5) How does our "super-rubber" ball model for gases account for the behavior of liquids?
(6) What modification in the gas model is needed to explain the properties of liquids?

Question (6) is the most significant. It can also be phrased: how must the model for gases be altered in order to explain or account for the nature of liquids? Let us suppose that a liquid is also composed of "super-rubber" balls, collected in the lower part of the container. Each ball still has kinetic energy since the liquid is at the same temperature as the gas from which it was formed. This means that the balls (or molecules) can vibrate back and forth and move around pushing the other balls about, but *some forces must be acting among the balls as a group to hold them together.*

Clearly, this is an important point. Our development of the kinetic theory for gases assumed that gas particles exert no real forces on each other. In contrast, we cannot understand the existence of the liquid phase unless we assume that real molecules *do exert* forces of attraction on each other. These forces are very small when the molecules are far apart (that is, when the gas is at low pressure). As we developed the model for gases, agreement between theory and experiment was good at low pressures, even though we did not consider intermolecular attractions. When forces are very small, we can ignore them. But as molecules are pushed closer and closer together at higher pressures, the forces of attraction between molecules become important. At intermediate pressures molecules are attracted to each other just a little; the volume is a little smaller than it would be if there were no attraction between molecules. Because the *volume is less* than it would be without molecular attraction, the PV product for NH_3 at 25 °C and pressures above 2 atm drops *below* 24.4. This is a reasonable answer to question (1).

When we tried to push the molecules close enough together to give a gas pressure higher than 9.8 atm at 25 °C, the forces acting between molecules became strong enough—because of the shorter distance—to pull the molecules together into liquid droplets. Condensation of the gas into liquid continued until the pressure of the remaining gas dropped again to 9.8 atm [question (2)]. The model describes the difference between liquid and gaseous phases. Intermolecular forces hold liquid molecules together [questions (3) and (5)]. Finally, we find that in explaining the relationship $PV = a$ constant for gases using the kinetic theory, we assumed that the molecules of gas were far apart and moved rapidly through open space. This is not so for liquids. Liquid molecules are actually held together in a movable mass where molecules touch each other [question (6)]. An increase in pressure does not bring about a corresponding decrease in volume because the molecules are already touching. It really is not strange that PV is *not* a constant for a liquid [question (4)].

Let us summarize what has been said. The kinetic theory for gases is based on an "ideal" gas—one in which the molecules exert no force on each other. Every gas approaches such "ideal" behavior when its pressure is low enough and temperature high enough. At very low pressures molecules are, on the average, so far apart that their attractive forces are negligible. An *ideal* or *perfect gas* obeys the ideal gas law ($PV = nRT$). Attractions between molecules first cause deviations from the ideal gas law and finally the formation of liquids. Most gases show some deviation from ideality. The larger the deviation from ideal behavior, the smaller the **molar volume** of the gas at STP and the easier the gas is to liquefy. (See data for ammonia in Table 5-1 on page 98.)

EXERCISE 5-1

The following table indicates the boiling points and the molar volumes (at 0 °C and 1 atm) of some common gases:

Gas	Formula	Boiling Point (°C)	Molar Volume (litres)
Helium	He	−269	22.426
Nitrogen	N_2	−196	22.402
Carbon monoxide	CO	−190	22.402
Oxygen	O_2	−183	22.393
Methane	CH_4	−161	22.360
Hydrogen chloride	HCl	−84.0	22.248
Ammonia	NH_3	−33.3	22.094
Chlorine	Cl_2	−34.6	22.063
Sulfur dioxide	SO_2	−10.0	21.888

(1) What regularity is suggested in the relationship between the boiling points and molar volumes? Plot the values. Choose a scale so that range 21.500-22.500 will occupy a full page in your notebook.

(2) Account for this regularity. (*Hint:* what does a high boiling point suggest about intermolecular forces?)

5-1.2 Liquid, Solid, or Gaseous States?— The Factors Involved

Although our description of pressure-volume relationships for ideal gases is fairly good, it is not very widely applicable. Only a handful of substances are gases under normal conditions of temperature and pressure. Of the hundred or so elements, eleven are gases* and two (bromine and mercury) are liquids at STP (0 °C and 1 atm). All the rest are solids. As for compounds, more than a million have been prepared. Yet more than 99 percent of these are liquids or solids at STP. Gases clearly are in the minority.

Look again at the data for ammonia in Table 5-1. Here we see that the classification of ammonia as a gas or a liquid does not really mean much unless we give the temperature and the pressure for the system. Ammonia is a gas at 25 °C and 1 atm; it is a liquid at 25 °C and 10 atm. Pure substances can be converted from gas to liquid in a process which we have called a **phase change** (see Section 1-4.2). Phase changes are familiar to you: ice melts to water and water boils to give steam (water vapor); solid iron melts to liquid iron; gaseous ammonia condenses to give liquid ammonia; candle wax melts to give liquid wax. These are only a few of the phase changes with which you are familiar.

In Section 1-4.2 we stated that the melting point of a pure substance is a characteristic property of that substance and can be used to identify the material. For example, if we know that a material melts at −8.6 °C, we know that it cannot be the explosive trinitrotoluene (TNT) which melts at 80.7 °C. It could, however, be oil of wintergreen which is known to melt at −8.6 °C. Pressure has a very small effect upon the melting point. For this reason, the melting point is precisely defined as the temperature at which a pure solid changes to a liquid under a given pressure (usually 1 atmosphere).

5-1.3 Energy Required for Phase Changes— The Heat of Vaporization

When a pan of water is warmed, the input of energy causes the water temperature to rise. At a certain temperature the water begins to boil. Gas bubbles form in the liquid and rise to the surface where they burst. Liquid water is being converted to gaseous water. If we place a thermometer in the boiling water, we find that the *temperature remains constant as long as any liquid water remains* (see Figure 5-2). *The energy added by the gas flame is being used to convert water in the liquid phase to water in the gas phase at constant temperature.* If we stop adding energy (turn off the gas flame), the boiling stops immediately. In summary we can say: *when water changes from the liquid phase to the gaseous phase at constant pressure, energy must be supplied; yet the boiling temperature remains constant.*

*The eleven gaseous elements at STP are hydrogen (H_2), helium (He), nitrogen (N_2), oxygen (O_2), fluorine (F_2), neon (Ne), chlorine (Cl_2), argon (Ar), krypton (Kr), xenon (Xe), and radon (Rn).

Fig. 5-2 Temperature of water above a flame as a function of time. (Pressure of atmosphere = 760 mm Hg.)

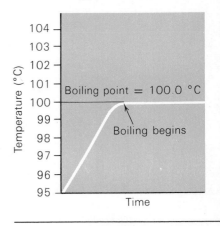

ENERGY REQUIRED
for PHASE CHANGES

Clearly, water in the gas phase has more energy than water in the liquid phase. The equation representing the change is

$$H_2O(\textit{liquid}) + \text{thermal energy} \longrightarrow$$

$$H_2O(\textit{gas}) \text{ at } 100 \text{ °C and 1 atm} \quad (1)$$

How much energy is involved in the process? Using a calorimeter like the one you used in the laboratory, we discover that it takes 9.70 kilocalories of energy to vaporize 1 mole of water (6.02×10^{23} molecules or 18.0 g). The equation can be written in somewhat abbreviated but more precise form as

$$H_2O(l) + 9.70 \text{ kcal} \longrightarrow H_2O(g) \text{ at } 100.00 \text{ °C and 1 atm} \quad (2)$$

Fig. 5-3 Schematic representation of the vaporization of 1 mole of liquid water.

The value 9.70 kcal is called the **molar heat of vaporization** of water. This is the energy required to separate 6.02×10^{23} molecules of water one from another, as pictured in Figure 5-3.

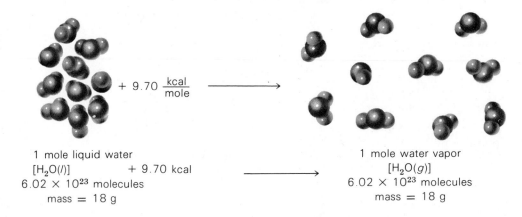

1 mole liquid water
[$H_2O(l)$]
6.02×10^{23} molecules
mass = 18 g

+ 9.70 kcal

1 mole water vapor
[$H_2O(g)$]
6.02×10^{23} molecules
mass = 18 g

EXERCISE 5-2

How much energy is required to evaporate 2.00 moles of water? 0.500 mole of water?

When water vapor condenses to liquid water, the molecules release the energy which was absorbed in separating them. One mole of gaseous water will release 9.70 kcal of energy (heat) when condensed to liquid water at the same temperature. The amount of heat energy released is numerically equal to the molar heat of vaporization.

The amount of energy required to evaporate 1 mole of pure liquid to give 1 mole of pure vapor (gas) varies over a wide range for different pure substances. Table 5-2 shows the boiling points and heats of vaporization of a variety of liquids. In each case, energy is absorbed by the liquid molecules as they separate into gaseous molecules.

Substance	Phase Change (*liquid*) $\longrightarrow$ (*gas*)	Boiling Point (K)	(°C)	Molar Heat of Vaporization (kcal/mole)
Neon	$Ne(l) \longrightarrow Ne(g)$	27.2	−245.8	0.405
Chlorine	$Cl_2(l) \longrightarrow Cl_2(g)$	238.9	−34.1	4.88
Water	$H_2O(l) \longrightarrow H_2O(g)$	373	100	9.7
Sodium	$Na(l) \longrightarrow Na(g)$	1162	889	24.1
Sodium chloride	$NaCl(l) \longrightarrow NaCl(g)$	1738	1465	40.8
Copper	$Cu(l) \longrightarrow Cu(g)$	2855	2582	72.8

We shall see in Chapter 8 that the extreme range of heats of vaporization shown in this table can be explained using rather simple principles. These principles provide a basis for qualitative predictions of boiling point, heat of vaporization, and other properties.

5-1.4 Liquid-Vapor Equilibrium—Vapor Pressure

We have been considering vaporization of a liquid at its usual boiling point. But liquids can vaporize at other temperatures. Let us consider this process, again beginning with liquid water.

A 50-ml sample of liquid water is placed in the flask shown in Figure 5-4.1. The liquid is frozen with a very cold refrigerant such as liquid nitrogen (−196 °C), and the air in the flask is pumped out using a vacuum pump. When the air has been removed as completely as possible, the glass tube is melted shut at the point indicated in the figure. We can now place the sealed flask in a series of constant temperature baths maintained at 0 °C, 25 °C, 50 °C, and 100 °C. The results are seen in Figure 5-4.2 (page 104).

Our observations indicate that

(1) *there is a pressure above the liquid even after the air has been removed,* and
(2) *the pressure above the liquid increases as the temperature is raised.*

The pressure reading in the flask will change when the flask is first put into the bath, but ultimately *many different sealed flasks of pure water give the same reading at the same temperature.* When the pressure reading does not change with time, we say that the liquid and its vapor are in **equilibrium.** The pressure reading is then the **equilibrium pressure.** The **equilibrium pressure reading** in the flask gives the **vapor pressure** of water at the temperature of the bath. In a more formal sense we can say: *the pressure exerted by a vapor in equilibrium with its pure liquid phase is the vapor pressure of the liquid at the temperature used.* At equilibrium no *net* evaporation or condensation is taking place. We are unable to detect measurable changes.

From the experiment just described, we can now tabulate the vapor pressure of water at four different temperatures as in Table 5-3. The experiment can be repeated using many liquids other than water.

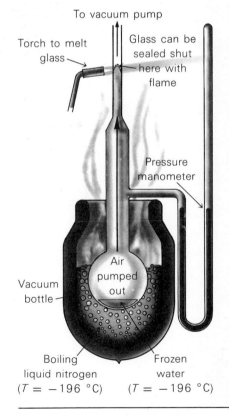

Fig. 5-4.1 Preparing a flask to study the vapor pressure of water.

To vacuum pump

Torch to melt glass

Glass can be sealed shut here with flame

Pressure manometer

Air pumped out

Vacuum bottle

Boiling liquid nitrogen (*T* = −196 °C)

Frozen water (*T* = −196 °C)

LIQUID-VAPOR EQUILIBRIUM—VAPOR PRESSURE

103

Fig. 5-4.2 Vapor pressure of water at four different temperatures.

In this way we learn a third fact: *different liquids at the same temperature give different vapor pressures*. For example, if liquid benzene is used in the experiment instead of water, the vapor-pressure values at 0 °C, 25 °C, 50 °C, and 100 °C are those in Table 5-4. A repetition of this type of experiment for many liquids indicates another generalization: *the vapor pressure of every liquid increases as the temperature is raised*.

TABLE 5-3 VAPOR PRESSURE OF WATER

Temperature (°C)	Vapor Pressure (mm Hg)
0	4.6
25	23.8
50	92.5
100	760.0

TABLE 5-4 VAPOR PRESSURE OF BENZENE

Temperature (°C)	Vapor Pressure (mm Hg)
0	27
25	94
50	271
100	1,360

Our knowledge of vapor pressure can now be summarized:

(1) The pressure exerted by a vapor in equilibrium with its liquid phase at constant temperature is the vapor pressure of the liquid at that temperature.
(2) The vapor pressure of a liquid is dependent only upon the nature of the liquid and the temperature.
(3) Different liquids at any one temperature have different vapor pressures.
(4) The vapor pressure of every liquid increases as the temperature is raised.

EXERCISE 5-3

Watch water boil in a pan or beaker. What is inside the bubbles that rise from the bottom and sides during boiling?

5-1.5 The Kinetic Theory for the Vapor Pressure of a Liquid—Partial Pressures

Does the **kinetic theory** (or "super-rubber" ball model) for liquids and gases explain what we have seen? Let us put it to the test.

We suggested earlier that molecules attract each other as they are pushed closer together. At some point this attraction is great enough to pull the molecules together into droplets or aggregates which we call liquids. We noted that molecules in liquids have kinetic energy too; they are in motion. At any instant some move rapidly, some move slowly. If a given molecule near the surface begins a rapid movement away from the surface of the liquid, it may have enough kinetic energy to overcome the forces of attraction which hold it to the liquid. It then leaves the liquid and enters the vapor (gas) phase (Figure 5-5). In the vapor phase it behaves like any other gas molecule; its collisions with the walls produce pressure. The model tells us that if a liquid has strong forces of attraction between molecules, then only a few molecules will have enough energy to overcome the forces of attraction and escape. Relatively few molecules will be able to evaporate. Thus, *liquids with strong attractive forces between molecules will have* lower *vapor pressures at any given temperature than will liquids with weak intermolecular forces.*

EXERCISE 5-4

Which liquid has the stronger intermolecular forces, water or benzene?

Clearly, different liquids at the same temperature should have different vapor pressure values. (See Table 5-5, page 106). So far, so good. The model is in agreement with observation. What about temperature effects? An increase in temperature of liquid or gas is associated with an increase in the average kinetic energy of the molecules. As the average kinetic energy increases, a larger number of molecules

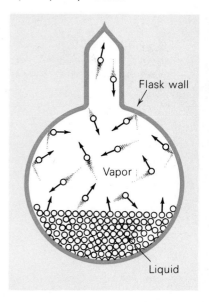

Fig. 5-5 Kinetic theory view of liquid-vapor equilibrium.

Flask wall

Vapor

Liquid

The KINETIC THEORY—
PARTIAL PRESSURES

will have enough kinetic energy (*i.e.*, are moving fast enough) to overcome the forces of attraction in the liquid and escape into the vapor (Figure 5-5). At higher temperatures there will be more molecules in the vapor phase. Hence, vapor pressure will increase with temperature.

TABLE 5-5 VAPOR PRESSURES OF LIQUIDS

Temp (°C)	Water (mm Hg)	Ethyl Alcohol (mm Hg)	Carbon Tetrachloride (mm Hg)	Methyl Salicylate (mm Hg)	Benzene (mm Hg)
−10	2.1	5.6	19		15
−5	3.2	8.3	25		20
0	4.6	12.2	33		27
5	6.5	17.3	43		35
10	9.2	23.6	56		45
15	12.8	32.2	71		58
20	17.5	43.9	91		74
25	23.8	59.0	114		94
30	31.8	78.8	143		118
35	42.2	103.7	176		147
40	55.3	135.3	216		182
45	71.9	174.0	263		225
50	92.5	222.2	317		271
55	118.0	280.6	379		325
60	149.4	352.7	451	1.41	389
65	190.0	448.8	531	1.90	462
70	233.7	542.5	622	2.52	547
75	289.1	666.1	720	3.40	643
80	355.1	812.6	843	4.41	753
85	433.6	986.7	968	5.90	877
90	525.8	1187	1122	7.63	1020
95	633.9	1420	1270	9.93	1180
100	760.0	1693.3	1463	12.8	1360

Fig. 5-6 Vapor pressure versus temperature for some common liquids.

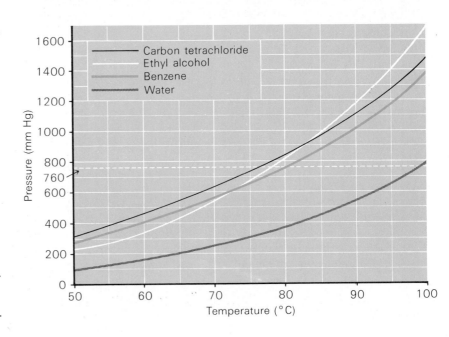

What happens as time passes? Some molecules leave the liquid and go into the vapor. Some molecules in the vapor collide with the liquid surface and return to the liquid phase. Soon a condition will exist where the number of molecules leaving the liquid in any one second is just equal to the number of molecules returning to the liquid in any one second. To the observer on the outside, no measurable changes are taking place. We say that the system is at **equilibrium**: the *rate* at which molecules leave the liquid phase is equal to the *rate* at which they return to the liquid phase.

So far we have been concerned only with the vapor pressure produced by a pure liquid in a flask from which all other gases have been removed. What will happen if other gases are present? Surely, other gas molecules above the surface will collide with molecules escaping from the liquid surface (see point *A* in Figure 5-7). After the collision, the escaping molecule may well bounce back into the liquid. The *rate* at which molecules escape from the surface is *reduced* by the presence of another gas above the liquid. If this were the only consequence of other gases being above the liquid, the vapor pressure would fall; but *we find that the vapor pressure does not fall*. The explanation lies in the fact that molecules *returning to the surface* are also blocked to some degree by collisions with the inert* gas molecules (see point *B* in Figure 5-7). In short, *the "inert" gas has just as much effect on the rate of return of molecules as it does on their rate of escape*. The presence of an "inert" gas above the liquid does not alter the *partial pressure* of the vapor (gas from the liquid) above that liquid. *The equilibrium partial pressure due to gaseous water molecules above a liquid water surface is independent of the presence of air or other gas above that surface.* The measured pressure due to air and water above the water surface will be the *sum* of the *partial pressures* of the gaseous water and the other gases which make up the air. For example, if a flask originally contained no measurable amount of air (it was evacuated as in the experiment), liquid water placed in the flask at 20 °C would evaporate until the pressure rose from 0.0 mm to 17.5 mm. If the flask originally contained dry air at 750.0 mm, liquid would evaporate until the total pressure rose from 750.0 mm to 767.5 mm (the partial pressure of water vapor changing from 0.0 to 17.5 mm in both cases). Experiment fully confirms this prediction.

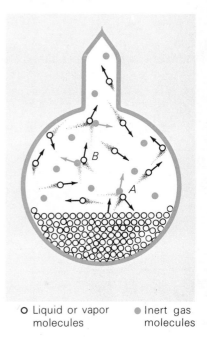

Fig. 5-7 Effects of an "inert" gas on liquid-vapor equilibrium.

○ Liquid or vapor molecules　● Inert gas molecules

5-1.6　The Kinetic Theory and the Heat of Vaporization

We are all familiar with the cooling effect a breeze has when it blows over a person wearing a wet bathing suit. A person can feel cold even on a very hot day. Why? It is convenient to say that the evaporation of water has a "cooling effect" and that the breeze increases the rate of evaporation of water, but this does not really provide a fundamental answer. What does the kinetic theory tell us about this question? According to the kinetic theory, those molecules in the liquid surface with the highest kinetic energy will have the greatest *probability* of overcoming the intermolecular forces of attraction and escaping at any

---

*"Inert gas" as used here refers to any gas which does not react with the liquid being vaporized.

instant. In short, the more energetic or more rapidly moving molecules will escape, while the less energetic, more slowly moving molecules will remain. The molecules remaining will thus have lower kinetic energy on the average than did molecules of the original liquid. Since temperature is directly proportional to the average kinetic energy of the molecules, the temperature of the remaining liquid is lower. In a simpler but less accurate way, we can say: the faster moving, "hot" molecules go to the vapor; the slower moving, "cold" molecules remain in the liquid. The liquid cools. If we want the temperature to remain constant, external energy—the **heat of vaporization**—must be added to supply the energy lost in overcoming the intermolecular forces of attraction between molecules in the liquid phase.

5-1.7 The Boiling Point

The model tells us that the vapor pressure of a liquid increases as temperature rises (Section 5-1.5). If a liquid in an open dish is heated, its temperature will go up and its vapor pressure will rise until bubbles appear in the liquid and boiling begins. The temperature and vapor pressure will then remain constant as the liquid boils (Figure 5-2).

Separate experiments show that when the liquid boils, the vapor pressure of the liquid is just equal to the pressure of the atmosphere. Why is the pressure of the atmosphere important to boiling? The kinetic theory provides the answer. Consider the bubble just below the liquid surface in Figure 5-8. Vapor molecules from vaporization of the liquid are present inside the bubble. These vapor molecules bombard the bubble walls and tend to push them outward. At the same time the atmosphere pushes downward on the surface of the liquid. The push of the atmosphere is transmitted equally in all directions throughout the liquid and tends to collapse the bubble. If the atmospheric pressure is greater than the vapor pressure of the liquid,

Fig. 5-8 Bubble in a boiling liquid.

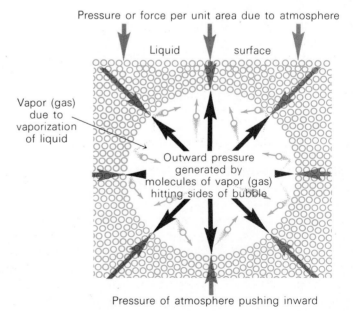

Pressure or force per unit area due to atmosphere

Liquid surface

Vapor (gas) due to vaporization of liquid

Outward pressure generated by molecules of vapor (gas) hitting sides of bubble

Pressure of atmosphere pushing inward

the bubble collapses. If the pressure inside the bubble (due to vapor pressure of liquid at that temperature) is very slightly higher than atmospheric pressure, the bubble grows and rises to the surface where it breaks. Bubble formation is characteristic of the boiling process.

The boiling point of a liquid is the temperature at which the vapor pressure of the liquid is equal to the pressure of the atmosphere above the liquid. If atmospheric pressure is 760.0 mm Hg, water boils at 100.0 °C. At 100.0 °C the vapor pressure of water is 760.0 mm Hg. If the atmospheric pressure is 750 mm Hg, water boils at 99.6 °C, because the vapor pressure of water is 750 mm Hg at 99.6 °C.

The **normal boiling point** of a liquid is defined as the temperature at which the vapor pressure of the liquid is exactly 1 standard atm or 760.0 mm Hg.

EXERCISE 5-5

What is the normal boiling point of ethyl alcohol (see Figure 5-6)?

EXERCISE 5-6

Suppose a closed flask containing liquid water is connected to a vacuum pump and the pressure over the liquid is gradually lowered. If the water temperature is kept at 20 °C, at what pressure will the water boil?

EXERCISE 5-7

Answer Exercise 5-6 substituting ethyl alcohol for water. Repeat for carbon tetrachloride at 40 °C.

EXERCISE 5-8

A thermometer in a pot of boiling water on a mountain reads 95.0 °C. What is the atmospheric pressure on the mountain? The rule of thumb for altitude-pressure correlations is that the pressure falls about 25 mm for every 305 metres (1,000 feet) of elevation. Estimate the height of this mountain.

5-1.8 Solid-Liquid Phase Changes

According to the model just developed, molecules in solid and liquid phases (called *condensed phases*) are held together by intermolecular attraction. In liquids, molecules are irregularly spaced, randomly oriented, and reasonably free to move over each other. In crystalline solids, the molecules occupy regular positions and are held together more firmly (see Figure 5-9, page 110). One mole of a pure solid has lower energy than 1 mole of its liquid phase at the same temperature.

The difference between the energy of a substance in liquid form and its energy in solid form is usually much smaller than the difference between the energies of the liquid and gaseous forms. For ice we can write

$$H_2O(solid) + 1.440 \text{ kcal} \longrightarrow H_2O(liquid) \text{ at } 0 \text{ }°C \qquad (3)$$

or, 1.440 kcal of energy would be required to convert 1 mole of ice (18.0 g) to 1 mole of liquid water at 0 °C. This is much less than the 9.7 kcal required to convert 1 mole of water to vapor at 100 °C. The energy of melting per mole is known as the **molar heat of melting** or the **molar heat of fusion.** Table 5-6 compares melting points of various substances with their molar heats of melting.

We find an extreme range for the heats of melting of these substances. The molar heats of melting may vary from 0.080 kcal/mole for neon to 6.8 kcal/mole for sodium chloride (common table salt). The value for sodium chloride is 85 times that for neon. As you may well suspect, there are very great differences in the forces that bind solids together. These forces affect many properties other than melting point and heat of melting. We shall consider them in more detail later.

Fig. 5-9 Schematic representation of the melting of 1 mole of ice.

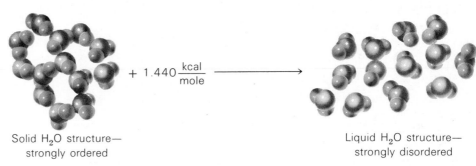

Solid H_2O structure—
strongly ordered

$+ 1.440 \dfrac{\text{kcal}}{\text{mole}} \longrightarrow$

Liquid H_2O structure—
strongly disordered

TABLE 5-6 THE MELTING POINTS AND HEATS OF MELTING OF SOME PURE SUBSTANCES

Substance	Phase Change (solid) ⟶ (liquid)	Melting Point (K)	(°C)	Molar Heat of Melting (kcal/mole)
Neon	$Ne(s) \longrightarrow Ne(l)$	24.6	−248.4	0.080
Chlorine	$Cl_2(s) \longrightarrow Cl_2(l)$	172	−101	1.53
Water	$H_2O(s) \longrightarrow H_2O(l)$	273	0	1.44
Sodium	$Na(s) \longrightarrow Na(l)$	371	98	0.63
Sodium chloride	$NaCl(s) \longrightarrow NaCl(l)$	1081	808	6.8
Copper	$Cu(s) \longrightarrow Cu(l)$	1356	1083	3.11

5-2 SOLUTIONS

Sodium chloride, sugar, ethyl alcohol, and water are four **pure substances.** Each is characterized by definite properties such as vapor pressure, melting point, molar heat of melting, boiling point at a given pressure, and density at a given temperature. Suppose we mix some of these pure substances. Sodium chloride dissolves when placed in contact with water. The solid disappears, becoming part of the liquid. Similarly, sugar in contact with water dissolves. When ethyl alcohol is added to water, the two substances mix to give a liquid similar in appearance to each of the original liquids.

The salt-water mixture, the sugar-water mixture, and the alcohol-water mixture are all *homogeneous*. Each mixture has only a single liquid phase. Such homogeneous mixtures are called **solutions.** In the laboratory we shall handle solutions frequently. Solutions of many types surround us. Filtered seawater is a solution of salts in water; the air we breathe (on smogless days, if any) is oxygen and other gases dissolved in nitrogen; soft drinks are solutions made by dissolving sugar, flavoring, carbon dioxide, and occasionally other ingredients in water; even the gasoline we burn in our cars is a solution made by mixing organic compounds called *hydrocarbons* with various antiknock agents, and other soluble special purpose ingredients.

Solutions differ from pure substances in that their properties vary, depending upon the relative amounts of the pure substances present. The behavior of a solution during a phase change is dramatically different from the behavior of a pure substance. For this reason it is useful to make a distinction between pure substances and solutions. These differences provide a basis for deciding whether a given material is a pure substance or solution. For example, suppose we compare salt water and distilled water. (Each sample is a homogeneous system.) How do we know which one, if either, is a pure substance? We cannot tell just by looking at them. True, there are differences such as taste, density, and so on, but these differences considered separately do not tell us which sample is a pure substance and which a mixture. More sophisticated observation is needed. Let us look further.

5-2.1 Solutions and Phase Changes

A sample of water freezes at 0 °C (at 760 mm Hg). If we freeze 10 ml out of a 100-ml sample of water, a 10-ml ice cube and 90 ml of pure water will remain. If we continue this process, separating ice and water each time, ten ice cubes will result—all the same size and composition, all pure water. In a similar way we can boil the original sample of water (at 100 °C) until 10 ml have vaporized and condensed (Figure 5-10, page 112). A 90-ml sample of hot water and a 10-ml sample of freshly distilled water result. If the boiling process is continued, nine more 10-ml quantities of freshly distilled water will be obtained. The properties of the different samples of a pure substance, separated through freezing or boiling, remain unchanged. A pure substance has a definite and reproducible melting point and boiling point at a given pressure. In fact, chemists use both melting and boiling points of pure substances to identify compounds.

Solutions behave differently. Suppose that we start with a 100-ml sample of a salt solution. We have made the solution by dissolving a convenient amount (say, 1 g) of sodium chloride in the water. This solution is not very different from the pure water, but the difference is important. We are not surprised to find that it begins to boil close to, but not exactly at, 100.0 °C. If we collect the steam (gaseous water) from the salt solution and condense it in a separate vessel (see Figure

5-10), we find that the resulting liquid behaves like pure water rather than like the solution from which it came. Furthermore, after a 10-ml sample of water has been vaporized, we are left with 90 ml of a solution whose composition is not the same as the original. It is saltier: the same amount of salt is present in the solution containing less water. The first solution had 1 g of salt dissolved in 100 ml of solution; the second solution has 1 g of salt dissolved in 90 ml of solution.

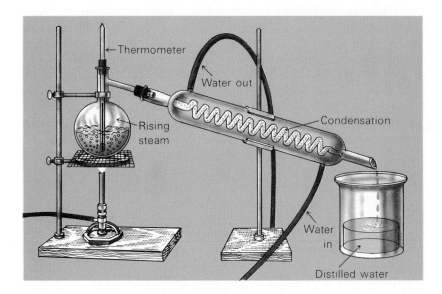

Fig. 5-10 A distillation unit.

This difference results in different properties for the two solutions. Figure 5-11 contrasts the behavior of pure water and a concentrated salt-water solution during boiling. As the amount of water per gram of salt decreases, the boiling point of the salt solution increases. The salt solution starts to boil at a temperature which is somewhat higher than the boiling point of pure water. As the boiling continues, the temperature of the pure water remains constant whereas the temperature of the salt solution keeps rising. If we boil off all the water, solid salt remains.

Fig. 5-11 Behavior on boiling.

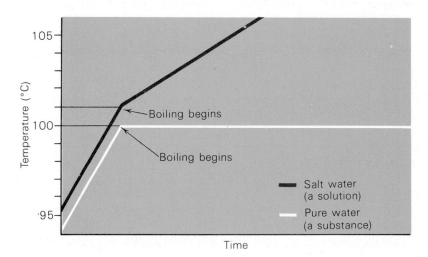

Thus, by **distilling**—that is, by *evaporating and recondensing the resulting vapor in a separate vessel*—we can frequently separate a pure liquid from a solution; and by **crystallizing**—that is, by *forming a crystalline solid*—we can frequently obtain a pure solid from a solution. We usually call the pure substances making up the solution (such as salt and water) the **components** of the solution. It should be obvious that crystallization or distillation will *not* separate a pure substance into components. *A pure substance consists of only one component.* The more closely alike the components of a solution are, the harder it is to separate them.

In nature, solutions are much more common than pure substances, and heterogeneous systems (systems containing more than one phase, such as muddy water) are much more common than homogeneous systems such as solutions. When we want pure substances, we often must prepare them from solutions through successive phase changes.

Although our main interest is in liquid solutions, gas and solid solutions are also important for certain situations. We shall consider them briefly and then return to liquid solutions, which are the most important of the three from a chemist's point of view.

5-2.2 Gaseous Solutions

All gas mixtures are homogeneous; hence, all gas mixtures are solutions. Air is an example. There is only one phase—the gas phase—and all the molecules behave as gas molecules. The molecules themselves may have come from gaseous, liquid, or solid substances. Whatever the source of the components, this gaseous solution—air—is a single, homogeneous phase. As with other solutions, the components of air can be separated by phase changes. Through an exotic low-temperature distillation process, liquid air can be separated into liquid oxygen (boiling point -182 °C), liquid nitrogen (boiling point -196 °C), and other substances such as argon.

5-2.3 Solid Solutions

Solid solutions are not often considered in an elementary laboratory study in chemistry, but they are very common in nature. Many of our common minerals and gem stones, such as emeralds, sapphires, rubies, and amethysts, are solid solutions which have always fascinated people. Steel contains a solid solution (Section 20-5). Similarly, gold atoms can replace some of the copper atoms in a copper crystal to give a gold-copper alloy. The alloy is a solid solution. In the same manner, copper atoms can replace gold atoms in a gold crystal to give another solid solution, a copper-gold alloy. Many other metal alloys are solid solutions. Solid solutions are extremely important today in transistors and in so-called solid-state radios, amplifiers, record players, and television units.

5-2.4 Liquid Solutions

In your laboratory work you will deal mostly with liquid solutions. Liquid solutions can be made by mixing two liquids (*e.g.*, alcohol and water), by dissolving a gas in a liquid (*e.g.*, carbon dioxide in water to give "soda water"), or by dissolving a solid in a liquid (*e.g.*, sugar in water). The result is a homogeneous, transparent system containing more than one substance. By definition, the result is a solution.

In such a solution, each component is diluted by the other. The effects of this dilution process are usually fairly easy to see. Consider for a moment the vapor pressure of a salt solution. Since the solution contains salt, which does not vaporize, and water, which does, there will be fewer vaporizable water molecules per unit of volume than in pure water. Furthermore, water molecules that are present in solution may well be restricted in their movement by their attraction for the dissolved salt. The net effect is that the "escaping tendency" of the water in the solution will be *lower* than the "escaping tendency" of the pure water. As a result the *vapor pressure* due to gaseous water above the solution will be lower than the vapor pressure due to gaseous water above pure water at the same temperature. We know that pure water has a vapor pressure of 760 mm Hg at 100 °C. It is necessary to heat a salt solution *above* 100 °C to reach this same vapor pressure. For this reason the boiling point of salt water at a given pressure is higher than the boiling point of pure water at the same pressure. The amount by which the boiling point is raised is dependent upon the relative amounts of water and salt present in the solution. The more salt in a given volume of solution, the less pure water and the higher the boiling point.

Correspondingly, a lower temperature is required to crystallize ice from salt water or from an alcohol-water solution than is required to crystallize ice from pure water. "Antifreeze" substances added to an automobile radiator act on this principle. They dilute the water in the radiator and lower the temperature at which ice can crystallize from the solution. Again, the amount that the freezing temperature is lowered depends on the relative amounts of water and antifreeze.

In general, the properties of a solution depend upon the relative amounts of the components. It is important to be able to specify quantitatively what is present in a solution; that is, to specify its **composition**—the relative amounts of the components, or pure substances, that were mixed to form the solution. If there are two components, one is called the **solvent** and the other is called the **solute.** *These are merely terms of convenience.* Since both components must intermingle to form the final solution, we cannot make any important distinction between them. When a liquid solution is made from a pure liquid and a solid, it is usually convenient to call the liquid component the solvent.

5-2.5 Expressing the Composition of Solutions

To indicate the composition of a particular solution we must know *relative amounts,* as well as the *kinds,* of components used. When we specify the relative amounts of each component present in the solution, we have specified the **concentration** of the solution. Chemists have many different ways of expressing concentration. The choice of method depends upon the way in which the solution will be used. We shall need only one method of expressing solution concentration in this course. That method will be described below.

In laboratory work it is convenient to measure out a given quantity of a reagent by using a *measured volume of a solution of known concentration*. Rapid measurement of reagents represents one of the most important uses we shall have for solutions in our work. Further, reagents dissolved in solution will frequently react more rapidly and completely than will the pure reagents. This is a welcome bonus resulting from using solutions.

How can a solution be used to measure out a given quantity of reagent? Let us see how this works. Suppose we weigh out carefully 1 mole of table salt. (From the formula this is 23.0 g Na + 35.5 g Cl or 58.5 g of NaCl per mole.) The salt is dissolved in about 500 ml of water; then the resulting solution is transferred completely to the 1,000-ml volumetric flask shown in Figure 5-12. Water is added, the flask is shaken, and more water is added until the volume of the solution is 1 litre (at the mark on the flask) at 25 °C. The solution is now shaken to be sure that liquid and solid are thoroughly mixed. In the final solution we have 1 mole of solute (salt) per litre of solution.*

If we now pour a $\frac{1}{2}$-litre quantity (500 ml) of this solution into a beaker, the beaker will contain $\frac{1}{2}$ mole of the salt. If we measure out 0.1 litre of solution into a beaker, the beaker will contain 0.1 mole of salt. In short, the number of moles of reagent is given by the expression:

$$\left\{\begin{matrix} \text{number of moles} \\ \text{of solute} \end{matrix}\right\} = \left\{\begin{matrix} \text{concentration} \\ \text{of solution in} \\ \text{moles per litre} \end{matrix}\right\} \times \left\{\begin{matrix} \text{volume of} \\ \text{solution in} \\ \text{litres} \end{matrix}\right\} \quad (4)$$

or

$$\left\{\begin{matrix} \text{number of moles} \\ \text{of solute} \end{matrix}\right\} = \frac{1.000 \text{ mole}}{\text{litre}} \times 0.500 \text{ litre} = 0.500 \text{ mole}$$

It is frequently convenient to indicate the number of moles per litre by a number followed by a capital M. Thus, a solution containing 2 moles per litre is designated as 2 M.

5-2.6 Solubility

When sugar is added to water in a beaker, it dissolves. As more sugar is added, the concentration increases until the sugar begins to accumulate on the bottom of the beaker. From this point on, so long as the temperature remains constant, *the concentration of sugar in the solution will not change*. This solution, containing all of the sugar that it will hold at equilibrium at a given temperature, is called a **saturated solution.** A solution in equilibrium at a given temperature with excess solid is said to be saturated. The solution and solid are in equilibrium

Fig. 5-12 Volumetric flask.

---

*A solution containing 1.000 mole of solute in a litre of solution has long been called a 1 molar solution by chemists. By international agreement, concentration is now defined as moles per cubic metre, which is more useful when very precise measurements are being made. However, concentration in moles per litre is a very useful means of expressing concentration for chemists and will be used in this text.

(solution is saturated) if a small crystal added to the solution neither increases nor decreases in volume. In a saturated solution the net volume of the added crystal will remain constant.

When a fixed amount of liquid has dissolved all the solid it can hold at equilibrium at a given temperature, the concentration reached is called the **solubility** of that solid in the liquid. For example, a saturated solution of sodium chloride in water at 20 °C has a concentration of about 6 moles NaCl per litre of water solution (6 M). In contrast, a saturated solution of NaCl in ethyl alcohol at 20 °C has a concentration of only 0.009 mole NaCl per litre of alcohol solution (0.009 M). The solubility of lead nitrate [$Pb(NO_3)_2$] in water is greater than 1 mole per litre (1 M). In contrast, lead chromate ($PbCrO_4$) has a solubility in water of only 10^{-7} mole per litre. You used these facts in the laboratory in Experiment 7. The $Pb(NO_3)_2$, having good solubility in water, dissolved easily to form a solution which reacted with the K_2CrO_4 solution. The low solubility of the resulting $PbCrO_4$ enabled you to separate it as a solid from the remaining solution.

The solubilities of solids in any solvent will change with temperature. An increase in temperature will sometimes increase solubility, sometimes reduce it.

Because of this range of solubilities, the word *soluble* does not have a precise meaning. There is frequently an upper limit to the solubility of even the most soluble solid, while even the least soluble solid yields a few dissolved particles per litre of solution. If a compound has a solubility of more than $\frac{1}{10}$ mole per litre (0.1 M), most chemists usually say it is *soluble*. When the solubility is below 0.1 M (10^{-1} M), most chemists usually say the compound is *slightly soluble*. Compounds with solubility below about 10^{-3} M are sometimes said to be *very slightly soluble*. With solubility much below about 10^{-4} M, a substance is described as *insoluble*. We use glass containers for pure water because glass has a negligible solubility in water.

EXERCISE 5-9

Classify the solubility in water of the following substances that you have used in your experiments: copper, magnesium, silver nitrate, sodium iodide, ammonia (*g*), and carbon dioxide (*g*).

5-2.7 Variations in the Properties of Solutions

Though many solutions are colorless and closely resemble pure water in appearance, the differences between solutions are great. Furthermore, the ability of apparently similar solvents to dissolve different solids varies widely. For example, pure sugar dissolves in both pure water and in pure (ethyl) alcohol. Sodium chloride or table salt dissolves in water but not noticeably in ethyl alcohol. Iodine does not dissolve in water even enough to color the water. It is, however, quite soluble in ethyl alcohol. Solubility is determined by the nature of both solute and solvent.

The examples just described give us four solutions containing a substantial amount of solute:

(1) sugar in water	(3) sodium chloride in water
(2) sugar in ethyl alcohol	(4) iodine in ethyl alcohol

Solution (4) is readily distinguishable by its dark brown color. The other three are colorless, but they can be identified easily by taste. Chemists, however, have safer and more meaningful ways of distinguishing them: *these solutions differ markedly in their ability to conduct an electric current*. Solution (3) conducts an electric current much more readily than does pure water. In contrast, solutions (1) and (2) conduct the electric current no better than does pure water.

Differences in solubility and electrical conductivity are very important in chemistry. We shall investigate electrical conductivity and the electrical nature of matter in the next chapter.

5-3 HIGHLIGHTS

Liquids and solids (condensed phases) exist because molecules attract each other when they are close together. These forces of attraction can be ignored in a study of gases because gas molecules are separated by large distances; but in liquids and solids molecules are close together and the forces of attraction between them, therefore, are important.

In changing a liquid to a gas at constant temperature, energy from the outside is needed to separate the liquid molecules one from another. The energy required to convert 1 mole of liquid to 1 mole of vapor at constant temperature is called the **molar heat of vaporization** of the liquid. The model for liquids can be used to rationalize the fact that all liquids show a **vapor pressure** which is dependent only on the nature of the liquid and its temperature. A liquid boils when its vapor pressure is equal to the confining or atmospheric pressure.

The energy required to convert 1 mole of solid to 1 mole of liquid is the **molar heat of melting** or the **molar heat of fusion.** As we might expect, it is less than the molar heat of vaporization since molecules do not have to be separated so far.

Solutions are homogeneous mixtures. The concentration of a solute in a liquid solution is described most easily in terms of the number of moles of solute per litre of solution. Solutions have properties that differ from the properties of the pure components which made up the solutions. Some solutions conduct electricity; others do not.

QUESTIONS and PROBLEMS

1 Why is the expression $PV = k$ (developed in Chapter 2) obeyed better by gases at low pressures than at high pressures?

2 Consider some boiling water in a beaker: (a) Is energy being absorbed or released? (b) If the heat of vaporization of water is 9.70 kcal/mole, how much energy is involved in changing 45.0 g of water at its boiling point to water vapor at the same temperature?

3 Explain why a burn from water vapor at 100 °C (such as that from a steam iron) is more severe than a burn from an equal quantity of boiling water at 100 °C.

4 Evaporation of water also takes place at temperatures below 100 °C. If a swimmer emerges from water with 90 g of water clinging to him, (a) why does the swimmer feel cold, even though the day may be hot? (b) How much heat energy is necessary to evaporate the water clinging to him?

5 An actively sweating person, such as a laborer or an athlete, on a hot day may lose as much as 3 gallons, or about 11 kg, of water through the skin. (a) How many kilocalories are required to evaporate 11 kg of water? (b) Explain, in terms of regulating body temperature, why sweating is more profuse on hot days than on cold days.

6 Mercury vapor is a substance which is a cumulative poison; that is, repeated small doses of mercury vapor add up to a seriously disabling condition. Explain why, although the boiling point of mercury is 357 °C, it is important to clean up mercury spills thoroughly and promptly.

7 Carbon tetrachloride is another vapor which is poisonous. Its boiling point is 76.8 °C. Explain the following: (a) Carbon tetrachloride poisoning can result from relatively short exposure to its vapor. (b) Spilled carbon tetrachloride can be removed from a room by thorough airing, while spilled mercury must be cleaned up.

8 Fog is composed of tiny droplets of *liquid* water suspended in air. Explain, in terms of the relationship between temperature and the vapor pressure of water, why fog is commonly present during early mornings and late afternoons rather than at the middle of the day.

9 Refer to Figure 5-6 to answer the following questions. (a) What is the normal boiling point of each of the substances listed? (b) At a temperature of 80 °C, which liquids would be boiling? (c) Of all the liquids listed, which has the strongest intermolecular forces?

10 A flask containing ethyl alcohol is attached to a vacuum pump and the pressure is reduced to 12 mm Hg. If the flask is maintained in an ice-water bath at 0 °C, (a) will the alcohol boil? (b) Which, if any, of the other substances listed in Table 5-5 would boil at 0 °C if exposed to this same vacuum pump?

11 Atmospheric pressure falls about 25 mm Hg for every 300 metres above sea level. (a) What would be the boiling temperature of water near the top of Pike's Peak, which has an altitude of about 4,300 metres (over 14,000 feet)? (b) Explain why the comforts of a hot cup of tea or soup are difficult for climbers to obtain near the top of Mount Everest (8,839 metres). (c) Suggest a means of obtaining hot water under such conditions.

12 (a) Explain why food cooks more rapidly in a pressure cooker than in an open pan. (b) Explain why a pressure cooker is more effective in sterilizing baby bottles and surgical instruments than is boiling water in an unpressurized container.

13 What good reason is there for "pressurizing" automobile cooling systems?

14 Liquid sodium has been proposed as a coolant in nuclear power plants to replace water, which is used as a coolant in conventional power plants. Sodium has a melting point of 98 °C and a boiling point of 889 °C. (a) Which would have the higher vapor pressure at 99 °C, sodium or water? (b) Are the intermolecular forces in sodium stronger or weaker than those in water? How can you tell? (c) Which would you expect to have the higher heat of vaporization, liquid sodium or liquid water? Why? (d) Which would you predict to have the higher molar volume in the gaseous phase at, for instance, 1000 °C and 1 atm pressure? Why? (Consider small differences carefully.)

15 Butane, a gas used as a fuel in camping equipment, has a melting point of −138.3 °C and a boiling point of −0.5 °C. Methane, another common fuel, has a melting point of −182 °C and a boiling point of −161 °C. Predict whether the following physical properties will be higher or lower for butane than methane: (a) intermolecular attraction; (b) heat of vaporization; (c) molar heat of melting; (d) vapor pressure at any given temperature.

16 How much heat must be removed from an ice cube tray full of water at 0 °C to freeze it if the tray holds 450 g of water?

17 Explain, in terms of molecular activity, why the molar heat of vaporization of a substance is higher than its molar heat of melting.

18 Consider a stoppered flask partially filled with salt water, in which there is undissolved salt at the bottom of the flask even after several days of shaking and swirling. (a) How many phases are present in the flask? (b) Describe the components of each phase. (c) Which phases are pure substances and which are solutions? (d) How could you separate the solutions into their component pure substances? (e) Would you expect the liquid phase to boil at 100 °C, a temperature higher than 100 °C, or a temperature lower than 100 °C? (f) Would you expect the liquid phase to freeze at 0 °C, a temperature higher than 0 °C, or a temperature lower than 0 °C?

19 Ethylene glycol is a substance used as an antifreeze in automobile radiators. Why is this substance added to automobile radiators even in very hot climates when there is no chance of encountering freezing temperatures?

20 Rock salt (NaCl) is frequently scattered on icy streets to melt the ice and permit traffic to flow safely. Explain how the addition of salt causes ice to melt even if the temperature remains below the freezing point of water.

21 Explain how to make the following solutions: (a) 1.00 litre of 1.00 M NaCl (b) 0.500 litre of 1.00 M $AgNO_3$ (c) 0.100 litre of 0.500 M K_2CO_3 (d) 0.250 litre of 0.100 M $Pb(NO_3)_2$.

22 How many grams of solute are necessary to make each of the following? (a) 250 ml of 0.010 M Na_2CrO_4 (b) 100 ml of 0.050 M $CoCl_2$ (c) 500 ml of 0.250 M NaBr (d) 100 ml of 0.50 M KCl.

23 How many millilitres of a 0.100 M solution contain each of the following? (a) 0.100 mole of NaCl (b) 0.010 mole of HCl (c) 0.050 mole of $Zn(NO_3)_2$ (d) 0.075 mole of NaI.

24 How many millilitres of 0.200 M solution contain each of the following? (a) 8.40 g of $NaHCO_3$ (b) 5.95 g of KBr (c) 1.17 g of NaCl (d) 1.01 g of KNO_3.

25 What is the concentration, in moles per litre, of solutions made as described below? (a) 5.85 g of NaCl dissolved in water to make 250 ml total volume (b) 4.25 g of $NaNO_3$ dissolved in water to make 100 ml total volume (c) 4.17 g of KBr dissolved in water to make 500 ml total volume (d) 1.90 g $SnCl_2$ dissolved in water to make 1,000 ml total volume.

26 What is the concentration, in moles per litre, of solutions made as described below? (a) 4.00 g of NaOH dissolved in water to make 500 ml total volume (b) 1.06 g of LiCl dissolved in water to make 1.00 litre total volume (c) 1.31 g of $Ba(NO_3)_2$ dissolved in water to make 250 ml total volume (d) 9.20 g of CH_3CH_2OH dissolved in water to make 500 ml total volume.

It is the glory of a good bit of work that it opens the way for better things and thus rapidly leads to its own eclipse.

SIR ALEXANDER FLEMING (1881–1955)

WHY WE BELIEVE IN ATOMS

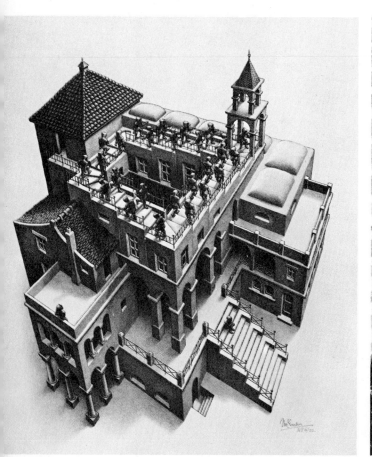

M. C. Escher; Escher Association

Some things, we see clearly, like these two pictures, are not believable. Other things we cannot see, like atoms, are quite believable.

"GREAT FLEAS HAVE LITTLE FLEAS UPON THEIR BACKS TO BITE 'EM, and little fleas have lesser fleas, and so *ad infinitum.*"

To explain what we encountered in Chapter 3 we found it necessary to subdivide molecules into smaller particles called atoms. Now we find that in order to explain the fact that some substances in solution conduct an electric current we must think of them as comprised of still smaller subdivisions which are electrically charged. Electric charge is familiar to anyone who has ever combed their hair, scuffed their feet across deep carpet and touched their little brother, or who unsuspectingly stuck a paper clip into an electrical outlet. The relationship between atoms and electric charge is explored in this chapter.

So far we have found it convenient to postulate the existence of rapidly moving molecules in order to explain the behavior of gases. An expansion of the model to include intermolecular attraction helped us to understand the behavior of liquids and solids. Chemical evidence suggested that many molecules divide in a number of chemical processes, hence they must consist of at least two or more parts called atoms. By postulating the existence of such atoms, we could explain the law of combining volumes for gases provided that we were willing to assume the validity of Avogadro's hypothesis. So far then our belief in the atomic theory seems to hinge on the validity of Avogadro's hypothesis. Indeed, if this were the only reason for believing in atoms, modern science would be built on a shaky foundation. There must be more evidence!

6-1 OBSERVATION AND CONCLUSION

The atom is so incredibly small that direct observation of it in a conventional sense is out of the question, yet our belief in atoms is strong. Why? It is one thing to ask, "do we believe in atoms?" and quite another to ask, "why do we believe in atoms?" In this chapter we shall begin to consider the second and harder question: why do we believe in atoms? Strangely enough, most of the evidence upon which our belief in atoms is based arose from *many* simple chemical observations rather than from one conclusive experiment.

The atomic theory was a topic of conversation among the ancient Greek philosophers. The observations upon which the original atomic theory was based were made in the eighteenth and nineteenth centuries by investigators who used equipment less sophisticated than that found in the average high school laboratory today.

6-1.1 Why We Believe in Garbage Collectors

Let us approach our study of atoms using a rather transparent—even ridiculous—example of how we arrive at conclusions in day-to-day living. This example parallels very closely the scientific account which follows it. Look for the connections.

A new tenant is told by his neighbor that the garbage collector comes every Thursday, early in the morning. Later, in answer to a question from his wife about the matter, the tenant says, "I have been told that there is a garbage collector and that he comes early Thursday morning. We shall see if this is true." The tenant, if he behaves like a true scientist, accepts the statement of the neighbor (who has had opportunity to make observations on the subject). However, he accepts it *tentatively* until he himself knows the evidence for the conclusion; he remembers that this same neighbor gave him some stock market tips.

After a few weeks, the new tenant has made a number of observations consistent with the existence of a Thursday-morning garbage collector. Most importantly, the garbage does disappear every Thursday morning. Secondly, the tenant receives a bill from the city once a month for municipal services. There are several supplementary observations that could corroborate the garbage collector's existence. The tenant is sometimes awakened at 5:00 A.M. on Thursdays by a loud banging and the sound of a truck. Occasionally the banging is accompanied by happy whistling; sometimes it is accompanied by a dog's bark.

The tenant now has many reasons to believe in the existence of the garbage collector, *yet he has never seen him*. Being a curious man, he sets his alarm clock on Wednesday night for 5:00 A.M. Looking out the window Thursday morning, his first observation is that it is surprisingly dark and things are difficult to see (an observation made frequently in scientific research also). However, he sees a shadowy form pass by, a form that looks like a man carrying a large object.

Seeing is believing—or is it? Which of these pieces of evidence really constitutes "seeing" the garbage collector? The answer is that *all* of the evidence taken together furnishes the basis for accepting the "garbage collector theory of garbage disappearance." The direct vision of a shadowy form at 5:00 A.M. would not constitute "seeing" a garbage collector if the garbage did not disappear at that time; the form might have been the paper boy or the milkman. Neither would the garbage disappearance *alone* constitute "seeing" the garbage collector; perhaps an opossum or a large dog eats the garbage and drags the cans away. (Remember, a dog's bark was heard.) No, the tenant is convinced that there is a garbage collector because the conviction is consistent with many observations and is inconsistent with none. Other explanations fit the observations too, but not as well. (The tenant has never heard a dog or an opossum whistle gaily.) The garbage collector theory passes the test of a good theory—that is, it is useful in explaining a large number of experimental observations. This was true even before the tenant set eyes on the shadowy form at 5:00 A.M.

Yet, we must agree, there are advantages to the "direct vision" type of experiment. Often more detailed information can be obtained in this way. Is the garbage collector tall? Does he have a mustache? Could the garbage collector be a woman? This type of information is less easily obtained from indirect methods of observation, although you will remember the amazing ability of Sherlock Holmes to draw conclusions from such indirect observations (Chapter 1). If we ordinary observers want answers to these questions, it may be worthwhile to set the alarm clock and go outside at 5:00 A.M. on a Thursday morning, even if we are absolutely convinced that there is a garbage collector.

Earlier in our study you were a new tenant. You were told that chemists believe in atoms because it helps to explain the chemical combination of gases. You were asked to accept that explanation *tentatively* and you were promised, indirectly, that other evidence would be made available to you.

Now we are going to review additional types of evidence that form the basis for belief in the atomic theory. Our belief will be further strengthened by successful application of the model throughout the remainder of the course.

But belief in atoms is not enough. We shall find many experiments which can be most successfully explained by assuming that atoms themselves have substructures, that atoms can be broken into smaller particles. We shall therefore expand the model to include the structure of the atom.

6-2 OBSERVATION AND BELIEF IN ATOMS

It was noted earlier that Higgins and Dalton were guided by the chemical evidence of the late eighteenth century in their formulation of the atomic theory. What kind of evidence for atoms is provided by chemistry today? We shall consider in turn the definite composition of compounds, the simple mass relations among compounds, and, in review, the combining volumes of gases. Such information provides a chemical basis for believing in atoms.

6-2.1 The Law of Definite Composition

Compounds are found to have definite composition, no matter how they are prepared. For example a 2.016-g sample of hydrogen gas combines with 16.000 g of oxygen gas to produce 18.016 g of liquid water. If a sample of water from the Pacific Ocean is distilled several times, the resulting product will contain 2.016 g of hydrogen for each 16.000 g of oxygen. Water of exactly the same composition will be obtained by distilling water samples from the Great Salt Lake, from the English Channel, or from a snow drift in Antarctica. The percent composition by mass for a pure compound is always the same.*

The atomic theory provides a ready explanation for the definite composition of chemical compounds. It says that compounds are composed of atoms, and every sample of a given compound must contain the same relative number of atoms of each of its elements. Since the atoms of each element have a characteristic mass, the mass composition of a compound is always the same. Thus the definite composition of compounds provides experimental support for the atomic theory. Further, it provides us with the key used today in determining the formula of a compound from laboratory analytical data.

---

*This statement applies if the naturally occurring distribution of isotopes is not disturbed. More will be said about isotopes and their influence on chemical composition.

6-2.2 The Law of Simple Multiple Proportions

In many cases, two elements brought together under different conditions can form two or more different compounds. For example, hydrogen and oxygen can form both water and another compound called hydrogen peroxide in which the mass of hydrogen is one-sixteenth the mass of oxygen. If the hydrogen mass in hydrogen peroxide is 1.008, the oxygen mass is 16.000. In water, 2.016 g of hydrogen combine with 16.000 g of oxygen. The same relationship is true on a molar basis. In hydrogen peroxide, *1* mole of hydrogen atoms combines with *1* mole of oxygen atoms to give a compound. In water, *2* moles of hydrogen atoms combine with *1* mole of oxygen atoms to give a different compound. Water contains *exactly twice* as many hydrogen atoms per oxygen atom as does hydrogen peroxide. Such simple numerical mass and atom relationships are almost always found when two or more elements form more than one pure compound. Indeed, these observations, identified as the law of multiple proportions, are summarized easily in atomic terms by the formulas H_2O and $(HO)_2$, or H_2O_2.

In fact, the atomic theory was first deduced from evidence of this very type. Chemists had found that the law of definite composition was obeyed whenever compounds were formed. In searching for an explanation for this and related facts, John Dalton proposed the atomic theory. Its value in explaining many additional phenomena such as the data leading to the law of multiple proportions soon led to general acceptance of the theory in chemistry.

Fig. 6-1 Simple multiple proportions of oxygen to hydrogen in H_2O and H_2O_2.

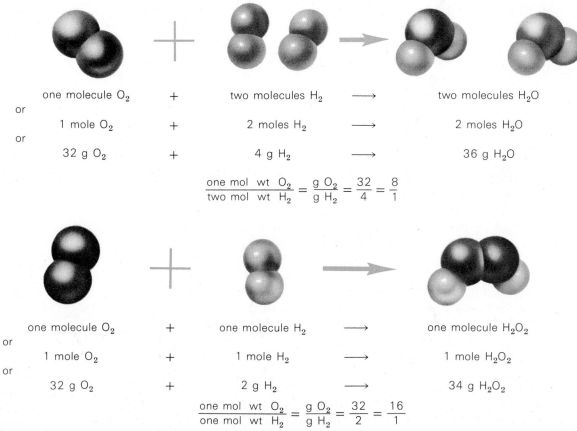

one molecule O_2	+	two molecules H_2	⟶	two molecules H_2O
or 1 mole O_2	+	2 moles H_2	⟶	2 moles H_2O
or 32 g O_2	+	4 g H_2	⟶	36 g H_2O

$$\frac{\text{one mol wt } O_2}{\text{two mol wt } H_2} = \frac{\text{g } O_2}{\text{g } H_2} = \frac{32}{4} = \frac{8}{1}$$

one molecule O_2	+	one molecule H_2	⟶	one molecule H_2O_2
or 1 mole O_2	+	1 mole H_2	⟶	1 mole H_2O_2
or 32 g O_2	+	2 g H_2	⟶	34 g H_2O_2

$$\frac{\text{one mol wt } O_2}{\text{one mol wt } H_2} = \frac{\text{g } O_2}{\text{g } H_2} = \frac{32}{2} = \frac{16}{1}$$

EXERCISE 6-1

Two compounds are known that contain only nitrogen and fluorine. Careful analysis shows that 23.67 g of compound I contain 19.00 g of fluorine and that 26.00 g of compound II contain 19.00 g of fluorine.

(1) For each compound, calculate the mass of nitrogen combined with 19.00 g of fluorine.

(2) What is the ratio of the calculated mass of nitrogen in compound II to that in I?

(3) Compound I is NF_3. This compound has one atom of nitrogen per three atoms of fluorine. How many atoms of nitrogen are there per three atoms of fluorine for each of the molecular formulas N_2F_2 and N_2F_4? Compare these atom ratios to the mass ratio obtained in part (2) and convince yourself that compound II could have the formula N_2F_4 but not N_2F_2.

6-2.3 The Law of Combining Volumes

In Chapter 3 the fundamental argument for believing in atoms centered on the fact that 1 litre of hydrogen will combine with 1 litre of chlorine to give 2 litres of hydrogen chloride. Avogadro's hypothesis (*i.e.*, equal volumes of gases measured at the same temperature and pressure contain equal numbers of molecules) then led to the conclusion that each molecule of hydrogen chloride must contain one half of a molecule of chlorine and one half of a molecule of hydrogen. Each molecule of hydrogen and each molecule of chlorine is broken into two pieces in forming hydrogen chloride. This suggestion is consistent only if chlorine and hydrogen molecules contain sub-units or atoms. Similar observations were made for many other reactions involving gases. Such observations on the combining volumes of gases suggested the existence of atoms of many different kinds.

6-3 THE ELECTRICAL NATURE OF MATTER AND THE MAKEUP OF ATOMS

In Chapter 5 it was noted that some solutions conduct electricity. This raises an interesting "wondering why" question. What is there about a salt solution which makes it conduct electricity? In fact one can ask an even more fundamental question: *how does the salt solution conduct electricity?* To answer such a question we need to know more about electrical phenomena in general. We shall then be able to explore the connection between electrical conductivity and the nature of atoms.

6-3.1 Some Simple Electrical Phenomena

Electrical phenomena are so common that we often take them for granted. Some, like the electric charge we generate when combing our hair, have been known for centuries. Others are comparatively new to us. Try to name five you have seen, before reading on. Does your list include the following:

(1) the attraction of a comb for your hair on a dry day;
(2) the flash of a bolt of lightning;
(3) the shock you get if you touch a bare wire in a radio set or other electrical appliance;
(4) the heat generated by an electric current passing through the heating element of an electric stove;
(5) the light emitted by the filament of a light bulb as electric current is passed through it;
(6) the magnetic field generated by a current passing through a coil of wire;
(7) the work done by an electric motor when a current passes through its coils; or
(8) the emission of "radio waves" by the antenna of a radio or television station?

How are these facts interconnected? What is the relationship between the attraction of a comb for your hair and the current passing through the electric motor? What does it mean to say that an electric current "passes through" a coil of wire? Even more basically, what is an electric current?

6-3.2 Detection of Electric Charge

To begin answering these questions, it will be helpful to work with an electrometer, a device for detecting and measuring electric charge. Figure 6-2 shows a simple electrometer. It consists of two spheres of very light weight, each coated with a thin film of metal. The spheres are suspended near each other by fine metal threads in a box closed to exclude air drafts. Each suspending thread is connected to a brass terminal. Next to the box is a "battery," or another source of electrical voltage. There are two terminal posts on the battery. We shall call these posts P_1 and P_2. If post P_1 is connected by a copper wire to the left terminal of the electrometer and post P_2 is connected to the right terminal, we observe that the two spheres move toward each other. Evidently the wires have transmitted to the spheres the property of exerting force on each other—an attractive force. The force is still present when the air in the electrometer is removed with a vacuum pump. The spheres react to each other "across space." They "feel" force at a distance.

If the wires are now disconnected, the attractive force remains. However, if the two electrometer terminals are connected by a copper wire, the spheres return to their original positions and hang vertically again. The attraction is lost.

We see that the battery transfers to the electrometer spheres the property of attracting each other. It is natural to imagine that something has been transferred from the battery to the spheres. This "something" is called **electric charge.** The movement of this electric charge from the battery through the metal threads to the spheres is called an **electric current.** This electric charge is lost when the two electrometer terminals are connected by a copper wire.

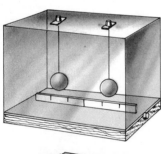
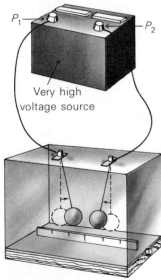

Fig. 6-2 A simple electrometer.

P_1 — — P_2

Very high voltage source

We can learn more about electric charge by another use of the electrometer. Connect one wire from the battery (say, post P_2) to the base of the electrometer and the other wire (from post P_1) to both terminals, as in Figure 6-3. This time the two spheres move apart—they repel each other! When both spheres are given electric charge from the battery post labeled P_1, they repel instead of attract. In Figure 6-2 we saw that when one sphere received charge from post P_1 and the other sphere received charge from post P_2, the two spheres attracted. There must be at least two kinds of charge!

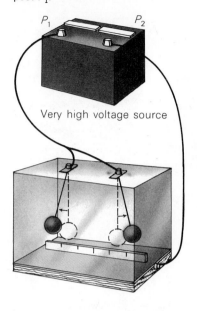

Very high voltage source

Now let us reverse the wires so that both spheres are charged from battery post P_2. This time P_1 is connected to the base of the electrometer. Again we observe that the spheres move apart. *When both spheres are connected to the same battery post, the two spheres repel each other.*

This represents a large gain in our knowledge of electric charge. One kind of charge comes from battery post P_1. Until we have reason to do otherwise, we shall call this kind of charge C_1. The other kind of charge comes from battery post P_2; we shall call this kind of charge C_2. The spheres attract or repel each other when they carry charge according to the following pattern:

$$\begin{aligned} &C_1 \text{ attracts } C_2 &&\textit{Unlike charges attract} \\ &C_1 \text{ repels } C_1 &&\textit{Like charges repel} &&(1) \\ &C_2 \text{ repels } C_2 &&\textit{Like charges repel} \end{aligned}$$

We have one more observation to formulate. When the spheres were given different charges (as in Figure 6-2), the charges could be removed by connecting the two terminals by a copper wire. Then the spheres lost all attraction for each other. We interpret this behavior to mean that either C_1 or C_2 (or both) has moved through the wire so as to join the other kind of charge. When C_1 and C_2 are united, no charge remains. Symbolically we can say

$$C_1 + C_2 = \text{no charge} \qquad (2)$$

Our accumulated evidence shows that there are at least two kinds of electric charge, which we have symbolized as C_1 and C_2. We may wonder whether or not there are other kinds of charge. For example, charge is frequently generated when two surfaces are rubbed together. A charge is left on a comb as it is pulled through dry hair. The hair is then attracted to the comb. The charge on the comb is found to be identical to C_1; that on the hair is C_2. If a hard rubber rod is rubbed with cat's fur, the rubber rod carries charge C_1 and the cat's fur carries charge C_2. If a glass rod is rubbed with silk, the glass rod will carry charge C_2 and the silk will carry charge C_1. No matter how an electric charge is produced, we always find these same two types, C_1 and C_2 and *only* these two. Any method of producing C_1 always produces an equivalent amount of C_2.

6-3.3 The Effect of Distance

Figure 6-4 shows two electrometers with different distances between the two pairs of spheres. Though the charges on the spheres come from

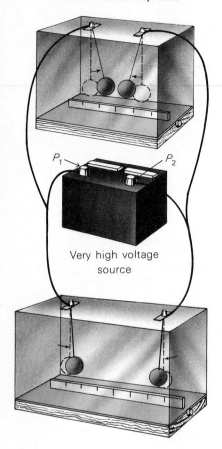

the same battery, there is more deflection of the spheres when they are closely spaced (the top of Figure 6-4) than when they are widely spaced. *When the spheres are closer together, the deflection is larger.* We might conclude that the force of attraction varies with distance and is stronger when the charges are closer together. Careful quantitative studies show that the force is inversely proportional to the square of the distance d between the two spheres:

$$\text{electric force} \propto \frac{1}{d \times d} \text{ or } \frac{1}{d^2} \tag{3}$$

where d is the distance between the centers of the two spheres.

6-3.4 Electric Force—A Fundamental Property of Matter

We have learned that a battery can transfer to the spheres of an electrometer a property called electric charge. When this happens, the spheres exert force on each other. The discussion brings up two "wondering why" questions.

The first is: how does a battery generate and transfer electric charge to the spheres? Let us delay this question until we come to Chapter 15. It will be examined in detail there. For the present we shall just recognize that operation of the battery generates charge.

The second question probes deeper: what is electric charge? Why do the two electrometer spheres attract or repel each other? No one really has a good explanation for this second question. Without an answer we say: it is a fundamental property of matter that it can acquire electric charge, and, when it does, it will then exert force on other charged bodies. Such a statement may be taken as a definition of the term *fundamental property*—a property which is generally observed but for which diligent search has failed to yield a useful model. Without an explanation of a property, we call the property *fundamental*. It is a curious fact that when a property has resisted explanation for quite a time and it becomes classified as a fundamental property, an explanation no longer seems to be necessary. Sometime in the future, though, someone who is unwilling to accept this may succeed in explaining a fundamental property in still more "fundamental" terms.

6-4 THE ELECTRICAL PROPERTIES OF CONDENSED PHASES

We mentioned very briefly that a salt solution conducts electric current, while a sugar solution does not. An electric current has been defined as the movement of electric charge. Hence, when we say that an electric current flows through a salt solution, we mean that there is a movement of electric charge through the solution. We shall be concerned here with the nature of charged particles in solution, the manner in which charge moves through the solution, and the relationship of these questions to the nature of atoms.

6-4.1 Electrolysis and the Particulate Nature of Electric Charge

In the early 1830's Michael Faraday, a distinguished British physicist, was interested in the passage of an electric current through salt solutions—the process of electrolysis. To understand the full impact of Faraday's work on the development of the atomic theory, we must turn back the scientific clock to the view held in the nineteenth century. At that time the atomic theory had been proposed by both Higgins and Dalton, but no one had yet suggested the existence of electrons. (Atoms were "fundamental.") Faraday's work focused attention on the close relationship between matter and electric charge; it provided compelling evidence in support of the idea that electricity comes in units or packages which we now call electrons. It is worthwhile to examine the information which can be derived from two experiments comparable to those of Faraday.

In the first experiment an electric current is passed in series through two solutions containing different compounds of mercury. The first solution contains dissolved mercurous nitrate and the second, dissolved mercuric nitrate.* Mercury is deposited from both solutions as electrolysis proceeds and an extremely important fact emerges. No matter how much electricity is passed through the solutions, the mass of mercury metal deposited from the mercurous nitrate solution is *always twice as great* as the mass deposited from the mercuric nitrate solution. This is a simple and far-reaching observation. It suggests that electricity, like matter, might come in units. During electrolysis these units would be parcelled out to convert mercury in solution to metallic mercury. One unit of electricity would be needed to convert a mercury "atom" in mercurous nitrate to metallic mercury while *two* units would be needed to convert a mercury "atom" in mercuric nitrate to metallic mercury. If this is true, a given quantity of electricity would give twice as much mercury metal from a mercurous nitrate solution as it would from a mercuric nitrate solution.

In the second experiment an electric current is passed through the three electrolysis cells in Figure 6-5 (page 130). The two ammeters have the same reading, showing that the current entering the cell at the right is identical to that leaving the cell at the left. Thus, the electric circuit guarantees that the same amount of electricity passes through each of the three cells. Note also that two of these cells contain a molten compound which carries the electric current while the third cell contains mercuric nitrate in water solution. This suggests that the process by which current is carried in the cells containing molten material is the same as that which was considered in the first experiment above.

In the first cell, containing mercuric nitrate, the net reaction is the production of metallic mercury and gaseous oxygen. After current has passed through the cell for a definite time, the mass of the mercury

*The formulas for the actual compounds which can be used are mercur*ous* nitrate, $Hg_2(NO_3)_2$, and mercur*ic* nitrate, $Hg(NO_3)_2$. Note that the first contains twice as many mercury atoms in its formula as does the second.

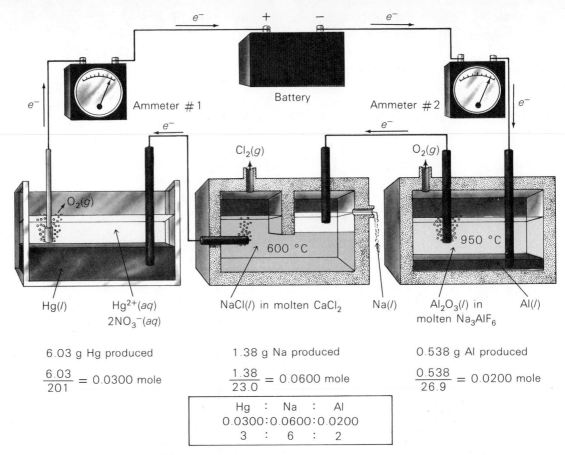

6.03 g Hg produced

$$\frac{6.03}{201} = 0.0300 \text{ mole}$$

1.38 g Na produced

$$\frac{1.38}{23.0} = 0.0600 \text{ mole}$$

0.538 g Al produced

$$\frac{0.538}{26.9} = 0.0200 \text{ mole}$$

Hg	:	Na	:	Al
0.0300	:	0.0600	:	0.0200
3	:	6	:	2

Fig. 6-5 Masses of three different elements deposited by a given amount of electricity.

produced is found to be 6.03 g. In the second cell metallic sodium and gaseous chlorine are formed.* The same current that produced 6.03 g of metallic mercury produces 1.38 g of molten sodium. The third cell gives metallic aluminum and gaseous oxygen,† but at the temperature used the oxygen attacks the carbon electrode to give CO_2 gas. The same current that produced 6.03 g of mercury produces 0.538 g of aluminum. The amount of oxygen produced in cell 3 can be determined from the amount of CO_2 or other products formed. The total oxygen produced is equivalent to the amount produced in cell 1. We also find that the volume (number of moles) of chlorine produced is twice the volume (number of moles) of the oxygen generated. In summary, we note that the same amount of electricity produced 6.03 g Hg, 1.38 g Na, and 0.538 g Al.

How are these masses related? If each mass is divided by the appropriate atomic weight, the numbers of moles of each kind of atom are obtained:

$$\frac{\text{mass Hg}}{\text{at. wt Hg}} = \frac{6.03 \text{ g Hg}}{201 \text{ g Hg/mole Hg}} = 0.0300 \text{ mole Hg atoms}$$

*In practice, calcium chloride must be added to such a cell to lower the melting point of the salt and, even then, the temperature must be high (600 °C). This is the commercial method for manufacturing metallic sodium.
†This is the basis for the commercial manufacture of aluminum. Another salt is added as solvent to lower the melting point. A mixture of Al_2O_3 and Na_3AlF_6 (cryolite) can be electrolyzed at 950 °C.

$$\frac{\text{mass Na}}{\text{at. wt Na}} = \frac{1.38 \text{ g Na}}{23.0 \text{ g Na/mole Na}} = 0.0600 \text{ mole Na atoms}$$

$$\frac{\text{mass Al}}{\text{at. wt Al}} = \frac{0.538 \text{ g Al}}{26.9 \text{ g Al/mole Al}} = 0.0200 \text{ mole Al atoms}$$

These numbers are related to each other as shown by the ratios

Hg		Na		Al
0.0300 mole	:	0.0600 mole	:	0.0200 mole
3 moles Hg atoms	:	6 moles Na atoms	:	2 moles Al atoms

A given quantity of electric current deposited six atoms of Na for every three atoms of Hg and two atoms of Al. Our results are quite clear: *a certain amount of electricity will deposit a fixed number of atoms, or some simple multiple of this number, regardless of which element is chosen.* Stated another way, twice as much current is required to deposit one mole of mercury as one mole of sodium. Three times as much current is required to deposit one mole of aluminum.

The results of the second experiment are also consistent with the hypothesis that electric charge comes in packages! An atom can carry one, two, or three packages of charge, but *cannot* carry 1.5872 or 1.4301 packages. Whatever the package of charge is, it is the same for all atoms, and it is not subject to subdivision under the experiments used here.

Historically, the idea that electric charge comes in packages led to the proposal that electricity is composed of particles. It was convenient to attach the name electron to the unit of charge of type C_1. The name proton was given to the other unit of charge, type C_2.

6-4.2 The Electrical Conductivity of Water Solutions

The number of moles of products generated in electrolysis experiments was of interest to us in the preceding section. Let us now examine the way in which charge moves through a solution during electrolysis, and summarize more effectively the processes which occur.

Water is a very poor conductor of electricity. Yet when sodium chloride dissolves in water, the solution conducts readily. The dissolved sodium chloride must be responsible. How does the dissolved salt permit charge to move through the liquid? One hypothesis consistent with our observations is that when salt dissolves in water, particles with electric charge are produced. The movement of these charged particles through the solution would account for the current. Since sodium chloride is electrically neutral and has the formula NaCl, and since it is responsible for carrying the current in the solution, perhaps charged particles of two different types appear in the solution when sodium chloride dissolves in water. A logical possibility would be that sodium chloride breaks into an atom of sodium which carries one kind of charge and an atom of chlorine which carries a different kind of charge. These two charges of opposite type, when taken together, would give an electrically neutral molecule (see page 127). It would be convenient to indicate the type of charge on the sodium atom (C_2) by the symbol + or positive and the type of charge on the chlorine atom (C_1) by the symbol − or negative. These are symbols of convenience only. The sodium atom with a positive or + charge would then be symbolized as Na^+; the chlorine atom with a negative or − charge would be symbolized as Cl^-. Atoms or groups of atoms that carry electric charge are called **ions.**

With these symbols, we can write the equation for the reaction that occurs when sodium chloride dissolves in water:

$$NaCl \ (solid) + \text{water} \longrightarrow Na^+ \ (in \ water) + Cl^- \ (in \ water) \quad (4)$$

This equation shows that when solid sodium chloride dissolves in water, Na^+ ions (sodium ions) and Cl^- ions (chloride ions) are present in the solution. It is convenient to abbreviate equations as much as possible while still keeping all the essential information. On the left side of the equation, the term *water* is usually not written since its presence is implied by the symbols on the right.

$$NaCl \ (solid) \longrightarrow Na^+ \ (in \ water) + Cl^- \ (in \ water) \quad (5)$$

We have already used the abbreviations for solid (s), liquid (l), and gas (g). Now we need an expression for *in water* when we deal with solutions. The term used is *aqueous,* abbreviated *aq.* Thus the usual form of the above equation is

$$NaCl(s) \longrightarrow Na^+ \ (aq) + Cl^- \ (aq) \quad (6)$$

Here is a model of a salt solution that will aid in discussing electrical conductivity. The solid dissolves, forming the charged particles $Na^+(aq)$ and $Cl^-(aq)$; the charges can move about in the solution. An electric current can pass through the solution by the movement of these ions. The $Cl^-(aq)$ ions move in one direction, carrying negative charge. The $Na^+(aq)$ ions move in the opposite direction, carrying positive charge. As we shall show in more detail later, these movements carry charge through the solution and the current flows.

Sugar dissolves in water, but the resulting solution conducts an electric current no better than does pure water. We conclude that when sugar dissolves, no charged particles result, that no ions form. Sugar must be quite different from sodium chloride!

Calcium chloride ($CaCl_2$) is another crystalline solid that dissolves readily in water. A one molar $CaCl_2$ solution conducts an electric current even better than does a one molar sodium chloride solution. Calcium chloride is, in this regard, like sodium chloride and unlike sugar. The equation for the reaction is

$$CaCl_2(s) \longrightarrow Ca^{2+}(aq) + 2Cl^-(aq) \quad (7)$$

The equation shows that when calcium chloride dissolves, $Ca^{2+}(aq)$ and $Cl^-(aq)$ ions appear in the solution. In this case, each calcium ion has twice the positive charge held by a sodium ion, $Na^+(aq)$; hence it is written as $Ca^{2+}(aq)$. The chloride ion that forms, $Cl^-(aq)$, is the same negative ion that is present in the sodium chloride solution; both calcium chloride solid and sodium chloride solid contain identical chloride ions. One mole of $CaCl_2$ contains twice as many chloride ions as does 1 mole of NaCl.

Silver nitrate ($AgNO_3$) is a third solid substance that dissolves in water to give a conducting solution. The reaction is

$$AgNO_3(s) \longrightarrow Ag^+(aq) + NO_3^-(aq) \qquad (8)$$

This time the ions formed are silver ions, $Ag^+(aq)$, and nitrate ions, $NO_3^-(aq)$. The silver ion is a silver atom* with a positive charge; it carries the same charge as an aqueous sodium ion. The aqueous nitrate ion carries a negative charge, the same charge as the aqueous chloride ion. This time, however, the negative charge is carried by four atoms, one nitrogen and three oxygen atoms, that remain together. Since this group, NO_3^-, remains together and acts as a unit, it has a distinctive name, the **nitrate ion.**

These three solids—sodium chloride, calcium chloride, and silver nitrate—all dissolve in water to form aqueous ions and to give conducting solutions. These solids are called **ionic solids.**

EXERCISE 6-2

Each of the following ionic solids dissolves in water to form a conducting solution. Write the equation for each reaction.

(1) potassium chloride (KCl)
(2) sodium nitrate ($NaNO_3$)
(3) calcium bromide ($CaBr_2$)
(4) lead nitrate [$Pb(NO_3)_2$]
(5) copper chloride ($CuCl_2$)
(6) potassium chromate (K_2CrO_4)
(7) mercuric nitrate [$Hg(NO_3)_2$]

6-4.3   Effect of Concentration—Insoluble Ionic Solids

A solution containing 0.1 mole per litre of NaCl conducts much better than a solution containing 0.01 mole per litre of NaCl. Conductivity depends not only on the presence of ions but also upon the number of ions per litre of solution.

Silver chloride is a solid that shows the concentration effect rather dramatically. This solid does *not* dissolve appreciably in water. In fact, it is frequently classed as insoluble. When solid silver chloride is placed in water, very little solid enters the solution and there is only a *very slight* increase in the conductivity of the solution over that of pure water. Yet there is a real and measurable increase—a few ions are formed. Careful measurements show that even though silver chloride is much less soluble in water than sodium chloride, it is like sodium

---

*As you shall see shortly, the positive charge arises because a *neutral* silver atom has lost an electron to give an *ion* with a positive charge.

chloride in that all of the solid that does dissolve forms ions in solution—aqueous ions. The reaction is

$$AgCl(s) \longrightarrow Ag^+(aq) + Cl^-(aq) \qquad (9)$$

Silver chloride, like sodium chloride, is an ionic solid.

6-5 THE ELECTRICAL CONDUCTIVITY OF SOLUTIONS AND AN ELECTRICAL MODEL FOR ATOMS

A number of separate observations have been made:

(1) chemical observations that suggest atoms;
(2) the behavior of spheres carrying electric charge; and
(3) the ability of some aqueous solutions to conduct electric current.

We recall the analogy:

(1) the garbage disappears every Thursday morning;
(2) a loud banging is heard along with the barking of a dog; and
(3) a bill from the city is received.

In each of these cases, the problem is: how can we interpret the facts? In one case we made an effort to "see" the garbage collector. Let us concentrate on "seeing" atoms. Our "first glance" will suggest many other experiments.

6-5.1 Electrons and Protons

In discussing the ability of a solution to conduct electricity, we suggested a new idea. Particles exist which carry the property called electric charge. Two kinds of particles and two kinds of charge exist; one kind of particle is represented by the symbol $+$, the second by the symbol $-$. It was convenient to give names as well as symbols to these charges. The following statements concerning names and properties summarize our current position.

(1) Matter includes particles, each of which carries a unit of electric charge. These particles are called **electrons** and **protons.**
(2) Each *electron* carries one unit of charge C_1. This has the symbol $-$.
(3) Each *proton* carries one unit of charge C_2. This has the symbol $+$.
(4) These particles exert force at a distance on each other in accordance with the electrical behavior we have observed.
  (a) Since C_1 repels C_1, minus repels minus, or electrons repel electrons.
  (b) Since C_2 repels C_2, plus repels plus, or protons repel protons.
  (c) Since C_1 attracts C_2, minus attracts plus, or electrons attract protons.
  (d) Since $C_1 + C_2 =$ no charge, $(+) + (-) = 0$, or one electron $+$ one proton $=$ no charge, or one unit $C_1 +$ one unit $C_2 =$ no charge.

With this expanded version of the particle model of matter, it is much easier to talk about electrical phenomena.

If a piece of matter (such as one of the electrometer spheres) has the same number of electrons and protons, there are just as many units of charge of type C_1 as of type C_2. Since $C_1 + C_2 =$ no charge, the sphere will have no charge. A body with no net charge (with equal numbers of protons and electrons) is said to be **electrically neutral.** If we remove some of the electrons from the sphere, it will then have an excess of protons, hence a net charge of type C_2. If we add an excess of electrons to the sphere, it will have a net charge of type C_1. The amount of **net charge** is the difference between the amount of charge C_1 and charge C_2.

It is a mathematical convenience to express the net charge in terms of algebraic symbols. For this reason, we identified the type of charge called C_1 as "negative charge" and the type called C_2 as "positive charge" in our earlier discussion. Notice the advantages. The combination of five units of C_1 and three units of C_2 leaves a net of two units of C_1. This can now be expressed

$$5(-1) + 3(+1) = -5 + 3 = -2$$

EXERCISE 6-3

There was a time when atoms were said to be the fundamental particles of which matter was composed. Now we describe the structure of the atom in terms of the fundamental particles we have just named, protons and electrons, plus another kind of particle called the neutron. Why are atoms no longer said to be fundamental particles (see Section 6-3.4)?

EXERCISE 6-4

Suppose ten protons and eleven electrons are brought together. These charges, grouped together, have the same net charge as how many electrons? Remember that one proton plus one electron gives no charge. Write an algebraic expression to show the answer.

6-5.2   An Electrical Model for Electrode Processes

The model for an atom has been allowed to "grow" to include gain or loss of positive or negative charge—ions result. The electrical conductivity of solutions has been interpreted in terms of the movement of these ions through the solution, and we have seen metals appear at one electrode while oxygen or chlorine gas appears at the other electrode. We have made progress, but the picture is still incomplete. A number of "wondering why" questions still seem very important. For example, we might ask

(1) What is the detailed process which occurs where the **electrode** (the wire dipping into the solution) meets the liquid?

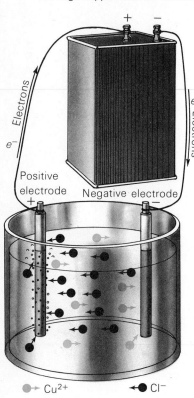

Fig. 6-6 Schematic representation of passage of electric current through copper chloride solution.

Electrons

e^- Electrons

e^- Electrons

Positive electrode +

Negative electrode −

Cu²⁺   Cl⁻

(2) Does electricity move through the metal wires as it does through the solution—by movement of ions?

(3) Since ions have + and − charges, can we really separate them so that the positive ions gather around one electrode and the negative ions around the other electrode? (See Figure 6-6.)

A more detailed model for electrical conductivity will help us to find an answer for all of these questions. Question (1) is the easiest since it can be answered by careful experimental observation. Let us start with the question: what happens when the wire meets the liquid?

Consider for the moment a dilute water solution of copper(II)* chloride ($CuCl_2$). Since the solution is known to be an electrical conductor, analogy to the case of NaCl and $CaCl_2$ suggests the following equation for the solution process:

$$CuCl_2(s) \longrightarrow Cu^{2+}(aq) + 2Cl^-(aq) \qquad (10)$$

The ions present in the solution are $Cu^{2+}(aq)$ and $Cl^-(aq)$. According to our earlier model, the $Cu^{2+}(aq)$ ions should move toward the **negative electrode** and the $Cl^-(aq)$ ions toward the **positive electrode.** Let us watch the platinum wire hooked up to the negative terminal of the battery. (This is the negative electrode.) We shall pay particular attention to the wire under the solution. *A coating of neutral, red copper metal forms over that surface of the silvery platinum wire which is under the surface of the liquid.* A *chemical process* seems to be taking place on the wire. Copper ions, $Cu^{2+}(aq)$, are being converted to copper metal (see Figure 6-6).

If we remember the experiments of Faraday and the charged particles which they suggested, it is easy to write an equation to explain the observed transformation of copper ions to copper metal at the negative electrode:

$$Cu^{2+}(aq) + 2e^- \longrightarrow Cu(\textit{solid metal})† \qquad (11)$$

At the positive electrode (this is the wire in the solution which is attached to the positive terminal of the battery) bubbles of chlorine gas grow, break away from the metal, and rise to the surface. Again a chemical process must be taking place; negatively charged chloride ions, $Cl^-(aq)$, are being converted to neutral chlorine gas (Cl_2). An equation for this process could be written:

$$2Cl^-(aq) \longrightarrow Cl_2(g) + 2e^-‡ \qquad (12)$$

Note that electrons are included among the products.

*The symbol (II) following the word copper indicates $CuCl_2$. Copper(I) chloride is CuCl.
†Loss of two positive charges would also give a neutral system; but this possibility is tentatively rejected since later arguments (Chapter 7) will show that gain of the electrons is the only acceptable process. Since the positively charged protons are present *in the nucleus,* they are held firmly and are not easily lost. Protons also have a large mass compared to the electron, so the loss of two protons from the copper would give a nucleus of lower mass and different properties.
‡Again, a gain of two positive charges would meet all algebraic requirements for giving us neutral chlorine atoms, but this possibility is tentatively rejected. Evidence considered in Chapter 7 will justify the choice used here.

The model for conductivity of solutions can now be made more detailed. Postulate: electrons given up by the chloride ions flow through the wire to the battery (which really serves as an "electron pump"), then over to the negative electrode where copper ions are converted to copper metal (see Figure 6-6). This postulate has many consequences. It suggests that electric current moves in the wire by a net flow of electrons, whereas electric current moves in the solution by migration of ions. Conductivity in a wire differs from that in solution! Bulky ions move in solution; only electrons move in the wire.

The postulate says that as ions carrying one kind of charge are removed at the electrode, the companion ion of opposite charge moves out toward the opposite electrode. As a result, though ions of opposite charge move in opposite directions, we do not build up a large excess of either positive or negative ions in any part of the solution or around the electrode. This is comforting since accumulation of an excess of ions of the same charge at any point would be very difficult and would require a very high electrical voltage.

EXERCISE 6-5

Remember that in the electrolysis described in Section 6-4.1, 0.0600 mole of sodium, 0.0300 mole of mercury, and 0.0200 mole of aluminum were produced.

(1) How many moles of Cl_2 will be generated in the NaCl(l) cell for each mole of sodium? Write the equation for the process.
(2) How many moles of chlorine will be given off in liberating 0.0600 mole of sodium?
(3) What volume will this chlorine occupy at STP?

[*Answers:* (1) $\frac{1}{2}$ mole Cl_2/mole Na, (2) 0.0300, (3) 0.672 litres Cl_2 at STP.]

EXERCISE 6-6

If the overall reaction for the deposition of mercury is given by the equation

$$2Hg^{2+}(aq) + 4NO_3^-(aq) + 2H_2O \xrightarrow[\text{energy}]{\text{electrical}}$$
$$2Hg(l) + O_2(g) + 4H^+(aq) + 4NO_3^-(aq)$$

what volume of oxygen (at STP) will be generated in the electrolysis experiment of Exercise 6-5? (*Answer:* 0.336 litre oxygen at STP.)

EXERCISE 6-7

Applying Avogadro's hypothesis, explain how the results of Exercises 6-5 and 6-6 show that atoms are "counted" by the electric current.

6-5.3 Measuring a Mole of Electrons

In the electrolysis operation just described, we made no effort to "count" electrons by use of conventional electric meters. Usually the electrician measures the flow of electricity in **amperes.** If our model is correct, *the number of amperes tells us how many electrons flow past a given point per second*. Additional experiments show that if *6.25 × 10^18 electrons flow past per second, we have 1 ampere*.* This number of electrons, 6.25×10^{18}, is called the **coulomb**—it is a quantity of electrons just like a litre is a quantity of water. We find that 96,500 coulombs of electricity are the same as 1 mole of electrons:

$$96{,}500 \; \text{\sout{coulombs electricity}} \times \left(6.25 \times 10^{18} \; \frac{\text{electrons}}{\text{\sout{coulomb electricity}}} \right)$$

$$= 6.02 \times 10^{23} \text{ electrons}$$

We thus can summarize the above discussion in several concise mathematical statements:

$$1 \text{ ampere (or amp)} = 6.25 \times 10^{18} \; \frac{\text{electrons}}{\text{sec}}$$

Thus, 1 amp flowing for 1 sec gives 6.25×10^{18} electrons = 1 coulomb of electricity. Therefore, **amps × sec = coulombs.**

$$96{,}500 \text{ coulombs} = 1 \text{ mole of electrons}$$

We can then write

$$\frac{\text{\sout{coulombs}}}{96{,}500 \; \text{\sout{coulombs}}/\text{mole of electrons}} = \text{moles of electrons}$$

Thus,

$$\frac{\text{\sout{amps × sec}}}{96{,}500 \; \text{\sout{coulombs}}/\text{mole of electrons}} = \text{moles of electrons} \qquad (13)$$

This is a useful relationship. It can be used, for example, to answer the question: how many moles of silver atoms will be deposited by a current of 2 amps flowing for 30 minutes? Since our equation is

$$\text{Ag}^+(aq) + \text{e}^- \longrightarrow \text{Ag}(metal) \qquad (14)$$

1 mole of electrons will deposit 1 mole of silver atoms. Our question could then be rephrased by asking how many moles of electrons flow in a current of 2 amps flowing for 30 minutes. The answer is

$$\frac{2 \; \text{\sout{amps}} \times 30 \; \text{\sout{min}} \times 60 \; \text{\sout{sec/min}}}{96{,}500 \; \text{\sout{amps}} \times \text{\sout{sec}}/\text{mole of electrons}} = 0.0373 \text{ mole of electrons} \qquad (15)$$

or 0.0373 mole of silver atoms.

How many moles of copper will be deposited from a solution of $CuSO_4$ by this same current? The answer is obtained in a similar fashion:

$$\frac{2 \; \text{\sout{amps}} \times 30 \; \text{\sout{min}} \times 60 \; \text{\sout{sec/min}}}{96{,}500 \; \text{\sout{amps}} \times \text{\sout{sec}}/\text{mole of electrons}}$$

$$= 0.0373 \text{ mole of electrons} \qquad (15)$$

---

*An ampere is actually defined in terms of deposition of silver. One ampere is that steady-state flow of direct current which will deposit 0.001118 g of silver metal per second from a silver nitrate solution.

But 2 moles of electrons deposit only 1 mole of copper:

$$Cu^{2+}(aq) + 2e^- \longrightarrow Cu(metal) \qquad (16)$$

Thus,

$$\frac{0.0373 \text{ mole of electrons}}{2 \text{ moles of electrons/mole Cu deposited}}$$

$$= 0.0186 \text{ mole of Cu atoms} \quad (17)$$

6-6 OTHER CONSEQUENCES OF THE EXISTENCE OF IONS

The concept of ions appears in many segments of chemistry, not just in a study of the passage of electric current through solutions. A few of these are described below.

6-6.1 Precipitation Reactions in Aqueous Solutions

Though both silver nitrate and sodium chloride have high solubility in water, silver chloride is almost insoluble. What will happen if we mix solutions of silver nitrate and sodium chloride? The solution obtained immediately after mixing will contain both $Ag^+(aq)$ and $Cl^-(aq)$ in high concentration! The $Ag^+(aq)$ came from the reaction

$$AgNO_3(s) \longrightarrow Ag^+(aq) + NO_3^-(aq) \qquad (8)$$

and the $Cl^-(aq)$ came from the reaction

$$NaCl(s) \longrightarrow Na^+(aq) + Cl^-(aq) \qquad (6)$$

The concentrations of $Ag^+(aq)$ and $Cl^-(aq)$ far exceed the solubility of silver chloride. The result is that a solid will be formed.

The formation of solid from a solution is called **precipitation:**

$$Ag^+(aq) + Cl^-(aq) \longrightarrow AgCl(s) \qquad (18)$$

Notice that the equation indicates the change that takes place when silver nitrate solution and sodium chloride solution are mixed. We could have written a more complete equation:

$$Ag^+(aq) + NO_3^-(aq) + Na^+(aq) + Cl^-(aq) \longrightarrow$$
$$AgCl(s) + NO_3^-(aq) + Na^+(aq) \quad (19)$$

However, the two ions $NO_3^-(aq)$ and $Na^+(aq)$ do not play an active role in the reaction, nor do they influence the reaction that does occur. Consequently, they are frequently omitted from the equation for the reaction. It is convenient to have the balanced chemical equation show only the species which actually participate in the reaction. The resulting equation is called the **net ionic equation.** The net ionic equation for the precipitation process giving AgCl is

$$Ag^+(aq) + Cl^-(aq) \longrightarrow AgCl(s) \qquad (18)$$

> (1) Write the complete equation for the reaction of Experiment 12, the precipitation of PbI_2. Include all reactants and products.
> (2) Rewrite the above equation eliminating those ions which are not active in the reaction. That is, write the net ionic equation.

6-6.2 Balancing Equations Involving Ions

The above equations involve charged species called ions. When we considered how to balance equations for chemical reactions (Section 3-3.2), we dealt with reactions involving electrically neutral particles. We were guided by the rule that atoms are conserved. This principle is still applicable to reactions involving ions. In addition, we must consider the balance of charges. *A chemical reaction does not change the total electric charge.* Consequently, the sum of the electric charges on the reactants must be the same as the sum of the electric charges on the products. Calcium chloride dissolves to give aqueous Ca^{2+} and Cl^- ions. The balanced equation tells us that the neutral solid, calcium chloride, dissolves to give one Ca^{2+} ion for every two Cl^- ions. Summing these electric charges,

$$(\text{charge on } CaCl_2 \text{ solid}) = (\text{charge on } Ca^{2+} \text{ ion}) + 2(\text{charge on } Cl^- \text{ ion})$$
$$\underline{\qquad 0 \qquad = \qquad (+2) \qquad + \qquad 2(-1)}$$
$$\text{SUM} \qquad 0 \qquad = \qquad 0$$

In a balanced equation for a chemical reaction, charge is conserved.

EXERCISE 6-9

> Balance the equations for the reactions given below. For each of the balanced equations, sum up the charges of the reactants and compare to the sum of the charges of the products.
>
> (1) $PbCl_2(s) \longrightarrow Pb^{2+}(aq) + Cl^-(aq)$
> (2) $K_2Cr_2O_7(s) \longrightarrow K^+(aq) + Cr_2O_7^{2-}(aq)$
> (3) $Cr_2O_7^{2-}(aq) + H_2O \longrightarrow CrO_4^{2-}(aq) + H^+(aq)$

6-7 HIGHLIGHTS

Many different facts justify our belief in atoms. Though no one fact is convincing in itself, the entire array of facts provides a most convincing case.

Among the facts reviewed here are

(1) the law of definite composition;
(2) the law of multiple proportions;
(3) the law of combining volumes for gases;
(4) Faraday's laws of electrolysis; and
(5) the behavior of ions.

To understand ions and the electric current, we took a side road and examined the behavior of an electrometer and the nature of electric charge. We found that *ions* are important in many aspects of chemistry, including precipitation processes. Our efforts have placed additional experimental supports around the model for matter. As the model continues to "grow," it becomes more detailed and more powerful. Further development promises to be worthwhile.

QUESTIONS and PROBLEMS

1 The Santa Claus Theory of Appearing Christmas Presents is another theory, familiar to everyone, which is built on indirect evidence. What observations lead a child to believe in the existence of Santa Claus? What theory is built? How is the theory modified in the light of more mature observations?

2 In a compound containing only carbon and hydrogen, there are 4.0 g of carbon present for every 1.0 g of hydrogen. (a) What is the *atomic* ratio of hydrogen to carbon in this substance? (b) What is the simplest chemical formula for this substance? (c) If the molecular weight of this substance is 30.0, what must the true formula for the substance be?

3 Determine the simplest formula for each of the following compounds: (a) 85.63 g of carbon atoms combine with 14.37 g of hydrogen atoms. (How many moles of carbon atoms are present? Of hydrogen atoms? Write the formula.) (b) 100.0 g of a compound contain 26.58 g of potassium atoms, 35.35 g of chromium atoms, and 38.07 g of oxygen atoms. (c) A 2.500-g sample of uranium was heated. The resulting uranium oxide had a mass of 2.949 g.

4 There are two known compounds containing only nitrogen and hydrogen. In the first, there are 4.67 g of nitrogen for each 1.00 g of hydrogen. In the second, there are 7.00 g of nitrogen for each 1.00 g of hydrogen. (a) Determine the simplest formula for each of these compounds. (b) Given the further information that the first compound can be synthesized directly from its elements, write the balanced equation for the reaction. (c) Explain why the existence of these two compounds illustrates (i) the law of definite composition; (ii) the law of multiple proportions; (iii) the law of combining volumes.

5 Name two forces other than electric force that are felt at a distance.

6 Why do scientists claim that there are only two kinds of electric charge?

7 Why do electrically neutral objects with large mass (such as stars and planets) attract each other?

8 Consider the examples of charged particles separated by a given distance, shown in Figure 6-7. (a) Identify each case as either attraction or repulsion. (b) In which case is the attractive force the largest? (c) The force in example A is how many times greater than the force in example D?

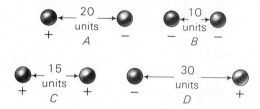

Fig. 6-7

9 Explain the following conductivity observations: (a) Distilled water conducts an electric current very poorly. (b) Tap water conducts an electric current slightly. (c) Salt water conducts an electric current very well. (d) A solution of sugar in distilled water conducts an electric current no better than does distilled water alone. (e) Solid silver nitrate is a very poor conductor of an electric current, but silver nitrate in solution is a good conductor. (f) Solid salt (NaCl) is a poor conductor, but molten salt is a very good conductor.

10 The following ionic solids dissolve in water. Write the equation for each reaction. (a) sodium chloride, $NaCl$ (b) potassium bromide, KBr (c) silver nitrate, $AgNO_3$ (d) potassium chromate, K_2CrO_4 (e) aluminum nitrate, $Al(NO_3)_3$ (f) ferric chloride, $FeCl_3$ (g) potassium phosphate, K_3PO_4.

11 The following ionic solids dissolve in water. Write the equation for the reaction. (a) tin(II) chloride, $SnCl_2$ (b) aluminum acetate, $Al(CH_3COO)_3$ (c) sodium chlorate, $NaClO_3$ (d) barium nitrate, $Ba(NO_3)_2$ (e) lithium sulfide, Li_2S (f) calcium nitrate, $Ca(NO_3)_2$.

12 What is the net charge of a system containing each of the following? (a) 9 protons and 10 electrons (b) 8 protons and 8 electrons (c) 12 protons and 10 electrons.

13 Copy the following table and enter the missing information.

Number of Protons	Number of Electrons	Net Charge
6	6	
8	10	
20		2+
9		1−
	18	1−
	18	1+

14 Each of the following substances dissolves in water to form ions. Write the equation for each reaction and calculate the concentration of *each ion* prepared as follows: (a) 0.50 mole of NaCl is dissolved in water to make 1.0 litre of solution. (b) 0.10 mole of $Ca(NO_3)_2$ is dissolved in water to make 1.0 litre of solution. (c) 0.10 mole of K_2CrO_4 is dissolved in water to make 500 ml of solution. (d) 0.10 mole of $Al(NO_3)_3$ is dissolved in water to make 250 ml of solution.

15 One litre of solution contains 0.100 mole of ferric nitrate [$Fe(NO_3)_3$] and 0.200 mole of calcium nitrate [$Ca(NO_3)_2$]. Calculate the concentrations of the Fe^{3+}, Ca^{2+}, and NO_3^- ions.

16 A current of 1.0 amp is passed for 30.0 minutes through two cells. In one cell, 0.60 g of copper is deposited; in the second, 2.05 g of silver are deposited. (a) How many coulombs of electricity pass through the circuit? (b) Calculate the number of moles of electrons that pass through the circuit. (c) Calculate the number of moles of silver that are deposited. (d) From your answers to (b) and (c), write the equation for the deposition of silver. (e) Will this reaction occur at the positive or negative electrode of the cell? (f) Calculate the number of moles of copper deposited. (g) From your answers to (b) and (f), write the equation for the deposition of copper. (h) Will this reaction occur at the positive or negative electrode of the cell? (i) What is the ratio of moles of silver deposited to moles of copper deposited? (j) How do the results of this experiment show that copper, silver, and electrons must exist as discrete particles?

17 A current of 10.7 amps is run for 30.0 minutes through a cell whose reaction at the negative electrode is

$$Ag^+ + e^- \longrightarrow Ag(s)$$

(Assume that the reaction is 100 percent efficient.) (a) How many coulombs of electricity pass through the cell? (b) How many moles of electrons pass through the cell? (c) How many moles of silver atoms will be deposited? (d) What will the mass of the deposited silver be? (e) If the same current is passed through a cell whose reaction at the negative electrode is

$$Cu^{2+} + 2e^- \longrightarrow Cu(s)$$

how many moles of copper will be deposited on the electrode?

18 How many moles of X^{3+} ion will be deposited as $X(s)$ in a cell if 1.93×10^7 coulombs of electricity pass through the cell?

19 (a) How many litres of chlorine gas (at STP) will result from passing 5.0 amps for 5 hours 22 minutes through a cell if the reaction at the positive electrode is

$$2Cl^- \longrightarrow Cl_2(g) + 2e^-$$

(b) How long must the cell run at 2.00 amps to produce 3.55 g of Cl_2?

20 (a) How many coulombs of electricity must pass through a cell to produce 135 g of aluminum if the cell reaction at the negative electrode is

$$Al^{3+} + 3e^- \longrightarrow Al(s)$$

(Assume that the reaction is 100 percent efficient.) (b) How many hours would a 100-amp current have to flow through the cell in order to produce this amount of electricity? (c) If the reaction were to be completed in an hour, what amperage must be used?

21 An electric current was passed through a solution containing silver nitrate ($AgNO_3$) and then through a solution containing an ion, X^{2+}. A 2.16-g sample of silver was deposited and a 0.63-g sample of the other metal, X, was deposited by the same current. What is the atomic weight of X?

22 Write (a) the complete equation (showing *all* ions present) and (b) the net ionic equation for each of the following solution reactions: (i) Silver nitrate ($AgNO_3$) and potassium bromide (KBr) react to form the precipitate silver bromide (AgBr). (ii) Sodium chromate (Na_2CrO_4) and lead nitrate $[Pb(NO_3)_2]$ react to form the precipitate lead chromate $(PbCrO_4)$. (iii) Barium nitrate $[Ba(NO_3)_2]$ and sodium sulfate (Na_2SO_4) react to form the precipitate barium sulfate $(BaSO_4)$. (iv) Sodium phosphate (Na_3PO_4) and calcium nitrate $[Ca(NO_3)_2]$ react to form the precipitate calcium phosphate $[Ca_3(PO_4)_2]$.

23 When silver nitrate $(AgNO_3)$ and sodium chloride (NaCl) are mixed in solution silver chloride (AgCl) is precipitated. (a) Write the overall and net ionic equations for this reaction. (b) If 1.0 litre each of 1.0 molar solutions of $AgNO_3$ and NaCl are mixed, what is the final concentration of each ion after mixing? (Assume that the solubility of AgCl is negligible.)

24 When solutions of copper(II) chloride and lead nitrate are mixed a precipitate of lead chloride $(PbCl_2)$ forms. (a) Write the overall ionic and the net ionic equations for this

reaction. (b) If 0.200 litre of the $CuCl_2$ solution contains 0.300 mole of the compound, what is the concentration of each ion? (c) If 0.300 litre of the $Pb(NO_3)_2$ solution contains 0.150 mole of the compound, what is the concentration of each ion? (d) If the 0.200 litre of $CuCl_2$ solution is added to the 0.300 litre of $Pb(NO_3)_2$ solution, what is the concentration of *each ion* after the precipitate forms? (Assume that the solubility of $PbCl_2$ is negligible.)

25 When solutions of sodium phosphate (Na_3PO_4) and magnesium sulfate $(MgSO_4)$ are mixed, a precipitate of magnesium phosphate $[Mg_3(PO_4)_2]$ is formed. (a) Write the overall and the net ionic equations for this reaction. (b) If each of the separate solutions contains 0.50 mole of the dissolved substance in a volume of 5.0 litres, what is the concentration of each of the four ions? (c) If 1.0 litre of each of the solutions is added together, what is the concentration of *each ion* after the precipitation has occurred?

THE STRUCTURE OF THE ATOM

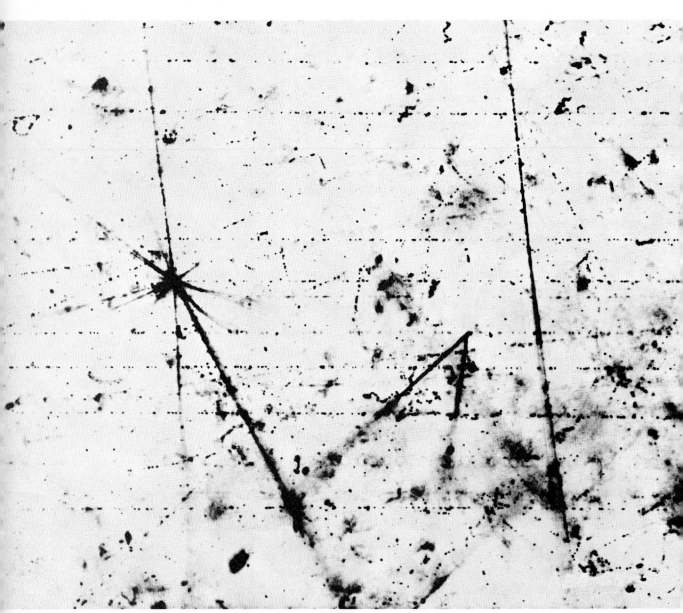

This photographic record of an atomic disintegration guides us in formulating our ideas of atomic structure.

SUBDIVISION OF ATOMS INTO POSITIVELY AND NEGATIVELY CHARGED particles leads us into a number of questions. Are there any other kinds of particles in the atom? How big are these particles? How much mass do they have? How are they arranged in the atom? Can subatomic particles themselves undergo changes?

Although investigating something as tiny as an atom and its sub-particles has many of the same difficulties as knitting with boxing gloves on, experiments have been devised which at least partially answer these questions about atomic architecture. In hindsight, these classic experiments are beautifully simple. All that was needed was someone to think them up.

May we remind you that there are still many unanswered questions waiting for a beautifully simple experiment?

Observations summarized in Chapter 6 provide additional reasons for believing in atoms. In addition, charged particles called ions were needed to explain electrical conductivity, precipitation reactions, and electrochemical processes at electrodes. Electrometer experiments provided evidence for positive and negative charges which seemed to be very much involved in the makeup of ions and atoms. The positive particles were called protons; the negative particles, electrons. How are protons and electrons used in the construction of the atom?

A closer approach to a "direct-vision" type of experiment is needed to obtain such detailed information. In the earlier garbage-collector analogy we were almost convinced that there was a garbage collector even before any attempt was made to see him. Details about him were obtained as we progressively "saw" him. The more clearly we saw him, the more clearly the details were defined.

We now believe in atoms, but we lack detail. It is now time to set our scientific alarm clock for five o'clock in the morning and look closely at matter to try to "see" the atom. More and more of our questions seem to point to the details of atomic structure. For example, why does salt give ions in solution while sugar does not? Why does sodium give a positive ion while chlorine gives a negative ion? Why do hydrogen gas and chlorine gas combine explosively when exposed to bright light? Why is diamond hard while white phosphorus is relatively soft? These questions are not easily answered, and in some cases the answers remain incomplete despite the best efforts of brilliant chemists. Still, progress has been made. The road to understanding these "wondering why" questions leads us into the world of atomic and nuclear structure.

In contrast to the experiments supporting our belief in atoms (review Section 6-2), many of the key experiments on atomic and nuclear structure involve complex instrumentation and reasonably sophisticated physical concepts. For these reasons, only an abbreviated presentation of experiments supporting our belief in the nuclear atom is given in the next section. Additional detail is given in Chapter 16 and in the appendices. As you will see in Chapter 8 and later, a large amount of chemistry can be correlated by a relatively simple model of the nuclear atom. These useful correlations save much wear and tear on the memory and strengthen our belief in the nuclear model for atomic structure. We shall use the nuclear model to correlate some chemical facts and then proceed with a more careful examination of the details of electron arrangements in atoms in Chapter 16.

7-1   ELEMENTARY ATOMIC ARCHITECTURE

7-1.1   The Components of the Atom

Experiments on the electrical conductivity of solutions suggested that molecules can be broken into charged particles or ions. Ions seemed to involve protons and electrons. Combination of equal numbers of protons and electrons would give a neutral particle (review Section 6-5.1). Perhaps atoms are made up of equal numbers of protons and electrons. Let us investigate this possibility.

By means of an instrument known as a mass spectrometer (described in Appendix 3), it is possible to determine the mass of the proton on the atomic weight scale. The value to two significant figures is 1.0. The mass of an electron determined on this same scale to two significant figures is 0.000 55 or 5.5×10^{-4} (see Section 7-2.3). Can protons and electrons combine to make gold, the alchemist's dream? Let us add up the parts.

Rather sophisticated experiments of the type done by Rutherford (see Section 7-2.5) and Moseley (see Appendix 4 for greater detail) indicate that each gold atom contains 79 protons. Since gold atoms are electrically neutral, each gold atom must also contain 79 electrons. Adding up the parts for a gold atom, we find $(79 \times 1.0) +$ $[79 \times (5.5 \times 10^{-4})]$. The second number $[79 \times (5.5 \times 10^{-4})]$ is only 0.04. This value is beyond the limit of significance in our first measurement; hence, the total mass of the gold atom should be 79. Measurement of the actual mass of a gold atom by chemical methods or by a mass spectrometer gives a value of about 197 on the atomic weight scale. If we compare 197 with 79, it is clear that each gold atom must contain something *in addition* to the protons and electrons counted. Experiments beyond those we are concerned with here identify that extra something as the **neutron.** *The neutron has zero charge and a mass of 1.0* on the atomic weight scale. Thus, a neutral gold atom must contain 79 protons, 118 neutrons, and 79 electrons.

The properties of the particles used to construct this picture of the gold atom are summarized in Table 7-1. These three particles—electron, proton, and neutron—are arranged in different combinations to give the more than 100 different elements known.

TABLE 7-1 APPROXIMATE CHARGE AND MASS OF SOME FUNDAMENTAL PARTICLES

Particle	Charge	Approximate Mass (Relative to the Mass of a Proton)
Electron	1−	0.000 55
Proton	1+	1
Neutron	0	1

7-1.2 A Model for an Atom: The Nuclear Atom

How are these fundamental particles arranged to give an atom? This question was a perplexing one at the turn of the century. The answer to it came from unexpected sources. The English physicist J. J. Thomson (1856–1940) was studying the passage of electricity through gases held in a tube at very low pressures (described in Section 7-2.1). His experiments showed that positive and negative particles were always produced in the tube as electricity passed through the gas. The negative particles were identified as electrons regardless of the gas in the tube, while the positive fragment varied according to the gas in the tube. These experiments suggested to Thomson that a neutral gas atom might be a sphere of positive electricity in which separate negative electrons were imbedded like plums in a pudding. Thomson's "plum-pudding model" seemed reasonable. Then in 1909 Ernest Rutherford,* H. Geiger, and E. Marsden began a series of experiments which led to an amazing conclusion: Dalton's atoms (Section 6-2.2) are *not* like plum puddings, nor are they hard little spheres. Instead, each atom contains an unbelievably small and positively charged nucleus which contains almost all of the mass of the atom.

This nucleus occupies approximately *one* part in 10^{13} of the total volume of a typical atom such as copper. In the relatively large volume of space outside this nucleus, electrons of low relative mass move about. These are referred to as **extranuclear electrons.** Strange as it may seem, *Dalton's atoms are mostly empty space, not hard little spheres.* (The experiments are described in Section 7-2.5.)

A hydrogen atom, the lightest atom known, contains one proton in the nucleus and one electron outside the nucleus. The nuclei of all other known elements have nuclear charges that are whole-number multiples of the positive charge on the proton. For example, the helium nucleus contains two protons and has a total positive charge of 2. Outside this nucleus there are two electrons. Hence, the overall atom is neutral. The neutral lithium atom has three protons in the nucleus (charge of 3 +) and three electrons outside. Neutral beryllium has four protons in the nucleus and four electrons outside. As these examples show, the number of protons in the nucleus determines the nuclear charge and the nuclear charge determines the identity of the atom. The number of protons in the nucleus gives the **atomic number** of the element. Thus, hydrogen has an atomic number of 1; helium, an atomic number of 2; lithium, an atomic number of 3; and carbon, an atomic number of 6. It is important to remember that *the number of protons in the nucleus determines the identity of the atom.*

Section 7-1.1 showed that protons and electrons alone do not account for the mass of a gold atom. Neutrons in the nucleus make up the additional mass required. Thus, a helium atom with an atomic number of 2 and an atomic mass of 4 has two protons plus two neutrons in the nucleus and two electrons outside the nucleus. We say it has a mass of 4 because it contains two protons (mass 1 each) and two neutrons (mass 1 each). The electron mass is negligible. Lith-

---

*Ernest Rutherford (1871–1937) was a distinguished British physicist and former student of Thomson. Although he originally subscribed to the "plum-pudding" model, additional evidence led him to the nuclear model.

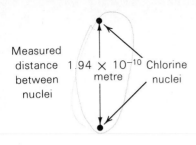

Measured distance between nuclei 1.94×10^{-10} metre Chlorine nuclei

Fig. 7-1.1 Results of experimental measurement of distance between two chlorine nuclei in a gaseous chlorine molecule.

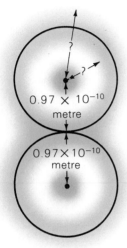

0.97×10^{-10} metre

0.97×10^{-10} metre

Fig. 7-1.2 The chlorine radius is half the distance between nuclei, or 0.97×10^{-10} metre. The fact that there is no definite "edge" to the atom prevents a meaningful measurement of size.

ium, with an atomic number of 3 and an atomic mass of 7, has three protons plus four neutrons in the nucleus and three electrons outside the nucleus. Again, the mass of the electrons is negligible. Carbon, with an atomic number of 6 and an atomic mass of 12, has six protons plus six neutrons in the nucleus and six electrons outside the nucleus.

EXERCISE 7-1

(1) What is the atomic number of boron, the element just before carbon? of beryllium, the element right after lithium?
(2) What is in the nucleus of the nitrogen atom, atomic mass 14? What is in the nucleus of the boron atom, atomic mass 11?

7-1.3 The Size of an Atom and of a Nucleus

How large is an atom? This would be an easy question to answer if atoms were like billiard balls and had well-defined outer surfaces. Unfortunately, atoms do not have well-defined boundaries; they have very fuzzy, indistinct boundaries so that it is impossible to tell where the surface of the atom really is. This strange property is a result of the wave nature of the electron and will be considered in more detail in Chapter 16.

For the present, let us define very carefully what we mean by atomic size. It is possible to devise experiments permitting accurate measurement of the distance between each of the nuclei in a molecule. Because these experiments involve rather complicated concepts and ideas, we shall postpone a description of them and use only the results of such experiments here. One important result gives the distance between the two chlorine nuclei in Cl_2 as 1.94×10^{-10} metre.* If the chlorine molecule consists of two spheres (atoms), then each sphere has a radius equal to half the distance between the two nuclei (see Figure 7-1). We could then assign a radius of 0.97×10^{-10} metre to each chlorine atom. This is a well-defined experimental quantity based on specific measurements.

EXERCISE 7-2

(1) The measured distance between the carbon nucleus and the chlorine nucleus in carbon tetrachloride is 1.76×10^{-10} metre. Using this value and information given in Figure 7-1.1, calculate the radius of a carbon atom.
(2) If the distance between a carbon nucleus and a bromine nucleus in CBr_4 is 1.94×10^{-10} metre, what is the radius of a bromine atom?
(3) What is the distance between nuclei in Br_2?

An atomic radius, as we have defined the term above, will vary from approximately 4×10^{-11} metre (0.000 000 000 04) to about 2.5×10^{-10} metre. A nucleus is much smaller. A typical nuclear diameter is about 10^{-14} metre or about $\frac{1}{10,000}$ of the diameter of an

*This value in older units is 1.94×10^{-8} cm or 1.94 ångstroms, where 1 ångstrom is 10^{-8} cm. We are using the units of the SI system.

atom. Suppose we represent a nucleus by a dot this big: (•). The atomic diameter (as defined above) would then be a circle 10 metres (32 feet) in diameter, or about the size of an "average" classroom. Another analogy may be helpful. Suppose a chlorine atom were expanded until the diameter of the atom were as large as a very large university football stadium, The University of Michigan stadium, for example, which seats 101,000 people. From the outer row of seats on the east side to the outer row of seats on the west side is about 187 metres or about 600 feet. On this scale the nucleus of the chlorine atom would be a sphere on the 50-yard line which is as large as the one shown in the margin. The electrons could be pictured as birds flying constantly in the stadium. The nucleus is truly very small compared to the size of the atom.

7-1.4   Mass Numbers and Isotopes

All the atoms of a given element have the same number of protons in the nucleus, hence the *same nuclear charge* and the same atomic number. Do all the atoms of an element have the same mass (or same atomic weight)?* Almost all hydrogen atoms do have the same mass. Their mass is equal to the mass of the single nuclear proton (1.0 on the atomic weight scale) plus that of the single extranuclear electron (0.000 55 on the atomic weight scale).

EXERCISE 7-3

What atomic weight for a hydrogen atom is indicated if the precise mass of a proton is 1.0075 units and the electron is 5.5×10^{-4}? Does this check the experimental atomic weight of hydrogen as shown in Table 3-1?

A few hydrogen atoms are different, however. About 0.015 percent of all hydrogen atoms in ordinary hydrogen have a nucleus whose mass is approximately twice as great as that of an ordinary hydrogen atom. Each such heavy hydrogen nucleus is composed of one proton (charge 1, mass 1) plus one neutron (charge 0, mass 1). The total mass of each such nucleus on the atomic weight scale is 2! This heavy hydrogen atom is called hydrogen-2 or, alternatively, **deuterium.** It has a **mass number†** of 2 (one proton plus one neutron). The two kinds of hydrogen atoms, having the same atomic number but different mass numbers, are called **isotopes.** All the elements have a number of isotopes. For example, *ordinary oxygen* contains three kinds of oxygen atoms. *All* have eight protons in the nucleus, making them oxygen atoms. The most common isotope in ordinary oxygen is oxygen-16. Oxygen-16 makes up 99.76 percent of ordinary oxygen. Its atoms have eight neutrons in the nucleus in addition to the eight protons. The total mass of such oxygen atoms is 8 + 8 or 16. A second isotopic species with

*While chemists for historical reasons still speak of atomic weight, the mass of the atom is really implied. Remember, *mass* refers to the actual amount of material, while *weight* represents the Earth's attraction for this quantity of material.
†The mass number is the mass of the nucleus to the nearest *whole* number.

eight protons and nine neutrons is known as oxygen-17 (about 0.04 percent of all oxygen). The third isotopic variety (about 0.20 percent of all oxygen) has a nucleus containing eight protons and ten neutrons and is, therefore, oxygen-18. The makeup of a number of the isotopes of different elements is summarized in Table 7-2. In short, *atoms which have the same atomic number but different numbers of neutrons in the nucleus are known as isotopes of the same element.*

TABLE 7-2 COMPOSITION OF ISOTOPES

Isotope of Element	Abundance in Nature (%)	Symbol	Protons in Nucleus	Neutrons in Nucleus	Electrons in Neutral Atom	Atomic Number	Atomic Mass or Mass Number
Hydrogen-1	99.985	^{1}H	1	0	1	1	1
Hydrogen-2	0.015	^{2}D	1	1	1	1	2
Helium-3	1.34×10^{-4}	^{3}He	2	1	2	2	3
Helium-4	100	^{4}He	2	2	2	2	4
Lithium-6	7.5	^{6}Li	3	3	3	3	6
Lithium-7	92.5	^{7}Li	3	4	3	3	7
Beryllium-9	100	^{9}Be	4	5	4	4	9
Boron-10	19.8	^{10}B	5	5	5	5	10
Boron-11	80.2	^{11}B	5	6	5	5	11
Carbon-12	98.89	^{12}C	6	6	6	6	12
Carbon-13	1.11	^{13}C	6	7	6	6	13
Nitrogen-14	99.64	^{14}N	7	7	7	7	14
Nitrogen-15	0.36	^{15}N	7	8	7	7	15
Oxygen-16	99.76	^{16}O	8	8	8	8	16
Oxygen-17	0.04	^{17}O	8	9	8	8	17
Oxygen-18	0.20	^{18}O	8	10	8	8	18

EXERCISE 7-4

(1) Fluorine-19 (atomic number 9) makes up 100 percent of natural fluorine. Give information like that in Table 7-2 for fluorine-19.
(2) Gold-197 (atomic number 79) makes up 100 percent of natural gold. Give information like that in Table 7-2 for gold-197.
(3) Uranium-235 (atomic number 92) makes up 0.71 percent of natural uranium; the remainder is uranium-238. Give information like that in Table 7-2 for uranium-235 and uranium-238.

7-1.5 Ion Formation

How do ions fit into this more detailed view of the atom? Earlier studies with the electrometer verified that positive charges attract negative charges. The picture just outlined indicates that the positive charge on the nucleus due to protons is just neutralized by electrons outside the nucleus. The result is a neutral atom. Consider the sodium atom:

$$\overset{\displaystyle\binom{11\ p^+}{12\ n}}{\text{NUCLEUS}} \qquad \overset{\displaystyle 11\ e^-}{\text{ELEVEN EXTRANUCLEAR ELECTRONS}}$$

Symbolically we can write $(11+) + (11-) = 0$. A neutral atom is formed. If one electron is removed from the sodium atom we can write

$$\left[\ \overset{\displaystyle\binom{11\ p^+}{12\ n}}{\text{NUCLEUS}} \qquad \underset{\text{TEN EXTRANUCLEAR ELECTRONS}}{10\ e^-}\ \right]^+ \quad \begin{array}{l}\text{One}\\ \text{electron}\\ \text{removed}\end{array}$$

Symbolically this gives $(11+) + (10-) = (1+)$. *A sodium atom which lacks one electron gives a sodium ion with a charge of 1+.* If two electrons are removed from a sodium atom, a sodium ion with a charge of $2+$ is formed.

Negative ions are formed by adding electrons to neutral atoms. Consider a neutral fluorine-19 atom:

$$\overset{\displaystyle\binom{9\ p^+}{10\ n}}{\text{NUCLEUS}} \qquad \overset{\displaystyle 9\ e^-}{\text{NINE EXTRANUCLEAR ELECTRONS}}$$

If an extra electron is added to a fluorine atom we have

$$\left[\ \overset{\displaystyle\binom{9\ p^+}{10\ n}}{\text{NUCLEUS}} \qquad \underset{\text{TEN EXTRANUCLEAR ELECTRONS}}{10\ e^-}\ \right]^- \quad \begin{array}{l}\text{One}\\ \text{electron}\\ \text{added}\end{array}$$

Symbolically this gives $(9+) + (10-) = (1-)$. A fluorine atom containing one extra electron is a negatively charged fluoride ion. *Positively charged ions are formed by removing electrons from neutral atoms. Negatively charged ions are formed by adding electrons to neutral atoms. Groups of atoms* can also lose electrons to give positively charged ions. Notice the ammonium ion (NH_4^+). Similarly, *groups of atoms* can pick up extra electrons to give negatively charged ions such as nitrate (NO_3^-) and sulfate (SO_4^{2-}).

7-1.6   Energy Relations in Ion Formation

Under what conditions are ions produced? In general, positive ions are produced under conditions in which large amounts of energy are available. For example, atoms in a flame will lose electrons as will atoms in the path of an electrical discharge. Thus, a lightning flash or a beam of high-energy electrons will produce ions. Equations representing this process for Na and Ca atoms can be written as

$$Na(g) + \text{energy} \longrightarrow Na^+(g) + e^- \qquad\qquad (1)$$

$$Ca(g) + \text{energy} \longrightarrow Ca^+(g) + e^- \qquad\qquad (2)$$

$$Ca^+(g) + \text{energy} \longrightarrow Ca^{2+}(g) + e^- \qquad\qquad (3)$$

Note the energy terms in these equations. Why are they necessary? Since a positively charged nucleus attracts a negatively charged electron, work must be done or energy must be used to *pull* the electron away from the atom. A positive ion and a free electron result. *Work* and *energy* are the same here; the statement indicates that an external agent must exert force on the electron to pull it away from the neutral atom.

In a few cases neutral atoms release energy when they pick up an electron to form a negative ion. Thus, when fluorine is converted to fluoride ion,

$$F(g) + e^- \longrightarrow F^-(g) + energy \qquad (4)$$

energy is released. This is not a very common situation, but is observed when certain negative ions are formed. On the other hand, energy is *always* absorbed when a neutral atom is converted to a *positive ion* and an *electron*.

In Chapter 6 we wrote ion-electron equations to describe reactions occurring at each electrode when electricity is passed through an electrochemical cell. We arbitrarily rejected a model in which a neutral copper atom would be obtained by loss of positive charges from Cu^{2+}, as in the following:

$$Cu^{2+} \longrightarrow Cu + two\ positive\ charges \qquad (5)$$

The reason becomes clearer now. Protons are very heavy particles compared to electrons and are bound in the small central nucleus. Electrons, on the other hand, are held on the outside of the nucleus. Furthermore, the *addition or subtraction of a whole proton from the nucleus would change the identity of the atom.*

7-1.7   A Summary of Information on Atomic Architecture

Let us summarize the present state of our knowledge of the atom.

(1) The *nucleus* of the atom consists of very tiny and very dense,* positively charged protons plus equally tiny and equally dense, neutral neutrons confined in a very small volume.
(2) The *number of protons in the nucleus* gives the *atomic number* of the element and thus the *positive charge* on the nucleus.
(3) The positive charge on the nucleus is compensated completely in a neutral atom, partially in a positive ion, and excessively in a negative ion by very light electrons which move in a relatively large volume outside the nucleus.
(4) Since electrons are *attracted* to the positively charged nucleus, work is *always* required to pull an electron away from a neutral atom or positive ion.
(5) *The atomic number of an element is an indication of its chemistry.* The nuclear charge (atomic number) and the electrons which it attracts are of major importance in determining the way in which an atom will behave toward another atom.

*"Dense" means large mass per unit of volume.

(6) Atoms having the same atomic number but different numbers of neutrons in the nucleus are known as *isotopes* of that element. Mass differences cause only minor chemical differences in atoms. Only the most precise measurements will indicate the very slight chemical differences between different isotopes of the same element. Thus, we can speak of the chemistry of oxygen without specifying which isotopes are being used.

(7) The mass of a given isotope is given to an accuracy of better than ±0.1 of a mass unit by adding up the number of protons plus the number of neutrons in the nucleus. The mass of the isotope is called its *mass number*. *The mass number for an isotope is equal to the number of protons plus the number of neutrons.*

7-2 "SEEING" PARTS OF ATOMS

In Section 7-1 many assertions about the details of atomic structure were made. In general the evidence presented was meager or nonexistent. Some of the classic experiments supporting the earlier statements are described here. Most require some knowledge of physics. It is not necessary for you to understand all these experiments in detail in order to use the nuclear model of the atom; however, a study of this section should be of assistance in learning how a more detailed view of the atom was obtained.

7-2.1 "Seeing" Electrons

Passing electricity through solutions of salts led us to the conclusion that an electric current consists of moving ions in solutions and moving electrons in the wires outside the solution. Passing electricity through gases gives a more detailed view of these electrons. We are all familiar with the red glow of a neon sign. Closer examination of one of the segments of a neon sign shows that it has much in common with the apparatus shown in Figure 7-2. This is a glass tube fitted with electrodes so that a potential

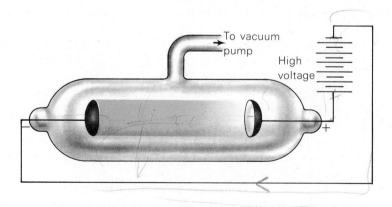

Fig. 7-2 An electric discharge through a gas.

of about 10,000 volts can be applied across the space between the electrodes. Let us fill the original tube with neon, then gradually begin to pump the gas out. When the pressure reaches 0.01 atm, the familiar red glow of the neon sign appears. The color depends on the gas selected. Different gases give different colors. If the vacuum pump continues to operate, the color will gradually disappear when the pressure reaches 10^{-6} atm and a fluorescent glow will appear on parts of the tube wall. This glow is of particular interest to us.* To study it more carefully, a new tube is made which has a metal disk placed in front of the negative electrode. A triangular hole has been cut out of this metal disk (Figure 7-3). The end of the tube

Fig. 7-3.1 An electric discharge tube, very low pressure. Some electrons leaving the negative electrode pass through the triangular hole to produce a triangular spot on the screen.

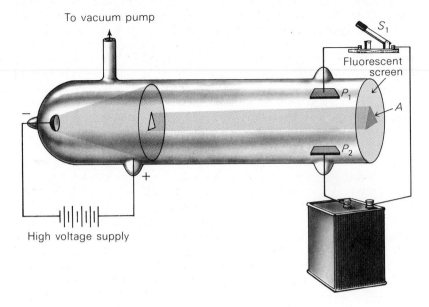

Fig. 7-3.2 Deflection of beam of electrons by electric charge on plates P_1 and P_2.

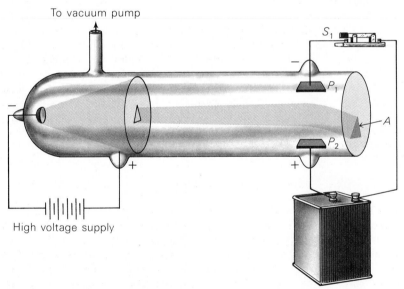

is covered with a thin layer of a material such as zinc sulfide. When the tube operates, a sharp triangular image appears on the tube wall opposite the disk (see A on diagram). It appears that the radiation is traveling in straight lines from the negative electrode to the opposite wall. This behavior is characteristic of light. If we now bring an ordinary magnet near the tube,

---

*In actual operation the glow on glass is faint and difficult to see. On the other hand, if the glass is covered with a thin layer of a compound such as zinc sulfide or similar fluorescent material, the glow is bright and easily seen. You see this phenomenon every time you look at a television screen. The fluorescent coating on the tube makes the picture brighter.

the beam of "light" can be bent and moved around. No one ever saw a light beam which could be moved around by a magnet of this type. The beam is clearly *not* ordinary light. Let us now bring the battery circuit of our apparatus into action by closing switch S_1. Plate P_1 becomes negatively charged (hooked to the negative pole of the battery or electrical generator) and P_2 positively charged (hooked to the positive pole of the battery or generator). Immediately the beam bends toward the positive electrode. Further, *the behavior of the beam is independent of the kind of gas in the tube.* Something in the beam is negatively charged! It is reasonable to suggest that the beam is a stream of the same kind of negative particles (or electrons) which we dealt with in our electrolysis experiments. Such a suggestion has been adequately verified by many other observations.

Have we really "seen" an electron? No, not really; but the experiment does have some features of a direct-vision experiment in that it gives us direct and detailed information about the beam. We know, for example, that it is negatively charged; a more careful study of the bending of the beam by a magnet and by the electrically charged plates P_1 and P_2 would permit us to measure the ratio of electron charge to electron mass. (The value of e/m, where e = charge and m = mass, is 1.759×10^8 coulombs*/g for the electron.) This experiment, though important, is omitted here and described in some detail in Appendix 2.

What have we really seen? We have *not* seen the electron directly; rather we have seen a burst of light on the fluorescent screen—damage resulting from the collision of the electron with the zinc sulfide on the glass screen. We have seen, to expand our analogy, the footprints in the garden rather than the garbage collector. From certain properties of the footprints—size, shape, depth, and spacing—we decide that the garbage collector is a man. Perhaps we might even develop a detailed description of him, including his height, weight, and stride (remember Sherlock Holmes in Chapter 1).

You will find that this is typical of most of the experiments that allow us to "see" atoms and their components. What we actually see is their "footprints"—bursts of light on a screen, dark spots or lines on a photographic plate, and noise from a Geiger counter. It is from such footprints that the characteristics of particles in the atom have been established with great certainty.

7-2.2 The Charge on the Electron

In 1909 Robert Millikan (1868–1953), an American physicist, and his students determined the charge on an electron by using an apparatus similar to that shown schematically in Figure 7-4. Tiny droplets of oil were sprayed into the space above the metal plates in the figure. Now and then an oil droplet would fall through the tiny hole in the upper plate into the space between the plates. The rate at which this oil droplet fell was determined by watching it through a telescope. When the rate of fall was established, the upper plate of the apparatus was connected to the positive terminal of a high-voltage battery and the lower plate was connected to the negative terminal of this battery. Then a beam of X rays was passed through the chamber to ionize gases and provide a ready source of free electrons. After the passage of the X rays, the rate of fall of the droplet changed in sudden jumps. Millikan interpreted this as evidence for gain

*The **coulomb** is a unit of electric charge (6.25×10^{18} electrons). Its magnitude can be evaluated by its relation to the **ampere.** One coulomb of charge passing a point in a wire every second is a current of 1 ampere. One mole of electrons has, then, 96,500 coulombs of charge. In a wire carrying 10 amp, it takes about $2\frac{1}{2}$ hours for 1 mole of electrons to pass any point.

Fig. 7-4 Millikan's oil-drop apparatus for determining the electron charge.

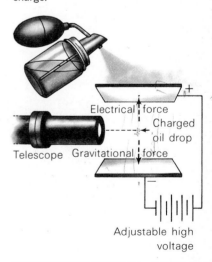

The CHARGE on the ELECTRON

or loss of one or more electrons by the oil droplet. If the oil droplet carried enough electrons and the charge on the plate were large enough, the fall of the droplet could be completely stopped. The droplet could even be made to rise. By balancing the electrical force which made the droplet rise against the known force of gravity, which made it fall, the amount of electric charge on the droplet could be estimated:

$$\begin{Bmatrix}\text{electrical}\\\text{force}\end{Bmatrix} = k\ \underbrace{\begin{Bmatrix}\dfrac{\text{voltage on plates}}{\text{distance between plates}}\end{Bmatrix}}_{\substack{\text{ELECTRIC}\\\text{FIELD}}} \times \underbrace{\begin{Bmatrix}\text{charge on}\\\text{electron}\end{Bmatrix} \times \begin{Bmatrix}\text{number of}\\\text{electrons}\\\text{on drops}\end{Bmatrix}}_{\substack{\text{AMOUNT OF ELECTRIC CHARGE}\\\text{ON DROP}}} \qquad (6)$$

The equation can be represented symbolically as

$$\text{electrical force} = E \times e \times n \qquad (7)$$

where E is the electric field. This is directly proportional to the voltage on the plates and is inversely proportional to the distance between the plates. The symbol e stands for the charge on the electron and n represents the number of excess electron charges on the drop. When the fall of the drop is stopped, the electrical force pulling up is just equal to the gravitational force pulling down. We can write

$$\text{electrical force pulling up} = \text{gravitational force pulling down} \qquad (8)$$
$$E \times n \times e = \text{gravitational force}$$

Since the gravitational force pulling down is known from other experiments and since E can be determined from the voltage on the plates and the distance between them, the charge on the drop ($n \times e$) can be determined.

Millikan made thousands of determinations of the charges on drops of oil, glycerine, and mercury. The charge on the drop was sometimes positive, as a result of the loss of an electron, or sometimes negative, as a result of the gain of an electron. Still, in every case the amount of charge was some whole number times a value which he assigned to the charge on the electron ($n \times e$). Today the accepted value for this charge, e, is 1.602×10^{-19} coulomb/electron (see Section 6-5.3). These experiments could then be combined with the electrolysis experiments, the neon electrical discharge-tube experiments, and with experiments giving e/m (Appendix 2) to give us a more detailed picture of the electron as a particle.

EXERCISE 7-5

Suppose five measurements of oil droplet charges give the values listed below:

$$4.83 \times 10^{-19} \text{ coulomb}$$
$$3.24 \times 10^{-19}$$
$$9.62 \times 10^{-19}$$
$$6.44 \times 10^{-19}$$
$$4.80 \times 10^{-19}$$

(1) Divide each charge by the smallest value to investigate the relative magnitudes of these charges.

Fig. 7-5 A mass spectrometer and the mass spectrum of neon: (a) a schematic drawing of a mass spectrometer, (b) an enlargement of the evacuated unit between the poles of the magnet, and (c) the photographic plate from (b).

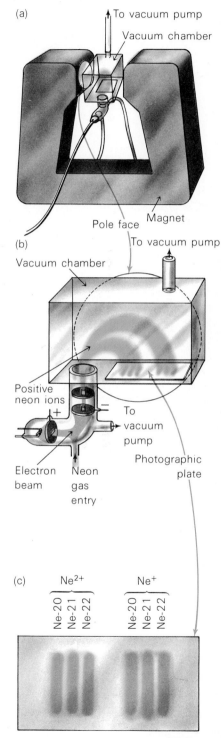

7-2.3 The Mass of the Electron

It was mentioned earlier that the ratio of electron charge to electron mass ($e/m = 1.759 \times 10^8$ coulombs/g) can be determined by an analysis of the deflection of a beam of electrons under the influence of a magnet and a pair of charged plates. We have also considered Millikan's experiment giving the charge on the electron as 1.602×10^{-19} coulomb/electron. The results of these two experiments can now be combined to give the *mass* of the electron.

$$\frac{e}{m} = 1.759 \times 10^8 \text{ coulombs/g} \qquad (9)$$

$$e = 1.602 \times 10^{-19} \text{ coulomb/electron} \qquad (10)$$

$$m = \frac{1.602 \times 10^{-19} \text{ coulomb/electron}}{1.759 \times 10^8 \text{ coulombs/g}} = 9.11 \times 10^{-28} \frac{\text{g}}{\text{electron}} \qquad (11)$$

7-2.4 "Seeing" Positive Ions

Experiments conducted in the evacuated neon gas discharge tube demonstrated that electrons are present and that all are the same regardless of the gas in the tube. On the other hand, a small amount of gas (10^{-6} atm) must be present in the tube for electrons to appear. If the gas is removed as completely as possible, no electron beam is seen. The electrons appear to come from the gas in the tube. We can write

$$\text{neon atom} = \text{neon ion}^+ + e^- \qquad (12)$$

We expect that a positively charged neon ion would be produced. It is possible to isolate a beam of these positive ions by constructing an apparatus similar to that shown in Figure 7-5. The beam of positive ions can be deflected in magnetic and electrostatic fields just as the electron beam could. Again, such deflection permits us to determine the ratio e/m for the positive ion just as was done for the electron. If we assume that the charge on the positive ion results from the loss of an electron from the atom, we can use the value for the charge on the electron and the ratio of e/m for the ion to determine the *mass* of the positive ion. Very precise mass determination for particles can be achieved in this way. An instrument to determine the mass of positive ions in this fashion has been mentioned earlier. It is known as a **mass spectrometer.** It is described in more detail in Appendix 3.

The results of measurements with the mass spectrometer reveal several very important points:

(1) The mass of the *positive ions* in a gas discharge tube changes if we change the gas in the tube. In contrast, the mass of the *electrons* in this same tube is independent of the type of gas present!
(2) Positive ions have a much higher mass than electrons. Thus, the observations support the model, which stated that the positive ions are fragments of gas which remain *after* electrons have been knocked off.

(3) Even a pure gas such as neon will give positive ions which differ somewhat in mass.

This last point is important. Let us examine it in more detail. When neon gas is put in the mass spectrometer, the bending of the positive ion beam shows that neon consists of atoms with three different masses—neon-20, neon-21, neon-22. *Neon is a mixture of three different isotopes.* The relative abundance of these isotopes in normal neon can be determined by measuring the intensity of the spots caused by each of the ion beams (see Appendix 3). This is a most important bit of information in support of the atomic model of the atom, since it permits independent determination of the apparent atomic weight for a mixture of isotopes.

EXERCISE 7-6

In a certain sample of neon in the mass spectrometer, 90.0 percent of the atoms have a mass of 20.0 and 10.0 percent have a mass of 22.0.

(1) Calculate the apparent atomic weight of this mixture.
(2) What would be the mass of 1.00 litre of this gas at 0 °C and 1.00 atm?

[*Answer to (1)*: 20.2 is the atomic weight.]

7-2.5 "Seeing" the Nucleus

We have described a nucleus which is about 10^{-14} metre in diameter. This number is so incredibly small that it is difficult to imagine, let alone see. Remember that if an *atom* were as big as a large football stadium, the nucleus would be about as big as a marble. How did Rutherford, Geiger, and Marsden go about "seeing" such a very small nucleus?

Let us consider a similar problem. Imagine that you are placed at the edge of a field covered with a large tent (Figure 7-6.1). The tent is empty except for a nonliving object of unknown size, shape, and composition placed near the center of the tent. You are to investigate this object using only a rifle and ammunition. You will fire bullets into the tent. By examining

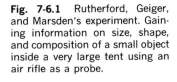

Fig. 7-6.1 Rutherford, Geiger, and Marsden's experiment. Gaining information on size, shape, and composition of a small object inside a very large tent using an air rifle as a probe.

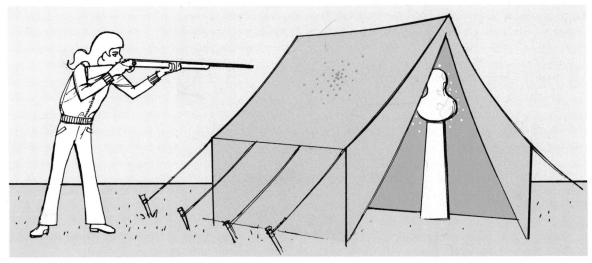

holes in the tent, you will be able to tell where each shot came out. If you stand at one point and fire a volley of shots, the bullets not hitting the object will pass right through the tent and emerge on the other side. Bullets hitting the unknown object will be deflected and will not arrive in the expected place at the opposite side of the tent. You could judge the size of the object by identifying the area from which bullets were deflected or scattered. Further, if the unknown object scatters a few of the bullets right back *toward* you, you would judge that it is heavy and made of a hard substance. A light or soft object might cause some deflection, but it could not exert the force needed to throw the bullet back in the direction from which it came.

In place of bullets the physicists Rutherford, Geiger, and Marsden used **alpha particles,** which are given off spontaneously from the radioactive decay of samples of radium (see Section 7-3). These alpha particles are nuclei of helium atoms with a mass number of 4 and a charge of 2+. They are emitted with a velocity of about 2×10^7 metres per second. A narrow beam of particles is obtained by placing the radium in a deep lead box with a small hole in the top; this is truly a nuclear rifle (see Figure 7-6.2). This nuclear rifle was fired at a thin sheet of gold foil (about 10,000 atoms thick). The alpha particles were detected by the light which they produced when they collided with plates covered with zinc sulfide. These so-called "scintillation screens" were much like the picture tube in a modern television set; such a screen gives off a burst of light when an alpha particle strikes it.

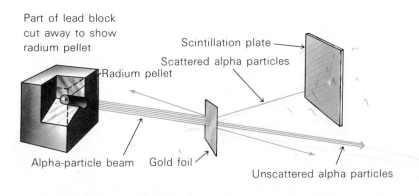

Part of lead block cut away to show radium pellet

Scintillation plate

Scattered alpha particles

Radium pellet

Alpha-particle beam   Gold foil

Unscattered alpha particles

Fig. 7-6.2 Rutherford's apparatus for observing the scattering of alpha particles by a metal foil. (The entire apparatus is enclosed in a vacuum chamber.)

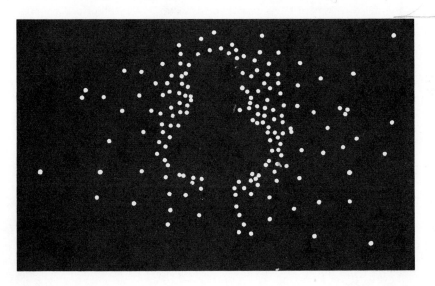

(The screen in a television set gives off a burst of light when an electron strikes it. These bursts give the image.) The scintillation screen could be moved in a circle so that particles coming off in any direction could be counted. The apparatus operated in a vacuum chamber so that no deflections would be caused by the impact of the alpha particles upon gaseous molecules.

The first observation made with this apparatus was that all the alpha particles appeared to pass through the foil undeflected. Let us see if this result is consistent with the model of the atom proposed by Thomson. What would happen to the alpha particles if they were shot into a solid made up of closely packed Thomson atoms? At first we might think that they would be stopped or deflected back after colliding with the atoms. However, it was observed that the alpha particles went straight through the metal foil; we must reconsider the problem. When we shoot at a paper target with a high-powered rifle, the projectile forces its way through the paper. The alpha particles produced by radium have very high kinetic energy and are very much like bullets from a high-powered rifle. Perhaps the very high kinetic energy allows an alpha particle to force its way right through the atoms of the metal foil. Since a rifle bullet fired into paper passes through undeflected, it seems reasonable to conclude that the alpha particle would also pass through the metal foil undeflected.

According to the Thomson model a metal foil is considered to have essentially uniform density. If this is true there is no way for bombarding alpha particles to be deflected through large angles. At best, the alpha particles might suffer slight deflections from many collisions with many atoms. The model predicts the scattering distribution shown in Figure 7-7.

The first result of Rutherford's experiments seemed to be quite consistent with the Thomson picture of the atom. On more careful examination, however, an astounding discovery was made. By moving the screen around the metal foil, Rutherford and his co-workers were able to see that some particles bounced back in the direction from which they came. It was as if some alpha particles had rebounded from a head-on collision with an immovable object. In describing his experiment Rutherford said: *"It is about as incredible as if you had fired a 15-inch shell at a piece of tissue paper and it came back and hit you."* It was impossible to explain the simultaneous observation of large-angle and small-angle deflections by using the Thomson atom.

To explain his experimental results, Rutherford designed a new picture of the atom which we have described in Section 7-1. Rutherford's model requires that most of the atom is almost empty space. However, the atom must contain a tiny, positively charged nucleus of very large density (see Figure 7-8).

If we allowed alpha particles to impinge upon a metal foil made up of Rutherford atoms, only a few of the particles would be appreciably deflected by the foil. The heavy, fast-moving alpha particles would brush past the lighter electrons without being deflected. Because most of the volume of the metal foil is relatively empty space, the greatest number of alpha particles would pass through the metal undeflected. It is possible, however, for a few particles to be scattered through very large angles. Since both the alpha particles and the nucleus of the atom are positively charged, they repel each other. This repulsion becomes large only when the alpha particles come quite close to the nucleus. Since the nucleus is much heavier than the alpha particles, the alpha particle bounces off, just as a steel post deflects a rifle bullet.

Besides providing a qualitative picture of the atom, Rutherford's experiments provided a method of measuring the charge of the nucleus. The repulsive force that a nucleus exerts on an alpha particle depends upon

Alpha particle

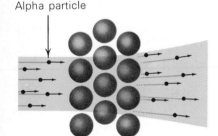

Fig. 7-7 The scattering of alpha particles by a metal foil made of Thomson atoms.

Alpha particle

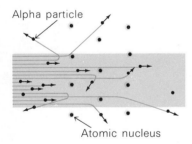

Atomic nucleus

Fig. 7-8 The scattering of alpha particles by a foil made of Rutherford nuclear atoms.

the magnitude of the charge on the nucleus. Rutherford was able to estimate nuclear charge from the pattern made by scattered alpha particles. The first measurements of the nuclear charge by this method were not very accurate. But by 1920 the alpha-particle scattering experiments were so refined that they could be used to determine nuclear charge accurately. Now a device based on this principle is used in space probes to analyze other planets.

7-3 PROPERTIES OF NUCLEI— RADIOACTIVITY AND NUCLEAR CHEMISTRY

You have been told that isotopes of the same element have almost identical chemical properties. We may then properly ask: how do different isotopes of the same element differ? Unless we have some way of measuring differences, a classification scheme for isotopes is neither useful nor philosophically appropriate. The nuclear model suggests the answer: *isotopes of the same element differ in those properties that are really properties of the nucleus itself.* For example, isotopes of the same element differ in mass because mass is essentially a nuclear property. The difference shows up in the mass spectrometer (see Appendix 3). On the other hand, since all isotopes of the same element have the same nuclear charge and the same number of electrons, their chemical properties are almost exactly the same. Probably the most dramatic difference between isotopes involves differences in **nuclear stability.** Some nuclei undergo spontaneous change to give new nuclei. Let us explore this process more carefully.

7-3.1 Nuclear Stability and Nuclear Decay Processes

If the compound zinc sulfide (ZnS) is mixed with a very small amount of radium salt, the mixture will glow in a dark room. Such mixtures are sometimes used in paints to make the hands and numbers of watch dials luminous. Look carefully at a luminous watch dial in a dark room. You will probably see some individual flashes of light on the paint surface. The flashes of light come at random and remind one of raindrops hitting the surface of a pond.

Indeed, the analogy is a happy one since the flashes result from alpha particles hitting the zinc sulfide surface. The alpha particles result from the spontaneous destruction of radium atoms. Occasionally a radium atom will explode and eject an alpha particle from its nucleus at high speed. Measurements of the mass and charge of such an alpha particle show that it has a mass number of 4 and a charge of 2. The *fragment* of the radium atom which remains after loss of the alpha particle must have a mass number that is four units *less than* the mass number of the original radium. Also, it must have a nuclear charge that is two units less than radium.

It would be convenient to have concise symbols that could be used to write an equation summarizing the process. Because each isotope is characterized by two important numbers—atomic number and mass number—the symbol for an atom of a given isotope should indicate what these numbers are. *A certain isotope is represented by the chemical symbol of the element with the atomic number at its lower left and the mass number at its upper left.* Radium of atomic number 88 and mass number 226 is written as

MASS NUMBER ⟶

$^{226}_{88}\text{Ra}$

ATOMIC NUMBER ⟶

Nitrogen-13, of atomic number 7 and mass number 13, is $^{13}_{7}\text{N}$. Plutonium of atomic number 94 and mass number 239 is $^{239}_{94}\text{Pu}$.

EXERCISE 7-7

How many protons and how many neutrons are contained in the nucleus of $^{239}_{94}\text{Pu}$?

The nuclear decay process for radium-226 can now be indicated by the equation

$$^{226}_{88}\text{Ra} \longrightarrow {}^{222}_{86}\text{Rn} + {}^{4}_{2}\text{He} \qquad (13)$$

Notice that both *electric charge* and *mass number* are conserved in the equation. The number of protons plus neutrons* is the same at the start and finish of the process. In nuclear processes, two elementary laws must be obeyed:

(1) *The total number of electric charges must be the same on both sides of the equation.*
(2) *Total mass numbers must be the same on both sides of the equation.*

Conservation of charge is indicated in the equation by the fact that 86 protons in radon plus 2 protons in the alpha particle ($^{4}_{2}\text{He}$) give the original 88 protons found in $^{226}_{88}\text{Ra}$. That is, the sums of numbers in the lower left-hand corners must be the same on both sides of the equation: $88 = 86 + 2$. Similarly, conservation of protons plus neutrons in the nucleus is indicated by the fact that the sum of the numbers in the upper left-hand corners is the same on opposite sides of the equation. That is, $226 = 222 + 4$. Mass is conserved to a good approximation.† The fate of extranuclear electrons is not specifically indicated in the equation. Still, the conservation of these electrons is indicated by the fact that when nuclear charge is conserved, electrons will be conserved since electrons counterbalance nuclear charge in neutral particles.

EXERCISE 7-8

Plutonium-238 ($^{238}_{94}\text{Pu}$) decays to give an α-particle and a new atom. What is the atomic number of the new atom? What is its mass number?

*Protons and neutrons together are called *nucleons*.
†This question will be considered with a higher degree of precision in Chapter 9.

Alpha-particle loss is not restricted to radium-226. Isotopes of many of the elements with an atomic number above 82 undergo alpha decay. Thus, alpha-particle loss is observed with bismuth-211 ($^{211}_{83}Bi$), polonium-208 ($^{208}_{84}Po$), radon-222 ($^{222}_{86}Rn$), uranium-238 ($^{238}_{92}U$), and many others.

None of the lighter elements (elements having atomic numbers below 82) show alpha activity, but some isotopes of the lighter elements have unstable nuclei. These nuclei emit **beta particles** rather than alpha particles. Mass and charge measurements on beta particles show that they are *electrons* traveling at high speed. With this information the beta decay process for strontium-90* can be represented by the equation

$$^{90}_{38}Sr \longrightarrow {}^{90}_{39}Y + {}^{0}_{-1}e \qquad (14)$$

Notice that the laws for both conservation of charge [38 = 39 + (−1)] and conservation of nuclear particles (90 = 90 + 0) are obeyed in this process too.

Beta decay is not limited to the light elements. Even a few of the isotopes of the heavier elements are beta-active. Thus, americium-242 undergoes beta decay to give curium-242:

$$^{242}_{95}Am \longrightarrow {}^{242}_{96}Cm + {}^{0}_{-1}e \qquad (15)$$

EXERCISE 7-9

Potassium-43, $^{43}_{19}K$, decays by beta-particle loss. Write the nuclear equation for the process.

Let us look a little more carefully at the process of β-particle loss. Notice that when strontium-90 is converted to yttrium-90, one of the neutrons in the nucleus is converted to a proton and an electron. The proton stays in the nucleus, but the electron is ejected. The equation for the process is

$$^{1}_{0}n \longrightarrow {}^{1}_{1}p + {}^{0}_{-1}e \qquad (16)$$

It is significant to note that *even the fundamental particles of the atom undergo change in nuclear processes*. This is never so in chemical processes. Thus, if a given nucleus has more neutrons and fewer protons than a stable isotope of the same element, β-particle loss is a logical way of increasing stability. Accordingly, those isotopes of a given element with the highest mass number have the highest probability of being beta-active. While carbon-12 is stable, carbon-14, of a higher mass number, decays by β-particle loss. Fluorine-19 is stable, but fluorine-20 is beta-active. The nucleus of highest mass number exhibits beta activity in each case.

*Because strontium-90 resembles calcium in its chemical properties, it is incorporated into bone tissue, where its radioactive nature creates a hazard for many years. Strontium-90 is a very serious environmental hazard which has found its way into the air as a result of nuclear explosions. Most civilized nations recognize the hazards and have banned tests of nuclear weapons in the air.

**GLENN T. SEABORG
(1912–   )**

Glenn T. Seaborg began life humbly in a small mining town, Ishpeming, Michigan. His Swedish-American parents moved to southern California, where, to finance his undergraduate education at the University of California, he worked as a stevedore, an apricot picker, a laboratory assistant in a rubber company, and a linotype apprentice. He received his Ph.D. from the Berkeley campus in 1937.

Along with Professor Edwin M. McMillan, Seaborg produced neptunium (atomic number 93) and plutonium (no. 94), for which they were awarded the Nobel Prize in 1951. During World War II Seaborg developed a method for extracting and purifying plutonium from uranium. From 1944 to 1953 he and research teams which he trained and supervised established the existence of elements 95-102, a truly remarkable achievement for one man's lifetime.

From 1958–1961 Seaborg was Chancellor of the University of California at Berkeley. In 1961 he was appointed Chairman of the Atomic Energy Commission. Now he is again a member of the faculty of the University of California where he is teaching chemistry.

NUCLEAR STABILITY and
NUCLEAR DECAY PROCESSES

Another type of nuclear decay is associated with isotopes which have *fewer* neutrons than do stable nuclei of that element. Such nuclear processes also involve changes in the fundamental particles in the nucleus. The nitrogen-14 nucleus is stable; it has seven protons and seven neutrons. The nitrogen-13 nucleus is radioactive; it has seven protons and six neutrons. A process which changes a proton to a neutron would help move the system toward stability. We might expect a special process resulting in loss of a positively charged particle of almost zero mass from a proton. Such a particle is called a **positron.** The positron is a particle with the same mass as an electron and a charge of the same size but *opposite* in sign. On the atomic scale it has a charge of $1+$ and a mass of approximately zero. The equation for the decay of nitrogen-13 is

$$^{13}_{7}N \longrightarrow {}^{13}_{6}C + {}^{0}_{1}e \qquad (17)$$

Notice that the conservation laws are obeyed here as well: conservation of charge—$7 = 6 + 1$; conservation of nuclear particles—$13 = 13 + 0$. Positrons are never seen in chemical processes. They occur only as a result of nuclear disintegration; a new element is always generated by positron-loss.

7-3.2   Rate of Nuclear Decay—Half-Life

Study of the rate of nuclear disintegration shows that in any period of time, a *constant fraction* of the nuclei will undergo decomposition. This observation allows us to characterize or describe the rate of nuclear decay in a very simple manner. It is customary to specify the length of time it takes for *half* the nuclei to decay; this length of time is known as the **half-life** of the nucleus. For example, measurements show that after 4.5×10^9 years, half the atoms in any sample of $^{238}_{92}U$ will decay to $^{234}_{90}Th$. The half-life of $^{238}_{92}U$ is 4.5×10^9 years. A nucleus is considered to be stable if its half-life is much longer than the age of the earth, which is now judged to be about 5×10^9 years. Nuclei that are very unstable are characterized by half-lives which are short, in some cases only a fraction of a second.

Consider the isotope $^{90}_{38}Sr$ which undergoes decay in accordance with the equation:

$$^{90}_{38}Sr \longrightarrow {}^{90}_{39}Y + {}^{0}_{-1}\beta \qquad (18)$$

Strontium-90 has a half-life of 28 years. This means that if we start with 100 g of strontium-90 we will have 50 g left after 28 years. After 28 more years (56 total) we will have 25 g. After another 28 years (84 total) we will have 12.5 g. It is not hard to see why people are concerned about the buildup of strontium-90 in the atmosphere. Because its half-life is relatively short (compared to atoms like radium), it is viciously radioactive. On the other hand, it stays on the earth for a distressingly long time.

7-3.3   Factors in Nuclear Stability

Our discussion on nuclear stability now leads us to one of the most significant "wondering why" questions in all science: what holds the nucleus together? Relatively simple calculations with Coulomb's law

$$\text{force} = \frac{\text{charge}_1 \times \text{charge}_2}{\text{distance}^2} \qquad (19)$$

show that the *repulsive* force between two protons in a helium nucleus is about ten billion times as great as the repulsive force between two protons in the hydrogen molecule (H_2), yet the helium nucleus itself is very stable. It is clear that *fantastically strong forces* must be overcoming the forces of repulsion between protons; they must be binding the protons and neutrons into a very stable unit, one which lasts indefinitely without undergoing a decay process. The nature of these forces is not understood and remains one of the most exciting problems in modern-day physics. Very large nuclear accelerators have been built to study this question.

7-4 HIGHLIGHTS

Experiments which come closer to giving a "direct view" of an atom and its components have been described. The mass of the proton and electron can be determined on the atomic weight scale. The mass of atoms is *not* obtained by adding up the masses of protons and electrons; additional particles with a charge of 0 and a mass of 1 (neutrons) are also required as a component of the **atomic nucleus.** Addition of, or removal of, electrons gives **ions.** Removal of electrons from a neutral atom or positive ion requires work. Defining the size of an atom is difficult. Approximate atomic diameters of 1×10^{-10} to 5×10^{-10} metre are given by experiments measuring the distance between nuclei of atoms in molecules. The nucleus of the atom has a diameter of about 10^{-14} metre or about $\frac{1}{10,000}$ the size of the atom. Most of the **mass** of the atom is concentrated in the nucleus and is equal to the sum of the masses of protons and neutrons which make up the nucleus. The **atomic number** gives the number of protons in the nucleus and the number of electrons outside the nucleus in the neutral atom. **Isotopes** of a given element are atoms of the same atomic number but of different mass. The atomic number determines the chemistry of the atom. Isotopes of a given element differ in mass; differences in their chemistry are trivial.

Isotopes of the same element vary in nuclear stability. Unstable nuclei undergo decay to form more stable nuclear arrangements. Alpha-particle loss, beta-particle loss, and positron-loss are ways in which the nucleus can obtain a more stable ratio of protons to neutrons. The stability of any radioactive isotope is described by its **half-life.** This is the length of time it takes for half the atoms in any sample of the isotope to decay. The longer the half-life, the more stable the isotope.

QUESTIONS and PROBLEMS

1 (a) The measured distance between the nuclei in a hydrogen molecule is 0.746×10^{-10} metre. What is the radius of the hydrogen atom? (b) If the distance between hydrogen and nitrogen nuclei in ammonia (NH_3) is 1.008×10^{-10} metre, what is the radius of the nitrogen atom in this compound? (c) If the distance between the nuclei in an iodine (I_2) molecule is 2.662×10^{-10} metre, what distance will there be between each nitrogen and each iodine atom in nitrogen triiodide (NI_3)?

2 If the distance between two chlorine nuclei in Cl_2 is 1.94×10^{-10} metre and the distance between two bromine nuclei is 2.28×10^{-10} metre, what will be the distance between the bromine and chlorine nuclei in ClBr?

3 The nucleus of an aluminum atom has a diameter of about 2.0×10^{-15} metre. The atom has an average diameter of about 3.0×10^{-10} metre. (a) What is the ratio of the diameter of the atom to the diameter of the nucleus? (b) What is the ratio of the volume of the atom to the volume of the nucleus? (The formula for the volume of a sphere is $\frac{4}{3}\pi r^3$.) (c) If 99.9 percent of the mass of the atom is contained in the nucleus, what is the ratio of the density of the extranuclear atom to the density of the nucleus?

4 Assume that the nucleus of the fluorine atom is a sphere with a radius of 5×10^{-15} metre. (a) Calculate the mass of the nucleus. (b) Calculate the volume of the nucleus. (c) Calculate the density (mass/volume) of the nucleus. Express your answer in tons per cubic metre. (One ton = 10^6 grams.)

5 (a) An oxygen atom contains 8 protons and 8 electrons. What other particles and how many of them are needed to account for oxygen with a mass of 16 u? (b) A fluorine atom contains 9 protons and 9 electrons. What other particles and how many of them are needed to account for the mass of 19 u for a fluorine atom?

6 Copy the table below into your notebook. Then fill in the blanks for the neutral atoms.

7 Atoms of a certain isotope have 73 neutrons and a mass number of 123. (a) What is the atomic number? (b) How many electrons are there? (c) What is the name of the element? (d) What is the nuclear charge?

8 Which of the following are isotopes of each other? (a) an atom with 17 protons and 18 neutrons; (b) an atom with atomic number 16 and atomic mass 32; (c) an atom with atomic number 16 and 18 neutrons; (d) an atom with 16 protons and 18 neutrons; (e) an atom with 17 protons and 20 neutrons; (f) an atom with atomic number 16 and atomic mass 33; (g) an atom with 15 protons and 16 neutrons.

9 A naturally-occurring sample of element X is found to contain 81.8 percent X-10 (*i.e.*, element X with a mass number of 10) and 18.2 percent X-11. Calculate the apparent atomic weight of this naturally-occurring sample of element X.

10 For which of the following processes will energy be required? (a) separating an electron from an electron; (b) separating an electron from a proton; (c) separating a proton from a proton; (d) removing an electron from a neutral atom.

11 Write balanced equations for each of the following. Include energy as part of the equation. (a) A neutral, gaseous potassium atom becomes a gaseous K^+ ion. (b) A neutral, gaseous magnesium atom becomes successively a gaseous Mg^+ ion and then a gaseous Mg^{2+} ion. (c) A neutral, gaseous

Element Name	Atomic Number	Number of Protons	Number of Electrons	Positive Charge on Nucleus	Mass Number	Number of Neutrons
Carbon					12	
	10					10
		1			1	
			3			4
				2	4	
Calcium						20
	11				23	
		18				22
			83		209	
				90		142

aluminum atom becomes successively a gaseous Al^+ ion, a gaseous Al^{2+} ion, and a gaseous Al^{3+} ion. (d) A neutral, gaseous fluorine atom becomes a gaseous F^- ion. (e) A neutral, gaseous chlorine atom becomes a gaseous Cl^- ion.

12 Figure 7-9 shows an electric discharge tube containing neon gas under low pressure. (a) When the switch leading to the battery is closed, what effect will this have on the electron beam? (b) What charge must the upper plate, P_1, have in order for the beam to be deflected downward? (c) What will happen if the terminals of the battery are reversed? (d) How would the results of this experiment be changed if argon gas rather than neon gas were used in the tube? (e) On the basis of the answer to (d), compare the charge/mass ratio of electrons of neon atoms to the electrons of argon atoms.

13 In the Millikan oil-drop experiment, the charge on a single electron is found to be 1.602×10^{-19} coulomb. (a) Explain why at the same time in the observation chamber, some droplets are stationary, some are moving upward, and some are moving downward. (b) Why is it not possible for an ion to have a charge of 2.00×10^{-19} coulomb?

14 Naturally-occurring magnesium consists of three isotopes with mass numbers of 24, 25, and 26. In the mass spectrometer, magnesium forms 1+ and 2+ ions. Draw a diagram of the mass spectrogram produced by magnesium. Label each line with the mass and charge of the ions producing it. (*Optional.*)

15 Platinum and zinc have the same number of atoms per cubic centimetre. Would thin sheets of these elements differ in the way that they scatter alpha particles? Explain. (*Hint:* although they have the same atomic volume, how do their nuclear volumes compare?)

16 What change in mass and atomic number results when an atom emits an alpha particle? A beta particle?

17 Write the equations for the nuclear reactions that occur when each of the following nuclei emits an alpha particle. (a) $^{238}_{92}U$ (b) $^{234}_{92}U$ (c) $^{230}_{90}Th$ (d) $^{226}_{88}Ra$ (e) $^{222}_{86}Rn$ (f) $^{218}_{84}Po$.

18 Write equations for the nuclear reactions that occur when each of the following nuclei emits a beta particle. (a) $^{234}_{90}Th$ (b) $^{234}_{91}Pa$ (c) $^{214}_{82}Pb$ (d) $^{214}_{83}Bi$.

19 A radioactive element, A, with mass 214 and atomic number 84 emits an alpha particle and changes to element B. Element B emits a beta particle and is converted into element C. What are the atomic masses and atomic numbers of elements A, B, and C?

20 Radioactive atoms of $^{216}_{85}At$ undergo a series of three spontaneous nuclear reactions before changing into stable atoms. These changes are (a) the atom disintegrates into an alpha particle and a second radioactive atom; (b) the second radioactive atom disintegrates into an alpha particle and a third radioactive atom; (c) this third atom then disintegrates into a beta particle, $^{0}_{-1}e$, and a stable atom which disintegrates no more. Write the three balanced nuclear equations for the changes involved. Include the atomic number, mass number, and symbol of each atom.

Fig. 7-9

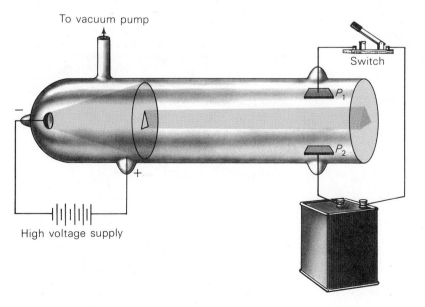

To vacuum pump

Switch

P_1

P_2

Δ

−

+

High voltage supply

The eighth element, starting from a given one, is a kind of repetition of the first, like the eighth note of an octave in music.

J. A. R. NEWLANDS (1838–1898)

ATOMIC STRUCTURE AND 8
THE PERIODIC TABLE

Таблица II.

Вторая нонытка Менделѣева найти естественную систему химическихъ элементовъ. Перепечатана безъ измѣненій изъ „Журнала Русскаго Химическаго Общества", т. III, стр. 31 (1871 г.).

	Группа I.	Группа II.	Группа III.	Группа IV.	Группа V.	Группа VI.	Группа VII.	Группа VIII, переходъ къ группе I.
	H=1							
Типическіе элементы.	Li=7	Be=9,4	B=11	C=12	N=14	O=16	F=19	
1-й періодъ. Рядъ 1-й.	Na=23	Mg=24	Al=27,3	Si=28	P=31	S=32	Cl=35,5	
— 2-й.	K=39	Ca=40	?=44	Ti=50?	V=51	Cr=52	Mn=55	Fe=56, Co=59 Ni=59, Cu=63
2-й періодъ. — 3-й.	(Cu=63)	Zn=65	?=68	?=72	As=75	Se=78	Br=80	
— 4-й.	Rb=85	Sr=87	Yt?=88?	Zr=90	Nb=94	Mo=96	— =100	Ru=104, Rh=104 Pd=104, Ag=108
3-й періодъ. — 5-й.	(Ag=108)	Cd=112	In=113	Sn=118	Sb=122	Te=128?	J=127	
— 6-й.	Cs=133	Ba=137	— =137	Ce=138?	—			— —
4-й періодъ. — 7-й.	—	—	—	—	—	—	—	
— 8-й.	—		—	—	Ta=182	W=184	—	Os=199?, Ir=198? Pt=197, Au=197
5-й періодъ. — 9-й.	(Au=197)	Hg=200	Tl=204	Pb=207	Bi=208	—		
—10-й.		—	—	Th=232	—	Ur=240	—	
Высшая соляная окись	R_2O	R_2O_2 или RO	R_2O_3	R_2O_4 или RO_2	R_2O_3	R_2O_6 или RO_3	R_2O_7	R_2O_8 или RO_4
Высшее водородное соединеніе . . .			(RH_3)	RH_4	RH_3	RH_2	RH	

The periodic table as originally published by Mendeleev.

WITH MORE THAN 100 ELEMENTS WITH DIFFERENT CHARACTERISTICS confronting us, the situation is rapidly getting out of hand. Organization is desperately needed. Perhaps we can sort the elements into groups with similar properties so we won't have to remember so much detail.

The property which we choose to measure is the amount of work necessary to remove electrons, one at a time, from the atoms of each kind of element. An unexpected dividend is that we discover that electrons are apparently arranged in levels outside the nucleus of each atom. By grouping elements according to ease of electron removal, we come up with just the device we were looking for—the periodic table. With it, we can approximately predict both the physical properties and chemical reactions of any element because of the family to which it belongs. What a relief!

Materials making up the world have strikingly different properties; they range from the glittering diamond to delights such as a thick juicy steak. One of the prime jobs of the scientist is to organize information about different materials. In this process, proper recognition must be given to both similarities and differences, even when such similarities and differences are not obvious to the casual observer. For example, little similarity is apparent between a chocolate cake and a high-energy rocket fuel, yet both are fuels; they differ only in the type of engine needed to utilize them properly. The energy content of each might be important in planning a space walk.

How do we proceed to organize information on chemical and physical properties of materials? In organizing information on gases, liquids, and solids, the molecular model was very useful. Growth of this model to include atoms and finally atomic structure permitted us to visualize processes ranging from the passage of an electric current through a salt solution to the radioactive decay of a sample of radium. What additional growth is needed in the atomic model to make it useful for organizing chemical information? Chapter 7 indicated that chemical properties are closely related to the arrangement of electrons outside the nucleus of the atom. Let us be like the new tenant hearing about the garbage collector for the first time—we shall accept this proposition *tentatively* while we make additional observations.

8-1 THE LOSS OF ELECTRONS FROM AN ATOM— THE IONIZATION ENERGY OF ATOMS

Perhaps clues to electron arrangement can be found by studying the loss of electrons from atoms. We already know that if an electron is to be pulled away from an atom, energy must be supplied (Chapter 7). We are interested in the process

$$\text{gaseous atom} + \text{energy} \longrightarrow \text{gaseous ion} + \text{gaseous electron}$$
$$\text{Na}(g) + \text{energy} \longrightarrow \text{Na}^+(g) + e^- \qquad (1)$$

The question of interest to us now is: how much energy is needed to remove an electron? This quantity of energy is worthy of a name and is worthy of measurement. The energy associated with the removal of an electron from a neutral *gaseous atom* to give a positively charged *gaseous ion* and an *electron* is known as the **ionization energy of the atom.** How are these ionization energies measured?

8-1.1 Determination of Ionization Energy

The ionization energy for certain atoms may be determined by bombarding the atomic vapor with electrons whose kinetic energy is accurately known. How do we obtain a beam of electrons of known kinetic energy? Section 7-2 stated that an electric discharge tube gives a beam of electrons. The kinetic energy of the electrons can be increased by increasing the voltage used on the tube. The adjustment is not too different from the adjustment for picture brightness on your television tube. (To get a brighter picture—more energetic electrons—you turn up the voltage on the picture tube.) When the kinetic energy of the bombarding electrons used in the measurement is increased to a certain critical value, singly charged positive ions can be determined electrically.* These ions result from collisions between the atoms being studied and the bombarding electrons. When the bombarding electrons have the same kinetic energy as the energy needed to separate the most loosely bound electron in the atom, a collision will knock the electron from the atom. The energy required to break an electron away from a given target atom is characteristic of that atom—it is a measure of the atom's ionization energy. We can read the voltage on the tube generating the electron beam as soon as positive ions are obtained. The value can be expressed in terms of electron volts or in other energy terms such as calories, kilocalories, or joules (see page 218).

Ionization energies can also be determined even more precisely by using methods of atomic spectroscopy described in Chapter 16. The method to be used is determined by the system studied.

8-1.2 Stable Electronic Patterns— Trends in Ionization Energies

Ionization energy measurements have been made for each of the elements. The results, in order of increasing atomic number for the first 20 elements, are shown in Table 8-1.

EXERCISE 8-1

Plot ionization energy against atomic number for the first 20 elements. At what atomic numbers do maxima appear? minima?

If you did Exercise 8-1 carefully, a number of regularities seem to jump at you from the paper! High ionization energies are seen for He (atomic number 2), Ne (no. 10), and Ar (no. 18). Low ionization energies are seen for Li (no. 3), Na (no. 11), and K (no. 19). Apparently, a large amount of energy is needed to pull an electron from the

*In actual operation such measurements are made in a mass spectrometer (Appendix 3), where somewhat more elaborate velocity selectors may be used.

configurations found in helium, neon, and argon. It seems reasonable to describe such electron patterns as stable. *If a large amount of energy is required to pull off an electron, the original configuration is said to be very stable.*

TABLE **8-1** FIRST IONIZATION ENERGIES OF ELEMENTS 1 TO 20

Atomic Number	Element	First Ionization Energy (kcal/mole)
1	Hydrogen (H)	313.6
2	Helium (He)	566.7
3	Lithium (Li)	124.3
4	Beryllium (Be)	214.9
5	Boron (B)	191.2
6	Carbon (C)	259.5
7	Nitrogen (N)	335.4
8	Oxygen (O)	313.8
9	Fluorine (F)	401.5
10	Neon (Ne)	497.0
11	Sodium (Na)	118.4
12	Magnesium (Mg)	175.2
13	Aluminum (Al)	137.9
14	Silicon (Si)	187.9
15	Phosphorus (P)	254.1
16	Sulfur (S)	238.8
17	Chlorine (Cl)	300.1
18	Argon (Ar)	363.2
19	Potassium (K)	100.0
20	Calcium (Ca)	141.0

The element Li (no. 3) follows He (no. 2); the element Na (no. 11) follows Ne (no. 10); and the element K (no. 19) follows Ar (no. 18). *Adding one more electron and proton to each of the stable atoms (He, Ne, and Ar) gives new atoms with electron arrangements of relatively low stability (Li, Na, and K).* A relatively small amount of energy is required to pull an electron from Li, Na, or K. The *ion* formed in each case has the same number of electrons as the stable element that precedes it. That is, the lithium *ion* (no. 3) has 2 electrons just like the helium *atom* (no. 2); the sodium *ion* (no. 11) has 10 electrons just like the neon *atom* (no. 10); the potassium *ion* (no. 19) has 18 electrons just like the argon *atom* (no. 18). We now wonder: does the lithium ion have a stable electron configuration like the helium atom? Does the sodium ion have a stable electron configuration like the neon atom? Does the potassium ion have a stable electron configuration like the argon atom?

These questions can only be answered by experiment. Let us look at the energies required to remove an electron from Li^+, Na^+, and K^+. These values are known as the **second ionization energies** of the atoms and are available from laboratory data. The equations are

$$Li^+(g) + 1{,}748 \text{ kcal/mole} \longrightarrow Li^{2+}(g) + e^- \qquad (2)$$

$$Na^+(g) + 1{,}090 \text{ kcal/mole} \longrightarrow Na^{2+}(g) + e^- \qquad (3)$$

$$K^+(g) + 730 \text{ kcal/mole} \longrightarrow K^{2+}(g) + e^- \qquad (4)$$

STABLE ELECTRONIC PATTERNS

The numbers given answer the earlier questions with a resounding yes! A very large amount of energy is required to pull an electron from each of the ions Li^+, Na^+, and K^+. The value for Li^+ is 15 times the value for Li; the value for Na^+ is more than 9 times the value for Na. These numbers suggest that the ions Li^+, Na^+, and K^+ have the same stable electron configurations that were found with the atoms He, Ne, and Ar. So far, stable electron patterns seem to appear if we have 2, 10, or 18 electrons outside the nucleus.

EXERCISE 8-2

Define the third ionization energy for sodium. Its value is 1.6×10^3 kcal/mole. Why is it larger than the value for the second ionization energy?

If the proposal just made is true, it should be easy to add an electron to an atom such as fluorine (atomic number 9) to obtain a pattern with 10 extranuclear electrons—the neon arrangement. It should be easy to add an electron to chlorine (no. 17) to obtain a pattern with 18 extranuclear electrons—the argon arrangement. For the processes involving fluorine (no. 9) and chlorine (no. 17), the equations are

$$
\begin{array}{cccccc}
F(g) & + & e^- & \longrightarrow & F^-(g) & + \ 79 \ \text{kcal/mole} \ (5) \\
\text{fluorine } atom & + & \text{electron} & \longrightarrow & \text{fluoride } ion \ + & \text{energy}
\end{array}
$$

$$
\begin{array}{cccccc}
Cl(g) & + & e^- & \longrightarrow & Cl^-(g) & + \ 85 \ \text{kcal/mole} \ (6) \\
\text{chlorine } atom & + & \text{electron} & \longrightarrow & \text{chloride } ion \ + & \text{energy}
\end{array}
$$

Energy is not required to add an electron to fluorine or chlorine; instead, energy is *released*. The process in each case goes by itself! The atoms move *spontaneously* toward the neon and argon configurations. This fact adds additional support to the proposal that arrangements of 10 and 18 electrons outside the nucleus represent very stable patterns.

The suggestion can be put to a further test. The next element after lithium is beryllium. Beryllium has two more electrons than the stable element helium. Perhaps beryllium will lose *two* electrons relatively easily to give the helium configuration (two electrons outside the nucleus). On the other hand, removing a third electron from beryllium and thus breaking the stable helium pattern should be very difficult if the helium pattern really has high stability. The appropriate equations and numbers are given below:

$$Be(g) + \quad 215 \ \text{kcal/mole} \longrightarrow Be^+(g) + e^- \qquad (7)$$

$$Be^+(g) + \quad 418 \ \text{kcal/mole} \longrightarrow Be^{2+}(g) + e^- \qquad (8)$$

$$Be^{2+}(g) + 3{,}532 \ \text{kcal/mole} \longrightarrow Be^{3+}(g) + e^- \qquad (9)$$

It takes almost twice as much energy to remove the second electron from beryllium as it does to remove the first, but it takes almost 8.5 times as much energy to remove the third electron as it does the second.

Again, *the pattern with two electrons outside the nucleus appears to be very stable.*

EXERCISE 8-3

How many electrons can be removed from a calcium atom (no. 20) before a big jump in ionization energy can be observed? an aluminum atom?

8-1.3   Other Stable Electron Arrangements

All of the foregoing facts support the postulate that 2, 10, or 18 extranuclear electrons represent stable numbers of electrons—these seem to be particularly stable groupings. We are now in a position to try to extend our generalizations. Atoms with atomic numbers 2, 10, and 18 have very high ionization energies. We see that $10 - 2 = 8$, and $18 - 10 = 8$. Do high ionization energies repeat after every eight elements? Will element 26 ($26 - 18 = 8$) have a very high ionization energy? Looking at the list of elements, we see that element number 26 is iron, with the relatively low ionization energy of 182 kcal/mole. On the other hand, krypton, element number 36, has an ionization energy of 320 kcal/mole—a value twice as high as the value given for iron. It is clear to even the most casual observer that our number 8 has lost its magic.

Our failure to predict the ionization energy for iron has additional meaning in the interpretation of data. Scientists have learned through experience that interpolation between points in a set of data on a curve is usually a fairly reliable procedure. For example, if we know that the ionization energy of aluminum (no. 13) is 137.9 kcal/mole and that phosphorus (no. 15) is 254.1 kcal/mole, the value for silicon should be about 189.8 kcal/mole. Fortunately, the experimental value is 187.9 kcal/mole, within range of the predicted value. On the other hand, extrapolation of the data—extending it well beyond the available information—is frequently hazardous. The value for iron was lower than predicted.

If extrapolation from limited data is hazardous, we need more data. Values for additional ionization energies are shown in Figure 8-1 (page 174). Maxima in the curve appear for elements 2, 10, 18, 36, 54, and 86. As we might expect, rubidium (no. 37) and cesium (no. 55) both have low ionization energies.

EXERCISE 8-4

(1) *Estimate* the ionization energy for element no. 85.
(2) Would you expect the addition of an electron to an atom of element no. 35 to give off or to absorb energy? Explain the basis for your choice.

Maxima in the curve of Figure 8-1 are summarized in Table 8-2. There is much food for thought in Table 8-2. First, each of the stable electron patterns involves an even number of electrons. Next, we see that there seems to be some regularity in the differences between the number of electrons possessed by a given stable pattern and the number of electrons possessed by its stable predecessor. The first two differences are 8 and the second two differences are 18. The third difference is 32. Would the next stable configuration be $86 + 32 = 118$ electrons? Extrapolation is still dangerous, but this extrapolation is founded on more data than our first. No one will really *know* the answer until element 118 is available for study.

Other even more interesting questions intrigue us. What is the special significance of the numbers 8, 18, and 32? Why do the values of ionization energy decrease in Table 8-2 as we go from He to Rn? What kind of a model for electron arrangement can be developed to "explain" the numbers in Table 8-2? The significance of the numbers 8, 18, and 32 will be explained in Chapter 16. The other questions can be considered here.

Fig. 8-1 Plot of ionization energy vs. atomic number.

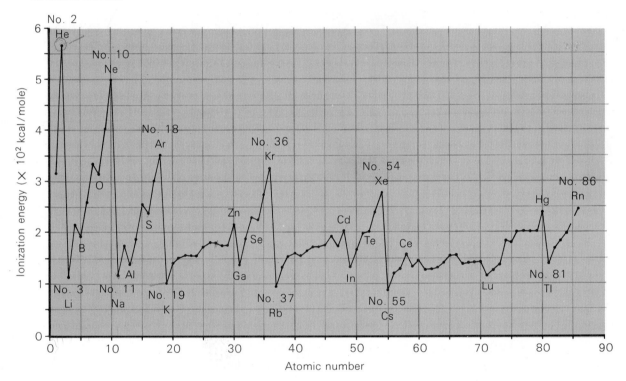

TABLE 8-2 STABLE ELECTRON ARRANGEMENTS—ATOMS WITH MAXIMA IN THE IONIZATION ENERGY CURVE

Element	Ionization Energy (kcal/mole)	Total Number of Electrons	Change in Number of Electrons
Helium	566.7	2	
Neon	497.0	10	$10 - 2 = 8$
Argon	363.2	18	$18 - 10 = 8$
Krypton	322.8	36	$36 - 18 = 18$
Xenon	279.7	54	$54 - 36 = 18$
Radon	247.8	86	$86 - 54 = 32$

In seeking an answer to the question of a model for electron arrangement, we return to a consideration of those forces that hold an electron in the atom. The electrons are held by the attraction between the positively charged nucleus and the negatively charged electron. In Section 6-3.3 we found that this force *decreases* as the distance between the charged objects *increases*. In quantitative terms, the relationship obeyed is

$$\begin{Bmatrix} \text{force of} \\ \text{attraction} \\ \text{between} \\ \text{nucleus and} \\ \text{electron} \end{Bmatrix} = \frac{\begin{Bmatrix} \text{total positive} \\ \text{charge on} \\ \text{nucleus} \end{Bmatrix} \begin{Bmatrix} \text{charge on} \\ \text{electron} \end{Bmatrix}}{\begin{Bmatrix} \text{distance from} \\ \text{electron to nucleus} \end{Bmatrix}^2} \qquad (10)$$

If we double the distance between nucleus and electron, the force of attraction drops to one-fourth its original value! We note again that *as we progress down in Table 8-2 from helium to radon, the ionization energy drops from 566.7 kcal to 247.8 kcal.* Perhaps the electron lost from radon is farther from the nucleus than the electron lost from helium. If this were true, radon would have a lower ionization energy. The expected trend is observed. This suggestion concerning distance between electron and nucleus was first made by the brilliant Danish physicist Niels Bohr in his original model for the atom. This particular postulate is still accepted in our present-day model for the atom. The electron lost from radon is farther from the nucleus than the electron lost from helium.

Another proposal is worth considering. Suppose electrons are arranged in levels going out from the nucleus as in Table 8-3 (page 176). Very near the nucleus the amount of room for electrons is limited. Perhaps two electrons would be the maximum number we could place very near the nucleus. After that, a new level would be needed at a larger average distance from the nucleus. The first electron added to this new level would be lost rather easily because it would be at a greater distance from the central positive charge. As extra protons are added to the nucleus to increase the atomic number of the elements (lithium ⟶ neon), the attraction between nucleus and electron would increase if electrons were added to this *same* level at nearly the same average distance from the nucleus. *As the nuclear charge increases, the ionization energy should increase if electrons are being added to the same level.* At neon this second level would be filled. At sodium a third level would be started. A drop in ionization energy would be expected when a new level is started because the next added electron would be at a greater distance from the nucleus. Indeed this drop appears at sodium. Our tentative model for the electronic arrangement of the first 20 elements can then be summarized as shown in Table 8-3.

The model suggested is consistent with all of the observations we have made. He, Ne, and Ar have electron levels that are full. Such completed levels are described as stable since it is difficult to remove electrons from them. The elements Li, Na, and K have an electron in the next level above He, Ne, and Ar, respectively. This electron can be pulled off relatively easily in each case to give *ions* having electron configurations which are like He, Ne, and Ar, respectively. If Be, Mg, and Ca each lose two electrons, the resulting *ions* have configurations like He, Ne, and Ar, respectively. In every case it is difficult to break up the 2, 10, or 18 pattern.

This crude model for atomic structure makes no effort to tell us precisely where the electrons are or what they are doing. Indeed, we will learn in Chapter 16 that such a question cannot really be answered. Rest assured, however, that the information given here is consistent with the general ideas of the modern atomic theory. It is supported by a tremendous amount of chemical and physical evidence. With this thought in mind, let us explore the chemical implications of the model summarized in Table 8-3.

TABLE 8-3 A PROPOSED ELECTRON ARRANGEMENT FOR THE FIRST 20 ELEMENTS

Atomic Number	Element	First Ionization Energy (kcal/mole)	Electrons in First Level	Electrons in Second Level	Electrons in Third Level	Electrons in Fourth Level
1	Hydrogen (H)	313.6	1			
2	Helium (He)	566.7	2 *(major level full)*			
3	Lithium (Li)	124.3	2	1 *(lost easily)*		
4	Beryllium (Be)	214.9	2	2		
5	Boron (B)	191.2	2	3		
6	Carbon (C)	259.5	2	4		
7	Nitrogen (N)	335.4	2	5		
8	Oxygen (O)	313.8	2	6		
9	Fluorine (F)	401.5	2	7		
10	Neon (Ne)	497.0	2	8 *(major level full)*		
11	Sodium (Na)	118.4	2	8	1 *(lost easily)*	
12	Magnesium (Mg)	175.2	2	8	2	
13	Aluminum (Al)	137.9	2	8	3	
14	Silicon (Si)	187.9	2	8	4	
15	Phosphorus (P)	254.1	2	8	5	
16	Sulfur (S)	238.8	2	8	6	
17	Chlorine (Cl)	300.1	2	8	7	
18	Argon (Ar)	363.2	2	8	8 *(major level full)*	
19	Potassium (K)	100.0	2	8	8	1 *(lost easily)*
20	Calcium (Ca)	141.0	2	8	8	2

8-3 THE CHEMICAL SIGNIFICANCE OF IONIZATION ENERGIES

The above pattern for electron arrangement offers some justification for the arrangement of atoms in the periodic table (pages 196–197). What are the chemical implications of this arrangement? First let us examine the elements that occupy the peak positions in the ionization energy curve (Figure 8-1). These are helium (no. 2), neon (no. 10), argon (no. 18), krypton (no. 36), xenon (no. 54), and radon (no. 86). They are called the **noble gases.**

8-3.1 The Noble Gas Family

All six of these elements (He, Ne, Ar, Kr, Xe, and Rn) are gases. In fact, they account for 6 of the 11 elements that are gases at STP. These gases are so strikingly similar that they are conveniently considered as a group called the noble gas family. If we look at the properties of other elements, we find that this recurrence of properties is usual. It is convenient to group all the elements into families or groups according to their chemistry. The elements in a particular group have similar properties. Knowledge about one element in a group then aids in understanding the chemistry of other elements in that group. In the periodic table (see Figure 8-15), each group appears in a vertical column.

As we have noted, all six members of the group with high ionization energies are gases. Each of the other five elements that are gases at STP have *two* atoms per molecule. The formulas are H_2, N_2, O_2, F_2, and Cl_2. In sharp contrast, *all members of the noble gas family have molecules that contain only a single atom*. Helium gas is made up of monatomic helium molecules—He, *not* He_2! Neon gas is made up of monatomic neon molecules—Ne, *not* Ne_2. Similarly, argon molecules have the formula Ar; krypton molecules, Kr; xenon molecules, Xe; and radon molecules, Rn.

EXERCISE 8-5

What is the mass of a 22.4-litre sample of xenon, measured at STP? of krypton?

The atoms of this family are remarkably self-sufficient. They show absolutely no measurable tendency to combine with each other under any conditions. *No real evidence for diatomic molecules in this family has ever been found.* Helium atoms also have little attraction for other atoms. *No stable compounds of helium have yet been found.* This fact, together with the fact that helium has the highest ionization energy of all of the atoms, suggests that the inert character of helium is related to its unusually stable electron configuration. Because helium atoms have such unusually stable electron configurations, they tend to have very little interaction with each other; the forces between the monatomic molecules are very low. We would therefore expect helium to have a low boiling point since little energy is needed to separate the molecules from the liquid and generate a gas. Such is the case. Helium boils at 4.2 K ($-268.9\,°C$) and cannot be solidified at any temperature unless pressure is applied. It becomes solid at 1.1 K ($-272.0\,°C$) under a pressure of 26 atm. It has the lowest boiling point and freezing point of any substance known.

The properties of the noble gases are summarized in Table 8-4 (page 178). Two points deserve comment. As the atomic number goes up and the ionization energy goes down, the boiling points and the freezing points of the noble gases go up (see Figure 8-3). Apparently, interactions between noble gas atoms, though never strong, become stronger as the atomic number increases and the stability of the electron arrangement decreases. Interactions become stronger as the ionization energy decreases.

Fig. 8-2 The noble gas family.

helium	2 He
neon	10 Ne
argon	18 Ar
krypton	36 Kr
xenon	54 Xe
radon	86 Rn

TABLE 8-4 SOME PROPERTIES OF THE NOBLE GASES

Element	Molecular Formula	Atomic Number	Atomic Weight	Boiling Point (K)	Melting Point (K)	Ionization Energy (kcal/mole)
Helium	He	2	4.00	4.2	—	566.7
Neon	Ne	10	20.18	27.2	24.6	497.0
Argon	Ar	18	39.9	87.3	83.9	363.2
Krypton	Kr	36	83.80	120	116	322.8
Xenon	Xe	54	131.30	165	161	279.7
Radon	Rn	86	222	211	202	247.8

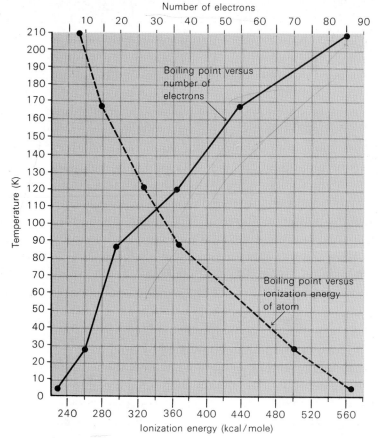

Fig. 8-3 Boiling points of noble gases plotted against number of electrons and against ionization energy.

NEIL BARTLETT (1932–)

A native of England, Neil Bartlett received his Ph.D. in chemistry from King's College, Newcastle-upon-Tyne, in 1957. Following a year as senior chemistry master at the Duke's School, Alnwick, he joined the faculty of the University of British Columbia. Since 1969, Bartlett has been a professor of chemistry at the University of California at Berkeley.

Thus far, Bartlett's outstanding contribution to chemistry is the preparation of the first compound of a noble gas, achieved in 1962. He observed an unknown compound which was produced when platinum was treated with fluorine in glass apparatus, rather than in the less reactive apparatus usually used for fluorine reactions. The development of special techniques of study led to the identification of the compound as an ionic salt, $O_2^+[PtF_6]^-$. The ability of PtF_6 to oxidize molecular oxygen to O_2^+ suggested further experiments with other species of high ionization energy. When PtF_6 was mixed with xenon gas at room temperature, xenon hexafluoroplatinate was formed, as described in Section 8-3.2.

8-3.2 The Non-Inert Noble Gases

Before 1962 all members of the noble gas family were considered inert and the family was called the "inert" gases. The inert character of the group was attributed to the presence of a very stable arrangement of electrons—eight electrons in the outer level. As we noted earlier, the belief that these gases are all inert—*i.e.*, formed no compounds at all—was destroyed in 1962 when Neil Bartlett first succeeded in preparing the yellow solid, xenon hexafluoroplatinate ($XePtF_6$). Bartlett described the experiment as follows:

The predicted interaction of xenon and platinum hexafluoride was confirmed in a simple and visually dramatic experiment. The deep red platinum hexafluoride vapor, of known pressure, was mixed, by breaking a glass diaphragm, with the same volume of xenon, the pressure of which was greater than that of the hexafluoride. Combination to produce a yellow solid was immediate at room temperature and the quantity of xenon which remained was commensurate with a combining ratio of 1:1. [Figure 8-4.]

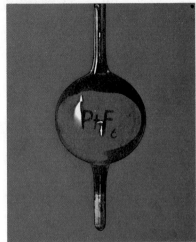

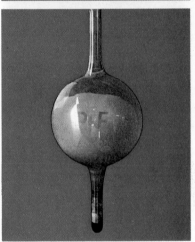

Fig. 8-4 The reaction of xenon with platinum hexafluoride. (Above: before reaction; below: after reaction.)

Following this observation, "inert gas" compounds were prepared in a number of laboratories.* Many xenon compounds are now known, including XeF_2, XeF_4, XeF_6, XeO_3, $XeOF_2$, $XeOF_3$, $XeOF_4$, $NaXeO_4 \cdot 6H_2O$, $K_4XeO_6 \cdot 2XeO_3$, $Ba_2XeO_6 \cdot xH_2O$, and $XeSbF_6$.

It is now fairly easy to rationalize the existence of these unstable compounds by looking at the ionization energies. The value for xenon is fairly high, but not exceptionally so in comparison to other elements around it (see Figure 8-1). Rationalization after the fact is easy. (Remember Mr. Wilson in the Sherlock Holmes tale.) On the other hand, a few men had used ionization energies to predict the possible existence of xenon compounds even before Bartlett's brilliant experiments.

EXERCISE 8-6

The compound KrF_2 is known. On the basis of the ionization energy data, would you expect KrF_2 to be more or less easily decomposed than XeF_2? Explain. (See Table 8-4.)

8-4 THE ALKALI METALS

The alkali metals are the six elements following the noble gases. They are lithium (Li), sodium (Na), potassium (K), rubidium (Rb), cesium (Cs), and francium (Fr). Their physical properties contrast sharply with the physical properties of the noble gases (see Table 8-5). All, when pure, are bright, shiny metals and conduct electricity very well. The one extra electron that differentiates the electronic structure of the alkali metals from the noble gases has a terrific effect upon the properties of the alkali metals. The structure of these metals and the role of this one electron will be considered in later sections of this chapter.

TABLE 8-5 PHYSICAL PROPERTIES OF ALKALI METALS

Element	Molecular Formula	Atomic Number	Atomic Weight	Boiling Point (°C)	Melting Point (°C)	Atomic Volume, Solid (cm³/mole of atoms)	Density of Solid at 20 °C (g/cm³)*
Lithium	Li	3	6.94	1326	180	13.0	0.535
Sodium	Na	11	23.00	889	98	23.7	0.971
Potassium	K	19	39.10	757	63.4	45.4	0.862
Rubidium	Rb	37	85.47	679	38.8	55.8	1.53
Cesium	Cs	55	132.90	690	28.7	70.0	1.87

*Density is usually given as kilograms per cubic metre in the SI system of units. Can you make this conversion?

*Research in this area was fast and dramatic. For example, three research teams reported the new and exciting compound XeF_6 almost simultaneously. The teams were headed by Dr. John Malm of Argonne National Laboratories, Dr. George Cady of the University of Washington, and Dr. Bernard Weinstock at the Research Laboratories of the Ford Motor Co.

Fig. 8-5 The alkali metals.

2 He	3 Li	lithium
10 Ne	11 Na	sodium
18 Ar	19 K	potassium
36 Kr	37 Rb	rubidium
54 Xe	55 Cs	cesium
86 Rn	87 Fr	francium

8-4.1 Reactions of the Alkali Metals with Chlorine

When an alkali metal such as sodium is brought into contact with chlorine gas, an alkali metal chloride is formed. For sodium the equation is

$$Na(s) + \tfrac{1}{2}Cl_2(g) \longrightarrow NaCl(s) + energy \qquad (11)$$

In Section 8-1 we saw that relatively little energy is required to remove an electron from a sodium *atom* to give a sodium *ion* (neon configuration). The alkali metals were characterized by the fact that they had lower first-ionization energies than any other group of atoms. We also noted that a chlorine atom with one electron less than the argon configuration will pick up an electron and release energy. Further, we know that when NaCl dissolves in water, $Na^+(aq)$ ions and $Cl^-(aq)$ ions are formed. We also know that molten NaCl conducts electricity. These facts suggest that NaCl(*s*) may well be built up from Na^+ and Cl^- units. This suggestion has been verified using X-ray diffraction methods (see Chapter 17).

Fig. 8-6 A representation of the formation of Na^+ and Cl^- ions.

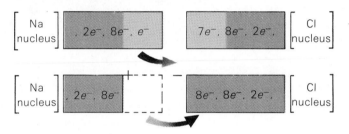

It then appears that one of the steps to be considered in the formation of NaCl involves the transfer of an electron from the outer level of a sodium atom to the incomplete level of a chlorine atom, as in Figure 8-6. Because of the low energy of ionization of sodium and the *release* of energy in the formation of Cl^-, the above process can be carried out at a low net energy cost. The two resulting ions of opposite charge, Na^+ and Cl^-, move toward each other with a large reduction in total energy. *The stability of the sodium chloride crystal depends upon the electrical attraction of the oppositely charged ions.* The crystal is held together by **ionic bonds.**

This chemistry is characteristic of all of the alkali metals. Each of them reacts with chlorine gas in a similar way:

$$Li(s) + \tfrac{1}{2}Cl_2(g) \longrightarrow LiCl(s) + energy \qquad (12)$$

$$Na(s) + \tfrac{1}{2}Cl_2(g) \longrightarrow NaCl(s) + energy \qquad (11)$$

$$K(s) + \tfrac{1}{2}Cl_2(g) \longrightarrow KCl(s) + energy \qquad (13)$$

$$Rb(s) + \tfrac{1}{2}Cl_2(g) \longrightarrow RbCl(s) + energy \qquad (14)$$

$$Cs(s) + \tfrac{1}{2}Cl_2(g) \longrightarrow CsCl(s) + energy \qquad (15)$$

In every case the alkali metal reacts to form a stable ionic solid in which the alkali is present as a noble-gas type positive ion. The product in each case is a crystalline substance with a high solubility in water.

8-4.2 The Nature of Solid Sodium Chloride

The formation of crystalline NaCl from gaseous Na^+ and Cl^- is the source of the energy released when sodium metal burns in chlorine. What is the nature of solid NaCl?

Studies of the crystal using X rays indicate that sodium ions and chloride ions are arranged in a regular geometric array or lattice. The packing arrangement can be seen in Figure 8-7. Each chloride ion is surrounded by six sodium ions, and each sodium ion is surrounded by six chloride ions. *Distinct ions of each element are clearly present.*

The positive and negative ions attract each other very strongly to give a solid with forces of attraction *extending through the entire solid. There are no separate NaCl molecules in a sodium chloride crystal.* The entire mass is a giant molecule; hence the formula NaCl is really just the simplest or empirical formula for the substance. Because the oppositely charged ions are strongly attracted to each other, bonds between ions are strong; the solid is hard with high boiling and melting points. These properties are characteristic of an ionic solid. Because ions cannot move in solid NaCl, it is a very poor conductor of electricity. On the other hand, if the solid is melted so that ions can move around, it becomes a good conductor of electricity.

The energy added to the crystal to melt the NaCl tears apart the regular lattice arrangement. When water dissolves NaCl, water molecules surround the Na^+ and Cl^- ions to supply the energy needed to tear apart the lattice.* In summary, ions with the configuration of neon and argon appear to be stable when they are in water solution. They are also stable in a solid ionic lattice of the type formed by NaCl.

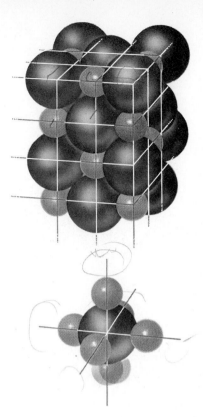

Fig. 8-7 The packing of ions in an ionic crystal.

8-4.3 Reactions of the Alkali Metals with Water

Sodium metal reacts vigorously with water to form hydrogen gas and an aqueous solution of sodium hydroxide (NaOH):

$$2Na(s) + 2H_2O(l) \longrightarrow 2Na^+(aq) + 2\,OH^-(aq) + H_2(g) + \text{energy.} \quad (16)$$

Energy is liberated, often so fast that the temperature rises sharply and the hydrogen, mixing with air, explodes. Thus, sodium metal is dangerous and must be handled with caution. Other alkali metals behave in a similar manner. K, Rb, and Cs are even more reactive with water.

In the reaction of an alkali metal with water, electron transfer from the metal to a water molecule or a hydrogen ion is important at some stage in the process.

We see that in this process as well as in the reaction of sodium and chlorine, the ease with which an electron can be removed from

*Electrical conductivity of an aqueous solution of a substance does *not* necessarily imply that the original material was ionic in form. For example, gaseous HCl will freeze to a solid at $-114\,°C$. This low-temperature solid is made up of (distinct) HCl molecules, yet it is pulled apart when dissolved in water to give $H^+(aq)$ and $Cl^-(aq)$. Thus, we cannot safely interpret the conductivity of an aqueous solution to mean that the original solid was made up of ions. We can, however, state the converse: when an ionic solid dissolves extensively in water, a conducting solution is obtained.

sodium contributes strongly to the reactivity characteristic of the system.

8-4.4 Summary of the Chemistry of the Alkali Elements

The alkali metals are extremely reactive. Thus, there is a dramatic change in chemistry as we pass from the noble gases to the alkali metal column in the periodic table. The chemistry of the alkali metals is interesting and often spectacular. These metals react with chlorine and water to form a stable 1+ ion. The 1+ ions, on the other hand, do not have a spectacular chemistry, but their importance and unique characteristics are displayed in more subtle ways. For example, potassium ions are essential to proper plant growth; hence, potassium salts are common constituents of most fertilizers. Similarly, sodium salts are essential to proper animal growth. Salt licks or blocks of salt are frequently supplied to range animals. Molecular biology is revealing interesting roles for alkali metal ions in nature.

8-5 THE ALKALINE EARTH METALS

The alkaline earth metals are the five elements following the alkali metals. They are beryllium (Be), magnesium (Mg), calcium (Ca), strontium (Sr), and barium (Ba). Radium, which follows francium, element no. 87, is radioactive and is more interesting from that standpoint than from its relationship to the other alkaline earth metals. It does, however, resemble the alkaline earth metals in its chemistry—a fact which made its initial isolation by Madame Curie possible. All of these elements are good conductors of electricity and are clearly metallic in appearance.

2 He	3 Li	4 Be	beryllium
10 Ne	11 Na	12 Mg	magnesium
18 Ar	19 K	20 Ca	calcium
36 Kr	37 Rb	38 Sr	strontium
54 Xe	55 Cs	56 Ba	barium
86 Rn	87 Fr		

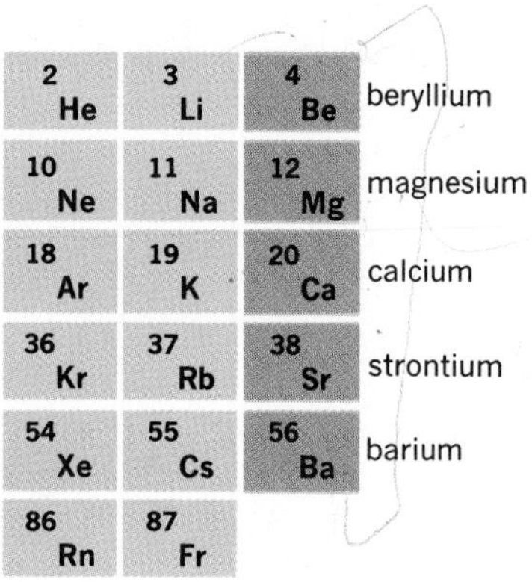

Fig. 8-8 The alkaline earth metals.

8-5.1 Chemical Reactions of the Alkaline Earth Family

The electron arrangement for the elements of the second column is of immediate interest to us. Notice that each element has *two more electrons* than the nearest noble gas. As expected from this fact and from the successive ionization energies shown in Table 8-6, the typical chemistry of this group involves the loss of two electrons from the atom to form a 2+ ion. For example, we can write

$$Mg(s) + energy \longrightarrow Mg^{2+} + 2e^- \qquad (17)$$

$$Ca(s) + energy \longrightarrow Ca^{2+} + 2e^- \qquad (18)$$

The metals react directly with chlorine to form the metal chlorides:

$$Ca(s) + Cl_2(g) \longrightarrow CaCl_2(s) \qquad (19)$$

$$Sr(s) + Cl_2(g) \longrightarrow SrCl_2(s) \qquad (20)$$

and with water, under the proper conditions, to form the metal hydroxide and hydrogen gas:

$$Ca(s) + 2H_2O(l) \longrightarrow Ca(OH)_2(s) + H_2(g) \qquad (21)$$

$$Ba(s) + 2H_2O(l) \longrightarrow Ba^{2+}(aq) + 2\,OH^-(aq) + H_2(g) \quad (22)$$

TABLE 8-6 IONIZATION ENERGIES OF THE ALKALINE EARTH ELEMENTS

Element	Ionization Energy (kcal/mole)		
	E_1	E_2	E_3
Beryllium	215	418	3,532
Magnesium	175	345	1,839
Calcium	141	273	1,175
Strontium	131	253	986
Barium	120	230	811

EXERCISE 8-7

For each alkaline earth metal, calculate the ratio E_2/E_1. (E_2 is the ionization energy of the second electron and E_1 is that of the first electron.) Account for the results in terms of the charges on the ions formed in the two ionization steps.

EXERCISE 8-8

If the ionization energy E_1 is regarded as a measure of the distance between the electron and the nuclear charge, what do the ionization energies of Be and Ba indicate about the relative sizes of the two atoms?

8-5.2 Physical Properties of the Alkaline Earth Family

The alkaline earth metals have higher ionization energies, higher melting and boiling points, and greater hardness than the corresponding alkali metals. This is due in part to the greater nuclear charge in the atoms of each alkaline earth metal as compared to those of the preceding alkali metal. Some other properties of this family are summarized in Table 8-7.

TABLE 8-7 PROPERTIES OF THE ALKALINE EARTH ELEMENTS IN THE METALLIC STATE

Element	Molecular Formula	Atomic Number	Atomic Weight	Melting Point (°C)	Atomic Volume, Solid, cm³/mole of atoms	Density of Solid at 20 °C (g/cm³)
Beryllium	Be	4	9.01	1283	4.87	1.85
Magnesium	Mg	12	24.3	650	14.0	1.74
Calcium	Ca	20	40.1	850	25.9	1.55
Strontium	Sr	38	87.6	770	34.5	2.54
Barium	Ba	56	137.3	704	39.2	3.50

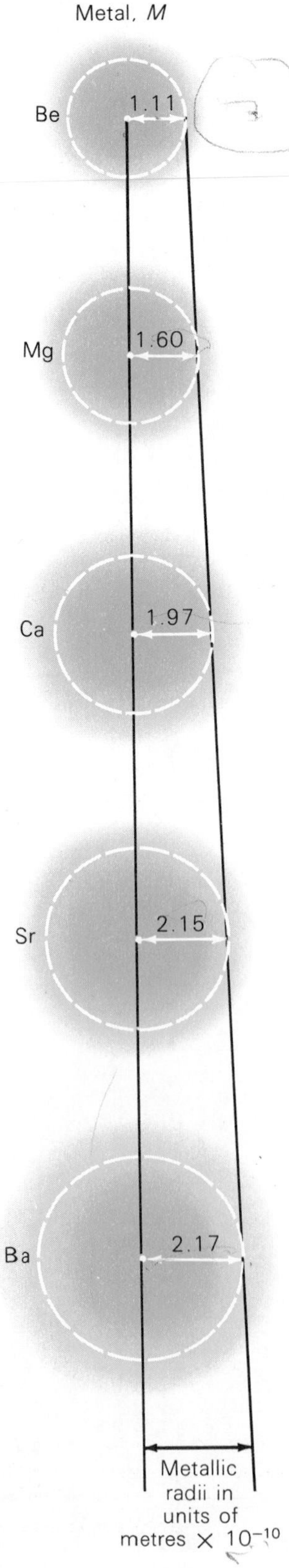

Fig. 8-9 Metallic radii of alkaline earth atoms.

Metal, M

Be 1.11

Mg 1.60

Ca 1.97

Sr 2.15

Ba 2.17

Metallic radii in units of metres $\times 10^{-10}$

8-5.3 Relative Sizes of the Alkaline Earth Metal Atoms

As you will recall from Section 7-1.3, atoms have no definite size. To assign a size, we must first decide where an atom "stops."

What kind of decisions do we make in assigning a radius value to a metal atom? The distance between magnesium nuclei in solid metallic magnesium can be determined by X-ray diffraction to be 3.20×10^{-10} metre. The radius of magnesium can be taken as half this value, or 1.60×10^{-10} metre. We designate this value as a metallic radius since these elements are metals. Interatomic distances in the metals and values for metallic radii of these elements are summarized in Table 8-8. Note that there is an increase in the size of metal atoms as we go down a column, which explains in part the downward trend in ionization energy noted earlier (Table 8-6). Electrons which are farther from the nucleus are lost more easily.

TABLE 8-8 METALLIC RADII FOR ALKALINE EARTH METALS

Element	Distance Between Atoms in Metal (metres)	Metallic Radius (metres)
Beryllium	2.23×10^{-10}	1.11×10^{-10}
Magnesium	3.20×10^{-10}	1.60×10^{-10}
Calcium	3.95×10^{-10}	1.97×10^{-10}
Strontium	4.30×10^{-10}	2.15×10^{-10}
Barium	4.35×10^{-10}	2.17×10^{-10}

8-6 THE HALOGENS

The lightest halogen, fluorine, occurs just before neon in the periodic table. Chlorine occurs just before argon; bromine appears just before krypton; iodine, just before xenon; and astatine, just before radon. Since astatine is very rare and little is published on its chemistry, our discussion will focus on fluorine, chlorine, bromine, and iodine (see Figure 8-10). We noted earlier that each of these elements has one less electron than the comparable noble gas atom; its outer electron level lacks one electron of being full. Much of the chemistry of this group of elements is concerned with ways of altering the outer electron configuration to obtain a more stable overall electron pattern.

8-6.1 Halogen Molecules and the Covalent Bond

Previously we saw that fluorine, chlorine, bromine, and iodine form diatomic molecules. A sizable amount of energy is needed to disrupt these molecules to give atoms. For chlorine the process is

$$Cl_2(g) + 57.8 \text{ kcal} \longrightarrow 2Cl(g) \qquad (23)$$

At extremely high temperatures, large numbers of chlorine molecules break into atoms. For example, near the surface of the sun at a temperature of 6000 K, chlorine is present as the monatomic gas Cl; but at room temperature and at most of our common laboratory temperatures, chlorine atoms combine with each other to give Cl_2 molecules.

How can we rationalize the formation of a bond between identical chlorine atoms? It is found that *a pair of electrons, shared between two positively charged nuclei, will be attracted by both nuclei* to give a chemical bond. Thus, in the case of two chlorine atoms, each atom can contribute one outer electron to make a pair which has a high probability of moving between the nuclei to make a chemical bond. We might represent our picture schematically as in Figure 8-11, where the two e^-'s represent *two electrons that spend a significant part of their time between the nuclei*. We do not have positive chlorine ions in the molecule, but unbalanced positive charges on the nucleus of each chlorine atom attract the electron pair between the nuclei to give a bond. We shall have more to say about the details of this bond in a subsequent chapter. A bond in which two atoms are held together by a shared pair of electrons is known as a **covalent bond**.

Fig. 8-10 The halogens.

		^{2} He	^{3} Li
fluorine	^{9} F	^{10} Ne	^{11} Na
chlorine	^{17} Cl	^{18} Ar	^{19} K
bromine	^{35} Br	^{36} Kr	^{37} Rb
iodine	^{53} I	^{54} Xe	^{55} Cs
astatine	^{85} At	^{86} Rn	^{87} Fr

EXERCISE 8-9

Two argon atoms will *not* form a covalent bond to give Ar_2. Why?

The consequences of molecule formation are reflected in the physical properties of the halogens shown in Table 8-9.

Fig. 8-11 A covalent bond: the bonding of chlorine atoms to give a chlorine molecule.

TABLE 8-9 PROPERTIES OF HALOGENS

Element	Molecular Formula	Atomic Number	Atomic Weight	Boiling Point (°C)	Melting Point (°C)	Atomic Volume, Solid, cm³/mole of atoms
Fluorine	F_2	9	19.0	−188	−218	14.6
Chlorine	Cl_2	17	35.5	−34.1	−101	18.7
Bromine	Br_2	35	79.9	58.8	−7.3	23.5
Iodine	I_2	53	127	184	114	25.7
Astatine*		85				

*Since there is probably less than 30 g of astatine in the entire crust of the earth, it has been studied very little and not much is known about its properties. All of its isotopes are radioactive, with the longest-lived one having a half-life of 8.3 hours.

8-6.2 The Chemistry of the Elemental Halogens

The reactions of the alkali metals with chlorine were used to show the similarities of the alkali metals. In a similar way the reactions of the halogens with one of the alkali metals, say sodium, show similarities within this group. The reactions that occur are as follows:

$$Na(s) + \tfrac{1}{2}F_2(g) \longrightarrow NaF(s) + energy \qquad (24)$$

$$Na(s) + \tfrac{1}{2}Cl_2(g) \longrightarrow NaCl(s) + energy \qquad (11)$$

$$Na(s) + \tfrac{1}{2}Br_2(g) \longrightarrow NaBr(s) + energy \qquad (25)$$

$$Na(s) + \tfrac{1}{2}I_2(g) \longrightarrow NaI(s) + energy \qquad (26)$$

These reactions all proceed readily. They produce ionic solids with the simplest formula NaX. Each of these solids has a crystal structure made up of positively charged sodium ions and negatively charged ions of the halogens. These negative ions—F^-, Cl^-, Br^-, and I^-—are called **halide ions.**

The halogens also react with hydrogen gas to form the covalent hydrogen halides:

$$H_2(g) + F_2(g) \longrightarrow 2HF(g) \qquad \text{HYDROGEN FLUORIDE} \quad (27)$$

$$H_2(g) + Cl_2(g) \longrightarrow 2HCl(g) \qquad \text{HYDROGEN CHLORIDE} \quad (28)$$

$$H_2(g) + Br_2(g) \longrightarrow 2HBr(g) \qquad \text{HYDROGEN BROMIDE} \quad (29)$$

$$H_2(g) + I_2(g) \longrightarrow 2HI(g) \qquad \text{HYDROGEN IODIDE} \quad (30)$$

The reaction of F_2 and H_2 will usually proceed explosively when the gases are just mixed at room temperature. Hydrogen and chlorine can be mixed at room temperature in the dark without reaction, but ultraviolet light will initiate an explosion. Why? Some thought tells you that the bonds holding atoms together in the hydrogen and chlorine molecules must be broken if new bonds are to form between hydrogen atoms and chlorine atoms. The first step in starting the reaction is the breaking of the bonds between like atoms. The breaking of bonds in the Cl_2 molecule is achieved by a beam of ultraviolet light or by high temperatures. This starts the reaction. Once started, the combination of hydrogen and chlorine tends to proceed rapidly or explosively without further addition of external energy. The reactions involving Br_2 and I_2 are similar but *much* less energetic than the chlorine reaction.

8-6.3 The Hydrogen Halides

Hydrogen chloride (HCl) and hydrogen fluoride (HF) are frequently prepared by the action of sulfuric acid on a metal salt of the halide:

$$NaCl(s) + H_2SO_4(conc) \longrightarrow HCl(g) + NaHSO_4(s) \qquad (31)$$

The HCl leaves the reaction mixture as a gas.

EXERCISE 8-10

Write an equation for the preparation of HF from CaF_2.

All the hydrogen halides are gaseous at room temperature, but hydrogen fluoride liquefies at 19.9 °C and 1 atm pressure. All the hydrogen halides dissolve in water to give solutions that conduct electric current. The reactions may be written

$$HF(g) + water \longrightarrow H^+(aq) + F^-(aq) \qquad (32)$$

$$HCl(g) + water \longrightarrow H^+(aq) + Cl^-(aq) \qquad (33)$$

$$HBr(g) + water \longrightarrow H^+(aq) + Br^-(aq) \qquad (34)$$

$$HI(g) + water \longrightarrow H^+(aq) + I^-(aq) \qquad (35)$$

The solutions have similar properties and are called **acid solutions.**
The common species in each case is the aqueous hydrogen ion, $H^+(aq)$,
and the properties of aqueous acid solutions are attributed to this ion.

8-6.4 Some Reactions of the Halide Ions

The halogens, because of their ability to form either stable ions or
covalent bonds, combine with most other elements. Thus, we have
$NaCl$, $MgCl_2$, HCl, and CCl_4. When magnesium metal reacts with
chlorine, each magnesium atom gives up two electrons to form a Mg^{2+}
ion and two Cl^- ions. (Remember that the Mg^{2+} ion has the neon
electron structure.) Calcium will form halides—CaF_2, $CaCl_2$, $CaBr_2$,
and CaI_2. Strontium and barium will also form MX_2 compounds where
M is the metal ion and X is a halide ion. Aluminum gives us a compound whose simplest formula is $AlCl_3$, but whose molecular formula
is Al_2Cl_6.

EXERCISE 8-11

Write the formula for the product expected when radium (same
family as calcium) combines with bromine. Repeat for the combination of radium with fluorine.

Most metal halides are water soluble. For example, NaCl (ordinary
salt), $CaCl_2$ (put on roads to lay dust), and KBr are easily dissolved
in water. A few halides such as AgCl, CaF_2, AgBr, and AgI are
different. They have a very low solubility in water. Silver bromide and
silver iodide are even less soluble than silver chloride. These low
solubilities provide a sensitive test for the presence of chloride ions,
bromide ions, and iodide ions in aqueous solutions. When silver nitrate
($AgNO_3$) is dissolved in water, the salt ionizes to give silver ions and
nitrate ions in solution:

$$AgNO_3(s) + \text{water} \longrightarrow Ag^+(aq) + NO_3{}^-(aq) \qquad (36)$$

If this solution is now added to a solution containing chloride ions,
a white precipitate of AgCl(s) forms:

$$Ag^+(aq) + Cl^-(aq) \longrightarrow AgCl(s) \qquad (37)$$
$$\text{WHITE SOLID}$$

Comparable reactions occur with bromide and iodide ions; we note
that while AgCl is white, AgBr is tan and AgI is yellow. Silver fluoride
is soluble; therefore, no precipitate forms when a solution containing
$Ag^+(aq)$ ions is added to a solution containing $F^-(aq)$ ions.

EXERCISE 8-12

Write the *ionic* equation for the process occurring when a solution
of $AgNO_3$ is added to a solution of potassium iodide (KI).

Devise a procedure for separating $F^-(aq)$ ions and $Br^-(aq)$ ions present in a water solution. Write appropriate equations.

8-6.5 Relative Sizes of the Halogen Atoms

In Section 7-1.3 we used an *operational definition* to define the size of a chlorine atom. First, we determined experimentally the distance between two chlorine nuclei in Cl_2. We then assigned half this distance to each chlorine as the radius of a chlorine atom. Because the chlorine molecule we used to determine this distance is held together by a covalent bond, the radius is called the **covalent radius** of the chlorine atom. It gives an estimate of the size of a chlorine atom in a covalently bonded situation. (See Figure 8-12.) As we might well expect, the covalent radii of the halogen atoms become greater as more electrons are added to the electron cloud outside the atomic nucleus. This corresponds nicely to the decrease in ionization energy shown in Table 8-10. The values for the covalent radii are 0.72×10^{-10} metre for F, 0.99×10^{-10} metre for Cl, 1.14×10^{-10} metre for Br, and 1.33×10^{-10} metre for I. Note that fluorine is *smaller* than we would have expected from a linear extrapolation of the sizes of the other atoms seen in Figure 8-12.

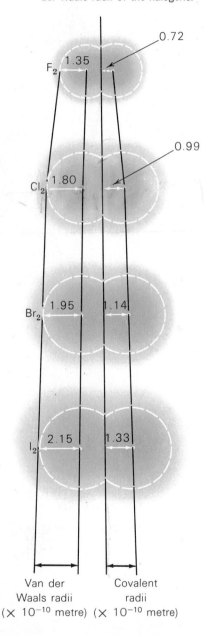

Fig. 8-12 Covalent radii and van der Waals radii of the halogens.

Van der Waals radii ($\times 10^{-10}$ metre)   Covalent radii ($\times 10^{-10}$ metre)

EXERCISE 8-14

Using the carbon atom covalent radius 0.77×10^{-10} metre and the covalent radii given above, predict the C—X bond length in the following molecules: CF_4, CBr_4, and CI_4. Compare your calculated bond lengths with the experimental values C—F in $CF_4 = 1.32 \times 10^{-10}$ metre, C—Br in $CBr_4 = 1.94 \times 10^{-10}$ metre, and C—I in $CI_4 = 2.15 \times 10^{-10}$ metre.

Another way of establishing a value for the atomic size of each halogen is to determine how closely the nuclei of the atoms *in two different molecules* approach each other during a molecular collision (see Figure 8-13). Half this distance could then be assigned as an atomic radius for each atom. These collision distances can be obtained by comparing pressure-volume data for the real gas with pressure-volume data for an ideal gas ($PV = nRT$). The real-gas values are related to attractions, repulsions, and distances between molecules at the time of the collision. Radii obtained by this method are called **van der Waals** radii, after the Dutch physicist who studied real gas behavior in 1873. Figure 8-12 compares the van der Waals and covalent radii for the halogens. Note specifically that van der Waals radii are always larger than covalent radii and that both the van der Waals and the covalent radii increase as the atomic number of the halogen becomes greater.

8-6.6 A Summary of Halogen Chemistry

Halogens have two atoms per molecule. Each atom shares its odd electron with the other atom to give a structure in which there is a high probability of finding the electron pair between the nuclei. Electrons between the nuclei give a bond between atoms, since both nuclei are attracted to the electron pair. This bond is called a **covalent bond.** Fluorine is the most reactive element known. Halogens frequently produce either an ionic structure containing the X^- ion or a covalent structure containing an electron-pair bond. Ionic solids dissolve in water to give solutions that conduct electric current. AgCl, AgBr, and AgI are insoluble in water; addition of silver nitrate to an acid solution can be used as a test for the presence of these halide ions in aqueous solution. The precipitates, AgX, and their colors have been described.

8-7 HYDROGEN—A FAMILY BY ITSELF

Perhaps you are wondering why the element hydrogen was not included among the halogens. It is, after all, an element with one less electron than its neighboring inert gas, helium. We did not consider the process $H + e^- \longrightarrow H^-$. On the other hand, the hydrogen atom has but one electron and, in a sense, it is like an alkali metal. The removal of one electron from an alkali metal atom leaves a very stable electron configuration—that of a noble gas. The removal of one electron from a hydrogen atom leaves it with *no* electrons; this also interacts to give stable species. We shall see both of these influences in the chemistry of hydrogen. This element forms a family by itself; it has some similarities to the halogens and some similarities to the alkalies.

8-7.1 The Properties of Hydrogen Gas

Hydrogen is a diatomic gas like the halogens rather than a metal like the alkalies. Its melting point is 15.9 K and its boiling point is 20.4 K, the lowest boiling point for any element except helium.

EXERCISE 8-15

Describe the bond that holds two hydrogen atoms together in the molecule H_2.

8-7.2 Some Chemistry of Hydrogen

One of the most distinctive reactions characterizing both the alkalies *and* the halogens is their reaction with each other. The example we have discussed most is the reaction between sodium and chlorine to give sodium chloride. Sodium chloride is an ionic solid that dissolves in water to give positively charged sodium ions, $Na^+(aq)$, and negatively charged chloride ions, $Cl^-(aq)$:

$$Na(s) + \tfrac{1}{2}Cl_2(g) \longrightarrow NaCl(s) + energy \qquad (11)$$

$$NaCl(s) + water \longrightarrow Na^+(aq) + Cl^-(aq) \qquad (38)$$

TABLE 8-10 IONIZATION ENERGIES OF THE HALOGENS

Element	Ionization Energy (kcal/mole)
Fluorine	402
Chlorine	300
Bromine	273
Iodine	241

Fig. 8-13 A collision of gaseous halogen molecules.

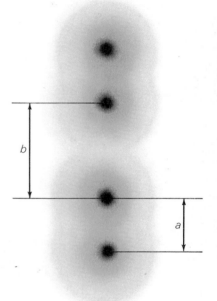

a = covalent bond length

Covalent radius = $\dfrac{a}{2}$

b = distance of closest approach of nuclei in molecular collision

Van der Waals radius = $\dfrac{b}{2}$

Does hydrogen react like sodium or chlorine? Experiments show that hydrogen can take *either* position; with chlorine the process is

$$\tfrac{1}{2}H_2(g) + \tfrac{1}{2}Cl_2(g) \longrightarrow HCl(g) \qquad (39)$$

With sodium the process is

$$Na(s) + \tfrac{1}{2}H_2(g) \longrightarrow NaH(s) \qquad (40)$$

The compound sodium hydride, formed in the reaction of hydrogen with sodium, is a crystalline compound with *physical* properties rather similar to those of sodium chloride. On the other hand, the *chemical* properties are very different. Whereas sodium burns readily in chlorine, sodium reacts with hydrogen only on heating to about 300 °C. While sodium chloride is a stable substance that dissolves in water to form $Na^+(aq)$ and $Cl^-(aq)$, sodium hydride is so reactive that it burns in air. In contact with water, sodium hydride gives a vigorous reaction to release hydrogen:

$$NaH(s) + H_2O(l) \longrightarrow H_2(g) + Na^+(aq) + OH^-(aq) \quad (41)$$

Thus, hydrogen reacts with sodium like a halogen does, but the product, sodium hydride, is very different in its chemistry from that of sodium chloride.

Hydrogen also reacts as does an alkali metal. Though the product, hydrogen chloride, is not an ionic solid like sodium chloride, it does dissolve in water to give aqueous ions.

$$HCl(g) + water \longrightarrow H^+(aq) + Cl^-(aq) \qquad (33)$$

The formation of $H^+(aq)$ and $Cl^-(aq)$ in water is strikingly like the formation of $Na^+(aq)$ and $Cl^-(aq)$ as salt dissolves in water.

$$NaCl(s) + water \longrightarrow Na^+(aq) + Cl^-(aq) \qquad (38)$$

In fact, the tendency of hydrogen to form a positively charged ion in water, $H^+(aq)$, and the absence of any evidence for a negatively charged ion in water, $H^-(aq)$, are two of the most significant differences between hydrogen and the halogens.

An overall view of the chemistry of hydrogen requires that it be classified alone—as a separate chemical family. There are some important similarities to halogens. For example, it is a stable diatomic gas. On the other hand, its chemistry is more like that of the alkalies. Hydrogen, therefore, is usually shown on the left side of the periodic table with the alkalies but separated from them to indicate its distinctive character.

8-8 THE ELEMENTS FROM THREE THROUGH TEN— THE SECOND ROW OF THE PERIODIC TABLE

When the first ionization energy for each element is plotted against its atomic number, a cyclic curve is obtained (Figure 8-1). By selecting the element with the maximum ionization energy for each cycle, it was possible to identify a group of relatively nonreactive gaseous elements called the noble gases. All members of this group or family had rather closely related properties. They were identified as a group of the periodic table. A second group was the reactive alkali metal family found at the *minimum* in each cycle of the ionization energy curve. Members of this group appear immediately after the noble gases (Figure 8-5) and exhibit strong similarities within the group. A third group studied was the halogens—the group of elements appearing just before the noble gases (Figure 8-10). Ionization energy values provided strong hints as to the type of chemistry that should be expected for each group, and the hints were fairly useful in considering the chemistry of alkalies and halogens.

Let us now examine the elements in a given cycle—for example, the elements from lithium (no. 3) through neon (no. 10) which make up the second cycle or the second row of the periodic table (Figure 8-14). We pass from Li with a minimum ionization energy to Ne with a maximum ionization energy. What happens in between? Let us examine the facts.

Fig. 8-14 The placement of the second row of the periodic table.

8-8.1 Trends in Physical Properties Across a Row of the Table—The Second Row

Lithium is a typical metal. It is bright and shiny in appearance (metallic luster); it can be rolled into sheets or formed into wire (malleable and ductile); it is a very good conductor of heat and electricity (one-sixth as good as copper); it has a low melting point and is soft enough to be cut with a knife (see Table 8-11, page 192). All these properties, except softness and low melting point, are characteristic properties by which we identify a metal. Lithium is truly metallic, yet because of its great chemical reactivity, it is not used as a metal in commerce. We never see objects made of metallic lithium.

Beryllium looks like a metal. It is steel gray in color and hard enough to scratch glass; it is very brittle. The brittle character is definitely not a metallic characteristic. Beryllium is a fair conductor of electricity—about half as good as lithium—and it combines with other metals to give metallic alloys. It is still quite metallic, although definitely less so than lithium.

TRENDS in PHYSICAL PROPERTIES

Description	Lithium	Beryllium	Boron	Carbon		Nitrogen	Oxygen	Fluorine
				Graphite	Diamond			
Form and appearance	silvery metal	steel-gray metal	black and red shiny crystals	gray-black plates	shiny diamond	colorless diatomic gas	colorless diatomic gas	yellow diatomic gas
Hardness (mohs scale)	very soft 0.6	scratches glass 6–7	very hard 9.3	soft 1.0	extremely hard 10 (std.)	gas —	gas —	gas —
Melting point (°C)	180	1283	2370	3600	3730 (est.)	−210	−218	−223
Boiling point (°C)	1326	2970	—	—	4830 (est.)	−196	−182	−188
*Electrical conductance (mhos)	excellent 10^5	good 5.4×10^4	poor† 2×10^{-5}	good 10^4	no	no	no	no
*Ductile and malleable‡	yes	no— brittle	no	no	no	no	no	no
*Metallic luster	yes	yes	yes	faint	no	no	no	no
Density (g/cm³)	0.53	1.86	2.30	2.1	3.5	0.96 (*solid*)	1.43 (*solid*)	1.1 (*liquid*)
Interesting properties	reactive metal	makes copper hard; alloys valuable	semi-conductor; useful in electronics; rods very strong	soft and slippery	hardest material known; nonmetal; low reactivity	nonmetal of low reactivity	moderately reactive nonmetal	most reactive non-metal known

*Characteristic of metal.
†Semiconductor of *p*-type (see Section 18-3.8).
‡Refer to property that permits substance to be drawn into wires or rolled into sheets.

With elemental or crystalline boron, most of the characteristics of a metal have disappeared. About the only metallic property remaining in boron is the metallic luster found on the red-to-black crystals. (Many forms of boron are known. One called α-T has red crystals; another, called β-R, has black crystals.) Boron is a semiconductor. This means that boron has potential value in electronics. On the other hand, it is a nonconductor compared to lithium. Its conductivity rises with temperature. Pure boron is very hard, being only slightly softer than diamond. It *cannot* be rolled into sheets or drawn into wires, but rods of boron can be amazingly strong and flexible and may find uses in commerce.

Carbon exists in two forms, diamond and graphite. You are all familiar with both of these. The diamond is strictly nonmetallic. It is the world's standard for hardness; it is brittle and a nonconductor of electricity. It has one of the highest melting and boiling points known to us (see Table 8-11). It is bright, sparkling, and romantic. Graphite, on the other hand, is drab. It is gray to black in color with a very weak metallic luster. It is used to make pencil "leads." It breaks into layers easily and is slippery. For this reason it is used as a dry lubricant and is added to oils. Graphite, in contrast to diamond, is a good conductor of electricity *along the layers,* but a poor conductor *at right angles to the layers.* You are probably familiar with other forms of carbon, such as lampblack, soot, and charcoal. These are composed, in large part, of very small crystals of graphite randomly arranged. Graphite has a few metallic characteristics such as electrical conductivity, but it really cannot be classed as a metal by any stretch of the imagination.

The elements nitrogen, oxygen, and fluorine are all low-boiling, diatomic gases. Fluorine is probably the prime example of a nonmetal. The transition from metallic lithium to nonmetallic fluorine has been made in distinct steps.

8-8.2 Trends in Chemical Properties Across the Second Row of the Periodic Table

What is the *chemistry* of this row like? Lithium is a very *reactive metal.* It burns vigorously in air, in chlorine gas, in fluorine gas, and in bromine vapor. It is this very reactivity that hides its metallic character. Typical compounds formed are listed in Table 8-12. At elevated temperatures lithium, like sodium, combines with H_2 to give LiH.

TABLE 8-12 FORMULAS OF SOME COMPOUNDS OF THE SECOND-ROW ELEMENTS

Group	I Li	II Be	III B	IV C	V N	VI O	VII F
Fluorides:	LiF	BeF_2	BF_3	CF_4	NF_3	OF_2	F_2
Ratio F/element	1	2	3	4	3	2	1
Chlorides:	LiCl	$BeCl_2$	BCl_3	CCl_4	NCl_3	OCl_2	ClF
Ratio Cl/element	1	2	3	4	3	2	1
Oxides:	Li_2O	BeO	B_2O_3	CO_2	N_2O_5	O_2	OF_2
Ratio O/element	0.5	1.0	1.5	2	2.5	1	0.5
Hydrides:	LiH	BeH_2	B_2H_6	CH_4	NH_3	H_2O	HF
Ratio H/element	1	2	3	4	3	2	1
Calcium:	—	—	—	CaC_2	Ca_3N_2	CaO	CaF_2
Ratio Ca/element	—	—	—	0.5	1.5	1.0	0.5

In general, beryllium has a much lower chemical reactivity than does lithium, but it does react with fluorine to give BeF_2, with Cl_2 to give $BeCl_2$, and with oxygen to give BeO. It does not combine directly with hydrogen, but a compound BeH_2 can be made by other means.

EXERCISE 8-16

How many electrons does oxygen need to achieve the neon structure? Justify the formula MgO.

Elemental boron is difficult to involve in a reaction. Does elemental boron represent a stable electron pattern like helium or neon? In considering this question, several facts are pertinent. First, boron, particularly if it is impure, will react at higher temperatures with fluorine, chlorine, and oxygen to give BF_3, BCl_3, and B_2O_3, respectively. Second, helium exists as isolated single atoms, not as helium clusters. Boron exists as a hard solid. *Boron atoms combine with themselves to give a stable, interlocked arrangement that is difficult to break up.* It appears that boron atoms, in contrast to helium atoms, are very reactive; however, boron atoms can react with other boron atoms to give a solid form of elemental boron that has low reactivity. Hence, the element *appears* to be inactive.

Pure crystalline diamond, like pure crystalline boron, is nonreactive; but it will burn in oxygen to give CO and CO_2 if heated to 800 °C. With Cl_2 and F_2, CCl_4 and CF_4 can be obtained, although not easily. Impure carbon or soot will react much more readily (compare with boron). Under appropriate conditions, carbon *atoms* are very reactive. They combine with hydrogen to give CH_4 and many other compounds. Chapter 19 is devoted to carbon chemistry. Carbon chemistry is one of the most important phases of modern science.

Nitrogen is a nonreactive gas at room temperature, but it becomes more reactive as the temperature rises. Its inert character is very important to us since it dilutes the oxygen of the air. Pure oxygen can have severe physiological effects if breathed for long periods of time. Since nitrogen is a gas, not a solid as is boron, we may properly ask: is the nitrogen electron configuration inert like helium and neon? Again, the answer is a definite and resounding "no"! Helium *atoms* are inert. They will not combine even with other helium atoms. On the other hand, nitrogen *atoms* are very reactive, but each combines so vigorously with another nitrogen atom that the resulting molecule, N_2, represents a very *stable* structure of relatively low reactivity. The large energy change associated with the formation of N_2 is shown by the equation:

$$2N(g) \longrightarrow N_2(g) + 225.8 \text{ kcal} \qquad (42)$$

Nitrogen will form a number of compounds with oxygen, including N_2O_3 and N_2O_5. The compounds NCl_3 and NF_3 can be produced by indirect methods. NCl_3 is a dangerously explosive material. NF_3 is more stable and has been considered as an oxidizer for rocket fuels; however, it has undesirable physical properties.

With hydrogen, under appropriate conditions, nitrogen forms the gaseous compound ammonia (NH_3):

$$N_2(g) + 3H_2(g) \longrightarrow 2NH_3(g) \qquad (43)$$

This is the equation for the Haber process, an extremely important commercial process that provides ammonia for everything from fertilizers to explosives, dyes, and nylon. With sodium, nitrogen forms the compound Na_3N.

Oxygen gas is much more reactive than nitrogen; we have already mentioned its combining with H, Li, B, Be, C, and N. It will also form compounds with F—for example, F_2O. The relatively high reactivity of oxygen, in comparison to that of nitrogen, can be attributed to the fact that two oxygen atoms combine with less vigor than do two nitrogen atoms. Let us compare the energies for the processes:

$$2N(g) \longrightarrow N_2(g) + 225.8 \text{ kcal} \qquad (42)$$

$$2O(g) \longrightarrow O_2(g) + 117 \text{ kcal} \qquad (44)$$

The fact that oxygen is more reactive than nitrogen reflects differences in the stabilities of the oxygen and nitrogen *molecules*—not necessarily differences in the stabilities of the electron patterns of the oxygen and nitrogen *atoms*. Oxygen gas is essential to most forms of life.

Fluorine is the most reactive element known. It combines directly at room temperature or above with all the elements except oxygen, nitrogen, and some gases of the helium family. As we have already noted, even the compounds OF_2 and NF_3 can be made indirectly, and a number of fluorides of the so-called "inert gas" or noble gas family are known (XeF_2, XeF_4, XeF_6). The energy for the reaction of two fluorine atoms is relatively low, as we might expect based on the trend across the table:

$$2F(g) \longrightarrow F_2(g) + 37.7 \text{ kcal} \qquad (45)$$

The very great reactivity of F_2 is closely related to this fact.

In summary, the metals from the left side of the table combine with the nonmetals from the right side of the table to give ionic solids. Ions such as M^+ and X^- suggest the stability and importance of the noble gas electron arrangements. This same stability is suggested by the next two elements, one from each side: Be forms Be^{2+} and oxygen forms O^{2-}. Be^{2+} has the helium configuration and O^{2-} has the neon configuration. An ionic lattice is formed. In CF_4, carbon *shares* its four electrons with four fluorine atoms to give four covalent bonds. Intermediate bond types lie between these extremes. The summary of formulas in Table 8-12 indicates the use of the table and of these concepts of bonding in writing formulas for compounds. The few cases such as CaC_2, which seem to be out of line, guarantee that we shall not run out of "wondering why" questions in the weeks ahead.

8-9 THE PERIODIC TABLE

The power of the **periodic table** is evident in the chemistry we have viewed. By arranging the elements as in Figure 8-15 (pages 196–197), we simplify the problem of understanding the variety of chemical characteristics found in nature. The elements grouped in a vertical column have pronounced similarities. General statements can be made about their chemistries and the compounds they form. Furthermore, the formulas of these compounds and the nature of the bonds that hold them together can be explained in terms of the especially stable electron arrangements of the noble gases.

The periodicity of chemical properties was discovered about 100 years ago. In 1828 J. W. Döbereiner, a German chemist, recognized similarities among certain elements (chlorine, bromine, and iodine;

lithium, sodium, and potassium; and so on). He grouped them as "triads." (Remember: "cylindrical objects burn.") J. A. R. Newlands, an English chemist, in 1864 was ridiculed for proposing a "law of octaves," which foresaw the differences of eight that we noted in Table 8-2. Simultaneously, Lothar Meyer, a German chemist and physicist, proposed a periodic table similar to Newlands'. Independently and in the same year (the time was ripe for the next step, "wooden objects burn"), D. I. Mendeleev, a Russian, framed the periodic table in more complete form. He even predicted both the existence and properties of elements not then known. The subsequent discovery of these elements and confirmation of their predicted properties solidified the acceptance of the periodic table. Mendeleev's table remains, 100 years later, as the most important single correlation of chemistry. It permits us to deal with the great variety of materials we find in nature.

8-10 MODELS AND PHYSICAL PROPERTIES—BONDING PATTERNS ACROSS THE SECOND ROW

It is relatively easy to understand the vaporization of the common gases O_2, N_2, and F_2. Separate, distinct, and self-sufficient molecules with

Fig. 8-15 The periodic table.

KEY

Atomic Number → 26 55.85 ← Atomic Weight
Symbol of Element → Fe
Iron ← Name of Element

IA	IIA							
1 1.0080 H Hydrogen								
3 6.941 Li Lithium	4 9.012 Be Beryllium							
11 22.990 Na Sodium	12 24.30 Mg Magnesium							
19 39.098 K Potassium	20 40.08 Ca Calcium	21 44.96 Sc Scandium	22 47.90 Ti Titanium	23 50.94 V Vanadium	24 52.00 Cr Chromium	25 54.94 Mn Manganese	26 55.85 Fe Iron	27 58.93 Co Cobalt
37 85.47 Rb Rubidium	38 87.62 Sr Strontium	39 88.91 Y Yttrium	40 91.22 Zr Zirconium	41 92.91 Nb Niobium	42 95.94 Mo Molybdenum	43 (97)▪ Tc Technetium	44 101.1 Ru Ruthenium	45 102.91 Rh Rhodium
55 132.90 Cs Cesium	56 137.34 Ba Barium	57–71 * below	72 178.49 Hf Hafnium	73 180.95 Ta Tantalum	74 183.85 W Tungsten	75 186.2 Re Rhenium	76 190.2 Os Osmium	77 192.2 Ir Iridium
87 (223)▪ Fr Francium	88 (226)▪ Ra Radium	89–103 ** below	104 (261)▪	105 (262)▪				
	* LANTHANIDE SERIES	57 138.91 La Lanthanum	58 140.12 Ce Cerium	59 140.92 Pr Praseodymium	60 144.24 Nd Neodymium	61 (145)▪ Pm Promethium	62 150.35 Sm Samarium	63 152.0 Eu Europium
	** ACTINIDE SERIES	89 (227)▪ Ac Actinium	90 232.04 Th Thorium	91 (231)▪ Pa Protactinium	92 238.03 U Uranium	93 (237)▪ Np Neptunium	94 (244)▪ Pu Plutonium	95 (243)▪ Am Americium

small forces of attraction acting between them make vaporization easy; boiling points and melting points are very low (Table 8-11). But what about the solid elements? How does their structure reflect the properties we summarized in Section 8-8.1? Let us begin with a view of the metals.

8-10.1 Metals

Metals, like ionic solids, have high boiling points. Lithium boils at 1326 °C, sodium at 889 °C, beryllium at 2970 °C, magnesium at 1110 °C, and aluminum at 2270 °C. These numbers indicate that forces between atoms extend over many atoms throughout the structure. Further, as we go across a row, boiling points for metals go up. Beryllium has a higher boiling point than lithium; magnesium (no. 12) is higher (1110 °C) than sodium (no. 11, 889 °C); and aluminum (no. 13) is higher (2270 °C) than magnesium. As more electrons become available in the bonding level, the boiling points go up. The forces between atoms get stronger. Further, the volume occupied by 1 mole of the metal gets smaller as we go from sodium to aluminum. The atoms are pulled more tightly together as more electrons are available in the bonding level. These facts, as well as the other physical

						VIIIA
						2 4.003 **He** Helium
IIIA	IVA	VA	VIA	VIIA		
5 10.81 **B** Boron	**6** 12.011 **C** Carbon	**7** 14.007 **N** Nitrogen	**8** 15.9994 **O** Oxygen	**9** 19.00 **F** Fluorine	**10** 20.179 **Ne** Neon	
13 26.98 **Al** Aluminum	**14** 28.09 **Si** Silicon	**15** 30.974 **P** Phosphorus	**16** 32.064 **S** Sulfur	**17** 35.453 **Cl** Chlorine	**18** 39.948 **Ar** Argon	

28 58.70 **Ni** Nickel	**29** 63.55 **Cu** Copper	**30** 65.38 **Zn** Zinc	**31** 69.72 **Ga** Gallium	**32** 72.59 **Ge** Germanium	**33** 74.92 **As** Arsenic	**34** 78.96 **Se** Selenium	**35** 79.904 **Br** Bromine	**36** 83.80 **Kr** Krypton
46 106.4 **Pd** Palladium	**47** 107.868 **Ag** Silver	**48** 112.40 **Cd** Cadmium	**49** 114.82 **In** Indium	**50** 118.69 **Sn** Tin	**51** 121.75 **Sb** Antimony	**52** 127.60 **Te** Tellurium	**53** 126.90 **I** Iodine	**54** 131.30 **Xe** Xenon
78 195.09 **Pt** Platinum	**79** 197.0 **Au** Gold	**80** 200.59 **Hg** Mercury	**81** 204.37 **Tl** Thallium	**82** 207.2 **Pb** Lead	**83** 208.98 **Bi** Bismuth	**84** (209)■ **Po** Polonium	**85** (210)■ **At** Astatine	**86** (222)■ **Rn** Radon

64 157.25 **Gd** Gadolinium	**65** 158.93 **Tb** Terbium	**66** 162.50 **Dy** Dysprosium	**67** 164.93 **Ho** Holmium	**68** 167.26 **Er** Erbium	**69** 168.93 **Tm** Thulium	**70** 173.04 **Yb** Ytterbium	**71** 174.97 **Lu** Lutetium
96 (247)■ **Cm** Curium	**97** (247)■ **Bk** Berkelium	**98** (251)■ **Cf** Californium	**99** (254)■ **Es** Einsteinium	**100** (257)■ **Fm** Fermium	**101** (258)■ **Md** Mendelevium	**102** (259)■ **No** Nobelium	**103** (260)■ **Lr** Lawrencium

Fig. 8-16 A segment of the structure of a metal.

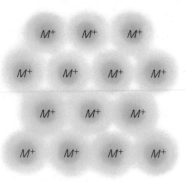

properties of a metal, are all consistent with a model in which we have metal ions arranged in a regular lattice with a "sea" of electrons moving among many atoms to hold them together in a giant structure (see Figure 8-16). Forces extend over many atoms. This sea of mobile electrons accounts for the electrical conductivity of the metal and for the ease with which it is deformed under pressure (easily deformed metals are said to be malleable and ductile). The more electrons available in the "sea," the stronger the bonds.

8-10.2 Network Solids

What about the diamond? The diamond represents a rigid network solid. Each atom is firmly bound by covalent bonds to four other atoms located at the corners of a regular tetrahedron (see Figure 8-17). This arrangement generates a giant, three-dimensional network; hence, the diamond is called a **network solid.** Because strong covalent bonds hold each atom in a rigid position, it is extremely difficult to break atoms away to obtain molecules or isolated atoms. Further, the structure is extremely hard since atoms are held firmly in a rigid position. Crystalline silicon is also a network solid with the same tetrahedral structure. But it does not have the hardness characteristic of diamond.

Beryllium and boron represent structures between these two extremes. Boron is closer to the network solid, and beryllium is closer to the metallic solid. We shall have more to say about such structures in Chapter 18.

Fig. 8-17 A segment of diamond structure.

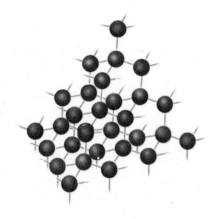

8-11 HIGHLIGHTS

The energy needed to separate one electron from a gaseous atom to give a singly charged gaseous ion and a free electron is the **first ionization energy** of the atom. The energy required to separate a second electron to get a doubly charged ion and a free electron is the **second ionization energy.** From values for ionization energies we identified stable electron patterns at elements no. 2, no. 10, and no. 18. This gave rise to a suggested model in which electrons for the first 20 elements are arranged in four general levels outside the nucleus. The first level contains two electrons, the second eight and the third eight, and the fourth has two, at which point we stopped development of the model. Using ionization energies as a guide, we could identify four families or groups of elements: the **noble gases,** the **alkali metals,** the **alkaline earth metals,** and the **halogens.** Elements in any group show remarkable similarities. These groups are the families of the **periodic table.** Members of these groups combine with themselves or other elements to form ionic, covalent, or metallic bonds.

In studying trends going across a row of the periodic table, we go from metals to nonmetals. The periodic table is very useful in correlating many facts on the chemical and physical properties of the elements. Proper use of the table and our electron model provides us with a basis for understanding the properties of gaseous elements such as N_2, O_2, and F_2; of metals such as Li, Be, Na, Mg, and Al; and of the network solids formed by such elements as C (diamond) and Si.

QUESTIONS and PROBLEMS

1 What does ionization energy measure? When we observe that an atom of one element has a higher ionization energy than an atom of another element, what does this mean about the two atoms being compared?

2 Why does it always take more energy to remove a second electron from an atom than it does to remove the first electron?

3 Which would you expect to have the *higher* first ionization energy in each of the following pairs of elements? Give reasons for each answer. (a) fluorine and chlorine (b) scandium and yttrium (c) rubidium and strontium (d) titanium and zirconium (e) sodium and cesium (f) potassium and calcium.

4 Elements 8, 9, and 10 (oxygen, fluorine, and neon) have first ionization energies of 314 kcal/mole, 402 kcal/mole, and 497 kcal/mole, respectively. (a) Explain this rather regular increase in ionization energy. (b) On the basis of the information given above *alone,* predict the ionization energy of element number 11 (sodium). (c) The actual ionization energy of sodium is 118 kcal/mole. Give a reason for the difference in this value from the value you predicted in (b) above.

5 The successive ionization energies for magnesium are 175 kcal/mole, 345 kcal/mole, 1,839 kcal/mole, and 2,512 kcal/mole. How many electrons does magnesium have in its outer energy level?

6 The successive ionization energies for aluminum are 137.9 kcal/mole, 432 kcal/mole, 653 kcal/mole, 2,753 kcal/mole, and 3,538 kcal/mole. How many electrons does aluminum have in its outer energy level?

7 Write the equation for the formation of the most stable ion from each of the elements listed below. Include energy as part of your balanced equation. (a) sodium (b) calcium (c) aluminum (d) rubidium (e) chlorine.

8 Which of the following combinations of atoms and ions do not *all* have the same number of electrons as a noble gas atom? (a) O^{2-}, Al^{3+}, F^- (b) Cs^+, Ba^{2+}, I^- (c) Na^+, O_2, Ne (d) Cl^-, Ca^{2+} (e) Br^-, Kr, Sr^{2+}.

9 On the basis of your knowledge of the periodic table, which of the following formulas are *not* reasonable? For any which are *not* reasonable, state the correct formula for the compound. (a) Na_2O (b) RbI (c) CaO (d) Mg_2O (e) Al_2O_3 (f) BaF_2 (g) BeCl (h) K_2S.

10 On the basis of your knowledge of the periodic table, determine which of the following are *not* reasonable reactions. For any which are *not,* rewrite the equation correctly.

(a) $K(g) + \text{energy} \longrightarrow K^+(g) + e^-$
(b) $F(g) + e^- \longrightarrow F^-(g) + \text{energy}$
(c) $Cl_2(g) \longrightarrow 2Cl^+(g) + 2e^- + \text{energy}$
(d) $Ne(g) + \text{energy} \longrightarrow Ne^+(g) + 2e^-$
(e) $Kr(g) + \text{energy} \longrightarrow Kr^-(g) + e^-$

11 Using the tables in this chapter, classify each of the following elements as a solid, liquid, or gas at (i) 25 °C and (ii) 100 °C. (a) sodium (b) bromine (c) iodine (d) neon (e) lithium (f) potassium.

12 Below are the physical properties of a family of elements. Estimate physical properties of the missing element, gallium.

	Boron	Aluminum	Gallium
Form and appearance	black and red shiny crystals	silvery-white metal	
Melting point, °C	2370	660	
Electrical conductivity	poor	excellent	
Ductile and malleable	no	excellent	
Metallic luster	no	yes	
Density, g/cm³	2.30	2.69	

13 On the basis of the information in Tables 8-5 and 8-9, predict the physical properties of astatine and francium. For each element, write three chemical reactions which are typical of the element.

14 Using the information in Table 8-12, write the chemical formulas for the fluorides of the third row elements.

15 Write balanced chemical equations for the following reactions: (a) lithium reacting with chlorine; (b) potassium reacting with water; (c) magnesium reacting with fluorine; (d) hydrogen reacting with liquid bromine.

16 To which chemical family (IA, IIA, VIA, VIIA, or VIII) must each of the following belong? (a) Element *A* combines with oxygen to form the compound *A*O. (b) Element *B* is gaseous and chemically nonreactive. (c) Element *C* combines with element *D* to form the compound *CD*. Element *C* also reacts vigorously with water, releasing hydrogen gas. (d) Element *E* reacts with element *C* to form a compound having the formula C_2E. (e) If these elements are found successively in the periodic table, what is their order?

Although a typical chemical reaction . . . may appear far removed from the working of an engine, the same fundamental principles of heat and work apply to both.

F. T. WALL (1912–   )

ENERGY CHANGES IN CHEMICAL 9 AND NUCLEAR REACTIONS

Chemical reactions such as this supply much of the world's energy.

WHY DOES A CANDLE GIVE OFF HEAT? WHERE DOES THE HEAT COME from? How does the heat get into the candle in the first place? And what relationship is there between these questions and the dull old saying, "You get out of something what you put into it"?

The most dramatic—and sometimes the most useful—chemical reactions are those which produce large amounts of energy. We use these reactions to heat our houses, alter our landscape, and run our factories and cars. The amount of energy available from a chemical reaction depends on how much energy is stored in the reactants and products of that reaction. This chapter will explore such energy relationships.

Every chemical reaction has energy changes associated with it. In many cases the energy changes are the most important feature of a chemical process. We have only to recall the fire that warmed Martin the Martian in our fable and the gasoline that powers our cars. The chemical process in each case is important only for the energy released by the reaction. In the automobile, a *mixture* of gasoline vapor and air is ignited in the cylinders, releasing a predictable amount of energy. How far the energy drives the car depends on the efficiency of the automobile, but the car will not move at all unless *gasoline and air react*. Both gasoline and oxygen are essential for combustion in the cylinders. Even a piece of chocolate cake is important ultimately because of its ability to provide energy to the "human machine." It is "burned" with oxygen in the cells of the body.

Energy changes in chemical processes are always important and frequently even critical. What can we learn about them? How much energy is associated with a given process? How is the energy change measured? Where does the energy come from? The questions come thick and fast. We have touched on some of these questions in earlier chapters. In this chapter we shall examine them in more detail.

9-1 ENERGY CHANGES AND CHEMICAL REACTIONS

In the laboratory we studied the heat* released when a given mass of our candle burned. Knowledge of the energy change associated with a laboratory process is helpful in understanding the process. Knowledge of the energy change associated with an industrial process is essential for economic survival.

The newspapers tell of an energy crisis and of a shortage of natural gas and oil. Soon we may be forced back completely to an old process for generating fuel gas from coal. Let us look in on the operation of this important industry in which coal is converted to a more convenient energy source—"water gas."

A jet of steam at 600 °C is forced through a bed of red-hot coke,† producing a mixture of carbon monoxide and hydrogen known as

---

*The common term for thermal energy released in a process is heat; however, we shall usually use the more precise terms thermal energy, electrical energy, and so on.
†Coke is almost pure carbon produced by heating coal.

"water gas." This is now an important industrial fuel. The gases coming out of the reactor first contain a high percentage of CO and H_2 and very little unreacted water vapor; but as the steam flow continues, the red-hot coke cools and the yield of water gas drops. Less and less CO and H_2 appear in the product gases, and more unreacted water vapor is found. At this point the operator turns off the steam and blows air through the coke bed. As the coke begins to burn in the air stream, it again becomes red hot. The operator now forces steam into the hot bed of coke and the cycle is repeated. Two qualitative observations seem to be clear.

(1) Energy (heat) is *absorbed* when steam or water vapor combines with hot coke to give water gas. (The coke cools off; therefore, heat is absorbed in water-gas production.)
(2) Energy (heat) is *liberated* when coke is burned in oxygen. (The coke heats up; therefore, heat is released.)

9-1.1 Some Quantitative Energy Relationships

Chemical engineers responsible for the manufacture of water gas cannot be as casual about the energy changes in each process as we have been. They must know how much energy (heat) is involved in each case if the employer is to remain in business. Let us check an engineer's lab notebook. The measurements show that in producing water gas 31.4 kcal of heat are absorbed for every mole of carbon converted to CO. All the observations can be summarized neatly by the equation

$$H_2O(g) + C(s) + 31.4 \text{ kcal} \longrightarrow CO(g) + H_2(g) \qquad (1)$$

We can represent the measurements on the combustion of coke by the equation

$$C(s) + O_2(g) \longrightarrow CO_2(g) + 94.0 \text{ kcal} \qquad (2)$$

A good chemical engineer will try to balance the two processes so that the heat given off in burning coke is just enough to supply the energy needed for the water-gas synthesis—the cycles must be properly timed. If excess coke is burned, valuable energy goes up the chimney or into the room. If the system is not hot enough, the yield of CO and H_2 drops.

The consumer's measurements on the burning of the water-gas fuel can best be summarized by two equations, one describing the burning of CO and the other describing the burning of H_2:

$$CO(g) + \tfrac{1}{2}O_2(g) \longrightarrow CO_2(g) + 67.6 \text{ kcal} \qquad (3)$$

$$H_2(g) + \tfrac{1}{2}O_2(g) \longrightarrow H_2O(g) + 57.8 \text{ kcal} \qquad (4)$$

If the water gas containing 1 mole of carbon is burned, the total heat released is 67.6 kcal + 57.8 kcal = 125.4 kcal. This is much more heat than can be obtained by burning 1 mole of carbon directly:

$$C(s) + O_2(g) \longrightarrow CO_2(g) + 94.0 \text{ kcal} \qquad (2)$$

The difference is $125.4 - 94.0 = 31.4$ kcal. The consumer seems to be doing better than the chemical engineer in obtaining energy from 1 mole of coke. The consumer obtains 31.4 kcal *more energy* from 1 mole of carbon as water gas than does the chemical engineer from 1 mole of carbon as coke. In comparing the skills of our engineer and consumer, the number 31.4 kcal suddenly seems familiar. This is the very number that appeared in the equation given earlier for the manufacture of water gas:

$$H_2O(g) + C(s) + 31.4 \text{ kcal} \longrightarrow H_2(g) + CO(g) \quad (1)$$

Refer to Table 9-1. The table shows that extra energy *stored* in the CO and H_2 became available to the consumer when the gas was burned. The chemical engineer obtained the extra energy from burning *extra* coke directly. (Remember: it was a two-cycle process—one cycle absorbed heat and one cycle gave off heat.) *The water gas released more energy per mole of carbon than did coke because extra energy was stored in the water gas when it was made.*

TABLE **9-1** SOME ENERGY CHANGES IN THE MANUFACTURE AND USE OF WATER GAS

Reaction	Debit	Credit
Energy absorbed: $H_2O(g) + C(s) + 31.4 \text{ kcal} \longrightarrow CO(g) + H_2(g)$	31.4 kcal	
Energy released: $CO(g) + \frac{1}{2}O_2(g) \longrightarrow CO_2(g) + 67.6 \text{ kcal}$		67.6 kcal
Energy released: $H_2(g) + \frac{1}{2}O_2(g) \longrightarrow H_2O(g) + 57.8 \text{ kcal}$		57.8 kcal
Overall reaction (total of above): $C(s) + O_2(g) \longrightarrow CO_2(g)$	31.4 kcal absorbed	125.4 kcal released
Net		125.4 -31.4 94.0
Experimental value for $C(s) + O_2(g) \longrightarrow CO_2(g)$		94.0 kcal released

9-1.2 Enthalpy or Heat Content of a Substance

The example just given shows that energy amounting to 31.4 kcal was stored in the water gas. We see also that the amount of energy stored per mole of carbon is constant. *We added a fixed amount of energy to coke and steam to make a specified amount of carbon monoxide and hydrogen.* The heat is retained by both the CO and H_2. We cannot decide how much of the heat is in the CO and how much is in the H_2 without doing additional laboratory work. However, we can say that the "heat content" of the gas mixture, 1 mole CO + 1 mole H_2, derived from 1 mole of coke and 1 mole of steam, is higher by 31.4 kcal than the "heat content" of 1 mole of coke and 1 mole of steam. With a little more work, we can find out how much of the energy is stored in the CO and how much is stored in the H_2. One mole of carbon monoxide has a characteristic "heat content" just as it has a characteristic mass. Similarly, 1 mole of H_2 has a characteristic heat content. Chemists call the energy stored in a substance the **heat content** or **enthalpy** of the substance. Thus 1 mole of any substance has a characteristic heat content or enthalpy.

This idea provides a good explanation of the energy changes associated with chemical reactions. If the reactants have more energy than the products, energy will be *released* during the reaction. Conversely, if the products have more energy than the reactants, energy will be *absorbed* during the reaction. These two statements can be put into one equation:

$$\begin{Bmatrix} \text{change in heat} \\ \text{content or enthalpy} \\ \text{of the system} \end{Bmatrix} = \begin{Bmatrix} \text{heat content} \\ \text{or enthalpy} \\ \text{of products} \end{Bmatrix} - \begin{Bmatrix} \text{heat content} \\ \text{or enthalpy} \\ \text{of reactants} \end{Bmatrix} \quad (5)$$

The enthalpy of a substance is represented by the letter H. The enthalpy of 1 mole of CO is then indicated as H_{CO}, that of H_2 as H_{H_2} and that of steam as H_{H_2O}. The change in enthalpy in a reaction is represented by ΔH where Δ signifies "difference" or "change." ΔH is often called the **heat of reaction.**

For the process $C(s) + O_2(g) \longrightarrow CO_2(g)$ we would write

$$\Delta H = H_{CO_2} - H_C - H_{O_2} \quad (6)$$

9-1.3 Additivity of Heats of Reaction

Let us apply our newly defined symbolism to the processes involved in the production and use of water gas. In terms of ΔH the energy changes can be summarized as follows: the manufacture of water gas absorbs energy; hence, the enthalpy (heat content) of the products is higher than the enthalpy of the reactants.

$$\Delta H = \text{enthalpy of products} - \text{enthalpy of reactants} \quad (5)$$

We see that ΔH for the process will be positive in this case. We can express this by writing

$$H_2O(g) + C(s) \longrightarrow CO(g) + H_2(g)$$
$$\Delta H = +31.4 \text{ kcal} \quad (1a)$$

The reaction as written is exactly equivalent to the earlier representation

$$H_2O(g) + C(s) + 31.4 \text{ kcal} \longrightarrow CO(g) + H_2(g) \quad (1)$$

If the value of ΔH is positive for a reaction, the process is **endo-thermic**—energy is absorbed during the process.

For an **exothermic** reaction—one evolving energy—ΔH is negative. In the burning of CO, energy in the form of heat is released. We write

$$CO(g) + \tfrac{1}{2}O_2(g) \longrightarrow CO_2(g) + 67.6 \text{ kcal} \qquad (3)$$

This has exactly the same meaning as

$$CO(g) + \tfrac{1}{2}O_2(g) \longrightarrow CO_2(g)$$
$$\Delta H = -67.6 \text{ kcal} \qquad (3a)$$

We see that the sign of ΔH is sensible. It is positive when the heat content or enthalpy of the system is rising (heat absorption), and it is negative when enthalpy is dropping (heat given off). This is shown diagrammatically in Figure 9-1.

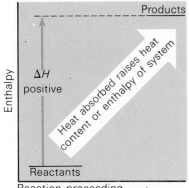

Reaction proceeding $\longrightarrow$
Energy is absorbed
ΔH is positive

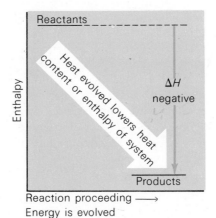

Reaction proceeding $\longrightarrow$
Energy is evolved
ΔH is negative

Fig. 9-1 Enthalpy changes during reactions.

Let us return to the debit and credit balance we found in our water-gas fuel problem. In terms of ΔH, the energy changes are as follows:

$$H_2O(g) + C(s) \longrightarrow CO(g) + H_2(g)$$
$$\Delta H_{1a} = +31.4 \text{ kcal} \qquad (1a)$$

$$CO(g) + \tfrac{1}{2}O_2(g) \longrightarrow CO_2(g)$$
$$\Delta H_{3a} = -67.6 \text{ kcal} \qquad (3a)$$

$$H_2(g) + \tfrac{1}{2}O_2(g) \longrightarrow H_2O(g)$$
$$\Delta H_{4a} = -57.8 \text{ kcal} \qquad (4a)$$

The overall reaction, $(1a) + (3a) + (4a) = (2a)$, is

$$C(s) + O_2(g) \longrightarrow CO_2(g)$$
$$\Delta H_{2a} = -94.0 \text{ kcal} \qquad (2a)$$

We discover that not only is reaction (2a) equal to the sum of reactions (1a) + (3a) + (4a) in terms of atoms, but also that

$$\Delta H_{2a} = \Delta H_{1a} + \Delta H_{3a} + \Delta H_{4a} \qquad (7)$$
$$= [31.4 + (-67.6) + (-57.8)] \text{ kcal}$$
$$= (31.4 - 67.6 - 57.8) \text{ kcal}$$
$$= -94.0 \text{ kcal}$$

We see that *when a reaction can be expressed as the algebraic sum of a sequence of two or more other reactions, then the heat of the reaction is the algebraic sum of the heats of these reactions.* This generalization has been found to be applicable to every reaction that has been tested. Because the generalization has been so widely tested, it is called a law—the **Law of Additivity of Heats of Reaction.***

9-1.4   The Measurement of Heats of Reaction

The measurement of the energy changes associated with a given process is achieved by the process of **calorimetry**—a name obviously related to one unit of thermal energy, the calorie. You already have some experience in calorimetry. In Experiment 9 you measured the heat of combustion of a candle and then the heat of solidification of several substances. Then in Experiment 17 you measured the energy evolved when NaOH reacted with HCl. The device you used was a simple calorimeter. Calorimeters vary in details and are adapted to the particular reaction being studied.

EXERCISE 9-1

If a 1.000-g sample of carbon is burned to CO_2 and liberates 7.833 kcal of energy, what is the heat of combustion of 1 mole of carbon atoms?

9-1.5   Predicting the Heat of a Reaction

The heats of many reactions have been measured. (A few are listed in Table 9-2.) With these measured values and the additivity principle, many unmeasured heats of reaction can be predicted.

Suppose we are interested in the heat of combustion of nitric oxide (NO). The appropriate equation is

$$NO(g) + \tfrac{1}{2}O_2(g) \longrightarrow NO_2(g) \qquad \Delta H_8 = ? \qquad (8)$$

Since the above equation can be obtained by combining two equations in Table 9-2, we can predict ΔH_8. In Table 9-2 we find the two reactions that involve the compounds $NO(g)$, $NO_2(g)$, and the element O_2:

*This generalization was first proposed in 1840 by G. H. Hess on the basis of his experimental measurements of reaction heats. It is sometimes called **Hess's Law of Constant Heat Summation.**

TABLE 9-2 HEATS OF REACTION BETWEEN ELEMENTS
($T = 25\,°C$, $P = 1$ atm)

| Elements | Compound (Product) | | Heat of Reaction (kcal/mole) of product) |
	Formula	Name	
$H_2(g) + \frac{1}{2}O_2(g) \longrightarrow$	$H_2O(g)$	water vapor	-57.8
$H_2(g) + \frac{1}{2}O_2(g) \longrightarrow$	$H_2O(l)$	water	-68.3
$S(s) + O_2(g) \longrightarrow$	$SO_2(g)$	sulfur dioxide	-71.0
$H_2(g) + S(s) + 2\,O_2(g) \longrightarrow$	$H_2SO_4(l)$	sulfuric acid	-194.0
$\frac{1}{2}N_2(g) + \frac{1}{2}O_2(g) \longrightarrow$	$NO(g)$	nitric oxide	$+21.6$
$\frac{1}{2}N_2(g) + O_2(g) \longrightarrow$	$NO_2(g)$	nitrogen dioxide	$+8.1$
$\frac{1}{2}N_2(g) + \frac{3}{2}H_2(g) \longrightarrow$	$NH_3(g)$	ammonia	-11.0
$C(s) + \frac{1}{2}O_2(g) \longrightarrow$	$CO(g)$	carbon monoxide	-26.4
$C(s) + O_2(g) \longrightarrow$	$CO_2(g)$	carbon dioxide	-94.0
$C(s) + 2H_2(g) \longrightarrow$	$CH_4(g)$	methane	-17.8
$2C(s) + 3H_2(g) \longrightarrow$	$C_2H_6(g)$	ethane	-20.2
$3C(s) + 4H_2(g) \longrightarrow$	$C_3H_8(g)$	propane	-24.8
$\frac{1}{2}H_2(g) + \frac{1}{2}I_2(g) \longrightarrow$	$HI(g)$	hydrogen iodide	$+6.2$

$$\frac{1}{2}N_2(g) + \frac{1}{2}O_2(g) \longrightarrow NO(g)$$
$$\Delta H_9 = +21.6 \text{ kcal/mole NO} \qquad (9)$$

$$\frac{1}{2}N_2(g) + O_2(g) \longrightarrow NO_2(g)$$
$$\Delta H_{10} = +8.1 \text{ kcal/mole NO}_2 \qquad (10)$$

Obviously, the addition of the above two equations will not give $NO(g) + \frac{1}{2}O_2(g) \longrightarrow NO_2(g)$. Since NO is a reactant in this process, we need the reverse of the reaction producing NO. Thus, if 21.6 kcal of heat are absorbed when 1 mole of NO is formed, then 21.6 kcal of heat will be released when 1 mole of NO is decomposed:

$$NO(g) \longrightarrow \frac{1}{2}N_2(g) + \frac{1}{2}O_2(g)$$
$$\Delta H_{11} = -21.6 \text{ kcal/mole NO} \qquad (11)$$

Adding the appropriate reactions does give the equation for oxidation of NO to NO_2.

$$\frac{1}{2}N_2(g) + O_2(g) \longrightarrow NO_2(g)$$
$$\Delta H_{10} = +8.1 \text{ kcal/mole NO}_2 \qquad (10)$$

$$NO(g) \longrightarrow \frac{1}{2}N_2(g) + \frac{1}{2}O_2(g)$$
$$\Delta H_{11} = -21.6 \text{ kcal/mole NO} \qquad (11)$$

The overall reaction is

$$NO(g) + O_2(g) + \frac{1}{2}N_2(g) \longrightarrow NO_2(g) + \frac{1}{2}O_2(g) + \frac{1}{2}N_2(g)$$
$$\Delta H_8 = 8.1 + (-21.6) \text{ kcal} \qquad (8a)$$

or

$$NO(g) + \frac{1}{2}O_2(g) \longrightarrow NO_2(g)$$
$$\Delta H_8 = -13.5 \text{ kcal/mole NO} \qquad (8)$$

EXERCISE 9-2

Predict the heat of the reaction

$$CO(g) + \tfrac{1}{2}O_2(g) \longrightarrow CO_2(g)$$

from two appropriate reactions listed in Table 9-2. Compare your results with ΔH_{3a} given in Section 9-1.3.

EXERCISE 9-3

Predict the heat of the reaction

$$CH_4(g) + 2\,O_2(g) \longrightarrow CO_2(g) + 2H_2O(g)$$

Which is the better fuel, 1 mole of CO or 1 mole of CH_4?

We can predict the heat of any reaction that can be obtained by adding two or more of the reactions in Table 9-2. *A given reaction can be obtained by adding reactions or appropriate multiples of reactions from Table 9-2, provided every compound in the reaction is included in the table.* If appropriate multiples are used, the elements involved in the reactions will appear in proper amounts.

Consider a more complicated example—the oxidation of ammonia (NH_3):

$$NH_3(g) + \tfrac{7}{4}O_2(g) \longrightarrow NO_2(g) + \tfrac{3}{2}H_2O(g) \qquad (12)$$

We find three compounds—$NH_3(g)$, $NO_2(g)$, and $H_2O(g)$. These are all found in Table 9-2. Consequently, we are able to calculate ΔH for the oxidation of ammonia.

EXERCISE 9-4

Show that the equation for ammonia oxidation is the result of adding the following equations, and that its $\Delta H = -67.6$ kcal.

$$NH_3(g) \longrightarrow \tfrac{1}{2}N_2(g) + \tfrac{3}{2}H_2(g) \qquad \Delta H = +11.0 \text{ kcal}$$

$$\tfrac{1}{2}N_2(g) + O_2(g) \longrightarrow NO_2(g) \qquad \Delta H = +8.1 \text{ kcal}$$

$$\tfrac{3}{2} \times [H_2(g) + \tfrac{1}{2}O_2(g) \longrightarrow H_2O(g)] \qquad \tfrac{3}{2} \times [\Delta H = -57.8 \text{ kcal}]$$

Thus, when we wish to predict the heat of some reaction, we refer to Table 9-2. If every *compound* in the reaction of interest is in the "compound" column of Table 9-2, then the prediction can be made. Of course, the list in Table 9-2 includes only a small fraction of the known values. Many more heats of reaction are tabulated in handbooks under "Heat of Formation." The heat of formation reported is the ΔH value for the formation of 1 mole of the compound from its elements taken at 25 °C and 1 atm. By convention, the ΔH value for the formation of *all elements* at 25 °C and 1 atm is taken as zero.

By now you have probably made an observation which leads to a shortcut. The result of adding the equations for compound formation together is identical to that obtained by adding the enthalpy of formation of all products together and subtracting the enthalpy of formation of all reactants. Let us see how this works. For equation (12) we can write

$$\Delta H_{\substack{\text{for oxidation} \\ \text{of ammonia}}} =$$

$$\left\{ \Delta H_{\substack{\text{formation} \\ \text{NO}_2(g)}} + \tfrac{3}{2}\Delta H_{\substack{\text{formation} \\ \text{H}_2\text{O}(g)}} \right\} - \left\{ \Delta H_{\substack{\text{formation} \\ \text{NH}_3(g)}} + \tfrac{7}{4}\Delta H_{\substack{\text{formation} \\ \text{O}_2(g)}} \right\} \qquad (13)$$

Or using values from Table 9-2, we write

$$\Delta H = [8.1 + \tfrac{3}{2}(-57.8)] - (-11.0 + 0) = -67.6$$

The general statement is

$$\Delta H_{\text{process}} =$$

$$\text{sum of } \Delta H_{\substack{\text{formation values} \\ \text{for products}}} - \text{sum of } \Delta H_{\substack{\text{formation values} \\ \text{for reactants}}} \qquad (14)$$

9-2 THE CONSERVATION OF ENERGY

The Law of Additivity of Heats of Reaction is a very useful and reliable generalization. But we wonder: why should this be so? The explanation, as usual, is found by examining a model system—a system of billiard balls.

9-2.1 Conservation of Energy in a Billiard-Ball Collision

In a billiard game the amount of kinetic energy received by the ball is fixed by the amount of work done on it. If the cue stick strikes the ball softly, the ball moves slowly; if the cue stick strikes it hard, the ball moves rapidly. The amount of work done on the ball (W) determines and equals the amount of kinetic energy (KE) which the ball will possess:

$$W = KE \qquad (15)$$

If this ball strikes another ball, the energy that it *loses* in the collision is exactly equal to the energy *gained* by the second ball. Even in a billiard parlor, energy is conserved.

9-2.2 Conservation of Energy in the Storage of Billiard Balls—Potential Energy

When billiard balls are stored, energy (work) is used to lift them from the billiard table to the shelf above. If the balls roll off the shelf, they gain speed, hence kinetic energy, as they fall. The **kinetic energy** (energy of motion) they possess just before hitting the table is equal to the energy used in lifting them to the shelf. While they are stored,

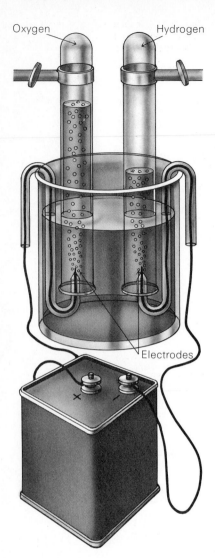

Oxygen   Hydrogen

Electrodes

Fig. 9-2 Apparatus for the electrolytic decomposition of water.

this same amount of energy is called **potential energy** (energy of position). When a ball falls from the shelf and strikes the table, the potential energy is converted to kinetic energy, which is in turn transformed into heat. The billiard ball and the table are both warmer after the collision than they were before. The amount of heat given to the ball and table is determined by the change in the kinetic energy of the ball. Again, energy is conserved throughout every operation.

EXERCISE 9-5

(1) A rubber band is stretched onto a toy gun. Work, W, is expended in the stretching. Is energy conserved? Explain.
(2) If a rubber band is stretched, then released, then stretched again and released, and the process is repeated many times, the band gets warm. Why?
(3) Why does an automobile tire heat up as it is driven on a bumpy road?

9-2.3 Conservation of Energy in a Chemical Reaction

Figure 9-2 shows an apparatus in which an electric current can be passed through water containing a few drops of sulfuric acid per litre. Under the conditions shown, the passage of the current causes the decomposition of the water. As electrical energy is supplied, hydrogen gas and oxygen gas are produced. Measurements of the electric current and voltage show that 68.3 kcal of electrical energy, E_1, must be expended to decompose 1 mole of water. The equation for the reaction is

$$\begin{Bmatrix} 68.3 \text{ kcal} \\ \text{electrical} \\ \text{energy} \end{Bmatrix} + H_2O(l) \longrightarrow H_2(g) + \tfrac{1}{2}O_2(g) \qquad (16)$$

Now suppose we measure the heat of the reaction of hydrogen and oxygen in a calorimeter. The results of many experiments show that 68.3 kcal of energy will be liberated for every mole of water formed. The equation for the reaction can then be written as

$$H_2(g) + \tfrac{1}{2}O_2(g) \longrightarrow H_2O(l) + 68.3 \text{ kcal}$$
$$\Delta H = -68.3 \text{ kcal} \qquad (17)$$

The energy recovered is exactly equal to that stored in the system when hydrogen and oxygen were generated from the water by the electric current. Symbolically, energy added by the electric current E_1 is equal to the energy $-\Delta H$ released in the combustion:

$$E_1 = -\Delta H = 68.3 \text{ kcal} \qquad (18)$$

Hydrogen and oxygen have more potential energy than water, just as the billiard ball on the shelf has more potential energy than the one on the table. As we shall see later, the energy stored in H_2 and O_2 is truly energy of position—energy due to the position of atoms in each substance. Energy is released when the atoms take up new positions to form water. The relationship between atom position and energy content of the system is illustrated in Figure 9-3. Note that H and O atoms have different relative positions after each process.

Fig. 9-3 Conservation of energy in a chemical reaction. The energy absorbed in reaction (a),

$$2H_2O(l) + E \longrightarrow 2H_2(g) + O_2(g)$$

equals the energy evolved in reaction (b),

$$2H_2(g) + O_2(g) \longrightarrow 2H_2O(l) + \Delta H$$

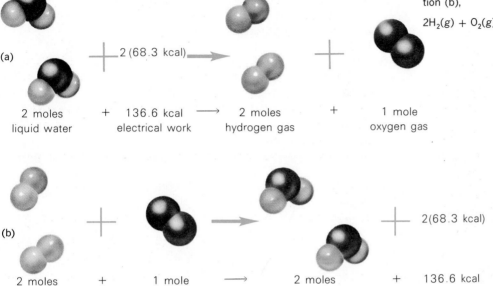

(a)

2 (68.3 kcal)

| 2 moles liquid water | + | 136.6 kcal electrical work | $\longrightarrow$ | 2 moles hydrogen gas | + | 1 mole oxygen gas |

(b)

2(68.3 kcal)

| 2 moles hydrogen gas | + | 1 mole oxygen gas | $\longrightarrow$ | 2 moles liquid water | + | 136.6 kcal Heat |

The relationships of Figure 9-3 can be represented schematically by another type of diagram shown in Figure 9-4. If the enthalpy of 2 moles of water is represented by a line on this diagram, then the energy of 2 moles of hydrogen plus 1 mole of oxygen should be represented by a line $2 \times 68.3 = 136.6$ kcal higher. The diagram shows that when water is decomposed, energy must be supplied to raise the enthalpy of the system to that of $2H_2$ plus O_2. When hydrogen burns in oxygen, the enthalpy of the system drops down to that for water. *Energy is released.*

Energy is conserved in chemical processes as well as in systems involving billiard balls (and rubber bands, Exercise 9-5). An important

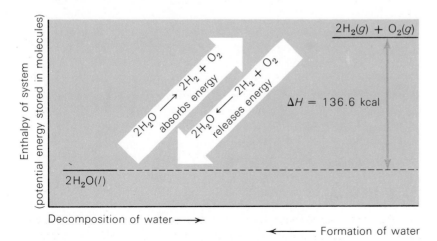

Enthalpy of system (potential energy stored in molecules)

$2H_2(g) + O_2(g)$

$2H_2O \longrightarrow 2H_2 + O_2$ absorbs energy

$2H_2O \longleftarrow 2H_2 + O_2$ releases energy

$\Delta H = 136.6$ kcal

$2H_2O(l)$

Decomposition of water $\longrightarrow$

$\longleftarrow$ Formation of water

Fig. 9-4 Enthalpy changes in the decomposition and formation of water.

CONSERVATION of ENERGY in a CHEMICAL REACTION

idea arises from this discussion. Each molecule has kinetic energy due to its movement through space (indicated by its temperature), and each molecule has potential energy due to the arrangement of atoms in the molecule. In short, each molecule has a certain capacity to store energy; it has a definite heat content or enthalpy at a given temperature. As the temperature is raised, more energy is stored.

9-2.4   The Law of Conservation of Energy

After we recognized both *kinetic* and *potential* energy, it was easy to see that energy was conserved in each of the systems we studied. Our specific observations can be generalized. For all systems studied* *energy is always conserved!* This is the Law of Conservation of Energy. It is based on thousands and thousands of experiments and can be used to make very accurate predictions. It requires only that we recognize both kinetic and potential energy and keep a careful balance on both.

The Law of Additivity of Heats of Reaction considered earlier for chemical systems is simply a special case of the more general Law of Conservation of Energy. Predictions based on the Law of Additivity of Heats of Reaction have always agreed with experiment. Conservation of energy has *always* been in agreement with experiment whenever a careful energy balance has been obtained.

9-3   THE ENERGY STORED IN A MOLECULE

In Sections 9-2.1 to 9-2.4 we considered energy changes associated with quantities of matter that we could handle in the laboratory. We found it useful to consider kinetic energy, the energy of motion, and potential energy, the energy of position. We also found it useful to use more common terms such as heat or thermal energy, chemical energy for energy stored in molecules such as H_2 and O_2, electrical energy, and mechanical energy associated with particle movement. In every case, special techniques were required to measure the energy changes in the system. For example, heat energy was measured in a calorimeter; electrical energy would be measured by using a voltmeter, an ammeter, and a watch.

Because different techniques were used in measuring each form of energy, our classification scheme was useful. On the other hand, when we wish to discuss matter and energy on the molecular level—by considering a few molecules rather than a few grams—we find that it is not necessary to use all these different forms of energy to describe molecular behavior. Only the first two forms of energy are needed— kinetic energy and potential energy. We can "explain" all the forms of energy by a molecular model that uses only the energy of motion (kinetic energy) and the energy of position (potential energy) for the molecules and their parts. Let us examine in more detail the ways in which a molecule can hold energy.

*For nuclear systems this statement is true when we recognize the equivalence of mass and energy. See Section 9-4.

9-3.1 The Energy of a Molecule

We shall represent a molecule such as carbon dioxide by three balls of comparable mass held together by springs (see Figure 9-5). The springs represent the bonds between the atoms. Let us start the springs vibrating, then toss the whole assembly through space in an end-over-end motion. There are now three kinds of motion associated with our molecule:

(1) There is the **energy of translation** associated with the motion of the entire molecular assembly through space [see Figure 9-5(a)]. (This is our original *gas-law kinetic energy*.)
(2) There is the **energy of rotation** associated with the end-over-end motion of the molecule as it twirls through space. This is the *rotational kinetic energy* [Figure 9-5(b)].
(3) There is the **energy of vibration** associated with the vibration of the balls on the springs, or the *vibrational kinetic energy* [Figure 9-5(c)].

The above model applies reasonably well to a molecule in the gaseous state, but in the liquid state and (even more so) in the solid state, all the molecular motions are restricted. In these condensed phases the translational molecular motion is restricted almost completely to a back-and-forth motion of the balls about a given point. Rotation and vibration are also frequently restricted.

In addition to these three kinds of kinetic energy, there is the potential energy related to the attractive forces acting between molecules. In the gaseous state (molecules far apart) these forces are small. In the liquid state (molecules closer together) the forces are relatively large. In the solid state the forces are even greater.

Next, there is present, within the molecule, chemical energy related to the forces holding the atoms together in the molecule. For example, there is the chemical bond energy—the energy of the covalent bond mentioned in Chapter 8 for H_2, Cl_2, and HCl; or that of the ionic bond mentioned for NaCl. When forces acting between atoms or ions are large, the potential energy of the system is usually low and the system tends to be stable. As we noted earlier, the energy associated with the chemical bond is the direct result of the attraction between nuclei and moving electrons.* Finally, there is present within the nucleus of each atom a store of energy. This energy is related to the forces holding the nuclear particles together (Section 9-4). Since each nucleus remains intact and is apparently unaffected by chemical reactions, this nuclear energy does not change. Hence, the amount of stored energy that the nucleus contributes to the molecular enthalpy does not usually concern us if no nuclear processes are being considered.

The sum of all these forms of molecular energy makes up the *molecular* enthalpy. If we add together the molecular enthalpy of

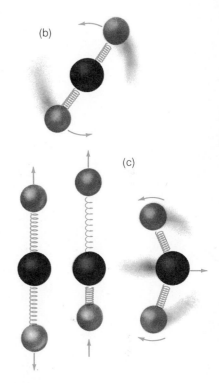

Fig. 9-5 Types of motion of a molecule of carbon dioxide, CO_2. (a) Translational motion; the molecule moves from place to place. (b) Rotational motion; the molecule rotates about its center of mass. (c) Vibrational motion; the atoms move alternately toward and away from the center of mass.

---

*As you recall, the ionization energy of an atom (Chapter 8) is a measure of the energy required to pull an electron away from an atom. If we assume that ion and electron have zero energy after separation, the ionization energy represents the sum of the kinetic and potential energies of the electron in the atom.

6.02×10^{23} molecules of a given kind, we obtain the *molar* enthalpy of that substance.

9-3.2 Energy Changes on Warming

In Chapter 5 we considered the general kinetic theory model for liquids and solids. We also used the model to interpret both the vaporization process and the freezing process for a liquid. Let us examine in more detail the heat effects associated with these processes and with the general heating of a solid.

When a solid is warmed, the atoms or molecules making up the solid bounce back and forth more vigorously around their regular crystal positions. The solid expands somewhat. As the temperature rises, these motions disturb the regularity of the crystal more and more. Too much of this random movement destroys the lattice completely. At a definite temperature the kinetic energy of the particles causes so much random movement that the lattice is no longer stable—the crystalline solid melts.

As you remember from Experiment 3, during the time that melting occurs, there is no increase in temperature—there was a plateau in the heating curve. Although energy was continually being supplied, there was no rise in temperature. Melting, then, must involve potential energy—the breaking up of the rigid crystal structure and the separation of molecules from each other.

In the liquid each molecule has considerably more freedom of movement, particularly for translation and rotation. Warming the liquid increases the amount of molecular movement. As molecular movement increases, more of the molecules have enough energy to overcome the forces of attraction holding them in the liquid and they move into relatively empty space above the liquid surface. Since there is no change in temperature as the liquid boils, the energy change is one of potential energy as the molecules become more randomly distributed. As the potential energy required for the change from liquid to vapor is supplied (heat of vaporization), the liquid vaporizes. The system is going from a state of lower potential energy to a state of higher potential energy. The factor most responsible for the change seems to be the tendency of the molecules to seek a more random arrangement—that is, their tendency to occupy the space above the liquid.

If we continue to warm the substance, we shall reach a point at which the kinetic energies of vibration, rotation, and translation become as large as the chemical bond energies. At this temperature complex molecules fall to pieces. For example, at the temperature of the sun's surface (6000 K), only monatomic and some diatomic molecules remain. All the more complicated structures have fallen to pieces.

This general discussion indicates that temperature and energy changes associated with chemical processes are usually significantly larger than temperature and energy changes associated with phase changes. In fact, they are usually larger by factors ranging from 10 to over 100. You saw this in the laboratory when you compared the heat released in burning 1 g of wax with that released in the freezing of 1 g of each of several molten materials.

9-4 THE ENERGY STORED IN A NUCLEUS

Our discussion in Chapter 7 indicated that a nucleus is built up of protons and neutrons, and that the number of neutrons per proton is important in determining nuclear stability. We noted earlier in this chapter that nuclei remain intact during even the most vigorous of chemical reactions. The energy involved in a nuclear process is usually at least one million times larger than the energy involved in any chemical process.

9-4.1 The Nuclear Fission Process

One of the first nuclear processes to be used on earth for the production of energy was the nuclear **fission** of uranium-235. Nuclear fission is a process in which a heavy nucleus splits to give two lighter nuclei of roughly comparable mass. If we utilize the symbolism* outlined in Chapter 7, a typical† fission process can be written as

$$^{235}_{92}U + ^{1}_{0}n \longrightarrow ^{141}_{56}Ba + ^{92}_{36}Kr + 3\,^{1}_{0}n + (\text{about})\ 4.5 \times 10^9 \text{ kcal} \quad (19)$$

We have conserved charge ($92 = 56 + 36$) and the number of nucleons (protons plus neutrons: $235 + 1 = 141 + 92 + 3$) in the process. For the process we are considering, one uranium-235 nucleus combines with one neutron, then *immediately* splits (undergoes fission) to give a barium nucleus, a krypton nucleus, and three neutrons. The released neutrons can also bring about the fission of more uranium nuclei. A **chain reaction** is set up. Each fission process provides neutrons to initiate the splitting of other $^{235}_{92}U$ nuclei. If neutron-loss to the outside is restricted, the process keeps itself going with a continual release of energy. The process can be controlled by regulating the number of neutrons lost or absorbed. Careful control is essential. If on the average each fission process provides neutrons that initiate only one new fission process, then the chain reaction will continue at a steady rate until the supply of fissionable nuclei becomes too small to keep the process going. This is what happens in a **nuclear reactor** (Figure 9-6). But if the neutrons from each fission process initiate

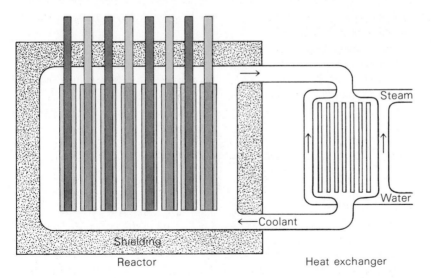

Fig. 9-6 A simplified diagram of a nuclear reactor. Gray rods are ^{235}U. Gold rods are Cd control rods.

Reactor

Heat exchanger

*Remember that a given isotope is represented by: (1) the symbol of the element, (2) the atomic number at the lower left-hand corner of the symbol, and (3) the mass number at the upper left-hand corner. For uranium the atomic number is 92 and the mass number is 235.

†This is a typical reaction. Many other pairs of products are also formed.

more than one new fission process, the chain reaction proceeds at an ever-increasing rate until the liberated heat blows the system to pieces—as in an atomic bomb.

Such a simple item as the size of a piece of uranium is important in determining the number of neutrons that can initiate a new fission process. If we have a large piece of uranium, a large number of uranium nuclei are confined in a unit with relatively *small* surface area per gram. Under these circumstances most of the neutrons released do not escape from the surface, but encounter other uranium nuclei and bring about new fission reactions. The process is self-sustaining. If, on the contrary, we have only a small piece of uranium with a relatively large surface area per gram of uranium, there is a high probability that the neutrons will escape from the uranium without encountering other uranium nuclei. These neutrons are wasted as far as the process is concerned, and the fission reaction is no longer self-sustaining. We say that a piece of fissionable material that is too small to maintain the fission process is below the **critical mass.**

The discussion on critical mass suggests that nuclear fission reactions can be controlled by controlling the number of neutrons available to initiate new fission processes. If we want to slow down or control nuclear fission, the number of neutrons available to initiate new fission reactions must be reduced. In a nuclear reactor, cadmium rods are used to control the number of neutrons. Cadmium nuclei are effective in absorbing neutrons without undergoing fission or without releasing other neutrons. One might say that they "soak up" neutrons and provide a means of reaction control.

It is frequently difficult to visualize the amount of energy represented by the amount 4.5×10^9 *kcal* in the fission equation. This analogy may help. The energy released in the fission of 235 g of uranium (about $\frac{1}{2}$ lb) is approximately equal to the energy released in the combustion of some 530,000 litres (140,000 gal) of gasoline. If your car is a gas-guzzling monster and uses as much as 100 litres (26 gal) per week, the 530,000 litres would solve your fuel problems for a little less than 100 years! In short, if we could properly harness the energy of this fission process and use uranium as an automobile fuel, $\frac{1}{2}$ lb of $^{235}_{92}U$ would keep an automobile going for about 100 years!

Where does all this energy come from? The answer is contained in the special theory of relativity, formulated first by Albert Einstein in 1905. One of the consequences of the theory of relativity was a suggestion that mass and energy are different forms of the same fundamental physical entity or "stuff." (We really do not have a good name for it.) The equation relating mass and energy

$$E = mc^2 \qquad (20)$$

is now familiar to most of us. In this equation E is the energy, m is the mass change equivalent to the energy E, and c is the velocity of light or 3.0×10^8 metres/sec. Because c^2 is so large (9.0×10^{16} metres^2/sec^2), a very small change in mass corresponds to a staggering change in energy. Conversely, the *mass change* associated with the energy change of a chemical reaction is too small to measure. Consider the mass change that should result from the burning of 1 mole of carbon (12 g) and 1 mole of oxygen (32 g):

$$C(s) + O_2(g) \longrightarrow CO_2(g)$$
$$\Delta H_{2a} = -94 \text{ kcal} \qquad (2a)$$

The 94 kcal of energy correspond to about 5×10^{-9} (0.000 000 005) g. Although the theory clearly predicts that the CO_2 should be 0.000 000 005 g *lighter* than the 12 g of carbon and 32 g of oxygen with which we started, the difference is just too small to measure at the present time. Nuclear reactions, in contrast to chemical reactions, do involve the conversion of measurable quantities of matter to energy, but simple, direct experiments to prove this are beyond our current experimental skills.

9-4.2 The Nuclear Fusion Process

We have just observed that energy is released when a heavy nucleus such as uranium-235 undergoes fission to give two lighter nuclei. Strangely enough, energy is also released when neutrons and protons combine to give the nuclei of somewhat heavier atoms such as helium or lithium. Let us examine mass relationships in the hypothetical process

$$2\,{}^{1}_{1}H + 2\,{}^{1}_{0}n \longrightarrow {}^{4}_{2}He \qquad (21)$$

Until now we have been content to write the mass of the proton or hydrogen atom as 1, the mass of the neutron as 1, and the mass of the electron as essentially 0. This was acceptable in calculations involving low precision, but if we are to accurately calculate mass-energy relationships, much more precise mass values must be used. Very careful measurements indicate that the hydrogen atom actually has a mass of 1.007 825 22 mass units. (How many significant figures are there in this value?) The neutron has a mass of 1.008 071 34 mass units, and the helium atom has a mass of 4.002 603 61. Let us check the mass balance. Two hydrogen atoms have a mass of

$$2 \times 1.007\ 825\ 22 = 2.015\ 650\ 44$$

Two neutrons have a mass of

$$2 \times 1.008\ 071\ 34 = 2.016\ 142\ 68$$

The total precision mass resulting from a combination of two hydrogen atoms and two neutrons should be

$$
\begin{array}{r}
2.015\ 650\ 44 \\
+2.016\ 142\ 68 \\
\hline
4.031\ 793\ 12
\end{array}
$$

The measured mass of the helium atom is $-4.002\ 603\ 61$*
The difference is $\underline{\ \ 0.029\ 189\ 51\ }$

In the hypothetical process cited, 0.029 189 51 units of mass are converted to energy. This is equivalent to 0.029 189 51 g per *mole* of helium formed, or 0.000 029 189 51 or $2.918\ 951 \times 10^{-5}$ kg per mole of helium formed. The arithmetic converting this quantity to a more easily recognized energy form is not hard when we apply $E = mc^2$ and convert to recognizable energy units. If we use 3.0×10^8 metres/sec as the velocity of light, and round off our mass difference to two significant figures, we can write

$$E = \left(\frac{2.9 \times 10^{-5}\ \text{kg}}{\text{mole}}\right)\left(\frac{3.0 \times 10^8\ \text{metres}}{\text{sec}}\right)^2$$

$$= \frac{2.6 \times 10^{12}\ \text{kg} \times \text{metres}^2}{\text{mole} \times \text{sec}^2} \qquad (22)$$

*This is the mass of a neutral helium atom—nucleus plus two electrons.

The unit of energy given above may be rather strange to you. It is the **joule.*** It can be converted to calories if we know that each calorie is 4.18 joules. We have

$$E = \frac{2.6 \times 10^{12} \text{ joules}}{\text{mole}} \times \frac{\text{cal}}{4.18 \text{ joules}} = 6.2 \times 10^{11} \text{ cal/mole} \quad (23)$$

$$E = 6.2 \times 10^8 \text{ kcal/mole or 620 million kcal/mole}$$

Thus, if 1 mole of helium were to be formed from 2 moles of protons and 2 moles of neutrons, 620 million kcal would be released. Conversely, the same amount of energy is required to break up 1 mole of helium nuclei into protons and neutrons. This quantity is called the **binding energy** of a mole of helium nuclei. Similar calculations can be made for other nuclei.

EXERCISE 9-6

If a nitrogen atom has a mass of 14.003 074 38 on the atomic weight scale, how much mass is converted to energy in the formation of 1 mole of nitrogen from hydrogen atoms and neutrons? If 1 g of mass is equivalent to 2.16×10^{10} kcal, what is the binding energy of the nitrogen nuclei per mole?

A significant comparison between nuclear binding energies can be made if we divide the total binding energy of each nucleus by the number of nucleons (protons plus neutrons) in the nucleus. This quantity, the binding energy per particle in the nucleus, varies systematically as the mass number of the nucleus increases. The variation is shown in Figure 9-7.

EXERCISE 9-7

The nuclear binding energy per nucleon does not vary in a periodic fashion like the ionization energies of the atoms. Why?

The nuclei with mass numbers around 60 have the highest binding energy per heavy nuclear particle, and are therefore the most stable nuclei. The graph in Figure 9-7 will help us understand the processes of nuclear **fusion** and nuclear **fission**. Nuclear fusion is a process in which nuclei of small mass fuse to give a nucleus of *greater* mass. When light nuclei such as ^1_1H or ^2_1H are fused together, the binding energy per nucleon increases and energy is released. We see from the graph that the energy released per nucleon is much greater in the fusion process than it is in the fission process (*i.e.*, the curve is much steeper on the left-hand than it is on the right-hand side). The calculation completed above indicates the energy changes expected for a fusion process. If the nuclei of the heavier elements, such as uranium and plutonium, are split into two smaller fragments, the binding energy per nucleon is greater in the lighter nuclei (the binding energy is a maximum near atomic number 60). As in every other reaction in which the products are more stable than the reactants, energy is evolved by this process of nuclear fission.

Fig. 9-7 The binding energy per nuclear particle.

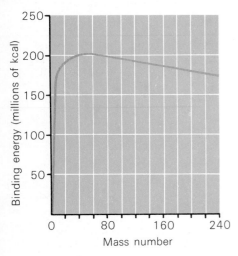

A graph with y-axis "Binding energy (millions of kcal)" ranging from 0 to 250, and x-axis "Mass number" ranging from 0 to 240 (marked at 80, 160, 240).

*The joule is the unit of energy in the internationally accepted SI system. It has the dimensions of $\text{kg} \times \dfrac{\text{metres}^2}{\text{sec}^2}$ or mass $\times$ velocity^2, the units of kinetic energy. One joule = 0.24 cal.

Unfortunately, it has not yet been possible to bring about the direct experimental combination of two protons and two neutrons on earth to give a helium nucleus. It has been possible, however, to bring about the combination of heavy hydrogen or hydrogen-2 ($_1^2H$) to give heavier nuclei. A typical reaction is

$$_1^2H + {_1^2H} \longrightarrow {_1^3H} + {_1^1H} + 7.5 \times 10^7 \text{ kcal} \qquad (24)$$

The hydrogen-3 nucleus can then combine with another hydrogen-2 nucleus to give helium:

$$_1^3H + {_1^2H} \longrightarrow {_2^4He} + {_0^1n} + 4.0 \times 10^8 \text{ kcal} \qquad (25)$$

The energy evolved is tremendous. It is very difficult to start these reactions; temperatures of 10 million to 100 million degrees are required. If a *fission* bomb reaction is used as a trigger, the fusion process can be initiated to give an uncontrolled *hydrogen* bomb explosion. Such weapons may produce unlimited explosive power, but they are of no value for the production of controlled power.

To achieve the much more difficult objective of a controlled release of energy from fusion demands alternative ways to heat, contain, and compress the hydrogen reactants. Very strong magnetic fields offer some hope. There is a long and difficult road ahead before we can use fusion energy in an effectively controlled manner.

EXERCISE 9-8

In the radioactive decomposition of radium-226, the equation for the nuclear process is

$$_{88}^{226}Ra \longrightarrow {_{86}^{222}Rn} + {_2^4He}$$

The mass of the $_{88}^{226}Ra$ atom is 226.025 360 mass units, the mass of $_{86}^{222}Rn$ 222.017 530, and the mass of $_2^4He$ 4.002 603 61. How much mass is converted to energy in the radioactive decay process? If 1 g of mass is equivalent to 2.16×10^{10} kcal, how many kilocalories of energy are released for every mole of $_2^4He$ liberated?

Let us review the difference between nuclear and chemical reactions. Referring to the fission of uranium-235, the symbol $_{92}^{235}U$ represents not an atom, but a nucleus. The equation for the fission process is written in terms of the nuclei and particles associated with them. A nuclear equation tells us nothing about what compounds were used or formed. We are summarizing only the nuclear changes. During the nuclear change there is much disruption of other atoms because of the tremendous amounts of energy liberated. We do not know in detail what happens, but eventually we return to electrically neutral substances (chemical compounds or elements) and the neutrons are absorbed by other nuclei. Thus, in nuclear reactions, changes in the nuclei take place. In chemical reactions, the nuclei remain intact and the changes are explainable in terms of the electrons outside the nucleus.

GERHARD HERZBERG
(1904–   )

Gerhard Herzberg was born in Hamburg, Germany, a few years after the discovery of the electron. After completing his studies in physics, he began independent research at the University of Gottingen. In the 1930's, Professor Herzberg joined the staff of the University of Saskatchewan in Canada. In 1945 he became professor at the Yerkes Observatory of the University of Chicago, where he applied spectroscopic techniques to astronomy. He returned to Canada in 1948 and is presently Distinguished Research Scientist of the National Research Council of Canada.

Professor Herzberg has made many major contributions to physics, chemistry, and astronomy. Early in his career, his studies of the structure of the nucleus led to the search for a new model of the nucleus. This was achieved only with the discovery of the neutron. In more recent years, he established the binding energy for hydrogen and helium.

Professor Herzberg is most noted for his spectroscopic studies of the electronic structure and geometry of molecules and of free radicals—important intermediates in many chemical reactions. For this work he was awarded the 1971 Nobel Prize in Chemistry.

9-5 HIGHLIGHTS

Every substance has a definite and characteristic **heat content** or **enthalpy** that varies with temperature. The change in enthalpy of the system is given by

$$\Delta H = \text{(enthalpy of products)} - \text{(enthalpy of reactants)}$$

A positive value of ΔH means that during the process, energy from the surroundings is stored in the products. The reaction is **endothermic.** A negative value of ΔH means that during the process energy is liberated to the surroundings so that the products have less energy than the original reactants. The process is **exothermic.** By proper addition of ΔH values for known reactions, ΔH values for new reactions can be predicted with a high degree of accuracy.

The energy for a system can be classified as kinetic and potential. The total energy for both mechanical and chemical systems is always conserved. Energy is stored in a molecule as **kinetic energy** (energy of motion) and as **potential energy** (energy of position). Potential energy is associated with attractions and repulsions of molecules, atoms, or charged particles making up the substance. Finally, in each nucleus there is a tremendous amount of stored energy.

The very large energy changes associated with nuclear processes have verified the Einstein relationship, $E = mc^2$.

QUESTIONS and PROBLEMS

1 In an experiment similar to Experiment 17, a 5.61 ± 0.02-g sample of solid potassium hydroxide (KOH) was dissolved in 100 ml of water. The temperature of the water rose 13.0 ± 0.4 °C. (a) Write the equation for the reaction. (b) Calculate the molar heat of solution of potassium hydroxide. The units are kcal/mole. (c) Rewrite the equation for the reaction, using the ΔH notation.

2 Convert each of the following equations to the ΔH notation. Indicate whether each reaction is exothermic or endothermic.

(a) $Cd(s) + \frac{1}{2}O_2(g) \longrightarrow CdO(s) + 62.3$ kcal

(b) $Cl_2(g) + \frac{7}{2}O_2(g) + 65$ kcal $\longrightarrow Cl_2O_7(g)$

(c) $2Au(s) + \frac{3}{2}O_2(g) \longrightarrow Au_2O_3(s) + 2$ kcal

(d) $2B(s) + \frac{3}{2}H_2(g) + 7.5$ kcal $\longrightarrow B_2H_6(g)$

(e) $\frac{1}{2}Br_2(l) + \frac{1}{2}Cl_2(g) + 3.5$ kcal $\longrightarrow BrCl(g)$

3 Identify each of the following reactions as exothermic or endothermic. Which processes store more energy in the products than in the reactants?

(a) $Hg(l) + \frac{1}{2}I_2(s) \longrightarrow HgI(g)$
$\Delta H = +33$ kcal

(b) $\frac{1}{2}N_2(g) + \frac{3}{2}F_2(g) \longrightarrow NF_3(g)$
$\Delta H = -27.2$ kcal

(c) $Si(s) + 2Br_2(l) \longrightarrow SiBr_4(l)$
$\Delta H = -95.1$ kcal

(d) $Na(s) \longrightarrow Na(g) \quad \Delta H = +25.98$ kcal

4 At 100 °C, solid ammonium nitrite decomposes to form nitrogen gas and gaseous water. At this temperature, the decomposition releases 53.5 kcal per mole of ammonium nitrite decomposed. (a) Write the balanced equation for this reaction including the energy term in the equation. (b) Write the balanced equation for the reaction and use the ΔH notation for the energy term.

5 At elevated temperatures, solid lead nitrate decomposes to form solid lead monoxide, oxygen gas, and gaseous nitrogen dioxide. This decomposition absorbs 69.6 kcal of energy per mole of lead nitrate decomposed. (a) Write the balanced equation for the reaction including the energy term in the equation. (b) Write the balanced equation for this reaction using the ΔH notation.

6 Given the following equation:

$$Na_2O(s) + 2HI(g) \longrightarrow$$
$$2NaI(s) + H_2O(l) + 120.0 \text{ kcal}$$

(a) If 9.00 grams of $NaI(s)$ are formed by the process, how much heat will be involved? (b) Is the heat absorbed or released in this reaction? Explain how you arrived at this conclusion.

7 When concentrated nitric acid (HNO_3) is added to water, heat is liberated. This "heat of dilution" is 7.2 kcal per mole of HNO_3 diluted. How many grams of nitric acid must be diluted to release 864 kcal of heat?

8 Given the following equation:

$$2NaHSO_4(s) \longrightarrow$$
$$Na_2SO_4(s) + H_2O(g) + SO_3(g)$$
$$\Delta H = +55.2 \text{ kcal}$$

If 3.60 grams of $NaHSO_4$ react, how much heat is involved?

9 Given the following equation:

$$C(s) + O_2(g) \longrightarrow CO_2(g)$$
$$\Delta H = -94.0 \text{ kcal}$$

(a) How many grams of carbon must be burned to produce 611 kcal of energy? (b) How many grams of oxygen will be consumed in the production of this energy?

10 Using the data from Table 9-2 (page 207), calculate ΔH for the reaction

$$H_2O(l) \longrightarrow H_2O(g)$$

11 Using the data from Table 9-2 and the following equation

$$S(s) + \tfrac{3}{2}O_2(g) \longrightarrow SO_3(g)$$
$$\Delta H = -94.4 \text{ kcal}$$

(a) Determine ΔH for the following reaction:

$$SO_2(g) + \tfrac{1}{2}O_2(g) \longrightarrow SO_3(g)$$

(b) Determine ΔH for the following reaction:

$$SO_3(g) + H_2O(l) \longrightarrow H_2SO_4(l)$$

12 If "water gas" is 50 percent hydrogen and 50 percent CO, calculate how much heat is liberated when 22.4 litres (at STP) of water gas are burned. Repeat for 22.4 litres (at STP) of "natural gas" or methane (CH_4). Which is the better fuel?

13 Using the data from Table 9-2 and the following equation:

$$4C(s) + 4H_2(g) + O_2(g) \longrightarrow$$
$$C_3H_7COOH(l)$$
$$\Delta H = -124.9 \text{ kcal}$$

calculate the heat of reaction for the following:

$$C_3H_7COOH(l) + 5\,O_2(g) \longrightarrow$$
$$4CO_2(g) + 4H_2O(l)$$

14 Use data from Table 9-2 and the following equation:

$$2C(s) + 2H_2(g) + O_2(g) \longrightarrow$$
$$CH_3COOH(l)$$
$$\Delta H = -116.4 \text{ kcal}$$

to calculate the heat of reaction for the following:

$$3CH_3COOH(l) + \tfrac{11}{2}O_2(g) \longrightarrow$$
$$5CO_2(g) + CO(g) + 6H_2O(l)$$

15 [Refer to Tables 5-2 and 5-6 (pages 103 and 110).] Consider the situation in which sodium chloride is heated from 500 °C and 1 atm pressure to 1600 °C and 1 atm. Describe what you would *see* as the system is heated and give the energy changes per mole occurring during the phase changes.

16 Use the same reference as in question 15. Chlorine is cooled from 25 °C and 1 atm to -50 °C and 1 atm. Describe what you would see during the change as well as the energy changes occurring.

17 How is energy stored when water is vaporized? Explain, using a molecular model.

18 Which molecule has the greater ability to store energy as it is heated, $CCl_4(g)$ or $Ar(g)$? Explain, indicating the kinds of motion by which each of these molecules can store energy.

19 Which of the following reactions is most likely to have a ΔH of -57.8 kcal? of -7.5×10^7 kcal? of $+10.5$ kcal?

(a) $H_2O(l) \longrightarrow H_2O(g)$

(b) $H_2(g) + \tfrac{1}{2}O_2(g) \longrightarrow H_2O(g)$

(c) $^2_1H + {}^2_1H \longrightarrow {}^3_1H + {}^1_1H$

20 If a hydrogen atom's mass is 1.007 825 22 u and a neutron's mass is 1.008 071 34 u:
(a) Predict the mass of a ^7_3Li atom. (b) If the actual ^7_3Li atom has a mass of 7.016 01 u, how much mass would be lost in the hypothetical construction of a mole of ^7_3Li atoms from hydrogen atoms and neutrons? (c) If 1 gram of mass loss produces 2.16×10^{10} kcal of energy, how much energy would be given off in the formation of 1 mole of ^7_3Li atoms from hydrogen atoms and neutrons?

21 When $^{235}_{92}U$ is struck by a neutron, the unstable isotope $^{236}_{92}U$ results.

$$^{235}_{92}U + {}^1_0n \longrightarrow {}^{236}_{92}U$$

When $^{236}_{92}U$ undergoes fission, there are numerous possible products. If strontium-90 ($^{90}_{38}Sr$) and 3 neutrons are the results of one such fission, what is the other product?

$$^{236}_{92}U \longrightarrow {}^{90}_{38}Sr + {}^?_? + 3\,{}^1_0n$$

> . . . a molecular system . . . [passes] . . . from one state of equilibrium to another . . . by means of all possible intermediate paths, but the path most economical of energy will be more often travelled.
>
> *HENRY EYRING (1901–   )*

THE RATES OF REACTIONS 10

A small difference in rate (metres/sec) may make the difference between a gold medal and none at all.

WHY DOESN'T A CANDLE BURN UNTIL LIT WITH A MATCH?
Why does it continue to burn after the match is taken away? Why, indeed, does a match not burn until you strike it on something? What is the difference between a candle, which burns fat or wax only at a high temperature and you, who "burn" fat at body temperature?

Why are some chemical reactions extremely rapid and others agonizingly slow? Why do we use a Bunsen burner so frequently in the laboratory and an ice bath so seldom? How can we change the rate of reactions to make them more useful to us?

There are lots of questions—and, theoretically at least—some amazingly simple answers.

A candle remains in contact with air indefinitely without observable reaction, but it burns when lighted by a match. A mixture of household gas and air in a closed room remains indefinitely without reacting, but it may explode violently if a glowing cigarette is brought into the room. Iron reacts quite slowly with air (it rusts), but white phosphorus in a very finely divided condition bursts into flame when exposed to air.* All are reactions with oxygen from the air, but they require very different amounts of time. *Reactions proceed at different rates.*† Reaction rates are important in strange and subtle ways. For example, oxides of nitrogen, produced by our automobiles and contaminating our air, will decompose spontaneously at room temperature to give gaseous oxygen and nitrogen. Still, the process is so *slow* at room temperature that oxides of nitrogen in the air constitute a serious pollution problem (Chapter 22). To solve the nitrogen oxides problem, we need to speed up the process by which they decompose. The decomposition

$$2NO \longrightarrow N_2 + O_2 + \text{energy} \qquad (1)$$

must be made faster.

Let us see what quantitative meaning is attached to the expression "rate of reaction." As an example, let us consider the reaction between carbon monoxide (CO) and nitrogen dioxide (NO_2). The equation for the reaction is

$$CO + NO_2 \longrightarrow CO_2 + NO \qquad (2)$$

If we heat a mixture of CO and NO_2 to 200 °C, we observe a gradual disappearance of the reddish-brown color of NO_2. Reaction is taking place. We can find the rate of the process by measuring the change in color during successive one-minute periods. Since the other gases are colorless, the color *change* is proportional to the *change* in the number of moles of NO_2 present in a litre. If we divide the change in the quantity of NO_2 per litre (change in concentration) by the time

---

*White phosphorus is a very dangerous material. Cases are known in which bulk phosphorus has ignited. It should be handled with great care.
†The study of reaction rates is called **chemical kinetics.**

interval (one minute), the quotient is the rate of the reaction. We can write symbolically

$$\text{rate of reaction} = \frac{\text{change in concentration } NO_2}{\text{time interval}}$$

We can express the rate of reaction in terms of the rate of consumption of either CO or NO_2, or in terms of the rate of production of either CO_2 or NO. Which we use depends upon convenience of measurement. If we prefer to measure the production of CO_2, we will express the rate in the form

$$\text{rate of reaction} = \frac{\text{increase in concentration } CO_2}{\text{time interval}}$$

The change in concentration can be expressed in any set of units which is convenient. If the substance is a gas, partial pressures are convenient; if it is in solution, moles per litre is usually used. The time measurement is also expressed in whatever units fit the reaction—microseconds for the explosion of household gas and oxygen, seconds or minutes for the burning of a candle, days or years for the rusting of iron.

10-1 FACTORS AFFECTING REACTION RATES

In the laboratory you observed the reaction of ferrous ion, $Fe^{2+}(aq)$, with permanganate ion, $MnO_4^-(aq)$, and also the reaction of oxalate ion, $C_2O_4^{2-}(aq)$, with permanganate ion, $MnO_4^-(aq)$. These studies show that *the rate of a reaction depends upon the nature of the reacting substances*. In Experiment 18, the reaction between IO_3^- and HSO_3^- shows that *the rate of a reaction depends upon concentrations of reactants and upon the temperature*. Let us examine these factors one at a time.

10-1.1 The Nature of the Reactants

Compare two reactions, both of which occur in water solutions:

$$5C_2O_4^{2-}(aq) + 2MnO_4^-(aq) + 16H^+(aq) \longrightarrow$$
$$10CO_2(g) + 2Mn^{2+}(aq) + 8H_2O \quad \text{SLOW} \quad (3)$$

$$5Fe^{2+}(aq) + MnO_4^-(aq) + 8H^+(aq) \longrightarrow$$
$$5Fe^{3+}(aq) + Mn^{2+}(aq) + 4H_2O \quad \text{VERY FAST} \quad (4)$$

Both ferrous ion, $Fe^{2+}(aq)$, and oxalate ion, $C_2O_4^{2-}(aq)$, are able to decolorize a solution containing permanganate ion at room temperature. Yet, there is a great contrast in the time required for the decoloration. The difference lies in specific characteristics of $Fe^{2+}(aq)$ and $C_2O_4^{2-}(aq)$.

Here are two reactions that take place in the gas phase:

$$2NO + O_2 \longrightarrow 2NO_2 \quad \text{MODERATE AT } 20\,°C \quad (5)$$

$$CH_4 + 2O_2 \longrightarrow CO_2 + 2H_2O \quad \text{EXTREMELY SLOW AT } 20\,°C \quad (6)$$

The *oxidation* of nitric oxide (NO), a reaction involved in smog production, is moderately fast at temperatures of 10–100 °C (Chapter 22).

The oxidation of methane (CH_4), household gas, however, occurs so slowly at room temperature that for all practical purposes there is no reaction. Again, the difference in the reaction rates must depend upon specific characteristics of the reactants, NO and CH_4.

The identification of those molecular characteristics which determine rate behavior is an interesting frontier of chemistry. Chemical reactions which involve the breaking of several chemical bonds and the formation of new chemical bonds tend to proceed slowly at room temperature. The reaction of $C_2O_4^{2-}(aq)$ and $MnO_4^-(aq)$ is of this type—many bonds must be broken in the five $C_2O_4^{2-}$ ions and the two MnO_4^- ions to form the $10CO_2$ and $2Mn^{2+}$. This reaction proceeds slowly, as we might expect. The reaction of CH_4 and O_2 also involves breaking bonds and forming new bonds; it is slow at room temperature. In contrast, the reaction of $Fe^{2+}(aq)$ and $MnO_4^-(aq)$ is very rapid, although it involves breaking chemical bonds and thus might be expected to be slow. We see that we cannot be certain of any prediction that a reaction might be slow.

You might properly ask: do not all reactions involve bond breaking? No, a few appear to proceed without bond breaking. For example, the reaction

$$Fe^{2+}(aq) + Ce^{4+}(aq) \longrightarrow Ce^{3+}(aq) + Fe^{3+}(aq) \qquad \text{VERY RAPID} \qquad (7)$$

appears to involve only the transfer of an electron between ions. We expect it to be very rapid—a prediction that is easily verified in solution. A prediction of this type is usually reliable. On the other hand, the reaction of NO with O_2 requires breaking one bond (O—O) and forming two new ones (N—O). It has a moderate reaction rate, rapid at high temperatures and slow at low temperatures.

These and other examples lead to the following rules:

(1) Reactions that do not involve bond rearrangements are usually rapid at room temperature.
(2) Reactions in which bonds are broken tend to be slow at room temperature.

We can say little more about how the nature of the reactants determines the reaction rate until we consider in detail how some reactions take place. For the time being, we shall just say that this is an active field of study and much remains to be learned.

EXERCISE 10-1

Are any of the following three reactions likely to be extremely rapid at room temperature? Are any likely to be extremely slow at room temperature? Explain.

(1) $Cr^{2+}(aq) + Fe^{3+}(aq) \longrightarrow Cr^{3+}(aq) + Fe^{2+}(aq)$
(2) $3Fe^{2+}(aq) + NO_3^-(aq) + 4H^+(aq) \longrightarrow$
$$3Fe^{3+}(aq) + NO(g) + 2H_2O$$
(3) $C_8H_{18}(l) + 12\frac{1}{2}O_2(g) \longrightarrow 8CO_2(g) + 9H_2O(g)$
    GASOLINE

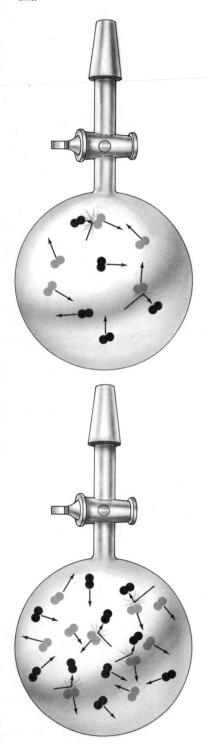

10-1.2 Effect of Concentration—Collision Theory

Henceforth we shall look at one reaction at a time. The nature of the reactants will be held constant while the other factors that affect rates are considered. The first of these factors is *concentration*. A great number of experiments have shown that, for many reactions, raising the concentration of a reactant increases the reaction rate. Still, this is not always true. For some reactions an increase in reactant concentration has no effect on the rate of the reaction. In this section we shall consider how a rate increase with rising reactant concentration is explained. In Section 10-1.3 we shall also explore why some reactions proceed at a rate independent of the concentrations of the reactants. Both explanations are based upon a molecular model for chemical reactions. In the molecular model, we assume that two molecules must come close together to react. Reaction at a distance seems rather unreasonable since atoms must usually be exchanged between molecules. For this reason, we postulate that chemical reactions depend upon collisions between the reacting particles—atoms, molecules, or ions. This model of reaction rate behavior is called the **collision theory** (see Figure 10-1).

The collision theory provides a successful framework for understanding the effect of concentration. Just as increasing the number of cars in motion on a highway leads to a higher rate of denting fenders, increasing the number of particles in a given volume gives more frequent molecular collisions. The higher frequency of collisions results in a higher rate of reaction.

Consider a homogeneous system, one in which all components are in the same phase. According to the collision theory, increasing the concentration of one or more reactants will result in an increase in the rate of the reaction. Lowering the concentration has the opposite effect. This is exactly the behavior found in the reaction between $HSO_3^-(aq)$ and $IO_3^-(aq)$ seen in Experiment 18. With gases (homogeneous systems), the concentration of an individual reactant can be raised by admitting more of that substance into the mixture. The concentrations of *all* gaseous components can be raised simultaneously by decreasing the volume occupied by the mixture. Decreasing the volume by compressing the gas raises the concentration of all reactants, hence increases the rates of reactions taking place. Increasing the volume by expanding the gas has the opposite effect on concentrations, hence decreases reaction rates.

In a heterogeneous reaction system, the components are in two or more different phases. As an example, consider

$$\text{wood } (s) + \text{oxygen } (g) \xrightarrow{\text{burning}} \text{carbon dioxide } (g) + \text{water } (g)$$

Here the rate of the reaction depends upon the area of contact between phases. For example, a log burns in air at a relatively slow rate. If the amount of exposed surface of the wood is increased by reducing the log to splinters, the burning is much more rapid. Further, if the wood is reduced to fine sawdust and the sawdust is suspended in a current of air, the combustion takes place explosively. Where one of the reactants is a gas, then, the concentration of the gas is also a factor.

A piece of wood burns much more rapidly in pure oxygen than it does in ordinary air. Remember that ordinary air is only about 20 percent oxygen.

We see that the collision theory provides a good explanation of reaction rate behavior. It is quite reasonable that the reaction rate should depend upon collisions involving the reactant molecules. In fact, it is so reasonable that we are left wondering why the concentrations of some reactants in some reactions do not affect the rate. The explanation is found in the detailed steps by which the reaction takes place, the reaction mechanism.

10-1.3 Reaction Mechanism

We have indicated that particles must collide before a reaction can occur. The particles may be atoms, molecules, or ions. As a result of collisions, there can be rearrangements of atoms, electrons, and chemical bonds, and subsequently production of new species. With this thought in mind, let us take another look at the reaction between Fe^{2+} and MnO_4^- in acid solution. The equation is

$$5Fe^{2+}(aq) + MnO_4^-(aq) + 8H^+(aq) \longrightarrow$$
$$5Fe^{3+}(aq) + Mn^{2+}(aq) + 4H_2O \quad (4)$$

This equation indicates that one MnO_4^- ion, five Fe^{2+} ions, and eight H^+ ions (a total of fourteen ions) must react with each other. If this reaction were to take place in a single step, these fourteen ions would have to collide with each other *simultaneously*. The probability of such an event occurring is extremely small, so small that a reaction which depended upon such a collision would proceed at a rate which would be immeasurably slow. Since the reaction does occur at an easily measured rate, it must proceed by some *sequence* of *steps,* rather than by a single step involving the simultaneous collision of fourteen ions. As a matter of fact, the collision of even four molecules or ions is an extremely improbable event if the molecules are at low concentration or if they are in the gas phase. We conclude that a complex chemical reaction which proceeds at a measurable rate must take place in a series of simpler steps.

Consider the oxidation of gaseous hydrogen bromide (HBr), a reaction that is reasonably rapid in the temperature range from 400 °C to 600 °C:

$$4HBr(g) + O_2(g) \longrightarrow 2H_2O(g) + 2Br_2(g) \quad (8)$$

By the collision theory, we expect that increasing the partial pressure (thus the concentration) of either the HBr or O_2 will speed up the reaction. Experiments show this is the case. Quantitative studies of the rate of the reaction of HBr and O_2 at various pressures and in varying proportions indicate that the reactants O_2 and HBr are equally effective in changing the reaction rate. However, this result raises a question. Since four molecules of HBr are required for every one molecule of O_2, why does a change in the HBr pressure have just the same effect as an equal change in the O_2 pressure?

Considering the details of the process by which the reaction of HBr and O_2 occurs gives us the explanation. The overall reaction brings together five molecules, four of HBr and one of O_2. Since there is very little chance that even five gaseous molecules will collide simultaneously, the reaction must occur in a series of simpler steps.

All the studies on this process are explained by the following series of simple reactions:

$$HBr + O_2 \longrightarrow \text{HOOBr} \qquad \text{SLOW} \quad (9)$$

$$\text{HOOBr} + HBr \longrightarrow \text{2HOBr} \qquad \text{FAST} \quad (10)$$

$$\text{2HOBr} + 2HBr \longrightarrow 2H_2O + 2Br_2 \qquad \text{FAST} \quad (11)$$

$$\overline{4HBr + O_2 \longrightarrow 2H_2O + 2Br_2 \qquad\qquad (8)}$$

Note that each step in the sequence requires the collision of only two molecules.* Finally, the proposal that the first step in the sequence is slow whereas the other steps are fast explains why HBr and O_2 have the same effect on the reaction rate.

The reaction giving HOOBr is a "bottleneck" in the oxidation of hydrogen bromide. As fast as HOOBr is formed by this slow reaction, it is consumed in the rapid reaction with more HBr. But no matter how rapid the latter reactions are, they can produce H_2O and Br_2 only as fast as the slowest reaction in the sequence. Hence, the factors that determine the rate of HOOBr formation determine the rate of the overall process.

The sequence of simple reactions, by which a complex process occurs, is called the **reaction mechanism.** In the example, the formation of HOOBr is the step that fixes the rate because it is the slowest reaction in the mechanism. *The slowest reaction in a mechanism is called the* **rate-determining step.**

There are two features of this example that are rather common. First, none of the steps in the reaction mechanism requires the collision of more than two particles. *Most chemical reactions proceed by sequences of steps, each involving only two-particle collisions.* Second, the overall or net reaction does *not* show the mechanism. In general, *the mechanism of a reaction cannot be deduced from the net equation for the reaction.* The various steps by which atoms are rearranged and recombined must be determined through separate experiments.

EXERCISE 10-2

Imagine that a telegram is to be sent on a winter night from New York City to a rancher who lives near the top of a mountain in Nevada. The steps in sending the telegram are the following: (a) The New Yorker calls the telegraph office and dictates a ten-word message. (b) The New York telegraph operator transmits the message to the Reno office. (c) The Reno office types out the message and hands it to a deliverer. (d) The deliverer gets into a car and struggles 20 miles up the snow-covered road to the rancher's house.

*Reaction (11) is the reaction $HOBr + HBr \longrightarrow H_2O + Br_2$ taking place twice.

How great an increase in the rate of transmitting a message would be observed if:

(1) The secretary receiving the message in New York could type twice as fast?
(2) Electricity (by some undefined and miraculous process) could move twice as fast in the wire?
(3) The Reno office could telephone the message to the rancher rather than send the deliverer?

What is the rate-determining step in the original process?

10-1.4 The Quantitative Effect of Concentration

Determining the effect of reactant concentration on the rate of a reaction is a relatively straightforward experimental procedure, but to establish the precise mechanism from this information is a much less certain process. Consider the reaction between gaseous hydrogen (H_2) and gaseous iodine (I_2):

$$H_2(g) + I_2(g) \longrightarrow 2HI(g) \qquad (12)$$

Since $I_2(g)$ is violet in color, we can follow the rate of the reaction under different conditions by measuring the change in color that takes place in a given time interval. (The color of the gas mixture is proportional to its iodine concentration.) Rate measurements show that doubling the concentration of I_2 doubles the reaction rate if the H_2 concentration is kept constant; tripling the concentration of I_2 increases the rate by a factor of three; and so on. The observations can be summarized by the statement: the rate at which I_2 disappears is proportional to I_2 concentration. This statement can be made in a somewhat more formal, mathematical way:

$$\text{rate} = k'[I_2] \quad \text{if } [H_2] \text{ is constant} \qquad (13)$$

In this equation $[I_2]$ is the concentration of I_2 vapor expressed as moles per litre, and k' is a constant indicating the rate of the reaction when $[I_2]$ is 1. We can also determine how the reaction rate changes if the H_2 concentration is changed while the I_2 concentration is held constant. It is found that the rate is proportional to the concentration of H_2. We can write

$$\text{rate} = k''[H_2] \quad \text{if } [I_2] \text{ is constant} \qquad (14)$$

Again, $[H_2]$ is the concentration of hydrogen in moles per litre, and k'' is a constant indicating the rate of the reaction when $[H_2]$ is 1.

If both $[H_2]$ and $[I_2]$ were to vary, the rate would be proportional to the product of their concentrations:

$$\text{rate} = k'[I_2] \cdot k''[H_2] = k'k''[I_2][H_2] \qquad (15)$$

or

$$\text{rate} = k[H_2][I_2] \qquad (16)$$

The constant k is a proportionality constant. It is equal to the measured rate when both H_2 and I_2 have a concentration of 1 mole per litre.

HENRY EYRING (1901–)

One of eighteen children, Henry Eyring was born in Chihuahua, Mexico, where his father was a cattle rancher and farmer. The Eyring family was forced to abandon this home in 1912 under threat of the revolutionist Salazar, moving first to Texas, then to Arizona.

Eyring first studied mining, then metallurgy, at the University of Arizona. In 1927 the University of California awarded him the Ph.D. in chemistry. Before becoming Dean of the graduate school and professor of chemistry at the University of Utah, Eyring served on the faculties of the University of Wisconsin, the University of California, and Princeton University.

Eyring's research has been original and frequently unorthodox. He was one of the first chemists to apply quantum mechanics to chemistry. He unleashed a revolution in the treatment of reaction rates by use of detailed thermodynamic reasoning. Having formulated the idea of the activated complex, Eyring proceeded to find a myriad of fruitful applications, from formation of artificial diamonds to conductance, adsorption, catalysis, and diffusion of liquids.

10-1.5 The Problems of Reaction Mechanism

The results just cited are those which would be expected for a reaction proceeding by a collision between an H_2 molecule and an I_2 molecule:

$$H_2(g) + I_2(g) \longrightarrow 2HI(g) \qquad (12)$$

For years chemists throughout the world have accepted and taught this simple mechanism for the reaction of H_2 and I_2. Most chemists were convinced that the reaction was simple; but a few rebels like Dr. Henry Eyring felt that certain details of the variation of the reaction rate with temperature implied a more complex process. Reports of work published in 1967 now show that the process is more complex than was originally thought. The best current conceptualization of the reaction mechanism suggests that I_2 molecules may undergo dissociation to iodine atoms just *before* reacting with H_2. The mechanism would then be

$$I_2 \longrightarrow 2I \qquad (17)$$

$$H_2 + 2I \longrightarrow 2HI \qquad (18)$$

This mechanism is consistent with all the rate measurements.

The abandonment of time-honored beliefs and concepts in the face of new data is the mark of a vigorous science. Remember Martin's generalization: cylindrical objects burn.

10-1.6 The Effect of Temperature on Reaction Rate— An Application of Collision Theory

In Experiment 18 you discovered that temperature has a marked effect upon the rate of chemical reactions. Thus, raising the temperature speeded up the reaction between IO_3^- and HSO_3^-. This is the same effect, qualitatively, that is observed in the reaction of a candle with air. The match "lighted" the wick by raising its temperature. Once started, the combustion process released enough heat to keep the temperature high, thus keeping the reaction going at a reasonable rate. Raising the temperature speeded up the reaction.

In all these reactions (and in almost all others), increasing the temperature has a very pronounced effect, always speeding up the reaction. Two questions come to mind: why does an increase in temperature speed up a reaction? And, why does the increase in temperature have such a large effect? Finding an answer leads us back to the collision theory.

Consider the gas phase reaction between CH_4 and O_2 at 25 °C, which is extremely slow. Assume both gases are present at a pressure of 1 atmosphere. From what we know about molecular sizes, we can calculate that a particular methane molecule (CH_4) collides with an oxygen molecule approximately once every one thousandth of a microsecond or once every nanosecond (10^{-9} sec). This means that in one second a methane molecule encounters 10^9 oxygen molecules! Yet the reaction does not proceed noticeably. If the collision theory is valid, most of these collisions do *not* lead to reaction. Why? To understand this, let us return to our analogy of cars bumping each other on a highway. In a line of heavy traffic one may receive gentle bumps from the car in front or the car behind. No damage is done to the cars, only to people's tempers. But occasionally a high-speed collision occurs. If this occurs with enough energy, a bumper may be knocked off a car and a fender may be collapsed. The geometry of the collision is important; a low-velocity collision with a bumper is much less effective than with a fender or door. For a really effective collision, a combination of high velocity and proper geometry is unbeatable.

Just as high-energy collisions at the proper site cause auto damage, high-energy molecular collisions occurring at a vulnerable site on the reacting molecules cause the molecular rearrangement we call a chemical reaction. Just as a certain amount of energy is required to break loose a bumper, a certain amount of energy is required to cause a chemical reaction. If there is more than this threshold energy, the reaction can occur. If there is less, it cannot occur. *Chemical reactions happen when collisions involving more than a certain amount of energy occur.*

This discussion of threshold energy causes us to wonder what energies are possessed by molecules at a given temperature. We have already compared the molecules of a gas with "super-rubber" balls rebounding in a room. When "super-rubber" balls bounce around and collide with each other, some move rapidly and some move slowly. Do molecules behave this way? Experiment provides the answer.

Velocity is commonly measured as the length of time it takes an object to travel a measured distance. In racing, for example, runners leave the starting blocks at the same moment, and are sorted out at the finish line on the basis of their speed. The faster runners arrive at the finish line first; the slower ones straggle in behind them. The average velocity of each runner can be calculated using the relationship: **velocity = distance/time.**

Similarly, the distribution of velocities of molecules or atoms can be measured using the device in Figure 10-2 (page 232). It has two disks, D_1 and D_2, rotating rapidly on a common axle, thus at the same speed. They rotate in a vacuum chamber in front of an oven containing molten tin held at a controlled temperature. Vapor streams out of the small opening in the oven; it strikes the rotating disk D_1, which lets molecules pass through in small bursts each time the slot passes the opening of the oven. This disk serves as the starting block for repeated "molecule races." When the disk has rotated to the position shown in Figure 10-2(b), a small amount of gas has passed the slot in disk D_1. No more gas can get through the slot until it has completed one full rotation and the slot is again opposite the opening of the oven.

A short time later [Figure 10-2(c)], the atoms of tin have traveled part of the way toward the second rotating disk, which is their target, and have spread out from their compact arrangement in Figure 10-2(b). The faster-moving atoms have traveled farther than the others, and are leading the way. The slower-moving atoms are beginning to lag behind. Still later, in Figure 10-2(d), the atoms are spread out in space even more; the faster atoms have already reached the second rotating disk, and have condensed on it. This disk sorts out the atoms on the basis of their velocity just as the timer in a race does. Since

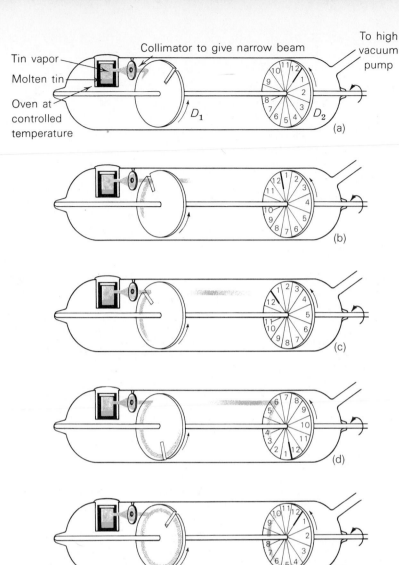

Tin vapor

Molten tin

Oven at controlled temperature

Collimator to give narrow beam

To high vacuum pump

D_1 D_2

(a)

(b)

(c)

(d)

(e)

Fig. 10-2 Rotating disk used to measure atomic or molecular velocities.

disk D_2 is rotating, the atoms condense at positions scattered along the edge of the disk, as shown in Figure 10-2(e). The position at which a given atom condenses on disk D_2 depends upon how long that atom took to travel from D_1 to D_2 and how fast D_2 is rotating.

As the slotted disk, D_1, lets through burst after burst of tin atoms, a layer of tin builds up on the surface of disk D_2. The pattern of this layer is determined by the distribution of velocities of the atoms escaping from the hot oven. Figure 10-3 shows the disk D_2 divided into sections, like slices of a pie. The fastest-moving atoms have condensed on "pie slices" 3, 4, and 5. The slowest-moving atoms have condensed on pie slices 10 and 11. If the disk is cut up and each slice weighed, the amount of tin can be determined. A plot of the mass of tin against the number of its pie slice indicates the distribution of atomic velocities.

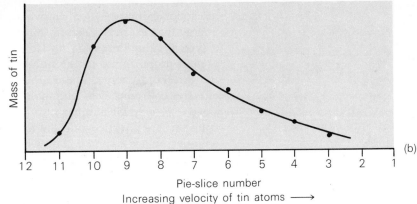

Disk D_2 after many revolutions

Pie-slice number

Increasing velocity of tin atoms $\longrightarrow$

Fig. 10-3 The relative distribution of atomic or molecular velocities obtained from the rotating disk.

EXERCISE 10-3

Why is there no tin deposited on pie slices 1 and 2? on slice 12? What would be the effect of speeding up the rotation of the disks on the amount of tin deposited on each slice? Which slices would have more tin deposited on them? which less? which the same?

We saw in Chapter 4 that the relationship between the velocity of a gas molecule, its mass, and its kinetic energy is expressed by the equation

$$KE = \tfrac{1}{2}mv^2 \qquad\qquad (19)$$

The plot of Figure 10-3 contains some information about the distribution of kinetic energies among the molecules which have condensed. From the rate of rotation of the disks and the distance between them, we can calculate the velocity which an atom must have to condense on any one pie slice.* From the atomic mass and our calculated velocity we learn the kinetic energy of the atom. Figure 10-4 shows the result. At temperature T_1 a few atoms have very low kinetic energies and some have very high kinetic energies. Most of them have intermediate kinetic energies, as shown by the black curve. At a higher temperature, T_2, the energy distribution is altered to that shown by the white curve. As can be seen, *increasing the temperature causes a general shift of the molecular distribution toward higher kinetic energies.* Moreover, in going from T_1 to T_2 there is a large increase in the number of molecules having kinetic energies above a certain value, E.

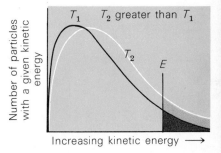

Fig. 10-4 Effect of temperature on relative distribution of atomic or molecular kinetic energies.

*Here is an example. Suppose the disks are 1.0 cm apart and are rotating at a rate of 1,200 revolutions per minute or $1{,}200/60 = 20$ revolutions per second. One-twentieth of a second is required for a complete revolution. There are 12 sections on the disk; hence each section will be in the target area for $1/12 \times 20 = 1/240$th second. The atoms collecting on slice 1 require 1/240th second to travel the distance of 1.0 cm between disks. Their average velocity will be

$$\frac{1.0 \text{ cm}}{1/240 \text{ sec}} = \frac{240 \text{ cm}}{\text{sec}}$$

Those on 2 require 2/240th of a second; they are going 120 cm/sec. And so on.

We can apply these curves to our reaction rate problem. Suppose a reaction can proceed only if two molecules collide with a total kinetic energy that exceeds a certain threshold energy, E. Figure 10-4 shows a typical situation. At T_1, the lower temperature, the darkly shaded area is proportional to the number of molecules possessing at least the threshold energy. These molecules have enough energy to stage effective collisions even with molecules of very low kinetic energy. But since only a small number of molecules have this much energy, few collisions are effective, and the reaction is slow. Some molecules with energies below E may collide with each other to give a total energy above the threshold, but the probability is rather small. However, if we raise the temperature to T_2, the number of molecules with energy E or greater is raised in proportion to the lightly shaded area. *Only a small temperature change is needed to make a large change in the area out on the tail of the energy distribution curve.* Consequently, the reaction rate is very sensitive to change in temperature.

This argument is based on the "typical" situation in which E is well out on the tail of the curve. Suppose it is not, but is near the maximum of the curve at T_1 or is even to the left of it. Then a large number of molecules have the necessary energy to react, even at the lower temperature T_1. Since collisions occur so rapidly (remember, one every 10^{-9} seconds or so), the reaction is over in less than the blink of an eye. The circumstances shown in Figure 10-4 are most important in considering a slow reaction.

It should be noted that raising the temperature also increases the reaction rate by increasing the frequency of the collisions. This is, however, a very small effect compared with that caused by the increase in the number of molecules with sufficient energy to cause reaction.

10-2   THE ROLE OF ENERGY IN REACTION RATES

Now that we see the effect of temperature in increasing the fraction of molecular collisions having a total energy greater than the threshold energy, our understanding of the role of energy in fixing reaction rates can be expanded. Let us consider a simple analogy.

10-2.1   Pole-Vaulting and Potential Energy Barriers— The Activation Energy

Suppose it is your ambition to be a great pole-vaulter. To achieve this goal, you must take a running start and then raise your body to an altitude of at least eight feet, go over the bar, and drop into the sandpit, as illustrated in Figure 10-5. Of course, it is in getting over the bar that the difficulties develop. Almost anyone can make a running start and achieve some altitude, but not everyone can get over the bar. Some individuals will clear the bar with room to spare, some will barely squeak over, and many will have to go back and try the running start again. Happiness is getting over the bar. If the bar is high, you will have to increase your distance from the earth; hence, your potential energy will increase. If the bar is high, few individuals will get over. If the bar is low, everyone will meet with success. It is the bar that

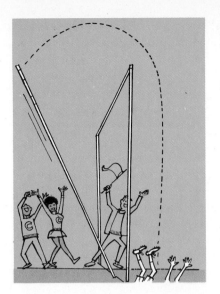
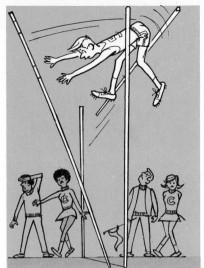
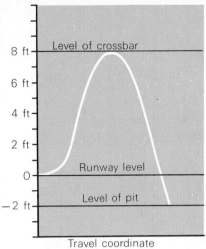

Fig. 10-5 A strong pole-vaulter with adequate height (potential energy) can jump over the crossbar (the activation energy). A weak pole-vaulter without adequate height cannot jump over the crossbar. Height (potential energy) of successful pole-vaulter vs. distance traveled.

defines the barrier; if you do get over it, the remainder of the process, falling from the bar to the sandpit, is sure to follow.

Chemical reactions are similar. As molecules collide and a reaction takes place, the atoms must momentarily take up bonding arrangements that are less stable than either reactants or products. Atoms are separated (as were the earth and the jumper) and the potential energy of the system goes up. These high-energy molecular arrangements are like the bar in Figure 10-5—they place an energy "barrier" between reactants and products. Only if the colliding molecules have enough energy to overcome the barrier imposed by the unstable arrangements can reaction take place. This barrier determines the "threshold energy" or minimum energy necessary to permit a reaction to occur. It is called the **activation energy.** If the activation energy is high, few molecules possess enough energy to react, and the reaction proceeds slowly. If the activation energy is low, more molecules have enough energy to get over the barrier, and the reaction tends to proceed rapidly.

Here again, the geometry of the colliding molecules is involved. Just as the pole-vaulter can get over the bar with a lower jump if he learns the proper position for just slipping over the bar, some collision patterns permit reaction at a lower energy. The activation energy is *the lowest energy necessary to cause a reaction between two molecules which collide in the best geometric arrangement for a reaction to occur* (see Figure 10-6, page 236).

This barrier can be shown graphically in Figure 10-7, which shows the relative energies of reactants and products. The diagram becomes the equivalent of the route the pole-vaulter takes in our analogy. This diagram applies to the reaction between carbon monoxide (CO) and nitrogen dioxide (NO_2). The horizontal axis of the diagram, called the **reaction coordinate,** shows the progress of the reaction. Proceeding from left to right along this reaction coordinate, we see the CO and NO_2 molecules approaching each other, colliding, and going through an intermediate process that results in the formation of CO_2 and NO. The vertical axis represents the total potential energy of the system. Thus, the curve provides a history of the potential energy change

The ACTIVATION ENERGY

Fig. 10-6 A pole-vaulter needs at least eight feet of height to clear the bar. Anything less than eight feet is not enough.

Fig. 10-7 Potential energy diagram for the reaction

$$CO + NO_2 \longrightarrow CO_2 + NO$$

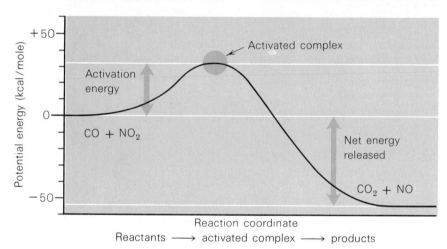

Reactants $\longrightarrow$ activated complex $\longrightarrow$ products

during a collision which results in a reaction. The energy required to overcome the potential energy barrier is usually provided by the kinetic energies of the colliding particles. The kinetic energies of the particles are determined by the temperature of the two reactants, CO and NO_2.

Let us move from left to right along this curve and describe the events which occur. Along the flat region at the left, CO and NO_2 are approaching each other. In this region, they possess kinetic energy and their total potential energy shows no change. The beginning of the rise in the curve signifies that the two molecules have come sufficiently close to have an effect on each other. During this approach, the molecules slow down as their kinetic energies convert to potential energy to climb the curve. If they have sufficient kinetic energy, they can ascend the left side of the barrier all the way up to the summit. Attaining this point is interpreted as follows: CO and NO_2 had sufficient kinetic energy to overcome the mutually repulsive forces between nuclei and between negative electron clouds. Here at the summit the molecular cluster, like the suspended pole-vaulter, is unstable with respect to either the forward reaction (giving CO_2 and NO) or the reverse reaction (restoring CO and NO_2). This transitory arrangement is of prime importance (its potential energy fixes the activation energy). It is called the **activated complex.**

Now there are two possibilities:

(1) the activated complex may separate into the two original CO and NO_2 molecules, which would then retrace their former path on the curve; or
(2) the activated complex may separate into CO_2 and NO molecules.

The latter possibility is represented by moving down the right side of the barrier. In the flat region at the right, CO_2 and NO have separated beyond the point of having any effect on each other; the potential energy of the activated complex has become kinetic energy again.

In the event that the CO and NO_2 molecules do not have sufficient energy to attain the summit, they reach a point only part of the way up the left side of the barrier. Then, repelling one another, they separate, going downhill to the left.

We have labeled the difference between the high potential energy at the activated complex and the lower energy of the reactants as the activation energy. *The activation energy is the energy necessary to transform the reactants into the activated complex.* This may involve weakening or breaking bonds, forcing reactants close together in opposition to repulsive forces, or storing energy in a vibrating molecule so that it reacts on collision. *Increasing the temperature affects reaction rate by increasing the number of molecular collisions having sufficient energy to form this activated complex.* The magnitude of the activation energy for a reaction can be determined by measuring experimentally the change in reaction rate associated with a known change in temperature.

10-2.2 Heat of Reaction

We can deduce the heat of reaction from Figure 10-7. In our example, the reactants are at a higher total energy than are the products. This means that in the course of the reaction there will be a net *release* of energy. This reaction is **exothermic.** Figure 10-7 shows that the reaction releases 54 kcal of heat per mole of carbon monoxide consumed. Notice that the height of the energy barrier between reactants and products has no effect on the net heat release. We must put in an amount of energy equal to the activation energy to get to the top of the barrier, but we get it all back on the way down the other side.

Now let us consider the reverse reaction. We need not draw another reaction diagram, since Figure 10-7 will suffice. Now we are interested in the reaction between CO_2 and NO to produce CO and NO_2:

$$CO + NO_2 \longleftarrow CO_2 + NO \qquad (2a)$$

This reaction begins at the lower energy appropriate to the chemical stability of CO_2 + NO (at the right side of Figure 10-7); it ends at the higher energy appropriate to the chemical stability of $CO + NO_2$ (at the left side of Figure 10-7). The difference in energy—the heat of this reaction—is just equal to that of the reverse reaction but is opposite in sign. This reaction *absorbs* 54 kcal of heat per mole of carbon monoxide produced. It is **endothermic.**

Figure 10-7 contains one other very interesting piece of information concerning the rate of the reverse reaction between CO_2 and NO. This reaction rate is controlled by the energy barrier confronting the colliding molecules of CO_2 and NO. We see from the diagram that the activation energy for this reaction is higher than that for the reaction we studied earlier. Further, it is higher by exactly the heat of reaction. We conclude that the reaction between CO_2 and NO will be slower, at any given temperature, than the reverse reaction between CO and NO_2, if the rates are compared at the same concentrations.

The relationship between activation energies for the forward and reverse reactions can be expressed mathematically. The activation energy is denoted by the symbol $\Delta H^{\ddagger}$ (read "delta-*H*-cross") and the heat of reaction by ΔH. Hence, we may write

$$\Delta H^{\ddagger}_{forward} = \Delta H^{\ddagger}_{reverse} + \Delta H \qquad (20)$$

where

(1) $\Delta H^{\ddagger}_{forward}$ = activation energy for reaction proceeding to the right (energy absorbed);
(2) $\Delta H^{\ddagger}_{reverse}$ = activation energy for reaction proceeding to the left (energy absorbed); and
(3) ΔH = heat absorbed during reaction proceeding left to right (ΔH is positive if endothermic, negative if exothermic).

The heat of reaction, ΔH, is positive if heat is absorbed as the reaction proceeds, left to right. It is negative if heat is evolved. In our example

$$CO + NO_2 \longrightarrow CO_2 + NO \qquad (2)$$

$\Delta H^{\ddagger}_{forward} = +32$ kcal/mole, $\Delta H^{\ddagger}_{reverse} = +86$ kcal/mole, and $\Delta H = -54$ kcal/mole. We see that

$$32 = 86 + (-54)$$

which is in accordance with equation (*20*). This relationship is important because it implies that we need only *two* of the three quantities $\Delta H^{\ddagger}_{forward}$, $\Delta H^{\ddagger}_{reverse}$, and ΔH, to calculate the third.

10-2.3 Action of Catalysts

Many reactions proceed quite slowly when the reactants are mixed alone, but can be made to take place much more rapidly by the introduction of other substances. These substances, called **catalysts,** are not used up in the reaction. The process of increasing the rate of a reaction through the use of a catalyst is referred to as **catalysis.** You have seen at least one example of catalytic action, the effect of $Mn^{2+}(aq)$ in speeding up the reaction between $C_2O_4^{2-}(aq)$ and $MnO_4^-(aq)$. The decomposition of hydrogen peroxide to give H_2O and $\frac{1}{2}O_2$ is also strongly catalyzed by MnO_2.

The action of a catalyst can be explained in terms of our pole-vaulting analogy. In Figure 10-5 we saw a formidable obstacle between our hopeful pole-vaulter and a successful landing in the sandpit. Most people simply cannot get over a bar eight feet high, no matter how many running starts they make. But the coach can help even these people to a successful landing in the pit simply by lowering the bar (Figure 10-8). The return trip (from sandpit, over the bar, and back to the starting line) would also be much easier if the bar were lowered.

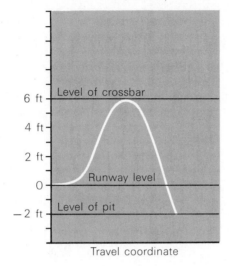

Fig. 10-8 With the coach's help (catalysis) the weak pole-vaulter can clear the crossbar.

Figure 10-9 shows the same situation for a chemical reaction. The potential energy of the system is plotted against the reaction coordinate. The solid curve shows the activation energy barrier that must be overcome for a reaction to take place. When a catalyst is added, there is a new reaction path, hence a different activation energy barrier. The dashed curve shows this situation. This new reaction path corre-

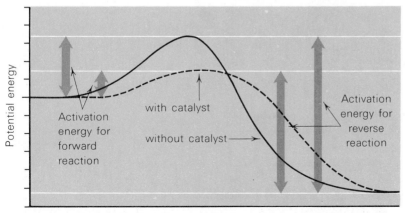

Fig. 10-9 Effect of a catalyst on a reaction and its reverse.

ACTION of CATALYSTS

Fig. 10-10 A model of formic acid, HCOOH.

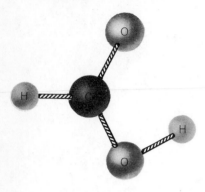

Ball-and-spring model

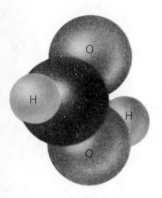

Space-filling model

sponds to a new reaction mechanism that permits the reaction to occur via a different activated complex. Hence, more particles can get over the new, lower-energy barrier and the rate of the reaction is increased. The activation energy for the reverse reaction is lowered by exactly the same amount as the forward reaction. This accounts for the experimental fact that a catalyst for a reaction has an equal effect on the reverse reaction. If a catalyst doubles the rate in one direction, it also doubles the rate in the other direction.

10-2.4 Examples of Catalysts

In all cases of catalysis, the catalyst acts by inserting intermediate steps in a reaction, steps that would not occur without the catalyst. *The catalyst itself must be regenerated in a subsequent step.* (An added substance that is continuously used up by a reaction is a *reactant,* not a catalyst.) An example is the catalytic action of acid on the decomposition of formic acid (HCOOH). Figure 10-10 shows a model of formic acid. To the carbon atom is attached a hydrogen atom, an oxygen atom, and an OH group.

Figure 10-11 shows how this molecule might decompose. If the hydrogen atom attached to carbon migrates over to the OH group, the carbon-oxygen bond can break to give a molecule of water and a molecule of carbon

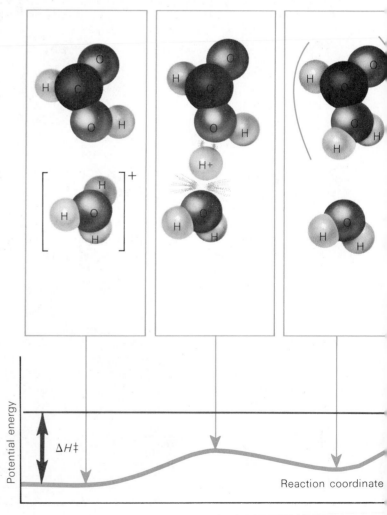

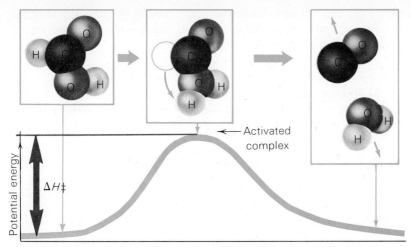

Fig. 10-11 Potential energy diagram for the uncatalyzed decomposition of formic acid.

Activated complex

$\Delta H\ddagger$

Potential energy

Reaction coordinate for uncatalyzed decomposition

Fig. 10-12 Potential energy diagram for the catalyzed decomposition of formic acid.

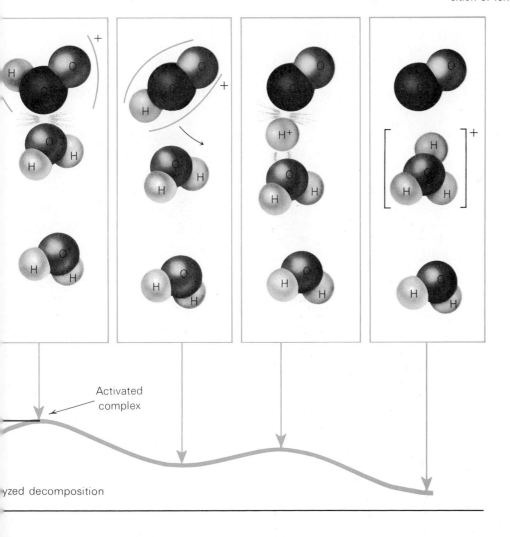

Activated complex

yzed decomposition

monoxide. This migration, shown in the center of the drawing, requires a large amount of energy. There is a high activation energy. Hence, the reaction below occurs very slowly.

$$HCOOH \longrightarrow H_2O + CO \qquad (21)$$

If sulfuric acid (H_2SO_4) is added to an aqueous solution of formic acid, carbon monoxide bubbles out rapidly. This also occurs if phosphoric acid (H_3PO_4) is added instead. The common factor in both cases is that both H_2SO_4 and H_3PO_4 give the ion $H^+(aq)$. On the other hand, careful analysis shows that the concentration of $H^+(aq)$ is constant during the rapid decomposition of formic acid; $H^+(aq)$ is not used up in the reaction. Evidently, hydrogen ion acts as a catalyst in this decomposition. In the presence of $H^+(aq)$, a new reaction path is available. The new reaction mechanism begins with the addition of a hydrogen ion to formic acid, as shown in Figure 10-12. Thus, the catalyst is consumed at first, forming a new species, $(HCOOH_2)^+$. In this new species, one of the carbon-oxygen bonds is weakened. With only a small expenditure of energy, the next reaction shown in Figure 10-12 can occur, producing $(HCO)^+$ and H_2O. Finally, $(HCO)^+$ decomposes to produce CO and H^+. This last reaction of the sequence regenerates the catalyst, $H^+(aq)$.

Each of the steps in this new reaction mechanism is governed by the same principles that govern a simple reaction. Each reaction has an activation energy. The overall reaction has a potential energy diagram that is merely a composite of the simple energy curves of each of the succeeding steps.

The highest energy required in this new reaction path is only 18 kcal, much lower than the activation energy shown in Figure 10-11 for the uncatalyzed reaction. The rate of decomposition, then, is much faster when acid is present.

Notice that the catalyst does not *cause* the reaction. A catalyst can *speed up* a reaction which might be very slow in its absence.

In some cases, the catalyst is a solid substance on whose surface a reactant molecule can be held (adsorbed) in a position favorable for reaction. When a molecule of another reactant reaches the same point on the solid, reaction occurs. Metals such as iron, nickel, platinum, and palladium seem to act in this way in reactions involving gases. There is evidence that in some cases bonds of reactant particles are weakened or actually broken. Such a particle will then react more easily with another reactant particle.

A very large number of catalysts, called enzymes, are found in living tissues. Among the best known examples are the digestive enzymes, such as ptyalin in saliva and pepsin in gastric juice. A common function of these two enzymes is to hasten the breakdown of large molecules, such as starch and protein (Chapter 19), into simpler molecules that can be utilized by body cells. In addition to the relatively small number of digestive enzymes, many other enzymes are involved in biochemical processes (Chapter 21).

The specific methods by which catalysts work are not clearly understood in most cases. Finding a catalyst suitable for a given reaction usually requires a long period of laboratory experimentation. Yet, we can look forward to the time when a catalyst can be tailor-made to fit a particular need. This exciting prospect accounts for the great activity on this chemical frontier.

10-3 THE RATE OF NUCLEAR PROCESSES

The rate of a nuclear process, like the rate of a chemical process, is described as the number of particles that undergo change per unit of time. Let us consider the decay of radium-226. The equation for this process is

$$^{226}_{88}\text{Ra} \longrightarrow {}^{222}_{86}\text{Rn} + {}^{4}_{2}\text{He} \qquad (22)$$

The amount of ${}^{4}_{2}\text{He}$ produced per hour is proportional to the number of radium-226 atoms present. We can write the equation

rate of helium-4 production $= k \cdot$ number of radium-226 nuclei

or

$$\text{rate of } {}^{4}_{2}\text{He formation} = k \cdot {}^{226}_{88}\text{Ra} \qquad (23)$$

where k is the proportionality constant and ${}^{226}_{88}\text{Ra}$ is the number of radium-226 nuclei present. The equation simply states that in a given time period, let us say one hour, a given fraction of the radium-226 nuclei will undergo decomposition. If we double the number of nuclei present, the number of nuclei decomposing will double; the rate is doubled. As we noted earlier, the time required for one half of the nuclei of a given radioactive isotope to decompose will be characteristic of that isotope. It is known as the half-life of the isotope (see page 164).

Scientists who first studied the rate of nuclear processes were surprised to find that the rate of a nuclear process is not altered by a change in temperature. We may well wonder: if the decay process follows the same concentration-dependence as does a typical chemical reaction, why does it not follow the same temperature-dependence? Why does an increase in temperature not accelerate a nuclear process? The answer lies in the energetics of nuclear processes. We noted in Chapter 9 that energy terms associated with a nuclear reaction are usually millions of times larger than energy terms associated with a chemical process. As you will recall, this is the very reason why the world has such a strong interest in "atomic energy." It is not unreasonable to guess that nuclear processes would also have activation energies millions of times larger than chemical activation energies. In fact, we have evidence to prove that this is so. You recall that fusion reactions can only be initiated at temperatures of 10 million degrees to 100 million degrees. This means that a very high activation energy is involved. In view of this fact, it is not surprising that temperature differences of 100 °C or even 500 °C have no observable effect on a nuclear process.

10-4 HIGHLIGHTS

Factors determining reaction rate are (1) temperature, (2) concentration of reactants, and (3) kind of reactants. The rate expression *cannot* be obtained from the equation for the process, only from experiment. The rate expression can be used to suggest a **reaction mechanism.**

Reactions occur when molecules collide. Not all collisions result in reaction; only those collisions of molecules with total energy above the **activation energy** and with proper orientation give rise to reaction.

Catalysts increase the reaction rate by making possible a new mechanism with a lower activation energy. Enzymes are catalysts for life processes.

QUESTIONS and PROBLEMS

1 The rate of movement of a bicycle can be measured in miles per hour. In what units would you express the rate at which (a) a family consumes eggs; (b) you spend money; (c) a propeller turns; (d) a dieter loses weight; (e) traffic passes an intersection; (f) planes take off from an airport?

2 In general, what effect does an increase in the concentration of the reactants have upon the rate of the reaction? Explain, using the "collision theory." Are there exceptions? Explain. (*Hint:* what happens if the reactant is not involved in the rate-determining step?)

3 In Experiment 10, hydrogen gas was produced by the reaction of magnesium ribbon with 15 ml of 3 M hydrochloric acid added to about 40 ml of water. What effect would there be on the rate of the reaction if 6 M HCl were used?

4 Consider the reaction which occurs when an aqueous solution of silver nitrate (a conducting solution) is added to an aqueous solution of sodium chromate (also a conducting solution). A precipitate of silver chromate (Ag_2CrO_4) is formed. (a) Write the overall ionic equation for this reaction. (b) Would you expect this reaction to be slow or fast at room temperature? (c) Explain your answer to (b).

5 In Experiment 8, the reaction

$$Cu(s) + 2Ag^+(aq) \longrightarrow Cu^{2+}(aq) + 2Ag(s)$$

required half an hour to complete, while in Experiment 12 the reaction

$$Pb^{2+}(aq) + 2I^-(aq) \longrightarrow PbI_2(s)$$

was nearly instantaneous. Explain this difference on the basis of the nature of the reactants.

6 Which of the following reactions would you expect to be rapid at room temperature? which slow? Explain your answer in each case.

(a) $PbO_2(s) \longrightarrow PbO(s) + \frac{1}{2}O_2(g)$

(b) $Ag^+(aq) + Cl^-(aq) \longrightarrow AgCl(s)$

(c) $C_6H_{12}O_6(s) + 6\,O_2(g) \longrightarrow$
$$6CO_2(g) + 6H_2O(g)$$

(d) $Ba^{2+}(aq) + SO_4^{2-}(aq) \longrightarrow BaSO_4(s)$

(e) $C(s) + O_2(g) \longrightarrow CO_2(g)$

7 If you know that one of the following equations represents a reaction mechanism, which one would it likely be? Explain your answer.

(a) $C_{25}H_{52}(s) + 38\,O_2(g) \longrightarrow$
$$25CO_2(g) + 26H_2O(g)$$

(b) $3Fe^{2+}(aq) + NO_3^-(aq) + 4H^+(aq) \longrightarrow$
$$3Fe^{3+}(aq) + NO(g) + 2H_2O(l)$$

(c) $Ag^+(aq) + I^-(aq) \longrightarrow AgI(s)$

(d) $2H_2(g) + O_2(g) \longrightarrow 2H_2O(l)$

8 Consider the following sequence of reactions. A person drives to the grocery store; parks the car; selects a shopping cart; fills the cart with groceries; pays for the groceries at the checkout counter; has the groceries bagged and put in the car. Under less than perfect conditions any of these steps can become the rate-determining step of buying groceries. (a) Which step usually is the rate-determining step of buying groceries? (b) Under what conditions could each of the other steps *become* the rate-determining step?

9 What effect does an increase in temperature have upon the rate of a reaction? Explain your answer (a) using the collision theory; (b) by drawing a kinetic energy distribution curve.

10 Given the kinetic energy distribution curves and the threshold energy for each reaction shown in Figure 10-13: (a) Which reaction will be faster at room temperature? (b) Which reaction will show the greater increase in rate if the temperature is raised 10 °C?

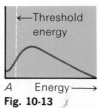

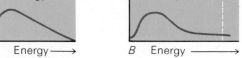

A Energy $\longrightarrow$ B Energy $\longrightarrow$

Fig. 10-13

11 Why does milk sour less rapidly in a refrigerator than at room temperature? Explain, using a kinetic energy distribution curve.

12 Why is lump sugar satisfactory for use in hot coffee but granulated sugar preferable for use in iced tea?

13 What is the function of the pilot light in a gas stove? Explain by drawing the approximate potential energy diagram for the reaction

$$CH_4(g) + 2 O_2(g) \longrightarrow CO_2(g) + 2H_2O(g)$$

and indicating with an arrow the function of the pilot light.

14 Given the potential energy diagram in Figure 10-14: (a) Is this reaction exothermic or endothermic? (b) Would you expect this reaction to occur rapidly at room temperature? Why or why not? (c) What is ΔH for this reaction? (d) What is $\Delta H^\ddagger$ for the forward reaction? (e) At what point on the graph might an activated complex exist? (f) Of the reactions you did in the laboratory in Experiment 16, which one would this diagram most likely represent?

(i) $H_2SO_4(l) \xrightarrow{H_2O} 2H^+(aq) + SO_4{}^{2-}(aq)$

(ii) $NH_4Cl(s) \xrightarrow{H_2O} NH_4{}^+(aq) + Cl^-(aq)$

(iii) $(NH_4)_2Cr_2O_7(s) \longrightarrow$
$\qquad N_2(g) + Cr_2O_3(s) + 4H_2O(g)$

Explain your reasoning in each case.

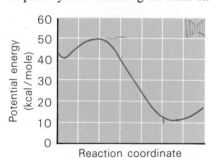

Fig. 10-14

15 Consider the potential energy diagram in Figure 10-15: (a) Is this reaction exothermic or endothermic? (b) Would you expect this reaction to occur rapidly at room temperature? Explain your answer. (c) Of the following reactions, which one might this diagram represent?

(i) $H_2SO_4(l) \longrightarrow 2H^+(aq) + SO_4{}^{2-}(aq)$
(ii) $NH_4Cl(s) \longrightarrow NH_4{}^+(aq) + Cl^-(aq)$
(iii) $CH_4(g) + 2 O_2(g) \longrightarrow$
$\qquad CO_2(g) + 2H_2O(g)$

(iv) $C(graphite) \longrightarrow C(diamond)$
$\qquad \Delta H = +0.45 \text{ kcal}$

This reaction takes place only at high temperatures and pressures.

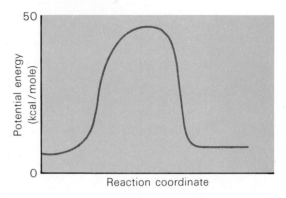

Fig. 10-15

16 Given the potential energy diagrams for processes A, B, C, and D (Figure 10-16): (a) Which process will be fastest at room temperature? (b) Which will be fairly fast at room temperature? (c) Which will be extremely slow at room temperature?

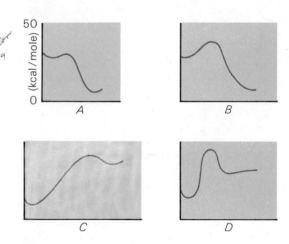

Fig. 10-16

17 For a particular reaction, $\Delta H = -60 \text{ kcal}$ and $\Delta H^\ddagger = +30 \text{ kcal}$ (for the forward reaction). (a) Draw the potential energy curve for the reaction. Be sure to label the axes and to put a scale on the potential energy axis. (b) Label the parts of the curve representing (i) the reactants; (ii) the products; (iii) the activation energy of the forward reaction; (iv) the activated complex; (v) the net energy absorbed or released (give amount and tell which).

245

> . . . by . . . equilibrium, we mean a state in which the properties of a system, as experimentally measured, would suffer no further observable change even after the lapse of an indefinite period of time. It is not intimated that the individual particles are unchanging.

G. N. LEWIS (1875–1946) and MERLE RANDALL (1888–1950)

EQUILIBRIUM IN PHASE CHANGES AND IN CHEMICAL REACTIONS 11

The rate of the forward reaction equals the rate of the reverse reaction.

EVERYONE HAS HAD THE FEELING OF BEING PULLED IN TWO directions at once and having to settle for some sort of compromise between alternatives. Strangely enough, chemical reactions sometimes have the same problem. They do not always march neatly down the path of the equation, converting reactants to products in a tidy manner.

Fortunately, the driving forces in chemistry are better understood than those in life situations. One is the tendency to exist in the lowest energy state possible, which is easy to understand by anyone who has frequently fallen *down* but never *up*. The second is the universal tendency toward maximum disorder. Disorder is a much more natural state than order. This may give you some much-needed ammunition the next time you are told to clean up your room, but don't count on it.

In chemistry, the proper combination of these two forces gives rise to the condition known as chemical EQUILIBRIUM.

In Chapter 10 we discussed the rate of the reaction between CO and NO_2,

$$CO(g) + NO_2(g) \longrightarrow CO_2(g) + NO(g) \qquad (1)$$

and the rate of the reverse reaction between CO_2 and NO,

$$CO_2(g) + NO(g) \longrightarrow CO(g) + NO_2(g) \qquad (2)$$

It is only fair to ask: which reaction *really* goes? In this chapter we shall investigate this and related questions. We shall try to set up procedures for deciding what happens when various reagents are mixed.

If we start by mixing NO_2 and CO, the red-brown color caused by NO_2 fades as the reddish NO_2 is converted into colorless NO. Clearly, reaction (1) giving colorless NO is taking place. The equation suggests that the color will continue to fade until the system is colorless and all NO_2 has been used up, but this does *not* happen. Instead, the system reaches a light, red-brown color and the color changes no further. The reaction seems to have stopped; relative amounts of NO_2 and NO are no longer changing. In Chapter 5 we said that a liquid and its vapor are at *equilibrium* when the pressure created by the vapor above the liquid stops changing. If the same criterion—*i.e.*, that the system is not undergoing observable change—is applied here, we would say that our chemical system has reached a state of equilibrium.

Many questions cross our minds.

(1) How do we recognize equilibrium?
(2) What are the molecules doing at equilibrium?
(3) How can we change the equilibrium condition?
(4) How do we define the composition of the gas mixture at equilibrium?
(5) Can equilibrium be treated in a quantitative manner?

Let us explore these questions.

Fig. 11-1 Exchange of molecules between liquid and gas. (a) At equilibrium—rate of evaporation is equal to rate of condensation. (b) When the partial pressure of vapor is *below* the vapor pressure—rate of evaporation is above rate of condensation. (c) When the partial pressure of vapor is *above* the vapor pressure—rate of condensation is above rate of evaporation.

11-1 EQUILIBRIUM IN PHASE CHANGES

Let us begin our study by reviewing the use of the word *equilibrium* as we applied it to phase changes.

11-1.1 Vapor-Liquid Equilibrium—Vapor Pressure

In Chapter 5 a model was constructed to explain the vapor pressure of a liquid. We visualized a system in which some molecules leave the liquid and enter the vapor phase while other molecules in the vapor phase return to the liquid surface. We defined equilibrium as the condition existing in this system when the *rate* at which molecules leave the surface is just equal to the *rate* at which they return. By this definition vigorous molecular activity goes on *even after all external signs of change have disappeared.* But we cannot *see* molecules; nor can we measure their rate of leaving or entering the liquid. How do we recognize the equilibrium condition?

In our earlier study, we agreed that when the vapor pressure of the liquid becomes constant over a long period of time (when there is no observable change in the system) the system is at equilibrium. In short, equilibrium is characterized by *constancy of observable properties.* However, constancy of properties can be difficult to recognize, particularly when a system is changing very slowly. For this reason we shall return frequently to the question of how to recognize the equilibrium condition.

Now let us examine the molecular model a little more closely. In Figure 11-1(a), a perfect balance between rates of evaporation and condensation is observed. The system is at equilibrium and no external changes can be seen. The partial pressure of the vapor is *equal to* the equilibrium value. What happens if the partial pressure of the vapor is *less than* the equilibrium value? As Figure 11-1(b) shows, the rate of evaporation exceeds the rate of condensation. As the concentration of molecules in the vapor phase builds up, the rate of condensation builds up; finally, the rate of condensation becomes equal to the rate of evaporation. At that point equilibrium, represented by Figure 11-1(a), is reached. Suppose the equilibrium is disturbed in another way. If we inject an excess of vapor into the bottle or compress the vapor above the liquid, the concentration of molecules in the vapor phase suddenly rises and the rate of condensation increases [Figure 11-1(c)]. As the excess vapor molecules return to the liquid phase, the rate of condensation falls off until finally *the rate of condensation equals the rate of evaporation*—the system is at equilibrium and the vapor pressure is the same as in Figure 11-1(a). At equilibrium, *microscopic processes continue* but balance each other so that no obvious changes can be observed.

If we now look closely at the method we used to recognize equilibrium in these cases, we see that we have observed a constancy of properties with time [Figure 11-1(a)]. This is our standard procedure for defining the equilibrium condition. In addition, we have disturbed the equilibrium system and approached it from two different sides. In Figure 11-1(b), the pressure of the vapor will build *up* to the equilibrium value from a pressure which is *below* the vapor pressure

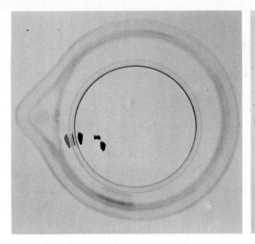

of the system. In Figure 11-1(c), the pressure of the vapor will drop to the equilibrium value from a pressure which is *above* the vapor pressure of the system. In all three cases the same equilibrium value will be obtained. *If the same pressure is reached when the system approaches equilibrium from a pressure either above or below the equilibrium vapor pressure, the vapor pressure obtained is the equilibrium value.* (Temperature is assumed constant throughout.)

The above discussion answers several of our original questions about vapor-liquid equilibrium. We know what the molecules are doing and we know how to recognize equilibrium. Other questions remain. For example, how can we change the equilibrium condition? We learned in Chapter 5 that we can change the vapor pressure above a given liquid by changing the temperature. As we raise the temperature, the vapor pressure rises; as we lower the temperature, the vapor pressure falls. *Temperature* is an important variable in controlling the equilibrium condition. The vapor pressure is determined by the nature of the liquid and the temperature. The *nature of the liquid (or of the system)* is obviously an important factor in determining the equilibrium condition.

11-1.2 Solubility (Solid-Solution Equilibrium)

In Figure 11-2 we see the sequence of events that occurs if several crystals of iodine are dissolved in a mixture of water and alcohol. At first the liquid is colorless, but very quickly a reddish color appears near the solid. Stirring the liquid causes swirls of the reddish color to move out; solid iodine is dissolving to become part of the liquid. Changes are evident: the liquid takes on increasing color and the pieces of solid iodine diminish in size as time passes. Finally, however, the color stops changing. Solid remains, but the pieces no longer diminish in size. By our earlier operational definition of equilibrium, the solution appears to be in equilibrium with the solid iodine crystals.

What does this process look like on the molecular level? Iodine molecules leave the surface of the crystal at a given rate as the crystals are first placed in the water-alcohol solution. The rate at which molecules return to the surface is low at first, since there are very few molecules of I_2 in solution (no color) and there is very low probability that

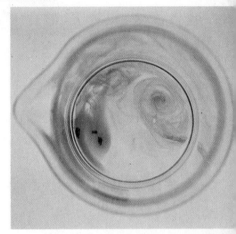

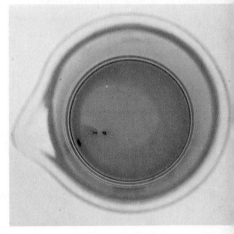

Fig. 11-2 Iodine dissolving in an alcohol-water mixture. Equilibrium is recognized by constant color of the solution.

those just leaving will return immediately. As time passes, however, more and more I_2 molecules enter the solution phase; there is a greater probability that a molecule in the solution will encounter the surface of an iodine crystal and become bonded to the crystal. As a result, the *rate of crystallization** increases until finally it is just *equal to* the *rate of solution*. The system is then at equilibrium. No net change is apparent even though action on the molecular level is vigorous.

In Chapter 5 we found that solubilities ranged from very low (lead chromate in water) to very high (sugar in water). Clearly, the *type of solid and liquid* will be important in determining the concentration at which solubility equilibrium is established. Further, we found that solubilities vary with temperature. *Temperature* is important in determining the equilibrium concentration.

Our analysis of physical systems at equilibrium has given us a start toward answering our original five questions about chemical equilibrium (page 247). Let us review these answers.

(1) *How do we recognize equilibrium?* Equilibrium is recognized by the constancy of observable properties in a closed system at a uniform temperature. It is important that we specify a *closed* system. The evaporation of water from an open dish does *not* represent equilibrium even though the *rate* of evaporation is *constant*. Further, we found that the equilibrium condition is the same regardless of the side from which it is approached. This knowledge helps greatly in recognizing equilibrium.

(2) *What are the molecules doing at equilibrium?* The molecules participate in both forward and reverse reactions. *At equilibrium the rate of the forward reaction is equal to the rate of the reverse reaction.*

(3) *How can we change the equilibrium condition?* So far, we have identified temperature and the nature of the reactants as two of the important variables determining the equilibrium condition.

The remaining questions, (4) and (5), will take on more significance as we proceed with a discussion of *chemical* equilibrium.

11-2 EQUILIBRIUM IN CHEMICAL SYSTEMS

11-2.1 The N_2O_4-NO_2 Equilibrium

Can our observations on physical equilibrium be carried over to chemical systems? Suppose we fill two identical bulbs with equal amounts of red-brown nitrogen dioxide (NO_2). Now let us immerse the first bulb (bulb *A*) in an ice bath and the second bulb (bulb *B*) in boiling water (see Figure 11-3). The bulb at 0 °C (ice bath) becomes lighter in color while the bulb at 100 °C (boiling water) turns deep red-brown. The deep red-brown color suggests a high concentration of NO_2 molecules, but why is the bulb at 0 °C so light in color? If we determine the molecular weight of the colorless vapor or nearly colorless liquid present at even lower temperatures, we find a value

*Rate of crystallization** is the rate at which molecules or ions bond to crystals.

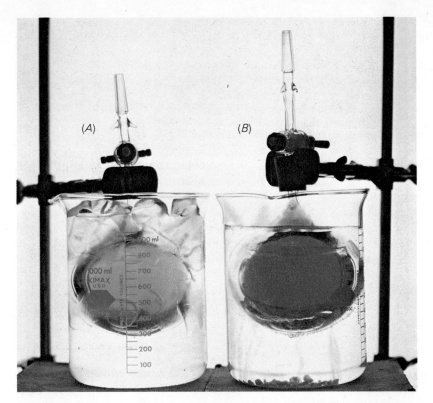

Fig. 11-3 Nitrogen dioxide gas at different temperatures. Bulb *A*: N₂O₄ at 0 °C (almost colorless). Bulb *B*: NO₂ at 100 °C (red-brown).

equal to *twice* the molecular weight of NO_2. It has the formula $(NO_2)_2$ or N_2O_4. The N_2O_4 is colorless; the NO_2 is red-brown in color.

Now let us transfer these two bulbs to a bath at room temperature as shown in Figure 11-4 (page 252). Immediately bulb *A* (cold bulb) becomes a darker brown while bulb *B* (hot bulb) becomes lighter in color. Our observations can be summarized by two equations:

BULB *A* (COLD BULB WARMING UP)

$$N_2O_4(g) \longrightarrow 2NO_2(g) \qquad (3)$$

BULB *B* (WARM BULB COOLING OFF)

$$2NO_2(g) \longrightarrow N_2O_4(g) \qquad (4)$$

Finally, as the two bulbs approach the same temperature, the colors stop changing. The bulbs are now *identical* in color; both have the same shade of brown—the system is at chemical equilibrium. If we now heat the bulb that was cold and cool the bulb that was hot, we can repeat the cycle.

We have watched the two bulbs approach the equilibrium condition from opposite directions. As bulb *A* was warmed, equilibrium was approached by the dissociation of N_2O_4 to give NO_2; as bulb *B* was cooled, equilibrium was approached by NO_2 molecules combining to give N_2O_4. If we join the two equations, we can write

$$N_2O_4(g) \longrightarrow 2NO_2(g) \qquad (3)$$

$$N_2O_4(g) \longleftarrow 2NO_2(g) \qquad (4)$$

$$\overline{N_2O_4(g) \rightleftharpoons 2NO_2(g)} \qquad (5)$$

COLORLESS   RED-BROWN

The N_2O_4-NO_2 EQUILIBRIUM

Fig. 11-4 Nitrogen dioxide gas at room temperature. Bulb *A* and bulb *B* after transfer to water bath at 25 °C.

(A) *(B)*

The double arrows indicate that both *dissociation* and *formation* of N_2O_4 are taking place and, hence, chemical equilibrium prevails.* Just as with phase changes at equilibrium, the *microscopic* processes of chemical reactions at equilibrium continue at the same rates, but no observable or *macroscopic* changes are apparent.

As we noted earlier, equilibrium is approached very rapidly in some systems, while in others it may be approached so slowly that years are required to reach the equilibrium condition. In the latter case, it is difficult to be sure that a system is really at equilibrium. Small changes are hard to recognize. How can we be sure, then, that a chemical system is really at equilibrium and is not just changing very slowly? *One of the best ways to be sure that we have a true equilibrium condition is to show that we can get the same equilibrium point from either the reactants or the products—that is, we can arrive at the same equilibrium value by starting from either side.* This is what we have done for the N_2O_4-NO_2 system.

CO₂ and air

Electric furnace

CaCO₃ and CaO

Hot air blast

Electric power supply

Fig. 11-5.1 *Open system not at equilibrium.* Calcium carbonate heated in stream of hot air. CO_2 generated is swept out of vessel. Recombination of CaO and CO_2 prevented.

11-2.2 The CaCO₃-CO₂ Equilibrium

This point can be illustrated further by considering the formation of quicklime or calcium oxide (CaO). Millions of tons of CaO are made in the United States each year for plaster, mortar, and agriculture. If limestone, known chemically as calcium carbonate ($CaCO_3$), is heated in a blast of hot air (800 °C), CaO and CO_2 are formed:

$$CaCO_3(s) \xrightarrow{\text{heat}} CaO(s) + CO_2(g) \qquad (6)$$

*In some cases an equal sign (=) replaces the double arrow to indicate equilibrium.

Calcium carbonate breaks down into solid CaO and gaseous CO_2. Since the $CO_2(g)$ is carried away from $CaO(s)$, their recombination to give $CaCO_3$ is prevented. In this dynamic system there is little opportunity for the reverse reaction to occur:

$$CaO(s) + CO_2(g) \longrightarrow CaCO_3(s) \qquad (7)$$

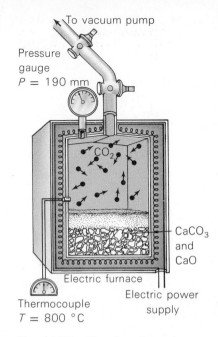

The system *cannot* reach equilibrium (see Figure 11-5.1).

The commercial production of CaO is based on the prompt removal of CO_2 from the system. Since fresh $CaCO_3$ is fed in at the bottom of the furnace and newly generated CaO is removed at the top, while CO_2 is swept away rapidly, we might think that the contents of the reactor do not change with time. Is this chemical equilibrium? *No!* We say that the system has reached a **steady state,** but this is *not* equilibrium. It is clear that our steady-state system depends upon the addition of fresh $CaCO_3$ at a constant rate and the removal of the resulting CaO at an appropriate constant rate. If we look beyond the reactor and watch the shrinking pile of $CaCO_3$ and the growing pile of CaO, it is now clear that macroscopic or visible changes *are* taking place. The apparent constancy of conditions in the reactor is a result of adding $CaCO_3$ and removing CaO at identical rates (measured in moles per minute).

Fig. 11-5.2 *Closed system at equilibrium.* Calcium carbonate heated in evacuated and closed vessel. Pressure reaches a constant value at a given temperature.

How does equilibrium differ from a steady state for a dynamic process? If this system is to reach equilibrium, the reactor must be *closed* so that CO_2 can no longer escape. A suitable vessel is shown in Figure 11-5.2. $CaCO_3$ is placed in the vessel, which has an attached pressure gauge. The air in the vessel is pumped out; then the gas exit valve is closed. If the $CaCO_3$ and container are now heated to 800 °C, the pressure of CO_2 inside the vessel builds up until the pressure gauge reads 190 mm. As long as the temperature is held constant at 800 °C, the pressure will remain steady at 190 mm. The system appears to be at equilibrium since no changes in macroscopic properties can be detected and the system is closed.

If we wanted to be sure that the system is at equilibrium when the pressure is at 190 mm, we could carry out the reverse reaction in the closed vessel. CaO would be placed in the reactor; air would be removed; then CO_2 would be pumped into the system until the pressure read well above 190 mm. For example, suppose CO_2 is added until the pressure is 400 mm. (The exact value is not important.) The valve is now closed to seal the system and the temperature is raised. Pressure begins to fall and finally at 800 °C, the pressure gauge again becomes steady at 190 mm. *The same equilibrium pressure of CO_2 has been reached starting with either $CaCO_3$ or with CaO plus CO_2 (Figure 11-5.3).*

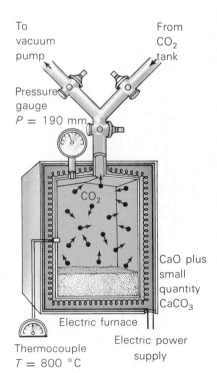

Both the decomposition and formation of $CaCO_3$ are taking place in the container:

$$CaCO_3(s) \longrightarrow CaO(s) + CO_2(g) \qquad (6)$$

$$CaCO_3(s) \longleftarrow CaO(s) + CO_2(g) \qquad (7)$$

$$\overline{CaCO_3(s) \rightleftharpoons CaO(s) + CO_2(g)} \qquad (8)$$

Fig. 11-5.3 CO_2 added to CaO in closed system. Equilibrium established between CaO, CO_2, and $CaCO_3$.

The system is at equilibrium at 800 °C when the pressure of CO_2 above the $CaCO_3$ is 190 mm. This is truly an equilibrium, *not* a steady-state, system: the system is closed; no observable changes, such as growing piles of CaO, are seen; and the constancy of the system is *not* dependent upon the addition or subtraction of reagents at a constant rate. Rates of both forward and reverse reactions are controlled by the environmental and physical conditions such as temperature and nature of the system.

EXERCISE 11-1

Which of the following systems constitute steady-state situations, and which are at equilibrium? For each, a constant property is indicated.

(1) An open pan of water is boiling on a stove. The temperature of the water is constant.
(2) A balloon contains air and a few drops of water. The pressure in the balloon is constant.
(3) A colony of ants is going about its daily routine in an anthill. The population of the anthill is constant.
(4) A Bunsen burner burns in the laboratory to give a well-defined flame. Supplies of gas and air are constant.

11-2.3 The Equilibrium Condition and the Meaning of an Equation

Much of our work in chemical equilibrium utilizes chemical equations. Let us review what is meant by an equation such as the one we discussed in Section 11-2.1:

$$N_2O_4(g) \rightleftharpoons 2NO_2(g) \qquad (5)$$

The equation tells us that *one* molecule of N_2O_4 can decompose to give two molecules of NO_2. It also tells us that two molecules of NO_2 can combine to give one molecule of N_2O_4. The equation does *not* tell us anything about the *relative amounts* of NO_2 and N_2O_4 present in a vessel at equilibrium! It definitely does *not* say that at equilibrium there will be 2 moles of NO_2 for each mole of N_2O_4.

These statements can be illustrated by a commonplace example. Consider the "reaction" that takes place at a "mixer" at the beginning of any school year. One of the equations for this system might be

$$\text{boy}(s) + \text{girl}(s) \rightleftharpoons \text{dancing couple}(s) \qquad (9)$$

What does this equation tell us? It tells us that a boy (if he knows what is good for him) asks one and only one girl to dance at any one time. It tells us that a girl (if she knows what is good for her) accepts the invitation of one and only one boy at any one time. And it tells us that a dancing couple consists of one boy and one girl. It does *not* say that at any dance there will be equal numbers of boys and girls. It does *not* say that the number of dancing couples will always be equal to the number of nondancing boys in the room. In short, our equation tells us nothing about the **equilibrium condition**—the number of dancing couples and the number of nondancing boys and girls. Experimental conditions such as the quality of the music, the size of the dance hall, the temperature in the room, the age of the group, and even the weather outside must be carefully defined before we can speak with any confidence about the equilibrium condition in the system.

Let us consider a chemical system comparable to the boy-plus-girl reaction—namely, phosphorus trichloride (PCl_3) plus chlorine (Cl_2) to give phosphorus pentachloride (PCl_5). The equation is

$$boy(s) + girl(s) \longrightarrow dancing\ couple(s) \qquad (9)$$

$$PCl_3(g) + Cl_2(g) \longrightarrow \qquad PCl_5(g) \qquad (10)$$

We still have no idea how completely PCl_3 and Cl_2 combine to give PCl_5 at equilibrium. All we know is that every mole of phosphorus trichloride that does react will combine with 1 mole of chlorine to give 1 mole of phosphorus pentachloride. All reagents and products are gases at 250 °C. However, if we start with 1 mole of PCl_3 and 1 mole of Cl_2 in a vessel under a pressure of 1 atm and a temperature of 250 °C, we may bring the system to equilibrium; then we can measure the moles of free PCl_3, the moles of free Cl_2, and the moles of free PCl_5 present *at equilibrium*. At 250 °C and 1 atm pressure, such measurements will show 0.71 mole of PCl_3, 0.71 mole of Cl_2, and 0.29 mole of PCl_5. If this is a true equilibrium, we shall obtain exactly the same mixture by starting with 1 mole of PCl_5 instead of 1 mole of PCl_3 and 1 mole of Cl_2. We do, in fact, observe this. All these observations may be summarized by a table:

	$PCl_3(g)$ +	$Cl_2(g)$ ⇌	$PCl_5(g)$
↓ Initial moles	1.0	1.0	0.0
Moles at equilibrium	0.71	0.71	0.29
↑ Initial moles	0.0	0.0	1.0

The composition of the equilibrium mixture is *not* dependent upon the direction from which equilibrium is approached. Further, the equation does *not* indicate relative concentrations at equilibrium.

11-3 ALTERING THE EQUILIBRIUM CONDITION OR THE STATE OF EQUILIBRIUM

We have seen that qualitatively the state of equilibrium for a system is characterized by the relative amounts of products and reactants present. In the decomposition of PCl_5, any change in conditions causing a larger percentage of the PCl_5 to dissociate would shift the state of equilibrium in favor of the formation of more PCl_3 and Cl_2.

$$PCl_5(g) \rightleftharpoons PCl_3(g) + Cl_2(g) \qquad (10a)$$

What conditions might alter the equilibrium state? *Concentration* and *temperature,* factors that affect the rate of reaction! Equilibrium is attained when the rates of opposing reactions become equal. Any condition that changes the rate of one of the reactions involved in the equilibrium may affect the chemical composition of the system at equilibrium.

11-3.1 Concentration

Consider the reaction between ferric ion (Fe^{3+}) and thiocyanate ion (SCN^-) which was demonstrated in the laboratory:

$$Fe^{3+}(aq) + SCN^-(aq) \rightleftharpoons FeSCN^{2+}(aq) \qquad (11)$$

We have visual evidence of concentration at equilibrium, since the intensity of the color is fixed by the concentration of the $FeSCN^{2+}$ ion. Increasing either the ferric ion—by adding a soluble salt such as ferric nitrate, $Fe(NO_3)_3$—or thiocyanate ion—by adding, say, sodium thiocyanate, NaSCN—changes the concentration of one of the reactants (see Figure 11-6). Immediately, the color of the solution darkens, indicating an increase in the amount of the colored ion $FeSCN^{2+}$. *The equilibrium concentrations are affected if the concentrations of reactants (or products) are altered.*

EXERCISE 11-2

Does the "dancing-couple equilibrium" respond to concentration changes in the same way? What happens if a large group of boys enters the dance hall?

11-3.2 Temperature

We have already considered an example of a change in an equilibrium system as temperature is altered. The relative amounts of NO_2 and N_2O_4 are readily and obviously changed by a change in temperature. *The equilibrium concentrations are changed if the temperature is altered.*

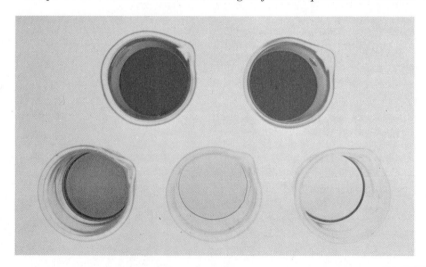

Fig. 11-6 Equilibrium concentrations are affected by the reactant concentrations. As the concentration of $FeSCN^{2+}$ decreases, the color of the solution lightens. Top row, left, 0.0010 *M* KSCN, 0.10 *M* $Fe(NO_3)_3$; right, 0.0010 *M* KSCN, 0.040 *M* $Fe(NO_3)_3$. Bottom row, left, 0.0010 *M* KSCN, 0.016 *M* $Fe(NO_3)_3$; center, 0.0010 *M* KSCN, 0.0064 *M* $Fe(NO_3)_3$; right, 0.0010 *M* KSCN, 0.0026 *M* $Fe(NO_3)_3$.

11-3.3 Catalysts Do *Not* Alter Equilibrium

Although catalysts increase the rate of reactions, it is found experimentally that *adding a catalyst to a system at equilibrium does not alter the equilibrium state*. Hence, it must be true that any catalyst has the same relative effect on the rate of the forward and the rate of the reverse reactions. You will recall that the effect of a catalyst on reaction rates can be discussed in terms of lowering the activation energy. This lowering is effective in increasing the rate in both forward and reverse directions. Thus, a catalyst produces no *net* change in the equilibrium concentrations, even though the system may reach equilibrium much more rapidly.

11-4 ATTAINMENT OF EQUILIBRIUM

We have already noted that some reactions reach equilibrium slowly and that this fact may make it difficult for us to recognize equilibrium. It is very important for us to recognize the distinction between a system *at* equilibrium and a system *approaching* equilibrium extremely slowly. In both cases, we may see little in the way of visible change. Consider, for example, the reaction between H_2 and O_2:

$$2H_2(g) + O_2(g) \rightleftharpoons 2H_2O(g) + 115.6 \text{ kcal} \qquad (12)$$

There is a large quantity of heat given off. Experiments such as those described for PCl_5 show that as temperature is raised to a very high level (3000 °C), a small amount (0.6 percent) of water decomposes to give H_2 and O_2; as temperature is *lowered,* essentially all the H_2 and O_2 combine to give H_2O. Yet a mixture of pure hydrogen and oxygen can remain at room temperature for a long period without apparent reaction or change. *Equilibrium is not attained in this system because hydrogen and oxygen react very slowly at room temperature.* This statement can be checked easily. Let us pass a spark through the H_2 and O_2 mixture. The resulting explosion is dramatic proof that something has happened. The system went rapidly to equilibrium once the process was properly initiated by a spark. Apparently, nothing was observed earlier because the initial process was slow.

This distinction between the conditions in a chemical system at equilibrium and the rate at which equilibrium is attained is very important in chemistry. By arguments that we shall consider later, one can decide with confidence whether equilibrium favors reactants, products, or neither. One cannot predict, however, how rapidly a system will approach equilibrium. This is a matter of reaction rates; separate experiments must be performed to learn whether a given reaction is rapid or slow.

11-5 PREDICTING NEW EQUILIBRIUM CONCENTRATIONS—LE CHATELIER'S PRINCIPLE

We are not satisfied with the conclusion that certain changes affect equilibrium concentrations. We would also like to predict the *direction* of the effect (does the change favor products or reactants?) and the

LARS ONSAGER (1903–   )

A native of Norway, Lars Onsager received his chemical engineering degree from the Norwegian Technical Institute in 1925. He came to the United States in 1928, and studied at Johns Hopkins and Brown Universities before going to Yale University in 1933. Onsager received the Ph.D. degree in 1935 and has been a member of the faculty of Yale since. In 1931 he published the work for which he received the 1968 Nobel Prize in Chemistry.

Onsager's interest has centered on the thermodynamics or energy relationships of chemical reactions. He has developed a set of equations expressing the heat relationships between various forms of activity (such as voltage and temperature) in reactions *before* equilibrium is reached, or when equilibrium is disturbed. Onsager has made many other contributions to chemistry, including the development of the gaseous diffusion process which is used to separate different isotopes of the same element.

magnitude of the effect (how much does it favor products or reactants?). The first desire, to know the qualitative effects, is satisfied by a generalization first proposed by a French chemist, Henry Louis Le Chatelier (1850–1936). It is now called **Le Chatelier's principle.**

Le Chatelier looked for regularities in a large amount of experimental data on equilibrium systems. Summarizing the regularities, he made this generalization: *if an equilibrium system is subjected to a change, processes occur that tend to counteract partially the imposed change.* To make the meaning of this generalization or principle crystal-clear, we shall restate it as it applies to changes in temperature, concentration, and pressure.

11-5.1 Temperature and Le Chatelier's Principle

Le Chatelier's principle, as it applies to temperature is: *if the temperature of a system at equilibrium is raised by adding heat (thermal energy), that reaction will take place which will absorb energy. If the temperature of a system at equilibrium is lowered by removing heat, that reaction will take place which will give off energy.*

How does this generalization apply to a specific system? Consider the reaction of N_2O_4 to give NO_2:

$$14.1 \text{ kcal} + N_2O_4(g) \rightleftharpoons 2NO_2(g) \tag{13}$$

Our experimental observations indicated that warming a bulb containing NO_2 and N_2O_4 causes a shift of the equilibrium state in favor of the formation of NO_2 (the reddish-brown color deepened). It is easy to see that this is in accord with Le Chatelier's principle. An increase in temperature gives more NO_2. The formation of NO_2 from N_2O_4 *absorbs* heat. An increase in the temperature of the equilibrium system results in the formation of more NO_2 by the reaction that absorbs heat. The reverse process, the formation of more N_2O_4 as the temperature is lowered, liberates heat. This is also in accord with the principle of Le Chatelier.

In the water vapor equilibrium, raising the temperature of liquid water raises its vapor pressure. This is also in accord with Le Chatelier's principle, since heat is absorbed as the liquid vaporizes. This absorption of heat, which accompanies the change to the new equilibrium condition, *partially* counteracts the temperature rise causing the change. This is seen in the equation

$$H_2O(l) + 9.7 \text{ kcal} \longrightarrow H_2O(g) \tag{14}$$

As heat is added to a closed system, more $H_2O(g)$ is formed *and* the temperature goes up, but less than it would if water did not vaporize.

11-5.2 Concentration Changes and Le Chatelier's Principle

Le Chatelier's principle can be stated specifically for changes in concentration. *If a reactant or product is added to a system at equilibrium, that reaction will occur which partially uses up the added reactant or product. If a reactant or product is removed, that reaction will occur which produces more of the removed reactant or product.*

We have considered this principle in laboratory experiments. If a solution containing $SCN^-(aq)$ ions is added to an equilibrium solution containing both $Fe^{3+}(aq)$ and $SCN^-(aq)$ ions, the color of the solution deepens:

$$Fe^{3+}(aq) + SCN^-(aq) \rightleftharpoons FeSCN^{2+}(aq) \qquad (11)$$
$$\text{COLORLESS} \qquad\qquad\qquad \text{RED}$$

A new state of equilibrium is then attained in which more $FeSCN^{2+}$ is present than before the addition of SCN^-. Increasing the concentration of SCN^- has increased the concentration of the $FeSCN^{2+}$ ion. This agrees with Le Chatelier's principle. The change imposed on the system was an increase in the concentration of SCN^-. This change can be counteracted in part by some Fe^{3+} and SCN^- ions reacting to form more $FeSCN^{2+}$. Some of the added SCN^- was used up! The same argument applies to an addition of a solution containing $Fe^{3+}(aq)$ ions. In each case, the formation of $FeSCN^{2+}$ *uses up* a *portion* of the added reactant, *partially* counteracting the change.

Le Chatelier's principle can also be applied to gaseous systems. Consider the equilibrium system

$$PCl_3(g) + Cl_2(g) \longrightarrow PCl_5(g) \qquad (10)$$

If we were to add more Cl_2 while the volume and temperature of the system were held constant, the pressure would go up, the concentration of Cl_2 would go up, and more $PCl_5(g)$ would be produced. This observation would be in complete accord with Le Chatelier's principle: when a reactant is added, that reaction occurs which uses up the reactant. Similarly, if more PCl_5 were added at fixed volume and temperature, additional PCl_3 and Cl_2 would be produced. Although pressure would go up in both these systems as more reagents were added, the direction of the equilibrium shift would be determined by the changes in *concentration* resulting from added reagents.

11-5.3 Effect of Volume Changes

Is adding or subtracting a reagent the only way to change concentration? If we remember that concentration is number of moles *per unit volume,* we see that changes in the volume also change the concentrations in a gaseous system. Consider again the PCl_3-Cl_2-PCl_5 equilibrium. Suppose the volume of the equilibrium system were to be reduced suddenly to *half* its original volume. The pressure on this system would go up. The reduction in volume would double the initial concentration of the $PCl_3(g)$ and the $PCl_5(g)$. These concentration changes would then just compensate because they appear on opposite sides of the equation. We have, however, an additional concentration change which is not compensated. The change in volume would also double the concentration of Cl_2. This additional increase in concentration would have the effect of shifting the equilibrium toward the production of more PCl_5. The expected formation of PCl_5 does indeed occur. Changes in *volume* of gaseous systems bring about changes in concentrations that then shift the equilibrium.

11-5.4 Pressure As a Variable and Its Relation to Concentration Changes

Changes in volume always bring about changes in the *pressure* of closed gaseous systems; for this reason, people sometimes prefer to consider that pressure causes a shift in equilibrium. *Pressure effects are always those which result from changes in effective concentration.*

It is possible, however, to analyze the set of changes in the gaseous PCl_3-Cl_2-PCl_5 system in a somewhat different (and perhaps easier) manner if we apply Le Chatelier's principle while considering for convenience that pressure is the cause of the shift in equilibrium. The answer must be the same as that given for concentration changes, since pressure is really a variable which is proportional to gas concentrations. When we increased the pressure on the system by reducing the volume, the number of moles per unit volume was greater than it had been under the original equilibrium condition. This increase in moles per unit volume could be counteracted in part if some PCl_3 and Cl_2 were to combine to give PCl_5 (if 2 moles were to combine to give 1 mole). Hence, since Le Chatelier's principle tells us that the process which will occur is the one that tends to counteract the imposed change, we expect that PCl_3 and Cl_2 will combine to give PCl_5. The overall conversion of two molecules to one molecule would tend to reduce the number of molecules per unit volume (and thus the pressure), counteracting in part the effects of increased pressure. Our observations on pressure can be summarized in another special statement of Le Chatelier's principle. If pressure is *increased* on a system at equilibrium, that reaction takes place that tends to give a *decrease* in total volume. In the case just discussed an increase in pressure resulted in the reaction occurring that converts 1 mole of PCl_3 (22.4 litres at STP) and 1 mole of Cl_2 (22.4 litres at STP) to 1 mole of PCl_5 (22.4 litres at STP). The converse of this statement is also true. If pressure is *reduced* on a system at equilibrium, that reaction takes place which tends to give an *increase* in the total volume of the system. A decrease in pressure should favor the conversion of $PCl_5(g)$ to $PCl_3(g)$ and $Cl_2(g)$.

What happens if the reaction does not involve an increase or decrease in the total volume of the system? Our statement would seem to indicate that no change is to be expected. Experiment confirms such a prediction. Consider the first reactions mentioned in this chapter:

$$CO(g) + NO_2(g) \rightleftharpoons CO_2(g) + NO(g) \qquad (1, 2)$$

If we increase the pressure on this system by reducing the volume, the concentrations of all four gases would go up, but the composition of the gaseous mixture would not change. The total number of moles of gas is not altered by this chemical reaction; hence, nothing is observed as pressure is increased.

11-6 APPLICATION OF EQUILIBRIUM PRINCIPLES— THE HABER PROCESS

Knowledge of chemical principles pays off! The control of equilibrium by the application of Le Chatelier's principle is literally feeding and clothing a large segment of the population of the world. The large-scale production of ammonia (NH_3) is possible today because we can apply the principles of Le Chatelier. Liquid ammonia for fertilizer, as well as ammonia for the synthesis of nylon and hundreds of other chemicals can be obtained from the air. Before people learned to control equilibrium, they were dependent upon the erratic whims of nature and international politics for their essential nitrogen compounds.

We observed in Chapter 8 that the nitrogen of the earth's atmosphere is relatively inert at low temperatures. The nitrogen atoms combine so strongly with each other that the N_2 molecule has low reactivity at room temperature. Under proper conditions we can, however, make nitrogen molecules combine with hydrogen molecules to give ammonia:

$$N_2(g) + 3H_2(g) \rightleftharpoons 2NH_3(g) + 22 \text{ kcal} \qquad (15)$$

Can our knowledge of equilibrium and kinetics (Chapter 10) be used to decide what conditions would give the ammonia? First, what about pressure? In the formation of ammonia *one* volume of nitrogen and *three* volumes of hydrogen give *two* volumes of ammonia (four volumes go to two volumes). Le Chatelier's principle tells us that high pressure (small volume, thus high concentration) should favor the production of ammonia. What about temperature? We note that heat is *given off* when ammonia is formed from N_2 and H_2. Le Chatelier's principle tells us that low temperatures will favor a reaction liberating heat; therefore, we want low temperature. It begins to look as though our preferred reactor should be a *refrigerated* tank containing N_2 and H_2 under thousands of pounds of *pressure*. If such a tank is prepared and the N_2-H_2 mixture is allowed to stand for several days, *no NH_3 is found*. If the mixture is allowed to stand for several weeks, *no NH_3 is found*. Even after several years the yield of NH_3 cannot be detected. Apparently N_2 reacts *very* slowly with H_2 at the low temperature which favors production of NH_3. The situation reminds us of the reaction of H_2 and O_2 mentioned earlier. In the H_2-O_2 case, a spark made the reaction proceed explosively. We have no such good luck when we pass a spark through the N_2-H_2 mixture. Other ways must be found to accelerate the process.

We remember from Chapter 10 that reactions can be made to go faster by raising the temperature. We are now face to face with a compromise. Low temperature is required for a desirable equilibrium state and high temperature is necessary for a satisfactory rate. The compromise used industrially involves an intermediate temperature, about 400 °C; even then the success of the process depends upon the presence of a suitable catalyst to achieve a reasonable reaction rate.* Very high pressures are desirable, but equipment that will stand up under both high pressure and high temperature is expensive to build. A pressure of about 300 atm is actually used. Under these conditions, 300 atm and 400 °C, only slightly more than 30 percent of the reactants

---

*As catalysts for the process get better, the conditions needed for the conversion get milder; that is, lower temperatures and pressures can be used. Since high temperature and pressure are expensive, better catalysts give less expensive ammonia.

are converted to NH_3. The NH_3 is removed from the mixture by liquefying it under conditions at which N_2 and H_2 remain as gases. The unreacted N_2 and H_2 are then recycled until the total percentage conversion of expensive hydrogen to ammonia is very high.

Prior to World War I the principal sources of nitrogen compounds were some nitrate deposits in Chile. Fritz Haber, a German chemist, successfully developed the process we have just described, thus allowing the world to use its almost unlimited supply of nitrogen in air. The world eats better and is clothed better because of Fritz Haber.

EXERCISE 11-3

An American corporation is now making nitrogen compounds directly from the reaction of nitrogen with oxygen. The essential equation is

$$N_2(g) + O_2(g) + 21.5\, kcal \longrightarrow 2NO(g)$$

Using Le Chatelier's principle, select conditions that would give the best yields of $NO(g)$.

11-7   QUANTITATIVE ASPECTS OF EQUILIBRIUM

Le Chatelier's principle permits us to make qualitative predictions about equilibrium states. For example, we know that raising the pressure will favor the production of NH_3 from N_2 and H_2. The next question is: by *how much* will an increase in pressure favor NH_3 formation? Will the yield change by a factor of 10 or by only 0.01 percent? To control a reaction, we need *quantitative* information about equilibrium. Experiments show that quantitative predictions are possible. Furthermore, we are delighted to learn that they can be explained in terms of our models for the reaction of materials on the molecular level.

11-7.1   The Equilibrium Constant

By means of laboratory colorimetric observations (based on estimation of color) you measured the concentration of $FeSCN^{2+}$ in solutions containing ferric and thiocyanate ions, Fe^{3+} and SCN^-. The reaction is

$$Fe^{3+}(aq) + SCN^-(aq) \rightleftharpoons FeSCN^{2+}(aq) \qquad (11)$$

From $[FeSCN^{2+}]$* and the initial values of $[Fe^{3+}]$ and $[SCN^-]$ you calculated the values of $[Fe^{3+}]$ and $[SCN^-]$ at equilibrium. You then made calculations for various combinations of these values. Many experiments just like these show that the ratio

$$\frac{[FeSCN^{2+}]}{[Fe^{3+}][SCN^-]} \qquad (16)$$

*Hereafter we shall regularly use the square bracket notation $[M^+]$ to indicate concentration of the substance inside the bracket. We read "$[FeSCN^{2+}]$" as *concentration of* $FeSCN^{2+}(aq)$ ions in solution.

TABLE 11-1 EQUILIBRIUM CONCENTRATION AT 698.6 K
OF HYDROGEN, IODINE, AND HYDROGEN IODIDE*

Expt. No.	[H₂] (moles/litre)	[I₂] (moles/litre)	[HI] (moles/litre)
1	1.8313×10^{-3}	3.1292×10^{-3}	17.671×10^{-3}
2	2.9070×10^{-3}	1.7069×10^{-3}	16.482×10^{-3}
3	4.5647×10^{-3}	0.7378×10^{-3}	13.544×10^{-3}
4	0.4789×10^{-3}	0.4789×10^{-3}	3.531×10^{-3}
5	1.1409×10^{-3}	1.1409×10^{-3}	8.410×10^{-3}

*Values above the line were obtained by heating hydrogen and iodine together; values below the line, by heating pure hydrogen iodide.

comes closest to being a fixed value. Notice this ratio carefully. The reaction product is on top.

Colorimetric analysis is not very exact. More accurate data on another system at equilibrium are shown in Table 11-1. The reaction is

$$2HI(g) \rightleftharpoons H_2(g) + I_2(g) \qquad (17)$$

The data have been expressed in concentrations, although pressure units would be equally good for a reaction involving gases.

EXERCISE 11-4

For experiments 4 and 5 in Table 11-1, why is [H₂] equal to [I₂]? For experiment 1 in Table 11-1, what were the concentrations of H₂ and I₂ before the reaction occurred to form HI?

Let us work with these data to compute the value of the ratio

$$\frac{[H_2][I_2]}{[HI]} \qquad (18)$$

Note again that the products are on top. We obtain the numbers in Table 11-2. In view of the precision of the data from which these ratios are derived, the ratios are far from constant. Now let us try the ratio

$$\frac{[H_2][I_2]}{[HI]^2} \qquad (19)$$

These calculations are summarized in Table 11-3. The results are most encouraging. They imply that with a fair degree of accuracy we can write

$$\frac{[H_2][I_2]}{[HI]^2} = \text{a constant} = 1.835 \times 10^{-2} \text{ at } 698.6 \text{ K} \qquad (20)$$

Look at this ratio in terms of the reaction

$$2HI(g) \rightleftharpoons H_2(g) + I_2(g) \qquad (17)$$

TABLE 11-2 VALUES OF [H₂][I₂]/[HI] FOR DATA OF TABLE 11-1

Expt. No.	$\dfrac{[H_2][I_2]}{[HI]}$ (moles/litre)
1	32.429×10^{-5}
2	30.105×10^{-5}
3	24.866×10^{-5}
4	6.495×10^{-5}
5	15.477×10^{-5}

TABLE 11-3 VALUES OF [H₂][I₂]/[HI]² FOR DATA OF TABLE 11-1

Expt. No.	$\dfrac{[H_2][I_2]}{[HI]^2}$
1	1.8351×10^{-2}
2	1.8265×10^{-2}
3	1.8359×10^{-2}
4	1.8390×10^{-2}
5	1.8403×10^{-2}
Aver.	1.835×10^{-2}

The ratio is the product of the equilibrium concentrations of the substances produced in the reaction, $[H_2] \times [I_2]$, divided by the *square* of the concentration of the reacting substance, $[HI]^2$. The squaring of the $[HI]$ term may seem more reasonable if we rewrite equation (*17*) as

$$HI(g) + HI(g) \rightleftharpoons H_2(g) + I_2(g) \qquad (17a)$$

Just as it is the product of the concentrations of the products which determines the numerator in the equilibrium constant expression, it is the *product* of the concentrations of the reactants which determines the denominator. In this ratio, the power to which we raise the concentration of each substance is equal to its coefficient in the reaction.

11-7.2   The Law of Chemical Equilibrium

Let us summarize what we have learned. For the reaction

$$Fe^{3+}(aq) + SCN^-(aq) \rightleftharpoons FeSCN^{2+}(aq) \qquad (11)$$

we found that the concentrations of the molecules involved have a simple approximate relationship:

$$\frac{[FeSCN^{2+}]}{[Fe^{3+}][SCN^-]} = \text{a constant} \qquad (21)$$

Then we considered precise equilibrium data for the reaction

$$2HI(g) \rightleftharpoons H_2(g) + I_2(g) \qquad (17)$$

The concentrations of the molecules in the reaction of $2HI$ to give H_2 and I_2 (*17*) were found to have a simple relationship:

$$\frac{[H_2][I_2]}{[HI]^2} = \text{a constant} \qquad (20)$$

In each of our simple relationships, (*20*) and (*21*), the concentrations of the products appear in the numerator. In each relationship the concentrations of reactants appear in the denominator. In the reaction for the decomposition of HI (*17*), 2 moles of hydrogen iodide react. This influences the ratio (*20*) because it is necessary to square the concentration of hydrogen iodide, $[HI]$, in order to obtain a constant ratio.

These observations and many others like them lead to the generalization known as the **Law of Chemical Equilibrium** (or of **Mass Action**). For a reaction

$$aA + bB \rightleftharpoons eE + fF \qquad (22)$$

when equilibrium exists there will be a simple relation between the concentrations of products, $[E]$ and $[F]$, and the concentrations of reactants, $[A]$ and $[B]$:

$$\frac{[E]^e[F]^f}{[A]^a[B]^b} = K = \text{a constant} \quad \text{(at constant temperature)} \quad (23)$$

In this generalized equation (23), we see again that the numerator is the product of the equilibrium concentrations of the species formed, each raised to the power equal to the number of moles of that species in the chemical equation. The denominator is again the product of the equilibrium concentrations of the reacting species, each raised to a power equal to the number of moles of the species in the chemical equation. The quotient of these two remains constant. The constant K is called the **equilibrium constant.** This generalization is one of the most useful in all chemistry. From the equation for any chemical reaction we can immediately write an expression, in terms of the concentrations of reactants and products, that will be constant at any given temperature. If this constant is known (from measuring concentrations in a particular equilibrium system), then it can be used in calculations for any other equilibrium state of that system at that same temperature.

Table 11-4 (page 266) lists some reactions along with the equilibrium-law relationships and the numerical values of the equilibrium constants. First, let us verify the forms of the equilibrium-law relationships for the concentrations. The very first has an unexpected form. For this reaction,

$$Cu(s) + 2Ag^+(aq) \rightleftharpoons Cu^{2+}(aq) + 2Ag(s) \quad (24)$$

you do not find

$$\frac{[Cu^{2+}][Ag]^2}{[Ag^+]^2[Cu]} = K \quad (25)$$

but rather, you find

$$\frac{[Cu^{2+}]}{[Ag^+]^2} = K \quad (26)$$

This occurs because the concentrations of solid copper and solid silver are incorporated into the equilibrium constant. The concentration of solid copper (moles of copper per litre) is fixed by the density of the metal—it cannot be altered either by the chemist or by the progress of the reaction. The same is true of the concentration of solid silver. Since neither of these concentrations varies (no matter how much solid is added), there is no need to write them each time an equilibrium calculation is made. Equation (26) will suffice.

TABLE 11-4 SOME EQUILIBRIUM CONSTANTS

Reaction	Equilibrium-Law Relationship	K at Stated Temperature
$Cu(s) + 2Ag^+(aq) \rightleftharpoons Cu^{2+}(aq) + 2Ag(s)$	$K = \dfrac{[Cu^{2+}]}{[Ag^+]^2}$	2×10^{15} at 25 °C
$Ag^+(aq) + 2NH_3(aq) \rightleftharpoons Ag(NH_3)_2^+(aq)$	$K = \dfrac{[Ag(NH_3)_2^+]}{[Ag^+][NH_3]^2}$	1.7×10^7 at 25 °C
$N_2O_4(g) \rightleftharpoons 2NO_2(g)$	$K = \dfrac{[NO_2]^2}{[N_2O_4]}$	0.87 at 55 °C
$2HI(g) \rightleftharpoons H_2(g) + I_2(g)$	$K = \dfrac{[H_2][I_2]}{[HI]^2}$	0.018 at 423 °C
$HSO_4^-(aq) \rightleftharpoons H^+(aq) + SO_4^{2-}(aq)$	$K = \dfrac{[H^+][SO_4^{2-}]}{[HSO_4^-]}$	0.013 at 25 °C
$CH_3COOH(aq) \rightleftharpoons H^+(aq) + CH_3COO^-(aq)$	$K = \dfrac{[H^+][CH_3COO^-]}{[CH_3COOH]}$	1.8×10^{-5} at 25 °C
$AgCl(s) \rightleftharpoons Ag^+(aq) + Cl^-(aq)$	$K = [Ag^+][Cl^-]$	1.7×10^{-10} at 25 °C
$H_2O \rightleftharpoons H^+(aq) + OH^-(aq)$	$K = [H^+][OH^-]$	10^{-14} at 25 °C
$AgI(s) \rightleftharpoons Ag^+(aq) + I^-(aq)$	$K = [Ag^+][I^-]$	10^{-16} at 25 °C

EXERCISE 11-5

If we assign the equilibrium constant K' to expression (25) and K to expression (26),

$$K' = \frac{[Cu^{2+}][Ag]^2}{[Ag^+]^2[Cu]} \qquad K = \frac{[Cu^{2+}]}{[Ag^+]^2}$$

show that

$$K = K' \times \frac{[Cu]}{[Ag]^2}$$

Another equilibrium constant of unexpected form applies to the reaction

$$H_2O \rightleftharpoons H^+(aq) + OH^-(aq) \qquad (27)$$

For this reaction we might have written

$$\frac{[H^+][OH^-]}{[H_2O]} = K \qquad (28)$$

Instead, Table 11-4 lists the equation as

$$[H^+][OH^-] = K \qquad (29)$$

The concentration of water does not appear in the denominator of expression (29). Water is frequently omitted in treating aqueous reactions that consume or produce water. It is justified because the variation in the concentration of water during reaction is very small in dilute aqueous solutions. We can treat $[H_2O]$ as a concentration that does not change. Hence, it can be incorporated into the equilibrium constant.

EXERCISE 11-6

Water has a density of 1 g/ml. Calculate the concentration of water (expressed in moles/litre) in pure water. Now calculate the concentration of water in 0.10 M aqueous solution of acetic acid (CH_3COOH), assuming each molecule of CH_3COOH occupies the same volume as one molecule of H_2O.

In summary, the concentrations of solids, of pure liquids, and of solvent (frequently water) can be and usually are incorporated in the equilibrium constant, so they do not appear in the equilibrium-law relationship.

Now look at the numerical values of the equilibrium constants in Table 11-4. The K's listed range from 10^{+15} to 10^{-16}, so we see there is a wide variation. We want to acquire a sense* of the relation between the size of the equilibrium constant and the state of equilibrium. *A large value of K must mean that in the system at equilibrium there are much larger concentrations of products than of reactants.* Remember that the numerator of our equilibrium expression contains the concentrations of the products of the reaction. The value of 2×10^{15} for the K for the reaction of $Cu(s) + Ag^+(aq)$ certainly indicates that if a reaction is initiated by placing metallic copper in a solution containing Ag^+—for example, in silver nitrate solution, as in Experiment 8—silver metal will plate out. When equilibrium is finally reached, the concentration of copper ion, $[Cu^{2+}]$, will be very much greater than the square of the concentration of silver ion, $[Ag^+]^2$.

A small value of K for a given reaction implies that very little of the products have to be formed from the reactants before equilibrium is attained. The value of $K = 10^{-16}$ for the reaction

$$AgI(s) \rightleftharpoons Ag^+(aq) + I^-(aq) \qquad (30)$$

indicates that very little solid AgI can dissolve before equilibrium concentrations are attained. Silver iodide has extremely low solubility. Conversely, if 0.1 M solutions of KI and $AgNO_3$ are mixed, the values of $[Ag^+]$ and $[I^-]$ are large; an equilibrium state cannot be reached until the $[Ag^+]$ and $[I^-]$ have been greatly reduced by the precipitation of AgI.

---

*Because equilibrium constants differ in the powers to which numbers are raised, one can get only rough indications of the equilibrium condition from the size of constants. If quantitative comparisons are wanted, concentrations should be calculated.

11-7.3 The Law of Chemical Equilibrium Derived from Rates of Opposing Reactions

In discussing the equilibrium between a liquid and its vapor, we described the equilibrium state as a dynamic balance between the rate of evaporation and the rate of condensation. An understanding of the law of chemical equilibrium can also be built on this basis if the reaction-rate balance is applied to *each step* in the mechanism for the process. We cannot, however, use the rate data for only the slow step in a process and arrive at a proper expression for the equilibrium constant.

11-8 THE FACTORS DETERMINING EQUILIBRIUM

At the beginning of this chapter, we raised a number of questions about equilibrium. Some of those questions have been answered. We are now able to recognize equilibrium by the fact that the system does not seem to change. As a double check to differentiate slow change from true equilibrium (remember H_2 and N_2), we found that the concentrations in the system in true equilibrium are identical regardless of the side from which equilibrium is approached. We have a picture of equilibrium activity on the molecular level: at equilibrium the rate of the forward reaction is equal to the rate of the reverse reaction. We know how to shift an equilibrium through control of such variables as temperature and concentration. Finally, we know how to express equilibrium relationships in a quantitative fashion through the use of the equilibrium constant.

Although many questions have been answered, the key "why" questions remain. What determines the equilibrium constant? Why does one reaction favor products while another favors reactants? Why does iron react with oxygen to give Fe_2O_3 while gold does not? These are hard questions, but a great deal of help can be obtained by considering some "common sense" analogies.

11-8.1 Energy and the Equilibrium Condition

We are not surprised, for example, when a skier goes downhill. He or she moves spontaneously from a condition of *higher* potential energy to a condition of *lower* potential energy (the energy of position is less at the bottom of the hill). Similarly, we know in advance that a skateboard will spontaneously carry a rider down a long, smooth hill if the rider can stay on the board. Our everyday experience tells us that systems tend to move spontaneously from a condition of higher potential energy to a condition of lower potential energy. The potential energy is changed to kinetic energy and ultimately to heat in the process. "Burned" elbows and knees offer grim proof of the conversion of kinetic energy to heat in skateboarding. We even pick up "floor burns" from a fall in the gymnasium.

Chemical systems are not too different from the skateboard or the skis. We saw in Chapter 9 that each chemical system has a given energy or heat content; furthermore, a portion of this chemical energy

is potential energy resulting from the *position* of atoms relative to each other. Chemical systems, like skateboards, tend to move toward a condition of lower energy; further, the chemical energy of chemical systems can be converted to molecular kinetic energy, *i.e.*, heat. These arguments seem to lead from an analogy to a generalization: *chemical systems—like skis and skateboards—proceed spontaneously from a state of higher energy to a state of lower energy.* The energy involved in the change appears as kinetic energy. We see it ultimately as heat. In short, a reaction will proceed spontaneously if the products will have lower energy than the reactants. This generalization is in accord with much of our experience; it is particularly true for reactions that release a large amount of energy.

Unfortunately, this logical generalization based on analogy soon runs into trouble. Like our earlier generalization—cylindrical objects burn—the generalization about energy conflicts with experiment. Our

Fig. 11-8 Potential energy is changed to kinetic energy and ultimately to heat as evidenced by burned elbows and knees.

ENERGY and the

EQUILIBRIUM CONDITION

generalization predicts that only exothermic reactions (reactions liberating heat) will be spontaneous, *yet many endothermic reactions are spontaneous*. We have only to recall the evaporation of a liquid such as water. This is clearly an endothermic process: the system moves spontaneously from a condition of lower potential energy to one of higher potential energy.

Our generalization encounters still another difficulty: *spontaneous chemical reactions do not always go to completion but proceed only until equilibrium is reached*. The system does not always go completely to the lower energy state but seems to stop at an intermediate equilibrium position. Why?

11-8.2 Randomness and the Equilibrium Condition

Perhaps a factor *in addition to* the energy of the system is important in determining the equilibrium position. What is this additional factor? It is more subtle than energy content as a driving force for a process and is harder to recognize, but it is still very familiar to you from your everyday experience. The new factor is simply the general tendency of objects or particles to get mixed up, to become more *randomly* arranged. One of the most fundamental laws of the universe is that a system tends to become disorganized, randomized, or mixed up, unless work is done on it. Look at your room; unless you or someone else does work to keep it neat, it will spontaneously approach a state of maximum disorder as you live in it. If you drop a handful of marbles from the top of a ladder, they will scatter all over the floor; they become randomly distributed. A small child, turned loose in a room, tends to "randomize" the contents.

This *tendency toward randomness* is a characteristic of chemical systems as well as of real-life situations. If a tank of nitrogen is connected to a tank of oxygen of equal pressure and the valve between the two is opened, the two gases will mix randomly until a uniform mixture of nitrogen and oxygen is obtained. The mixing process goes on spontaneously because of the random motion of the molecules.

Fig. 11-9 All systems tend toward a state of maximum disorder unless work is done on them. The universe tends to become more disordered.

Similarly, if we place a few drops of methyl violet solution in a test tube of water, the color will spread gradually through the test tube. Because molecular motion is increased by an increase in temperature, the system approaches the uniform color more rapidly as the temperature is raised. Further, we note that there is no tendency for the reverse process to occur spontaneously unless work is done on the system. We never see the nitrogen molecules going back into one tank and the oxygen molecules going back into the other tank spontaneously. Machines and work must be used to separate the components of the nitrogen-oxygen mixture; the process is *not* spontaneous. Similarly, methyl violet molecules, once distributed in the water, will have no tendency to reform crystals. Crystals will form only if external conditions are changed and work is done.

Fig. 11-10 A few drops of methyl violet in a test tube of water tend to become randomly distributed.

It appears that the natural tendency of the universe to approach a state of maximum disorder can be important in determining the equilibrium condition in a system. The degree of disorder is so important in science that it has been given a special name. A property known as **entropy** measures the randomness of the system on the atomic-molecular level. *As the degree of atomic-molecular disorder increases, the entropy of the system increases.* Indeed, the world and even the universe are proceeding toward a condition of complete disorder. When the heat of the universe becomes randomly distributed throughout the universe, all life will cease. This has led some astronomers to refer to our "dying universe." Fortunately, the universe is dying so slowly that we have little to worry about. Political and social problems are far more threatening.

How does entropy or disorder apply to an equilibrium system? Let us take our simplest example, the vaporization of a liquid. We notice that the vaporization of a liquid is both *spontaneous* and *endothermic*. Our "super-rubber" ball model for liquids indicated that the balls (or molecules) attract one another when close together in the liquid phase. Separating these balls and moving them into the vapor phase required work; each molecule had to be pushed out of the liquid phase and into the vapor phase, where molecules had higher potential energy. The energy to vaporize the liquid came from the kinetic energy of the molecules; the faster-moving molecules either flew off into the vapor phase or knocked other molecules into the vapor by collision. We noticed that if heat were not supplied from the outside, the liquid became colder; the faster-moving molecules left; the slower (colder) molecules remained in the liquid. Kinetic energy of the faster-moving liquid molecules was converted to the higher potential energy of gaseous molecules. Heat of vaporization had to be supplied to keep the temperature constant.

What is the real driving force in this vaporization process? It is clearly the tendency of the molecules to seek a more random distribution throughout all possible space—*i.e.*, a tendency of molecules to go into the space above the liquid and gain more space in which to move. In our vaporization example, the tendency to seek a random distribution is *opposed* by the energy effect; the process is endothermic.

In other cases, however, both energy effects and entropy effects (randomness) combine to drive a process. An example of such a reaction is the familiar burning of a candle. Energy is given off as the candle burns; randomness is increased as the solid candle is changed to hot gaseous products. Since there is *both* a lowering of energy *and* an increase in randomness as this reaction occurs, the formation of products is highly favored. Since the entropy effects are dependent upon the motion of molecules, we would expect entropy to become a more important factor in the equilibrium as the temperature is raised; more molecules will have the energy to move into the randomized vapor state as the temperature is raised. *Entropy effects become more important as temperature is raised.*

Let us summarize the generalizations our model suggests in relation to chemical equilibrium:

(1) All systems tend to approach the equilibrium state.
(2) The first factor important in determining the equilibrium state of a system is its *energy content*. As far as the energy criterion alone is concerned, systems tend to move toward a state of minimum potential energy. Water, for example, runs downhill and strongly exothermic reactions are spontaneous.
(3) The second factor important in determining the equilibrium state is *the degree of randomness or the entropy* of the system. In general, systems tend to move spontaneously toward a state of maximum randomness or disorder—toward maximum entropy.
(4) *The equilibrium state is a compromise between these two factors— minimum energy and maximum randomness, or, in the more sophisticated language of the laboratory, minimum enthalpy and maximum entropy.* At very low temperatures, energy tends to be the more important factor; then equilibrium favors the substance with lowest heat content or lowest energy. At very high temperatures, randomness becomes more important; then equilibrium favors a random distribution of reactants and products without regard to energy differences.

11-9 HIGHLIGHTS

The physical processes of liquid vaporization and solid solubility reach a state of equilibrium when the rate of the forward reaction is equal to the rate of the reverse reaction in each case. *At equilibrium, no macroscopic changes are visible.* Chemical systems also reach a condition of equilibrium *when the rate of the forward reaction is equal to the rate of the reverse reaction.* Again no macroscopic changes are visible.

Equilibrium states can be altered as predicted by **Le Chatelier's principle:** *if an equilibrium system is subjected to a change, processes occur that tend to counteract partially the imposed change.* Temperature and concentration are the two most important variables involved in determining the equilibrium condition.

Quantitative equilibrium relationships are obtained by use of the **equilibrium constant.** At any temperature, a fixed ratio relates concentrations of products and reactants. This ratio is known as the equilibrium constant, *K*. The numerator of the ratio is the product of the concentrations of all products, each product concentration being raised to the power corresponding to the number of the product molecules in the balanced equation. Similarly, the denominator is the product of the concentrations of all reactants, each reactant concentration being raised to the power corresponding to the number of the reactant molecules in the balanced equation.

Finally, the equilibrium state was shown to result from a balance of two factors. The first is the tendency of the system to reach minimum energy; the second is the tendency of the system to reach maximum disorder. In more sophisticated terms we might say that the system tends toward minimum **enthalpy** and maximum **entropy.** At low temperatures the tendency of the system to reach minimum energy predominates. At high temperatures the tendency of the system to reach maximum disorder predominates. At very high temperatures the tendency toward maximum disorder is so large that even the order and organization inherent in molecular formation is eliminated. At the temperature of the sun, molecules break up into atoms.

QUESTIONS and PROBLEMS

1 Consider a fire burning in a fireplace. Is equilibrium established? Explain.

2 Which of the following are equilibrium situations? Explain your answer in each case. (a) During a football game, 22 players are on the field and the rest are on the bench. (b) The student population of your high school is constant over a period of five years. (c) The mercury vapor in a thermometer when the temperature is constant. (d) A glass of iced tea which has undissolved sugar at the bottom of it after being stirred for half an hour. There is no ice remaining. (e) Today, during school hours, 15 percent of the students at your school are in physical education class.

(Disregard before and after school hours.) (f) A well-fed lion in his cage. The lion's weight is constant.

3 One drop of water may or may not establish a state of vapor-pressure equilibrium when placed in a closed bottle. Explain.

4 What do the following experiments (done at 25 °C) show about the state of equilibrium? (a) One litre of water is added, a few millilitres at a time, to a kilogram of salt, which only partly dissolves. (b) A large saltshaker containing 1 kg of salt is gradually emptied into 1 litre of water. The same amount of salt dissolves as in (a).

5 Consider the following reaction at equilibrium:

$$4NH_3(g) + 5 O_2(g) \rightleftharpoons$$
$$4NO(g) + 6H_2O(g) + 216.4 \text{ kcal}$$

(a) When equilibrium is attained, what observations concerning macroscopic (observable) properties could you make? Be specific. (b) Describe what is happening on the *molecular* level at equilibrium. (c) With the temperature and volume held constant, more $NH_3(g)$ is added to the system. When equilibrium is reestablished, what will be the equilibrium concentrations of *each* substance compared to what they were before the NH_3 was added? (d) If you wish to *decrease* the equilibrium concentration of NH_3, how would you change (increase or decrease) each of the following? (i) temperature of the system; (ii) pressure of the system; (iii) partial pressure of $H_2O(g)$; (iv) partial pressure of $NO(g)$; (v) partial pressure of $O_2(g)$.

6 Consider the reaction for the manufacture of water gas which you studied in Chapter 9:

$$C(s) + H_2O(g) \rightleftharpoons CO(g) + H_2(g)$$
$$\Delta H = +31.4 \text{ kcal}$$

Which of the following will *increase* the equilibrium yield of products? (a) Removing some of the H_2O using a dehydrating agent. (b) Increasing the temperature of the system. (c) Increasing the pressure on the system. (d) Removing the products as they are formed. (e) Using powdered instead of lump coal.

7 When some of the NO_2-N_2O_4 mixture shown in Figure 11-4 is placed in a syringe at room temperature, the following is observed: as the piston is gradually pushed in, the red-brown color of NO_2 first darkens and then becomes progressively lighter. It always, however, remains darker than it was originally. The equation for the equilibrium is

$$N_2O_4(g) \rightleftharpoons 2NO_2(g) \quad \Delta H = +14.1 \text{ kcal}$$
COLORLESS   RED-BROWN

Explain the experimental results, using Le Chatelier's principle.

8 Everyone knows that water expands when it freezes into ice. Will putting ice under pressure cause it to melt? Explain, using Le Chatelier's principle.

9 Explain, using Le Chatelier's principle, why increasing the pressure on boiling water causes it to stop boiling until a higher temperature is reached. The equation is

$$H_2O(l) \rightleftharpoons H_2O(g)$$
$$\Delta H = +9.7 \text{ kcal/mole}$$

10 Each of the following reactions has come to equilibrium. What will be the effect on the equilibrium concentration (increase, decrease, no change) of *each* substance in the system when the change described below is made?

(a) $2H_2(g) + 2NO(g) \rightleftharpoons$
$$N_2(g) + 2H_2O(g)$$
The pressure on the system is increased.

(b) $SO_2(g) + \frac{1}{2}O_2(g) \rightleftharpoons$
$$SO_3(g) + 23 \text{ kcal}$$
The temperature is increased.

(c) $P_4(g) + 6H_2(g) \rightleftharpoons 4PH_3(g)$
$H_2(g)$ is added.

(d) $FeO(s) + CO(g) \rightleftharpoons Fe(s) + CO_2(g)$
The $Fe(s)$ is removed as rapidly as it is formed.

(e) $N_2(g) + O_2(g) \rightleftharpoons 2NO(g)$
The pressure on the system is increased.

11 Write the equilibrium law expression for each of the following reactions:

(a) $N_2(g) + 2 O_2(g) \rightleftharpoons 2NO_2(g)$
(b) $2C(s) + 3H_2(g) \rightleftharpoons C_2H_6(g)$
(c) $NaOH(s) + H^+(aq) \rightleftharpoons$
$$Na^+(aq) + H_2O(l)$$
(d) $I_2(s) \rightleftharpoons I_2(aq)$

12 Write the equilibrium law expression for each of the following reactions:

(a) $3 O_2(g) \rightleftharpoons 2 O_3(g)$
(b) $MgCO_3(s) \rightleftharpoons MgO(s) + CO_2(g)$
(c) $SO_2(g) + NO_2(g) \rightleftharpoons$
$$SO_3(g) + NO(g)$$
(d) $2Bi^{3+}(aq) + 3H_2S(g) \rightleftharpoons$
$$Bi_2S_3(s) + 6H^+(aq)$$

13 Given that $K = 5.0 \times 10^{-5}$ for the reaction
$$2NO(g) + O_2(g) \rightleftharpoons 2NO_2(g)$$
Calculate the equilibrium concentration of oxygen gas if the NO and NO_2 concentrations are known to be equal at equilibrium. (Concentrations are given in moles/litre.)

14 Given the reaction at equilibrium
$$2A + B \rightleftharpoons C + 3D$$
Calculate the value of K if the equilibrium concentrations are found to be

$[A] = 10.0 \, M;$ $[B] = 15.0 \, M;$
$[C] = 5.0 \, M;$ $[D] = 25.0 \, M$

15 Reactants A and B are mixed, each initially at a concentration of 1.0 M. They react slowly to produce C according to the equation

$$2A + B \rightleftharpoons C$$

When equilibrium is established the concentration of C is found to be 0.30 M. Calculate the value of K.

16 Consider the reaction described by the following equation:

$$H_2(g) + CO_2(g) \rightleftharpoons H_2O(g) + CO(g)$$

One mole of $H_2(g)$ and 1 mole of $CO_2(g)$ are allowed to react in a 1-litre container until equilibrium is attained. If the equilibrium concentration of H_2 is 0.44 M, what is the equilibrium concentration of each of the other substances?

17 In the reaction

$$Fe^{2+}(aq) + Ag^+(aq) \rightleftharpoons Fe^{3+}(aq) + Ag(s)$$

at equilibrium the following concentrations were found: $[Fe^{2+}] = 0.50\ M$; $[Ag^+] = 1.0\ M$; $[Fe^{3+}] = 1.50\ M$. (a) Calculate the equilibrium constant, K, for the reaction. (b) If at equilibrium the concentration of $Fe^{2+}(aq)$ is found to be 0.20 M and the concentration of $Ag^+(aq)$ is 0.30 M, what must be the concentration of $Fe^{3+}(aq)$?

18 Select from each of the following pairs the more random system. (a) Your room just after you have cleaned it and your room a week later. (b) A beaker just before and just after you have dropped it. (c) Logs stacked in your fireplace and their combustion products after burning. (d) A cube of sugar before and after being dropped into hot coffee.

19 Consider the reaction

$$Y(s) + 2W(g) \rightleftharpoons 2Z(s)$$
$$\Delta H = -200\ \text{kcal}$$

(a) Which reaction (forward or reverse) is driven by the tendency toward minimum energy? (b) Which reaction is driven by the tendency toward maximum randomness?

20 For each of the following reactions, state (i) whether the tendency toward minimum energy favors reactants or products; (ii) whether the tendency toward maximum randomness favors reactants or products.

(a) $CO(g) + \frac{1}{2}O_2(g) \rightleftharpoons CO_2(g)$
$$\Delta H = -67.6\ \text{kcal}$$

(b) $Mg(s) + \frac{1}{2}O_2(g) \rightleftharpoons MgO(s)$
$$\Delta H = -146\ \text{kcal}$$

(c) $NaCl(s) \rightleftharpoons NaCl(aq)$
$$\Delta H = +0.4\ \text{kcal}$$

(d) $H_2SO_4(aq) \rightleftharpoons H_2SO_4(l)$
$$\Delta H = +19.0\ \text{kcal}$$

(e) $Pb^{2+}(aq) + 2I^-(aq) \rightleftharpoons PbI_2(s)$
$$\Delta H = -14.0\ \text{kcal}$$

(f) $Br_2(s) \rightleftharpoons Br_2(l)$ $\quad \Delta H = +16.2\ \text{kcal}$

21 For each of the following reactions, state (i) whether the tendency toward minimum energy favors reactants or products; (ii) whether the tendency toward maximum randomness favors reactants or products.

(a) $3C_2H_2(g) \rightleftharpoons C_6H_6(g)$
$$\Delta H = -142.6\ \text{kcal}$$

(b) $H_2(g) + F_2(g) \rightleftharpoons 2HF(g)$
$$\Delta H = -128.5\ \text{kcal}$$

(c) $CS_2(g) + 3\,O_2(g) \rightleftharpoons$
$$CO_2(g) + 2SO_2(g)$$
$$\Delta H = -265\ \text{kcal}$$

(d) $NaOH(s) \rightleftharpoons NaOH(aq)$
$$\Delta H = -10.2\ \text{kcal}$$

(e) $CO_2(g) \rightleftharpoons CO_2(aq)$
$$\Delta H = -4.8\ \text{kcal}$$

(f) $C_3H_8(l) \rightleftharpoons C_3H_8(g)$
$$\Delta H = +83.6\ \text{kcal}$$

> . . . solubility . . . depends fundamentally upon the ease with which . . . two molecular species are able to mix, and if the two species display a certain hostility toward mixing . . . saturation [is] attained at smaller concentration . . . .
>
> *JOEL H. HILDEBRAND (1881–   )*

SOLUBILITY EQUILIBRIUM 12

Limestone formations in caves result from the action of equilibrium processes.

SUGAR DISSOLVES IN WATER; ROCK DOESN'T. IN THE LABORATORY you have dissolved lead nitrate and sodium iodide in water to form colorless solutions, yet when you mixed these two solutions the yellow precipitate of lead iodide resulted.

Why do some substances dissolve in water readily, others hardly at all, and still others to a limited extent? Can the factors governing equilibrium be applied to solutions? The answer is an emphatic yes. Differences in solubility offer the chemist tools for identifying chemical substances and separating them from each other. Since chemicals seldom occur in nature in the pure form that we need for our stockroom shelves and industries, application of equilibrium principles to solubility is big business.

In Chapter 11 we saw that a proper application of equilibrium was important in the synthesis of ammonia from the air, a reaction which helps feed the world. Equilibrium would be an important topic even if its usefulness did not extend beyond the ammonia plant; but in actual fact, the principles of equilibrium are important throughout all nature. For example, the solubility of a gas in a liquid is determined by equilibrium principles, and the solubility of oxygen in water is essential to all fish life. Depletion of oxygen in water is a major problem in lake and stream pollution. The formation of limestone caves, the softening of hard water, the formation of Mammoth Hot Springs in Yellowstone Park, the dating of some ancient deposits by means of carbon-14 decay, indeed life itself, are all intimately affected by equilibrium processes involving solubility. In this chapter we shall concern ourselves with various **solubility equilibria**—the solution of a gas in a liquid, of a molecular solid in a liquid, and of an ionic solid in a liquid. The general concepts of equilibrium developed in the last chapter can be applied in detail to each of these specific systems.

Fig. 12-1 The growth of formations in limestone caves is a direct product of equilibrium processes.

12-1 SOLUBILITY: A CASE OF EQUILIBRIUM

In the last chapter we developed the idea of an equilibrium constant for a reaction which reaches equilibrium at a constant temperature. For the generalized reaction

$$aA + bB + \cdots \rightleftharpoons eE + fF + \cdots \qquad (1)$$

the equilibrium constant can be written

$$K = \text{a constant} = \frac{[E]^e[F]^f \cdots}{[A]^a[B]^b \cdots} \qquad (2)$$

Let us see how these generalized concepts can be applied to the dissolving of solid iodine in liquid ethyl alcohol. The equation for the process is

$$I_2(solid) \rightleftharpoons I_2(solution) \qquad (3)$$

An application of the general equilibrium law to the iodine-alcohol system gives the expression:

$$K' = \frac{[I_2(solution)]}{[I_2(solid)]} \qquad (4)$$

From Chapter 11 we remember that the concentration of a pure solid phase is constant. We then write

$$K'[I_2(solid)] = [I_2(solution)] \qquad (5)$$

Since $[I_2(solid)]$ is constant we can write

$$K'[I_2(solid)] = \text{constant} = [I_2(solution)] \qquad (6)$$

This formalized statement really tells us something that we knew all along: the concentration of I_2 in a *saturated* alcohol solution is constant at constant temperature. It is reassuring to find that a quantitative application of the equilibrium law gives a result in agreement with experiment.

EXERCISE 12-1

The density of solid iodine is 4.93 g/cm³. How many grams of iodine are present in a litre of actual crystals? How many grams of iodine are present in a mole of I_2 molecules? How many moles of I_2 molecules are present in a litre of iodine crystals?

We know from Chapter 11 that at equilibrium the rate of the forward reaction must equal the rate of the reverse reaction. This means that at equilibrium the rate at which I_2 molecules leave the crystal is exactly equal to the rate at which they return. By applying common sense and the ideas about reaction rates found in Chapter 10, it can again be shown that the concentration of I_2 in a saturated alcohol solution is constant at constant temperature. Our models are all consistent.

12-2 THE FACTORS THAT FIX THE SOLUBILITY OF A SOLID

The discussion of iodine dissolving in ethyl alcohol applies equally well to iodine dissolving in carbon tetrachloride (CCl_4). Iodine at room temperature dissolves in carbon tetrachloride at a certain rate. At equilibrium, precipitation occurs at a rate exactly equal to the rate of solution. As a result, the concentration of I_2 dissolved in carbon tetrachloride is constant:

$$K = [I_2(solution)] \qquad (7)$$

Despite this qualitative similarity in the equation, the solubility of I_2 in CCl_4 is very different from its solubility in alcohol. One litre of alcohol dissolves 0.84 mole of I_2, whereas 1 litre of CCl_4 dissolves only 0.12 mole at 20 °C:

$$K_{\text{alcohol}} = 0.84 \text{ mole/litre} \qquad (8)$$

$$K_{\text{CCl}_4} = 0.12 \text{ mole/litre} \qquad (9)$$

Why are these constants so different? To answer this question, we must turn again to the two factors that control every equilibrium—tendency toward minimum energy and tendency toward maximum randomness.

12-2.1 The Effect of Randomness

In a crystal of iodine, molecules are arranged in a highly regular and ordered pattern. The lattice is so regular that if we know the arrangement of one small segment, known as the unit cell, we can predict the arrangement of atoms in the whole crystal (see Figure 12-2). If we have a perfect crystal at 0 K, the system will have zero entropy—*i.e.*, it will have no randomness, it will be perfectly ordered. As we begin to warm up this crystal, the molecules vibrate back and forth and become disordered. The disorder (or entropy), then, increases as the temperature rises. If the crystal is now put into a liquid, where it dissolves, the beautiful, ordered arrangement of the crystal is destroyed; molecules wander away from the ordered crystal surface; the system becomes *highly randomized* as molecules wander aimlessly through the solution. It is also true that this disorder is greater for dilute than for concentrated solutions. Even the *liquid* arrangement is made more disordered by random injections of foreign molecules into it. The dissolving process *increases* the randomness of the system; hence, it *increases* the entropy of the system. This increase in randomness tends to favor the solution process.

12-2.2 The Effect of Energy

Experiment shows that heat is absorbed as iodine dissolves in alcohol or in carbon tetrachloride. The regular, ideally packed iodine crystal gives an iodine molecule a *lower* potential energy than does the loosely packed solvent environment. Thus, the tendency of a system to seek a minimum energy content (or minimum enthalpy) would favor the growth of iodine crystals.

Our equilibrium condition must now be determined by a balance between the tendency toward maximum randomness (favors solution) and the tendency toward minimum energy (favors crystalline solid). Equilibrium is reached when the concentration is such that these two opposing factors just balance each other.

How much the energy factor favors the crystal depends upon the change in enthalpy or energy content as a mole of solid dissolves (see Figure 12-3, page 280). This change is called the **heat of solution.** The heats of solution of iodine in these two solvents have been measured; they are as follows:

$$I_2(s) + 1.6 \text{ kcal} \rightleftharpoons I_2(\textit{in alcohol}) \qquad (10)$$

$$I_2(s) + 5.8 \text{ kcal} \rightleftharpoons I_2(\textit{in CCl}_4) \qquad (11)$$

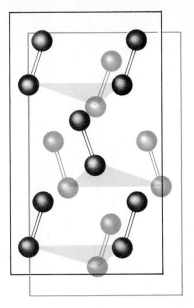

Fig. 12-2 A unit cell of an I_2 crystal.

Fig. 12-3 A large energy difference between solid and solution
lowers the solubility.

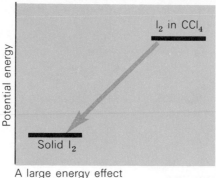

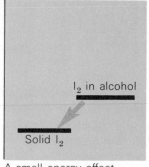

We see that more energy is required to dissolve I_2 in CCl_4 (5.8 kcal) than to dissolve it in alcohol (1.6 kcal). Thus, the energy factor favoring the crystal (and opposing solution) is much larger when the solvent is CCl_4 than when it is alcohol. As a consequence, the solubility of I_2 in CCl_4 is not as high as it is in alcohol.

12-2.3 The Effect of Temperature

In the processes considered, it was found that as the temperature increases, more and more of the *molecules* have enough energy to overcome the energy barrier and pass into the more random state (recall vaporization of a liquid). In short, the energy consideration becomes less restrictive and the randomization factor becomes relatively more important at higher temperatures. This means that higher solubility (increased randomness) is to be expected as the temperature is raised in both alcohol and CCl_4 solutions.

EXERCISE 12-2

The heat of solution of iodine in benzene is $+4.2$ kcal/mole (heat is absorbed). Assuming that the increase in randomness is the same when equal amounts of I_2 dissolve in equal volumes of either liquid benzene, ethyl alcohol, or CCl_4, justify the prediction that the solubility of I_2 in benzene is higher than in CCl_4 but lower than in alcohol.

12-3 THE FACTORS THAT FIX THE SOLUBILITY OF A GAS IN A LIQUID

Gases, too, dissolve in liquids. Let us apply our understanding of equilibrium to this type of system.

12-3.1 The Effect of Randomness

The gaseous state is more random than the liquid state since the molecules move freely through a much larger space as a gas. Hence, randomness *decreases* as a gas dissolves in a liquid. In this case, unlike solids, *the tendency toward maximum randomness favors the gas phase and opposes the dissolving process.*

12-3.2 The Effect of Energy

In a gas the molecules are far apart and they interact very weakly. As a gas molecule enters the liquid, it is attracted to the solvent molecules and the potential energy of the gas molecule is lowered. Again we find a contrast to the behavior of solids. *When a gas dissolves in a liquid, heat is evolved.* The tendency toward minimum energy favors the dissolving process.

Thus, we see that the equilibrium solubility of a gas involves a balance between randomness and energy as it does for a solid, but the effects are opposite. For a gas, the tendency toward maximum randomness favors the gas phase, opposing dissolving. The tendency toward minimum energy favors the liquid state, favoring dissolving.

As an example, consider the solubilities of the two gases oxygen (O_2) and nitrous oxide (N_2O) in water. The heats of solution have been measured and are as follows:

$$O_2(g) \rightleftharpoons O_2(aq) + 3.0 \text{ kcal} \qquad (12)$$

$$N_2O(g) \rightleftharpoons N_2O(aq) + 4.8 \text{ kcal} \qquad (13)$$

Assuming the randomness factor is about the same, the gas with the larger heat effect (favoring dissolving) should have the higher solubility. The measured solubilities at 1 atm pressure and 20 °C of O_2 and N_2O in water are, respectively, 1.4×10^{-3} mole/litre and 27×10^{-3} mole/litre. This is consistent with our prediction.

12-3.3 The Effect of Temperature

Raising the temperature always tends to favor the more random state. This means that less gas will dissolve, since the gas is more random than the liquid. The solubility of a gas *decreases* as temperature is raised (see Figure 12-4, page 282).

EXERCISE 12-3

From the heat of solution of chlorine in water ($\Delta H = -6.0$ kcal/mole, heat evolved), how would you expect the solubility of chlorine at 1 atm pressure and 20 °C to compare with that of oxygen (O_2) and nitrous oxide (N_2O)?

12-4 AQUEOUS SOLUTIONS

The expression "$K =$ concentration of solute in solution" is applicable to the solubility equilibria of some substances in water, but not to all. Contrast, for example, water solutions of sugar, salt, and hydrochloric acid. Sugar forms a molecular solid and, as it dissolves in water, the sugar molecules remain intact. These molecules leave the crystal and become a part of the liquid. This is exactly the situation we described for iodine in alcohol, and the expression "$K =$ concentration of sugar

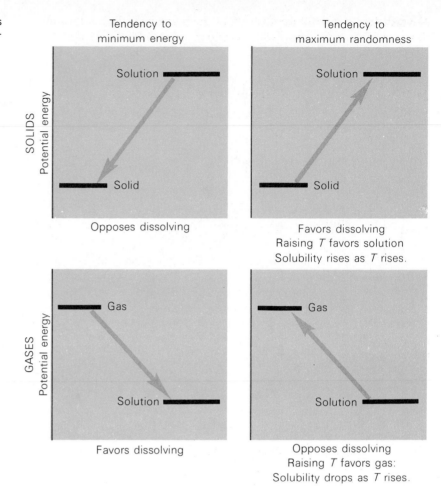

Fig. 12-4 Maximum randomness versus minimum energy; the solubility of solids and gases.

Tendency to minimum energy

Tendency to maximum randomness

SOLIDS

Potential energy

Solution

Solid

Opposes dissolving

Solution

Solid

Favors dissolving
Raising T favors solution
Solubility rises as T rises.

GASES

Potential energy

Gas

Solution

Favors dissolving

Gas

Solution

Opposes dissolving
Raising T favors gas:
Solubility drops as T rises.

in solution" is applicable to aqueous sugar solutions. But sodium chloride (NaCl) behaves quite differently. As we noted in Chapter 6, salt dissolves in water to form positively charged sodium ions and negatively charged chloride ions, each surrounded by water molecules:

$$\text{NaCl}(s) \longrightarrow \text{Na}^+(aq) + \text{Cl}^-(aq) \qquad (14)$$

The existence of these ions made the solution a conductor of electricity. We noticed further that both Na^+ ions and Cl^- ions have the electron configuration of a noble gas. We noticed in Chapter 8 that hydrogen chloride gas (HCl) dissolves in water to form $\text{H}^+(aq)$ and $\text{Cl}^-(aq)$ ions. The presence of ions makes the solution a conductor of electricity:

$$\text{HCl}(g) + \text{H}_2\text{O}(l) \longrightarrow \text{H}^+(aq) + \text{Cl}^-(aq) \qquad (15)$$

You will remember that substances which dissolve in water to give a conductor of the electric current are called *electrolytes* in water. The equation for the dissolving of an electrolyte is more complex than the equation for the dissolving of a non-electrolyte such as I_2 or sugar.

Nevertheless, a careful application of the principles of equilibrium to this more complex process will provide meaningful information about electrolytic solutions.

12-4.1 A Review of Electrolytic Solutions

In Chapters 6, 7, and 8, we discussed the removal of an electron from a metal atom (Na) to form a positive ion (Na^+); we also considered the acceptance of this electron by a nonmetal atom (Cl) to form a negative ion (Cl^-). We noted that these ions may combine to produce an *ionic solid*. It is only natural to expect that such ionic solids might well dissolve to form separate ions in solution. The equation for the solution of NaCl to form ions, then, is not completely unexpected. Further, we noted that such ionic solids would be expected from compounds formed from metals on the left-hand side of the periodic table (see page 196) and nonmetals on the right-hand side (*e.g.*, NaCl, CsBr, KI, $CaCl_2$). When these solids go into solution, ions are freed.

Conducting solutions are also formed when some substances which are themselves molecular, non-ionic solids, liquids, or gases *react* with water to give ions in solution. The mineral acids are particularly good examples. In addition to hydrogen chloride (HCl), which we know dissolves to give aqueous H^+ and Cl^- ions, other acids such as sulfuric acid (H_2SO_4), nitric acid (HNO_3), and perchloric acid ($HClO_4$) follow this pattern:

$$H_2SO_4(l) + H_2O \longrightarrow H^+(aq) + HSO_4{}^-(aq) \qquad (16)$$

$$HSO_4{}^-(aq) + H_2O \longrightarrow H^+(aq) + SO_4{}^{2-}(aq) \qquad (17)$$

$$HNO_3(l) + H_2O \longrightarrow H^+(aq) + NO_3{}^-(aq) \qquad (18)$$

$$HClO_4(l) + H_2O \longrightarrow H^+(aq) + ClO_4{}^-(aq) \qquad (19)$$

Particularly important in our treatment of ionic solutions is a recognition of the fact that a given kind of ion, once it is formed in solution, is the same as other ions of that kind. This is true regardless of the compound from which each ion originated. For example, if a solution is made by dissolving both NaCl and HCl in a single litre of water, the chloride ions are the same *whether they came from NaCl or HCl*. No ion "remembers" the compound from which it originated.

In considering solubility equilibria, it is convenient for us to use special terminology for positive and negative ions. First, we recall that positively charged ions in an electrolysis cell move toward the negative electrode, the cathode, and therefore are known as *cations* (pronounced cat-ions); the negatively charged ions move toward the positive electrode, the anode, and are called *anions* (pronounced an-ions). Further, we recall that the number of charges carried by anions in a solution just balances the number of charges carried by cations, so that our solution must be *electrically neutral*. With our memories briefly refreshed about ions in solution, we are ready to consider some qualitative and quantitative relationships involving equilibrium in ionic solutions.

12-4.2 A Qualitative View of Aqueous Solubilities

First, let us consider substances with high solubility. As was stated earlier, a substance is usually considered soluble if it dissolves giving a concentration in excess of one tenth of a mole per litre (0.1 M) at room temperature. Using this definition of *solubility,* we can say that a few cations (positive ions) form compounds soluble in water with nearly all anions (negative ions). These cations are the hydrogen ion, $H^+(aq)$; the ammonium ion, NH_4^+; and the alkali metal ions, Li^+, Na^+, K^+, Rb^+, Cs^+, and Fr^+. Figure 12-5 shows the placement of these ions in the periodic table.

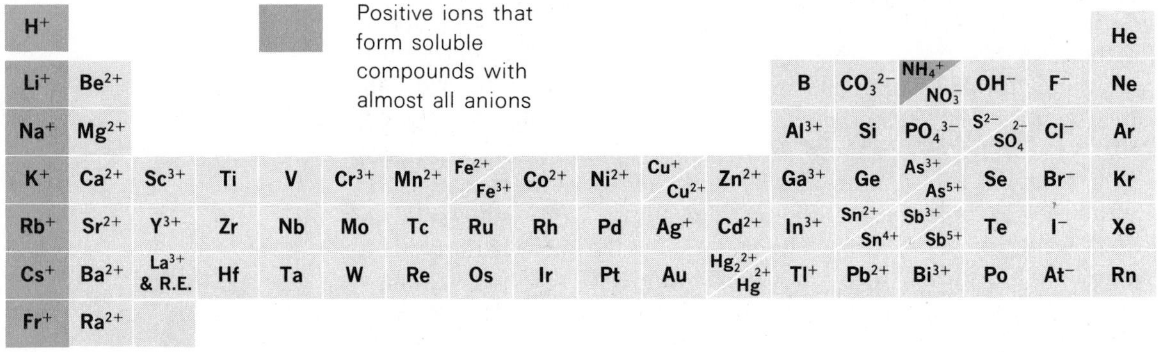

Positive ions that form soluble compounds with almost all anions

Fig. 12-5 Positive ions forming soluble compounds with almost all anions.

The same sort of remark can be made about three anions. Almost all compounds involving nitrate ion, NO_3^-; acetate ion, CH_3COO^-; and perchlorate ion, ClO_4^-, are soluble in water.*

Other anions (negative ions) form compounds of high solubility in water with some metal cations (positive ions) and compounds of low solubilities with others. Figure 12-6 indicates for five anions the metal ions that form compounds of *low* solubilities. Figure 12-6(a) refers to chlorides, Cl^-, bromides, Br^-, and iodides, I^-. Figure 12-6(b) refers to sulfates, SO_4^{2-}, and Figure 12-6(c), to sulfides, S^{2-}. Notice the difference between Figures 12-5 and 12-6. The dark gold shading in Figure 12-5 identifies metal ions that form *soluble* compounds. Figure 12-6 identifies those positive ions that form compounds of *low* solubility.

Figure 12-7 (page 286) continues this presentation of solubilities. Figure 12-7(a) shows the positive ions that form hydroxides of low solubility. Figure 12-7(b) shows the positive ions that have low solubility when combined with phosphate ion, PO_4^{3-}; carbonate ion, CO_3^{2-}; and sulfite ion, SO_3^{2-}.

These figures neatly summarize solubility behavior.

The information in Figures 12-5, 12-6, and 12-7 is summarized in Table 12-1 (page 287). These generalizations, like any generalizations, will have exceptions, but they can be used when quantitative information is not available.

---

*There are a few compounds of alkalies, nitrate, and acetate that have low solubilities, but most of them are quite complex in composition. For example, sodium uranyl acetate [$NaUO(CH_3COO)$] has low solubility. Silver acetate [$Ag(CH_3COO)$] and chromous acetate [$Cr(CH_3COO)_2$] have low solubilities, as does tetraphenyl arsonium perchlorate, [$(C_6H_5)_4As]ClO_4$.

EXERCISE 12-4

Use the information in Table 12-1 to determine whether each of the following compounds has high or low solubility in water solution. Write "sol" if the compound is soluble and "low" if it has low solubility.

Mg(NO$_3$)$_2$	MgCl$_2$	MgSO$_4$	Mg(OH)$_2$	MgCO$_3$
Ca(NO$_3$)$_2$	CaCl$_2$	CaSO$_4$	Ca(OH)$_2$	CaCO$_3$
Sr(NO$_3$)$_2$	SrCl$_2$	SrSO$_4$	Sr(OH)$_2$	SrCO$_3$

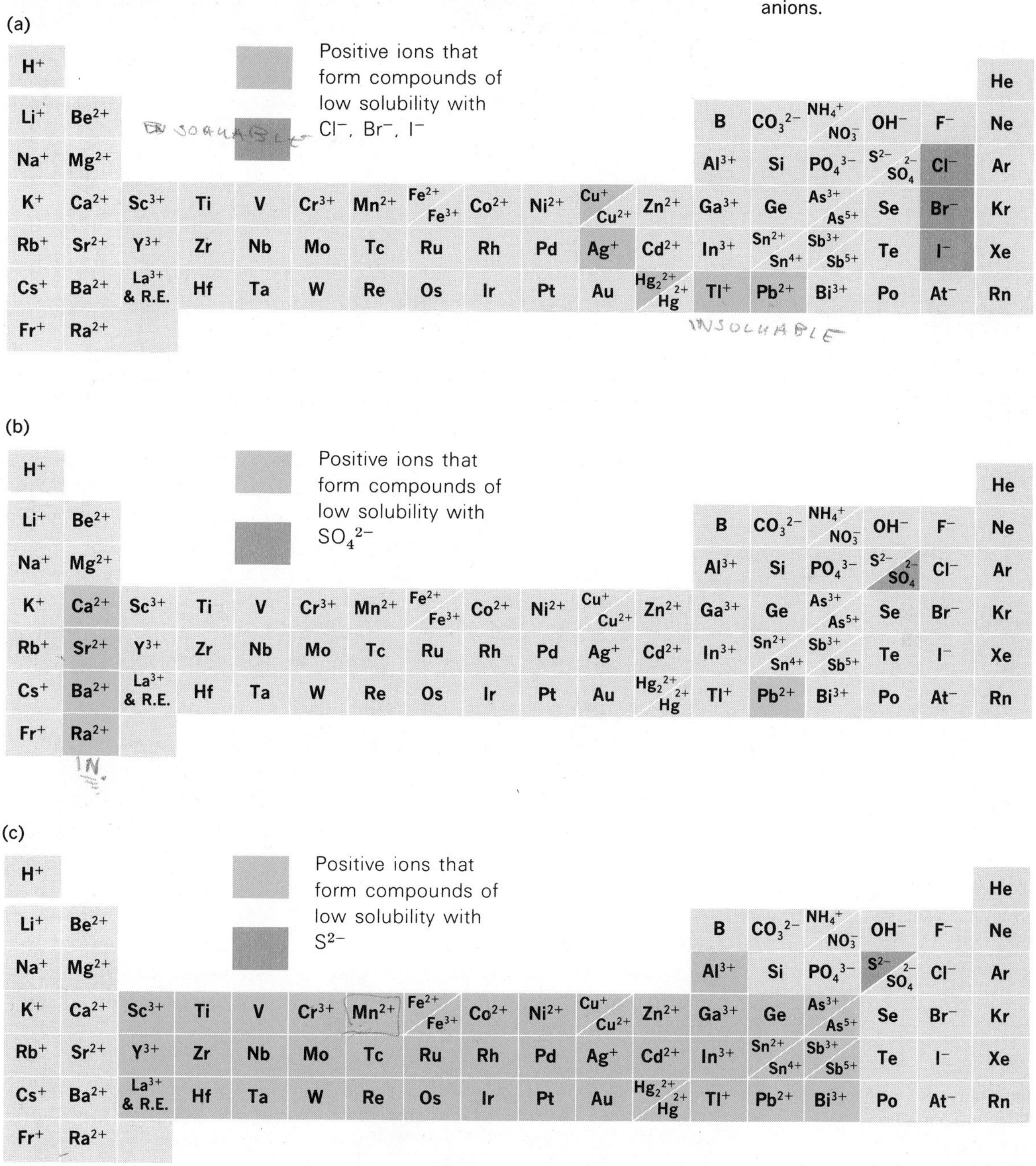

Fig. 12-6 Positive ions forming compounds of low solubilities with anions.

(a)

Positive ions that form compounds of low solubility with Cl$^-$, Br$^-$, I$^-$

(b)

Positive ions that form compounds of low solubility with SO$_4^{2-}$

(c)

Positive ions that form compounds of low solubility with S^{2-}

285

EXERCISE 12-5

Write formulas for each of the following compounds and decide whether the compound will be of high or low solubility in water.

silver carbonate	magnesium sulfate
aluminum hydroxide	rubidium iodide
cuprous (Cu^+) chloride	cesium nitrate
lead sulfate	barium sulfate
ammonium nitrate	silver iodide
silver sulfide	lead sulfite
calcium iodide	mercurous bromide

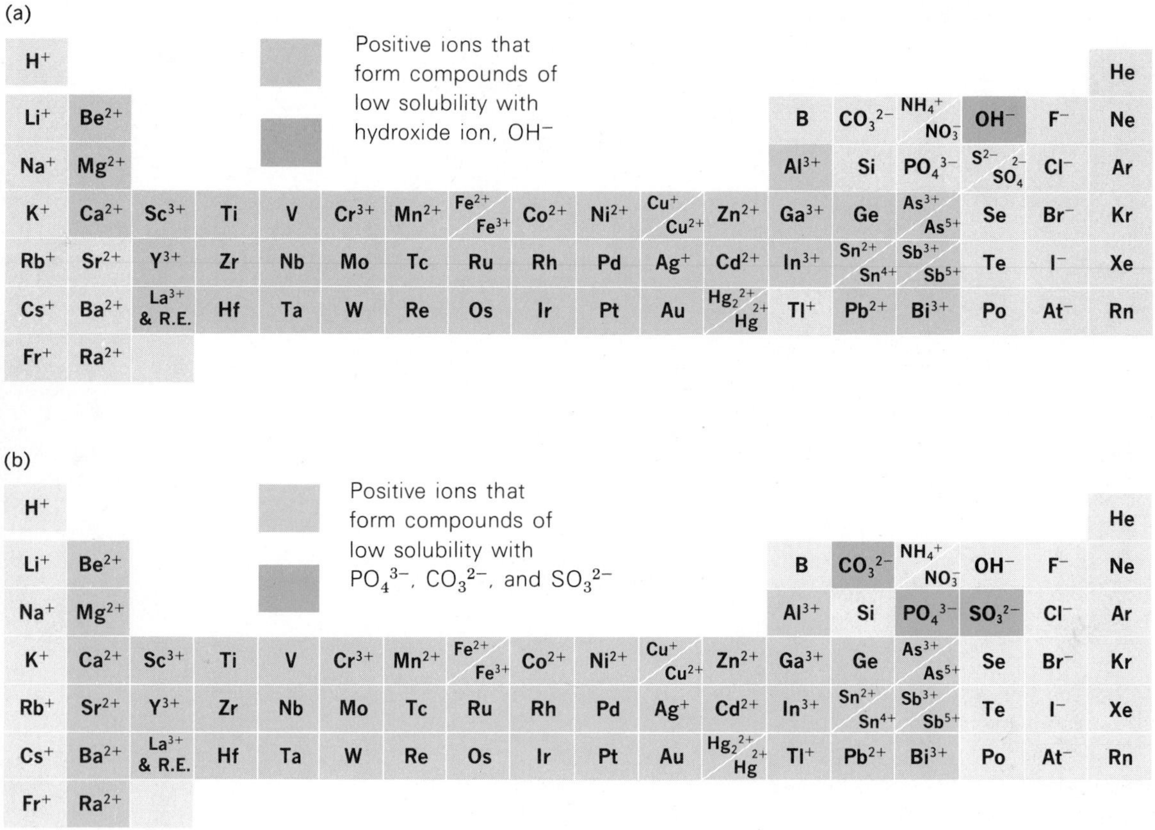

(a)

Positive ions that form compounds of low solubility with hydroxide ion, OH^-

(b)

Positive ions that form compounds of low solubility with PO_4^{3-}, CO_3^{2-}, and SO_3^{2-}

Fig. 12-7 More positive ions forming compounds of low solubilities with various anions.

EXERCISE 12-6

Write an equation for the process expected when a solution of sodium sulfate (0.5 *M*) is poured into a solution of strontium nitrate (0.5 *M*). Indicate precipitate formation of *MX* by writing *MX*(*s*). Repeat for the pouring of a solution of ammonium chloride into a solution of sodium nitrate. If no precipitate forms, show ions in solution as products.

TABLE 12-1 SOLUBILITY OF COMMON COMPOUNDS IN WATER

Negative Ions (Anions)	+	Positive Ions (Cations)	$\longrightarrow$	Compounds with the Solubility:
Essentially all		alkali ions (Li^+, Na^+, K^+, Rb^+, Cs^+, Fr^+)		soluble
Essentially all		hydrogen ion [$H^+(aq)$]		soluble
Essentially all		ammonium ion (NH_4^+)		soluble
Nitrate, NO_3^-		essentially all		soluble
Acetate, CH_3COO^-		essentially all		soluble
Chloride, Cl^- Bromide, Br^- Iodide, I^-		Ag^+, Pb^{2+}, Hg_2^{2+}, Cu^+, Tl^+		low solubility
		all others		soluble
Sulfate, SO_4^{2-}		Ca^{2+}, Sr^{2+}, Ba^{2+}, Pb^{2+}, Ra^{2+}		low solubility
		all others		soluble
Sulfide, S^{2-}		alkali ions, $H^+(aq)$, NH_4^+, Be^{2+}, Mg^{2+}, Ca^{2+}, Sr^{2+}, Ba^{2+}, Ra^{2+}		soluble
		all others		low solubility
Hydroxide, OH^-		alkali ions, $H^+(aq)$, NH_4^+, Sr^{2+}, Ba^{2+}, Ra^{2+}, Tl^+		soluble
		all others		low solubility
Phosphate, PO_4^{3-} Carbonate, CO_3^{2-} Sulfite, SO_3^{2-}		alkali ions, $H^+(aq)$, NH_4^+		soluble
		all others		low solubility

12-5 AN APPLICATION OF EQUILIBRIUM CONCEPTS TO IONIC SOLUTIONS

So far, we have organized our information in a more or less qualitative fashion so that we can make intelligent estimates of compound solubility. But *qualitative* answers are frequently not enough; we want to know *how much* of an ionic solid dissolves in a litre of water! *Quantitative* models of equilibrium are thus desired. Let us start with the equation for a solution process.

The low solubility of silver chloride (AgCl) has been considered earlier and makes a convenient place to start. If we write

$$AgCl(s) \rightleftharpoons Ag^+(aq) + Cl^-(aq) \qquad (20)$$

a general equilibrium constant for the system can be written as before:

$$K' = \frac{[Ag^+(aq)][Cl^-(aq)]}{[AgCl(s)]} \qquad (21)$$

Once again, we see the concentration of a solid—AgCl in this case—in the equilibrium constant. Our experience with solid iodine showed that *the concentration of a solid is constant;* therefore, if we consider the concentration of AgCl(s) as constant, we can write

$$K'[AgCl(s)] = \text{a constant} = [Ag^+(aq)][Cl^-(aq)]$$

We can now write

$$K = K'[AgCl(s)] = [Ag^+(aq)][Cl^-(aq)] \qquad (22)$$

This constant, K, which is defined by the relationship

$$K_{sp} = [Ag^+(aq)][Cl^-(aq)] \qquad (22)$$

is known as the **solubility product constant** for silver chloride (in a saturated aqueous solution). A low value of K_{sp} means that the concentration of ions is low at equilibrium; hence, the solubility of the compound must be low. Table 12-2 lists solubility product constants for a few common compounds.

EXERCISE 12-7

Show from the equation for the solution of lead chloride that K_{sp} for $PbCl_2$ is $K_{sp} = [Pb^{2+}(aq)][Cl^-(aq)]^2$. Write the equation for the dissolving of Ag_2CrO_4, silver chromate, and write the expression for K_{sp}.

TABLE 12-2

SOME SOLUBILITY PRODUCTS
AT ROOM TEMPERATURE

Compound	K_{sp}
TlCl	1.9×10^{-4}
CuCl	3.2×10^{-7}
AgCl	1.7×10^{-10}
TlBr	3.6×10^{-6}
CuBr	5.9×10^{-9}
AgBr	5.0×10^{-13}
TlI	8.9×10^{-8}
CuI	1.1×10^{-12}
AgI	8.5×10^{-17}
SrCrO$_4$	3.6×10^{-5}
BaCrO$_4$	8.5×10^{-11}
PbCrO$_4$	2×10^{-16}
CaSO$_4$	2.6×10^{-4}
SrSO$_4$	7.6×10^{-7}
PbSO$_4$	1.3×10^{-8}
BaSO$_4$	1.5×10^{-9}
RaSO$_4$	4×10^{-11}
AgBrO$_3$	5.4×10^{-5}
AgIO$_3$	2.1×10^{-8}

12-5.1 Calculation of the Solubility of Silver Bromide in Water

The solubility product is obtained from measurements of solubility. In turn, it can be used to make a quantitative estimate of solubility. In short, a solubility product provides *a method of summarizing very concisely a large amount of experimental information on the solubility of a given ionic substance.* Suppose we wish to know how much silver bromide (AgBr) will dissolve in 1 litre of water. How can this information be computed from the value for K_{sp} carried in handbooks and reference sources? We begin by writing the balanced equation for the reaction:

$$AgBr(s) \rightleftharpoons Ag^+(aq) + Br^-(aq) \qquad (23)$$

After a quick look at this equation, we can write the equilibrium expression:

$$K_{sp} = [Ag^+][Br^-] \qquad (24)$$

Now the numerical value of K_{sp} for silver bromide is found in Table 12-2:

$$K_{sp} = 5.0 \times 10^{-13} = [Ag^+][Br^-] \qquad (25)$$

The equation for the dissolving process (23) indicates that silver bromide (AgBr) continues to dissolve until the product of the molar concentrations of silver ion, Ag^+, and bromide ion, Br^-, is equal to 5.0×10^{-13}.

Now is the time to put our algebra to work. Suppose we designate the solubility of silver bromide in water by a symbol, s. This symbol s equals the number of moles of solid silver bromide that dissolve to produce 1 litre of saturated silver bromide solution. Remembering the equation for the solution process, we see that s moles of solid silver bromide will produce s moles of silver ion, Ag^+, and s moles of bromide ion, Br^-. Hence these concentrations must be equal:

$$[Ag^+] = [Br^-] = s \text{ moles/litre} = s \text{ moles/litre AgBr dissolved} \quad (26)$$

Substituting this equality into the K_{sp} expression and then solving for s, we have

$$
\begin{aligned}
K_{sp} &= 5.0 \times 10^{-13} \text{ moles}^2/\text{litre}^2 = (s) \times (s) = s^2 \\
s^2 &= 5.0 \times 10^{-13} \text{ moles}^2/\text{litre}^2 = 50 \times 10^{-14} \text{ moles}^2/\text{litre}^2 \\
s &= \sqrt{50 \times 10^{-14} \text{ moles}^2/\text{litre}^2} = 7.1 \times 10^{-7} \text{ mole/litre} \\
&= 0.000\,000\,71 \, M \quad (27)
\end{aligned}
$$

EXERCISE 12-8

Calculate the solubility in moles per litre of thallium iodide (TlI) in water using the solubility product given in Table 12-2.

12-5.2 Will a Precipitate Form?

In Exercise 12-6, we asked for a qualitative answer to the question: what happens when a solution (0.5 M) of sodium sulfate is poured into a solution (0.5 M) of strontium nitrate? For rather concentrated solutions the answer is clear. A precipitate of insoluble strontium sulfate appears. But is this always true? What happens if the solutions are more dilute? How insoluble does a solid have to be before the precipitate appears? These questions require a more quantitative application of the equilibrium concept. Let us consider quantitative relationships for two examples of mixing solutions of thallium nitrate ($TlNO_3$) and sodium chloride (NaCl).

Example (1) If equal volumes of 0.02 M $TlNO_3$ and 0.004 M NaCl are mixed, will a precipitate form?

The balanced equation for the solution or precipitation of thallium chloride in water is

$$TlCl(s) \rightleftharpoons Tl^+(aq) + Cl^-(aq) \quad (28)$$

The K_{sp} value for TlCl in Table 12-2 is 1.9×10^{-4}. We can write

$$K_{sp} = 1.9 \times 10^{-4} \text{ moles}^2/\text{litre}^2 = [Tl^+(aq)][Cl^-(aq)] \quad (29)$$

We must now calculate the concentrations of $Tl^+(aq)$ and $Cl^-(aq)$ immediately after mixing and before any reaction has had a chance to occur. Since we are mixing *equal volumes* of the two solutions, each ion will be present in twice as much volume; hence, its concentration will be only *half* as great as it was before the solutions were mixed. This being true, we can write

Ion	Concentration Before Mixing	Concentration After Mixing
$Tl^+(aq)$	0.02 M	$\frac{0.02\ M}{2} = 0.01\ M$
$NO_3^-(aq)$	0.02 M	$\frac{0.02\ M}{2} = 0.01\ M$
$Na^+(aq)$	0.004 M	$\frac{0.004\ M}{2} = 0.002\ M$
$Cl^-(aq)$	0.004 M	$\frac{0.004\ M}{2} = 0.002\ M$

We must ask next: is the product $[Tl^+(aq)][Cl^-(aq)]$ in the solution, after mixing, *larger* or *smaller* than the value of K_{sp} for TlCl? If the product is *larger* than K_{sp}, *a precipitate will form*: ions will be removed through precipitation until the ion product becomes equal to K_{sp}. If the product $[Tl^+(aq)][Cl^-(aq)]$ is *smaller* than K_{sp}, *no precipitate will form*. In our case, $[Tl^+(aq)] = 0.01\ M$ and $[Cl^-(aq)] = 0.002\ M$; we can write

$$[Tl^+(aq)][Cl^-(aq)] = 0.01 \times 0.002 = 2 \times 10^{-5}\ moles^2/litre^2 * \quad (30)$$

Since 2×10^{-5} is *less than* 1.9×10^{-4}, *no precipitate will form*. This is true since we also know that $NaNO_3$ is water soluble.

Example (2) Equal volumes of 0.08 M $TlNO_3$ and 0.2 M NaCl are mixed. Will a precipitate form?

Again, we may write

Ion	Concentration Before Mixing	Concentration After Mixing
$Tl^+(aq)$	0.08 M	$\frac{0.08\ M}{2} = 0.04\ M$
$NO_3^-(aq)$	0.08 M	$\frac{0.08\ M}{2} = 0.04\ M$
$Na^+(aq)$	0.2 M	$\frac{0.2\ M}{2} = 0.1\ M$
$Cl^-(aq)$	0.2 M	$\frac{0.2\ M}{2} = 0.1\ M$

The trial ion product relationship gives

$$[Tl^+(aq)][Cl^-(aq)] = 0.04 \times 0.1 = 4 \times 10^{-3}\ moles^2/litre^2 \quad (31)$$

*This value, the product of ion concentrations, is sometimes called the **trial ion product.**

This value is obviously larger than K_{sp}; hence, a precipitate of TlCl will form. Precipitation will occur until the concentrations of $Tl^+(aq)$ and $Cl^-(aq)$ are reduced to a point at which their product is no longer larger than the value of K_{sp}.

EXERCISE 12-9

A 50-ml volume of 0.04 M $Ca(NO_3)_2$ solution is added to 150 ml of 0.008 M $(NH_4)_2SO_4$ solution. Show that a trial value of the calcium sulfate ion product is 6×10^{-5} moles²/litre². Will a precipitate form?

EXERCISE 12-10

Would a precipitate form if 100 ml of 0.04 M $TlNO_3$ were mixed with 300 ml of 0.008 M NaCl? Watch the dilution ratios.

The formation of precipitates from solution is of tremendous importance in nature and industry. The oyster, in growing its shell, must adjust conditions so that the concentration of CO_3^{2-} is large enough to precipitate calcium carbonate ($CaCO_3$) from the surrounding seawater. Coral reefs grow in the same way. Limestone caves are carved out of limestone rock by water in which the concentrations of $Ca^{2+}(aq)$ and $CO_3^{2-}(aq)$ have a product below the K_{sp} for $CaCO_3$. Many beautiful pigments such as "cadmium reds" (cadmium selenide-cadmium sulfide) are prepared by a careful application of the principles of precipitation equilibrium. Failure to pay strict attention to data summarized in values of a K_{sp} table can result in loss of large amounts of expensive raw materials and the contamination of rivers and streams. Chemical engineers cannot afford the luxury of ignoring K_{sp} values.

12-5.3   Precipitations Used for Separations

A chemist is often interested in separating substances present in solution. The commercial preparation of magnesium metal starts with the separation of magnesium salts from seawater or other brine. Such a problem is solved by applying equilibrium considerations. Suppose we have a solution known to contain both lead nitrate [$Pb(NO_3)_2$] and magnesium nitrate [$Mg(NO_3)_2$]. The lead and magnesium can be separated by removing from the solution almost all the lead ion (Pb^{2+}) as a solid lead compound. We must avoid precipitation of any magnesium compound. Consulting Figure 12-6(b) or Table 12-1, we see that lead ion and sulfate ion form a compound with low solubility. If enough sodium sulfate (Na_2SO_4) is added, lead sulfate ($PbSO_4$) will precipitate. Since Figure 12-6(b) and Table 12-1 indicate that magnesium sulfate ($MgSO_4$) is soluble, there will be no precipitation of $MgSO_4$. The solid can be removed from the liquid by filtration producing the desired separation. Magnesium could then be precipitated as the carbonate.

EXERCISE 12-11

Use Figures 12-6 and 12-7 or Table 12-1 to decide which of the following soluble salts would permit a separation of magnesium and lead through a precipitation reaction: sodium iodide, NaI; sodium sulfide, Na_2S; sodium carbonate, Na_2CO_3.

Let us consider a somewhat more complicated separation. Suppose a solution contains silver nitrate ($AgNO_3$), copper(II) nitrate [$Cu(NO_3)_2$], and magnesium nitrate [$Mg(NO_3)_2$]. How can a separation of the metal ions be achieved? In such a case, the reagents used and the order in which they are added are both important. Referring to Figure 12-7, we see that Ag^+, Cu^{2+}, and Mg^{2+} all form insoluble carbonates (CO_3^{2-}), phosphates (PO_4^{3-}), and hydroxides (OH^-). Clearly, salts with these anions would *not* be helpful to us in accomplishing a separation. From Figure 12-6(a), we see that Ag^+ forms an insoluble chloride while Cu^{2+} and Mg^{2+} ions form soluble chlorides. This information is useful. Addition of a solution of ammonium or sodium chloride will precipitate AgCl, which can then be filtered off.

We now have only Cu^{2+} and Mg^{2+} ions to separate. Figure 12-6(b) shows that $MgSO_4$ and $CuSO_4$ are both water soluble: addition of Na_2SO_4 will not help us. Figure 12-6(c) provides the answer. MgS is soluble while CuS is insoluble. Adding Na_2S solution to the mixture containing Mg^{2+} and Cu^{2+} will precipitate CuS and leave $Mg^{2+}(aq)$ in solution. The $Mg^{2+}(aq)$ can then be removed as $MgCO_3$ by adding Na_2CO_3 solution.

The order in which the reagents are added is important. If we had added Na_2S solution before we added NaCl solution, both Ag_2S and CuS would have precipitated immediately. If we had added Na_2CO_3 solution at the beginning, $MgCO_3$, $CuCO_3$, and Ag_2CO_3 would have precipitated. Thus, both *the selection of reagents* and *the order in which they are added* is of concern. The segment of chemistry which deals with separations of this type is called **qualitative analysis.** More detailed qualitative-analysis schemes for more difficult separations could be worked out with a knowledge of acids and bases.

EXERCISE 12-12

A liquid contains the following salts in solution: potassium nitrate (KNO_3), lead nitrate [$Pb(NO_3)_2$], copper nitrate [$Cu(NO_3)_2$], and barium nitrate [$Ba(NO_3)_2$]. Show that the addition of the following salts in order would leave only KNO_3 in solution. Identify the precipitate coming out after the addition of each reagent. The order in which they are added is (1) KCl solution, (2) K_2SO_4 solution, and (3) K_2CO_3 solution. Would other orders work as well?

12-6   HIGHLIGHTS

The extent to which a substance will dissolve depends upon two factors:

(1) the tendency of the system to achieve maximum randomness—a process which favors the solution process for solids and opposes the solution process for gases, and

(2) the tendency of the system to achieve minimum energy content.

Energy changes may favor either the solid or the solution. Energy changes always favor gas solubility. When randomness and energy are balanced, equilibrium is achieved.

General concepts of equilibrium can be applied to problems of solubility. Since concentration of a pure solid phase is constant, this value is conventionally included in the equilibrium constant so that the equilibrium expression takes a rather unexpectedly simple form. For the dissolving of non-electrolytes such as I_2 in a solvent such as alcohol at a constant temperature, the equilibrium constant takes the very simple form

$$K = [I_2(solution)]$$

For ionic materials such as AgCl dissolving in water at a constant temperature, the equilibrium constant takes the form

$$K_{sp} = [Ag^+(aq)][Cl^-(aq)]$$

where K_{sp} is known as the **solubility product constant.**

QUESTIONS and PROBLEMS

1 Sugar is added to a vigorously stirred cup of coffee until no more sugar will dissolve. Does addition of another spoonful of sugar increase the rate at which the sugar molecules dissolve? Will the sweetness of the coffee be increased by this addition? Explain.

2 Enough copper sulfate ($CuSO_4$) is put into water to make a saturated solution. The blue solution is found to conduct an electric current. (a) Write the net ionic equation for the equilibrium reaction that is established. (b) Describe the process in terms of molecular motion.

3 Explain, using the tendencies toward minimum energy and maximum randomness, the following observations: (a) Lead iodide has low solubility in water. The ΔH of solution is $+14.0$ kcal/mole. (b) Sodium hydroxide has high solubility in water. The ΔH of solution is -10.3 kcal/mole.

4 Liquid chloroform ($CHCl_3$) and liquid acetone (CH_3COCH_3) dissolve each other in all proportions. (a) When pure $CHCl_3$ is mixed with pure CH_3COCH_3, is randomness increased or decreased? (b) Does the tendency toward maximum randomness favor reactants or products in the reaction

$$CHCl_3(l) + CH_3COCH_3(l) \longrightarrow$$
$$\text{1:1 solution}$$
$$\Delta H = -0.5 \text{ kcal}$$

(c) Considering the sign of ΔH shown in (b), does the tendency toward minimum energy favor reactants or products? (d) In view of your answers to (b) and (c), why are these two liquids soluble in all proportions?

5 Carbon dioxide is soluble in water at $0\,°C$ to the extent of 0.0087 mole/litre. Sulfur dioxide is soluble at $0\,°C$ to the extent of 0.36 mole/litre. (a) If the randomness considerations in the dissolving of the two gases are approximately equal, which gas must have the greater ΔH of solution? (Both reactions are exothermic.) (b) CO_2 and SO_2 are both less soluble in hot water than in cold water. Explain.

6 Given:
$$Ba(ClO_3)_2(s) \longrightarrow Ba^{2+}(aq) + 2ClO_3^-(aq)$$
$$\Delta H = +6.69 \text{ kcal}$$

If the temperature of the water is increased, would a greater or lesser amount of barium chlorate dissolve in a given amount of water? Briefly explain your answer in terms of Le Chatelier's principle. stress - heating

7 Assume that each of the following compounds forms separate, mobile ions in solution. Write the equation for the dissolving of each of the following substances in water. (a) $HCl(g)$ (b) $NaNO_3(s)$ (c) $H_2SO_4(l)$ (d) $(NH_4)_3PO_4(s)$ (e) $K_2CO_3(s)$.

293

8 Write the equation for the dissolving of each of the following in water. Be sure that your equation indicates whether or not ions are formed as each substance goes into solution. (a) $NaCl(s)$ (b) $HBr(g)$ (c) $CH_4(g)$ (d) $C_{12}H_{22}O_{11}(s)$ (e) $HNO_3(l)$.

9 Refer to the tables and figures on pages 284–287 of the text. Write the formula for each of the following compounds and indicate which have low solubility in water: (a) mercury(II) phosphate (b) aluminum sulfate (c) nickel chloride (d) sodium acetate (e) calcium sulfite.

10 Refer to the tables and figures on pages 284–287 of the text. Write the formula for each of the following compounds and indicate which have low solubility in water: (a) chromium(II) chloride (b) ammonium phosphate (c) lead bromide (d) aluminum sulfide (e) sodium sulfate (f) thallium(I) hydroxide (g) potassium carbonate (h) cobalt(II) sulfate (i) rubidium sulfite (j) barium hydroxide.

11 How could you separate each of the following pairs of ions from each other?

(a) $Pb^{2+}(aq)$ and $Ca^{2+}(aq)$

(b) $Mg^{2+}(aq)$ and $Ba^{2+}(aq)$

(c) $Ni^{2+}(aq)$ and $Na^+(aq)$

(d) $Mg^{2+}(aq)$ and $Ca^{2+}(aq)$

(e) $Ag^+(aq)$ and $Pb^{2+}(aq)$

12 A solution contains the following ions, each in $0.1\ M$ concentration: $Tl^+(aq)$, $Ba^{2+}(aq)$, $Al^{3+}(aq)$. Refer to the solubility tables on pages 284–287 in the text. Write a procedure by which these ions may be separated *from each other* and *from the solution*. Clearly indicate the order of separation and when filtration should be carried out.

13 Repeat question 12 for a solution containing the following: $Ag^+(aq)$, $Ca^{2+}(aq)$, $Ni^{2+}(aq)$.

14 What ions could be present in a solution if samples of it gave (a) a precipitate when either $Cl^-(aq)$ or $SO_4^{2-}(aq)$ is added? (b) a precipitate when $Cl^-(aq)$ is added but none when $SO_4^{2-}(aq)$ is added? (c) a precipitate when $SO_4^{2-}(aq)$ is added but none when $Cl^-(aq)$ is added?

15 Write the solubility product expression for each of the following reactions:

(a) $PbSO_4(s) \rightleftharpoons Pb^{2+}(aq) + SO_4^{2-}(aq)$

(b) $Mg(OH)_2(s) \rightleftharpoons Mg^{2+}(aq) + 2OH^-(aq)$

16 Write the solubility product expression for the dissolving of each of the following substances in water: (a) silver chloride (b) nickel sulfide (c) chromium hydroxide (d) calcium sulfite (e) barium phosphate.

17 $PbCrO_4$ dissolves in water to the extent of 7×10^{-5} *gram* per litre at 20 °C. Calculate the value of K_{sp} at 20 °C.

18 The solubility of cobalt sulfide (CoS) is 3.8×10^{-3} *gram* per litre at 18 °C. Calculate the value of K_{sp} for this reaction.

19 The solubility of silver sulfide (Ag_2S) is 1.3×10^{-6} mole per litre at 20 °C. (a) Write the equation for the dissolving of Ag_2S in water. (b) Write the solubility product expression for the reaction. (c) Calculate the value of K_{sp} for the reaction.

20 The solubility product of CuS is 4×10^{-38} at 25 °C. (a) Calculate the number of moles of CuS that will dissolve in 1.0 litre of solution at 25 °C. (b) Calculate the number of *grams* of CuS that will dissolve in 1.0 litre of solution at 25 °C.

21 The solubility product of $BaCO_3$ at 25 °C is 8.1×10^{-9}. Calculate the mass (in grams) of barium carbonate that will dissolve in 0.100 litre of solution at 25 °C.

22 The K_{sp} of MnS is 4.9×10^{-9} at 18 °C. Calculate the mass (in grams) of MnS that will dissolve in 1.0 litre of solution.

23 If 0.010 mole of $AgNO_3$ and 0.00052 mole of $NaIO_3$ are dissolved in enough water to make a final volume of 2.00 litres, will a precipitate form? Justify your answer with the necessary calculations. The K_{sp} for $AgIO_3$ is 2.1×10^{-8}.

24 The K_{sp} for CuS is 2.5×10^{-41} at 18 °C. If 2×10^{-6} mole of $Cu(NO_3)_2$ and 2×10^{-6} mole of Na_2S are mixed in enough water to give a total volume of 10 litres, will a precipitate form? Justify your answer. Moles/litre

25 If 0.0010 mole of $AgNO_3$ is added to 0.500 litre of a $0.00050\ M$ solution of $NaBrO_3$, will a precipitate of $AgBrO_3$ form? Justify your answer by showing your calculations. K_{sp} for $AgBrO_3 = 5.4 \times 10^{-5}$.

26 If 0.010 mole of $Sr(NO_3)_2$ is added to 1.0 litre of $0.10\ M\ Na_2CrO_4$, will a precipitate form? The K_{sp} for $SrCrO_4$ is 3.6×10^{-5}.

27 The K_{sp} for $CaSO_4$ is 2.6×10^{-4}. If 1.0 litre of 2.0×10^{-3} M $Ca(NO_3)_2$ is added to 1.0 litre of 2.0×10^{-3} M H_2SO_4, will a precipitate form? (Remember that each solution is being diluted by the other.) Justify your answer by showing your calculations.

28 If 50.0 ml of a 0.050 M $AgNO_3$ solution is added to 50.0 ml of 0.00020 M KIO_3 solution, will a precipitate form? Justify your answer by showing your calculations.

29 What volume of water is necessary to dissolve 0.010 mole of AgCl entirely? The K_{sp} for AgCl is 1.7×10^{-10}.

Out of the simplest things ye shall know the truth.

GREGOR JOHANN MENDEL (1822–1884)

Ionic Equilibrium: 13
Acids and Bases

Most common fruits that we eat are acidic.

ACIDS HAVE QUITE A REPUTATION, BUT THEIR BARK IS USUALLY worse than their bite. If you're naturally curious, you may already have asked your teacher which acid is strongest. It's a common question. Everyone knows that acids must be handled with great care, yet oranges contain citric acid, and boric acid is so mild that it is used as an eyewash! What gives? What makes some acids dangerous and others tame? And what is a base? You guessed it—it's all a matter of equilibrium. Read on!

We have investigated equilibrium as it applies to gaseous systems and have learned that the commercial preparation of ammonia (NH_3) is based on an application of equilibrium principles. We were able to use equilibrium concepts in discussing solubility relationships. For the solubility of an ionic solid we wrote

$$AgCl(s) \rightleftharpoons Ag^+(aq) + Cl^-(aq) \qquad (1)$$

Since the concentration of $AgCl(s)$ is constant in the above system, the equilibrium constant has a particularly simple form at any given temperature. It is known as the **solubility product constant,** K_{sp}, and is written as

$$\underbrace{K'[AgCl(s)]}_{\text{CONSTANT}} = K_{sp} = [Ag^+(aq)][Cl^-(aq)] \qquad (2)$$

You may now wonder: what about an ionic equilibrium which does not involve a solid phase? In Experiment 20 we considered such an equilibrium involving the red $FeSCN^{2+}(aq)$ ion. We wrote

$$Fe^{3+}(aq) + SCN^-(aq) \rightleftharpoons Fe(SCN)^{2+}(aq) \qquad (3)$$

and

$$K = \frac{[Fe(SCN)^{2+}(aq)]}{[Fe^{3+}(aq)][SCN^-(aq)]} \qquad (4)$$

In this chapter we shall consider additional ionic equilibria. The discussion will lead us naturally into a study of acids and bases, a topic of great importance to chemists, biologists, physicians, and engineers.

13-1 ELECTROLYTES—STRONG AND WEAK

Our model describing the electrical conductivity of aqueous solutions pictured positive and negative ions moving through the liquid to carry the electric current (Chapter 6). Such a model suggested that electrical conductivity would rise as the concentration of ions increased and would drop to zero if no ions were present. On the basis of this model we can infer that those solutions having very good electrical conductivity contain a large supply of ions. For example, NaCl and HCl appear to dissolve to give *only* ions in dilute solution. These solutions are very good conductors. A solution of sodium hydroxide (NaOH) is also a good conductor. Its ionization in dilute solution to give $Na^+(aq)$ and $OH^-(aq)$ is essentially complete:

$$NaOH(s) \longrightarrow Na^+(aq) + OH^-(aq) \qquad (5)$$

There is no clear experimental evidence for the presence of a significant fraction of NaOH *molecules* in a dilute solution of NaOH in water or for a significant fraction of HCl molecules in a dilute solution of HCl in water. *A substance which breaks up almost completely to give ions in water solution is known as a* **strong electrolyte** *in water.* (See Figure 13-1.)

Fig. 13-1 Conductivity of (a) a strong electrolyte and (b) a weak electrolyte.

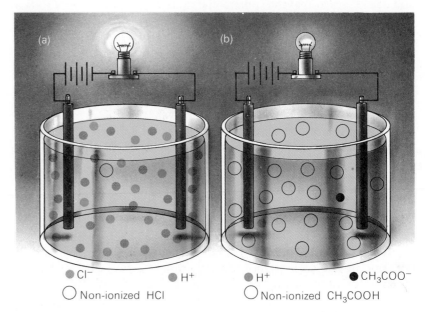

●Cl⁻   ●H⁺   ●H⁺   ●CH₃COO⁻
○ Non-ionized HCl   ○ Non-ionized CH₃COOH

The very name "strong electrolyte" suggests that we may have weak electrolytes too—substances which ionize to only a limited extent when they are dissolved in water. Acetic acid, found in vinegar, is such a material. A 0.1 M acetic acid solution is a *much poorer* conductor of electricity than a 0.1 M hydrochloric acid solution. This can be understood most easily by assuming that acetic acid does not ionize completely when dissolved in water. Our proposal can be summarized by an equation:

$$CH_3COOH(aq) \xmapsto{H_2O(l)} H^+(aq) + CH_3COO^-(aq) \qquad (6)$$

The long arrow pointing to the left tells us that very little of the acetic acid ionizes to give hydrogen ions, $H^+(aq)$, and acetate ions, $CH_3COO^-(aq)$. In contrast, our equation for HCl in water would be written as

$$HCl(g) \xrightarrow{H_2O(l)} H^+(aq) + Cl^-(aq) \qquad (7)$$

The reverse process to give HCl is too small to indicate with an arrow. *A substance like acetic acid which dissolves in water, yet which breaks up only partially into ions, is called a* **weak electrolyte** *in water.* (See Figure 13-1.)

13-1.1 The Dissociation of Water, a Very Weak Electrolyte

Relatively crude measurements show that pure water does *not* conduct electric current. If, however, the conductivity of pure water is measured with an extremely sensitive meter, a tiny electrical conductivity is found in even the purest water.* Such an observation suggests that water itself forms a few ions by the process

$$H_2O(l) \rightleftharpoons H^+(aq) + OH^-(aq) \tag{8}$$

The concentration of ions is *very* small and the equilibrium lies well toward non-ionized water. The equilibrium constant can be written

$$K' = \frac{[H^+(aq)][OH^-(aq)]}{[H_2O(l)]} \tag{9}$$

Since only the *tiniest trace* of water is ionized, essentially all the water is present as $H_2O(l)$. In 1 litre of water we have 1,000 g. Since 1 mole of water has a mass of 18.0 g $(16 + 1 + 1)$, we have

$$\frac{1,000 \text{ g } H_2O}{18.0 \text{ g } H_2O/\text{mole}} = 55.6 \text{ moles } H_2O$$

In most water solutions the concentration of water is virtually constant at 55.6 M; consequently, we can incorporate this number into the constant, just as we did when we considered the solubility of a solid. We can write

$$\underset{\text{CONSTANT}}{K'[H_2O]} = [H^+(aq)][OH^-(aq)] \tag{10}$$

The value $K'[H_2O]$ is a constant since $[H_2O]$ is constant. We thus write

$$K'[H_2O] = K_w = [H^+(aq)][OH^-(aq)]$$
$$= 1.00 \times 10^{-14} \text{ mole}^2/\text{litre}^2 \text{ at } 25 \text{ °C} \tag{11}$$

13-1.2 The Nature of Li$^+$(aq) and H$^+$(aq) and a Comment on the Symbols Used

When we consider the ionization of water and the existence of H$^+$ in solution, questions about the actual nature of H$^+$(aq) arise. What is really known about the nature of the proton in aqueous solution?

Let us approach this problem by considering the behavior of a related species in aqueous solution. Lithium chloride provides a good example. As we noted in Chapter 8, lithium chloride is composed of lithium cations, Li$^+$, and chloride anions, Cl$^-$, held together in a rigid lattice by electrostatic forces of attraction. If we heat this solid to a sufficiently high temperature, 613 °C, the kinetic energy of the ions is large enough to overcome the attraction of the positively and negatively charged particles. Under these circumstances, the tendency of a system to achieve maximum randomness

---

*The fact that pure water ionizes to a small degree can be shown qualitatively by the use of a 2-watt neon glow lamp in a conductivity apparatus.

Fig. 13-2 Hydration of Li$^+$ and Cl$^-$ ions from LiCl.

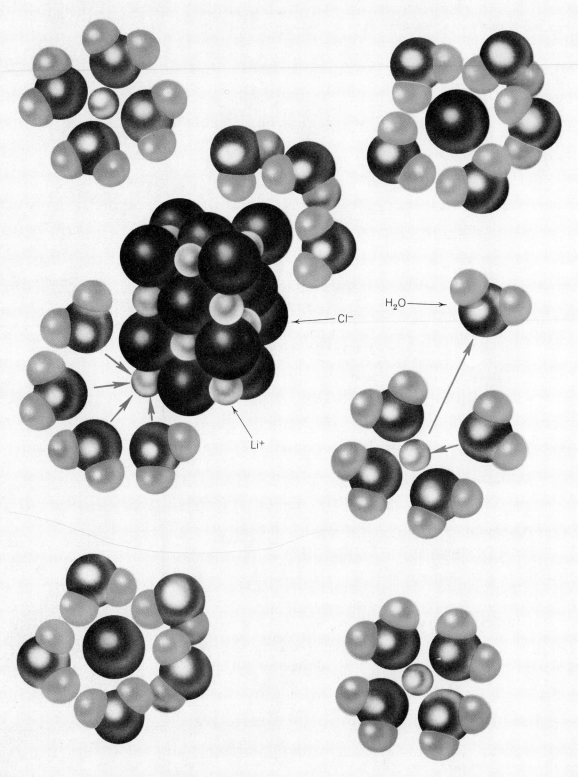

Cl$^-$

H$_2$O

Li$^+$

takes over. The ions scatter in helter-skelter fashion; in short, the solid LiCl melts and Li^+ and Cl^- ions are freed. These ions can then carry current through the molten mass.

In contrast to the high temperature required to produce ions in a molten salt, lithium chloride dissolves in water at 25 °C to produce $Li^+(aq)$ and $Cl^-(aq)$ ions in aqueous solution (see Figure 13-2, page 300). Where does the energy to separate the ions come from? What takes the place of the large amounts of energy required in the melting process (system heated to 613 °C)? The most reasonable assumption is that Li^+ and Cl^- interact very strongly with water. It is known that each water molecule has a negative end and a positive end (we use the symbols " − " and " + " for these poles) and therefore is known as a **polar molecule.** The negative end of this polar molecule will be attracted toward the positively charged Li^+ ion, while the positive end will be attracted toward the negative Cl^- ion. The interaction between the positive Li^+ and the negative end of the water molecule releases energy. Similarly, the interaction between the negative Cl^- and a positive end of the water molecule releases energy. This energy, known as the **energy of hydration,** provides the energy required to break up the lattice of Li^+ ions and Cl^- ions, even at room temperature.

When we write $Li^+(aq)$ in solution, we indicate that many water molecules are grouped around the Li^+ ion and that their negative end is pointing inward in a manner that releases energy. At present, there is no completely reliable way of counting the number of water molecules around any single Li^+ ion in solution. Water molecules seem to move in and out around the Li^+ with considerable ease, and different methods of estimating numbers provide different answers. One of the best estimates, based on the size of Li^+, the size of water molecules, and the formulas for salts such as $LiCl \cdot 4H_2O$, places four water molecules around each Li^+ (as in Figure 13-3). We could write $Li(H_2O)_4^+$, but we really are not sure $4H_2O$ is right! It is easier to hide our ignorance by using a less definite symbolism,

$$LiCl(s) \xrightarrow{H_2O(l)} Li^+(aq) + Cl^-(aq) \qquad (12)$$

$Li^+(aq)$ indicates lithium ions surrounded by properly oriented water molecules; $Cl^-(aq)$ indicates chloride ions surrounded by properly oriented water molecules. Water molecules interact strongly with Li^+ and Cl^- to liberate enough energy to break up the crystal.

The solution of HCl in water is only slightly different. Liquid HCl is not a good conductor of electricity; it contains no sizable concentration of ions in the liquid. Similarly, if HCl is dissolved in benzene, the system is a nonconductor—no ions are formed. The HCl in both cases is present as HCl molecules. As in the lithium chloride case, a very large amount of energy is required to pull a proton away from the Cl^- ion to give H^+ and Cl^-. In the gaseous state, temperatures far in excess of 1000 °C are required. Since this process proceeds readily in water at 25 °C, it is logical to conclude that the protons and the chloride ions interact strongly with water molecules to provide the required energy. A real chemical reaction to produce ions from HCl and water takes place.

As in the case of Li^+, we cannot really determine how many water molecules surround a proton. We might write $H(H_2O)_4^+$ by analogy to $Li(H_2O)_4^+$ (Figure 13-3). But there is a big difference: the H^+ ion is a bare proton—it has no external electrons and differs markedly from the much larger Li^+ ion. This fact has led many chemists to suggest that the proton attaches itself rather strongly to a *single* water molecule to give H_3O^+, and that this positive ion then interacts with additional water molecules to give $H_3O^+(aq)$. As seen in Figure 13-4, all three protons of H_3O^+ would be equivalent, and the positive ion would resemble in some ways the well

Fig. 13-3 Possible tetrahedral arrangements of water molecules around Li^+ and H^+ ions.

$Li^+(aq)$
$Li^+ \cdot 4H_2O$

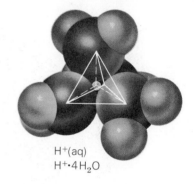

$H^+(aq)$
$H^+ \cdot 4H_2O$

Fig. 13-4 A model for the hydronium ion, H_3O^+.

The NATURE of
$Li^+(aq)$ and $H^+(aq)$

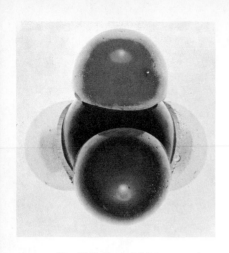

Fig. 13-5 A model for ammonium ion, NH_4^+.

known NH_4^+ ion (Figure 13-5), where a single proton is added to a neutral NH_3 molecule. It is further argued that there is structural evidence for the ion H_3O^+ in crystalline $HClO_4 \cdot H_2O$.

Despite these arguments, we still do not *know* how many water molecules surround a proton. Many models, each with different numbers of water molecules, are possible; hence, we again find it convenient to hide our ignorance by using a noncommittal symbol, $H^+(aq)$. As an additional convenience in notation, we shall indicate concentration of $H^+(aq)$ in solution as $[H^+]$. The concentration of $OH^-(aq)$ will be written as $[OH^-]$. The fact that ions are hydrated is implied by the symbols.

A little later we shall want to emphasize the fact that water *has* actually served to break off a proton from a molecule. In these cases we shall find it more convenient to specify one molecule of water as one of the reactants and write

$$HX(aq) + H_2O(l) \longrightarrow H_3O^+(aq) + X^-(aq) \qquad (13)$$

Remember that this is a matter of convenience only; it does not really say anything about the true condition of the proton in water solution.

One other point of notation is important. In the introduction we indicated by relative arrow lengths the predominating species in a solution. While this scheme is helpful in a general sense, it is not quantitative and is inconvenient in repeated use. For this reason we shall simply use *double arrows of equal length* to indicate a system at equilibrium. As we shall see later, *the size of the equilibrium constant will indicate which species predominates in the container.* With these conventions, the ionization of water is now indicated as

$$H_2O(l) \rightleftharpoons H^+(aq) + OH^-(aq) \qquad K_w = 1.00 \times 10^{-14} \quad \text{at 25 °C} \quad (14)$$

13-1.3 The Size and Significance of K_w— Its Variation with Temperature

So far we have considered the process

$$H_2O(l) \rightleftharpoons H^+(aq) + OH^-(aq)$$
$$K_w = 1.00 \times 10^{-14} \quad \text{at 25 °C} \quad (14)$$

What happens to the value of K_w if the temperature of the system is raised to 30 °C? What happens if the temperature is lowered to 20 °C? Experiments show that the ionization reaction for water absorbs energy:

$$H_2O(l) + 13.7 \text{ kcal} \rightleftharpoons H^+(aq) + OH^-(aq)^* \qquad (14a)$$

The measured energy term can now be used to predict how K_w changes with temperature. According to Le Chatelier's principle, an increase in temperature shifts the equilibrium in the direction of the process which absorbs heat. In this case, an increase in temperature should give a larger concentration of ions; hence, K_w should *increase* as the temperature rises. Experimental values given in Table 13-1 show that K_w does in fact increase with an increase in temperature. Conversely, decreasing the temperature should reduce the number of ions. This is also observed.

TABLE 13-1 VALUES OF K_w AT VARIOUS TEMPERATURES

Temperature (°C)	K_w
0	0.114×10^{-14}
10	0.295×10^{-14}
20	0.676×10^{-14}
25	1.00×10^{-14}
60	9.55×10^{-14}

*It is usually most convenient to measure the value 13.7 kcal by measuring the energy released in the reverse process when 1 mole of water is formed from 1 mole of $H^+(aq)$ and 1 mole of $OH^-(aq)$. (Refer to Experiment 17.)

EXERCISE 13-1

Using the data in Table 13-1, show that the concentration of $H^+(aq)$ in pure water at 60 °C is 3.1×10^{-7} M. What is the concentration of $OH^-(aq)$ in this pure water at 60 °C?

13-1.4 Concentrations of $H^+(aq)$ and $OH^-(aq)$ in Pure Water

When *pure water* ionizes, one $H^+(aq)$ is produced for every $OH^-(aq)$. Hence, in *pure* water, where *the only source of ions is the ionization of water,* the concentrations of $H^+(aq)$ and $OH^-(aq)$ must be equal.* For *pure water* we can write

$$[OH^-] = [H^+] \tag{15}$$

If we combine this with our expression for K_w, we can write

$$K_w = [H^+][OH^-] = [H^+][H^+] = [H^+]^2 \tag{11a}$$

or

$$[H^+] = \sqrt{K_w} = \sqrt{1.00 \times 10^{-14}} \quad \text{at 25 °C}$$
$$[H^+] = 1.00 \times 10^{-7} M$$
$$[OH^-] = 1.00 \times 10^{-7} M$$

At equilibrium and 25 °C, the concentration $[H^+]$ in pure water is 1.00×10^{-7} mole per litre, and the concentration $[OH^-]$ is 1.00×10^{-7} mole per litre. *Solutions in which $[H^+] = [OH^-]$ are called* **neutral.**† In neutral solutions at 25 °C, $[H^+] = [OH^-] = 1.00 \times 10^{-7} M$. At any given time only approximately two per billion molecules are ionized. This should not surprise us because it explains the very low conductivity of pure water.

13-1.5 Concentrations of $H^+(aq)$ and $OH^-(aq)$ in Solutions of HCl and NaOH

Does the concentration of $H^+(aq)$ always have to equal the concentration of $OH^-(aq)$ in water solution? Let us investigate this question. Suppose we add a solution of HCl containing $H^+(aq)$ and $Cl^-(aq)$ to pure water.‡ The original equilibrium for the water alone was

$$H_2O(l) \rightleftharpoons H^+(aq) + OH^-(aq) \tag{14}$$

*This is the same as saying that at a formal party where only *couples* attend, the number of nondancing girls will be equal to the number of nondancing boys. This is not generally true of a dance for singles.
†This use of the word *neutral* for a solution with equal amounts of H^+ and OH^- has its disadvantages because the same word is used in reference to electrical neutrality. Aqueous solutions are *always* electrically neutral, whether there is an excess of either H^+ or OH^-. Other positive or negative ions always restore electrical neutrality.
‡This would be comparable to some boys coming without dates to the formal, "couple" party described earlier. The concentration of nondancing boys would be higher than the concentration of nondancing girls.

If we add $H^+(aq)$ to the equilibrium mixture, Le Chatelier's principle tells us that the reaction

$$H^+(aq) + OH^-(aq) \longrightarrow H_2O(l) \qquad (14)$$

will occur until enough of the $H^+(aq)$ and $OH^-(aq)$ are used up for the equilibrium relationship to be reestablished:

$$K_w = [H^+][OH^-] = 1.00 \times 10^{-14} \qquad (11)$$

Note, however, that in the new equilibrium $[H^+]$ is *not* equal to $[OH^-]$. The concentration of $H^+(aq)$ is *larger than* 1.00×10^{-7} and the concentration of $OH^-(aq)$ is much *smaller* than 1.00×10^{-7} since much of the $OH^-(aq)$ has been converted into water in reacting with the excess $H^+(aq)$.

Similarly, if we add NaOH, containing $Na^+(aq)$ and $OH^-(aq)$, $H^+(aq)$ will be used up until the equilibrium relationship is again attained. *In both these cases the concentration of H^+(aq) is no longer equal to the concentration of OH^-(aq). $[H^+]$ is equal to $[OH^-]$ only in neutral solutions.*

Let us consider some actual examples of systems containing HCl or NaOH. Suppose 0.10 mole of HCl is dissolved in enough water to give 1.0 litre of solution at 25 °C. Since HCl is completely ionized to give $H^+(aq)$ ions and $Cl^-(aq)$ ions, 0.10 mole of HCl in 1.0 litre will give 0.10 mole of $H^+(aq)$ and 0.10 mole of $Cl^-(aq)$ per litre. $[H^+]$ is 1.0×10^{-1} mole/litre.* The concentration of $OH^-(aq)$ at equilibrium with the $H^+(aq)$ can be calculated easily from the equilibrium law

$$[H^+][OH^-] = 1.00 \times 10^{-14} \text{ mole}^2/\text{litre}^2$$

or

$$\begin{aligned}
[OH^-] &= \frac{1.00 \times 10^{-14} \text{ mole}^2/\text{litre}^2}{[H^+]} \\
&= \frac{1.00 \times 10^{-14} \text{ mole}^2/\text{litre}^2}{1.0 \times 10^{-1} \text{ mole/litre}} \\
&= 1.0 \times 10^{-13} \text{ mole/litre}
\end{aligned}$$

Addition of 0.10 mole of HCl lowered the $[OH^-]$ from 10^{-7} to 10^{-13} mole/litre by the reaction

$$H^+(aq) + OH^-(aq) \longrightarrow H_2O(l)$$

This is a decrease by a factor of one million. Strangely enough, a solution of HCl in water still contains a measurable concentration of $OH^-(aq)$ ions, as demanded by water's ionization equilibrium.

Let us look at another experiment. Suppose we add 0.10 mole of NaOH to enough water to give 1.0 litre of solution at 25 °C. Since sodium hydroxide is a strong electrolyte—almost 100 percent ionized

*The original $[H^+]$ in pure water, 1.00×10^{-7} M, is trivial in comparison to the new $[H^+]$ of 1.0×10^{-1} M, and is ignored.

into $Na^+(aq)$ and $OH^-(aq)$—the concentration of both $Na^+(aq)$ and $OH^-(aq)$ will be 0.10 mole per litre. Since water is the solvent, the water equilibrium must be established:

$$H_2O(l) \rightleftharpoons H^+(aq) + OH^-(aq) \qquad (14)$$

$$K_w = [H^+][OH^-] = 1.00 \times 10^{-14} \text{ mole}^2/\text{litre}^2 \quad (11)$$

$$[OH^-] = 0.10 \text{ mole/litre}$$

Hence,

$$K_w = [H^+] \times 0.10 \text{ mole/litre} = 1.00 \times 10^{-14} \text{ mole}^2/\text{litre}^2$$

$$[H^+] = \frac{1.00 \times 10^{-14} \text{ mole}^2/\text{litre}^2}{0.10 \text{ mole/litre}} = 1.0 \times 10^{-13} \text{ mole/litre}$$

In these two ordinary laboratory solutions, the concentration of $H^+(aq)$ has varied from 0.1 mole per litre to 10^{-13} mole per litre. The range is almost too large to comprehend. This would just be a chemical curiosity but for one fact: *the ions H^+(aq) and OH^-(aq) take part in many important reactions that occur in aqueous solution.* Many biological processes in solution are extremely sensitive to the concentration of $H^+(aq)$. For example, human blood must be kept very close to the $H^+(aq)$ concentration of 6.0×10^{-8} mole per litre or severe damage and even death may result. In many solution reactions either the $H^+(aq)$ or the $OH^-(aq)$ ions take part as reactants. It is not hard to see that a million-fold or a trillion-fold change in concentration of one of the reactants could have a serious effect on the equilibrium and the course of the reaction. Furthermore, there are many reactions for which either the hydrogen ion or the hydroxide ion is a catalyst. For example, catalysis of the decomposition of formic acid by $H^+(aq)$ was discussed in Chapter 10. Formic acid is reasonably stable until the $H^+(aq)$ concentration is raised; then the rate of decomposition becomes very rapid. The concentration of $H^+(aq)$ is one of the most important variables in the study of aqueous solutions.

EXERCISE 13-2

Show that the addition of 0.010 mole of $NaOH(s)$ to enough water to give 1 litre of solution reduces the $[H^+]$ to 1.0×10^{-12} M.

EXERCISE 13-3

Suppose that 3.65 g of HCl are dissolved in enough water to give 10.0 litres of solution. What is the value of $[H^+]$? Use the expression

$$K_w = [H^+][OH^-] = 10^{-14}$$

to show that $[OH^-] = 1.00 \times 10^{-12}$ M.

CONCENTRATIONS of

H^+(aq) and OH^-(aq)

EXERCISE 13-4

In the laboratory you saw that the color of a solution of potassium chromate (K_2CrO_4) changes to the color of a solution of potassium dichromate ($K_2Cr_2O_7$) when we add a few drops of HCl solution. Write the balanced equation for the reaction between $CrO_4^{2-}(aq)$ and $H^+(aq)$ to produce $Cr_2O_7^{2-}(aq)$ and H_2O. Then explain the color change on the basis of Le Chatelier's principle.

13-2 EXPERIMENTAL INTRODUCTION TO ACID AND BASE SYSTEMS

13-2.1 Experimental Identification of Acids

In trying to classify materials they found around them, early experimenters identified a group of substances having some common properties. These materials dissolved in water to give solutions which

(1) were electrical conductors;
(2) reacted with an active metal such as Zn to liberate hydrogen gas;
(3) turned blue litmus solution red and altered the color of many organic dyes, including such common liquids as the juice of red cabbage; and
(4) had a sour taste.*

Substances having these experimental properties were called **acids.**

13-2.2 A Model for Explaining the Properties of Acids

What makes an acid behave as it does? What common characteristic or structural feature can account for the properties of an acid? Let us investigate this question more carefully.

You are familiar with hydrochloric acid (HCl), nitric acid (HNO_3), acetic acid (CH_3COOH), sulfuric acid (H_2SO_4), and phosphoric acid (H_3PO_4). These acids all contain hydrogen atoms in combined form. Is hydrogen important to the behavior of acids? It might be, since Zn gives hydrogen gas in reacting with acids. Since acids conduct electric current, it is reasonable to propose that acids produce ions when dissolved in water. Since all acids have a similar group of properties, we might suggest that all contain a common ion. Based on the evidence before us, the ion $H^+(aq)$ is a likely choice. We postulate: *a substance has the properties of an acid if it can release hydrogen ions in water solution.*

13-2.3 Experimental Identification of Bases

Another group of materials identified by early experimenters resemble acids in a few ways, but most of their properties contrast sharply with the properties of acids. For example, many compounds of this group

*Many chemicals, however, are poisonous. Hydrogen cyanide, one of the most poisonous materials, is an acid. Obviously, taste should *not* be used by chemists to identify a substance.

resemble acids in that they contain combined hydrogen and dissolve in water to give solutions that conduct electricity. On the other hand, these materials change red litmus to blue and cause many dyes to assume a color quite different from that found in acidic solution. The substances have a bitter rather than a sour taste* and feel slippery. (Like acids, these substances are corrosive to the skin.) Finally, when we add one of these compounds to an acid, the identifying properties of both acid and the compound disappear; only electrical conductivity remains as a characteristic property of the mixture.

Materials in this second class are called **bases.** Typical bases include sodium hydroxide (NaOH), potassium hydroxide (KOH), calcium hydroxide [$Ca(OH)_2$], magnesium hydroxide [$Mg(OH)_2$], sodium carbonate (Na_2CO_3), and ammonia (NH_3).

13-2.4 A Model for Explaining the Properties of Bases

Using the line of reasoning we applied to acids, we seek a common factor that accounts for the similarities of bases. Because of their electrical conductivity, we might look for an ion. Because of their ability to counteract the properties of acids, we might look for an ion that can remove the acidic hydrogen ion, $H^+(aq)$.

Sodium hydroxide (NaOH), when dissolved in water, gives a solution having basic properties. The hydroxides of many elements from the left side of the periodic table behave in the same way. Perhaps they dissolve to form ions of the sort

$$NaOH(s) \rightleftharpoons Na^+(aq) + OH^-(aq) \qquad (16)$$

$$KOH(s) \rightleftharpoons K^+(aq) + OH^-(aq) \qquad (17)$$

$$Mg(OH)_2(s) \rightleftharpoons Mg^{2+}(aq) + 2\,OH^-(aq) \qquad (18)$$

$$Ca(OH)_2(s) \rightleftharpoons Ca^{2+}(aq) + 2\,OH^-(aq) \qquad (19)$$

The hydroxide ion, $OH^-(aq)$, could react with hydrogen ion to account for the second property of bases, the removal of acidic properties:

$$OH^-(aq) + H^+(aq) \rightleftharpoons H_2O(l) \qquad (14)$$

The similarities among the hydroxides are obvious. Let us compare sodium carbonate (Na_2CO_3) and ammonia (NH_3). Na_2CO_3 dissolves in water to give a solution having the properties of a base. Quantitative studies of the solubilities of carbonates show that the carbonate ion, CO_3^{2-}, reacts with water. The reactions are

$$Na_2CO_3(s) \rightleftharpoons 2Na^+(aq) + CO_3^{2-}(aq) \qquad (20)$$

$$CO_3^{2-}(aq) + H_2O(l) \rightleftharpoons HCO_3^-(aq) + OH^-(aq) \qquad (21)$$

Equation (21) indicates that the presence of the carbonate ion, $CO_3^{2-}(aq)$, in water increases the hydroxide ion concentration, $[OH^-]$. The hydroxide ion is present in the solutions of NaOH, KOH, $Mg(OH)_2$, and $Ca(OH)_2$. We see that the existence of the stable bi-

*If you have forgotten the danger of tasting chemicals, reread the preceeding footnote.

carbonate ion, $HCO_3^-(aq)$,* produces the chemical species $OH^-(aq)$, the same ion found in solutions of the hydroxides. We can postulate that $OH^-(aq)$ accounts for the slippery feel and bitter taste of the basic solutions. The stability of the bicarbonate ion also explains the removal of acidic properties through direct reaction between the carbonate ion and a hydrated proton to give the bicarbonate ion:

$$CO_3^{2-}(aq) + H^+(aq) \rightleftharpoons HCO_3^-(aq) \qquad (22)$$

We have listed ammonia (NH_3) as a base. Ammonia readily forms ammonium ion, NH_4^+. Ammonia reacts with water,

$$NH_3(g) + H_2O(l) \rightleftharpoons NH_4^+(aq) + OH^-(aq) \qquad (23)$$

and with hydrogen ion,

$$NH_3(g) + H^+(aq) \rightleftharpoons NH_4^+(aq) \qquad (24)$$

The formation of $NH_4^+(aq)$ explains the fact that ammonia has basic properties. The reaction of ammonia with water produces hydroxide ion, which, by our postulate, accounts for the taste and feel of basic solutions. The direct reaction of an ammonia molecule and a proton to give the ammonium ion shows how ammonia can act to destroy the acidic properties of any solution which contains hydrogen ions.

Investigation of the reactions of other compounds having basic properties shows that each compound can produce hydroxide ions in water. The $OH^-(aq)$ ions may be produced directly [as when $NaOH(s)$ dissolves in water] or by adding a substance which reacts chemically with water [as when $Na_2CO_3(s)$ and $NH_3(g)$ dissolve in water]:

$$NaOH(s) \rightleftharpoons Na^+(aq) + OH^-(aq) \qquad (16)$$
$$CO_3^{2-}(aq) + H_2O(l) \rightleftharpoons HCO_3^-(aq) + OH^-(aq) \qquad (21)$$
$$NH_3(g) + H_2O(l) \rightleftharpoons NH_4^+(aq) + OH^-(aq) \qquad (23)$$

Furthermore, *any substance that can produce hydroxide ions in water also combines with hydrogen ions:*

$$OH^-(aq) + H^+(aq) \rightleftharpoons H_2O(l) \qquad (14)$$
$$CO_3^{2-}(aq) + H^+(aq) \rightleftharpoons HCO_3^-(aq) \qquad (22)$$
$$NH_3(g) + H^+(aq) \rightleftharpoons NH_4^+(aq) \qquad (24)$$

Since production of $OH^-(aq)$ and reaction with $H^+(aq)$ go hand-in-hand in aqueous solutions, we can describe a base *either* as a substance that produces $OH^-(aq)$ *or* as a substance that can react with $H^+(aq)$. In solvents other than water, the latter description is generally more useful. Therefore, the more general postulate is: *a substance has the properties of a base if it can combine with hydrogen ions.*

*Bicarbonate ion, HCO_3^-, is also termed "hydrogen carbonate" or "monohydrogen carbonate."

Sodium acetate (CH_3COONa) serves as a base in water solution.

(1) Write the equation by which sodium acetate (or its active component) removes hydrogen ions from water solution.
(2) Why is sodium acetate classed as a base?

13-3 CONCEPTUAL AND OPERATIONAL DEFINITIONS

Looking back on the earlier sections reveals that we have used two different definitions of an acid and two different definitions of a base. The first definition of each came from the laboratory; it told us what an acid or base will do and how to recognize each. We can summarize such descriptions by listing the properties. Let us compare acids and bases in terms of these properties:

Acid	*Base*
(1) electrical conductor	(1) electrical conductor
(2) reacts with Zn to give $H_2(g)$	(2) destroys the properties of acids
(3) makes blue litmus red	(3) makes red litmus blue
(4) tastes sour	(4) tastes bitter
(5) frequently corrosive to skin	(5) frequently corrosive to skin
	(6) feels slippery

These are called **operational definitions.** To understand this term, consider the meaning of the word *definition*. According to one dictionary, *definition* means "a statement of what a thing is." By using a definition, we can sort the universe into two piles, one containing those objects that fit the definition and another containing those that do not. Our *operational* definition gives the criteria by which this sorting process can be carried out. An operational definition is, then, one that lists the measurements or observations (the *operations*) by which we decide if an object belongs in a given group.

The second type of definition we have used is a **conceptual definition.** It is more concerned with the question "why?" It seeks to define the group in terms of an explanation of *why the class has its properties.* When we state that an acid is a substance that releases hydrogen ions to aqueous solution, we are using a *conceptual* definition. We are on less secure experimental ground than with the operational definition, but the conceptual definition is far more useful in the construction of chemical models and in *expansion of the definitions to solvents other than water*. Conceptual definitions lead to new research and to the development of hidden likenesses, or regularities.

Each type of definition has its merits; neither is *the* definition. We shall see that, as more and more complicated systems are considered, the operational and conceptual definitions of acids and bases must be expanded. The concept of an acid is a device used by chemists to correlate different kinds of observations. The definition of an acid has been expanded accordingly. We shall confine our attention to water solutions and to the operational and conceptual definitions given thus far. Remember, however, that there is no *absolute* definition of an acid; we use this classification scheme because it is appropriate to the system we are studying. Every musician knows that there is no *one* key in which a symphony must be written; the key is chosen to evoke the desired mood. Similarly, definitions of acids are selected by the chemist on the basis of their ability to explain or simplify the system under study.

13-4 ACID-BASE TITRATIONS

One of the observations we used in defining a base was that a base can neutralize or destroy certain properties characteristic of an acid. The conceptual definition we used explains this ability in terms of a simple reaction:

$$OH^-(aq) + H^+(aq) \longrightarrow H_2O(l) \qquad (14)$$
$$\text{BASE} \qquad \text{ACID} \qquad \text{WATER}$$

Let us see how this concept applies to mixing HCl and NaOH in the same solution.

13-4.1 HCl and NaOH in the Same Solution: Excess HCl

Suppose that to 0.100 litre of 1.00 M HCl solution we add 0.090 mole of NaOH(s). By adding solid NaOH we keep the volume of the solution essentially constant. Now we have both $H^+(aq)$ and $OH^-(aq)$ in relatively high concentrations in the *same* solution. What will happen? Immediately after the sodium hydroxide dissolves, the concentrations of $H^+(aq)$ and $OH^-(aq)$ far exceed the equilibrium values. The trial product $[H^+][OH^-]$ far exceeds 1.00×10^{-14} mole^2/litre^2:

$$\text{initial } [H^+] = 1.00 \ M$$
$$\text{initial } [OH^-] = \frac{0.090 \text{ mole}}{0.100 \text{ litre}} = 0.90 \ M$$
$$\text{trial product} = [H^+] \times [OH^-] = 9.00 \times 10^{-1} \text{ mole}^2/\text{litre}^2$$

The equilibrium relationship, $[H^+][OH^-] = 1.00 \times 10^{-14}$, can be achieved most easily by removing both $H^+(aq)$ and $OH^-(aq)$. The reaction of these two ions to form water is clearly indicated.

$$OH^-(aq) + H^+(aq) \longrightarrow H_2O(l) \qquad (14)$$

Since K_w is so small, almost all the $OH^-(aq)$ is consumed when the HCl is present in excess. In our example $[H^+]$ initially exceeds $[OH^-]$ by 0.10 mole per litre:

$$\text{initial } [H^+] - \text{initial } [OH^-] = \text{excess } [H^+]$$
$$1.00 \ M \quad - \quad 0.90 \ M \quad = \quad 0.10 \ M$$

If [H$^+$] is 0.10 mole per litre, then

$$[H^+][OH^-] = 1.00 \times 10^{-14} \text{ mole}^2/\text{litre}^2$$

$$[OH^-] = \frac{1.00 \times 10^{-14} \text{ mole}^2/\text{litre}^2}{1.0 \times 10^{-1} \text{ mole/litre}}$$

$$= 1.0 \times 10^{-13} \text{ mole/litre}$$

The concentration of OH$^-$(aq), 10^{-13} mole per litre, is a million times smaller than the OH$^-$(aq) concentration of pure water. Nearly all the OH$^-$(aq) has been *neutralized* or removed by the HCl present.

EXERCISE 13-6

Suppose that 0.099 mole of NaOH(s) is added to 0.100 litre of 1.00 M HCl.

(1) How many moles of ionized HCl are present in the final solution?

(2) From the moles of HCl and the volume, calculate the concentration of excess H$^+$(aq).

(3) Calculate the concentration of OH$^-$(aq) at equilibrium (see your calculations for Exercise 13-3).

13-4.2   HCl and NaOH in the Same Solution: Excess NaOH

Returning to our original 0.100 litre of 1.00 M HCl, let us now consider the addition of 0.101 mole of NaOH(s). Again, we have added both H$^+$(aq) and OH$^-$(aq) to the *same* solution, and the concentrations immediately after mixing do not satisfy the equilibrium expression:

$$\text{initial } [H^+] = 1.00 \ M$$

$$\text{initial } [OH^-] = \frac{0.101 \text{ mole}}{0.100 \text{ litre}} = 1.01 \ M$$

$$\text{initial product} = [H^+] \times [OH^-] = 1.01 \text{ moles}^2/\text{litre}^2$$

far exceeding 1.00×10^{-14} mole^2/litre^2.

This solution contains excess hydroxide ion, OH$^-$(aq); therefore, essentially all the H$^+$(aq) will be consumed, forming water:

$$\text{initial } [OH^-] - \text{initial } [H^+] = \text{excess } [OH^-]$$
$$1.01 \ M \quad - \quad 1.00 \ M \quad = \quad 0.01 \ M$$

In Exercise 13-2 we calculated the equilibrium concentration of H$^+$ in a solution containing [OH$^-$] = 0.010 M. You will recall that

$$[H^+] = \frac{1.00 \times 10^{-14} \text{ mole}^2/\text{litre}^2}{1 \times 10^{-2} \text{ mole/litre}} = 1 \times 10^{-12} \text{ mole/litre}$$

13-4.3 HCl and NaOH in the Same Solution: No Excess of Either

In each example used in this section, a number of moles of NaOH was added to 0.100 litre of 1.00 M HCl. Either HCl or NaOH was in excess. Reaction between $H^+(aq)$ and $OH^-(aq)$ consumes essentially all the constituent not in excess. Let us now consider the case in which there is an excess of *neither* HCl nor NaOH.

Suppose we add 0.100 mole of NaOH to 0.100 litre of 1.00 M HCl. The initial values of $[H^+]$ and $[OH^-]$ are equal and their product far exceeds 1.00×10^{-14}:

$$\text{initial } [H^+] = 1.00 \ M$$
$$\text{initial } [OH^-] = \frac{0.100 \text{ mole}}{0.100 \text{ litre}} = 1.00 \ M$$
$$\text{initial product} = [H^+] \times [OH^-] = 1.00 \text{ moles}^2/\text{litre}^2$$

Reaction between $H^+(aq)$ and $OH^-(aq)$ must again occur, forming water:

$$OH^-(aq) + H^+(aq) \rightleftharpoons H_2O(l) \qquad (14)$$

Since 1 mole of $OH^-(aq)$ consumes 1 mole of $H^+(aq)$, the concentrations $[H^+]$ and $[OH^-]$ remain equal as the neutralization reaction between $H^+(aq)$ and $OH^-(aq)$ proceeds. When equilibrium is reached, they will still be equal. This is exactly the situation in pure water. As we saw in Section 13-1.4,

$$[H^+] = [OH^-] = \sqrt{K_w} = 1.00 \times 10^{-7} \ M \qquad (15a)$$

A solution containing exactly equivalent amounts of acid and base is neither acidic nor basic; it is neutral. *If equal numbers of moles of HCl and NaOH are added to water, the final solution is neutral.*

13-4.4 Progressive Addition of NaOH to HCl: A Titration

Now we will consider the progressive addition of NaOH to a fixed amount of HCl solution. The results are compiled in Table 13-2. We see that $[H^+]$ changes by a factor of 10^{10} as the initial $[OH^-]$ is changed from 0.99 M to 1.01 M. Since $[H^+]$ can be easily followed experimentally, it provides a sensitive means of observing the mixing of an acid and a base. The process is called a **titration,** *the progressive addition of a base to an acid.**

In an acid-base titration, carefully measured amounts of a basic solution of known concentration are added to a known volume of an acidic solution. The acidic solution contains some substance that provides visual evidence of the magnitude of $[H^+]$. The dye litmus is one such substance. As mentioned in Sections 13-2.1 and 13-2.3, litmus is red in solutions with excess $H^+(aq)$ and blue in solutions with excess $OH^-(aq)$. Fortunately, the dye color is extremely sensitive to very small

*The addition of an acid to a base is also a titration.

amounts of $H^+(aq)$. In solutions containing $[H^+]$ of $10^{-6} M$, the dye is red. In solutions containing $[H^+]$ of $10^{-8} M$, the dye is blue. As we see in Table 13-2, the *slightest* addition of excess OH^- causes a great change in $[H^+]$ and a marked change in color.

There are many dyes whose color is very sensitive to the concentration of $H^+(aq)$. Such dyes are called **acid-base indicators.** All do not change color where $[H^+] = [OH^-]$. Some change on the acidic side, some on the basic side. Litmus and bromthymol blue change at the neutral point. In Figure 13-6 (on next page), the colors of other acid-base indicators in solutions of different $[H^+]$ are shown.

13-5 THE *p*H SCALE

Chemists and biologists have found it convenient to use a quantity known as the pH for indicating in shorthand form the hydrogen-ion concentration in any solution. The pH is officially defined by the expression

$$pH = -\log_{10} [H^+] \qquad (25)$$

The pH values for the solutions we have been dealing with are very easily obtained from values for $[H^+]$. Consider the following example: if the solution contains $0.01 M$ HCl (100 percent ionized), we write $[H^+] = 0.01 M = 10^{-2} M$. Once the hydrogen-ion concentration has been expressed in this exponential form (10^{-2}), the pH is easily obtained by simply taking the exponent of 10 (-2, in this case) and changing its sign: $pH = 2$. Values of pH for solutions in Table 13-2 are shown in that table. Note that:

(1) A pH value of 7 is neutral.
(2) pH values less than 7 are acidic.
(3) pH values greater than 7 are basic or alkaline.

13-6 STRENGTHS OF ACIDS

Earlier in this chapter we noted that HCl ionizes almost completely in water solution:

$$HCl(aq) \longrightarrow H^+(aq) + Cl^-(aq) \qquad (7)$$

TABLE 13-2 CONCENTRATIONS OF H^+ AND OH^- IN SOLUTIONS CONTAINING HCl AND NaOH

Initial $[H^+]$ (M)	Initial $[OH^-]$ (M)	Excess $[H^+]$ or $[OH^-]$ (M)	Calc $[H^+]$ (M)	Calc $[OH^-]$ (M)	Acidic or Basic	log $[H^+]$	pH	Color of Solution (litmus)
1.00	none	1.00 H^+	10^0 or 1.00	10^{-14}	acidic	0	0	red
1.00	0.90	0.10 H^+	10^{-1}	10^{-13}	acidic	-1	1	red
1.00	0.99	0.01 H^+	10^{-2}	10^{-12}	acidic	-2	2	red
1.00	1.00	none	10^{-7}	10^{-7}	neutral	-7	7	purple
1.00	1.01	0.01 OH^-	10^{-12}	10^{-2}	basic	-12	12	blue

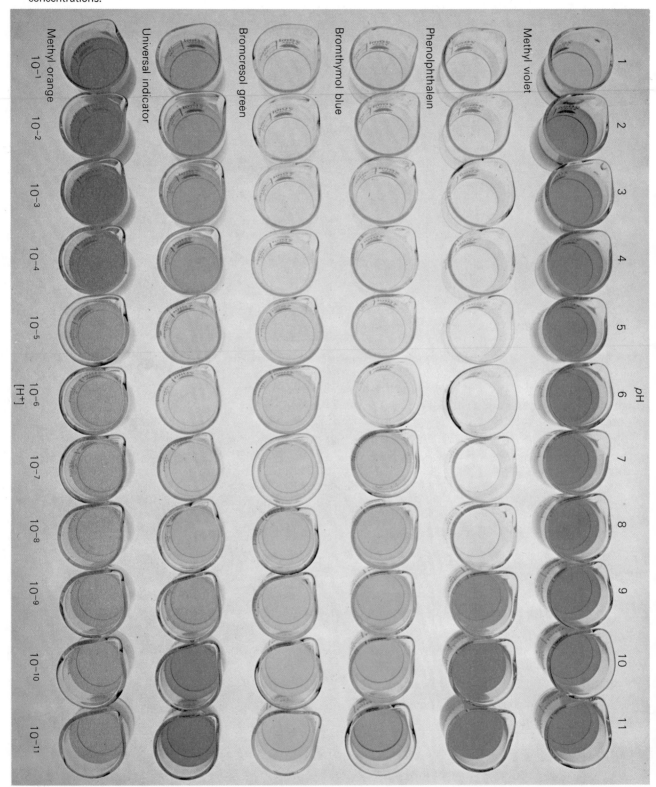

For all practical purposes, the reaction goes completely to $H^+(aq)$ and $Cl^-(aq)$. The concentration of $HCl(aq)$ remaining in the solution is *extremely small*. Because the concentration of $HCl(aq)$ is so small, the equilibrium constant for HCl ionization is *very large*.

$$K_{HCl} = \left.\frac{[H^+(aq)][Cl^-(aq)]}{[HCl(aq)]}\right\} = \text{VERY LARGE} \qquad (26)$$

An acid which gives a large equilibrium constant is known as a strong acid.

We also considered the ionization of acetic acid, which ionizes to a much smaller degree. We wrote

$$CH_3COOH(aq) \rightleftharpoons H^+(aq) + CH_3COO^-(aq) \qquad (6)$$

Conductivity studies showed that very little acetic acid was ionized. The equilibrium constant for this process takes the form

$$K_{CH_3COOH} = \frac{[H^+][CH_3COO^-]}{[CH_3COOH]} = 1.8 \times 10^{-5} \qquad (27)$$

The *small value* of the equilibrium constant means that very little acetic acid is ionized. As we noted earlier, this value, sometimes called K_A or the **acid equilibrium constant,** is a precise way of indicating acid strength. It is a most useful number for characterizing an acid.

If we now compare quantitatively the electrical conductivity of 0.1 M solutions of CH_3COOH and HF, we find that HF has about ten times as many ions present as acetic acid (ten times the conductivity). HF is a stronger acid than CH_3COOH. The equilibrium constant reveals this fact:

$$K_{HF} = \frac{[H^+][F^-]}{[HF]} = 6.7 \times 10^{-4} \qquad (28)$$

The value 6.7×10^{-4} is significantly larger than 1.8×10^{-5}.

We can express these ideas in terms of a general acid, HB:

$$HB(aq) \rightleftharpoons H^+(aq) + B^-(aq) \qquad (29)$$

where

$$K_A \text{ for acid } HB = K_{HB} = \frac{[H^+(aq)][B^-(aq)]}{[HB(aq)]} \qquad (30)$$

Values of K_A for a number of acids are listed in Table 13-3. The strong acids have large values of K_A; the weak acids have small values of K_A.

Acid	Strength	Reaction	K_A
HCl	very strong	$HCl(l) \longrightarrow H^+(aq) + Cl^-(aq)$	very large
HNO_3	↓	$HNO_3(l) \longrightarrow H^+(aq) + NO_3^-(aq)$	very large
H_2SO_4	very strong	$H_2SO_4 \longrightarrow H^+(aq) + HSO_4^-(aq)$	very large
HSO_4^-	strong	$HSO_4^-(aq) \longrightarrow H^+(aq) + SO_4^{2-}(aq)$	1.3×10^{-2}
HF	weak	$HF(aq) \longrightarrow H^+(aq) + F^-(aq)$	6.7×10^{-4}
CH_3COOH	↓	$CH_3COOH(aq) \longrightarrow H^+(aq) + CH_3COO^-(aq)$	1.8×10^{-5}
H_2CO_3 ($CO_2 + H_2O$)	↓	$H_2CO_3(aq) \longrightarrow H^+(aq) + HCO_3^-(aq)$	4.4×10^{-7}
H_2S	weak	$H_2S(aq) \longrightarrow H^+(aq) + HS^-(aq)$	1.0×10^{-7}
NH_4^+	↓	$NH_4^+(aq) \longrightarrow H^+(aq) + NH_3(aq)$	5.7×10^{-10}
HCO_3^-	↓	$HCO_3^-(aq) \longrightarrow H^+(aq) + CO_3^{2-}(aq)$	4.7×10^{-11}
H_2O	very weak	$H_2O(l) \longrightarrow H^+(aq) + OH^-(aq)$	$1.8 \times 10^{-16*}$

*The acid equilibrium constant, K_A, for water equals

$$\frac{K_w}{[H_2O]} = \frac{1.00 \times 10^{-14}}{55.6} = \frac{[H^+][OH^-]}{[H_2O]} = 1.8 \times 10^{-16}$$

(See Section 13-1.1.)

EXERCISE 13-7

Which of the following acids is the strongest acid and which the weakest?

Nitrous acid (HNO_2) $K_{HNO_2} = 5.1 \times 10^{-4}$
Sulfurous acid (H_2SO_3) $K_{H_2SO_3} = 1.7 \times 10^{-2}$ (1st proton)
Phosphoric acid (H_3PO_4) $K_{H_3PO_4} = 7.1 \times 10^{-3}$ (1st proton)

13-6.1 Determination of K_A

How do we determine values of this useful number, K_A, from labora-tory data? The experiments must provide a measurement of hydro-gen-ion concentration. A number of procedures are available. One of the most precise methods involves a careful measurement of cell voltage. The method will be discussed in Chapter 15. Acid-sensitive dyes (see Figure 13-6) offer the easiest estimate of $H^+(aq)$ when electronic meters are not available. Let us consider a specific example.

Benzoic acid (C_6H_5COOH) is a white solid with only moderate solubility in water. The aqueous solution has all the characteristic properties of acids listed in Section 13-2.1. The ionization equation and acid equilibrium constant, $K_{C_6H_5COOH}$, are

$$C_6H_5COOH(aq) \rightleftharpoons H^+(aq) + C_6H_5COO^-(aq) \qquad (31)$$

$$K_{C_6H_5COOH} = \frac{[H^+][C_6H_5COO^-]}{[C_6H_5COOH]} \qquad (32)$$

To determine $K_{C_6H_5COOH}$, we need to obtain experimental values for the concentrations of $H^+(aq)$, $C_6H_5COO^-(aq)$, and $C_6H_5COOH(aq)$ in a given water solution. Once these values are obtained, the calcula-tion of the equilibrium constant is simple. The following experiment gives us all the information needed.

A 1.22-g sample of solid benzoic acid is dissolved in enough water to give 1.00 litre of solution at 25 °C. Several drops of methyl orange acid-base indicator are added to this solution; the color of the resulting liquid is compared to those of solutions containing methyl orange and known concentrations of $H^+(aq)$ (see Figure 13-6). The best color match is obtained with a known solution containing 8×10^{-4} mole $H^+(aq)$/litre. We can therefore conclude that the $H^+(aq)$ concentration of the benzoic acid is about 8×10^{-4} M. We write

$$[H^+] = 8 \times 10^{-4}\ M$$

Equation (31) tells us that when pure benzoic acid is dissolved in water, the concentration of $H^+(aq)$ is the same as that of the benzoate ion, $C_6H_5COO^-(aq)$,* since each mole of benzoic acid produces 1 mole of $H^+(aq)$ and 1 mole of $C_6H_5COO^-(aq)$ when it ionizes. We now have

$$[H^+] = 8 \times 10^{-4}\ M$$

and

$$[C_6H_5COO^-] = 8 \times 10^{-4}\ M$$

The only information still needed is the concentration of non-ionized $C_6H_5COOH(aq)$. We dissolved 1.22 g of benzoic acid to make 1 litre of solution. Since the molecular weight of benzoic acid is 122, the number of moles of benzoic acid is

$$\frac{1.22\ \text{g benzoic acid}}{122\ \text{g}\ \dfrac{\text{benzoic acid}}{\text{mole}}} = 0.0100\ \text{mole}$$

We have, then, 0.0100 mole of benzoic acid in 1.00 litre of solution. The original benzoic acid concentration is 0.0100 M. To generate an $H^+(aq)$ concentration of 8×10^{-4} mole per litre, we had to have 8×10^{-4} mole per litre of the original benzoic acid ionize. [See equation (31) for the ionization process.] The final concentration of non-ionized benzoic acid in the solution will be

$$\left\{\begin{matrix}\text{original concn}\\ \text{benzoic acid}\\ \text{in solution}\end{matrix}\right\} - \left\{\begin{matrix}\text{concn}\\ \text{benzoic acid}\\ \text{lost by}\\ \text{ionization}\end{matrix}\right\} = \left\{\begin{matrix}\text{final}\\ \text{equilibrium}\\ \text{concn}\\ \text{benzoic acid}\end{matrix}\right\} \quad (33)$$

or

$$0.0100\ M \quad - \quad 0.0008\ M \quad = \quad 0.0092\ M$$

We can now write

$$[H^+] = 8 \times 10^{-4}\ M$$
$$[C_6H_5COO^-] = 8 \times 10^{-4}\ M$$
$$[C_6H_5COOH] = 0.0092 = 9 \times 10^{-3}\ M$$

*A solution containing only pure benzoic acid may be compared to the formal dance involving *only couples,* where the concentration of nondancing boys equals the concentration of nondancing girls.

Then $K_{C_6H_5COOH}$ is

$$K_{C_6H_5COOH} = \frac{(8 \times 10^{-4})(8 \times 10^{-4})}{9 \times 10^{-3}} = 7 \times 10^{-5}$$

Since the concentration of $H^+(aq)$ was measured to only one significant figure, the answer can have no more than one significant figure.

13-6.2 The Use of K_A Values—The Calculation of $[H^+]$ in an Acid Solution

Let us use the value of K_A we just measured to determine the $[H^+]$ in a solution that contains 0.41 g per litre of benzoic acid. In this solution (pure benzoic acid in water), the concentration of $H^+(aq)$ is again equal to the concentration of benzoate ion, $C_6H_5COO^-(aq)$.

$$[H^+] = [C_6H_5COO^-] \qquad (34)$$

The concentration of benzoic acid before ionization took place was 0.0033 mole/litre (0.41 g/122 g/litre). If we remember the relationship

$$\begin{Bmatrix} \text{original concn} \\ \text{benzoic acid} \\ \text{in solution} \end{Bmatrix} - \begin{Bmatrix} \text{concn} \\ \text{benzoic acid} \\ \text{lost by} \\ \text{ionization} \end{Bmatrix} = \begin{Bmatrix} \text{final} \\ \text{equilibrium} \\ \text{concn} \\ \text{benzoic acid} \end{Bmatrix} \quad (33)$$

and the relationship from equation (34),

$$\begin{Bmatrix} \text{concn} \\ \text{benzoic acid} \\ \text{lost by} \\ \text{ionization} \end{Bmatrix} = \begin{Bmatrix} \text{concn } H^+(aq) \\ \text{formed in} \\ \text{solution} \end{Bmatrix} \quad (34a)$$

we can write

$$\begin{Bmatrix} \text{original concn} \\ \text{benzoic acid} \\ \text{in solution} \end{Bmatrix} - \begin{Bmatrix} \text{concn} \\ \text{benzoic acid} \\ \text{lost by} \\ \text{ionization} \end{Bmatrix} = \begin{Bmatrix} \text{final} \\ \text{equilibrium} \\ \text{concn} \\ \text{benzoic acid} \end{Bmatrix} \quad (33)$$

$$0.0033\ M \qquad\qquad [H^+(aq)] \qquad\qquad [C_6H_5COOH(aq)]$$

We can then write

$$\frac{[H^+][C_6H_5COO^-]}{[C_6H_5COOH]} = 7 \times 10^{-5} = \frac{[H^+][H^+]}{0.0033 - [H^+]}$$

The equation

$$\frac{[H^+]^2}{0.0033 - [H^+]} = 7 \times 10^{-5}$$

can be solved, but the algebra can be greatly simplified by making an assumption that permits us to obtain an approximate answer easily. The quantity $0.0033 - [H^+]$ is probably not too different from 0.0033, since a relatively small percentage of benzoic acid is lost by ionization. As you will remember, in our calculation of K_A we found that $0.0100 - 0.0008 = 0.0092\ M$ benzoic acid at equilibrium. The final value of 0.0092 differs from the original value 0.0100 by less than 10 percent! Let us then assume as a reasonable approximation that $0.0033 - [H^+]$ is very close to 0.0033.

We can then write

$$\frac{[H^+]^2}{0.0033} = 7 \times 10^{-5}$$

$$[H^+]^2 = 23 \times 10^{-8}$$

$$[H^+] \approx 5 \times 10^{-4}\ M$$

The concentration of H^+ is about 5×10^{-4} mole per litre. To complete the calculation we must check our assumption. We see that 0.0005 is small compared to 0.0033. The assumption is a reasonably good one.

13-6.3 Another Example of the Calculation of [H⁺]

Other calculations using K_A are frequently made. As an example, suppose we need to know the hydrogen-ion concentration in a solution containing both 0.010 M benzoic acid (C_6H_5COOH) and 0.030 M sodium benzoate (C_6H_5COONa). Of course, we could go to the laboratory and investigate the colors of indicator dyes placed in the solution. However, it is easier to calculate the value of [H⁺] using the accurate value of K_A listed in Appendix 6.

Sodium benzoate is a strong electrolyte; its aqueous solutions contain sodium ions, $Na^+(aq)$, and benzoate ions, $C_6H_5COO^-(aq)$. Hence, the equilibrium involved is the same as before:

$$C_6H_5COOH(aq) \rightleftharpoons H^+(aq) + C_6H_5COO^-(aq) \quad (31)$$

At equilibrium, the concentrations must be in accord with the equilibrium expression. That is,

$$K_A = \frac{[H^+][C_6H_5COO^-]}{[C_6H_5COOH]} = 6.6 \times 10^{-5} \quad (32)$$

In Section 13-6.2, we calculated the [H⁺] in a solution of benzoic acid. We noted that the concentration of undissociated benzoic acid was

$$\begin{Bmatrix} \text{original concn} \\ \text{benzoic acid} \\ \text{in solution} \end{Bmatrix} - \begin{Bmatrix} \text{concn} \\ \text{benzoic acid} \\ \text{lost by} \\ \text{ionization} \end{Bmatrix} = \begin{Bmatrix} \text{final} \\ \text{equilibrium} \\ \text{concn} \\ \text{benzoic acid} \end{Bmatrix} \quad (33)$$

Again, we shall neglect the concentration of benzoic acid lost through ionization and write

$$[C_6H_5COOH] \approx \begin{Bmatrix} \text{original concn} \\ \text{benzoic acid} \\ \text{in solution} \end{Bmatrix} = 0.010 \ M$$

In the same way we can write for C_6H_5COONa

$$\begin{Bmatrix} \text{final} \\ \text{equilibrium} \\ \text{concn} \\ C_6H_5COO^- \end{Bmatrix} = \begin{Bmatrix} \text{original concn} \\ C_6H_5COONa \\ \text{in solution} \end{Bmatrix} + \begin{Bmatrix} \text{concn } C_6H_5COO^- \\ \text{gained from} \\ \text{ionization} \\ \text{benzoic acid} \end{Bmatrix} \quad (35)$$

The concentration of $C_6H_5COO^-(aq)$ from ionization of benzoic acid will be very small because benzoic acid is a weak acid. Thus, we can write

$$[C_6H_5COO^-] \approx \begin{Bmatrix} \text{initial concn} \\ C_6H_5COONa \end{Bmatrix} = 0.030 \ M$$

We can then use the expression for the acid ionization constant:

$$K_A = 6.6 \times 10^{-5} = \frac{[H^+][C_6H_5COO^-]}{[C_6H_5COOH]} = \frac{[H^+][0.030]}{0.010} \quad (32)$$

Multiplying both sides of the equation by 0.010 and dividing both sides by 0.030, we obtain

$$[H^+] = \frac{6.6 \times 10^{-5} \times 0.010}{0.030} = 2.2 \times 10^{-5} \ M$$

The calculation is not completed until we validate the assumption. Was it reasonable to assume that the concentrations of benzoate ion and benzoic acid were not changed by the ionization of benzoic acid? Let us put some numbers into equation (33) for the concentration of undissociated benzoic acid:

$$\begin{Bmatrix} \text{final} \\ \text{equilibrium} \\ \text{concn} \\ C_6H_5COOH \end{Bmatrix} = \begin{Bmatrix} \text{original concn} \\ C_6H_5COOH \end{Bmatrix} - \begin{Bmatrix} \text{concn } C_6H_5COOH \\ \text{lost by} \\ \text{ionization} \end{Bmatrix} \quad (33)$$

$$\begin{Bmatrix} \text{final} \\ \text{equilibrium} \\ \text{concn} \\ C_6H_5COOH \end{Bmatrix} = \quad 0.010 \ M \quad - \ 0.000022 \ M \approx 0.010 \ M$$

The concentration loss due to ionization is equal to the concentration of $H^+(aq)$, since every $H^+(aq)$ formed by ionization takes away one molecule of C_6H_5COOH. The final concentration of C_6H_5COOH is then 0.010 M within the limits of measurement. The correlation is less than the uncertainty in the measured value of the original $[C_6H_5COOH]$.

EXERCISE 13-8

Show that the concentration of benzoate ion is determined to a good approximation by the sodium benzoate added.

13-7 AN EXPANSION OF ACID-BASE CONCEPTS

13-7.1 The Proton-Transfer Concept of Acids and Bases

We have explained the properties of acids in terms of their ability to release hydrogen ions, $H^+(aq)$. Thus, acetic acid is a weak acid because the ionization reaction releases $H^+(aq)$ only slightly:

$$CH_3COOH(aq) \rightleftharpoons H^+(aq) + CH_3COO^-(aq) \quad (6)$$

We have explained the properties of bases in terms of their ability to react with hydrogen ion. Ammonia is therefore a base:

$$NH_3(aq) + H^+(aq) \rightleftharpoons NH_4^+(aq) \quad (24)$$

Now consider the result of mixing aqueous solutions of acetic acid and ammonia. The reaction that occurs can be broken down into a sequence of reactions:

$$CH_3COOH(aq) \rightleftharpoons H^+(aq) + CH_3COO^-(aq) \quad (6)$$
$$NH_3(aq) + H^+(aq) \rightleftharpoons NH_4^+(aq) \quad (24)$$

The net reaction is

$$CH_3COOH(aq) + NH_3(aq) \rightleftharpoons CH_3COO^-(aq) + NH_4^+(aq) \quad (36)$$

Practically, the sum of reactions (*6*) and (*24*) is reaction (*36*). *Acetic acid acts as an acid* in giving a proton to ammonia to form the ammonium ion, $NH_4^+(aq)$, just as it gives a proton to water to form the hydronium ion, $H_3O^+(aq)$. In either case, acetic acid releases hydrogen ions: in its ionization in water, acetic acid releases hydrogen ions and forms $H^+(aq)$; and in its reaction with ammonia, acetic acid releases hydrogen ions to NH_3, forming NH_4^+. Similarly, *ammonia acts as a base* by reacting with the hydrogen ion released by acetic acid. The reaction between acetic acid and ammonia is, then, an acid-base reaction, although the net reaction, (*36*), does not explicitly show $H^+(aq)$.

By going one step further, we can view acid-base reactions more broadly. Suppose we mix aqueous solutions of ammonium chloride (NH_4Cl) and sodium acetate (CH_3COONa). One sniff tells us that ammonia has been formed. The following reaction has occurred:

$$NH_4^+(aq) + CH_3COO^-(aq) \rightleftharpoons CH_3COOH(aq) + NH_3(aq) \quad (37)$$

This is exactly the reverse of reaction (*36*). We see that it, too, is an acid-base reaction! Once again there is an acid that releases H⁺, NH₄⁺, and a base that accepts H⁺, CH₃COO⁻. Once again, the net effect of the reaction is transfer of a hydrogen ion from one species to another.

We see that the acid-base reaction between acetic acid and ammonia gives two products—one an acid, NH_4^+, and the other a base, CH_3COO^-. A little thought will convince you that every acid-base reaction does so. The transfer of a hydrogen ion from an acid to a base necessarily implies that it might be "handed back." The reaction of "handing it back," the reverse reaction, is just as much a **hydrogen-ion transfer,** or an **acid-base reaction,** as is the original transfer.

Notice that we are now referring to reactions in which a hydrogen ion is transferred from an acid to a base without specifically involving the aqueous species $H^+(aq)$. A hydrogen ion, H^+, is nothing more than a proton. Consequently, we can frame a more general view of acid-base reactions in terms of **proton transfer.** The main value of this view is that it is applicable to a wider range of chemical systems, *including nonaqueous systems.*

Let us generalize our view of the acid-base reaction. In our example, the following equation applies:

$$CH_3COOH + NH_3 \rightleftharpoons NH_4^+ + CH_3COO^- \qquad (36)$$
$$\text{ACID} \qquad\quad \text{BASE} \qquad\quad \text{ACID} \qquad\quad \text{BASE}$$

The acetic acid acts as an acid, giving up its proton, to form acetate, CH_3COO^-, a substance that can act as a base. We can write the acetic acid-ammonia reaction in a general form:

$$HB_1 + B_2 \rightleftharpoons HB_2 + B_1$$
$$\text{acid}_1 + \text{base}_2 \rightleftharpoons \text{acid}_2 + \text{base}_1 \qquad (38)$$

We see that *an acid and a base react, through proton transfer, to form another acid and another base.**

We can use this more general view to discuss the strengths of acids. In our generalized acid-base reaction, the proton transfer implies that the chemical bond in HB_1 must be broken and that the bond in HB_2 must be formed. If the HB_1 bond is easily broken, then HB_1 will be a strong acid. Equilibrium will then tend to favor a proton transfer from HB_1 to some other base, B_2. If, on the other hand, the HB_1 bond is extremely stable, HB_1 will be a weak acid. Equilibrium will tend to favor a proton transfer from some other acid, HB_2 to base B_1, forming the stable HB_1 bond. *A reaction between an acid and a base results in a weaker acid and a weaker base.*

13-7.2 Hydronium Ion in the Proton-Transfer Theory of Acids and Bases

In the proton-transfer view of acid-base reactions, an acid and a base react to form another acid and another base. Let us see how this theory

---

*This more general view of acids and bases is named the **Brønsted-Lowry theory** after the two scientists who proposed it independently in 1923, J. N. Brønsted (1879–1947) and T. M. Lowry (1847–1939).

encompasses the elementary reaction between $H^+(aq)$ and $OH^-(aq)$ and the reaction in which acetic acid ionizes:

$$H^+(aq) + OH^-(aq) \rightleftharpoons H_2O(l) \qquad (14)$$

$$CH_3COOH(aq) \rightleftharpoons H^+(aq) + CH_3COO^-(aq) \qquad (6)$$

It does so by making a specific assumption about the nature of the species $H^+(aq)$. It assumes that $H^+(aq)$ is more properly written with the molecular formula $H_3O^+(aq)$. Thus, when HCl dissolves in water, the reaction is written

$$HCl(g) + H_2O(l) \rightleftharpoons H_3O^+(aq) + Cl^-(aq) \qquad (39)$$

instead of

$$HCl(g) \rightleftharpoons H^+(aq) + Cl^-(aq) \qquad (7)$$

Whenever $H^+(aq)$ might appear in an equation for a reaction, it is replaced by the **hydronium ion,** H_3O^+, and a molecule of water is added to the other side of the equation. We write the ionization equation in the form

$$CH_3COOH(aq) + H_2O \rightleftharpoons H_3O^+(aq) + CH_3COO^-(aq) \qquad (40)$$

Now the ionization of acetic acid can be regarded as an acid-base reaction. The acid CH_3COOH transfers a proton to the base H_2O forming the acid H_3O^+ and the base CH_3COO^-. The neutralization of $H^+(aq)$ by $OH^-(aq)$ now takes the form

$$H_3O^+(aq) + OH^-(aq) \rightleftharpoons H_2O + H_2O \qquad (41)$$

The acid H_3O^+ transfers a proton to the base OH^-, forming an acid, H_2O, and a base, H_2O. We see that within the proton-transfer theory, the molecule H_2O must be assigned the properties of an acid as well as a base.

No definite experimental evidence demands that we write $H^+(aq)$ as $H_3O^+(aq)$. Nevertheless, the *convenience* of this assumption amply justifies its use in this representation of acid-base reactions.

13-7.3 Other Extensions of Acid-Base Theory

We noted earlier that by a slight redefinition of terms, we could expand our concept of acids and bases to include solutions using liquids other than water as a solvent. This idea has been extensively applied by chemists so that we now have at least four additional definitions of acids and bases.

One of the more useful acid-base definitions is that suggested by G. N. Lewis. A *base* is defined as *an electron-pair donor* and an *acid* as *an electron-pair acceptor*. Using these definitions, the concept of acids and bases can be extended to systems not involving protons. As an example, it is convenient to consider the reaction between the fluoride ion and the BF_3 molecule. Electronically the fluoride ion can be written as

$$:\overset{..}{\underset{..}{F}}:^-$$

where F represents the fluorine nucleus plus the two electrons in the first electron level. Each dot represents an electron. Remember that this gives an *ion* with the same electron configuration as neon. The compound boron trifluoride (BF_3) can be represented as

$$\begin{array}{c} :\overset{..}{F}: \\[2pt] \overset{..}{\underset{..}{B}}:\overset{..}{\underset{..}{F}}: \\[2pt] :\overset{..}{\underset{..}{F}}: \end{array}$$

where B represents the boron nucleus plus the two electrons of the first electron level and F again represents the fluorine nucleus plus two electrons. We see immediately that boron in BF_3 has only six electrons around it rather than the eight electrons characteristic of a stable configuration for elements in the second row of the periodic table. We wonder: can the fluoride *ion* share two of its electrons with the boron of BF_3 to give a more stable structure? The resulting structure would be

$$\left[\begin{array}{c} :\overset{..}{F}: \\[2pt] :\overset{..}{\underset{..}{F}}:\overset{..}{\underset{..}{B}}:\overset{..}{\underset{..}{F}}: \\[2pt] :\overset{..}{\underset{..}{F}}: \end{array} \right]^-$$

This is just what happens; this complex negative ion known as the fluoroborate ion forms. Of course, once the bond between the fluoride ion and boron is formed, all fluorines become equivalent. There is no way to tell which fluorine originated in the fluoride ion.

The fluoroborate ion can be pictured as a tetrahedral arrangement of four F^- ions which have interacted strongly with a central B^{3+} ion. In this process *the fluoride ion is an electron-pair donor. By the Lewis definitions, F^- is a base.* The boron of BF_3 *accepts* the electron pair. We say that BF_3 is an acid; it is an electron-pair acceptor. Using this definition, the concept of acids and bases can be extended to systems not involving protons.

We shall not pursue these ideas further here, but it is worthwhile to note that the best definition of an acid is dependent upon the system being studied and upon the ideas being considered.

13-8   HIGHLIGHTS

It is reasonable to write equilibrium constants (also called **ionization constants**) for ionization processes. **Strong electrolytes** have *very large* equilibrium constants, whereas **weak electrolytes** have *small* equilibrium constants. About two water molecules in every billion ionize to give $H^+(aq)$ and $OH^-(aq)$. In every water solution the concentration of non-ionized water is almost constant so we can write

$$[H^+][OH^-] = K_w \tag{11}$$

At 25 °C, $K_w = 1.00 \times 10^{-14}$. Le Chatelier's principle can be used to show that K_w should increase as the temperature rises. The value of

K_w can be used to calculate concentrations of $OH^-(aq)$ in acidic solutions and of $H^+(aq)$ in basic solutions.

Acids and bases can be defined using both operational and conceptual definitions. **Operational definitions** list the observations defining the group. **Conceptual definitions** explain why the group has its properties. *There is no one best definition of an acid or a base.*

The **hydrogen-ion concentration** of aqueous solutions is an extremely important property. It can be measured by organic dyes whose color is sensitive to the concentration of $H^+(aq)$ (see Figure 13-6). Such dyes are useful in experimentally determining acid-equilibrium constants.

The *p*H value is a convenient shorthand representation of the concentration of $H^+(aq)$. It is defined as $pH = -\log_{10}[H^+]$. If $H^+(aq)$ has a concentration of 10^{-7} *M*, the *p*H is 7. In the process of **titration,** acids and bases are mixed and the neutralization process occurs. A number of useful quantitative relationships can be based on equilibrium constants.

Other acid-base definitions can be used. A base can be defined as a species which *receives* a proton; an acid can be defined as a species which *donates* a proton. Other definitions of acids and bases can also be used, depending upon the system under study.

QUESTIONS and PROBLEMS

1 Sulfuric acid is a *strong* electrolyte when it dissolves in water. Write an equation to show what this means. Suggest at least one experiment which you could do to show that sulfuric acid *is* a strong electrolyte.

2 Can we have a strong electrolyte in dilute solution? Explain and contrast the terms strong and weak electrolyte and dilute and concentrated solution.

3 Write the equilibrium constant expression for the ionization of water. Show how this expression is converted into the important relationship

$K_w = 1.00 \times 10^{-14} = [H^+][OH^-]$ at 25 °C

4 Why is molten LiCl an electrolyte while solid LiCl is not? Explain, using a suitable model.

5 What does the term $Li^+(aq)$ mean? Why is it used? What does the term $H^+(aq)$ mean? What is indicated when we write $[H^+]$?

6 When the NH_3 molecule accepts a proton, what is the formula of the cation which is formed? When an H_2O molecule accepts a proton, what is the formula of the cation which is formed? The compound formed between NH_3 and HCl is NH_4Cl. What is the formula of the corresponding water-HCl compound?

7 The $[H^+]$ of a dilute hydrochloric acid solution is 0.001 *M*. What is the $[OH^-]$ of the solution?

8 The $[OH^-]$ of a sodium hydroxide solution is 1×10^{-2} *M*. What is the $[H^+]$ of the solution?

9 Calculate the $[H^+]$ and $[OH^-]$ for a solution in which 0.96 gram of lithium hydroxide is dissolved in enough water to make 1,500 ml of solution.

10 One mole of nitric acid (HNO_3) and 0.10 mole of sodium hydroxide (NaOH) are added to 1.0 litre of water. (a) Explain why the following statement is false. "The $[H^+]$ of the solution is 1 *M* and the $[OH^-]$ is 0.1 *M*." (b) Calculate the actual $[H^+]$ and $[OH^-]$ of the solution.

11 If 0.0200 mole of HCl is dissolved in 4.00 litres of water, the $[OH^-]$ is decreased to 2.00×10^{-12} *M*. Explain why this reduction of $[OH^-]$ takes place, using Le Chatelier's principle.

12 Suppose 1.00×10^{-2} mole of KOH and 1.0×10^{-4} mole of HCl are both added to a litre of water. Calculate the final $[H^+]$ and $[OH^-]$ of the resulting solution.

13 A student is given three solutions: an acid, a base, and one which is neither acidic nor basic. The student performs tests on these solutions and records their properties. For each property listed below, tell whether it is the property of an acid, the property of a base, the property of neither an acid nor a base, or whether there is insufficient evidence to decide. (a) The solution has $[H^+] = 10^{-7} M$. (b) The solution has $[OH^-] = 10^{-2} M$. (c) The solution turns litmus paper red. (d) The solution is a good conductor of electricity.

14 Explain, using Le Chatelier's principle, what happens to the $[H^+]$ of a $1.0 M$ solution of acetic acid when one drop of $1.0 M$ NaOH is added.

15 To 50.0 ml of $0.10 M$ HCl are added 50.0 ml of $1.0 M$ NaOH. Find the $[H^+]$ and $[OH^-]$ of the resulting solution.

16 Find the $[H^+]$ and $[OH^-]$ of a solution made by mixing 25 ml of $0.100 M$ NaOH and 75 ml of $0.010 M$ HCl.

17 Thirty ml of $0.0200 M$ NaOH are added to 70 ml of $0.0100 M$ HCl solution. Calculate the $[H^+]$ and $[OH^-]$ of the resulting solution.

18 Ten ml of $0.100 M$ HCl are titrated with a base of unknown concentration. If 40.0 ml of the base are needed to reach the end-point, what is the concentration, in moles/litre, of the base?

19 Exactly 12 ml of $0.0240 M$ NaOH are required to neutralize (i.e., completely react with) 20.0 ml of HCl solution. What is the concentration, in moles/litre, of the HCl solution?

20 To 20.0 ml of $0.200 M$ nitric acid (HNO_3) are added successive amounts of a base of unknown concentration. Neutrality is reached after the addition of 40.0 ml of the base. (a) What was the $[OH^-]$ of the original base solution? Assume that it was 100 percent ionized. (b) Calculate the $[H^+]$ and $[OH^-]$ of the solution when exactly 10.0 ml of the base had been added during the titration. (c) Calculate the $[H^+]$ and $[OH^-]$ of the solution when exactly 20.0 ml of the base had been added during the titration.

21 What volume of $0.200 M$ NaOH solution will be needed to neutralize each of the following: (a) 10.0 ml of $0.10 M$ HCl (b) 5.0 ml of $0.010 M$ HNO_3 (c) 15.0 ml of $0.050 M$ HCl?

22 A solution has a pH of 12. (a) Calculate the $[H^+]$ of the solution. (b) Calculate the $[OH^-]$ of the solution. (c) Predict the result of adding a drop of phenolphthalein indicator to the solution. (d) Identify the solution as acidic or basic.

23 Consider a $0.0010 M$ solution of HCl. (a) What is the $[H^+]$ of the solution? (b) What is the $[OH^-]$ of the solution? (c) What is the pH of the solution?

24 What is the pH of a solution that contains 1×10^{-9} mole of OH^- ion per litre?

25 Solution X has a pH of 2. Solution Y has a pH of 4. On the basis of this information, which of the following is true: (a) The $[H^+]$ of X is one-half that of Y. (b) The $[H^+]$ of X is twice that of Y. (c) The $[H^+]$ of X is 100 times that of Y. (d) The $[H^+]$ of X is $\frac{1}{100}$ that of Y.

26 Write the chemical equation for the ionization of one proton from H_2SeO_3. Write the K_A expression for this reaction.

27 Using Le Chatelier's principle, explain the effects on the following concentrations which result from adding one drop of $1 M$ HCl to a $1 M$ solution of acetic acid (CH_3COOH). (Remember that acetic acid is a weak acid.) (a) $[H^+]$ (b) $[CH_3COOH]$ (c) $[CH_3COO^-]$ (d) $[OH^-]$.

28 One drop of $1 M$ OH^- ion is added to a $1 M$ solution of nitrous acid (HNO_2). What will be the effect on each of the following: (a) $[OH^-]$ (b) $[H^+]$ (c) $[NO_2^-]$ (d) $[HNO_2]$?

29 List the following acids in order of increasing strengths (weakest to strongest): nitrous acid, ferric ion, hydrogen peroxide, acetic acid, and hydrogen sulfite ion. Give a quantitative reason for your ranking.

30 The pH of a $0.1 M$ solution of cyanic acid (HCNO) is found to be 3. (a) Write the equation for the ionization of cyanic acid. (b) Write the K_A expression for this reaction. (c) Calculate the value of K_A for this reaction.

31 The K_A for hypoiodous acid (HOI) is approximately 2.5×10^{-11}. What would you expect the $[H^+]$ of a $0.010 M$ solution of this acid to be?

32 Calculate the $[H^+]$ in 1.00 litre of a solution in which there have been dissolved 0.20 mole of formic acid (HCOOH) and 0.40 mole of

sodium formate (HCOONa). The value of K_A for formic acid is 1.8×10^{-4}. State any assumptions made in your calculations and show whether your assumptions are valid.

33. Calculate the [H^+] in 1.00 litre of a solution in which there have been dissolved 0.10 mole of hydrofluoric acid (HF) and 0.50 mole of sodium fluoride (NaF). The K_A for hydrofluoric acid is 6.7×10^{-4}.

34. (a) Write the equation that shows the acid-base reaction between hydrogen telluride (H_2Te) and the sulfide ion (S^{2-}). (b) What are the two acids competing for H^+? (c) From the values of K_A for these two acids (see Appendix 6), predict whether the equilibrium favors reactants or products.

35. Consider the acid-base reaction between benzoic acid (C_6H_5COOH) and dihydrogen phosphate ion ($H_2PO_4^-$). (a) Write the balanced equation for this reaction. (b) Label *each* reactant and product as either an acid or a base. (c) Predict whether the products

or reactants would be favored at equilibrium. (d) Explain your answer in (c) quantitatively.

36. Write the equations for the reactions between each of the following acid-base pairs. For each reaction, predict whether reactants or products are favored. (a) $HBr(aq) + SO_4^{2-}(aq)$ (b) $H_3PO_4(aq) + NO_3^-(aq)$ (c) $NH_4^+(aq) + S^{2-}(aq)$.

37. When excess ammonia is added to a solution of $AgNO_3$ in water, the complex ion $Ag(NH_3)_2^+(aq)$ is formed. Write the equation for this process. Which reagent is the Lewis base? Which is the Lewis acid? Explain.

38. Ether ($CH_3CH_2OCH_2CH_3$) will react with BF_3 to give a 1:1 compound. Write out the formula of ether and show how it can undergo an acid-base reaction with BF_3.

39. Is the SCN^- ion a Lewis acid or a Lewis base when it reacts with $Fe^{3+}(aq)$ to give the familiar red solution, $FeSCN^{2+}(aq)$?

Be patient now, my soul; thou hast endured still worse than this.

ODYSSEUS *IN* **THE ODYSSEY**

OXIDATION AND REDUCTION

One person in four in the steel industry works to replace iron lost by corrosion—a form of oxidation.

ONE OF THE THINGS THAT YOU NEVER KNEW AND WERE afraid to ask about atoms is that they have a competitive nature. Although seldom awarded scholarships, given trophies, or even making headlines, atoms go about their daily business of competing industriously for electrons. If chemists had their way, "Copper takes two from zinc!" would be an everyday stock market report.

We have used the principles of equilibrium in two general types of reactions. First, we took up the question of equilibrium reactions involving a solid and a solution. In Chapter 13 we turned to reactions occurring entirely in solution and involving proton transfer. Now we shall examine reactions involving electron transfer. Since such processes can involve solids as well as solutions, a more general view of equilibrium is needed—a view provided by an investigation of **oxidation-reduction** reactions. Such reactions are extremely important in chemistry in both a theoretical and an applied sense. Properly harnessed oxidation-reduction reactions provide power for your automobile storage battery, your flashlight battery, and even your car itself. How did the term *oxidation* arise? A little background will help.

14-1   OXIDATION-REDUCTION PROCESSES

14-1.1   Some Important Terms

It is almost obvious that the term oxidation is tied in a very direct way to the element oxygen. When magnesium metal burns in air, it combines with oxygen:

$$2Mg(s) + O_2(g) \longrightarrow 2MgO(s) \qquad (1)$$

We say that magnesium is **oxidized** in the process. For reasons given in Chapter 8, we can picture this reaction as a transfer of two electrons from each magnesium atom to each oxygen atom. Ions of charge $2+$ and $2-$ are formed. X-ray studies reveal an ionic arrangement similar to that of NaCl. We can then say that *a magnesium atom loses two electrons to an oxygen atom when it is oxidized.* From this fact it is logical to describe oxidation of magnesium as a loss of electrons. Magnesium also loses electrons, or is oxidized, when it combines with chlorine:

$$Mg(s) + Cl_2(g) \longrightarrow MgCl_2(s) \qquad (2)$$

Positively charged magnesium ions are again formed. The same type of electron-transfer reaction goes on in both cases. It was thus logical for earlier chemists to define **oxidation** *as a loss of electrons* and **reduction** *as a gain of electrons.*

EXERCISE 14-1

When a zinc metal strip is placed in a copper sulfate solution, zinc goes into solution as $Zn^{2+}(aq)$ and copper deposits out as copper metal. What is oxidized in this process? What is reduced?

Further names were also used. Chemists called oxygen the *oxidizing agent* because it oxidized the magnesium. Since chlorine also oxidized the magnesium, it was also called an oxidizing agent. We can now state that an **oxidizing agent** *brings about the oxidation of another species*. The same line of reasoning identifies the reducing agent. Magnesium atoms reduce oxygen; two magnesium atoms give four electrons to an O_2 molecule to generate two O^{2-} ions. Similarly, magnesium *reduces* chlorine (Cl_2) to give $2Cl^-$. In each case magnesium serves as the reducing agent. A **reducing agent** *brings about the reduction of another species*.

EXERCISE 14-2

An oxidation-reduction reaction is represented by the equation

$$Fe^{3+} + Cu^+ \longrightarrow Fe^{2+} + Cu^{2+}$$

Identify the oxidizing agent in this process.

14-1.2 Oxidation Numbers

Arguments given above show that magnesium has an apparent charge of $2+$ in MgO and oxygen has an apparent charge of $2-$. Since these came about in an oxidation-reduction process, it is logical to call these numbers **oxidation numbers.** *The oxidation numbers add to zero* in MgO. *Electrons lost equal electrons gained;* charge is conserved. By convention we say that the oxidation number of any element is zero. Thus, the oxidation number of metallic magnesium is zero. Similarly, oxygen in gaseous O_2 and chlorine in gaseous Cl_2 have zero oxidation number.

EXERCISE 14-3

What is the oxidation number of lithium (atomic number 3) in Li_2O? of iron in Fe_2O_3? of titanium in TiO_2?

Can the idea of oxidation numbers be extended beyond ionic solids? Let us try. If elemental sulfur is burned in air, the equation for the process is

$$S(s) + O_2(g) \longrightarrow SO_2(g) \tag{3}$$

Remembering what happened with magnesium, it is tempting to suggest that each sulfur atom donates, or shares, a pair of electrons with each of the two oxygen atoms. Extrapolating from the magnesium oxide case, we can *assign* each oxygen atom an oxidation number of $2-$ and the sulfur an oxidation number of $4+$. As in MgO, the oxidation numbers add to zero.

$$\begin{Bmatrix} \text{oxidation} \\ \text{number} \\ \text{sulfur} \end{Bmatrix} + 2 \begin{Bmatrix} \text{oxidation} \\ \text{number} \\ \text{oxygen} \end{Bmatrix} = \text{zero} \tag{4}$$

$$[4+] \quad + \quad [2 \times (2-)] \ = \ [0]$$

Does this notation mean that each sulfur has given away four electrons and is now a 4+ ion and that each oxygen is a 2− ion? Not at all! SO_2 is a gas, not an ionic solid like MgO. *The oxidation number is just a convenient number for electron bookkeeping*. It suggests here that four of the six outermost electrons of sulfur are involved in the formation of SO_2.

If four out of six electrons are involved, can we involve the other two electrons and use six out of six electrons? As usual, experiment gives the answer. Under the influence of a catalyst such as NO_2, gaseous SO_2 will combine with oxygen to give SO_3, a liquid whose boiling point is 45 °C:

$$SO_2(g) + \tfrac{1}{2}O_2(g) \xrightarrow{\;NO_2\;} SO_3(l) \tag{5}$$

The SO_2 is oxidized in the classical sense. Again, extrapolation from the simpler cases suggests that we can assign an oxidation number of 6+ to the sulfur of SO_3 if each oxygen is assigned its regular number of 2−.

$$\begin{Bmatrix} \text{oxidation} \\ \text{number} \\ \text{sulfur} \end{Bmatrix} + 3 \begin{Bmatrix} \text{oxidation} \\ \text{number} \\ \text{oxygen} \end{Bmatrix} = \text{zero} \tag{6}$$

$$[6+] \quad + \quad [3 \times (2-)] \;=\; [0]$$

Again, the oxidation numbers add to zero in a neutral molecule. The oxidation number of sulfur goes from 4+ in SO_2 to 6+ in SO_3 when SO_2 is oxidized to SO_3 by elemental oxygen. *Apparently, oxidation produces an increase in oxidation number.*

If SO_3 is allowed to react with calcium oxide, the following process takes place:

$$CaO(s) + SO_3(g) \longrightarrow CaSO_4(s) \tag{7}$$

or

$$Ca^{2+},\ :\!\ddot{O}\!:^{2-} +\ \overset{\displaystyle :\ddot{O}:}{\underset{\displaystyle :\ddot{O}:}{S\!:\!\ddot{O}\!:}} \longrightarrow Ca^{2+},\ \overset{\displaystyle :\ddot{O}:}{\underset{\displaystyle :\ddot{O}:}{:\!\ddot{O}\!:\!S\!:\!\ddot{O}\!:}}{}^{2-}$$

Has sulfur changed its oxidation number in this case? We can check. Calcium, like magnesium, should have an oxidation number of 2+. (Why?) According to the rule carried over from the MgO and SO_2 cases, each oxygen should have an oxidation number of 2−. What is then left for sulfur? (Remember, the sum of the oxidation numbers in electrically neutral $CaSO_4$ must be zero.)

$$\begin{Bmatrix} \text{oxidation} \\ \text{number} \\ \text{calcium} \end{Bmatrix} + \begin{Bmatrix} \text{oxidation} \\ \text{number} \\ \text{sulfur} \end{Bmatrix} + 4 \begin{Bmatrix} \text{oxidation} \\ \text{number} \\ \text{oxygen} \end{Bmatrix} = \text{zero} \tag{8}$$

$$[2+] \quad + \quad x \quad + \quad [4 \times (2-)] \;=\; [0]$$
$$[2+] \quad + \quad x \quad + \quad [8-] \quad\;=\; [0]$$
$$x \;=\; [6+]$$

Sulfur did not change its oxidation number when SO_3 combined with CaO. This makes sense, since sulfur had already used all its six outer electrons in SO_3. The oxide ion which combined with sulfur had two electrons from calcium to complete its octet. Sulfur trioxide plus calcium oxide exhibits *Lewis acid-base behavior, not* oxidation-reduction. The assignment of oxidation numbers to molecules or ions enables us to keep track of electrons and to identify an oxidation process. *Oxidation causes an increase in oxidation number. Reduction causes a decrease in oxidation number.*

Based on arguments of the type outlined above, a set of rules has been developed for assigning oxidation numbers. We should emphasize that these numbers do not represent ionic charges, since it is quite probable that ions of the type required by oxidation numbers such as 6+ do *not* exist in compounds—there is no S^{6+} in SO_3, for example. Nevertheless, oxidation numbers provide a convenient basis for keeping track of electrons in oxidation-reduction reactions. Here are the rules. You will realize that many were derived from ion-formation studies such as that discussed for MgO.

(1) *The oxidation number of a monatomic ion is equal to the charge on the ion.* Chloride (Cl^-), for example, has an oxidation number of 1−; oxide, O^{2-}, an oxidation number of 2−; phosphide in Na_3P, an oxidation number of 3−; Fe^{2+}, 2+; Fe^{3+}, 3+.

(2) *The oxidation number of any element is zero.* The oxidation number of elemental chlorine (Cl_2) is zero; of oxygen gas (O_2), zero; of magnesium metal (Mg), zero.

(3) *The oxidation number of members of the alkali metal family (Li, Na, K, Rb, Cs, and Fr) in compounds is 1+.* Sodium is 1+ in NaCl and lithium is 1+ in Li_2O. Both are zero in the metallic form.

(4) *The oxidation number of Be, Mg, Ca, Sr, Ba, and Ra in compounds is 2+.* Calcium is 2+ in CaO; Mg is 2+ in $MgCl_2$; Ba is 2+ in $BaCl_2$.

(5) *The oxidation number of oxygen in compounds is taken to be 2−* (except in peroxides and superoxides, which contain an oxygen-oxygen bond).

(6) *The oxidation number of hydrogen in compounds is taken to be 1+* (except in a few hydrides such as NaH). Hydrogen is 1+ in HCl, H_2O, H_2S, and so on.

(7) *The oxidation numbers of any other element or elements in a molecule or ion are selected to make the sum of the oxidation numbers equal to the charge on the molecule or ion.* You will recall that for SO_3 we had

$$\begin{Bmatrix} \text{oxidation} \\ \text{number} \\ \text{sulfur} \end{Bmatrix} + 3 \begin{Bmatrix} \text{oxidation} \\ \text{number} \\ \text{oxygen} \end{Bmatrix} = \begin{Bmatrix} \text{charge on} \\ \text{molecule} \\ \text{or ion} \end{Bmatrix} \qquad (6a)$$

$$[6+] \quad + \quad [3 \times (2-)] = \quad [0]$$

For the SO_4^{2-} ion, with a charge of $2-$, the rule can be written as

$$\left\{\begin{array}{l}\text{oxidation}\\\text{number}\\\text{sulfur}\end{array}\right\} + 4 \left\{\begin{array}{l}\text{oxidation}\\\text{number}\\\text{oxygen}\end{array}\right\} = \left\{\begin{array}{l}\text{charge on}\\SO_4^{2-} \text{ ion}\end{array}\right\} \qquad (9)$$

$$[6+] \quad + \quad [4 \times (2-)] \quad = \quad [2-]$$

For the ammonium ion (NH_4^+), the rule takes the form

$$\left\{\begin{array}{l}\text{oxidation}\\\text{number}\\\text{nitrogen}\end{array}\right\} + 4 \left\{\begin{array}{l}\text{oxidation}\\\text{number}\\\text{hydrogen}\end{array}\right\} = \left\{\begin{array}{l}\text{charge on}\\NH_4^+ \text{ ion}\end{array}\right\} \qquad (10)$$

$$[3-] \quad + \quad [4 \times (1+)] \quad = \quad [1+]$$

The next rule is simply a statement of the principle that charge is conserved.

(8) *In any overall reaction the net change in oxidation numbers must be zero.*

$$2Mg(s) + O_2(g) \longrightarrow 2MgO(s) \qquad (1)$$

Mg changes from 0 to $2+$ = $(2+) \times 2$
O_2 changes from 0 to $2-$ = $\underline{(2-) \times 2}$
Net change = $\quad 0$

$$SO_2(g) + \tfrac{1}{2}O_2(g) \rightarrow SO_3(l) \qquad (5)$$

Sulfur changes from $4+$ to $6+$ = $2+$
One oxygen changes from 0 to $2-$ = $\underline{2-}$
Net change = 0

Do not worry about the exceptions in rules (5) and (6). Your attention will be called to them later when substances involving them are considered.

EXERCISE 14-4

Use the above rules to obtain the oxidation numbers of

(a) P in Na_3PO_4 (d) Br in NaBr
(b) Cr in K_2CrO_4 (e) S in S_8
(c) N in HNO_3 (f) Cr in $Cr_2O_7^{2-}$

[*Answers:* (a) $5+$, (c) $5+$, (e) 0, (f) $6+$.]

14-1.3 Oxidation-Reduction Reactions in a Beaker

The rules considered above apply to electron-transfer or oxidation-reduction reactions which occur in solution. In Experiment 8, a copper wire was placed in a silver nitrate solution. We found that the copper wire lost mass and the solution turned blue. At the same time, a loose deposit of silver crystals appeared on the wire. When we determined the mass of the copper which went into solution and the mass of the silver deposited, we found two moles of silver atoms deposited for every mole of copper lost from the wire. These observations are all neatly summed up by the net ionic equation

$$Cu(s) + 2Ag^+(aq) \longrightarrow Cu^{2+}(aq) + 2Ag(s) \qquad (11)$$

COLORLESS   BLUE

In this process the copper atom has lost 2 electrons to form $Cu^{2+}(aq)$. *Copper has been oxidized.* Two silver ions have gained the two electrons to form two silver atoms. *Silver has been reduced.* (In general, a metal is formed from its cation by a reduction process.) Copper goes from an oxidation number of zero to $2+$. Silver goes from $1+$ to zero. In order to make the net change in oxidation number zero [rule (8)], two silver ions were reduced. Rule (8) (page 333) agrees with experiment.

Other oxidation-reduction reactions in solution are already familiar to us. In discussing acids we found that acids are characterized by their ability to react with some metals to liberate H_2. The reaction with zinc is a typical one:

$$Zn(s) + 2H^+(aq) \longrightarrow Zn^{2+}(aq) + H_2(g) \qquad (12)$$

Each zinc atom loses two electrons in changing to a zinc ion—*zinc is oxidized.* Each hydrogen ion gains an electron in changing to a hydrogen atom—*hydrogen is reduced.* After reduction, two hydrogen atoms combine to give hydrogen gas, H_2. Zinc changes from zero to $2+$ in oxidation number and hydrogen changes from $1+$ to zero. By rule (8), two hydrogen ions are needed for each zinc atom. The prediction is in agreement with experiment.

Not all metals react with aqueous acids. Of the common metals, magnesium, aluminum, iron, and nickel liberate H_2 as zinc does. Other metals, including copper, mercury, silver, and gold, do not produce measurable amounts of hydrogen, even though we make sure that the equilibrium state has been attained. Apparently, some metals release electrons to H^+ (as zinc does) and others do not (see Figure 14-1).

For a third example of oxidation-reduction, let us place a strip of metallic zinc in a solution of copper nitrate [$Cu(NO_3)_2$]. The strip becomes coated with reddish metallic copper and the blue color of the solution disappears. The presence of zinc ion, Zn^{2+}, among the products can be shown by passing hydrogen sulfide (H_2S) gas into the final colorless solution. White zinc sulfide (ZnS) precipitates if the solution is neutral. The reaction between metallic zinc and the aqueous copper nitrate is

$$Zn(s) + Cu^{2+} \longrightarrow Zn^{2+} + Cu(s)* \qquad (13)$$

Fig. 14-1 Some metals release electrons to H^+ and others do not.

Copper metal   Zinc metal

1 *M* HCl

EXERCISE 14-5

What is oxidized in equation (13)? What is reduced? Why? Show changes in oxidation numbers for both Zn and Cu, and show that rule (8) (page 333) applies.

*For the remainder of this chapter, we shall consider only aqueous solutions and therefore not specify (*aq*) for each ion.

What about the state of equilibrium for the reaction of Zn and Cu^{2+}? Let us try the reverse process by placing a strip of metallic copper in a zinc sulfate solution. No visible reaction occurs. Attempts to detect the presence of cupric ion by adding H_2S to produce the black color of cupric sulfide (CuS) fail. Cupric sulfide has such low solubility that this is an extremely sensitive test; yet the amount of Cu^{2+} formed by the reverse process, $Cu(s) + Zn^{2+}$, cannot be detected. It appears that the state of equilibrium for reaction (13) greatly favors the products, $Cu(s)$ and Zn^{2+}, over the reactants, $Zn(s)$ and Cu^{2+}. Apparently zinc metal gives electrons to Cu^{2+}, but copper metal will not give electrons to Zn^{2+}.

14-2 COMPETITION FOR ELECTRONS

It appears that a zinc ion and a copper ion are competing for a single pair of electrons. The equation is

$$\underbrace{Zn^{2+} + 2e^-}_{\substack{\text{ZINC} \\ \text{METAL}}} + \underbrace{Cu^{2+}}_{\substack{\text{COPPER} \\ \text{ION}}} \rightleftarrows Zn^{2+} + Cu(s) \qquad (13a)$$

Copper ion is a better competitor and usually gets the electrons. Equilibrium is attained when a balance exists between opposing reactions. How can these observations be explained? What factors determine the point at which equilibrium is reached? We check randomness and energy. The number of particles is the same on both sides of the equation; hence, differences in randomness are relatively small. Since the equilibrium lies far to the side of the products, the energy term must favor products. Energy of the system decreases as electrons move from zinc metal to copper ion.

Is randomness ever important? To answer this question, let us examine another familiar process:

$$Cu(s) + 2Ag^+ \longrightarrow Cu^{2+} + 2Ag(s) \qquad (11)$$

The equation shows three particles on each side of the equation. It is again tempting to jump to the conclusion that randomness is *not* important. More careful analysis shows, however, that our conclusion is too hasty. We know that ions distributed randomly in solution have a greater degree of disorder than atoms in an ordered metal lattice. As reactants of the copper-silver nitrate process, we have two ions $(2Ag^+)$ in the random solution and only one atom (Cu) in the ordered metal. For the products we have *two* atoms in the ordered metal (Ag) and only one ion (Cu^{2+}) in the random solution. The reactants are more disordered than the products. Thus, the reactants, Cu and $2Ag^+$, are favored by our randomness criterion. The fact that the reaction goes well toward the products, Cu^{2+} and 2Ag, indicates that the energy term must favor the products. The system $Cu^{2+} + 2Ag$ must be much lower in energy than the system $2Ag^+ + Cu$. Silver ion is a better competitor for electrons than is copper ion.

By way of contrast, compare the reaction of metallic cobalt placed in a nickel sulfate solution:

$$Co(s) + Ni^{2+} \rightleftharpoons Co^{2+} + Ni(s) \qquad (14)$$

At equilibrium, chemical tests show that both Ni^{2+} and Co^{2+} are present in moderate concentrations. In this case, neither the reactants, $Co(s)$ and Ni^{2+}, nor the products, Co^{2+} and $Ni(s)$, are greatly favored. Randomness does not favor products or reactants (why?) and energy differences must be small.

This competition for electrons is reminiscent of the competition among bases for protons. The similarity suggests that we might develop a table in which metal ions are listed in order of their tendency to pick up electrons. This would resemble a list of bases arranged in order of their ability to pick up protons. We might begin by comparing Cu^{2+} and Ag^+. The results of the $Cu + Ag^+$ experiment (Experiment 8) show that Ag^+ is a much stronger competitor for electrons than Cu^{2+}. Further, we can compare Cu^{2+} and Zn^{2+}. The results of the $Zn + Cu^{2+}$ experiment show that Cu^{2+} is a much stronger competitor than Zn^{2+} for electrons. Finally, the $Zn + H^+$ experiment shows that H^+ is a better competitor for electrons than Zn^{2+}. All of these results can be summarized in an "electron competition list":

$$Ag^+ \left\{ \begin{matrix} \text{is} \\ \text{better} \\ \text{than} \end{matrix} \right\} Cu^{2+}, H^+ \left\{ \begin{matrix} \text{is} \\ \text{better} \\ \text{than} \end{matrix} \right\} Zn^{2+}$$

Is Cu^{2+} better than H^+? Data say, "yes," since we did notice that H^+ cannot take an electron away from metallic Cu. The final list would then be

$$Ag^+ \left\{ \begin{matrix} \text{better} \\ \text{than} \end{matrix} \right\} Cu^{2+} \left\{ \begin{matrix} \text{better} \\ \text{than} \end{matrix} \right\} H^+ \left\{ \begin{matrix} \text{better} \\ \text{than} \end{matrix} \right\} Zn^{2+}$$

BEST COMPETITOR $\longrightarrow$ POOREST COMPETITOR
FOR ELECTRONS   FOR ELECTRONS

The list permits predictions. If Ag^+ is a better electron competitor than Zn^{2+}, then Zn metal placed in an $AgNO_3$ solution should give up its electrons to the highly competitive Ag^+. The reaction expected *and observed* is

$$Zn(s) + 2Ag^+ \longrightarrow Zn^{2+} + 2Ag(s) \qquad (15)$$

We can also write

$$Ag(s) + H^+ \longrightarrow \text{no reaction} \qquad (16)$$

The list is useful, but not quantitative. The most useful list would be one which indicated relative electron-attracting ability by means of numbers. Such a list can be prepared; it will be considered in the next chapter.

14-3 BALANCING OXIDATION-REDUCTION REACTIONS THROUGH THE USE OF OXIDATION NUMBERS

In the two previous sections, we found that simple oxidation-reduction reactions were balanced when we applied rule (8) of our oxidation number list: *in any overall reaction the net change in oxidation numbers must be zero.* The rule is a powerful one and provides a procedure for balancing both simple and complex oxidation-reduction reactions. Here are some examples.

Before an equation can be balanced we must know the formulas for all reactants and products. As we have already seen, this information has been accumulated by direct laboratory observation. We find, for example, that when purple potassium permanganate is mixed with a water solution of hydrogen sulfide, the purple color fades and a milky suspension of elementary sulfur forms in the solution. Tests show Mn^{2+} in the final solution. These facts can be summarized by the *unbalanced* equation for the process:

$$MnO_4^- + H_2S(g) \longrightarrow S(s) + Mn^{2+} + H_2O \qquad (17)$$

Let us now apply oxidation number changes to balance the above equation. First, we assign oxidation numbers to each element, using rules (1)–(6). We find

$$MnO_4^- + H_2S(g) \longrightarrow S(s) + Mn^{2+} + H_2O \qquad (17)$$
$$7+,2- \quad 1+,2- \qquad 0 \quad 2+ \quad 1+,2-$$

Since manganese changes from an oxidation number of $7+$ to a new value of $2+$, it has undergone *a change of* $5-$. Sulfur, on the other hand, has undergone a change from $2-$ to 0, or *a change of* $2+$. If the net change in oxidation number for the overall process is to be zero, the gain in oxidation number by sulfur must be equal to the loss by manganese. We must take two MnO_4^- [net change $= 2 \times (5-) = 10-$] and five H_2S [net change $= 5 \times (2+) = 10+$] to make the net change zero:

$$2MnO_4^- + 5H_2S(g) \text{ gives } 5S(s) + 2Mn^{2+} \qquad (18)$$

Now we show conservation of oxygen atoms. There are eight oxygen atoms on the left side of the equation; hence, we must add eight molecules of H_2O to the right side. (The reaction occurs in aqueous solution, so there is a large quantity of H_2O.)

$$2MnO_4^- + 5H_2S(g) \text{ gives } 5S(s) + 2Mn^{2+} + 8H_2O \qquad (19)$$

Next we must show conservation of hydrogen atoms. There are ten hydrogen atoms on the left side of the equation (in $5H_2S$) and sixteen on the right (in $8H_2O$). In aqueous solutions (neutral or acidic), we assume that these six additional hydrogens on the left are provided by H^+:

$$2MnO_4^- + 5H_2S(g) + 6H^+ \longrightarrow 5S(s) + 2Mn^{2+} + 8H_2O \quad (20)$$

The equation is balanced now, but experience tells us that a check must always be made on the charge balance:

$$2(1-) + 5(0) + 6(1+) \longrightarrow 5(0) + 2(2+) + 8(0) \qquad (21)$$
$$(2-) \qquad\qquad (6+) \qquad\qquad (4+)$$
$$(4+) = (4+)$$

The oxidation number method provides a neat and effective method for balancing oxidation-reduction equations. Trial-and-error methods are frustrating and slow.

14-4 HIGHLIGHTS

When magnesium metal burns in air, it combines with oxygen—it is oxidized. In the process of combining with oxygen, magnesium loses electrons. Hence, we generalize our definition: **oxidation** *is a loss of electrons;* **reduction** *is a gain of electrons.* In many reactions, the "gain" or "loss" of electrons is not complete. In such cases, oxidation numbers can be assigned to each of the elements involved. They are helpful in keeping track of electrons during oxidation-reduction processes. Equations can be balanced by a proper application of oxidation numbers. Transfer of electrons between species can be visualized as a result of competition for electrons between the two species. Using this idea, we prepared a list of ions, arranged in decreasing order of their ability to attract electrons. The list is useful, but a quantitative list would be better. Can we prepare such a list? We can! Read on.

QUESTIONS and PROBLEMS

1 Identify each of the following as oxidation or reduction:

(a) $Na \longrightarrow Na^+ + e^-$

(b) $F + e^- \longrightarrow F^-$

(c) $Mg^{2+} + 2e^- \longrightarrow Mg$

(d) $2Cl^- \longrightarrow Cl_2 + 2e^-$

(e) $O_2^{2-} \longrightarrow O_2 + 2e^-$

(f) $Ti^{3+} \longrightarrow Ti^{4+} + e^-$

(g) $MnO_2 + 2e^- + 4H^+ \longrightarrow$
$$2H_2O + Mn^{2+}$$

(h) $PbO_2 + 2e^- + 4H^+ \longrightarrow Pb^{2+} + 2H_2O$

2 Why must oxidation and reduction occur together (as paired processes)?

3 In each of the following oxidation-reduction equations, identify (i) what is oxidized; (ii) what is reduced; (iii) the oxidizing agent; (iv) the reducing agent.

(a) $C + O_2 \longrightarrow CO_2$

(b) $Na + \frac{1}{2}Cl_2 \longrightarrow NaCl$

(c) $H_2 + \frac{1}{2}O_2 \longrightarrow H_2O$

4 When a substance serves as an oxidizing agent, some atom in the compound or element must undergo a change in oxidation number. Does such an atom in an oxidizing agent go from a more positive value to a less positive (or more negative) value or does the reverse type of change take place? Which would be more likely to serve as an oxidizing agent, Na_2CrO_4 or chromium metal? $SnCl_4$ or Sn metal? Explain. Why does chlorine with an oxidation number of zero serve as a common oxidizing agent? (*Hint:* what is the product when chlorine serves as an oxidizing agent?)

5 (a) Iron normally has oxidation numbers of $0, 2+,$ and $3+.$ Can $FeSO_4$ serve as an oxidizing agent? If so, what must the product containing iron be? (b) Tin normally has oxidation numbers of $0, 2+,$ and $4+.$ Would Sn^{2+} be an oxidizing agent, reducing agent, or both? What might the product containing Sn be in each case?

6 Which of the following reactions are oxidation-reduction processes and which are Lewis acid-base processes? How can you tell?

(a) $MgO + SO_2 \longrightarrow MgSO_3$

(b) $NO_2 + SO_2 \longrightarrow SO_3 + NO$

✗ (c) $MgF_2 + 2PF_5 \longrightarrow Mg(PF_6)_2$

(d) $NO_2 + sunlight \longrightarrow NO + O$
(This process is important in the formation of photochemical smog.)

7 Determine the oxidation number of manganese in each of the following compounds: $Mn(OH)_2$, MnF_3, MnO_2, K_2MnO_4, $KMnO_4$.

8 Determine the oxidation number of nitrogen in each of the following molecules or ions: N_2O, NO, NO_2, NO_3, NO_2^-, NO_3^-.

9 Suppose 1 mole of an oxide of iron was prepared by combining 1 mole of FeO with 1 mole of Fe_2O_3. What would the formula of this oxide be? What would the *average* oxidation number of iron be in the compound? What, in general, is implied by oxidation numbers which are not whole numbers?

10 In the following oxidation-reduction equation, identify (a) what is oxidized; (b) what is reduced; (c) the oxidizing agent; (d) the reducing agent.

$$PbO_2 + Pb + 2H_2SO_4 \longrightarrow 2PbSO_4 + 2H_2O$$

11 (a) Determine the average oxidation number of sulfur in each of the following molecules or ions: H_2S, SO_2, SO_3, SO_3^{2-}, SO_4^{2-}, S_8. (b) The compound $Na_2S_2O_3$ can be visualized as the product of a Lewis acid-base reaction in which 1 mole of Na_2S combines with 1 mole of SO_3 (see page 331). What is the *average* oxidation number of S in $Na_2S_2O_3$ if our usual rules are applied? What is the structural formula of $Na_2S_2O_3$ [see equation (7)]? What is the average oxidation number of S in $Na_2S_2O_5$? in $Na_2S_2O_7$?

12 What is the average oxidation number of carbon in table sugar ($C_{12}H_{22}O_{11}$) if we assume, as usual, that H is $1+$ and O is $2-$? What change in oxidation number does carbon undergo when a green plant in sunshine converts carbon dioxide of the air to sugar and oxygen:

$$12CO_2 + 11H_2O \xrightarrow[\text{sugar cane plant}]{\text{sunlight +}} C_{12}H_{22}O_{11} + 12\,O_2$$

Does the fact that oxygen is given off suggest that the process is reduction? Does the change in oxidation number confirm your conclusion? Explain.

13 Use oxidation numbers to balance the equations for the following reactions:

(a) $Fe + Cl_2 \longrightarrow FeCl_3$

(b) $Co + MnO_4^- + H^+ \longrightarrow Co^{2+} + Mn^{2+} + H_2O$

✗ (c) $Cl_2 + OH^- \longrightarrow ClO^- + Cl^- + H_2O$

(d) $I^- + IO_3^- + H^+ \longrightarrow I_2 + H_2O$

✳ (e) $Cr_2O_7^{2-} + SO_3^{2-} + H^+ \longrightarrow Cr^{3+} + SO_4^{2-} + H_2O$

(f) $I_2 + Cl_2 + H_2O \longrightarrow IO_3^- + Cl^- + H^+$

✳ (g) $S^{2-} + Cr_2O_7^{2-} + H^+ \longrightarrow S + Cr^{3+} + H_2O$

(h) $S^{2-} + NO_3^- + H^+ \longrightarrow SO_2 + NO_2 + H_2O$

(i) $H_2O_2 \longrightarrow O_2 + H_2O$

(j) $Fe_3O_4 + Al \longrightarrow Fe + Al_2O_3$

14 In an experiment similar to Experiment 27, strips of gold, silver, and tin were placed in beakers containing solutions of Au^{3+}, Ag^+, and Sn^{2+} ions. The following results were observed:

$Au^{3+} + Sn$: metallic gold was deposited on the tin strip.
$Au + Ag^+$: no reaction.
$Sn + Ag^+$: metallic silver was deposited on the tin strip.

Arrange the ions above in order of *decreasing* tendency to attract electrons (*i.e.,* the ion with the greatest attraction for electrons on top).

15 Another experiment similar to that in question 14 was run, and the following was found:

$Zn + Ni^{2+}$: metallic nickel is deposited on the zinc strip.
$Zn + Mn^{2+}$: no reaction.

Arrange these ions in order of decreasing tendency to attract electrons.

Chemical thermodynamics enables one to state what may happen when two substances react.

WENDELL M. LATIMER (1893–1955)

ELECTROCHEMICAL 15
CELLS: ELECTROCHEMISTRY

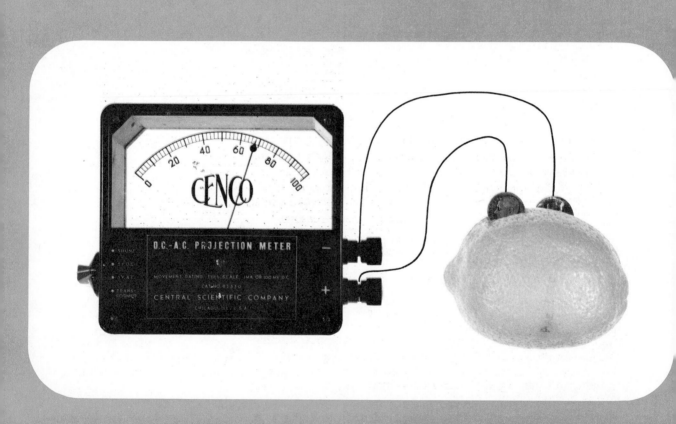

A piece of silver, a piece of copper, and a lemon make a simple electrochemical cell.

WHEN IT COMES TO THE BUSINESS OF CAPTURING ELECTRONS, some ions are lots better than others. What do we mean by "lots"? Only numbers will tell—numbers which must come from the laboratory.

If we carry oxidation-reduction reactions out in a special way, quantitative information about an ion's attraction for electrons can be obtained. The first step is to force the electrons to detour through a wire. Then we can measure "electron pressure" easily with a voltmeter. Comparing the voltages produced in different reactions gives us real insight into the "go power" of each. It's really rather similar to listing acids in order of strength, isn't it? Let's try.

In Chapter 14 we identified oxidation with electron loss and reduction with electron gain. We found that the transfer of electrons between a metal and a metal ion is determined by the relative ability of the two competing metal ions to attract electrons.

We made a qualitative list showing the relative ability of ions to attract electrons:

$$\text{Ag}^+ \begin{Bmatrix} \text{better} \\ \text{than} \end{Bmatrix} \text{Cu}^{2+} \begin{Bmatrix} \text{better} \\ \text{than} \end{Bmatrix} \text{H}^+ \begin{Bmatrix} \text{better} \\ \text{than} \end{Bmatrix} \text{Zn}^{2+}$$

BEST   POOREST

We even promised a quantitative listing of ions. In order to prepare such a quantitative list, **electrochemical cells** are helpful, since they allow us to compare electron-attracting ability by means of numbers. *The reaction in an electrochemical cell is just an oxidation-reduction reaction carried out in a very special way.* Such cells are all around us. One is found in our commercial auto batteries; another appears as a dry cell. Some future ones may even power our cars (Appendix 9). An electrochemical cell is worth studying for many reasons.

15-1 OXIDATION-REDUCTION AND ELECTROCHEMICAL CELLS

15-1.1 Half-Reactions in an Electrochemical Cell

Let us construct an electrochemical cell which uses the now familiar oxidation-reduction reaction between Cu and Ag^+:

$$\text{Cu}(s) + 2\text{Ag}^+ \longrightarrow \text{Cu}^{2+} + 2\text{Ag}(s)^* \qquad (1)$$

Fill a beaker (beaker A) with a dilute solution of silver nitrate (0.1 M) and another beaker (beaker B) with dilute copper sulfate (also 0.1 M). Put a *silver strip* in the $AgNO_3$ *solution* and a *copper strip* in the $CuSO_4$ *solution*. With a wire, connect the silver strip to one terminal of an **ammeter.** (Ammeters measure electric current.) Connect the other terminal of the ammeter to the copper strip. (See Figure 15-1.1.)

*In this chapter, we shall consider only aqueous solutions and therefore not specify (*aq*) for each ion.

Finally, connect the two solutions. One way to make this connection is by a salt bridge as shown in Figure 15-1.2. As you see, the bridge consists of a glass tube, plugged at each end with cotton, and containing a sodium nitrate ($NaNO_3$) solution. The "bridge" completes the electric circuit by furnishing a path for the ions in the solutions to move between the two beakers.

Fig. 15-1.1 An electrochemical cell with salt bridge removed.

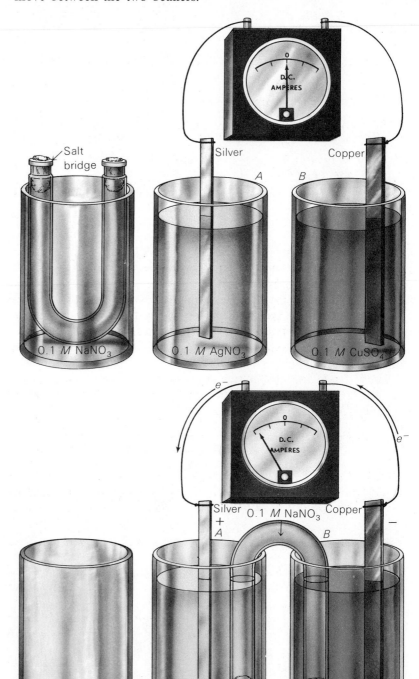

Fig. 15-1.2 An electrochemical cell with salt bridge in place.

As soon as the connection is made, the ammeter needle deflects —electric current is moving through the wires. The wires become warm; the cell is doing work as it forces electrons through the metal. In beaker B, the copper strip is dissolving and the copper sulfate solution is becoming a deeper blue. In beaker A, the silver strip is being covered with a loosely adhering deposit of metallic silver crystals.* As time goes by, the ammeter registers less and less current until finally there is none. Our cell is now "dead." What happened before it died?

The reaction generating current is obviously our old friend:

$$Cu(s) + 2Ag^+ \longrightarrow Cu^{2+} + 2Ag(s) \qquad (1)$$

but some things are different here. The *oxidation* process is taking place in *beaker B* and can be represented by the equation:

$$Cu(s) \longrightarrow Cu^{2+} + 2e^- \qquad (2)$$

The *reduction* process is taking place in *beaker A* and can be represented by the equation:

$$2Ag^+ + 2e^- \longrightarrow 2Ag(s) \qquad (3)$$

The electrons must then flow from copper to silver through the wire connecting the strips in the beakers. To prevent an accumulation of positive ions around the copper strip or negative ions around the silver strip (see equations), ions must be able to pass between beakers. Our salt bridge provides a path for such movement.

The overall process is a combination of the reactions in the individual beakers:

Beaker B	$Cu(s) \longrightarrow Cu^{2+} + 2e^-$	(2)
Beaker A	$2e^- + 2Ag^+ \longrightarrow 2Ag(s)$	(3)
Net reaction	$Cu(s) + 2Ag^+ \longrightarrow 2Ag(s) + Cu^{2+}$	(1)

We see that half the reaction is taking place in beaker A and half in beaker B; the overall reaction is the *sum* of the two **half-reactions.** The reaction in each beaker is called a **half-cell reaction** or a **half-reaction.**

There are several interesting features about these half-reactions:

(1) *The two half-reactions are written separately.* In this electrochemical cell, the half-reactions occur in separate beakers. As the name implies, there must be two such reactions.
(2) *Electrons are shown as part of the reaction.* The ammeter shows that electrons are involved. Electrons flow when the reaction starts and stop flowing when the reaction stops. Earlier arguments showed that electrons flow from copper to silver through the external wire.

*If the crystals are very small, the deposit may appear black in color; but it is still metallic silver.

Fig. 15-2 The operation of an electrochemical cell.

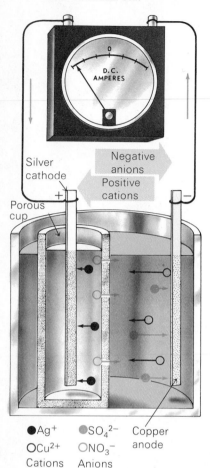

Silver cathode

Negative anions

Positive cations

Porous cup

● Ag^+ ● SO_4^{2-} Copper anode
○ Cu^{2+} ○ NO_3^-
Cations   Anions

Reduction reaction at silver cathode:
$$2Ag^+ + 2e^- \longrightarrow 2Ag(s)$$
Oxidation reaction at copper anode:
$$Cu(s) \longrightarrow Cu^{2+} + 2e^-$$

(3) *New chemical species are produced in each half of the cell*. The copper strip is converted to copper ions (the strip loses mass) and the silver ions are changed to metal (the silver strip gains mass). The new species can be explained in terms of *loss of electrons* (by copper) and *gain of electrons* (by silver ions).

(4) *The half-reactions, when combined, express the overall reaction*. As you see in equations (*2*), (*3*), and (*1*), electrons lost by copper must equal electrons gained by silver. Hence, electrons do not appear in our final overall equation.

15-1.2 Operation of an Electrochemical Cell— Some Terminology

A slightly modified electrochemical cell is better for the measurements which we plan. Figure 15-2 shows such a cell in cross section. The only difference between the new cell and that shown originally is that the salt bridge of Figure 15-1.2 has been replaced by a porous porcelain cup. The cup prevents bulk mixing of the silver nitrate and copper sulfate solutions, but permits ions to seep through its wall to prevent ion accumulation in either cell. The chemical processes are identical to those of our original cell.

Some names will help us to identify parts of the new cell and discuss its operation more easily. As you will recall, the metal strips of copper and silver dipping into the solution are called the **electrodes.** Electrons are left on the copper electrodes as copper atoms enter the solution to become ions:

$$Cu(s) \longrightarrow Cu^{2+} + 2e^- \qquad (2)$$

Note that this is an *oxidation* process because the copper metal *releases electrons* as it forms copper ions. *Chemists call the electrode at which oxidation occurs the* **anode.** Because extra electrons are being generated at the solution-electrode interface through the oxidation of copper, electrons cross into the copper electrode and flow down the wire (Figure 15-2). We call the copper electrode negative in such a commercial cell because it is the source of the negative electricity arising in the cell. In an electrochemical cell, experiment shows that the copper electrode is negatively charged relative to the silver electrode. At the silver electrode, *silver ions* make contact with the silver metal surface and pick up the needed electrons to become silver metal:

$$2Ag^+ + 2e^- \longrightarrow 2Ag(s) \qquad (3)$$

The process is a *reduction* reaction because the silver ions *gain electrons* to become silver metal. *Chemists call the electrode at which reduction occurs the* **cathode.** Because electrons are being generated at the copper electrode and are being used at the silver electrode, silver is less negative (or more positive) than copper. The silver electrode is usually marked with a plus (+). Electron flow in the wire is from copper to silver.

Now what happens in solution? Around the copper anode, positive copper ions are being generated. Around the silver cathode, positive silver ions are being used up. Consequently, positive ions show a net drift from around the copper electrode, where they are being formed, to around the silver electrode, where they are being used up. To help maintain electrical neutrality, the negative ions will also move in solution away from the region around the silver electrode where positive ions have been removed and toward the region around the copper electrode where positive ions are being generated. Notice that the movement of both positive and negative ions is a result of the accumulation of positive ions around one electrode and their removal at the other electrode. In this cell, ion movement has nothing to do with the signs on the electrodes. The whole process is driven by the oxidation-reduction reaction. Because the positive ions move toward the silver cathode where they are being used up, they are called **cations.** Because negative ions are attracted by excess copper ions around the copper electrode and move toward the copper anode, they are called **anions.** In short, *cations move toward the cathode; anions move toward the anode.* This is true both in an electrolysis cell (Chapter 6) and in an electrochemical cell as described here. This movement of ions in the solution completes the circuit; electrons move through the external wires; ions move through the solution. Exchange of electrons with ions must occur where the electrodes are in contact with the solution.

These processes and names are shown in Figure 15-2 and are summarized here:

(1) **Electrodes:** The solid conductors in a cell. At the surface of an electrode, reactions involving electron transfer between solid and solution occur.

(2) **Anode:** The electrode at which oxidation occurs.

(3) **Cathode:** The electrode at which reduction occurs.

(4) **Anion:** A *negatively charged* ion which moves toward the anode.

(5) **Cation:** A *positively charged* ion which moves toward the cathode.

EXERCISE 15-1

We wish to make an electrochemical cell using the reaction

$$Zn(s) + 2Ag^+ \longrightarrow Zn^{2+} + 2Ag(s)$$

Construct a diagram similar to Figure 15-1. Indicate the substances in each beaker, the direction of flow of electrons in the wire, the half-reactions at each electrode, and the direction of movement of both positive and negative ions in the solution. Identify the cathode and the anode in each cell. Which electrode is negative?

15-2 THE ELECTRON-ATTRACTING POWER OF IONS— HALF-CELL POTENTIALS

Voltages from electrochemical cells provide us with quantitative information about the ability of an ion to attract electrons.

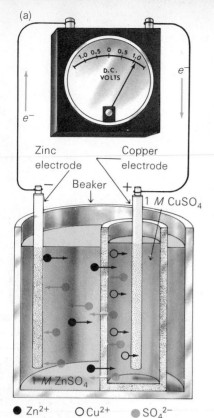

(a)

Zinc electrode | Copper electrode

Beaker

1 M CuSO$_4$

1 M ZnSO$_4$

● Zn^{2+} ○ Cu^{2+} ● SO$_4^{2-}$

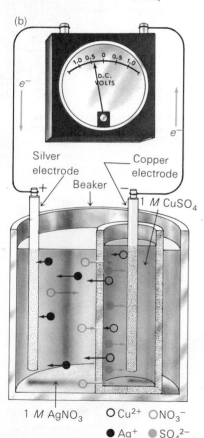

(b)

Silver electrode | Copper electrode

Beaker

1 M CuSO$_4$

1 M AgNO$_3$ ○ Cu^{2+} ○ NO$_3^-$

● Ag$^+$ ● SO$_4^{2-}$

15-2.1   The Voltage of an Electrochemical Cell

In some ways the cells we have constructed resemble cells that power flashlights and start cars. If we put a small light bulb of proper voltage in place of the ammeter of Figure 15-2, the bulb will glow, giving off heat and light. The cell is doing electrical work in forcing the electric current (stream of electrons) through the bulb. As the electrons leave the bulb, they must have lower potential energy than they had when they entered. This drop in potential energy appears as heat and light.* The potential-energy change associated with the chemical reaction of the cell is directly related to the voltage of the cell. *The voltage of a chemical cell measures its ability to force electrons through the circuit. As such, it serves as a measure of the tendency of the cell reaction to go in one direction.*

Different cells have different voltages (Experiment 28). Consider first the cell based on the reactions

$$Zn(s) \longrightarrow Zn^{2+} + 2e^- \qquad (4)$$

$$2e^- + Cu^{2+} \longrightarrow Cu(s) \qquad (5)$$

$$Zn(s) + Cu^{2+} \longrightarrow Zn^{2+} + Cu(s) \qquad (6)$$

The experimental arrangement is shown in Figure 15-3(a). It involves one half-cell consisting of a zinc rod dipping in 1 M ZnSO$_4$, and another half-cell consisting of a copper rod in 1 M CuSO$_4$ solution. The electron flow will be *from zinc,* through the meter, *to copper.* Current flowing in this direction causes the **voltmeter** to deflect to the *right* (clockwise), as shown. The voltmeter reads close to 1.1 volts when the zinc half-cell is connected. The value is recorded in Table 15-1.

One interesting feature of the cell we are using is that the Cu^{2+}–Cu half-cell is completely contained in the center porous cup, while the Zn^{2+}–Zn half-cell is completely contained in the beaker outside the porous cup. This arrangement makes it possible to unhook the copper electrode from the voltmeter and *to transfer the entire half-cell over to a Ag$^+$–Ag half-cell contained in a similar outer beaker.* The result of this transfer is shown in Figure 15-3(b). Our earlier analysis has shown that the reaction between copper metal and silver nitrate is given by the equations

$$Cu(s) \longrightarrow Cu^{2+} + 2e^- \qquad (2)$$

$$2e^- + 2Ag^+ \longrightarrow 2Ag(s) \qquad (3)$$

$$Cu(s) + 2Ag^+ \longrightarrow Cu^{2+} + 2Ag(s) \qquad (1)$$

We see now that electrons are given up by copper and the electron flow is *from copper,* through the meter, *to silver.* We observe that the

*Remember that when billiard balls fell off the high shelf in Chapter 9, the change in their potential energy appeared as heat after impact. The balls were warmer.

Fig. 15-3 Two electrochemical cells involving copper. In each case the porous cup containing the copper electrode can be removed and placed in another beaker.

meter deflects in the opposite direction, toward the *left* (counter-clockwise). The reading on the voltmeter is recorded as left 0.4 volt. This value is placed in Table 15-1. If our standard Cu^{2+}–Cu half-cell is placed in a beaker containing an identical Cu^{2+}–Cu half-cell, the voltmeter reads 0.0 and no deflection is observed. That observation is also recorded in the table. Table 15-1 can be expanded by systematically placing the standard Cu^{2+}–Cu half-cell in other half-cells contained in external beakers. With a Ni^{2+}–Ni half-cell, the reading is right 0.60 volt. Other cells can be constructed and the results added to Table 15-1.

TABLE 15-1 HALF-CELL VOLTAGES
AGAINST COPPER REFERENCE CELL

Half-Reaction in Outer Beaker	Voltmeter Reading
$Ag^+ + e^- \longrightarrow Ag(s)$	left 0.4 volt
$Cu^{2+} + 2e^- \longrightarrow Cu(s)$	0.00 (no deflection)
$2H^+ + 2e^- \longrightarrow H_2(g)$	right 0.3 volt
$Ni^{2+} + 2e^- \longrightarrow Ni(s)$	right 0.6 volt
$Zn^{2+} + 2e^- \longrightarrow Zn(s)$	right 1.1 volts

A special cell is required if we want to enter the value for the half-reaction

$$2e^- + 2H^+ \longrightarrow H_2(g) \tag{7}$$

because gaseous hydrogen does not give us a place to attach the wire as does metallic copper or silver. For this reason, an auxiliary platinum electrode is placed in the 1 *M* solution of H^+. Then, hydrogen gas at 1 atm pressure is bubbled around the platinum metal electrode. The arrangement is shown in Figure 15-4. When this electrode is hooked up to the Cu^{2+}–Cu standard, the reading is right 0.3.

15-2.2 Selection of a Standard Half-Cell for Comparison

Let us study the results summarized in Table 15-1. These numbers tell us, in effect, how each ion competes with Cu^{2+} for electrons. Silver is clearly a better competitor and is placed first. Instead of indicating "right" and "left" readings, perhaps we could designate "left" as "positive" and "right" as "negative." This is a reasonable but *arbitrary* choice. A positive value means that the metal *ion* is a better competitor than Cu^{2+} *ion* for electrons; a negative value, that Cu^{2+} is a better competitor for electrons than the metal ion being considered (for example, Zn^{2+}). The results appear in Table 15-2 (page 348).

If we review the last experiment, we realize that copper was chosen as a comparison electrode because copper and copper sulfate solution were on hand. Suppose we had chosen a Ni^{2+}–Ni half-cell for comparison. All half-cells in Table 15-2 would have had the same relative positions, but the numbers would have been different. The Ni^{2+}–Ni half-cell would obviously be 0.0 and the Cu^{2+}–Cu half-cell would read left 0.6 because the electrons would be flowing to copper from the new

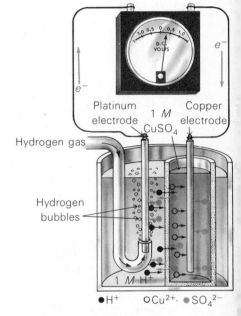

Fig. 15-4 An electrochemical cell made of a hydrogen half-cell and a copper half-cell.

TABLE 15-2 HALF-CELL VOLTAGES
AGAINST COPPER REFERENCE CELL

Half-Reaction in Outer Beaker	Voltmeter Reading
$Ag^+ + e^- \longrightarrow Ag(s)$	+0.4 volt (left)
$Cu^{2+} + 2e^- \longrightarrow Cu(s)$	0.0 volt (no deflection)
$2H^+ + 2e^- \longrightarrow H_2(g)$	−0.3 volt (right)
$Ni^{2+} + 2e^- \longrightarrow Ni(s)$	−0.6 volt (right)
$Zn^{2+} + 2e^- \longrightarrow Zn(s)$	−1.1 volts (right)

reference half-cell. This is just the reverse of when copper was in the porous cup and nickel outside. Values shown in Table 15-3 indicate that all readings would be just 0.6 volt more positive if the Ni^{2+}–Ni half-cell were our comparison standard. Any half-cell in the list could have been used as the standard reference for determining the half-cell voltage readings, but *we must use a standard half-cell. Without a standard half-cell, there is no place to fasten one voltmeter wire and the circuit cannot therefore be completed to get a reading!*

TABLE 15-3 HALF-CELL VOLTAGES
AGAINST NICKEL REFERENCE CELL

Half-Reaction in Outer Beaker	Voltmeter Reading
$Ag^+ + e^- \longrightarrow Ag(s)$	+1.0 volt (left)
$Cu^{2+} + 2e^- \longrightarrow Cu(s)$	+0.6 volt (left)
$2H^+ + 2e^- \longrightarrow H_2(g)$	+0.3 volt (left)
$Ni^{2+} + 2e^- \longrightarrow Ni(s)$	0.0 volt (no deflection)
$Zn^{2+} + 2e^- \longrightarrow Zn(s)$	−0.5 volt (right)

Faced with this situation, chemists have arbitrarily selected the H^+–H_2 half-cell as a standard and have compared all other half-cells to it. This means that a H^+–H_2 half-cell, measured against an identical H^+–H_2 half-cell used as a standard, generates 0.0 volt. Other half-cells will give the values shown in Table 15-4 (page 350), *if the measurement is properly made.*

EXERCISE 15-2

Suppose a Ag^+–Ag half-cell were chosen as the standard. What would all values in Table 15-3 read?

15-2.3 The Influence of Concentration on Voltage

The qualifier "if the measurement is properly made" suggests that in defining the reference half-cell and the measured half-cells, we must tell precisely how each half-cell is made! You remember from your laboratory work that the concentration of the solution surrounding the metal electrode is important in determining the cell voltage. You studied a cell based on the reaction

$$Zn(s) + Cu^{2+} \longrightarrow Zn^{2+} + Cu(s) \qquad (6)$$

If *more* $CuSO_4$ were dissolved in the solution surrounding the copper electrode, the cell voltage would *increase*. If a solution containing *less* $ZnSO_4$ were used around the zinc electrode, the voltage would *also increase*. A decrease in the concentration of Cu^{2+} or an increase in the concentration of Zn^{2+} would make the voltage drop. Are not these observations in complete agreement with predictions we would make on the basis of Le Chatelier's principle? The tendency of reaction (6) to go from left to right is measured by the *positive* voltage value for the cell. Le Chatelier's principle tells us that if the Cu^{2+} concentration is reduced (*e.g.*, by precipitation of Cu^{2+} as CuS), there will be less tendency for the reaction to go. (The equilibrium will shift toward $Zn + Cu^{2+}$.) The voltage should decrease—a prediction in complete agreement with experimental findings.

EXERCISE 15-3

A cell is based on the reaction

$$Ni(s) + 2Ag^+ \longrightarrow Ni^{2+} + 2Ag(s)$$

What would be the effect on cell voltage if

(1) more $AgNO_3$ were dissolved in the solution around the silver electrode?
(2) more $NiSO_4$ were dissolved in the solution around the nickel electrode?
(3) Ag_2S were precipitated by adding H_2S?

The effects of concentration changes on cell voltage are very familiar to you, although you probably were not aware of the meaning of your observations when you made them. You have all watched a flashlight go dim after continued use or heard the battery of a car gradually run down as someone tried to start it on a cold morning. What happens? Why does the cell or battery stop generating electrical energy?

To answer this question, let us first consider another question. What happens to any cell or battery as it operates? Reactants are used up and products accumulate around the electrodes. Observation shows that the *voltage also decreases* as the reactants convert to products. Finally the voltage of the cell reaches zero. We say that the cell is "dead." Equilibrium has been attained, and the reaction that has been producing the energy has the same tendency to proceed as does its reverse. Again, the observed voltage measures the *net* tendency for the reaction to occur. At equilibrium there is a balance between forward and reverse reactions; hence, there is *no* tendency for further reaction either way. The voltage of a cell at equilibrium is zero; the cell is "dead."

15-2.4 Standard Half-Cell Potentials—E^0

Since concentrations in a cell do influence its voltage, concentrations of all reagents in a cell should be specified if the measured voltages are going to have maximum value for predicting chemical reactions.

Because of this, chemists have introduced the idea of **standard state.** The standard state for gases is taken as a pressure of 1 atm at 25 °C; the standard state for ions is taken as a 1 M solution*; and the standard state for other pure substances is taken as the state in which the pure substance exists at 25 °C and 1 atm.

We can now specify more precisely how half-cell potentials should be measured. Values in Table 15-4 were obtained by measuring the cell voltages with all reagents in their standard state. Thus, if we set up a cell based on the reaction

$$Zn(s) + 2H^+ (1\ M) \longrightarrow Zn^{2+} (1\ M) + H_2\ (1\ atm) \qquad (8)$$

a reading of 0.76 (right) will be made on the voltmeter if the measurement is made at 25 °C. Results for a number of half-cells are listed in Table 15-4. This value of -0.76 volt for the zinc half-cell is known as the E^0 value for the reduction of Zn^{2+} ion. The E^0 **value** *is the potential associated with a half-reaction taking place between substances in their standard states.* (The superscript zero means standard state.) By international agreement,† the standard H^+–H_2 half-cell is always used as a reference and assigned an E^0 of zero.

TABLE 15-4 SELECTED STANDARD REDUCTION POTENTIALS FOR HALF-REACTIONS*

Half-Reaction		E^0 (volts)
Oxidized State	Reduced State	
$MnO_4^- + 8H^+ + 5e^- \longrightarrow Mn^{2+} + 4H_2O$		$+1.52$
$Cl_2(g) + 2e^- \longrightarrow 2Cl^-$		$+1.36$
$MnO_2(s) + 4H^+ + 2e^- \longrightarrow Mn^{2+} + 2H_2O$		$+1.28$
$Br_2(l) + 2e^- \longrightarrow 2Br^-$		$+1.06$
$Ag^+ + e^- \longrightarrow Ag(s)$		$+0.80$
$I_2(s) + 2e^- \longrightarrow 2I^-$		$+0.53$
$Cu^{2+} + 2e^- \longrightarrow Cu(s)$		$+0.34$
$2H^+ + 2e^- \longrightarrow H_2(g)$		0.00
$Ni^{2+} + 2e^- \longrightarrow Ni(s)$		-0.25
$Co^{2+} + 2e^- \longrightarrow Co(s)$		-0.28
$Zn^{2+} + 2e^- \longrightarrow Zn(s)$		-0.76

*A more complete list is given in Appendix 7.

A large number of standard half-cell potentials,‡ E^0 values, have been determined. A more complete list is shown in Appendix 7. What do they mean and what can they be used for? *The standard half-cell potential is a quantitative measure of the electron-attracting ability of an ion in its standard state in the half-cell. In all cases the electron-attracting ability of the hydrogen ion in the standard hydrogen reference*

*Some refinement is needed to define the standard state for ions precisely, but we shall not be concerned with that refinement here.
†The electrode signs used in this text are those adopted by the International Union of Pure and Applied Chemistry.
‡The term *potential* refers to the voltages we have been measuring. It emphasizes the relationship between voltage and potential energy. **Voltage** is the energy supplied per elementary charge in driving the charge around the circuit of the cell. Voltage multiplied by charge is electrical energy. One volt driving one electron is 1.6×10^{-19} **joule.** Remember that the joule is a work term.

half-cell is used as a basis for comparison. If the sign of E^0 is *positive,* it means that *the ion of the half-cell equation is better at attracting an electron than is the hydrogen ion.* Thus, an E^0 value of $+0.80$ volt for the half-cell defined by the equation $Ag^+ + e^- \longrightarrow Ag(s)$ means that silver ion ($1\ M$) in solution has a stronger attraction for electrons than does hydrogen ion ($1\ M$) in solution. We find that silver ions can pull electrons away from hydrogen gas to give hydrogen ions and silver metal. The overall process then goes spontaneously as written with a voltage of 0.80 volt:

$$2Ag^+ + H_2(g) \longrightarrow 2Ag(s) + 2H^+ \qquad E^0 = +0.80 \text{ volt} \qquad (9)$$

We have not added $1\ M$ for the concentration of each ionic species, nor have we indicated $25\ °C$ and 1 atm for H_2. All this is implied by the symbol E^0.

If the sign of a half-cell is *negative, the hydrogen ion has a stronger attraction for electrons than does the ion of the half-cell.* Thus, for the half-cell with the half-reaction

$$Zn^{2+} + 2e^- \longrightarrow Zn(s) \qquad E^0 = -0.76 \text{ volt} \qquad (10)$$

the negative sign means that Zn^{2+} has less attraction for electrons than does H^+. Accordingly, we would expect that H^+ would be able to take electrons away from metallic zinc to give hydrogen gas. The process has been observed in the laboratory:

$$Zn(s) + 2H^+ \longrightarrow H_2(g) + Zn^{2+} \qquad E^0 = +0.76 \text{ volt} \qquad (11)$$

For the reverse process we write

$$Zn^{2+} + H_2(g) \longrightarrow 2H^+ + Zn(s) \qquad E^0 = -0.76 \text{ volt} \qquad (12)$$

Thus, if the half-reaction only is written, for the two cases we have

$$Zn(s) \longrightarrow Zn^{2+} + 2e^- \qquad E^0 = +0.76 \text{ volt} \qquad (4a)$$
$$Zn^{2+} + 2e^- \longrightarrow Zn(s) \qquad E^0 = -0.76 \text{ volt} \qquad (10)$$

Note that when the direction of the equation is reversed, the sign of E^0 is reversed.

15-3 USES OF HALF-CELL POTENTIALS

15-3.1 Voltages of Electrochemical Cells

Since experimental cell voltage measurements were the source of our E^0 values, it is easy to determine cell voltages from tables of E^0 values. Consider the reaction between zinc metal and silver ion:

$$Zn(s) + 2Ag^+ \longrightarrow 2Ag(s) + Zn^{2+} \qquad (13)$$

The appropriate E^0 values are

$$Zn^{2+} + 2e^- \longrightarrow Zn(s) \qquad E^0 = -0.76 \text{ volt} \qquad (10)$$

$$Ag^+ + e^- \longrightarrow Ag(s) \qquad E^0 = +0.80 \text{ volt} \qquad (14)$$

Since Ag^+ has a larger positive E^0 value than Zn^{2+}, silver ion has a greater tendency to pick up electrons than does Zn^{2+}. The silver half-reaction will go as written above; the half-reaction for Zn^{2+} must be reversed:

$$2Ag^+ + 2e^- \longrightarrow 2Ag(s) \qquad\qquad E^0 = +0.80 \text{ volt} \qquad (3a)$$

$$Zn(s) \longrightarrow Zn^{2+} + 2e^- \qquad E^0 = +0.76 \text{ volt} \qquad (4a)$$

$$2Ag^+ + Zn(s) \longrightarrow Zn^{2+} + 2Ag(s) \quad E^0 = +1.56 \text{ volts} \qquad (13a)$$

Notice that we did *not* double E^0 for the reaction $Ag^+ + e^- \longrightarrow$ Ag in obtaining the voltage. The voltage of a half-reaction does *not* depend on how many moles we consider, but it does depend upon the concentration. Thus,

$$Ag^+ + e^- \longrightarrow Ag(s) \qquad E^0 = +0.80 \text{ volt} \qquad (14)$$

$$2Ag^+ + 2e^- \longrightarrow 2Ag(s) \qquad E^0 = +0.80 \text{ volt} \qquad (3a)$$

$$3Ag^+ + 3e^- \longrightarrow 3Ag(s) \qquad E^0 = +0.80 \text{ volt} \qquad (15)$$

This is simply a statement that the voltage of a cell is not determined by how big the cell is. A tiny cell (battery) for an electric watch can give a voltage as high as that of a massive storage battery based on the same reaction.

You might wonder what we would have learned if we had assumed that the cell operates in the reverse direction.

$$Zn^{2+} + 2Ag(s) \longrightarrow Zn(s) + 2Ag^+ \qquad (16)$$

Half-cell values show

$$Zn^{2+} + 2e^- \longrightarrow Zn(s) \qquad\qquad E^0 = -0.76 \text{ volt} \qquad (10)$$

$$2Ag(s) \longrightarrow 2Ag^+ + 2e^- \qquad E^0 = -0.80 \text{ volt} \qquad (17)$$

$$2Ag(s) + Zn^{2+} \longrightarrow 2Ag^+ + Zn(s) \quad E^0 = -1.56 \text{ volts} \qquad (18)$$

The process is spontaneous in the reverse direction since E^0 is negative.

15-3.2 Predicting Reactions from Table 15-4

Half-cell potentials can be used in general to predict what chemical reactions can occur spontaneously. Suppose someone wishes to know whether zinc can be oxidized when it is placed in contact with a solution of nickel sulfate. The values of E^0 help to decide. The standard half-cell potential, or E^0 value, for Zn^{2+}–Zn is -0.76 volt; that of Ni^{2+}–Ni, -0.25 volt. Apparently, Ni^{2+} has a stronger attraction for electrons than does Zn^{2+}. We predict from this information that zinc metal will react with nickel ion to give nickel metal and zinc ion. Zinc is oxidized and nickel is reduced. This is exactly what happens. Successful predictions save lots of hard work.

Suppose we want to know whether or not nickel metal will be attacked by chlorine water (Cl_2 gas dissolved in water). Table 15-4 provides the answer. The appropriate half-reactions are

$$Cl_2(g) + 2e^- \longrightarrow 2Cl^- \qquad E^0 = +1.36 \text{ volts} \qquad (19)$$

$$Ni^{2+} + 2e^- \longrightarrow Ni(s) \qquad E^0 = -0.25 \text{ volt} \qquad (20)$$

Since we are interested in the reaction of Cl_2 with metallic nickel, the second half-reaction should be turned around and the sign of E^0 should be reversed. Then:

$$Cl_2(g) + 2e^- \longrightarrow 2Cl^- \qquad E^0 = +1.36 \text{ volts} \quad (19)$$

$$Ni(s) \longrightarrow Ni^{2+} + 2e^- \qquad E^0 = +0.25 \text{ volt} \qquad (21)$$

$$\overline{Ni(s) + Cl_2(g) \longrightarrow Ni^{2+} + 2Cl^- \quad E^0 = +1.61 \text{ volts} \qquad (22)}$$

The answer is a resounding "yes"!

EXERCISE 15-4

Use the values of E^0 to predict whether cobalt metal will tend to dissolve in a $1\ M$ solution of acid, H^+. Now predict whether cobalt metal will tend to dissolve in a $1\ M$ solution of zinc sulfate (reacting with Zn^{2+}).

We can generalize now on the use of Table 15-4. A substance on the left in Table 15-4 reacts by gaining electrons. A substance on the right reacts by losing electrons. We may draw the following conclusions:

(1) *An oxidation-reduction reaction must involve a substance from the left side of the equations in Table 15-4 (something which can be reduced) and a substance from the right side (something which can be oxidized).*

(2) *A substance on the left side of the equations in Table 15-4 tends to react spontaneously with any substance on the right side which is lower in the table.*

Applying these rules, we would predict: copper metal could be oxidized to Cu^{2+} by $Br_2(l)$ or $MnO_2(s)$, but not by Ni^{2+} or Zn^{2+}. Of course, copper metal cannot be oxidized by either zinc metal or nickel metal because neither zinc metal nor nickel metal can accept electrons to be reduced.

EXERCISE 15-5

Use Table 15-4 to decide which of the following substances tend to oxidize bromide ion, Br^-, to give the element bromine: $Cl_2(g)$, H^+, Ni^{2+}, MnO_4^-.

EXERCISE 15-6

Use Table 15-4 to decide which of the following substances tend to reduce $Br_2(l)$ to $2Br^-$: Cl^-, $H_2(g)$, $Ni(s)$, Mn^{2+}.

15-3.3 Predictions and the Effect of Concentrations

The foregoing predictions have been based upon the values of E^0 and apply only to standard conditions. Yet we often wish to carry out a reaction at conditions other than standard ones. The prediction then must be adjusted in accord with Le Chatelier's principle.

For example, we might ask, will silver metal dissolve in $1\ M\ H^+$? According to Table 15-4, the data are

$$2Ag(s) \longrightarrow 2Ag^+ (1\ M) + 2e^- \quad E^0 = -0.80 \text{ volt} \quad (23)$$

$$2e^- + 2H^+ (1\ M) \longrightarrow H_2(g) \qquad\qquad E^0 = 0.00 \text{ volt} \quad (7a)$$

$$2Ag(s) + 2H^+ (1\ M) \longrightarrow 2Ag^+ (1\ M) + H_2(g)$$
$$E^0 = -0.80 \text{ volt} \quad (24)$$

The negative E^0 shows that the state of equilibrium favors the reactants rather than the products for reaction (24). For standard conditions, the reaction will not tend to occur spontaneously. However, if we place $Ag(s)$ in fresh $1\ M\ H^+$, the initial Ag^+ concentration will be zero, not $1\ M$. By Le Chatelier's principle, we know that this will increase the tendency to form products. Will this tendency be enough to counteract the E^0 prediction (no reaction)? Experiments show that some silver will dissolve, though only a *very small amount*. The tendency for silver metal to release electrons is much less than the tendency for H_2 to release electrons. *The equilibrium concentration of Ag^+ is so small that no silver chloride precipitate is formed* when chloride ions are present in the solution. Very little Ag^+ is present since silver chloride has a very low solubility.

That some silver does dissolve to form Ag^+ can be shown experimentally by adding a little KI to the solution. Silver iodide has an even lower solubility than does silver chloride. The experiment shows that the amount of dissolved silver is sufficient to precipitate some AgI but not AgCl. This places the equilibrium Ag^+ concentration below $10^{-10}\ M$ but above $10^{-17}\ M$. Either concentration is so small that we can consider our prediction for the standard state to be generally applicable. Silver metal does not dissolve in $1\ M$ HCl. In general, whether a prediction based upon the standard state can be applied to other conditions depends upon how large E^0 is. If E^0 for the overall reaction is only 0.1 or 0.2 volt (either positive or negative), then deviations from standard conditions may invalidate predictions if we do not consider concentration or temperature changes in arriving at our conclusions.

15-3.4 Reliability of Predictions

There is one more limitation on the reliability of predictions based upon E^0's. To see it, we shall consider the three reactions

$$Cu(s) + 2H^+ \longrightarrow Cu^{2+} + H_2(g) \quad E^0 = -0.34 \text{ volt} \quad (25)$$

$$Fe(s) + 2H^+ \longrightarrow Fe^{2+} + H_2(g) \quad E^0 = +0.44 \text{ volt} \quad (26)$$

$$3Fe(s) + 2NO_3^- + 8H^+ \longrightarrow 3Fe^{2+} + 2NO(g) + 4H_2O$$
$$E^0 = +1.40 \text{ volts} \quad (27)$$

The three values of E^0 are easily calculated from half-cell potentials. We can predict with confidence that the reaction of copper metal with dilute H^+ will not occur to any appreciable extent. The negative value of E^0 indicates that equilibrium strongly favors the reactants. Moreover, we can predict that the reaction of iron metal with dilute hydrochloric acid *might* occur, and that the reaction of iron metal with dilute nitric acid to give NO *might* occur. The fairly large positive values of E^0 for reactions (26) and (27) indicate that the products are strongly favored in equilibrium. Experiments are warranted. A piece of iron is immersed in dilute HCl. Bubbles of hydrogen appear; the reaction does occur. A piece of iron is immersed in a 1 M nitric acid solution. Although bubbles of hydrogen may appear initially, no nitric oxide (NO) gas appears. The reaction between iron and nitrate ion in acid solution to give NO does not occur immediately; the reaction rate is extremely slow. This slow rate could *not* be predicted from the E^0's.

So the equilibrium predictions based on E^0's do not eliminate the need for experiments. They provide no basis, for example, for anticipating reaction rate; only experiment provides this information. The E^0's do, however, provide definite and reliable guidance concerning the equilibrium state, thus eliminating the need for many experiments. A multitude of reactions do not need to be tried. We can predict their failure by considering the values of E^0.

15-4 E^0 AND THE FACTORS THAT DETERMINE EQUILIBRIUM

In Chapter 14, oxidation-reduction reactions were analyzed in terms of two factors: randomness and energy. We noted that randomness tends toward a maximum and energy toward a minimum. What is the connection between E^0 and these two factors?

Consider two oxidation-reduction reactions for which E^0 shows that products are favored, one exothermic and the other endothermic. For the exothermic reaction, reactants, having been mixed, are driven toward equilibrium by their tendency toward minimum energy. Contrast this with the endothermic reaction, for which E^0 shows that equilibrium favors products. When these reactants are mixed, they approach equilibrium *against* the tendency toward minimum energy (since heat is absorbed). This reaction is driven by the tendency toward maximum randomness. Neither the tendency toward minimum energy nor the tendency toward maximum randomness *considered alone* will give us a reliable guide to the direction in which a reaction will go. But E^0 does give us the experimental result obtained by combining these two tendencies.

In summary, E^0 *measures quantitatively a proper combination of the tendency toward minimum energy and the tendency toward maximum randomness under the standard-state conditions.*

15-5 THE BALANCING OF EQUATIONS THROUGH HALF-REACTIONS

In Chapter 14 we talked about balancing equations. Are half-reactions useful for balancing equations? It is worth a try. Let us consider a very simple example first.

Suppose we want to describe the process which occurs when pure lithium metal is added to a 1 M HCl solution. The appropriate half-reactions and E^0 values can be written as

$$\text{Li}(s) \longrightarrow \text{Li}^+ + e^- \qquad E^0 = +3.00 \text{ volts} \qquad (28)$$

$$2\text{H}^+ + 2e^- \longrightarrow \text{H}_2(g) \qquad E^0 = +0.00 \text{ volt} \qquad (7a)$$

Combination of these two half-reactions will leave one electron on the left-hand side. This is not appropriate for a net equation, only for a half-reaction. The problem is very easily solved by multiplying the top equation by 2.

$$2\text{Li}(s) \longrightarrow 2\text{Li}^+ + 2e^- \qquad E^0 = +3.00 \text{ volts}^* \qquad (29)$$

$$\underline{2\text{H}^+ + 2e^- \longrightarrow \text{H}_2(g) \qquad E^0 = +0.00 \text{ volt} \qquad (7a)}$$

$$2\text{Li}(s) + 2\text{H}^+ \longrightarrow 2\text{Li}^+ + \text{H}_2(g) \quad E^0 = +3.00 \text{ volts} \qquad (30)$$

As a more complex case we will consider the example which was used in Section 14-3. Hydrogen sulfide is bubbled into an acidified potassium permanganate solution. From Appendix 7, we see that permanganate is reduced in acid solution as indicated by the equation:

$$\text{MnO}_4^- + 8\text{H}^+ + 5e^- \longrightarrow \text{Mn}^{2+} + 4\text{H}_2\text{O} \qquad (31)$$

The oxidation of hydrogen sulfide is represented as:

$$\text{H}_2\text{S}(g) \longrightarrow 2\text{H}^+ + \text{S}(s) + 2e^-\dagger \qquad (32)$$

These two equations cannot be added directly as written, since charge would remain on the left-hand side.

---

*Note that multiplying the half-reaction by 2 to balance the equation does *not* change the size of the E^0 value (see page 352). Note that we have unbalanced positive charges on both right- and left-hand sides of the equation, and that all atoms are balanced.
†Equation in table turned around because $\text{H}_2\text{S}(g)$ is a reactant.

Balancing the electrons is the next step. Using 10 as the least common multiple for the numbers of electrons, we multiply equation (32) by 5 and equation (31) by 2:

$$5H_2S(g) \longrightarrow 5S(s) + 10H^+ + 10e^- \qquad (33)$$

$$10e^- + 16H^+ + 2MnO_4^- \longrightarrow 2Mn^{2+} + 8H_2O \qquad (34)$$

$$5H_2S(g) + 16H^+ + 2MnO_4^- \longrightarrow$$
$$5S(s) + 10H^+ + 2Mn^{2+} + 8H_2O \quad (35)$$

When we add equations (33) and (34), the ten electrons on each side add to zero. Both atoms and charges are properly balanced in equation (35), but there are excess H^+ ions included among the reactants as well as the products. Subtracting $10H^+$ from both sides of the equation, we obtain the final balanced reaction

$$5H_2S(g) + 2MnO_4^- + 6H^+ \longrightarrow 5S(s) + 2Mn^{2+} + 8H_2O \quad (36)$$

Before leaving the equation, let us check the electric-charge balance:

$$5H_2S(g) + 2MnO_4^- + 6H^+ \longrightarrow 5S(s) + 2Mn^{2+} + 8H_2O$$
$$5(0) \quad + \; 2(1-) \; + 6(1+) \qquad 5(0) + 2(2+) \; + 8(0)$$
$$(2-) \; + \; (6+) \qquad\qquad (4+)$$
$$(4+) = (4+)$$

Sometimes the overall equation to be balanced involves a half-reaction for which we do not have a balanced equation. A method for balancing such half-reactions is given in Appendix 8.

15-6 ELECTROLYSIS

Earlier in this chapter we dealt with spontaneous processes which released energy as electrical energy. In Chapter 6 we considered the reverse process, where an *externally generated electric current* (electrical energy) was passed through a solution to give products of higher potential energy. Let us compare and contrast the spontaneous process **(electrochemical** or **voltaic cell)** and the nonspontaneous one **(electrolytic cell).**

Many features of voltaic and electrolytic cells are the same. Each cell involves *both* oxidation and reduction processes. In both cells the *anode* is the electrode at which *oxidation* occurs and the *cathode* is the electrode at which *reduction* occurs. Electric current moves in the external wires of both cells as a result of net *electron* flow in one direction. In both cells electric current moves through the *solution* of the cell as a result of migrating ions. Because the mechanism for carrying the current through the solution differs from that for carrying the current in a wire, a chemical reaction must take place at *each* junction between metal electrode and solution. Oxidation or reduction processes occur at these junctions. In both cells, *cations* move through the solution toward the *cathode,* and *anions* move through the solution toward the *anode.*

Despite the many common features shared by electrochemical and electrolytic cells some real and significant differences exist between

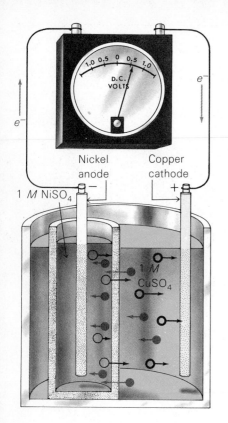

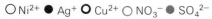

$\bigcirc$ Ni^{2+} $\bullet$ Ag$^+$ $\bigcirc$ Cu^{2+} $\bigcirc$ NO$_3^-$ $\bullet$ SO$_4^{2-}$

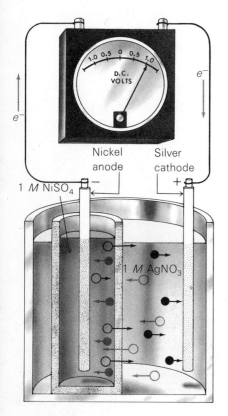

Fig. 15-5.1 (Top) A voltaic cell based on the reaction

$$\text{Ni}(s) + \text{Cu}^{2+} \longrightarrow \text{Cu}(s) + \text{Ni}^{2+} \qquad E^0 = 0.59 \text{ volt}$$

Fig. 15-5.2 (Bottom) A voltaic cell based on the reaction

$$\text{Ni}(s) + 2\text{Ag}^+ \longrightarrow 2\text{Ag}(s) + \text{Ni}^{2+} \qquad E^0 = 1.05 \text{ volts}$$

them. For example, in a voltaic cell, a *spontaneous chemical process* forces electrons around a system. In an electrolysis cell, a *dynamo* or external voltaic cell *forces* electrons through the system. Consider a cell based on the equation

$$\text{Ni}(s) + \text{Cu}^{2+} \longrightarrow \text{Ni}^{2+} + \text{Cu}(s) \qquad (37)$$

The half-reactions and the E^0 values are

$$\text{Ni}(s) \longrightarrow \text{Ni}^{2+} + 2e^- \qquad E^0 = +0.25 \text{ volt} \quad (21)$$

$$\underline{2e^- + \text{Cu}^{2+} \longrightarrow \text{Cu}(s) \qquad E^0 = +0.34 \text{ volt} \quad (5a)}$$

$$\text{Ni}(s) + \text{Cu}^{2+} \longrightarrow \text{Ni}^{2+} + \text{Cu}(s) \quad E^0 = +0.59 \text{ volt} \quad (37)$$

Nickel is the negative electrode and copper is the positive electrode. The observed voltage is 0.59 volt. The chemical process as written is spontaneous and will force electrons from the nickel electrode to copper with a voltage of 0.59 volt (Figure 15-5.1).

Now, what would happen if we hooked the electrodes up to a dynamo which pumps electrons toward the nickel with a potential far above 0.59 volt? Experiment shows that under these conditions the nickel cell would run backward; it would function as an electrolysis cell.

$$2e^- + \text{Ni}^{2+} \longrightarrow \text{Ni}(s) \qquad (20)$$

$$\underline{\text{Cu}(s) \longrightarrow \text{Cu}^{2+} + 2e^- \qquad (2)}$$

$$\text{Cu}(s) + \text{Ni}^{2+} \xrightarrow[\text{energy}]{\text{electrical}} \text{Cu}^{2+} + \text{Ni}(s) \qquad (38)$$

If another voltaic cell were used to drive the electrons instead of a dynamo, the results would be similar. Suppose we used a voltaic cell based on the reaction

$$\text{Ni}(s) + 2\text{Ag}^+ \longrightarrow \text{Ni}^{2+} + 2\text{Ag}(s) \qquad E^0 = +1.05 \text{ volts} \quad (39)$$

to power the electrolysis (Figure 15-5.2). The voltage observed in the circuit will be the difference between the voltages of the two cells:

$$E^0 = E^0_{\text{Ni-Ag}} - E^0_{\text{Ni-Cu}} = 1.05 - 0.59 = +0.46 \text{ volt} \quad (40)$$

This experimental observation can be understood by considering the net reaction taking place in the entire circuit (Figure 15-5.3). If the net reaction in the electrochemical cell and the net reaction in the electrolytic cell are added together, the net reaction for the combined process is obtained:

Voltaic $\qquad \text{Ni}(s) + 2\text{Ag}^+ \longrightarrow \text{Ni}^{2+} + 2\text{Ag}(s)$
$$E^0 = +1.05 \text{ volts} \quad (39)$$

Electrolytic $\quad \text{Cu}(s) + \text{Ni}^{2+} \longrightarrow \text{Ni}(s) + \text{Cu}^{2+}$
$$E^0 = -0.59 \text{ volt} \quad (38)$$

Net reaction $2\text{Ag}^+ + \text{Cu}(s) \longrightarrow \text{Cu}^{2+} + 2\text{Ag}(s)$
$$E^0 = +0.46 \text{ volt} \qquad (1a)$$

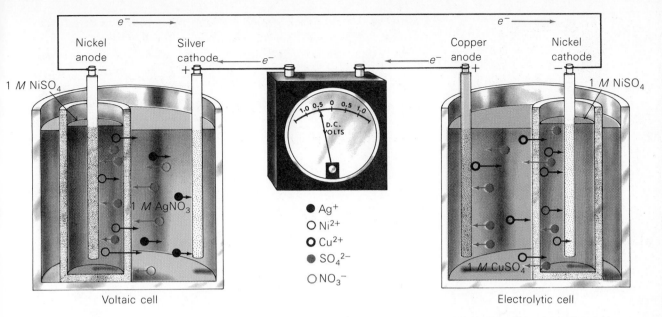

Fig. 15-5.3 Two electrochemical cells connected in opposition.

The E^0 value for the net reaction can be calculated separately from E^0 values for the silver and copper half-cells:

$$2e^- + 2Ag^+ \longrightarrow 2Ag(s) \qquad E^0 = +0.80 \text{ volt} \qquad (3)$$
$$Cu(s) \longrightarrow Cu^{2+} + 2e^- \qquad E^0 = -0.34 \text{ volt} \qquad (2)$$
$$\overline{2Ag^+ + Cu(s) \longrightarrow Cu^{2+} + 2Ag(s) \quad E^0 = +0.46 \text{ volt} \quad (1a)}$$

We see that:

(1) The E^0 value for the Ni^{2+}–Ni half-cell cancels out in considering the net reaction for the overall process.
(2) The measured voltage for the overall process involving two cells can be calculated from the net equation for the overall process.

Let us now focus our attention on the electrolytic cell, the cell containing nickel and copper half-cells. The process is in many ways like the electrolysis process discussed in Chapter 6. Electrons forced through the wire from the dynamo or voltaic cell make the nickel electrode negatively charged. At the nickel electrode, Ni^{2+} ions make contact and electrons are transferred to give nickel metal:

$$\text{Reduction} \qquad 2e^- + Ni^{2+} \longrightarrow Ni(s) \qquad (20)$$

At the copper electrode electrons flow out to the positive electrode of the voltaic cell:

$$\text{Oxidation} \qquad Cu(s) \longrightarrow Cu^{2+} + 2e^- \qquad (2)$$

ELECTROLYSIS

359

Positive ions that formed around the copper electrode now drift toward the negatively charged nickel electrode, while negative ions left in excess around the nickel electrode by removal of Ni^{2+} drift toward the positively charged copper electrode. *We see that an electrolytic cell is simply a voltaic cell forced to operate in the reverse direction by a voltage larger than that which the original cell could produce.*

If more than one reaction is possible in a cell, that reaction will take place which requires the lowest voltage. For example, in the electrolysis of a table salt solution, two reduction reactions are possible at the negative electrode:

$$Na^+ + e^- \longrightarrow Na(s) \qquad E^0 = -2.71 \text{ volts} \qquad (41)$$

$$2H^+ + 2e^- \longrightarrow H_2(g) \qquad E^0 = 0.00 \text{ volt} \qquad (7a)$$

Hydrogen gas is liberated much more easily than sodium if both ions are present at a 1 M concentration. Decreasing the concentration of hydrogen ion should make hydrogen formation more difficult; but because of the very high voltage needed for sodium deposition (-2.71 volts), hydrogen gas is still more easily produced than sodium metal in any water solution. For this reason, the electrolysis of NaCl in water solution, using platinum electrodes, gives H_2 and Cl_2, *not* Na and Cl_2.

EXERCISE 15-7

Which ion will be deposited first if a solution containing 1 M concentrations of Cu^{2+} and Ni^{2+} is electrolyzed?

15-7 HIGHLIGHTS

A chemical reaction involving electron transfer from one species to another can be broken down into two **half-reactions.** If **oxidation** (loss of electrons) is carried out in one part of a cell and **reduction** (gain of electrons) is carried out in another, *electrons* can be made to flow *through a wire* from the part of the cell where electrons are released to the other part where they are used. The resulting **electric current** can be made to do useful work. To prevent charge buildup at any point in the cell, *ions* must be able to *migrate in the liquid phase* from one part of the cell to the other. The entire device is called an **electrochemical** or **voltaic cell.**

During its operation, the **electrochemical** or **voltaic cell** passes from a state of higher energy to a state of lower potential energy and electrical work is done. The voltage generated by an **electrochemical cell** is a measure of the driving force for the cell reaction. If the voltage for the $H^+(aq)$–H_2 half-cell is taken as zero, the voltage associated with other half-cell reactions can be measured by using carefully defined experimental conditions.

E^0 **values** or standard half-cell potentials can be collected in a table such as that shown in Appendix 7. E^0 values are useful in estimating cell voltages and in deciding whether equilibrium favors a given reaction or its reverse. A positive E^0 value, favoring reaction as written, may not guarantee that the process will go as written, but a negative E^0 value indicates with certainty that the process will not go spontaneously as written.

In **balancing** oxidation-reduction reactions, both atoms and charge must be conserved. A method for balancing oxidation-reduction reactions can be based on half-cell reactions.

Finally, we saw that the process of **electrolysis,** first discussed in Chapter 6, involves a voltaic cell which is forced to run backward by an opposing potential larger than the potential of the cell.

QUESTIONS and PROBLEMS

1 An electrochemical cell is to be assembled using the overall reaction:

$$Cd(s) + 2AgNO_3 \longrightarrow Cd(NO_3)_2 + 2Ag(s)$$

(a) What is oxidized in this process? (b) Write the equation for that half-reaction which is an *oxidation process*. (c) Do the negative ions serve any useful purpose in the operation of the cell? Explain. (d) Diagram the half-cell in which oxidation occurs. Label the electrode and the solution around it. (It will be convenient here to use the porous cup as a container for the half-cell.) (e) What is the electrode called which is undergoing oxidation? (f) Write the equation for that half-reaction which is a *reduction process*. Diagram the half-cell for this process and identify the material used for the electrode and the compound dissolved in the solution. (g) What is the name of the electrode in the half-cell where reduction is occurring? (h) Combine the half-cells of parts (d) and (f) to give a complete cell; then indicate the direction of electron flow in the external circuit. Indicate the direction of movement of positive ions in the cell. Indicate the direction of movement of negative ions in the cell. Which half-cell electrode would be labeled negative? (i) Suppose 2 moles of silver atoms were deposited. How many moles of cadmium atoms would dissolve? How many grams of Cd would dissolve if 2.0 grams of silver metal plated out?

2 (a) In one step of the photographic "toning" process the following reaction takes place:

$$3Ag(s) + Au^{3+} \longrightarrow Au(s) + 3Ag^+$$

Could this reaction be used as the reaction for an electrochemical cell? If so, answer parts (a) to (h) of question 1 as they apply to this new process. (b) Could one use the reaction

$$Ag^+ + NO_3^- + K^+ + Cl^- \longrightarrow$$
$$AgCl(s) + K^+ + NO_3^-$$

for an electrochemical cell? If so, answer question 1 as it applies to this process. If not, indicate why the reaction cannot be used.

3 It is known that copper ion has a greater attraction for electrons than does cadmium ion. (a) Can this information be used to write the overall equation for the process in an electrochemical cell which uses strips of Cu, of Cd, and appropriate solutions of $Cu(NO_3)_2$ and $Cd(NO_3)_2$? If so, write the equation. (b) Diagram the electrochemical cell using the reaction in (a) and indicate the negative electrode or anode; the direction of flow of electrons in the external circuit; the direction of flow of positive ions in the cell; the direction of flow of negative ions in the cell; and the place where an oxidation reaction occurs. (c) If the cell is run until there is a mass change of 4.13 g in the copper electrode, what mass change will occur at the cadmium electrode? Indicate whether mass is gained or lost.

4 Can the reaction between iron metal and aqueous hydrochloric acid be used as the basis for an electrochemical cell? If so, diagram the cell and describe any special features which were not a part of the cells in questions 1, 2, and 3.

5 In a series of experiments comparable to those described in Section 15-2.1, the following observations were made: A standard cobalt half-cell (Co^{2+}–Co) was connected to a standard zinc half-cell. When the switch was first closed the voltmeter deflected to the right giving a voltage of $+0.48$ volt with zinc being oxidized. When the zinc half-cell was replaced by a standard tin half-cell (Sn^{2+}–Sn) the voltmeter deflected left to give a voltage of -0.14 volt. (Cobalt is now the anode.) (a) What would be the E^0 for the standard $Zn^{2+} + 2e^- \longrightarrow Zn(s)$ half-reaction if the standard $Co^{2+} + 2e^- \longrightarrow Co(s)$ half-cell were used as the reference electrode? (b) What would be the comparable E^0 for the $Sn^{2+} + 2e^- \longrightarrow Sn(s)$ half-reaction? (Cobalt is the reference standard.) (c) What would be the standard voltage of the cell using the reaction

$$Zn(s) + Sn^{2+} \longrightarrow Zn^{2+} + Sn(s)$$

(d) A Cu^{2+}–Cu half-cell is now connected to the Sn^{2+}–Sn half-cell and the voltmeter deflects to the right to give a voltage read as +0.48 volt. (Tin is dissolving, copper is plating.) What would the E^0 of the Cu^{2+}–Cu half-cell be if the Co^{2+}–Co cell were arbitrarily selected as zero?

6 What would the standard voltages of the Cu^{2+}–Cu, Co^{2+}–Co, and Sn^{2+}–Sn cells be if the Zn^{2+}–Zn half-cell were selected as zero?

7 The E^0 value for the half-reaction $Ag(s) \longrightarrow Ag^+ + e^-$ as written is -0.80 volt. What would happen to the measured half-cell value (H^+–H_2 reference) if a salt solution (NaCl) were added to the solution around the silver electrode? Which one of the following values would be most reasonable: -0.40; -0.80; -1.20? Explain.

8 (a) What would be the standard voltage (E^0) of a cell based on the reaction

$$Zn(s) + Cu^{2+} \longrightarrow Zn^{2+} + Cu(s)$$

(b) What would happen to the voltage of this cell if sodium sulfide solution were added to the solution around the zinc electrode? (Remember that ZnS is insoluble.) Explain your answer. (c) What would happen to the voltage if solid copper sulfate were dissolved in the solution around the copper electrode? (d) What would happen to the voltage if sodium sulfide were added to the solution around the copper electrode? (CuS is insoluble.)

9 The overall equation for a relative of the lead storage battery is

$$Pb(s) + PbO_2(s) + 4H^+ \longrightarrow$$
$$2Pb^{2+} + 2H_2O$$

(a) $Pb(ClO_4)_2$ is water-soluble and $PbSO_4$ is insoluble. Would $HClO_4$ be as useful as H_2SO_4 in making a lead storage battery? Explain, considering only the effect on cell voltage. (b) The E^0 half-cell potential for the reaction $Pb(s) \longrightarrow Pb^{2+} + 2e^-$ is +0.13 volt as written, while for the process $PbO_2(s) + 4H^+ + 2e^- \longrightarrow Pb^{2+} + 2H_2O$ the value is +1.46 volts. What voltage would be expected for the overall cell PbO_2–Pb?

10 A standard Pb^{2+}–Pb half-cell is connected to a standard Zn^{2+}–Zn cell and allowed to run spontaneously. (a) Write the two half-reactions and the net ionic equation for the overall reaction occurring in the cell. (b) Using E^0 values, predict the voltage as the cell first begins to operate. (c) Use Le Chatelier's principle to describe the effect on cell voltage of increasing the concentration of Zn^{2+} ions; of increasing the concentration of Pb^{2+} ions; of adding solid NaI to the Pb^{2+}–Pb

cell (remember that PbI_2 is insoluble); of doubling the size of the lead electrode; and of letting the cell run for half an hour.

11 Use the table of E^0 values in Appendix 7 and the information that many fruits and all carbonated drinks are quite acidic [containing $H^+(aq)$ ion] to explain the following: (a) Cavities in teeth are filled with gold or a silver-mercury amalgam rather than with aluminum or zinc. (b) An unpleasant sensation is felt when aluminum foil accidentally gets in the mouth. (c) Considering only its position in the table of E^0 values, would copper be a satisfactory material for dental fillings? Zinc? Lithium? Explain. Is electrical activity the only important property for filling materials?

12 What will happen if a solution of silver nitrate ($AgNO_3$) is prepared in an aluminum pan? Would it be satisfactory to prepare an aluminum nitrate [$Al(NO_3)_3$] solution in a silver container? Explain, using E^0 values.

13 Use E^0 values to predict which of the following equations should be spontaneous as written. Explain the basis for your choice in each case. (See Table 15-4.)

(a) $Zn(s) + I_2(aq) \longrightarrow Zn^{2+} + 2I^-$
(b) $Zn^{2+} + 2H^+ \longrightarrow Zn(s) + H_2(g)$
(c) $Ag(s) + H^+ \longrightarrow Ag^+ + \frac{1}{2}H_2(g)$
(d) $5Cu(s) + 2K^+ + 2MnO_4^- + 16H^+ \longrightarrow$
$$5Cu^{2+} + 2Mn^{2+} + 8H_2O + 2K^+$$
(e) $2Ag(s) + Br_2(aq) \longrightarrow 2AgBr(s)$

14 Calculate the E^0 value for each of the following processes. All products and reactants are assumed at standard concentration for E^0 measurement.

(a) $Co(s) + 2H^+ \longrightarrow H_2(g) + Co^{2+}$
(b) $Zn(s) + 2Cr^{3+} \longrightarrow Zn^{2+} + 2Cr^{2+}$
(c) $Cr(s) + 2H^+ \longrightarrow Cr^{3+} + H_2(g)$
(d) $2Cr^{2+} + 2H^+ \longrightarrow 2Cr^{3+} + H_2(g)$

15 A Ce^{4+}–Ce^{3+} half-cell when connected to a Fe^{3+}–Fe^{2+} half-cell has an overall voltage of +0.84 volt. The iron electrode is the anode in the cell. Determine the E^0 value of the Ce^{4+}–Ce^{3+} half-reaction, using the H^+–H_2 standard.

16 Would you expect the tin coating on a "tin can" to dissolve in 1 M HCl? Write the appropriate equation and calculate the E^0 value.

17 Hydrogen sulfide solution is poured into cold, concentrated laboratory nitric acid. The solution goes milky (S) and a brown gas (NO_2)

bubbles out. Write the equation which describes these observations and calculate E^0 for the process.

18 A set of reactants and a set of products are listed below for eight different systems. Write balanced equations for each system using half-cell reactions to balance the equations.

(a) $Cu(s) + NO_3^- + H^+$ gives
$$Cu^{2+} + NO_2(g) + H_2O$$

(b) $Fe^{2+} + MnO_4^- + H^+$ gives
$$Fe^{3+} + Mn^{2+} + H_2O$$

(c) $H_2S(g) + NO_3^- + H^+$ gives
$$S(s) + NO_2(g) + H_2O$$

(d) $Cl_2(g) + SO_2(g) + H_2O$ gives
$$SO_4^{2-} + Cl^- + H^+$$

(e) $Cr_2O_7^{2-} + I^- + H^+$ gives
$$Cr^{3+} + I_2(s) + H_2O$$

(f) $H_2O_2 + Cl^- + H^+$ gives $H_2O + Cl_2(g)$

(g) $MnO_2(s) + Fe^{2+} + H^+$ gives
$$Mn^{2+} + Fe^{3+} + H_2O$$

(h) $NO_3^- + Sn^{2+} + H^+$ gives
$$NO(g) + Sn^{4+} + H_2O$$

19 When copper is placed in concentrated nitric acid, vigorous bubbling takes place as a brown gas evolves. The copper disappears and the solution changes from colorless to a greenish-blue. The brown gas is nitrogen dioxide (NO_2) and the color of the solution

is caused by the presence of copper(II) ion, Cu^{2+}. Using half-reactions from Appendix 7, write the net ionic equation for this process.

20 Sodium metal and chlorine gas are produced by the electrolysis of molten sodium chloride (NaCl). (a) Draw a diagram of a cell for electrolysis of NaCl. Label the anode and cathode. (b) Write the equation for the anode and cathode half-reactions and the overall reaction. (c) Estimate the minimum voltage necessary for electrolysis to occur. (Use aqueous solution potentials as a basis for your estimate.) (d) Explain, using E^0 values, why a sodium chloride solution in water cannot be electrolyzed with platinum electrodes to give sodium and chlorine as products.

21 Estimate the voltage required to electrolyze a 1 M solution of $CuBr_2$.

22 In order to make $Na(s)$ and $Cl_2(g)$, an electric current is passed through $NaCl(l)$. What does the energy supplied to this reaction do?

23 Silver-plating of copper ornaments or utensils is done by electrolysis of a soluble silver compound with the object to be plated as one of the electrodes. (a) In silver-plating a copper ornament, should the ornament be the anode or cathode of the cell? (b) If 5.40 g of silver are deposited, how many moles of electrons must pass through the wires connecting the electrodes?

Treat electrons like light waves. Though they are bullets, they are also waves.

LOUIS de BROGLIE (1892–)

ELECTROMAGNETIC RADIATION 16
AND ATOMIC STRUCTURE

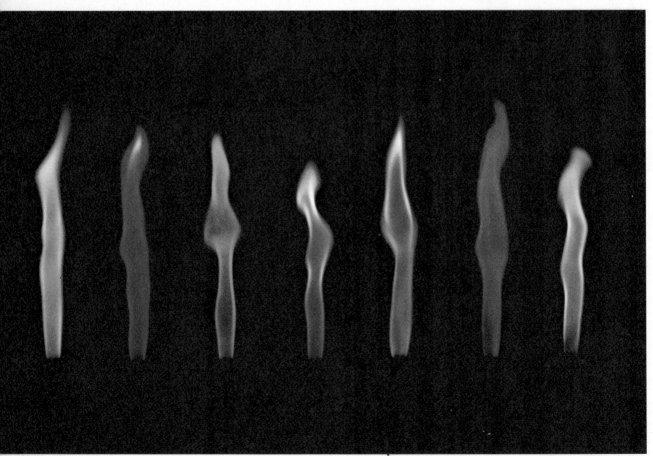

Flame tests for different ions; from left to right: Na^+ in NaCl, Li^+ in LiCl, Cu^{2+} in $CuCl_2$, K^+ in KCl, Ca^{2+} in $CaCl_2$, Sr^{2+} in $SrCl_2$, and Ba^{2+} in $BaCl_2$.

ONE OF THE CONCEPTS YOU'LL HAVE TO GIVE UP IN THIS CHAPTER is the belief that electrons are particles which whiz rapidly around the nucleus in discrete orbits. It's a nice, neat concept, but it doesn't happen to agree with the observed facts. So it's time to shed your security blanket, see what the facts are, and what new model we can build to agree with them. The clue here is in the similarity of the behavior of electrons to that of light, of all things. Good grief! But light at least is familiar to us; we can see it and measure it, and even though the idea of the electron behaving as a wave is foreign to us, we can come up with a model that leaves us somewhat less in the dark.

So far a relatively simple model of the atom has been adequate for all of our discussion of the properties of substances. Building on the original Rutherford model, we visualized a very small, very dense nucleus composed of protons and neutrons; surrounding this nucleus we pictured just enough electrons to neutralize the positive nuclear charge. On the basis of ionization-energy measurements, we were able to achieve a rough subdivision of the electrons of the atom into "energy groups"; but little detailed information on electronic arrangement was available.

Our situation is not too different from that facing the scientific community in 1912. Following Rutherford's proposal of a nuclear model for the atom (review Section 7-1.2), three questions arose:

(1) What is the detailed structure of the nucleus?
(2) What keeps the nucleus from exploding as a result of the mutual repulsion of its components? (It contains densely packed protons, all bearing the same positive charge.)
(3) How are the electrons arranged around the nucleus?

In 1974, the answers to questions (1) and (2) are still fuzzy, but a large amount of information is available on question (3). Since the electronic structure of the atom is of major importance in chemistry, we shall examine the evidence and the new ideas associated with the details of atomic structure.

The evidence for the electronic arrangement of atoms comes from a rather unexpected source—*a study of color*. What can be learned about light and color?

EXERCISE 16-1

Review electron groupings shown in Chapter 8.

(1) Complete the following table.

Noble Gas	Number Electrons in Atom	Electrons Needed to Give Next Noble Gas
—	0	2
Helium	2	
Neon	10	
___	___	
___	___	
___	___	

(2) Assume another noble gas were found. What would be a reasonable estimate of its atomic number? Explain.

(3) Can you predict the next number beyond 32 in the third column of the table? Explain how you did it.

16-1 LIGHT AND COLOR

The subject of color raises many "wondering why" questions in thoughtful minds. For example, we might ask: why is a copper sulfate solution blue? (See Figure 16-1.) Why does a sodium vapor lamp glow with a yellow light, while a neon sign is bright red? Why does a color television tube glow red, green, and blue? In seeking answers to these questions, scientists developed a more detailed model of the atom. Let us follow the trail.

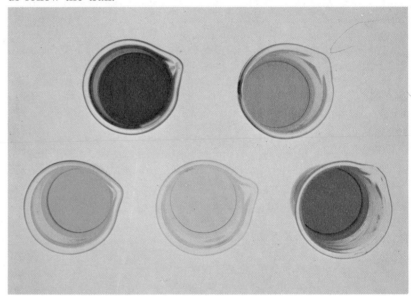

Fig. 16-1 The colored solutions of different compounds in water; from left to right: top row, $[Cu(NH_3)_4]SO_4$, $[Co(NH_3)_6]Cl_3$; bottom row, $CuSO_4$, $K[AuCl_4]$, $CoSO_4$.

All of us associate color with light; it is logical then to ask: what is the nature of light? Is it made up of little particles, or is it a continuous wavy stream? Is it a "solid ray," as a solid "beam" of sunlight might be? Be prepared for some exciting new thoughts and ideas as we explore these questions and the modern quantum theory. Its concepts revolutionized much of our view of nature.

16-1.1 The Nature of Light

Have you ever noticed the colors arising from an oil film on water? Or have you watched the rapidly changing colors in a soap bubble as it drifts in the sunlight? Perhaps you have seen diffraction jewelry (Figure 16-2). A sample may even be available in your classroom. The surface of such diffraction jewelry displays a variety of colors which change as you look at the jewelry from different angles. The surface is marked with many fine, closely spaced lines. The color arises from the interaction of white light with these closely spaced lines. The phenomena shown by the oil film, the soap bubble, and the jewelry

Fig. 16-2 A piece of diffraction jewelry.

are examples of what we call *diffraction* or *interference*. These phenomena can be best explained if we assume that light is a wavelike disturbance. By making this assumption, scientists during the last century developed an impressive wave theory of light. In modified form it is still in use. If light is to be described in terms of waves, it will be helpful to examine some of the characteristics of waves.

16-1.2 Waves and Their Characteristics

Have you ever watched waves rolling into the shore? If so, you have noticed that some waves are large, others are small. With large waves, the water surface at the top, or crest, is many feet above the water surface at the bottom, or trough. In technical language, we say that the large wave has a large **amplitude,** the *vertical distance from equilibrium point to crest;* small waves have a small amplitude. We could also measure the *horizontal distance between crests.* This is the **wavelength** (see Figure 16-3). For ocean waves, metres would be a suitable unit for wavelength.

We are interested in one other property of ocean waves—the **frequency.** It may be determined by counting the *number of crests* that pass a particular point *in a given period of time,* or by counting the waves that break on the shore during a given period of time. A suitable unit for the frequency of ocean waves would be wave crests per 15 minutes. We could describe the frequency of other waves such as light in terms of *vibrations per second* or in terms of *cycles per second,* where a cycle means a complete vibration. Note that the unit has time in the denominator in all cases.

Fig. 16-3 Amplitude, wavelength, and wave velocity for ocean waves.

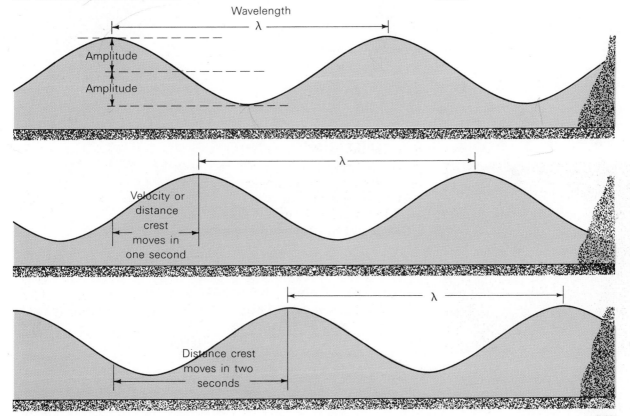

The frequency of light waves is given by the Greek letter nu (ν). Sometimes the word *vibration* in the expression for frequency is understood and the frequency, ν, is given in units of 1/sec or sec^{-1}. The wavelength of light is called lambda (λ) and is given in units of length. The metre or the nanometre (10^{-9} metre) is the preferred unit* for the short wavelengths found with light.

What is the relationship between frequency and wavelength? Consider a wave traveling from the sea toward the shore. The number of crests reaching the shore in a given period of time (frequency of wave) is determined by how fast the waves are coming in and by the distance between crests. If the waves are coming in at a fast rate, the number of crests reaching the shore per unit of time will be large. If, however, each crest is coming in fairly slowly, the number of crests reaching the shore in a given period of time will be smaller. Similarly, if the wavelength (distance between crests) is large, the number of crests reaching the shore in unit time will be less than if the wavelength is small. We can express this relationship as

$$\frac{\left\{\begin{array}{c}\text{number of crests}\\ \text{reaching shore}\end{array}\right\}}{\text{unit of time}} = \text{frequency} = \frac{\text{velocity of ocean wave}}{\text{wavelength of ocean wave}} \quad (1)$$

(See Figure 16-3.) For light this relationship is given in a very useful form by the equation

$$\text{frequency of light} = \frac{\text{velocity of light}}{\text{wavelength of light}} \quad (2)$$

or

$$\nu = \frac{c}{\lambda} = \frac{3.0 \times 10^8 \text{ metres/sec}}{\lambda} \quad (2a)$$

where c = velocity of light, ν = frequency of light, and λ = wavelength of light.

EXERCISE 16-2

What is the frequency of light with a wavelength of $5,000 \times 10^{-10}$ metre? (Remember, velocity of light is 3.0×10^8 metres/sec.)

16-1.3 What Waves in Light Waves?

In an ocean, water moves up and down to give *waves;* when a flag *waves* in the wind, the cloth moves back and forth; and so on. With these easily visualized waves, something moves. This seems to be common sense. If, then, light is a wave, what waves? What moves to define the wave of light? The answer to this question is not easily found, but an analogy based on a simple experiment may be helpful. First, we need some new concepts.

*Other units of length can also be used. For example, the centimetre (10^{-2} metre), the micron (10^{-6} metre), the millimicron (10^{-9} metre), and the ångstrom (10^{-10} metre) still appear in scientific literature.

16-1.4 Oscillating Magnetic and Electric Fields

Fig. 16-4 Deflection of a compass needle by a bar magnet.

If we bring the north pole of a bar magnet up to the north pole of a compass needle, the needle moves *away* from the bar magnet [Figure 16-4(b)]. If we turn the magnet over so that the south pole of the bar magnet is near the north pole of the compass needle, the needle moves *toward* the magnet [Figure 16-4(c)]. The needle is pushed or pulled by the bar magnet. The effect is the same whether air is present or absent from the system. *The attractive or repulsive force of a magnet is carried through empty space.*

Scientists are fond of giving names to phenomena when they cannot construct a simple model to describe what they see. Let us do that here. Although we cannot explain in a simple form *how* the magnet attracts the needle, we can assign a name to describe what we see. We say that there is a **magnetic field** arising and radiating from the bar magnet which pushes or pulls the compass needle. The field is strongest very near the end or pole of the magnet and rapidly grows weaker as we move away from the pole. If the bar magnet in Figure 16-4 is slowly rotated, we shall see that the needle is first pushed out from the bar magnet and then pulled toward it. The magnetic field is changing from a push to a pull and back again.

If we plot the position of the needle tip as a function of time, we find that it traces out a wavelike pattern. The changing magnetic field, which makes the needle move in a wavelike pattern, might be described as an "oscillating magnetic field" which swings from a push to a pull, or as a **magnetic wave.** The magnetic wave is being carried through empty space as an alternating push or pull, or as an **oscillating force field.** We can identify the **source** of the oscillating magnetic field as the moving magnet. The oscillating needle represents the **receiver** or detector. In many of our studies of light and other forms of radiation, we shall be able to identify a *source* (a light bulb for light, a broadcasting antenna for a radio or television station) and a *receiver* (the eye for light or your receiving set for radio and television).

Similar experiments in which a charged plate moves show that an oscillating electric field can be set up. The oscillating nature of the field is generated by the movement of the charged plate. We find further that whenever a charged body moves, it generates a magnetic field in addition to the electric field. This is the principle of the common and widely used electromagnet. *A moving charged particle has both electric and magnetic fields associated with it.* Let us now tie these observations to light and color.

16-1.5 Electromagnetic Radiation and Light

In the period 1864–1873, James Clerk Maxwell,* a gifted Scotsman, predicted that if a moving charged body is accelerated (speeded up or slowed down), oscillating electric and magnetic fields will radiate from the charged particles at a velocity of 3.0×10^8 metres/sec. Maxwell's prediction was verified by Heinrich Hertz (1857–1894) eight

*James Clerk Maxwell (1831–1879) was a Scotsman who served on the faculties of both Scottish and British universities. At the time of his death, he was Professor of Experimental Physics at Cambridge, England. His work on electromagnetic theory must surely stand as one of the most brilliant intellectual achievements in history.

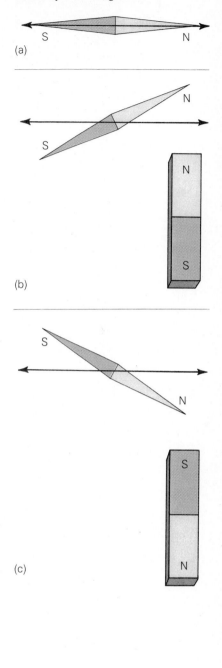

(a)

(b)

(c)

years after Maxwell's death. The oscillating fields constitute **electromagnetic radiation.** Light is one form of electromagnetic radiation. Radio waves are another. Both are made up of oscillating electric and magnetic force fields in which the push and pull of the magnetic field is at right angles to the push and pull of the electric field (Figure 16-5). These waves are transmitted through empty space at 3.0×10^8 metres/sec. This velocity of light is indicated by the letter c.

Fig. 16-5 The electric and magnetic force fields of electromagnetic radiation such as sunlight are at right angles to each other.

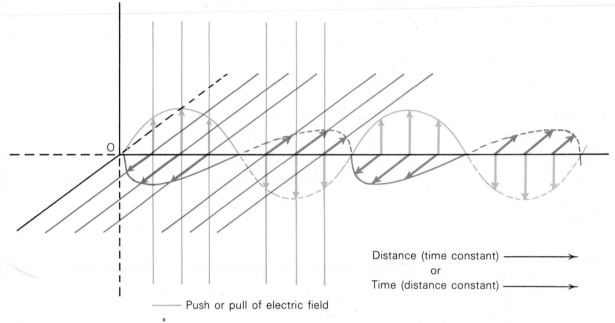

Distance (time constant) ⟶

or

Time (distance constant) ⟶

—— Push or pull of electric field

Push or pull of magnetic field

The simple facts we have just discussed stand at the core of our radio and television industries. A radio or television transmitting station pumps charges (electrons) along an antenna. (The charges speed up, slow down, stop, then speed up in the reverse direction.) Power from the station is used to pump the charges back and forth. As these change speed, electromagnetic radio waves break away from the antenna and travel through space at 3.0×10^8 metres/sec. The waves have the *frequency* of the oscillating charges in the antenna. Your radio or television set, when properly tuned, serves as the *detector*. It picks up the signal and converts the weak electromagnetic waves into sound or pictures.

The color of compounds has its origin in a surprisingly similar set of events. The movement of electrons from higher energy levels to lower ones generates electromagnetic waves of short wavelength. Light is emitted. Conversely, if energy is absorbed, electrons jump to a higher level.

16-1.6 The Electromagnetic Spectrum

Our description of electromagnetic radiation indicates that radio waves and visible light are different examples of the same fundamental phenomenon. How do these waves differ? Experiments on ordinary sunlight help provide the answer. If a very narrow "beam" of sunlight passes through a glass prism, it spreads out into a bright **spectrum** of colors—violet, indigo, blue, green, yellow, orange, red. The colors are those of the rainbow; they are best seen when displayed on a white screen (see Figure 16-6, following page). (The spectrum can be recorded on a photographic plate if study at a later date is desired.) Detailed studies of prism action indicate that the prism separates light of different wavelengths into different bands. Red light has the longest wavelength (λ) and the lowest frequency (ν) (remember: $\nu = c/\lambda$); a beam of red light is bent the least in going through the prism. Violet light has the shortest wavelength (λ) and the highest frequency (ν); a beam of violet light is bent the most in going through the prism. The wavelengths and frequencies of the visible spectral colors are shown in Table 16-1.

TABLE 16-1 SPECTRAL COLORS AND THE WAVELENGTHS OF VARIOUS REGIONS OF THE ELECTROMAGNETIC SPECTRUM

Color	Wavelength (λ) ($\times 10^{-7}$ metre)	Frequency (ν) (vibrations/sec)
Ultraviolet	2.0 to 4.0	15 to 7.5×10^{14}
Violet	4.0 to 4.2 (4.1)*	7.5 to 7.1×10^{14}
Blue	4.2 to 4.9 (4.7)	7.1 to 6.1×10^{14}
Green	4.9 to 5.8 (5.2)	6.1 to 5.2×10^{14}
Yellow	5.8 to 5.9 (5.8)	5.2 to 5.1×10^{14}
Orange	5.9 to 6.5 (6.0)	5.1 to 4.6×10^{14}
Red	6.5 to 7.0 (6.5)	4.6 to 4.3×10^{14}
Infrared	longer than 7.0	less than 4.3×10^{14}
Radio	2200	1.4×10^{12}

*The values in parentheses represent the wavelengths most characteristically recognized as the pure colors.

EXERCISE 16-3

The light produced by a sodium vapor lamp shows two lines with wavelengths of 5.89×10^{-7} metre and 5.90×10^{-7} metre. Identify the color of the sodium vapor lamp using the data assembled in Table 16-1. What color is the light from a potassium vapor lamp if the spectral lines for potassium have wavelengths of 4.044×10^{-7} metre and 4.047×10^{-7} metre? What color is a mercury vapor lamp if the frequencies of the lines are 6.6×10^{14} vibrations/sec and 5.5×10^{14} vibrations/sec? Estimate the wavelength of one of the most intense lines in the *neon* spectrum. Remember the color of neon light. (To check your answers, refer to the photograph at the beginning of the chapter.)

In order to resolve a beam of light into its spectral colors in the laboratory, a somewhat more elaborate prism arrangement is usually used. Such an instrument is known as a **spectrometer** (an instrument which measures spectra).

Even a casual inspection of Table 16-1 shows that the visible electromagnetic spectrum covers a very narrow range of frequencies. Examination of a photographic plate upon which the spectrum of sunlight has been registered shows dark regions at positions beyond

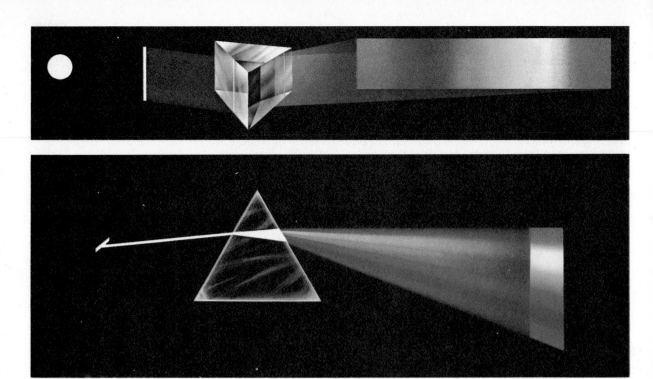

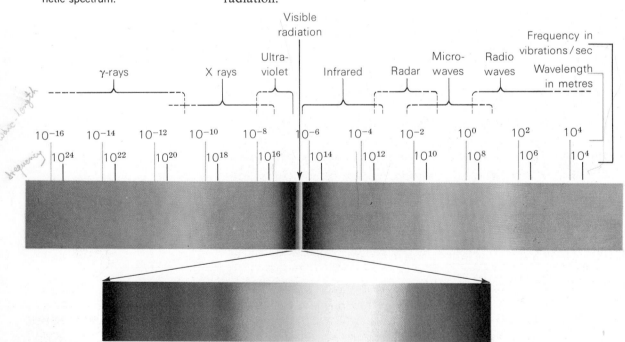

Fig. 16-6.1 (Top) The spectrum of visible light.

Fig. 16-6.2 (Bottom) The action of a prism on white light.

Fig. 16-7 The whole electromagnetic spectrum.

that of visible light in both directions. The dark area corresponding to frequencies higher than that of violet is called **ultraviolet.** The dark area corresponding to frequencies lower than that of red is called **infrared.** Still lower frequencies are called **radio** waves. The visible spectrum is only a part of the total electromagnetic spectrum, shown schematically in Figure 16-7 and summarized in Table 16-2. X rays have a very short wavelength while heat (infrared) is long-wavelength radiation.

TABLE 16-2 SPECTRUM OF ELECTROMAGNETIC RADIATION

Name of Radiation	Approximate Range of Wavelength
Radio waves	a few metres and up
Microwaves	a few millimetres to a few metres
Infrared waves	$7,500 \times 10^{-10}$ metre to 10^{-4} metre
Visible light	$4,000$ to $7,500 \times 10^{-10}$ metre
Ultraviolet light	100 to $4,000 \times 10^{-10}$ metre
X rays	0.1 to 500×10^{-10} metre
Gamma rays	less than 0.5×10^{-10} metre

16-1.7   A Summary of the Nature of Light

Light is a form of electromagnetic radiation which can be characterized by the radiation **frequency** (v), which is the number of field oscillations or vibrations per second, and by the **wavelength** (λ) of the radiation, which is the distance between wave crests. These numbers are related by a common-sense formula which can be verified on any good beach:

$$\text{frequency of light} = v = \frac{c}{\lambda} = \frac{\text{velocity of light}}{\text{wavelength}} \qquad (2b)$$

Red light has relatively low frequency and long wavelength. Violet light has high frequency and short wavelength. **Ultraviolet** radiation has higher frequency than violet; **infrared** radiation has lower frequency than red.

16-2   ENERGY AND AN INTERPRETATION OF THE HYDROGEN SPECTRUM

16-2.1   Electromagnetic Radiation and Energy

Sunlight is a form of energy. Remember how warm it gets in the sunshine, even on a cool day? The sun feels even warmer if you have on dark-colored clothes, which absorb the sunlight.*

The connection between light and kinetic energy is easy to visualize if we remember the simple experiment in which a fluctuating magnetic field made the compass needle move. The compass needle picked up kinetic energy (energy of motion) from the fluctuating magnetic field. In a similar manner, motions of electrons and of atoms in molecules may be induced by the fluctuating electromagnetic fields present in radiation. Under appropriate conditions radiation can increase the molecular energy very substantially.

How much energy is carried by light? The answer, as given by Max Planck (1858–1947), is: "it all depends on color or radiation frequency." Planck proposed that light is made up of bundles of energy called **quanta.** The energy in any one bundle is dependent upon the color of the light. Violet light has more energy per bundle than does red light; red light has more energy than does infrared; and infrared

---

*As we use up our fossil fuels and other forms of energy, we look more and more carefully at sunlight as a source of clean, abundant energy. This is one of the challenges of our age.

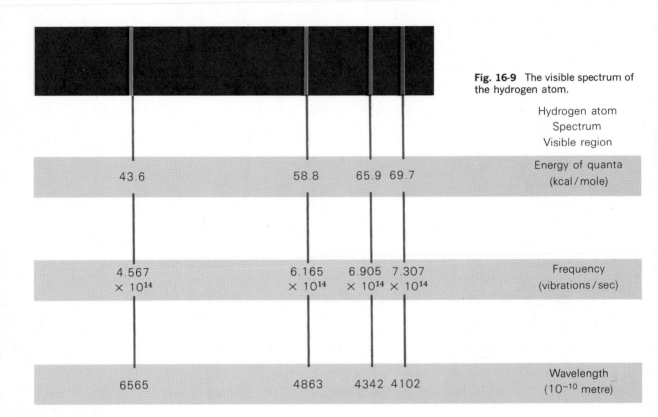

Fig. 16-8 The visible spectrum of neon.

Fig. 16-9 The visible spectrum of the hydrogen atom.

Hydrogen atom
Spectrum
Visible region

			Energy of quanta (kcal/mole)
43.6	58.8	65.9 69.7	

			Frequency (vibrations/sec)
4.567 × 10¹⁴	6.165 × 10¹⁴	6.905 × 10¹⁴ 7.307 × 10¹⁴	

			Wavelength (10⁻¹⁰ metre)
6565	4863	4342 4102	

has more energy than does a radio wave. Planck's proposal can be given in quantitative terms by a simple relationship between energy and frequency of the radiation:

$$\begin{Bmatrix} \text{energy per quantum} \\ \text{of light (or radiation)} \end{Bmatrix} = \begin{Bmatrix} \text{proportionality} \\ \text{constant} \end{Bmatrix} \times \begin{Bmatrix} \text{frequency} \\ \text{of light} \end{Bmatrix} \quad (3)$$

Using symbols, we write

$$E = h\nu \qquad (3a)$$

The letter h stands for a simple proportionality constant and is known as **Planck's constant of action.** It is equal to 1.58×10^{-37} kcal × sec.* This simple equation, $E = h\nu$, is one of the most important and powerful statements of modern science.

*Planck's constant is also expressed in other units as 6.63×10^{-34} joules × sec.

16-2.2 Energy Changes and the Hydrogen Spectrum

You may be wondering what light has to do with atomic structure. To answer such a question let us look at the light given off by a "hydrogen light." A hydrogen light is related to a neon light. You will recall that a tube containing low-pressure neon gas glows with a beautiful red color when electricity is passed through it. This red light is the heart of the electric sign business. If the light from the neon tube is passed through the spectrometer, bright red and even green lines appear. (A color photo of the spectrum of the neon light is shown in Figure 16-8.) If a tube containing low-pressure hydrogen is used instead of low-pressure neon, a light with a purplish color is emitted. When this light is passed through the spectrometer, the series of lines shown in Figure 16-9 appears. Each line in the spectrum corresponds to a given pure color or frequency given off by hydrogen atoms. Every hydrogen discharge lamp emits the same small group of "lines" or frequencies.

Let us now try to put our ideas about light and the observations on the hydrogen spectrum together to get a model for the hydrogen atom. Progress began when a physicist, J. R. Rydberg (1854–1919), found empirically that the frequency of all of the lines in the visible part of the hydrogen spectrum could be given by a simple relationship:

$$\nu = 3.287 \times 10^{15}\left(\frac{1}{2^2} - \frac{1}{n^2}\right) \text{ vibrations/sec} \qquad (4)$$

where n was 3, 4, 5, 6, and so on.

EXERCISE 16-4

(1) Calculate the frequency of the line where $n = 3$. Which one of the lines in Figure 16-9 does this represent? Repeat for $n = 4$ and $n = \infty$.

(2) Another set of frequencies exists where the formula is

$$\nu = 3.287 \times 10^{15}\left(\frac{1}{1^2} - \frac{1}{n^2}\right) \text{ vibrations/sec}$$

What frequency would be associated with the line where $n = 3$? Where would this line occur: visible, ultraviolet, or infrared? (See Table 16-1.)

(3) A formula

$$\nu = 3.287 \times 10^{15}\left(\frac{1}{3^2} - \frac{1}{n^2}\right) \text{ vibrations/sec}$$

also exists. Where would these lines appear: visible, ultraviolet, or infrared? (See Table 16-1.)

[*Answer to (2)*: ultraviolet. *Note:* all lines predicted by the Rydberg relationship can be found experimentally.]

As noted in Exercise 16-4, the Rydberg relationship could be expanded to predict many more spectral lines, all of which were found.

Now we need a model to account for the Rydberg equation. The equation is of the general form:

$$\nu = \frac{k}{n_1{}^2} - \frac{k}{n_2{}^2} \tag{5}$$

where $k = 3.287 \times 10^{15}$ vibrations/sec.

The original hydrogen atom has some definite amount of energy; let us call it $E_{initial}$. When light of frequency ν is emitted, energy, $h\nu$, is carried away. The hydrogen atom now has less energy than it did before; let us call this smaller amount of energy E_{final}. Since energy must be conserved in atomic physics, we say that the energy *given off* in the radiation must be exactly equal to the difference between initial and final energy states of the atom.

$$\left\{ \begin{matrix} \text{energy } \textit{given off} \\ \text{in radiation} \end{matrix} \right\} =$$

$$\left\{ \begin{matrix} \text{energy of atom } \textit{before} \\ \text{radiation emitted} \end{matrix} \right\} - \left\{ \begin{matrix} \text{energy of atom } \textit{after} \\ \text{radiation emitted} \end{matrix} \right\} \tag{6}$$

or, symbolically:

$$E_{given\ off} = h\nu = E_{initial} - E_{final} \tag{6a}$$

Perhaps the spectral lines for hydrogen can be interpreted if we assume that hydrogen atoms exist in distinct and reproducible energy states, where the initial energy state is $hk/n_1{}^2$ and the final energy state is $hk/n_2{}^2$. The energy given off is then

$$E_{given\ off} = \frac{hk}{n_1{}^2} - \frac{hk}{n_2{}^2} \tag{7}$$

Since $E_{given\ off} = h\nu$, we can write

$$h\nu = \frac{hk}{n_1{}^2} - \frac{hk}{n_2{}^2} \tag{7a}$$

or

$$\nu = \frac{k}{n_1{}^2} - \frac{k}{n_2{}^2} \tag{5}$$

The equation is identical to that of Rydberg.

16-2.3 The Quantum Model for the Hydrogen Atom

The light given off by an excited hydrogen atom corresponds to a change in the energy of the hydrogen atom from a condition of higher to a condition of lower energy. Since only certain lines appear in the spectrum, the hydrogen atom seems to be using only *a limited number of energy levels*. A model will help to make this point clearer. Let us assume that the modernistic bookcase shown in Figure 16-10 has been designed by an avante-garde artist. Let us now put a large paperweight on the bottom shelf of this bookcase. The paperweight cannot fall anywhere; the system is in its lowest energy state, or in its "ground state." If, however, we pick up the paperweight and place it on shelf 2 of the bookcase, work must be done to lift the weight from the bottom shelf, 1, to the next shelf, 2. If the paperweight falls from shelf 2 to shelf 1, energy will be released. The energy released will be exactly equal to the amount of energy used to raise the paperweight from shelf 1 to shelf 2. The kinetic energy of the paperweight just before it hits the bottom shelf will be equal to the difference in potential energy of the paperweight on shelves 2 and 1. There are no intermediate levels or shelves between shelves 2 and 1, so the paperweight can have only potential energy 2 or 1, so far. The weight will always gain the *same amount* of kinetic energy as it falls from level 2 to level 1. When the weight hits the floor and stops, its kinetic energy will be converted to heat. The weight and the floor will be a little warmer after collision than they were before.

Suppose we now raise the weight to level 3 and let it fall to level 1. The kinetic energy of the weight just before it hits the bottom shelf will be greater than it was when the weight only fell from level 2. The potential energy of the weight is greater in position 3 than in position 2, so more potential energy will be converted into kinetic energy as the weight falls from 3 to 1.

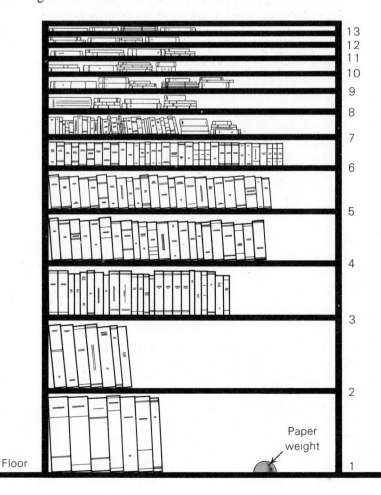

13
12
11
10
9
8
7
6
5
4
3
2
Paper weight
1
Floor

Fig. 16-10 A paperweight in a bookcase can rest only on the shelves and at no place in between.

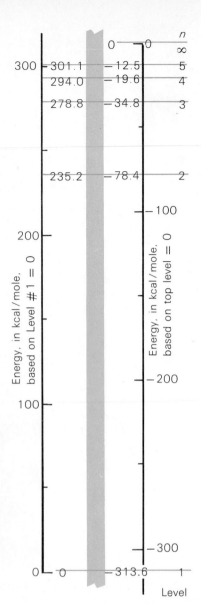

Fig. 16-11 The energy-level scheme of the hydrogen atom.

We can now write

$$\begin{Bmatrix} \text{thermal energy} \\ \text{released on} \\ \text{impact} \end{Bmatrix} = \begin{Bmatrix} \text{kinetic energy} \\ \text{of weight} \\ \text{before impact} \end{Bmatrix}$$

$$= \begin{Bmatrix} \text{potential energy} \\ \text{of weight on} \\ \text{top shelf (2 or 3)} \end{Bmatrix} - \begin{Bmatrix} \text{potential energy} \\ \text{of weight on} \\ \text{bottom shelf (1)} \end{Bmatrix} \quad (8)$$

or

$$\text{kinetic energy before impact} = E_2 - E_1 \quad (8a)$$

or

$$\text{heat released on impact} = E_2 - E_1 \quad (8b)$$

In general,

$$\text{energy released} = E_{shelf\,n} - E_{shelf\,1} = E_{initial} - E_{final} \quad (8c)$$

If the temperature increase of the weight is proportional to the heat released on impact, we see that *the same increase in temperature will always be observed as the weight falls from level 2 to level 1*. A different and higher temperature increase will be observed if the weight falls from level 3 to level 1.

Our picture of the hydrogen atom is much like our picture of the bookcase. The electron of the hydrogen atom can exist at different **energy levels** (see Figure 16-11). The electron can be placed in levels 1, 2, 3, 4, and so on, but *not* at intermediate points where no levels exist (just as with the bookcase shelves). When the electron falls from level 2 to level 1, it releases energy as electromagnetic radiation. The energy released is just equal to the difference in energy between level 2 and level 1.*

energy of electromagnetic radiation

= energy of level 2 − energy of level 1

Symbolically, we write

$$E_{released} = E_2 - E_1 = E_{initial} - E_{final} \quad (8d)$$

Since the energy released is proportional to the frequency of the radiation ($E_{released} = h\nu$), we can write

$$h\nu = E_2 - E_1 \quad (8e)$$

*There are some differences between our bookcase model and the hydrogen atom. The energy of the weight on different shelves of the bookcase is all potential energy. In contrast, the energy of the electron in level 1 or 2 of hydrogen is made up of both kinetic and potential energy.

Light of the same frequency (or color) will be given off every time an electron falls from level 2 to level 1. Light of a different frequency (or color) will be given off every time an electron falls from level 3 to level 1. Another spectral line will be seen.

The general form of the expression obtained from the "bookcase model" of the hydrogen atom,

$$h\nu = E_2 - E_1 \qquad\qquad (8e)$$

is identical to the expression obtained in the Rydberg representation of the data. So far, the bookcase model passes the first test of a good theory: it describes the experimental regularities quantitatively and in detail. If we assume that the energy of the hydrogen atom is quantized—that is, it exists in separate and distinct levels—we can "explain" the hydrogen spectrum.

16-3 ATOMIC MODELS—PROBLEMS WITH MECHANICAL MODELS

So far all we have done is state that the electron in a hydrogen atom can exist in *any one* of many different and distinct *energy levels*. This same conclusion was implied by regularities in ionization energies discussed in Chapter 8. So far the model has not been very specific about how the atom looks and how one energy level differs from another. A mechanical model with orbits and moving electrons would be helpful. Unfortunately, a fundamental philosophical principle known as the "uncertainty principle"* limits the amount of detailed information that we can have about the position and velocity of an electron in an atom. We have no way to determine exactly where it is and where it is going at the same time. In short, we cannot build a nice mechanical model which places electrons in neat little paths.†

16-4 WAVE MODELS FOR THE HYDROGEN ATOM

All attempts to build mechanical models of the hydrogen atom were discouraging. Basic philosophical conflicts barred the way without pointing to a solution. A new approach was needed—an approach which began as imaginative speculation on the part of a Frenchman, Louis de Broglie (1892–   ).

---

*The "uncertainty principle" states that in any measurement, the probe or measuring stick that we use must interact with the body being measured. Such interaction must change the property of the item being measured and cause real uncertainty in the accuracy of the result. This creates a very important philosophical limitation upon the accuracy of our knowledge. The smaller the body, the greater the relative uncertainty. For example, in trying to measure the position of an electron we use a probe such as a light beam. But this light beam makes the electron move significantly, so we always have a fundamental uncertainty as to its position.

†Before the development of the uncertainty principle and its limitation on mechanical models, a brilliant Dane, Niels Bohr, did imaginative pioneering work in building a mechanical model for the atom. His atom was based on the idea of quantized energy levels as circular orbits in which electrons moved. Although Bohr's model is no longer used today, he must be recognized as one of the major architects of modern atomic theory. He was truly a scientific giant. Perhaps your teacher will tell you Bohr's fascinating story.

Planck had adopted the notion that light is not only wavelike but particle-like in character—that is, it is made up of little bundles of energy called **photons.** After pondering Planck's suggestion that light has particle-like character, de Broglie asked a significant question: if waves have some particle character, do particles have some *wave* character? Do electrons, protons, baseballs, and freight trains have a wave nature as well as a particle nature? De Broglie concluded that particles do indeed have wavelike character and he derived the equation

$$\begin{Bmatrix} \text{wavelength of} \\ \text{the matter-wave} \\ \text{associated with} \\ \text{a particle} \end{Bmatrix} = \frac{\text{Planck's constant}}{\text{mass of particle} \times \text{velocity of particle}} \qquad (9)$$

or

$$\lambda = \frac{h}{mv} \; {}^{*} \qquad (9a)$$

This relationship was soon verified experimentally for electrons by Davisson and Germer, who showed in 1927 that electrons will give diffraction patterns like light. Perhaps the best description of the atom can be given in terms of waves rather than particles? Indeed, if we use the de Broglie relationship to calculate the wavelength of an electron in an atom, we find that the electron's wavelength is comparable to the size of the atom. *Wave properties are important for electrons in atoms!* To the atom the electron appears as a wave. On the other hand, if we use the de Broglie relationship to calculate the theoretical wavelength of a baseball, we find that its wavelength is very short because its mass is large. Apples, oranges, and baseballs have wavelengths which are far too short to see or detect. They appear only as particles, not as waves. On the other hand, electrons are very light and have wavelengths comparable to atomic sizes. Electrons in atoms can be explained best if the electron is treated as a wave.

16-5 THE QUANTUM THEORY

Atoms are described today by a new form of mechanics called **wave mechanics** or **quantum mechanics.** The origin of both names should now be apparent. One reflects the wavelike nature of the electron; the other, the quantization of energy in the atom. Unfortunately, quantum mechanics (or wave mechanics), unlike classical mechanics, is fundamentally mathematical, and the physical picture of the atom it suggests is far different from the mechanical models we would like. We shall try to summarize the results of the quantum-mechanical analysis without getting lost in the mathematical jungle.

*Your teacher can show you the logic which led de Broglie to this equation.

16-5.1 The Principal Quantum Number, n

One of the very significant results of **quantum theory** is that the distinct energy levels we have mentioned can be identified by numbers called **quantum numbers.** In our bookcase analogy, numbers increased as the shelves went from bottom to top. The shelf numbers so assigned would correspond to the **principal quantum numbers** in the bookcase model. Each principal quantum number corresponds to a particular energy level. It has been suggested (see page 376) that the energy of the initial state of an atom is $hk/n_1{}^2$ while the energy of the final state is $hk/n_2{}^2$. Thus, the number n in the denominator identifies the energy level and is called the *principal* quantum number. For the hydrogen atom, the formula below then gives the energy of level n:

$$E_n = -\frac{313.6}{n^2} \text{ kcal/mole} \qquad (10)$$

where E_n is the energy of the level with principal quantum number n.

The negative sign in front of 313.6 is significant and deserves comment. Simple algebra shows that as n becomes larger, the energy becomes less negative and as n approaches infinity, the energy approaches zero. Why is the energy of a hydrogen atom negative in its lowest state? To answer this question look at Figure 16-11. You will notice two energy scales; in the scale on the left, the bottom level is assigned the value zero; in the scale on the right, the top level is assigned the value zero. Choice of *either* assigned value would be understandable, but physical scientists have determined that calling the top level zero offers a number of advantages. Thus, *by definition, the hydrogen atom has zero energy when the electron and the nucleus are separated by an infinite distance.* As the electron approaches the proton, energy is released; the system has *less* energy than it did at the defined zero of energy. In view of this fact, all energies recorded for the hydrogen atom must carry the negative sign.

16-5.2 Orbitals

The principal quantum number, n, defines the energy and tells something about where the electron moves in space. But it does not describe an electron path.

In attempting to translate this mathematical picture of energy levels into physical terms, scientists have identified and named the region of space in which an electron in a given energy level is most likely to be found. This spatial distribution of an electron in a given energy level is called an **orbital.** An orbital, in contrast to an orbit, is not based on classical physics—it is based on probability. Let us be more specific about the quantum numbers and orbitals of the hydrogen atom.

The nature of the information furnished about an atom by quantum mechanics can be illustrated by the following analogy. Picture a bird-feeding station in a large, snow-covered park in the dead of winter. In this park there is a single bird (good chemistry but poor ornithology), whose movements we want to study. We have an excellent camera mounted on a very high platform, so that a picture of the entire park can be taken at any time during the day. Any one picture of the bird will not be very helpful in deciding where the bird spends most of its daylight hours. On the other hand, suppose we arranged to photograph the park and the bird every five minutes throughout the day. After we have done this several days, we can place the photographic negatives on top of each other so that the bird-feeding station in all pictures always appears at the same point. In this way a composite print is obtained. In those areas where the bird has spent the most time, the composite picture will be relatively dark in color. In those areas where the bird has appeared only infrequently, the photograph will be light in color. If the bird has behaved normally, the picture is darkest around the feeding station and fades out toward the edges of the park. The *probability* that the bird will be found in a given spot can be determined by how dark the film is at that spot. The composite picture tells us the *relative probability* that the bird will be present in a given spot at any given instant. (Figure 16-12.1 gives a representation of what this composite photograph would look like.)

Fig. 16-12.1 A composite picture of a bird at a bird-feeder.

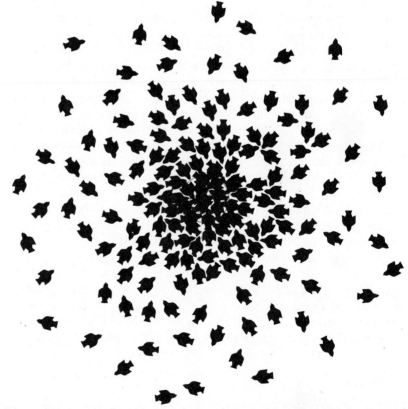

Quantum mechanics gives us the same type of information about an electron. *In the case of electron distribution, the properties of the orbital tell us the probability that an experiment designed to locate the electron will find it, in a given unit of volume, at a particular distance from the nucleus.* Our composite picture of the bird in the park does not tell us how the bird flies from spot to spot. Similarly, the quantum mechanical picture of the atom does *not* tell us *how the electron moves* from point to point, its **trajectory.**

Though quantum mechanics does not tell us the electron trajectory, it *does* tell us *how the orbital changes as* n *increases.* It also indicates that *for each value of* n *there are* n² *different orbitals.* If $n = 1$, there is one orbital; if $n = 2$, there are four orbitals. If $n = 3$, there are nine orbitals. For the hydrogen atom, the n^2 orbitals associated with a given n all have the same energy:

$$E_n = -\frac{313.6}{n^2} \text{ kcal/mole} \qquad (10)$$

In general, as n increases the electron is, on the average, farther from the nucleus.

How then do orbitals with the same value of n differ? They differ in the spatial distribution of electrons. Orbital "shapes" are quite different. Let us examine characteristic **orbital shapes** for the hydrogen atom.

s ORBITALS

Consider the lowest energy level of a hydrogen atom with $n = 1$. We have just learned that there are n^2 levels with this energy; then, since $n = 1$, there is only one level. This orbital corresponds to an electron distribution that is spherically symmetrical around the nucleus. A "composite picture" of this orbital is shown in Figure 16-12.2. Notice how closely it resembles the distribution for the bird in the park (Figure 16-12.1). We call this a **1s orbital.** An electron moving in an *s* **orbital** is called an *s* **electron.** *All s orbitals are spherically symmetrical* (like a ball). The probability of finding the electron in a given unit of volume decreases regularly in a spherical pattern as we go away from the nucleus. This is seen in Figure 16-12.2. The fact has an interesting consequence: *the atom does not have a definite size;* it tends to "fade away" as the distance from the nucleus increases. In short, a 1s electron has the *greatest probability* per unit of volume *at the nucleus.* The probability *decreases* as the distance from the nucleus increases.

The next energy level corresponds to $n = 2$. According to the rule, there are $n^2 = 2^2$ or four different spatial arrangements having the same energy. The energy value is $-313.6/4$ or -78.4 kcal/mole. One of these spatial arrangements or orbitals is again spherically symmetrical and is called the **2s orbital** (Figure 16-13). As we might have reasoned, the higher energy of the 2*s* electron results from the fact that it spends more time farther from the nucleus.

p ORBITALS

We have described the 2*s* orbital, which is just *one* of *four* orbitals having the principal quantum number 2. The other three orbitals are known as **2p orbitals.** Each *p* **orbital** tends to concentrate electron probability in the direction of one of the coordinate axes. As Figure 16-14 shows, a $2p_x$ orbital concentrates electron density along the x axis in a dumbbell-shaped pattern. Note that the probability of finding a *p* electron in a unit of volume at the nucleus is zero, whereas the probability of finding an *s* electron in a unit of volume at the nucleus is significant. As you might have guessed, we also have p_y and p_z

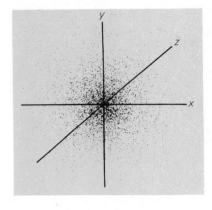

Fig. 16-12.2 A computer generated plot of a 1s orbital. A computer plotted the position of a 1s electron at 4,000 consecutive instants of time. This and the following five figures are courtesy of Don T. Cromer.

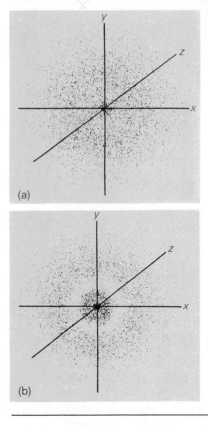

Fig. 16-13 Computer generated plots of (a) the 2s orbital and (b) the 3s orbital.

(a)

(b)

ORBITALS

383

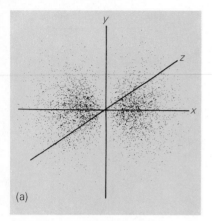

(a)

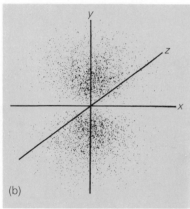

(b)

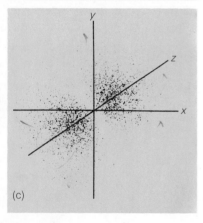

(c)

Fig. 16-15 The energy-level scheme of the hydrogen atom.

orbitals. They differ only in orientation of the dumbbell-shaped electron clouds. The p_y has the axis of the dumbbell along the y axis. The p_z has the axis of the dumbbell along the z axis. *Every energy level with n above 1 has three* p *orbitals.* These are np_x, np_y, and np_z. As n increases, electrons in p orbitals are, on the average, farther and farther from the nucleus; but the *overall shape* of the electron distribution along the x, y, and z axes does not change as n increases.

d ORBITALS

At this point we might summarize our information on orbitals by constructing the diagram shown in Figure 16-15. Each orbital is represented as a circle into which electrons may be placed. For a given value of n, there are n^2 total orbitals; for example, for $n = 3$, there are 3^2 or nine orbitals. We can immediately identify one **3s** and three **3p orbitals.** The five remaining orbitals are called **3d orbitals.** They have somewhat more complicated spatial distribution; their shape will not be considered here.

EXERCISE 16-5

How many orbitals would be expected for $n = 4$? How many orbitals are accounted for by the $4s$, $4p$, and $4d$ groups? The remaining electrons in the fourth quantum level are f electrons. How many $4f$ electrons are there?

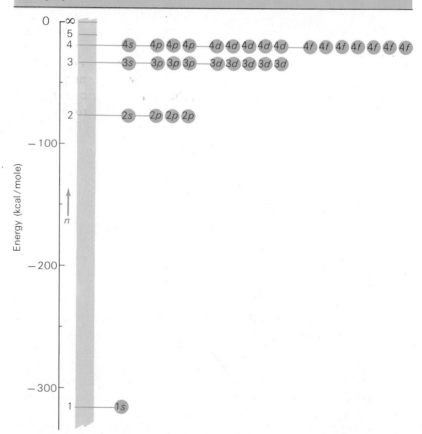

16-6 ELECTRONIC STRUCTURE AND THE PERIODIC TABLE

If the orbital picture for hydrogen were only useful in explaining the spectrum of hydrogen, we would expect to find the preceding discussion in a book on spectroscopy but not in a book on general chemistry. The fact that the discussion appears in a book on chemistry should suggest to you that the concept of orbitals can be extended well beyond hydrogen. Indeed, this idea can serve as the basis for constructing the entire periodic table; it can also provide a sound basis for understanding many of the chemical trends first summarized in Chapter 8.

16-6.1 Many-Electron Atoms

All atoms display line spectra. In general these spectra are much more complicated than the atomic hydrogen spectrum shown in Figure 16-9 on page 374, but they can be interpreted just as we interpreted the hydrogen spectrum, if certain reasonable assumptions are made. Such assumptions are logically supported by correlations with the periodic table. Let us list our assumptions:

(1) Atoms of all elements have orbitals and energy levels qualitatively like those of hydrogen.
(2) The lines in the spectra of all atoms can be understood in terms of an electron jumping between two definite energy levels. Such jumps are called **electronic transitions** between levels.
(3) The orbital energy-level diagrams for many-electron atoms resemble the hydrogen energy-level diagram *except that all orbitals with a given value of* n *no longer have the same energy.* For example, in many-electron atoms *s* orbitals are lower in energy than *p* orbitals. Figure 16-16 (next page) shows a schematic energy-level diagram of a many-electron atom for levels up through 6*p*. We sometimes speak of 2*s* and 2*p* sublevels. (Compare Figure 16-16 with 16-15. What differences do you see?)
(4) A single orbital of any atom can accommodate *no more than* two electrons.* Each electron in an orbital may be visualized as spinning around its own axis. The first electron in an orbital spins in one direction; the second must spin in the reverse direction. Such electrons are said to differ in spin or to have "paired spins." There are only two directions of spin; hence, each orbital can accommodate only two electrons.
(5) All orbitals of equal energy will acquire one electron before any orbital accepts two electrons.†

These five assumptions permit a sound interpretation of more complicated atomic spectra.

---

*This is just a statement, in its simplest form, of an empirical generalization known as the **Pauli Exclusion principle.**

†If two electrons are in the same orbital rather than in each of two equivalent orbitals, the electrons will repel each other to give a higher total energy for the atom.

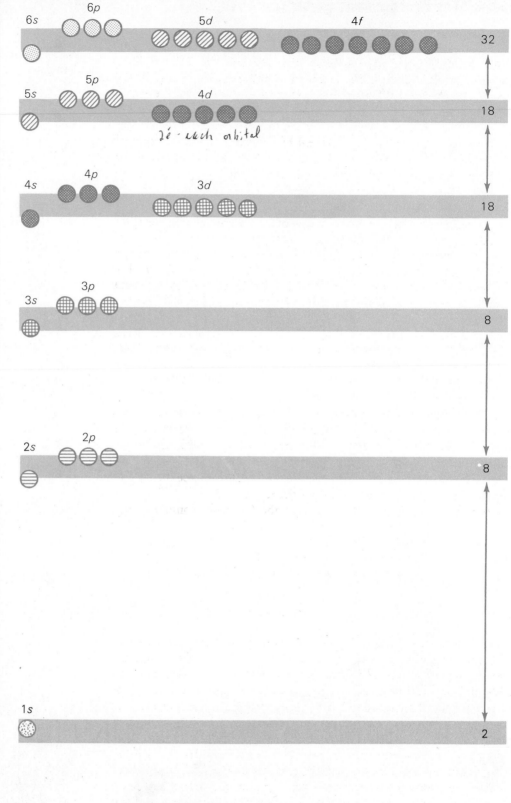

Fig. 16-16 The energy-level scheme of a many-electron atom.

2é · each orbital

why 3d

16-6.2 The First Eighteen Elements

Let us now use these assumptions to suggest the electron arrangement for an atom in the "ground" state or state of lowest energy for that atom. We do this by filling orbitals with electrons until the positive nuclear charge is just counterbalanced by the negative charge of the extranuclear electrons. We shall always place each additional electron in the lowest unfilled orbital available. Thus, in hydrogen with only a single electron, one electron is placed in the $1s$ level. The number of electrons in the level is designated by a superscript to the right of the orbital symbol. We write $1s^1$ as the **electron configuration** for hydrogen. In helium, with a nuclear charge of $2+$, we need two electrons. Both can be accommodated in the $1s$ orbital; hence, for helium we write $1s^2$.

For lithium, with a nuclear charge of $3+$, we need three electrons outside the nucleus. Two are placed in the $1s$ orbital. Since two electrons fill an orbital, the third electron must be placed in the $2s$ orbital. The electron configuration of Li is then $1s^2 2s^1$. Despite the nuclear charge of $3+$ in the lithium atom, the last electron is rather weakly bound because the $2s$ electron of lithium spends most of its time farther away from the nucleus than do the $1s$ electrons. The $2s$ electron should be fairly easily lost to give Li^+. Indeed, we have already noticed (Chapter 8) that gaseous alkali metal atoms lose electrons rather easily to give gaseous metal ions. Alkali metal atoms have a low **ionization energy.**

The beryllium atom has one more electron than the lithium atom. The fourth electron for beryllium is put in the $2s$ level; hence, its electron configuration is $1s^2 2s^2$. Removal of the two $2s$ electrons gives the Be^{2+} ion. The Be^{2+} ion has the same configuration as the noble gas helium.

With a boron atom five electrons are needed to balance the nuclear charge; hence, the configuration is $1s^2 2s^2 2p_x^1$.

Continuing this process, we obtain the following configurations:

Carbon atom	$1s^2$	$2s^2 2p_x^1 2p_y^1$
Nitrogen atom	$1s^2$	$2s^2 2p_x^1 2p_y^1 2p_z^1$
Oxygen atom	$1s^2$	$2s^2 2p_x^2 2p_y^1 2p_z^1$
Fluorine atom	$1s^2$	$2s^2 2p_x^2 2p_y^2 2p_z^1$
Neon atom	$1s^2$	$2s^2 2p_x^2 2p_y^2 2p_z^2$

We note that at the stable electron configuration of helium (high ionization energy), the level of principal quantum number 1 is completed. The two required electrons are present. The next configuration with high ionization energy is found at neon, where the levels of principal quantum number 2 as well as principal quantum number 1 are completed. Eight electrons go in the four orbitals (2^2) of principal quantum number 2; hence, neon has eight more electrons than helium. Argon represents completion of the one $3s$ and the three $3p$ orbitals. Also, argon has eight more electrons than neon. The "magic number" of eight electrons separating neon and helium and argon and neon is clearly tied to the eight electrons required to fill the one s and the three p orbitals.

The construction of the first 11 elements is shown schematically in Figure 16-17. Electrons spinning in one direction are shown by filling the upper half of the circle; electrons spinning in the opposite direction are shown by filling the lower half. Only two electrons are allowed per orbital. We made this assumption earlier, listing it as assumption (4).

If we proceed stepwise beyond neon, we come to sodium. Again, we are forced to use an orbital of higher quantum number, the 3s:

$$\text{Sodium atom} \qquad 1s^2 \quad 2s^2 2p_x{}^2 2p_y{}^2 2p_z{}^2 \quad 3s^1$$

The 3s electron spends more time away from the nucleus than does the electron in any other orbital; hence, it should be more easily removed to give Na^+. Perhaps the chemistry of sodium is like the chemistry of lithium. A review of Chapter 8 shows that this is so. In many other cases the properties of the first 20 elements are suggested by their electronic patterns. Electronic structure is based on available energy levels. The close agreement between the predicted chemical properties based on spectroscopy and the actual chemical properties found by experiment adds to our faith in these models.

EXERCISE 16-6

Magnesium has one more electron than sodium. Write the electron configuration for magnesium. What ion is suggested for magnesium? Write the electron configuration for argon (atomic number 18). Write the electron configuration for potassium (no. 19).

16-6.3 Elements Beyond Argon

For elements beyond argon we follow the same procedure. The only modification is in the appearance of the energy-level diagram used as we advance to higher levels (see Figure 16-16). Levels having the *same* principal quantum number are symbolized by the same type of interior pattern. As we go beyond the 3p orbitals, we find, to our surprise, that the 3d levels lie *above* the 4s levels but *below* the 4p levels.* If we continue to add electrons to the lowest available level, the first electron beyond the closed shell of argon goes into the 4s level. Thus, the potassium atom (atomic number 19) has the configuration

$$\text{Potassium atom} \qquad \underbrace{1s^2 \quad 2s^2 2p^6 \quad 3s^2 3p^6}_{\text{ARGON CONFIGURATION}} \quad 4s^1$$

Potassium is the first element of the fourth row of the periodic table. With the next element, calcium (no. 20), the twentieth electron is added to complete the 4s level; hence, its configuration is

$$\text{Calcium atom} \qquad \underbrace{1s^2 \quad 2s^2 2p^6 \quad 3s^2 3p^6}_{\text{ARGON CONFIGURATION}} \quad 4s^2$$

*The arrangement of levels shown in Figure 16-16 is an acceptable simplification. In actual fact, the relative position of levels changes as the nuclear charge and number of electrons change. The order given here accounts for the form of the periodic table.

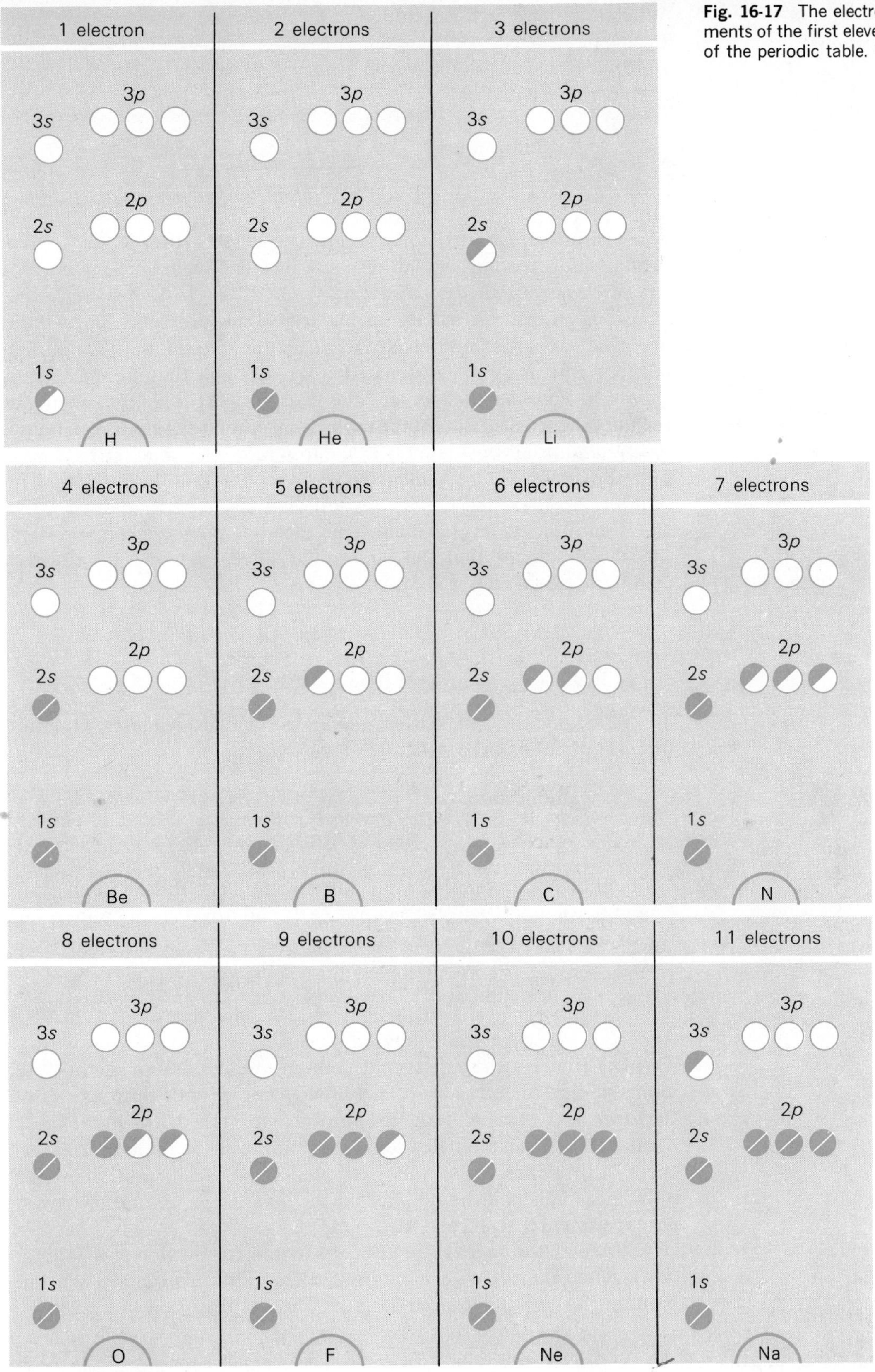

Fig. 16-17 The electron arrangements of the first eleven elements of the periodic table.

When another electron is added to form the next element, scandium, the available orbital of lowest energy is one of the $3d$ levels (remember, the $3d$ levels are a little lower in energy than the $4p$ levels). Scandium is thus represented as

Scandium atom $\underbrace{1s^2 \quad 2s^22p^6 \quad 3s^23p^63d^1}_{\text{ARGON CONFIGURATION}} \quad 4s^2$

As electrons are added to form other elements, they enter the $3d$ orbitals until the ten available spaces in these orbitals are filled.

The elements that are formed when the 3d electrons are added are called the **transition metals** *or the* **transition elements.** Since their chemical properties and electronic structures are unlike those of the lighter elements we have discussed, it is reasonable that these elements should be considered together. The first group of transition elements includes the ten elements of the table, from scandium to zinc: scandium (Sc), titanium (Ti), vanadium (V), chromium (Cr), manganese (Mn), iron (Fe), cobalt (Co), nickel (Ni), copper (Cu), and zinc (Zn).* In building up these ten elements additional electrons are added to $3d$ levels until the $3d$ level is filled. Zinc then has the same configuration as calcium except that the $3d$ level is filled in zinc. The electron configuration of zinc is

Zinc atom $\underbrace{1s^2 \quad 2s^22p^6 \quad 3s^23p^63d^{10}}_{\text{ARGON CONFIGURATION}} \quad 4s^2$

After zinc the $4p$ levels are the lowest orbitals available. Gallium (no. 31), then, has the structure

Gallium atom $\underbrace{1s^2 \quad 2s^22p^6 \quad 3s^23p^63d^{10}}_{\text{ARGON CONFIGURATION}} \quad 4s^24p^1$

Gallium has an outer electronic pattern similar to that of aluminum, except that outer electrons occupy the $4s$ and $4p$ levels in gallium but the $3s$ and $3p$ levels in aluminum:

Aluminum atom $1s^2 \quad 2s^22p^6 \quad 3s^23p^1$

Also, gallium has a completed $3d$ level.

The similarities suggest that gallium and aluminum might have many similar chemical properties; for example, both form oxides of the form M_2O_3 and halides of the empirical formula MX_3. On the other hand, the differences in electronic structure result in important differences in properties that cannot be overlooked. Such similarities and differences must still be established by experiment. Chemistry is still an experimental science!

When all the $4p$ levels have been completed, the elements gallium (Ga), germanium (Ge), arsenic (As), selenium (Se), bromine (Br), and krypton (Kr) will have been formed. The configuration of krypton is

*Occasionally people argue over the placement of zinc in the transition group. Its properties are not really those of the transition elements. It is in an intermediate region.

Krypton atom $\qquad$ $\underbrace{1s^2 \quad 2s^22p^6 \quad 3s^23p^63d^{10}}_{\text{ARGON CONFIGURATION}} \quad 4s^24p^6$

The eighteen elements running from potassium to krypton make up the fourth row of the periodic table. We see that this fourth row contains eighteen rather than eight elements because the five $3d$ orbitals have energies that are about the same as the energies of the $4s$ and $4p$ levels. Since ten electrons can be placed in the $3d$ levels, the fourth row has eighteen elements.

We might well guess that the fifth row could have a group of ten transition elements with the $4d$ level existing in varying stages of completion. Indeed, if we look at the periodic table, we see ten elements running from yttrium (Y) to cadmium (Cd), the second group of transition elements.

In the third group of transition elements, the $5d$ level is being filled. This group includes lanthanum (La), hafnium (Hf), tantalum (Ta), tungsten (W), rhenium (Re), osmium (Os), iridium (Ir), platinum (Pt), gold (Au), and mercury (Hg).

You will notice that we did not include the elements from lanthanum (no. 57, La) through lutetium (no. 71, Lu) in the transition metals. These fourteen elements result when the $4f$ levels start to fill. The $4f$ levels have about the same energy as the $5d$ and $6s$ levels; hence, they start to fill at the element having atomic number 57. The fourteen elements formed in the filling of the seven $4f$ levels are called the **inner transition elements.** Sometimes older names such as the **rare earths** or the **lanthanides** are used for these elements. They all have very similar chemistry and are usually placed at the bottom of the periodic table outside the normal arrangement.

16-6.4 The Periodic Table in Retrospect

We see that the rows of the periodic table arise from filling orbitals of approximately the same energy. When all orbitals of a given n value are filled (two electrons per orbital), the next electron must be placed in an s orbital of higher principal quantum number and a new row or *period* of the table starts. We can summarize the relation between the number of elements in each row of the table and the number of available orbitals of approximately equal energy by the information shown in Table 16-3.

TABLE 16-3 NUMBER OF ELEMENTS
IN EACH ROW OF THE PERIODIC TABLE

Row of Table	Number of Elements	Lowest Energy Orbitals Available to Be Filled			
1	2	1s			
2	8	2s,	2p		
3	8	3s,	3p		
4	18	4s,	3d,	4p	
5	18	5s,	4d,	5p	
6	32	6s,	4f,	5d,	6p
7		7s,	5f,	6d,	7p

16-7   IONIZATION ENERGIES, ENERGY LEVELS, AND THE PERIODIC TABLE

16-7.1   Ionization Energies of Atoms— The First Ionization Energy

On several occasions we have mentioned the ionization energies of the elements. Let us repeat our definition: *the* **first ionization energy** *of an atom is the amount of energy required to remove the most loosely bound electron from the gaseous atom.* It is the energy required for the process

$$\text{gaseous atom} + \text{energy} \longrightarrow \text{gaseous ion}^+ + \text{electron}^- \quad (11)$$

Since energy is involved in the definition of the ionization process, we should be able to represent ionization energy on the energy-level diagram. To do this, consider the energy-level diagram for the hydrogen atom (Figure 16-18). As our eye travels up the diagram, the levels become closer and closer together. As the principal quantum numbers grow larger, the differences between levels become smaller, until differences are too small to see on the diagram—the levels run together and the energy of the system approaches zero. Remember, the energy was negative in the original atom. As you will recall, zero was arbitrarily selected as the energy value for the state in which an electron is completely removed from the atom. Thus, if we put enough energy into the system to remove the electron from its "ground-state" orbital and raise it to the zero of energy, we shall have ionized the atom. In terms of the energy-level diagram, *the* **ionization energy** *is the energy necessary to lift an electron from the highest occupied orbital up to the limit corresponding to* n = *infinity* (∞).

For the hydrogen atom, we should be able to calculate the difference in energy between these two levels. The hydrogen electron in the ground state ($1s$ orbital) has energy given as

$$E = -\frac{313.6}{n^2} \text{ kcal/mole} = -\frac{313.6}{1^2} \text{ kcal/mole}$$
$$= -313.6 \text{ kcal/mole} \quad (10a)$$

The free electron with quantum number ∞ has energy given as

$$E = -\frac{313.6}{\infty^2} \text{ kcal/mole} = 0 \quad (10b)$$

The difference between these two states is then $E_{final} - E_{initial}$ or $0 - (-313.6) = 313.6$ kcal/mole. The ionization energy for the hydrogen atom is 313.6 kcal/mole, the quantity we have been using as the constant in our energy equation for hydrogen; a total of 313.6 kcal must be put into a mole of gaseous hydrogen atoms to remove electrons to infinity. The ionization energies of the first nineteen elements are shown in Table 16-4.

TABLE 16-4 IONIZATION ENERGIES OF THE ELEMENTS

Atomic Number	Element	Ionization Energy (kcal/mole)
1	H	313.6
2	He	566.7
3	Li	124.3
4	Be	214.9
5	B	191.2
6	C	259.5
7	N	335.4
8	O	313.8
9	F	401.5
10	Ne	497.0
11	Na	118.4
12	Mg	175.2
13	Al	137.9
14	Si	187.9
15	P	254.1
16	S	238.8
17	Cl	300.1
18	Ar	363.2
19	K	100.0

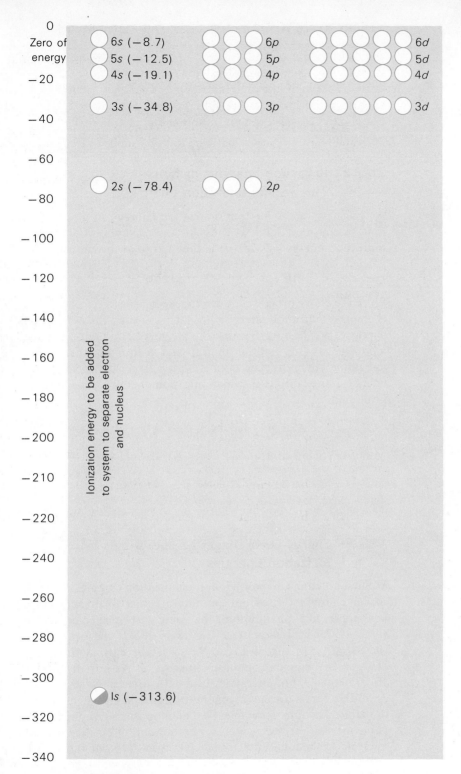

Fig. 16-18 The ionization energy and the energy-level diagram of the hydrogen atom.

EXERCISE 16-7

Sketch in qualitative form the energy-level diagram for lithium in its ground state (indicate individual electrons) and show its ionization energy on the diagram. What frequency of light ($E = h\nu$) would cause ionization of lithium ($h = 1.58 \times 10^{-37}$ kcal $\times$ sec)? See Table 16-4 for the ionization energy. (*Answer:* $\nu = 1.3 \times 10^{15}$ vibrations/sec.)

16-7.2 Ionization Energies of Ions—
The Second Ionization Energy

As you may recall, the term ionization energy can also be applied to ions (atoms that have already lost an electron). For example, the ionization energy of $Mg^+(g)$ is the energy in the process

$$Mg^+(g) + \text{energy} \longrightarrow Mg^{2+}(g) + e^-(g) \qquad (12)$$

Since the above process removes the *second* electron from a magnesium atom, the ionization energy of $Mg^+(g)$ is called the **second ionization energy** of magnesium. Because the second electron must be pulled from a *positive ion* (Mg^+) rather than from a *neutral atom* (Mg), the second ionization energy for an atom is *always larger* than its first ionization energy. For example, the first ionization energy for magnesium is 175 kcal/mole:

$$Mg(g) + 175 \text{ kcal} \longrightarrow Mg^+(g) + e^-(g) \qquad (13)$$

while its second ionization energy is 345 kcal/mole:

$$Mg^+(g) + 345 \text{ kcal} \longrightarrow Mg^{2+}(g) + e^-(g) \qquad (12a)$$

The effect of the positive charge on Mg^+ is clearly apparent.

16-7.3 Energy-Level Diagrams and Trends in
Ionization Energies

We first noted in Chapter 8 that the ionization energies of the elements in a given row will rise from a minimum for an alkali metal (Li = 124.3 kcal/mole) to a maximum for the noble gas which completes that row (Ne = 497.0 kcal/mole) (see Figure 16-19). If we focus attention on the second row—from Li to Ne—we find each atom is losing an electron of principal quantum number 2. As our diagram (Figure 16-20, page 397) of energy levels for the first ten elements shows, the $2s$ and $2p$ levels display a general decrease in energy as we go across the table. The ionization energies, then, must rise from Li to Ne. Such behavior can only be related to the buildup of positive charge in the nucleus. As the nuclear charge increases in the atom, it should become more difficult to remove an electron from a given quantum level. An ionization-energy curve should show a *general rise* from Li to Ne. Indeed, a general rise is seen in the values from Li to Ne. But this simple picture does not explain the irregularities seen at boron and oxygen. We shall consider some of these minor irregularities in the next section.

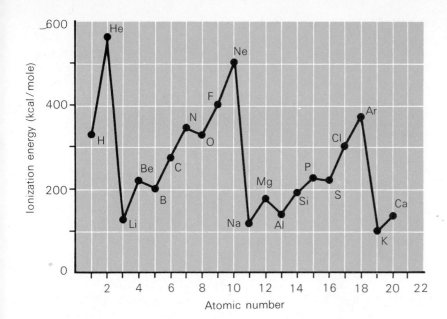

Fig. 16-19 Ionization energy as a function of atomic number.

16-7.4   Ionization Energies and Valence Electrons

In Chapter 8 we noted that the most loosely bound electrons can be lost or shared when one atom combines with another. These relatively loosely bound electrons are called **valence electrons.** A more detailed examination of the ionization energies of valence electrons will help us relate chemical properties to atomic structure.

Consider the elements lithium, beryllium, and boron. For each of these elements we know several ionization energies corresponding to processes such as

$$Li(g) \longrightarrow Li^+(g) + e^-(g)$$

first ionization energy = 124 kcal   *(14)*

$$Li^+(g) \longrightarrow Li^{2+}(g) + e^-(g)$$

second ionization energy = 1,748 kcal   *(15)*

TABLE 16-5 SUCCESSIVE IONIZATION ENERGIES
OF LITHIUM, BERYLLIUM, AND BORON

Element	Electron Configuration for Neutral Atom	Ionization Energy (kcal/mole)			
		E_1	E_2	E_3	E_4
Lithium	$1s^2$ $2s^1$	124	1,748	2,815	—
Beryllium	$1s^2$ $2s^2$	215	418	3,532	5,004
Boron	$1s^2$ $2s^22p^1$	191	577	872	5,964

The experimental values of these energies are shown in Table 16-5. Let us compare lithium and beryllium. For each, the first electron to be removed is a 2s electron. The attraction between the nucleus and the 2s outer electron will be higher for beryllium (four nuclear protons)

**LUIS W. ALVAREZ
(1911–   )**

The son of a prominent physician, Luis Alvarez was born in San Francisco and raised in Rochester, Minnesota. Educated at the University of Chicago, he received the Ph.D. in 1936. Most of his professional career has been spent at the University of California, where he is senior physicist of the Lawrence Radiation Laboratory.

Alvarez' scientific contributions are many and varied, ranging from the development of sophisticated atom accelerators to a color television system. Perhaps his most important work has been in the development of the hydrogen bubble chamber, with photographic processes and systems of data analysis, to study new subatomic particles. He has discovered a number of new particles, sometimes called "resonances" or higher energy levels of particles previously known.

For his many contributions to the sciences, Luis Alvarez was awarded the 1968 Nobel Prize in Physics.

than for lithium (three nuclear protons); hence, the higher first ionization energy of beryllium is understandable:

$$Li(g) + 124 \text{ kcal} \longrightarrow Li^+(g) + e^-(g) \qquad (14a)$$

$$Be(g) + 215 \text{ kcal} \longrightarrow Be^+(g) + e^-(g) \qquad (16)$$

The second ionization, however, reverses the situation; lithium has the higher second ionization energy:

$$Li^+(g) + 1,748 \text{ kcal} \longrightarrow Li^{2+}(g) + e^-(g) \qquad (15a)$$

$$Be^+(g) + 418 \text{ kcal} \longrightarrow Be^{2+}(g) + e^-(g) \qquad (17)$$

The energy required to remove the second electron from lithium is four times that of the energy required to remove the second electron from beryllium. Why? Why is the second ionization energy of lithium so much larger than the second ionization energy of beryllium? The answer is found in the energy-level diagram of Figure 16-20. *The second electron removed from beryllium is still a 2s electron, but the second electron removed from lithium is a 1s electron.* Notice how much lower in energy a 1s electron is than a 2s electron. (See Figure 16-20. The 1s levels run off the page.) The 1s electron is generally much closer to the nucleus than is the 2s electron.

Continuing to boron, we see that its first ionization energy is below that of beryllium, even though boron has a higher nuclear charge. The answer to this apparent deviation is also found in Figure 16-20. The first electron removed in boron is a 2p electron, which lies well above the 2s energy level. It is easier to remove a 2p electron from boron than it is to remove a 2s electron from beryllium, even though boron has the higher nuclear charge.

If we continue to remove electrons from boron, we discover a *very large increase* in ionization energy when the fourth electron is removed. We can understand this large jump in view of the fact that all electrons with quantum number 2 have been removed from boron when the third electron has gone. The fourth electron must come from the very low-energy 1s level. The energy jump from 1s to infinity is enormous.

By remembering how we placed electrons in the lowest empty orbitals, we can draw up a guideline for determining the number of valence electrons a given atom possesses. The number of electrons placed in the orbitals that form the *highest partially filled* cluster of energy levels is the number of valence electrons. These electrons are most easily removed or shared. Lithium has one valence electron; beryllium has two; boron, three; carbon, four; and nitrogen, five. In short, for this group the valence electrons are the electrons in the second level. These numbers will help us understand the chemistry of these elements.

EXERCISE 16-8

Explain why chemists say that aluminum has three valence electrons and chlorine seven. How many valence electrons does sodium have? magnesium?

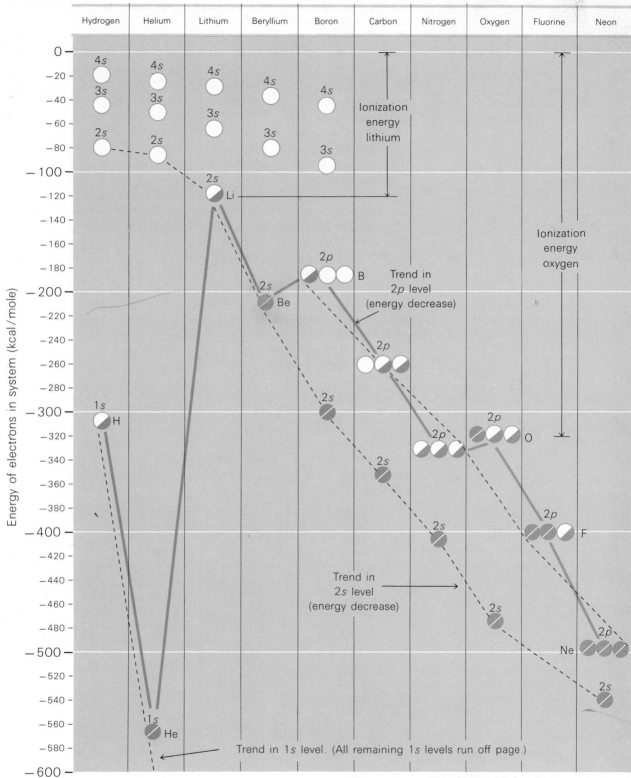

Fig. 16-20 Energy levels and atomic number for the first ten elements.

16-8 HIGHLIGHTS

Light is a form of **electromagnetic radiation.** As such, it is also a form of energy which can be propagated across empty space as **oscillating electric** and **magnetic fields.** A study of the light given off by hydrogen gas in a discharge tube led to a model with definite energy levels.

A *mathematical model* for the hydrogen atom based on the **wave** nature of the electron gave a reasonable description of the energy levels in the hydrogen atom. As a result of work in atomic spectroscopy, an energy-level diagram suitable for considering elements in general was obtained. By using this energy-level diagram and a few additional rules, the form of the periodic table can be understood.

Ionization energies, first considered in Chapter 8, can be represented on energy-level diagrams. Many of the details of ionization energies are understandable in terms of the energy-level diagram. The **valence electrons** of an atom are the electrons in an incompletely filled cluster of energy levels of roughly comparable energy.

A number of useful and significant relationships have been given. These are summarized here. For light:

$$\nu = \frac{c}{\lambda}$$

where $c = 3.0 \times 10^8$ metres/sec. For light quantization:

$$E = h\nu$$

For frequency of lines in the hydrogen spectrum:

$$\nu = 3.287 \times 10^{15} \left(\frac{1}{n_1{}^2} - \frac{1}{n_2{}^2} \right) \text{ vibrations/sec}$$

The road to our understanding of the atom has been a winding and tortuous one. Today we are sure of only one thing: there are still many curves ahead. You are certain to meet them as you advance in science.

QUESTIONS and PROBLEMS

1 In what way is the "heat" given off by an infrared lamp similar to the X rays used in the dentist's office? In what way does the "heat" differ from the X rays?

2 For each of the following wavelengths of light, determine the frequency and identify the region of the electromagnetic spectrum to which it belongs. (a) 2.0×10^{-14} metre (b) 4.0×10^{-9} metre (c) 6.0×10^{-7} metre (d) 1.00 metre.

3 For each of the following frequencies of visible light, determine the wavelength, λ, and identify the color of light associated with each frequency. (a) 6.4×10^{14} vib/sec (b) 5.5×10^{14} vib/sec (c) 5.0×10^{14} vib/sec.

4 A chemist is using radiation with a frequency of 6×10^{13} vibrations/second. What is the wavelength of this radiation in metres? Use Tables 16-1 and 16-2 to identify this radiation as red, blue, infrared, ultraviolet, and so on. Estimate the energy in kcal for one photon of this radiation. Planck's constant is 1.58×10^{-37} kcal $\times$ sec. The velocity of light is 3.00×10^8 metres/sec.

5 Carbon monoxide absorbs light at frequencies near 1.2×10^{11}, near 6.4×10^{13}, and near 1.5×10^{15} vibrations/second. It does not absorb at intermediate frequencies. (a) Name the spectral regions in which it absorbs (see Figure 16-7). (b) Explain why carbon monoxide is colorless.

6 The oxygen molecule undergoes molecular vibrations at a frequency of 2.4×10^{13} vibrations/sec. If the pressure is such that an oxygen molecule has about 10^9 collisions per second, how many times does the molecule vibrate between collisions?

7 Use Planck's constant (1.58×10^{-37} kcal × sec) to determine the energy which corresponds to the following frequencies of light. To obtain the energy per mole of photons, multiply the values by 6.02×10^{23} photons per mole. Compare your results with the energies of light in the visible spectrum produced by the hydrogen atom (Figure 16-9 and Exercise 16-4).

(a) 4.567×10^{14} vib/sec
(b) 6.165×10^{14} vib/sec
(c) 6.905×10^{14} vib/sec
(d) 7.307×10^{14} vib/sec
(e) 7.550×10^{14} vib/sec
(f) 7.707×10^{14} vib/sec

8 Use the energy-level diagram in Figure 16-11 to calculate the energy required to raise the electron in a hydrogen atom from level 1 to level 2, from level 1 to level 3, and from level 1 to level 4. Compare these energies with the spectral lines shown in Figure 16-9.

9 Use the Rydberg equation to calculate the frequency of a line in the hydrogen spectrum corresponding to a transition from $n = 5$ to $n = 4$. Identify the spectral region or color which corresponds to this frequency.

10 If the energy difference between two electron states is 7.66×10^{-23} kcal, what will be the frequency of light emitted when the electron drops from the higher to the lower state? Planck's constant $= 1.58 \times 10^{-37}$ kcal × sec.

11 According to the quantum mechanical description of the $1s$ orbital of the hydrogen atom, what relation exists between the surface of a sphere centered about the nucleus and the location of an electron?

12 What must be done to a $2s$ electron to make it a $3s$ electron? What happens when a $3s$ electron becomes a $2s$ electron?

13 Determine the value of E_n for $n = 1, 2, 3,$ and 4 for a hydrogen atom using the relation $E_n = -313.6$ kcal/mole/n^2. For each E_n, indicate how many orbitals have this energy.

14 The quantum mechanical description of the $1s$ orbital is similar in many respects to a description of the holes in a much-used dart board. For example, the "density" of dart holes is constant anywhere on a circle centered about the bullseye, and the "density" of dart holes reaches zero only at a distance very far from the bullseye (effectively, at infinity). What are the corresponding properties of a $1s$ orbital?

In view of your answer, point out erroneous features of the following models of a hydrogen atom (both of which were used before quantum mechanics demonstrated their inadequacies): (a) a ball of uniform density, (b) a "solar system" atom with the electron circling the nucleus at a fixed distance.

15 Make a table listing the principal quantum numbers (through 3), the types of orbitals, and the number of orbitals of each type.

16 Name the element which corresponds to each of the following electron configurations.

(a) $1s^1$
(b) $1s^2 \quad 2s^2 2p_x{}^1$
(c) $1s^2 \quad 2s^2 2p_x{}^2 2p_y{}^1 2p_z{}^1$
(d) $1s^2 \quad 2s^2 2p^6 \quad 3s^2 3p_x{}^1 3p_y{}^1$
(e) $1s^2 \quad 2s^2 2p^6 \quad 3s^2 3p^6 \quad 4s^2$

17 Use Figure 16-16 to determine the orbital occupancy of the following neutral atoms. Write the electron configuration for each. (a) oxygen (b) aluminum (c) scandium (d) bromine (e) zinc (f) strontium (g) cadmium (h) arsenic.

18 What trend is observed in the first ionization energy as you move from lithium down the first-column metals? On this basis, can you suggest a reason why potassium or cesium might be used in preference to sodium or lithium in photoelectric cells?

19 The first four ionization energies of boron atoms are as follows: $E_1 = 191$ kcal/mole, $E_2 = 577$, $E_3 = 872$, and $E_4 = 5,964$. Explain the magnitudes in terms of the electron configuration of boron and deduce the number of valence electrons of boron.

20 How many valence electrons has hydrogen? nitrogen? silicon? magnesium?

21 Explain in terms of orbital occupancy why boron has a lower ionization energy than beryllium and oxygen a lower ionization energy than nitrogen.

For the nature of the chemical bond is the problem at the heart of all chemistry.

BRYCE CRAWFORD, JR., (1914–   )

MOLECULAR ARCHITECTURE: 17
GASEOUS MOLECULES

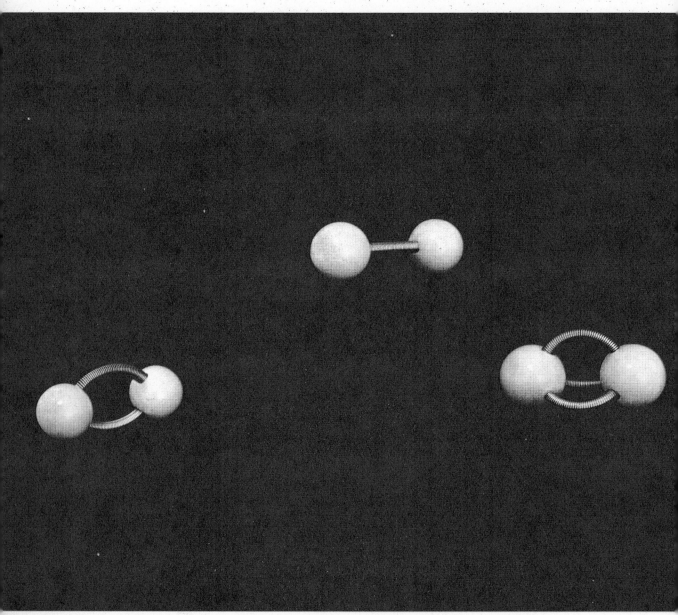

These models are one representation of the single, double, and triple bonds frequently found in gases.

BY NOW, YOU ARE WELL AWARE OF THE ATOM AS A POSITIVELY charged nucleus surrounded by negatively charged electrons. Since electrons repel each other, the prospect of two atoms approaching each other seems exceedingly remote. But take heart. Under that repulsive exterior beats an attractive nucleus! Molecules do exist! The attractive forces between atoms overcome the repulsions to form a chemical bond.

In this chapter we explore the attractive and repulsive forces within molecules and their relationship to the geometry of gaseous molecules.

In Chapter 8 we discussed the bonding in some molecules in a rather simplified manner. Since then we have learned much more about atomic structure and about the fundamental particles making up atoms. We must now apply the newly developed concepts of atomic structure to obtain a more detailed view of the chemical bond.

We shall now consider two important questions:

(1) Why does the cluster of atoms persist?
(2) Why does the cluster have characteristic properties?

In this chapter we shall restrict our attention to molecules as they exist in the gaseous phase. Then, in Chapter 18, we shall consider the additional ideas needed to understand the forces causing the formation of liquids and solids.

17-1   THE COVALENT BOND

In Chapter 8 the connection between the atoms in H_2 or F_2 was identified as an electron pair shared between atoms. This linkage was called a **covalent bond.** Let us examine the covalent bond in gaseous H_2 molecules more carefully.

17-1.1   The Covalent Bond in the Hydrogen Molecule

Under normal conditions of temperature and pressure, hydrogen forms diatomic molecules. At a temperature of several thousand degrees, highly energetic intermolecular collisions knock hydrogen molecules apart:

$$H_2(g) + 103.4 \text{ kcal} \rightleftharpoons H(g) + H(g) \qquad (1)$$

Since energy is absorbed in the separation process, the molecule H_2 is more stable (has a lower energy) than a system containing two separate hydrogen atoms.* To learn why the energy is lower when the atoms are near each other, we must examine interactions among the electric charges of the atoms.

Quantum mechanics tells us that the $1s$ orbital of an isolated hydrogen atom has spherical symmetry *before reaction*. On the other

---

*The film "Chemical Bonding" shows that the combination of hydrogen atoms liberates enough energy to make platinum foil red hot.

hand, if two hydrogen atoms (atoms 1 and 2) are brought together, the electron of atom 1 will be pulled toward the nucleus of atom 2. Similarly, the electron of atom 2 will be pulled toward the nucleus of atom 1. Both electrons 1 and 2 will spend a sizable fraction of their time in the space *between the two nuclei.* In this region each electron is attracted to *both* nuclei. Such *attraction* is the "glue" which holds two atoms together. *The chemical bond in H_2 forms because each of the two electrons is attracted to two protons simultaneously. This arrangement is energetically more stable than the separated atoms in which each electron is attracted to only one proton.*

But it is well to remember that there are also *repulsions* caused by the approach of the two atoms. The two electrons repel each other, as do the two protons. These repulsions tend to push the two atoms apart.

Which are more important, the attraction or the repulsion terms? Experiment shows that the attraction terms are greater—a stable chemical bond is formed. Why is this so? We find an explanation in the mobility of the electrons. The electrons do not occupy fixed positions but move about the molecule. The electrons move away from positions in which they would be near each other, although they still occupy positions between two nuclei. They are said to "correlate" their motion so as to remain apart. In this way electron-electron repulsion is minimized while proton-electron attraction remains high. The stable bond length in the hydrogen molecule is determined by a balance between the forces of attraction and the forces of repulsion.

We can also represent the chemical bond in the hydrogen molecule by using the visual representations of quantum mechanics. In Figure 17-1(a), we picture the electron distribution of an isolated atom in cross section. The electron distribution extends far from the nucleus; it is uniform in all directions but concentrated near the nucleus. Therefore, we should focus attention on the center region of the 1s orbital. We do this by representing the 1s orbital by a circle having a radius large enough to contain most of the electron distribution.* An orbital can accommodate either one or two electrons but no more. Figure 17-1(b) offers a way of showing a 1s orbital empty, with one electron, and with two electrons.

Now, in Figure 17-1(c), consider the interaction of two hydrogen atoms. Each atom has a single electron in a 1s orbital. As the two hydrogen atoms approach, the circles are distorted and tend to overlap each other. *In this region of overlap the two electrons are shared by the two protons* (as shown by the crosshatched and shaded area). If this sharing occurs, the two electrons can be near *both* protons a good part of the time. This causes the chemical bond. *When a bond arises from equal sharing, it is called a* **covalent bond.**

17-1.2 Interaction Between Helium Atoms— No Bond Formation

A measurement of the density of helium gas shows that it is a monatomic gas. Molecules of He_2 do *not* form. What difference between

*The fraction of the total electron cloud enclosed within the circle increases as the circle is made larger.

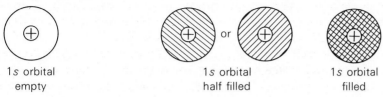

can be shown as — with the addition of shading to indicate occupancy

(a) A simplified representation of a 1s orbital

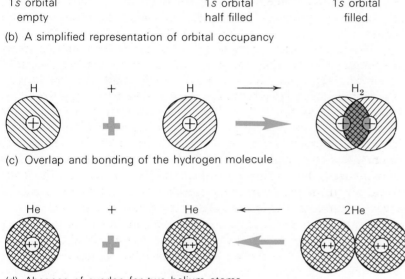

1s orbital
empty

or

1s orbital
half filled

1s orbital
filled

(b) A simplified representation of orbital occupancy

H + H ⟶ H₂

(c) Overlap and bonding of the hydrogen molecule

He + He ⟵ 2He

(d) Absence of overlap for two helium atoms

hydrogen and helium atoms accounts for the absence of bonding in helium? The answer to this question also must lie in the attractive and repulsive electrical interactions between two helium atoms when they approach. Each separate helium atom has two electrons attracted to its nucleus. This gives two attractive interactions for each helium atom. Further, *each* atom has two electrons repelling each other to give one repulsive interaction in *each* helium atom. In two separate He atoms there are four attractive interactions and two repulsive interactions. Now what happens if two atoms are brought together? Taking score, we find eight attractive interactions, four more than in the two separated atoms, and seven repulsive interactions, five more than in the two separated atoms.* Again appealing to experiment, we learn that the four new attractive terms are *not* sufficient to counterbalance the five new repulsive terms. A chemical bond does *not* form.

*The details of the interactions can be summarized as follows.

For the attractive interactions, nucleus of atom 1 attracts all four electrons; similarly, nucleus of atom 2 attracts all four electrons; thus, there are a total of eight attractive interactions.

In counting repulsive interactions, we start with the fact that the two nuclei repel each other. This gives one repulsive interaction. The repulsive interactions between electrons can best be schematized by numbering the electrons from 1 to 4. The repulsions are then given as 1–2, 1–3, 1–4, 2–3, 2–4, and 3–4. Notice that there are six electron interactions, giving a total of seven repulsive interactions.

Thus, the explanation of bonding for H_2 and the absence of it for He_2 lies in the *relative magnitudes* of attractive and repulsive terms. Quantum mechanics can be put to work with the aid of advanced and difficult mathematics to calculate these relative magnitudes. Unfortunately, the mathematics is so difficult that only a handful of the very simplest molecules have been treated with high accuracy. Nevertheless, for some time chemists have been able to decide whether chemical bonds can form without appealing to a digital computer. They use simple models.

Refer to Figure 17-1(d), which is a simplified diagram of the interaction of two helium atoms. Unlike the diagram for hydrogen [Figure 17-1(c)], each helium atom is crosshatched *before* the two atoms approach. This indicates there are *already* two electrons in the $1s$ orbital. The rule for orbital occupancy tells us that the $1s$ orbital can contain *only* two electrons. Consequently, when the two helium atoms approach, their valence orbitals cannot overlap significantly because each orbital is already filled. Filled orbitals *cannot* overlap enough to share electrons. As a result the helium atom forms no chemical bonds.

17-1.3   Representations of Chemical Bonding

We propose, then, that *chemical bonds can form if two atoms can share valence electrons using partially filled orbitals.* We need a shorthand notation which aids in the use of this rule. Such a shorthand notation is called a **representation of the bonding.**

Our rule about covalent bond formation can be shown quite simply for H_2 and He_2 through an **orbital representation:**

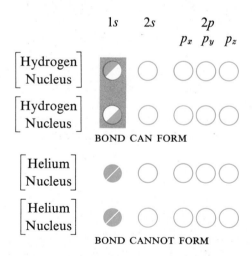

With this representation we need not consider the next higher energy-level clusters—the $2s$ and $2p$ orbitals—which for hydrogen and helium are much higher in energy and can only give rise to extremely weak attractions.

The sharing of electrons can be shown by representing valence electrons as dots placed between the atoms:

$$H\cdot \; + \; H\cdot \; \longrightarrow \; H\!:\!H \tag{2}$$

With this notation the symbol H must represent a bare proton. *The symbol of the atom as it appears in dot formulas represents the atomic core—the atom minus the valence electrons.* Valence electrons are shown by the dots. We shall use both **orbital** and **electron dot representations** to show chemical bonding.

17-1.4   Fluorine Atoms and Fluorine Molecules

A fluorine atom has seven valence electrons; that is, seven electrons occupy the outermost, partially filled cluster of energy levels. Using the electron dot method for representing the atom, we write fluorine as

$$\cdot \ddot{\underset{\cdot\cdot}{F}} :$$

You will recall from Chapter 8 that a gaseous fluorine atom *releases* energy when it picks up an electron to give a gaseous fluoride ion:

$$\cdot \ddot{\underset{\cdot\cdot}{F}} : + \, e^- \longrightarrow : \ddot{\underset{\cdot\cdot}{F}} :^- + \, 79 \pm 2 \text{ kcal/mole of F atoms} \qquad (3)$$

The energy change associated with this process is known as the **electron affinity** of the fluorine atom; it is symbolized here by the letter E.

$$\Delta H = -E \qquad (4)$$

The fact that energy is released tells us in experimental terms that the *attraction* between the fluorine nucleus and the extra electron *is greater than* the *repulsion* between electrons of the fluorine atom and the added electron. Indeed, this energy release suggests that there is some stability associated with completing the valence shell of fluorine. A fluoride *ion,* with a *completed* 2 level, is lower in energy than a fluorine *atom,* with an *incomplete* 2 level. In our analysis of the bonding of fluorine atoms, we shall be concerned with discovering the different ways in which some or all of the stability resulting from a completed 2 level can be gained in the bonding of two fluorine atoms.

Let us examine the bonding of two fluorine atoms with this thought in mind. A fluorine atom has the orbital configuration

Each atom has a valence electron in a half-filled p_z orbital. Suppose two gaseous fluorine atoms (atoms 1 and 2) collide. We can imagine these two atoms orienting so that the half-filled p_z orbitals overlap in space. The half-filled valence orbital of atom 1 shares one valence electron with atom 2. Thus, *part of the electron affinity of fluorine atom 1 is satisfied without pulling the electron away from fluorine atom 2. Meanwhile, atom 2 derives the same *energy benefit* from the valence electron of atom 1. Each fluorine atom has acquired *part interest* in another electron. The *most* energy we could expect to be released by such an electron-sharing procedure would be double the electron affinity of fluorine, or $2 \times 79 = 158$ kcal/mole of F_2. But this value does not take into account the amount of work done in bringing the two positive nuclei near each other. Nor can we expect to gain the whole electron affinity under conditions of electron sharing. We would be lucky to gain half since each atom has only a half interest in the electron pair. Experimentally, the energy released when two fluorine atoms form a bond is only 37.7 kcal/mole of F_2 formed—a reasonable fraction of the maximum energy possible.

The orbital representation for the two fluorine atoms in the F_2 molecule is

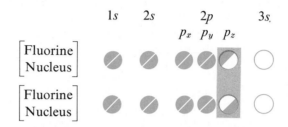

The overlapping half-filled p_z orbitals are enclosed in the shaded area. Now we can see why the chemical bond forms between two fluorine atoms. The electron affinity of a fluorine atom indicates that it is energetically favorable for a fluorine atom to acquire one more electron. Two fluorine atoms can realize a part of this energy decrease by *sharing* electrons. *All chemical bonds form because one or more electrons are placed so that they are attracted to two or more positive nuclei simultaneously.*

The interaction can also be represented easily by using the electron dot model of the atom. The electron-sharing is seen in Figure 17-2. In this discussion of covalent bonding in F_2, we have properly assumed that the $1s$ orbital in the fluorine atom is so tightly bound that it plays little role in the chemistry of fluorine. Only electrons in the 2 level

Fig. 17-2 Sharing of electrons in the fluorine molecule. The rings shown here do not represent discrete electron orbits, but rather indicate a volume region in which electrons spend about 90 percent of their time.

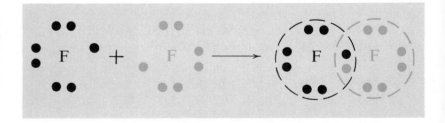

Fig. 17-3 Sharing of electrons in hydrogen fluoride.

are important. In the fluorine *molecule* each separate fluorine atom has two electrons in the $2s$ and six electrons in the three $2p$ orbitals. Some of the stability associated with a completed 2 level has been gained in the formation of the fluorine molecule from two fluorine atoms.

All methods of representation show that when two atoms of fluorine share electrons, they each have "filled" all their valence orbitals and they have no additional bonding capacity. Hence, F_2 does not add a third or fourth atom to form F_3 or F_4. Fluorine is **univalent.**

Hydrogen fluoride can also be represented by the electron dot and orbital notations (see Figure 17-3). A census of the number of electrons near each atom in the molecule shows that the hydrogen atom has only two electrons nearby, whereas fluorine has eight. This is energetically desirable, however, because hydrogen has only one valence orbital, the $1s$ orbital. Two electrons just fill this orbital. A chemical bond results.

EXERCISE 17-1

Using the orbital representation, explain the fact that no compound H_3F is formed.

17-2 THE BONDING CAPACITY OF THE SECOND-ROW ELEMENTS

In Chapter 8 a number of compounds of the second-row elements were identified. Formulas such as H_2O, NH_3, CH_4, CCl_4, and BF_3 were written. Now we have a basis for explaining in more detail why these compounds are formed.

17-2.1 The Bonding Capacity of Oxygen Atoms

The neutral oxygen atom has eight electrons. Six of these electrons occupy the $2s$ and $2p$ orbitals. They are much more easily removed than the two electrons in the $1s$ orbital because they are in the outer energy level, which is not yet filled. Oxygen, then, has six valence electrons. The $2s$ and $2p$ orbitals are the valence orbitals. They can accommodate the valence electrons in two ways, as follows:

or

Since electrons repel each other, that electron configuration which keeps the electrons farther apart will be the lower in energy. A configuration with one electron in each of two separate orbitals (different regions in space) keeps the electrons farther apart than a configuration with two electrons in a single orbital (same region in space). We would expect the configuration for the oxygen atom having two unpaired electrons to be lower in energy than the configuration having all electrons paired. Experiment confirms this prediction. Much of the chemistry of oxygen can be interpreted more easily using the orbital model having two unpaired electrons in separate, half-filled orbitals:

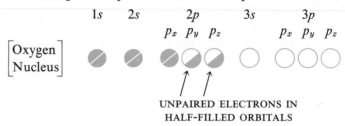

UNPAIRED ELECTRONS IN
HALF-FILLED ORBITALS

The differences in configuration between the two models are easily represented by the electron dot method. The arrangement below

$$\cdot \ddot{\text{O}} :$$

has a significantly lower energy than this configuration

$$\ddot{\underset{..}{\text{O}}} :$$

Suppose a single hydrogen atom approaches an oxygen atom in the lower energy state. Each atom has partially filled valence orbitals. Electron sharing can occur, placing electrons close to two nuclei simultaneously; hence, a stable bond can occur:

$$\text{H}\cdot + \cdot\ddot{\text{O}}: \longrightarrow \text{H}:\ddot{\underset{.}{\text{O}}}:^{*} \tag{5}$$

HALF-FILLED ORBITAL

We see that the species HO† has one unpaired electron left. Combination of HO with another hydrogen atom gives water:

$$\text{H}\cdot + \text{H}:\ddot{\underset{.}{\text{O}}}: \longrightarrow \text{H}:\underset{\text{H}}{\overset{..}{\ddot{\text{O}}}}: \tag{6}$$

The electron model suggests that the residual bonding capacity of HO has now been used up. We are not surprised to find that H_2O is very stable; it stands in striking contrast to the very reactive HO molecule. Oxygen is said to be **divalent** in water. Each atom in H_2O has filled its valence orbitals by electron sharing.

What happens if the HO unit combines with another HO unit? The electron dot diagram indicates the formula and the way the atoms are joined in the resulting compound. The equation is

$$:\underset{\text{H}}{\ddot{\text{O}}}\cdot + \overset{\text{H}}{\cdot\ddot{\text{O}}}: \longrightarrow \left(:\underset{..}{\ddot{\text{O}}} :\underset{\text{H}}{:} \overset{\text{H}}{\ddot{\text{O}}}: \right) \tag{7}$$

---

*Electron color is convenient for purposes of electron bookkeeping. Remember all electrons in the molecule are indistinguishable except for their energy.

†A molecular species with a half-filled valence orbital is frequently called a **free radical**. The HO· unit is called the **hydroxyl radical**. It has been identified and studied as an intermediate in many reactions, such as those taking place in high temperature flames.

The compound produced by two HO units combining is the well-known and very reactive bleaching agent hydrogen peroxide (H_2O_2). The model accurately predicts the existence of an O—O bond in H_2O_2.

EXERCISE 17-2

Predict the structure of the compound S_2Cl_2 from the electron dot representation of the atoms.

These analyses of the chemistry of oxygen and fluorine can be used to predict the compound F_2O. The electron dot representation is

Again oxygen is divalent.

EXERCISE 17-3

Draw orbital and electron dot representations of each of the following molecules: OF, F_2O_2, HOF, and HFO_2. Which of these would you expect to be the most reactive? H_2O_2 decomposes easily to give H_2O and O_2. Why?

17-2.2 The Bonding Capacity of Nitrogen Atoms

As with the oxygen atom, the nitrogen atom is most stable when it has the maximum number of partially filled valence orbitals because the electrons are then as far apart as possible. The most stable state of the five valence electrons of the nitrogen atom is

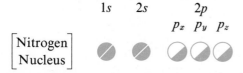

It is straightforward to predict that nitrogen will form a stable hydrogen compound with formula NH_3. The similar compound NF_3 will also be formed. The electron dot formula for NH_3 is

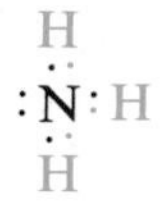

and the formula for NF_3 is

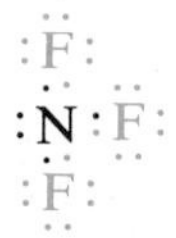

Nitrogen is **trivalent.**

EXERCISE 17-4

The molecule NH_2 has residual bonding capacity and is extremely reactive. The hydrazine molecule (N_2H_4) is much more stable. Draw an electron dot representation of the bonding of hydrazine. Draw its structural formula, showing which atoms are bonded to each other.

17-2.3   The Bonding Capacity of Carbon Atoms

Like oxygen and nitrogen, the carbon atom also is most stable when it has the maximum number of partially filled p orbitals. It has been experimentally shown that the lowest state for the carbon atom has a configuration of one electron in each p_x and p_y orbital. In this way electrons achieve a maximum average distance of separation.

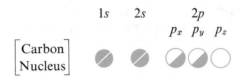

Now we can predict the chemistry of the carbon atom in this state. It should be divalent, forming CH_2 and CF_2. Let us consider CH_2:

$$H : \overset{..}{C} : H$$

The orbitals used are

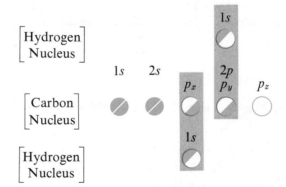

Here is a situation we have not yet met. After using the two available partially filled orbitals to form covalent bonds with hydrogen atoms, one vacant p orbital remains, and there is a filled, nonbonding s orbital.

What are the experimental consequences of this arrangement? It is found that both CH_2 and CF_2 can form as reaction intermediates at high temperatures, *but neither molecule has ever been obtained in a pure state. Both CH_2 and CF_2 are very reactive molecules.* This experimental fact can best be understood if we picture one of the electrons in the carbon $2s$ orbital as moving up to the $2p_z$ orbital with only a slight increase in the energy of the system. This process is called **promoting the electron.** As a result of the promotion process, the carbon atom has two more half-filled orbitals and thus the capacity to form *two* more covalent bonds.

$$\overset{\cdot}{\underset{\underset{H}{\cdot}}{C}}{:}H + 2H\cdot \longrightarrow H\overset{H}{\underset{\underset{H}{\cdot\cdot}}{:C:}}H \qquad (8)$$

Each covalent bond formed increases the stability of the system significantly. The decrease in the energy of the system due to new bond formation more than compensates for the small energy required to promote the $2s$ electron to the $2p_z$ level. The net result is that carbon is **tetravalent.**

EXERCISE 17-5

Draw the electron dot representation of the reaction between CF_2 and two F atoms. How would the CF_2 molecule be pictured in the electron dot formulation *prior to* and *after* electron promotion?

EXERCISE 17-6

Draw electron dot formulas for the molecules CH_3, CF_3, CHF_3, CH_2F_2, and CH_3F. Which will be extremely reactive?

EXERCISE 17-7

Draw an electron dot and a structural formula for the ethane molecule (C_2H_6), which forms when two CH_3 molecules are brought together. Explain why C_2H_6 is much less reactive than CH_3.

17-2.4 The Bonding Capacity of Boron Atoms

The boron atom presents the same sort of option in orbital occupancy as does carbon:

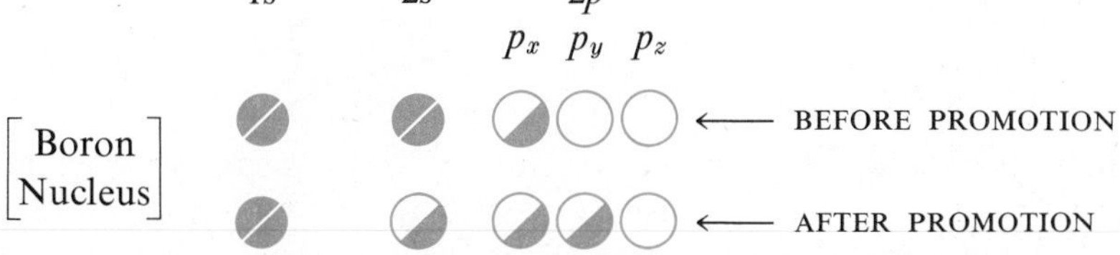

The promoted electron configuration is somewhat higher in energy than the lower electron state, in which full use is made of the low-energy $2s$ orbital. In return for this higher energy the boron atom gains bonding capacity from promotion. Whereas a boron atom can form only one covalent bond in the configuration before promotion, it can form three covalent bonds in the configuration after promotion. Since each bond lowers the energy, the chemistry of boron is determined by the promoted electron configuration.

Now we can expect that boron will be trivalent. We predict that there should be a molecule such as BF_3:

$$\ddot{:}\overset{\displaystyle ..}{\underset{\displaystyle ..}{F}}\ddot{:}$$
$$B:\ddot{F}:$$
$$\ddot{:}\overset{\displaystyle ..}{\underset{\displaystyle ..}{F}}\ddot{:}$$

Furthermore, the fact that there is one *empty* orbital left in BF_3 suggests possible additional reactivity for this species. What kind of reactivity is expected? In BF_3 there is *an empty orbital but no unused full orbital.* Thus, it is *not* possible for BF_3 to generate half-filled orbitals by electron promotion. The result is that BF_3 is a stable molecule which does *not* add other fluorine atoms to form additional covalent bonds.

Let us review and contrast the reactions of CF_2 and BF_3. In CF_2 we have a structure with *one unused orbital* and *one unused electron pair* on carbon. When one electron of the unused pair moves into the unused orbital, *two half-filled orbitals are obtained.* These half-filled orbitals make CF_2 very reactive toward any species having one half-filled orbital. For example, it combines with F atoms or other CF_2 groups. In contrast, BF_3 has *one empty orbital* but *no unused electron pair* on boron. Therefore, it is *not* possible to obtain half-filled orbitals by promoting an unused electron. We find that BF_3 is *not* readily attacked by F atoms, H atoms, or even other BF_3 molecules. BF_3 can be obtained as a pure compound of relatively high stability. But the compound BF_3 is *not inert;* it combines readily with molecules or ions, such as NH_3 or F^-, which can share a complete electron pair. This point is discussed in Chapter 13.

You may be wondering about the hydrides of boron. The line of reasoning we used in considering compounds of hydrogen with fluorine, oxygen, nitrogen, and carbon suggests that hydrogen and fluorine behave similarly. A compound BH_3 should exist just as does BF_3. We had H_2O, F_2O, HF, F_2, CH_4, CF_4, and so on. Why have we not discussed BH_3? Strangely enough, no stable BH_3 species is known. The simplest boron hydride is B_2H_6, known as diborane. This molecule and other boron hydrides in the series challenged many chemical theories. It is only recently that progress in understanding these molecules has been made. We shall discuss them briefly in the next chapter.

EXERCISE 17-8

What reaction, if any, would you expect between an HO molecule and a CH_3 molecule?

17-2.5 The Bonding Capacity of Beryllium Atoms

The beryllium atom in its lowest energy configuration shows two electrons in the $2s$ orbital. All $2p$ orbitals are vacant. Like boron and carbon, beryllium can promote a $2s$ electron to a $2p$ level:

After promotion we would expect the compound BeF_2, which is indeed found at temperatures above 1000 K. At lower temperatures, experiment shows that BeF_2 molecules tend to combine with each other to give a three-dimensional polymeric solid structure. BeH_2 is also a solid. It can best be explained in subsequent chemistry courses.

17-2.6 The Bonding Capacity of Lithium Atoms

The bonding capacity of a lithium atom is almost predictable from the foregoing arguments. Since the Li atom has just one valence electron, an LiF molecule might be expected to form at very high temperatures. Observation confirms the prediction.

17-3 TREND IN BOND TYPE AMONG THE SECOND-ROW FLUORIDES

All chemical bonds occur because electrons can be placed simultaneously near two nuclei. Yet, it is often true that this electron sharing is not exactly *equal* sharing. Sometimes the electrons tend to distribute somewhat nearer to one of the nuclei. We can understand this by comparing chemical bonding in gaseous fluorine (F_2) and in gaseous lithium fluoride (LiF).

17-3.1 The Bonding in Gaseous Lithium Fluoride

We have already treated the bonding in an F_2 molecule (Section 17-1.4). Since neither fluorine atom can completely pull an electron away from the other, they compromise and share a pair of electrons equally in a covalent bond. How does the chemical bonding in the lithium fluoride molecule compare?

As we have said, the Li atom has one valence electron, hence can share a pair of electrons with one fluorine atom. Thus, we can expect a stable gaseous molecular species, LiF.

$$\text{Li}\!:\!\ddot{\text{F}}\!:$$

However, the Li and F atoms attract electrons differently. This is shown by the ionization energies of these two atoms and the electron affinity of F.

$$401.5 \text{ kcal} + \text{F}(g) \longrightarrow \text{F}^+(g) + e^-(g) \qquad (9)$$

$$124.3 \text{ kcal} + \text{Li}(g) \longrightarrow \text{Li}^+(g) + e^-(g) \qquad (10)$$

$$\text{F}(g) + e^- \longrightarrow \text{F}^-(g) + 79 \text{ kcal} \qquad (11)$$

Clearly, the F atom holds electrons much more strongly than does the Li atom. As a result, the electron pair in the gaseous LiF bond is more strongly attracted to the F than to the Li atom. The energy is lowered when the electrons spill toward the F atom. *When the bonding electrons move closer to one of the two atoms, the bond is said to have* **ionic character.**

In the most extreme situation, the bonding electrons move so close to one of the atoms that this atom has virtually the electron distribution of the negative ion. This is the case in gaseous LiF. Using an electron dot representation, we might write

$$\text{Li}^+ \; :\!\overset{\displaystyle ..}{\underset{\displaystyle ..}{\text{F}}}\!:^-$$

or

$$\text{Li}^+ \quad \text{F}^-$$

When a formula showing ions provides a useful basis for discussing the properties of a molecule, the bond in that molecule is said to be an **ionic bond**.

Fig. 17-4 Electron distribution in various bond types.

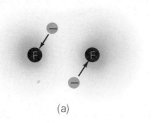

(a)

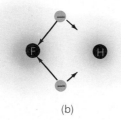

(b)

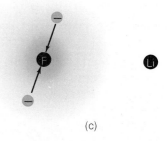

(c)

Remember that there is but one principle governing the formation of a chemical bond between two atoms: *all chemical bonds form because electrons are placed simultaneously near two positive nuclei.* The term **covalent bond** indicates that the most stable distribution of the electrons (in terms of *energy*) between the two atoms is symmetrical. When the bonding electrons are somewhat closer to one of the atoms, the bond is said to have **ionic character.** The term **ionic bond** indicates the electrons are displaced so much toward one atom that the bonded atoms must be considered a pair of ions that are near each other. Figure 17-4 shows schematically how the valence electron distributions are pictured in covalent (F—F), partially ionic (F—H), and ionic (F—Li) bonds. Figure 17-4 also shows how the valence electrons might look in an instantaneous snapshot. In each type of bond, the electron-nucleus attractions account for the energy stability of the molecule.

17-3.2 The Electric Dipole of the Ionic Bond

The spilling of negative electric charge toward one of the atoms in the ionic bond causes a charge separation. This can be represented crudely as in Figure 17-4(c). The LiF molecule is electrically positive at the lithium end and electrically negative at the fluorine end. It is said to possess an **electric dipole** and the molecule is called a **polar molecule.** The forces between polar molecules are much stronger than those between nonpolar molecules. The arrow representation of Figure 17-5 is commonly used and it is the simplest way of showing a bond dipole. The arrow indicates that the negative charge is mainly at one end of the bond. This means that the force this molecule exerts on another molecule depends upon the direction of approach of the second molecule.

Fig. 17-5 Representations of the electric dipole of gaseous lithium fluoride.

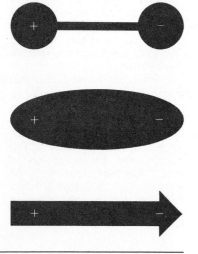

17-3.3 Ionic Character in Bonds to Fluorine

We can expect the effects just discussed in LiF to be at work in other fluorides. Ionization energies give us a rough clue to the electron-nucleus attractions in these bonds. Table 17-1 compares the ionization energies of each element of the second row with that of fluorine. The last column describes in appropriate terms the type of chemical bond.

The trend from covalent to ionic-bond type shown in Table 17-1 greatly influences the trend in properties of the fluorine compounds. This trend is caused by the increasing difference between ionization energies of the two bonded atoms.

TABLE 17-1 BOND TYPES IN SOME FLUORINE COMPOUNDS

Compound	Bond	Ionization Energies (kcal/mole)		Bond Type
		Element Bonded to F	Fluorine	
FF	F—F	F	401.5	401.5	COVALENT
OF_2	O—F	O	313.8	401.5	increasing ionic character
NF_3	N—F	N	335.4	401.5	
CF_4	C—F	C	259.5	401.5	
BF_3	B—F	B	191.2	401.5	increasing covalent character
BeF_2	Be—F	Be	214.9	401.5	
LiF	Li—F	Li	124.3	401.5	IONIC

17-3.4 Ionic Character in Bonds to Hydrogen

In Chapter 8 the element hydrogen was characterized as a family by itself. Often its chemistry distinguishes it from the rest of the periodic table. We find this is the case when we attempt to predict the ionic character of bonds to hydrogen.

The ionization energy of the H atom, 313.6 kcal/mole, is quite close to that of the F atom; so we expect a covalent bond between these two atoms in HF. Actually, the properties of HF show that the molecule has a significant electric dipole, indicating significant ionic character in the bond. The same is true in the O—H bonds of water and, to a lesser extent, in the N—H bonds of ammonia. Examination of the properties of a number of compounds involving hydrogen indicates that the ionic character of bonds to hydrogen is roughly like that of bonds to an element having an ionization energy near 200 kcal/mole. *We cannot predict, then, the ionic character of bonds to hydrogen from its measured ionization energy.* The C—H bond has only a slightly ionic character. At the other end of the periodic table, gaseous lithium hydride is known to have a significant electric dipole, but with the electric dipole turned around. In LiH the electrons are spilled toward the H atom, leaving the Li atom with a partial positive charge. This is in accord with the low ionization energy of Li, 124.3 kcal/mole, which is well below the value of 200 kcal/mole that we have assigned

LINUS C. PAULING
(1901–   )

The ideas of Linus C. Pauling pervade every aspect of chemistry. They have won him many high awards, including the 1954 Nobel Prize in Chemistry.

Born in Portland, Oregon, Pauling received his Ph.D. from the California Institute of Technology, where he pursued his illustrious career. In his early years, Pauling was quick to recognize the importance of quantum mechanics in any study of the chemical bond; he was one of the pioneers in the use of quantum mechanics to explain the facts of chemistry. His work has included definitive studies on hydrogen bonding, metallic bonding, effective sizes of atoms in molecules and crystals, and protein structure. The latter has been important in biochemistry.

Pauling has worked energetically to awaken the conscience of society to its new responsibilities in the nuclear age. His activities have at times attracted ridicule, when fear made his cause an unpopular one. In recognition of them, however, Pauling was awarded the 1962 Nobel Peace Prize, and thus became the second person in history to receive the Nobel Prize twice.

IONIC CHARACTER

in BONDS to HYDROGEN

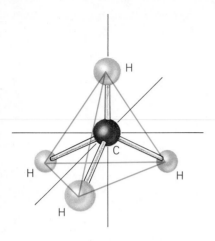

Fig. 17-6.1 The geometry of the methane molecule, CH_4.

Fig. 17-6.2 A space-filling model of the methane molecule.

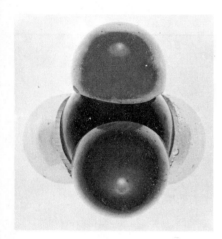

to hydrogen. For our purposes, *it suffices to discuss the bonding of hydrogen in terms of an apparent and arbitrary ionization energy near 200 kcal/mole.*

17-4 MOLECULAR GEOMETRY

Molecular properties result from both the identity of the atoms in the molecule and their geometrical arrangement. Shapes of many molecules have been determined experimentally using methods summarized briefly in the last section of this chapter. On the basis of this structural information, a number of different electron models have been proposed to help us understand and even predict molecular geometry.*

Chemists disagree rather vigorously over the relative values of these models. Some like one model; some like another. The plain truth of the matter is that we do not have a "correct" model for a system as complicated as a many-electron atom. In every case a general theoretical picture is constructed *after* a large amount of experimental information about structure has been accumulated. The theory is then used to predict an unknown structure. Experimental information about structure for the particular molecule is obtained and compared with that predicted by the general theory. The value of the theory is judged by its ability to correlate and anticipate the new experimental results. In this book we shall focus our attention on a relatively simple, but very effective, old theoretical model which has been vigorously revived recently.† The effectiveness of this model is matched only by its simplicity.

17-4.1 Arrangement of Electrons in Orbitals

In our discussion of orbital shapes for the gaseous hydrogen *atom*, we recognized one spherical 2s and three dumbbell shaped 2p orbitals. The 2p orbitals were at 90° angles to each other. This known orbital geometry is restricted to the hydrogen atom because of its makeup— one proton and one electron. Additional electrons and protons create electrical fields which greatly distort the electron or orbital arrangement. For example, in CH_4 we might expect an H—C—H angle of 90° since the 2p carbon orbitals forming the C—H bonds presumably make a 90° angle. (Section 17-2.3.) In fact the experimental H—C—H bond angle is 109°28′, not the 90° predicted by p-orbital geometry. Further, we do not find that the three hydrogen atoms bound to p orbitals differ from the hydrogen bound to an s orbital. *Experiment shows that every hydrogen atom in CH_4 is the same. All H—C—H angles in the molecule CH_4 are 109°28′.* The molecule has four hydrogen atoms arranged at the corners of a regular tetrahedron. The carbon atom is in the center of the tetrahedron. (See Figure 17-6.) What kind of model can interpret these and related observations?

*The *Journal of Chemical Education* for December, 1968, contains two papers describing different approaches to molecular geometry. See L. S. Bartell, page 754, and H. S. Bent, page 768. Molecular geometry is still an area of active research.
†Two of the most articulate and able spokesmen for this point of view are Professor R. J. Gillespie of McMaster University in Canada and the late Professor R. Nyholm of University College, London, England. See *J. Chem. Ed.*, **40**, 295 (1963).

The theory we shall consider proposes that *the arrangement of atoms around any given central atom is determined primarily by the repulsive interactions between electron pairs in the valence shell of that central atom.* For example, the geometry of CH_4 would be determined by the repulsion between electron pairs making up each of the four C—H bonds. The electron pairs move as far apart as possible and the tetrahedron results.*

The geometry of CH_4 is fairly obvious. Can the theory work to give us the structure of a less obvious molecule such as H_2O? In visualizing the geometry of water, let us start with an imaginary oxide ion containing eight valence electrons. Since only two electrons can exist in any one orbital, we must have four orbitals. Thus, for an oxide ion the one $2s$ and three $2p$ orbitals would combine or be "hybridized" to give *four identical orbitals,* each containing two electrons. These four identical orbitals, as in carbon, are called sp^3 hybrids. We know that electron clouds repel each other; hence, it would seem logical to assume that the electron clouds defining these four identical orbitals of O^{2-} would assume a position with a maximum distance between the clouds. The line defining the central axis of each orbital would make an angle of 109°28′ with the central axis of every other orbital in that atom. We would expect an essentially spherical distribution of electron charge around the oxygen core in O^{2-}. Theory and experiment agree for those structures with eight electrons in the outer level. As far as our experiments can determine, free oxide ions are spherically symmetrical!

17-4.2 The Introduction of Protons into Orbitals— The Geometry of Water

Now what happens if a proton is made to approach an oxide *ion?* As the proton approaches, two of the electrons in one of the orbitals will be pulled toward the approaching proton. *The formerly spherical electron cloud is distorted.* The electron cloud which represented this particular "hybrid orbital" will stretch out toward the proton and shrink downward toward the line between O and H nuclei. The electron cloud of the bonding orbital will become longer and thinner as the proton approaches. As the orbital shrinks in diameter, the other electron clouds expand to utilize the newly available space (see Figure 17-7.1, page 418).

Let us now bring a second proton toward the OH^- unit just formed. Again, an electron pair in one of the three unused orbitals will become involved in bond formation with the proton. Again, the electron cloud in this newly utilized bonding orbital will stretch out toward the proton and become thinner. The free electron pairs will force together the two somewhat shrunken bonding orbitals linked to each of the two protons (Figure 17-7.2, page 419).

The introduction of the proton causes a contraction in the angle defined by the H, O, and H atoms. The two electron clouds forming bonds with protons are contracted and forced together. The resulting H—O—H angle in water should be *less than* 109°28′. The experimental

---

*The four bonding orbitals are identical and are called sp^3 hybrids. They are made by mixing or "hybridizing" the s and the three valence p orbitals to obtain four orbitals pointing toward the corners of a regular tetrahedron.

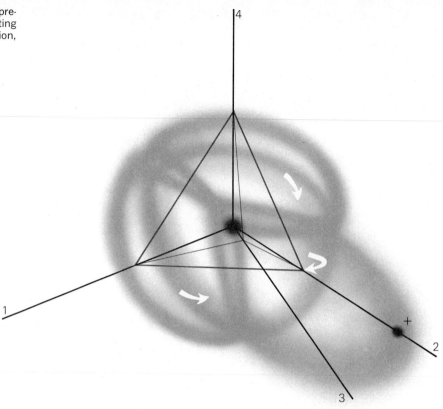

value is 104°30′. (See Figure 17-7.2.) Theory and experiment are in qualitative agreement because the theory was constructed from the observed facts.

This discussion tells us what the process might be when a water molecule is formed from an oxide ion and two protons; yet the final geometry is the same, no matter how the water molecule is formed. We note that the geometry of water can be understood in terms of the repulsion of the four pairs of valence electrons around the oxygen core (O^{6+}). Two pairs of electrons are used in binding protons and two pairs are free. The free pairs are the largest in size.

17-4.3 The Geometry of F_2O

It seems quite clear that if the approaching atom or ions attract electrons more strongly than does a proton of water, the electron cloud will stretch out and shrink in diameter to an even greater degree than in the case of water. If the electron clouds used in bonding are contracted more during bond formation, they can be pushed closer together by the expanding clouds of the unused electron pairs. This argument leads us to believe that if we visualize interaction of an F^+ ion with an O^{2-} ion, the bonding electron cloud will be compressed somewhat more along the bond axis. Electrons will then actually move well out toward F^+. This follows because of the very great attraction of F^+ for electrons. (Remember that the fluorine atom has an ionization energy of 402 kcal/mole. This value is second only to neon in the

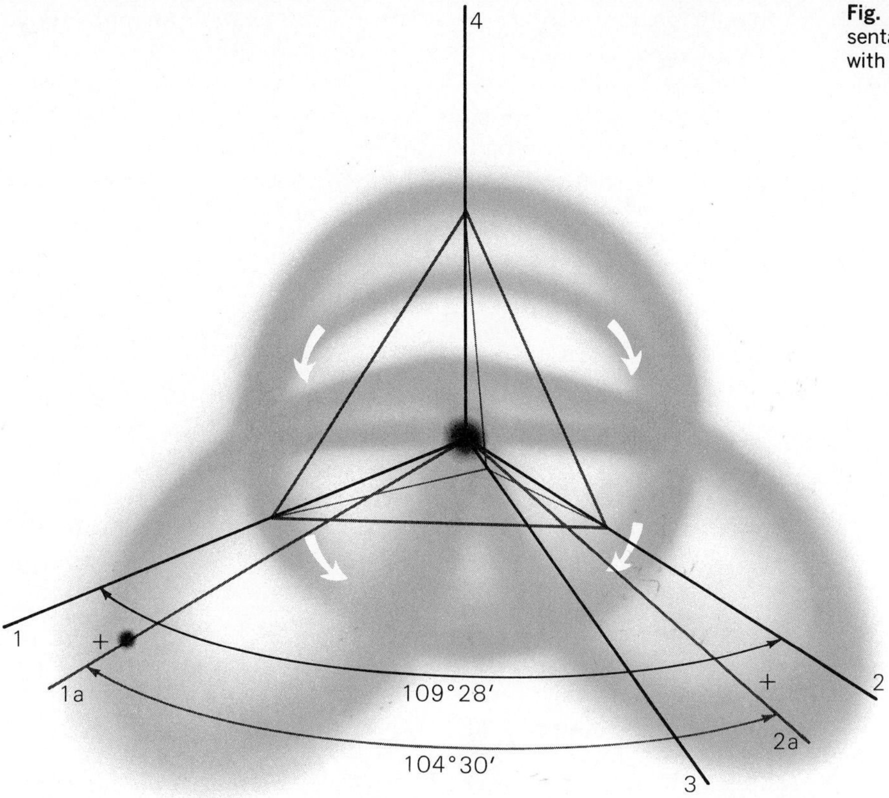

Fig. 17-7.2 A schematic representation of a proton interacting with the hydroxide ion, OH^-.

second row of the periodic table.) The electron-cloud model then suggests that the electron cloud as it moves out toward F^+ will become thinner and longer. It will then be pushed together by the expanding free electron clouds. An angle of even less than $104°30'$ is expected. The experimental value is $103°$. While a contraction in angle is observed, the change is so small that its significance may be questioned.

The molecules can be conveniently represented using these models:

$$H \overset{O}{\longleftrightarrow} H \qquad \angle H\text{—}O\text{—}H = 104°30'$$

$$F \overset{O}{\longleftrightarrow} F \qquad \angle F\text{—}O\text{—}F = 103°$$

A line is drawn between the oxygen atom and each hydrogen atom in water to indicate that a chemical bond holds these two atoms together. No line is drawn between the two hydrogen atoms since we think they are not directly bonded to each other. The same is true of F_2O.

17-4.4 The Geometry of NH_3 and of NF_3

In considering the geometry of NH_3 and NF_3, it is convenient to imagine the interaction of protons or of *positive* fluorine *ions** with

---

*This does not imply that we have F^+ ions or N^{3-} ions in the final molecule. Electrons move out to form a covalent bond. The cloud ultimately is probably closer to the fluorine than the nitrogen.

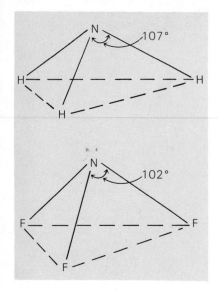

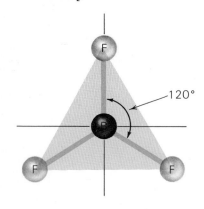

Fig. 17-8 The geometries of NH₃ and NF₃.

Fig. 17-9 The structures of BF₃ and BeF₂.

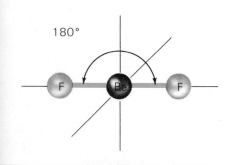

a hypothetical nitride ion, N^{3-}. If three protons were to approach the nitride ion one at a time, electron clouds in three orbitals would shrink in diameter around each N—H bond. *The unused electron pair would then expand, pushing the compressed electron clouds together.* The H—N—H angle in ammonia (NH_3) should be less than the 109°28' predicted by identical sp^3 hybrid orbitals. The experimental value is 107°.

Identical arguments indicate that NF_3, having three fluorine-nitrogen bonds and one free electron pair, should have a bond angle smaller than 107° (Figure 17-8). The experimental value is 102°, almost equal to the F—O—F angle in F_2O. One prediction of the theory—a smaller angle in NF_3 than in NH_3—is verified.

17-4.5 The Geometry of CH₄ and CF₄

In both CH_4 and CF_4 all four orbitals are identical. We are not surprised that in CH_4 the angle between *any two* C—H bonds is 109°28' and in CF_4 the angle between *any two* C—F bonds is 109°28'. This structure is called **tetrahedral** because the four hydrogen atoms occupy the positions at the corners of a *regular tetrahedron*. The structure is shown in Figure 17-6.

17-4.6 The Geometry of BF₃ and of BeF₂

In BF_3 we have to consider only three pairs of electrons around boron. Each electron pair is involved in forming a bond with fluorine. The arrangement permitting maximum distance between three electron pairs would be a **planar molecule** with a fluorine at each vertex of an *equilateral triangle*. Experiment confirms this. All atoms of the molecule lie in a plane. (See Figure 17-9.)

In gaseous BeF_2 there are only two electron pairs to keep apart and no free electron pairs. Of course, each electron pair is involved in a bond to fluorine. The arrangement giving maximum distance between electron clouds would be that of the linear molecule shown in Figure 17-9. Gaseous BeF_2 is a **linear molecule.**

17-4.7 A Summary of Molecular Geometry

In summary, the structure of most molecules can be derived by using the **valence-shell electron-pair repulsion theory.** The following procedure permits application of the theory.

(1) Write an electron dot formula for the molecule showing electron pair bonds (electron pairs bonded between atoms) and free electron pairs.

(2) Count the number of electron pair bonds and the number of free electron pairs around the central atom.

(3) If the molecule contains only two atoms, it must be linear. If the molecule contains three atoms and the number obtained in (2) is 2, the molecule is linear [Figure 17-10(a)]. If the molecule has three atoms and the number obtained in (2) is 3, the angle is 120° or perhaps a little less [Figure 17-10(b)].

Shapes corresponding to various numbers of atoms (X) and electron pairs (E) around a central atom (A) are shown in Figure 17-10.*

17-4.8 A Comment on Notation

As you will remember, the orbital description of the beryllium atom used in forming BeF_2 showed one electron in a $2s$ orbital and one electron in a $2p$ orbital. Experiment shows that the BeF_2 molecule is linear. Chemists sometimes summarize these facts by saying that the combination of one s and one p orbital gives two **linear orbitals.** The bonding is sometimes called **sp bonding.** A linear molecule is implied by the sp notation.

In considering boron bonding, we noted that the promoted boron atom has one electron in a $2s$ orbital and two electrons in two $2p$ orbitals. This combination of one s and two p orbitals gave a molecule with triangular geometry. For this reason the bonding is sometimes called **sp² bonding.** The sp^2 notation implies **planar triangular geometry.**

In forming CH_4 we had to use one s and three p orbitals. As pointed out earlier, this leads to the designation **sp³ bonding** for **tetrahedral geometry.** Nitrogen and oxygen are also considered to have modified sp^3 bonding, with one or two orbitals containing free electron pairs.

17-5 MOLECULAR SHAPE AND ELECTRIC DIPOLES

Consider the fluorides of the second-row elements. There is a continuous increase in ionic character of the bonds formed by fluorine with elements F, O, N, C, B, Be, and Li. (Look up the ionization energies of these elements in Table 17-1.) This ionic character results in an electric dipole in the bond. The *molecular dipole* will be determined by the sum of the dipoles of all bonds if this addition takes into account the geometry of the molecule. Since the properties of the molecule are strongly affected by the molecular dipole, we shall investigate its relationship to the molecular architecture and the ionic character of the individual bonds. For this study we shall begin at the left side of the periodic table. Information on geometry and bonding is summarized in Table 17-2 (page 422).

17-5.1 The Molecular Dipole of LiF

The lithium fluoride bond is highly ionic in character because of the large difference in ionization energies of lithium and fluorine. Consequently, gaseous lithium fluoride has an unusually high electric dipole.

*In Figure 17-10, each circle represents an atom; each line represents a bonded electron pair; and each gold cloud represents a free electron pair.

Fig. 17-10 The general shapes of molecules of the nontransition elements.

(a)

(b)

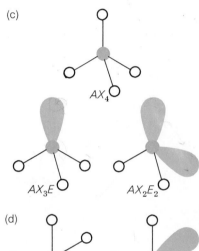

(c)

(d)

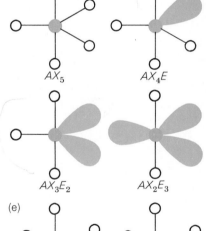

(e)

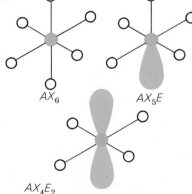

TABLE 17-2 BONDING AND MOLECULAR GEOMETRY FOR SOME FLUORINE COMPOUNDS

Element	Bonding Orbitals	Bonding Capacity	Number of Free Electron Pairs in Valence Shell	Shape of Fluoride Molecule	Formula
He	none	0	0	no fluoride known	He
Li	s	1	0	linear, diatomic	LiF
Be	sp	2	0	linear, triatomic	BeF_2
B	sp^2	3	0	planar, triangular	BF_3
C	sp^3	4	0	tetrahedral	CF_4
N	sp^{3*}	3	1	pyramidal	NF_3
O	$sp^3\dagger$	2	2	angular, bent	OF_2
F	p	1	3	linear	F_2
Ne	none	0	4	no fluoride known	Ne

*Nearly sp^3 with one orbital containing a free pair of electrons.
†Nearly sp^3 with two orbitals containing free pairs of electrons.

17-5.2   The Molecular Dipole of BeF_2

The beryllium-fluorine bond is also highly ionic in character. However, there are two such Be—F bonds, and the electrical properties of the entire molecule depend upon how these two bonds are oriented to each other. We must find the "geometrical sum" of these two bond dipoles. The geometrical sum of two arrows can be understood with the aid of Figure 17-11. Figure 17-11(a) shows how two arrows that point in the same direction combine to give a longer arrow. Figure 17-11(b) shows how two arrows that point in opposite directions combine to give a shorter arrow. Figure 17-11(c) shows how two arrows that are not parallel add to give an arrow in a new direction. In the linear, symmetrical BeF_2 molecule, the two bond dipoles point in *opposite* directions. Since the two bonds are equivalent, their sum is zero, as shown in Figure 17-12; hence, the molecule has no *net* dipole; the molecular dipole is zero.

Fig. 17-11 The geometrical sum of dipoles.

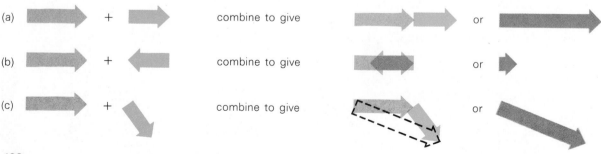

(a)   +   combine to give   or

(b)   +   combine to give   or

(c)   +   combine to give   or

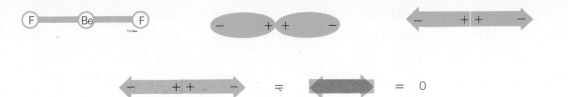

Fig. 17-12 The absence of a molecular dipole in BeF_2.

17-5.3 The Molecular Dipoles of BF_3 and CF_4

Both these molecules are thought to have moderate amounts of ionic character in each bond. Yet each molecular dipole is exactly zero. Careful consideration of the molecular geometry shows that there is a complete cancellation of the bond dipoles. This cancellation is shown in Figure 17-13 for BF_3.

Fig. 17-13 The absence of a molecular dipole in BF_3.

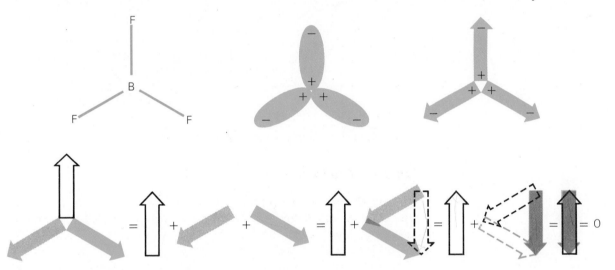

17-5.4 The Molecular Dipole in F_2O

Since F_2O is a bent molecule, the two bond dipoles do not cancel each other as they do in BeF_2 (Figure 17-12). On the other hand, the ionization energies of oxygen and fluorine are not very different, so the electric dipole of each bond is small in magnitude. These add together, according to their geometry or the "direction" of their "arrows," to give a polar molecule, as shown in Figure 17-14. (The polar molecule has a net molecular dipole.)

Fig. 17-14 The molecular dipole of F_2O.

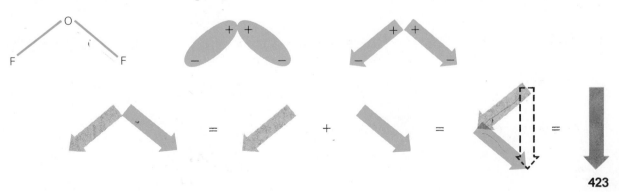

423

Water has a high molecular dipole while CO_2 has zero molecular dipole. Can you rationalize these facts?

17-6 MULTIPLE BONDS

In determining the bonding capacity of a given atom from the second row, we counted the number of hydrogen or fluorine atoms with which the atom will combine. Oxygen combines with *two* hydrogen atoms to give water; oxygen is described as **divalent.** Carbon combines with *four* hydrogen atoms to give methane (CH_4); carbon is described as **tetravalent.** In each case, the bond formed between the hydrogen atom and the central element is a single bond—two atoms share an electron pair. Similarly, one can recognize a single-bonded structure, giving C—H and C—C bonds, in the structure of the compound ethane (C_2H_6). Its structure is represented as

$$
\begin{array}{cc}
\text{H} & \text{H} \qquad * \\
\text{H}\!:\!\overset{..}{\underset{..}{\text{C}}}\!:\!\overset{..}{\underset{..}{\text{C}}}\!:\!\text{H} \\
\text{H} & \text{H}
\end{array}
$$

Note that all bonds are single bonds; they are made with a *single* electron pair.

17-6.1 The Carbon-Carbon Double Bond

Another compound containing hydrogen and two carbon atoms is ethylene (C_2H_4). Note that it has *two* hydrogen atoms *less than* does ethane (C_2H_6). Suppose we write an electron dot representation of ethylene following the pattern established for ethane:

$$
\begin{array}{cc}
\text{H} & \text{H} \\
\text{H}\!:\!\overset{..}{\text{C}}\!:\!\overset{..}{\text{C}}\!:\!\text{H} \\
\cdot & \cdot
\end{array}
$$

TWO HYDROGEN ATOMS REMOVED LEAVE
TWO HALF-FILLED ORBITALS

This formula has two unpaired electrons, thus unused bonding capacity. This objectionable situation could easily be rectified by the pairing of the unused electrons, thus forming an additional shared-electron pair bond. Now the carbon atoms are joined by a double bond:

$$
\begin{array}{cc}
\text{H}\cdot & \cdot\text{H} \\
\overset{..}{\text{C}}\!:\!:\!\overset{..}{\text{C}} \\
\text{H} & \text{H}
\end{array}
$$

Much evidence supports this proposal. The carbon-carbon bond length in C_2H_4 is 1.34×10^{-10} metre while that in C_2H_6 is 1.54×10^{-10} metre. The bond in C_2H_4 is 0.20×10^{-10} metre shorter as a result of increased electron density between carbons. The vibrational frequency of the $\text{C}{=}\text{C}$ bond (4.950×10^{13} vibrations/sec or $1,650$ cm^{-1}) is

*Remember again that color is only a bookkeeping convenience. All H atoms are identical and all C atoms are identical.

higher than that of the $-\overset{|}{\underset{|}{C}}-\overset{|}{\underset{|}{C}}-$ bond (3.600×10^{13} vibrations/sec or $1,200$ cm^{-1}). If we remember the relationship $E = h\nu$, we shall see that a higher vibrational frequency corresponds to the utilization of more energy in the vibration of carbon atoms joined by a double bond. *The $C{=}C$ double bond in C_2H_4 is stronger than the $C{-}C$ single bond in C_2H_6.* More energy is required to break the $\overset{\diagdown}{}C{=}C\overset{\diagup}{}$ bond in C_2H_4 (146 kcal/mole) than the $-\overset{|}{\underset{|}{C}}-\overset{|}{\underset{|}{C}}-$ bond in C_2H_6 (83 kcal/mole). On the other hand, we shall find that although the breaking of a $\overset{\diagdown}{}C{=}C\overset{\diagup}{}$ bond to give $\overset{\diagup}{}C{:}$ fragments requires much energy, the $\overset{\diagdown}{}C{=}C\overset{\diagup}{}$ bond is readily attacked and *opened up by many reagents* to give a more stable molecule. Such a new molecule contains two *new covalent $C{-}X$* bonds instead of the one extra $C{-}C$ bond. Consider, for example, the reaction with hydrogen:

$$\underset{H}{\overset{H}{\diagdown}}C{=}C\underset{H}{\overset{H}{\diagup}} + H{-}H \longrightarrow H{-}\overset{\overset{\displaystyle H}{|}}{\underset{\underset{\displaystyle H}{|}}{C}}{-}\overset{\overset{\displaystyle H}{|}}{\underset{\underset{\displaystyle H}{|}}{C}}{-}H \qquad (12)$$

The formation of two new $C{-}H$ bonds more than compensates for the destruction of one of the two $C{-}C$ bonds in ethylene and of the $H{-}H$ bond in gaseous hydrogen.

For this reason, *the double bond is a source of reactivity* in a molecule. In ethane (C_2H_6) all bonds are normal single bonds. Experiment shows that ethane is fairly unreactive. It reacts only when treated with quite reactive species (such as free chlorine atoms), or when it is raised to excited energy states by heat (as in combustion). Ethylene (C_2H_4), on the other hand, reacts readily with many chemical reagents. Any reagent which can utilize electrons from one of the double-bond pairs to form two new covalent bonds will attack ethylene very readily. Chlorine or bromine, for example, will be picked up very easily by ethylene to give dichloroethane or dibromoethane:

$$\underset{H}{\overset{H}{\diagdown}}C{=}C\underset{H}{\overset{H}{\diagup}} + Cl{-}Cl \longrightarrow H{-}\overset{\overset{\displaystyle H}{|}}{\underset{\underset{\displaystyle Cl}{|}}{C}}{-}\overset{\overset{\displaystyle H}{|}}{\underset{\underset{\displaystyle Cl}{|}}{C}}{-}H \qquad (13)$$

The electrons of the double bond seem to be accessible. We find that the typical reactions of ethylene are with those reagents which *seek* electrons, oxidizing agents. The double bond is readily oxidized by such oxidizing agents as potassium permanganate or potassium dichromate at ordinary temperatures. But at ordinary temperatures ethane, *without* the double bond, is completely unreactive to the same reagents.

17-6.2 The Geometric Consequences of the Carbon-Carbon Double Bond—Structural Isomers

Experiment shows that the ethylene molecule is planar—the four hydrogen atoms and the two carbon atoms all lie in one plane. The

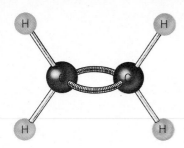

Fig. 17-15.1 A model of an ethylene molecule, C_2H_4.

Fig. 17-15.2 A model of an ethane molecule, C_2H_6.

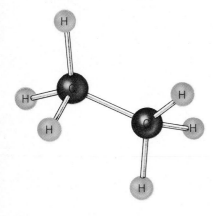

twisting of CH_2 groups around the C—C axis is difficult; otherwise, the molecule would not retain its flat form. The ball, spring, and stick model shown in Figure 17-15 shows the rigidity of the double-bonded structure. Compare it with the ball-and-stick model for ethane, in which rotation around the C—C bond is relatively easy.

It is possible to replace hydrogen atoms of ethylene with halogen atoms. One such compound has the formula $C_2H_2Cl_2$. Examination of the model for ethylene suggests three possible ways in which the two chlorine atoms can be arranged in $C_2H_2Cl_2$. This is shown in Figure 17-16. Experimentally, three different compounds with this formula are found, and structural studies confirm the existence of these three configurations. Note that all three compounds have the same formula, $C_2H_2Cl_2$. All are called dichloroethylene. *Different compounds with the same formula are called* **isomers.**

In one $C_2H_2Cl_2$ molecule two chlorines are attached to the *same* carbon [Figure 17-16(a)]. In the remaining two molecules [Figure 17-16(b) and (c)] chlorines are attached to *different* carbon atoms. Isomers in which the actual bonding arrangements among atoms differ—for example, two chlorines to a single carbon in one case, and one chlorine to each of two carbons in the other—are called **structural isomers.** The structural isomer with chlorines attached to two different carbons has two different forms—the *cis*-form—two chlorines on the *same side* of the double bond [Figure 17-16(b)]—and the *trans*-form—chlorine atoms on *opposite sides* of the double bond [Figure 17-16(c)].

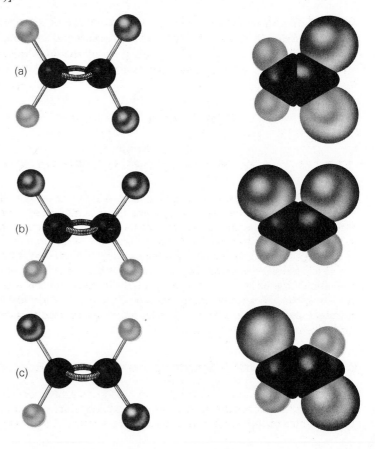

Fig. 17-16 Models of the three isomers of dichloroethylene, $C_2H_2Cl_2$.

17-6.3 The Triple Bond in Nitrogen

Multiple bonds are not restricted to carbon compounds. Let us investigate this by writing an electron dot formula for nitrogen. Suppose nitrogen had a single bond; the structure would be

$$:\overset{\cdot}{N}:\overset{\cdot}{N}:$$

The problem we recognized in C_2H_4 is present here, only it is worse because each nitrogen atom has *two* half-filled orbitals. The solution suggested for ethylene can be applied here to give a **triple bond:**

$$:N:::N:$$

or N≡N. The triple bond between nitrogen atoms in elemental nitrogen is very strong and accounts for the very high dissociation energy of N_2.

$$N_2(g) + 226 \text{ kcal} \longrightarrow 2N(g) \qquad (14)$$

The energy of dissociation is six times larger than the energy of the single N—N bond in hydrazine:

$$H_2N\text{—}NH_2 + 38 \text{ kcal} \longrightarrow 2H_2N \qquad (15)$$

Indeed, we can understand the very inert nature of nitrogen at low temperatures in terms of the very strong triple bond in the elemental nitrogen molecule. Similarly, a good part of the high reactivity of fluorine can be ascribed to the very weak single bond between two fluorine atoms:

$$F_2(g) + 37 \text{ kcal} \longrightarrow 2F(g) \qquad (16)$$

17-7 METHODS OF STRUCTURE DETERMINATION

Much has been said about molecular structure in earlier parts of this book. How do scientists know just where atoms are in a molecule? How sure are we that the models constructed really represent molecular geometry? Many types of experiments give structural information. Most such experimental techniques are so complex that a detailed study of them here is impossible. We shall, however, summarize the general ideas associated with several well-known methods for establishing structure. Some of these techniques will be applied to specific compounds in Chapter 19. Chemical evidence, infrared spectroscopy, and nmr spectroscopy will be used to establish the structure of an organic molecule.

17-7.1 Structural Information from Chemical Reactions

You learned in Section 17-6.2 that three distinct substances of formula $C_2H_2Cl_2$ could be formed. You also saw that the model for ethylene indicates the existence of three and only three distinct isomers. Agreement between

**DOROTHY C. HODGKIN
(1910–   )**

Dorothy C. Hodgkin was born in Cairo, Egypt. After receiving her B.Sc. degree from Somerville College in England, she pursued her doctoral studies at the crystallographic laboratory at Cambridge University. She received her Ph.D. in 1937.

Dr. Hodgkin's work using X-ray crystallography to determine the structures of complex biochemical substances is considered classic. In the 1950's, she determined the structure of vitamin B_{12}, an extremely complex coordination compound which is larger than any other known vitamin. It includes a trivalent cobalt and a cyano (C≡N) group, and has an empirical formula of $C_{63}H_{88}N_{14}O_{14}PCo$. For her work in determining the structure of vitamin B_{12} and other biochemical substances, including penicillin, Dr. Hodgkin was awarded the 1964 Nobel Prize in Chemistry.

At the present time, Dr. Hodgkin is Professor of Molecular Biophysics in the Department of Zoology at Oxford University.

chemical fact and structural prediction based on a given model (*i.e.*, number of isomers) provides experimental support for the model. Indeed, most early information on structure in chemistry was obtained using this very method. Today the chemical information is usually supplemented by more direct physical methods which can reveal actual atomic positions and identify individual isomers.

17-7.2   X-Ray Diffraction Methods

As you will remember from Chapter 16, X rays are light waves of frequencies near 10^{18} vibrations/sec and wavelengths near 10^{-10} metre. Such X-ray waves, when reflected from the surface of a crystal, give patterns on a photographic film. The appearance of the pattern is determined by the spacings of the atoms in the crystal and their geometric arrangement. The pattern is obtainable only with X rays because it results from scattering effects that occur only if the wavelength of the light is close to the atomic separations within the crystal. Therefore, a knowledge of the wavelength of the X-ray light permits an interpretation of the pattern in terms of atomic packing.

This method of study, when properly conducted, provides final evidence of molecular structure. After a proper single crystal X-ray study, atomic arrangement, bond angles, and bond distances are known with a high degree of certainty. The method is particularly applicable to crystalline solids. X-ray methods established the structure of NaCl, diamond, graphite, and recently, many biologically important substances.

17-7.3   Electron Diffraction

As you will recall from Chapter 16, moving electrons have wave character and will undergo diffraction just like X rays. Electron-diffraction methods are particularly appropriate to a study of gases and give the same type of structural information for gases that X rays give for solids.

17-7.4   Infrared Spectroscopy

Again, you will recall from Chapter 16 that light of longer wavelength than red light is called infrared radiation. Frequencies of infrared radiation range from about 2×10^{13} to 12×10^{13} vibrations/sec. When photons with this much energy* are absorbed by molecules, the atoms vibrate back and forth against each other.† The specific frequency needed to set a system in motion is determined by the type of atomic motion, the mass of the atoms, the shape of the molecule, and the strength of the chemical bonds linking the atoms. Through a study of the precise frequencies at which absorption occurs, it is often possible to obtain structural information. Infrared data are easy to obtain but provide less detailed structural information than do X-ray data.

Infrared spectra are very widely used for compound identification. Each molecule has a characteristic spectrum, which can be used to recognize molecular species. In Figure 17-17(a), we see the spectrum of carbon tetrachloride (CCl_4); in Figure 17-17(b), the spectrum of carbon disulfide (CS_2); and in Figure 17-17(c), that of a mixture containing 95 percent CCl_4 and 5 percent CS_2. As you can easily see, the presence of CS_2 in CCl_4 is not difficult to recognize.

*Remember that $E = h\nu$, where E is the energy of a photon, h is Planck's constant, and ν is light frequency.
†Remember that a fluctuating magnetic field can make a compass needle vibrate.

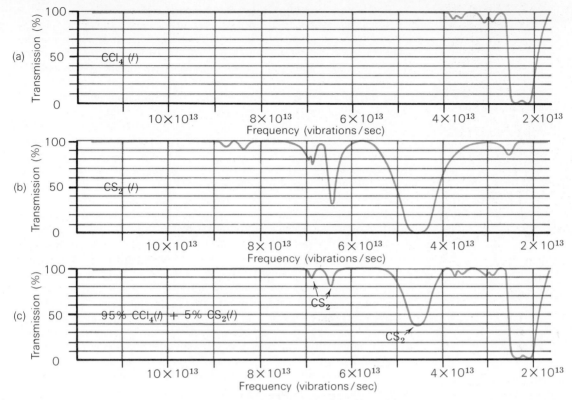

The value of infrared spectra in identifying substances, verifying purity, and quantitative analysis rivals their usefulness in learning about molecular structure. The infrared spectrum is even more important than melting point in characterizing a pure substance. Thus, infrared spectroscopy has become an important addition to the many techniques used by the chemist.

Fig. 17-17 Infrared absorption spectra of liquid carbon tetrachloride, CCl_4, carbon disulfide, CS_2, and a mixture of the two.

17-7.5 Microwave Spectroscopy

If you check the electromagnetic spectrum in Table 16-2 on page 373, you will find a group of *wavelengths* longer than infrared but shorter than radio waves. This region of the spectrum, known as the **microwave region,** covers frequencies from about 3×10^9 to 3×10^{11} vibrations/sec. Photons of this frequency carry enough energy to make a gaseous molecule *rotate* around various axes, but not quite enough energy to induce molecular *vibrations*. Precise knowledge of the microwave absorption frequencies permits identification of a geometric pattern which can be associated with the observed energy of rotation (see Figure 17-18). Very precise information on both the structure and electric dipole of a molecule can be obtained from microwave spectroscopy, but the technique is applicable only to a limited number of gaseous molecules.

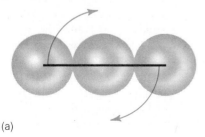

(a)

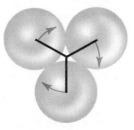

(b)

Fig. 17-18 The energy required to rotate a molecule is larger in the extended form (a) than in the compact form (b).

Fig. 17-19 A small bar magnet in a large magnetic field.

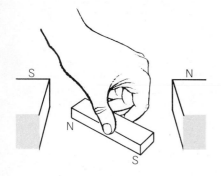

17-7.6 Nuclear Magnetic Resonance

In the past fifteen years another spectroscopic technique has found extensive use in structural studies and compound identification. This is the technique called **nmr,** or **nuclear magnetic resonance** spectroscopy. A nucleus is a charged body. *If a charged body moves, it becomes a small electromagnet.* Since some nuclei appear to spin, they behave as small electromagnets and will interact with an applied magnetic field. Consider that the nucleus is a small bar magnet which can be placed between the poles of a very strong, large magnet. The small bar magnet will orient itself with the north pole pointing toward the south pole of the big magnet and the south pole pointing toward the north pole (see Figure 17-19). If we want to turn the little magnet around, we must grasp it and turn it—energy is expended; work is done on the system.

In dealing with a nucleus, our hand is replaced by radiation of appropriate frequency. Hence, one examines the frequencies of the electromagnetic radiation which will flip over the nuclear magnet (make it change energy levels). This is the **resonance absorption frequency** of the nucleus. This frequency is dependent upon the strength of the field of the large magnet, the nature of the small nuclear magnet, and the arrangement of other nuclei and electrons in the region of the nucleus under study. The fact that the frequency is partially dependent upon the nuclei and electrons in the region of the nucleus under study makes the technique of great value in determining molecular structure and in identifying compounds. Nuclear magnetic resonance is now as widely used as infrared spectroscopy in most chemical laboratories. Its application will be illustrated in Chapter 19.

17-8 HIGHLIGHTS

We have explored the nature of that interaction between atoms giving rise to a chemical bond. A **covalent bond** results from a shared electron pair. When an electron is transferred more or less completely from one atom to another, ions are formed. Electrostatic attraction between ions gives an **ionic bond.** All chemical bonds form because one or more electrons are placed so as to "feel" electrostatic attraction of two or more positive nuclei simultaneously. Using either an **orbital representation** or an **electron dot representation** of bonding, the bonding capacity of the second-row elements can be discussed and their chemistry rationalized.

Unequal sharing of electrons between atoms gives rise to charge separation; a **bond dipole** is created. Proper addition of bond dipoles gives the **molecular dipole.** Such addition must take account of both size and orientation of the bond dipoles. Molecular geometry for simple molecules can be understood using a model which maximizes the distance between electron pairs. Both free pairs and pairs involved in bond formation must be considered. A **single bond** results from the sharing of an electron pair between two atoms; a **double bond,** when two electron pairs are shared; and a **triple bond,** when three electron pairs are shared.

Methods of structure determination include chemical reactions, X-ray diffraction, electron diffraction, infrared spectroscopy, microwave spectroscopy, and nuclear magnetic resonance spectroscopy.

QUESTIONS and PROBLEMS

1 (a) Which has the lower energy—two hydrogen atoms or a hydrogen molecule? Two helium atoms or a molecule of He_2? (b) What energy condition must exist for a bond to form between two atoms? (c) Can you relate these facts to the number of attractive and repulsive forces in H_2 and He_2?

2 Determine the number of attractive and repulsive forces that must exist in a Li atom. Repeat for a hydrogen atom. Repeat for LiH.

3 State in the simplest possible terms why *any* chemical bond forms. (*Hint:* consider changes in probable positions of electrons before and after bonding.)

4 Show by means of orbital diagrams and their degree of electron occupancy why H_2 is stable but He_2 is not.

5 Draw orbital electron configurations for each of the following elements in its lowest energy state. (a) potassium (b) phosphorus (c) chlorine (d) aluminum (e) calcium (f) silicon (g) sulfur.

6 Draw orbital and electron dot representations for each of the following, first in the unpromoted and then in the promoted state. (a) beryllium (b) boron (c) carbon. Explain what is gained in each case by electron promotion.

7 Draw orbital and electron dot representations for each of the following compounds. (a) NaF (b) MgF_2 (c) AlF_3 (d) SiH_4 (e) PH_3 (f) H_2S (g) Cl_2.

8 Draw the electron dot notation for the following molecules: (a) CO_2 (b) C_2H_6 (c) BrI (d) $Ca(OH)_2$ (e) GeH_4 (f) N_2H_4 (g) NaOH.

9 Draw the electron dot notation for each of the following ions. (a) NH_4^+ (b) OH^- (c) Cl^- (d) S^{2-} (e) HS^- (f) OH (g) OH^+.

10 Show by electron dot representations why CH_3OCH_3 is known as a stable species, but CH_3O is not. What are the chances that the molecule $(CH_3)_2O_2$ could be formed? Would you expect it to decompose fairly easily? (See Section 17-2.1.) Explain.

11 Would you expect N_2H_4 to react with BF_3? Explain using an electron dot representation.

12 Suppose that by some mysterious process* you were able to obtain a large number of

*Such molecules are formed at temperatures near 1500 K.

CH_2 molecules in a given container. What reaction would you anticipate?

13 Use ionization energy (see Figure 8-1, page 174) to determine the direction of the bond dipole in each of the following compounds. Use an arrow to indicate each bond dipole. (a) KCl(g) (b) HF(g) (c) CaO(g) (d) $KCH_3(g)$. (Consider the K—C bond only.)

14 In general, what conditions cause two atoms to combine to form (a) a bond that is mainly covalent? (b) a bond that is mainly ionic? (c) a polar bond?

15 Use ionization energy (see Figure 8-1, page 174) to determine which of the following will have predominantly ionic and which predominantly covalent bonds. Which molecules will have a dipole? (a) LiF(g) (b) MgO(g) (c) $Cl_2(g)$ (d) $NO_2(g)$ (e) NaBr(g) (f) $CCl_4(g)$ (g) HCl(g).

16 What will be the shape of each of the following molecules or ions? (a) LiH (b) H_2S (c) CO_2 (d) $SiBr_4$ (e) PH_3 (f) BCl_3 (g) MgI_2 (h) H_3NBF_3 (i) NH_4^+ (j) BF_4^-.

17 Considering comparable oxygen compounds and the electron-pair repulsion model, predict the shape of H_2S and H_2S_2. Which should have the larger bond dipole, HO or HS? The dipole of H_2O is approximately twice that of H_2S. Is this in agreement with your theoretical predictions?

18 Which of the following molecules will have a molecular dipole? (a) NaF(g) (b) MgO(g) (c) $MgI_2(g)$ (d) $GaCl_3(g)$ (e) $CO_2(g)$ (f) $H_2S(g)$ (g) $CCl_4(g)$ (h) $PF_3(g)$.

19 Consider the following series: CH_4, CH_3Cl, CH_2Cl_2, $CHCl_3$, and CCl_4. In which case(s) will the molecule have an electric dipole? Support your answer by considering the bonding orbitals of carbon, the molecular shape of the molecules, and the resulting symmetry.

20 Draw the structural isomers of $C_2H_2F_2$. Identify the *cis* and *trans* isomers and indicate which isomers will have a molecular dipole.

21 What orbital hybridization notation can be used to represent the orbitals from carbon in CI_4? The orbitals from boron in BF_3?

22 Nitrogen will form a stable triple N—N bond. Phosphorus will not. How can this be used to rationalize the fact that N_2 exists as a stable molecular species but P_2 does not? **431**

We are all agreed that the theory is crazy. The question that divides us is whether it is crazy enough to have a chance of being correct.

NIELS BOHR (1885–1962)

MOLECULAR ARCHITECTURE: 18
LIQUIDS AND SOLIDS

The natures of familiar liquids and solids are determined by their molecular architecture.

THE ARCHITECTURE OF GASEOUS MOLECULES, AS DISCUSSED in Chapter 17, leaves us, as usual, with a few answers and a lot of new questions. We now have knowledge of the forces *within* molecules in the gas phase in terms of our model of electron arrangement in orbitals. Can we apply this model to the forces *between* molecules in the liquid and solid phases? You bet! Distribution of the electron population in valence orbitals turns out to be a valuable key to understanding the bonding in metals, molecular solids, network solids, and ionic solids—and why each type of substance has its own characteristic properties.

In Chapter 8 a rather primitive model was used to describe the bonding in network solids, metals, and ionic solids. How does this model change as more sophisticated ideas of atomic structure are applied to these materials? Let us examine bonding between atoms in solids in more detail.

Two or more atoms remain near each other in a particular arrangement because energy is lowest in that arrangement. This is true whether the cluster of atoms is strongly or weakly bound, whether it contains a few atoms or 6.02×10^{23} atoms, whether the arrangement is regular (as in a crystal) or irregular (as in a liquid). The cluster of atoms is stable if, and only if, the energy is lower when the atoms are together than when they are apart. Remember that randomness always favors the breaking up of clusters.

18-1 MOLECULAR SOLIDS—VAN DER WAALS FORCES

In Chapter 17 you were told that the diatomic molecule of fluorine (F_2) does not form larger molecules such as F_3 or F_4. We explained this by noting that each fluorine atom has only *one* partially filled valence orbital. When two atoms combine by sharing electrons from the two formerly half-filled orbitals, the valence orbitals in both fluorine atoms are completely filled. A very stable electron configuration has been achieved. The stable F_2 molecule exists as a unit.

But at sufficiently low temperatures fluorine molecules condense to give a liquid! And at still lower temperatures a solid may form! The observation is general. *Any pure gas, when cooled sufficiently under appropriate pressure, will condense to give a liquid; at lower temperatures it will give a solid.* Even helium gas will condense to liquid helium.

The same forces that cause molecular fluorine to condense at 85 K cause noble gases such as helium to condense. These forces are named **van der Waals forces,** after the Dutch physicist Johannes D. van der Waals (1837–1923), who studied them. They are weak and poorly understood, but are very important. Gasoline is a liquid because of van der Waals forces. Molecules with filled valence orbitals, such as Cl_2, F_2, or C_8H_{18} (one component of gasoline), cannot interact strongly with each other because the electrons of one molecule cannot approach the nuclei in another molecule closely. All outer valence orbitals are filled in the separate molecules. On the other hand, weak interactions which lower the energy of the system by a few tenths of a kilocalorie

Fig. 18-1 Elements that form molecular crystals bound by van der Waals forces.

Fig. 18-2 Melting and boiling points of noble gases and halogens.

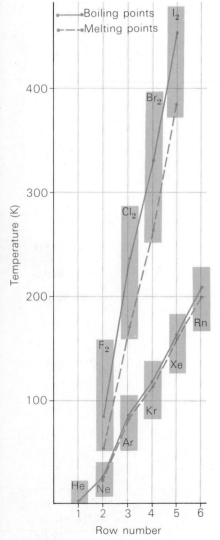

per mole are possible. Liquids or molecular crystals with low melting points will result. We can state a generalization: *van der Waals forces are the basic attractive forces among molecules in which all valence orbitals of all atoms are filled.* The *elements* forming van der Waals liquids and solids are concentrated in the upper right-hand corner of the periodic table (see Figure 18-1). We recognize old friends such as N_2, O_2, and F_2.

18-1.1   Van der Waals Forces and the Number of Electrons

In Chapter 8 we noticed that the boiling points of the noble gases increase as their atomic numbers increase. Boiling points range from 4.2 K for helium (atomic number 2) to 211 K for radon (no. 86). Furthermore, the boiling points of the halogens increase from 85 K for F_2 to 457 K for I_2. These data, along with corresponding melting points, are plotted in Figure 18-2. The horizontal axis shows the row number, which is an index of the total number of electrons per element. In Figure 18-3 the same type of information is plotted for compounds having the formula CX_4. The horizontal axis shows the row number of the periodic table for the outermost atoms in the molecule, since these are the atoms that "rub shoulders" with neighboring molecules. As far as van der Waals forces are concerned, it is quite important that CBr_4 has atoms from the fourth row (bromine) on the outer "surface" of the molecule, and it is somewhat less important that the central atom is carbon from the second row. The outermost atoms are the most influential in determining intermolecular forces because these forces act over very short distances. The data indicate that for substances in closely related groups, van der Waals forces increase as the number of electrons in the molecule increases.

A further and closely related generalization can be made. If we compare similar molecules, we find that the larger the molecule, the higher its boiling point. For example, if we compare methane (CH_4) and ethane (C_2H_6), the exterior atoms are the same—hydrogen atoms. Still, the boiling point of C_2H_6, 185 K, is higher than that of CH_4, 112 K. This difference can be attributed to the fact that there must be greater contact surface between two C_2H_6 molecules than between two CH_4 molecules. The same effect is found for C_2F_6 (boiling point, 195 K) and CF_4 (145 K).*

*Notice that these two factors, number of electrons and molecular size, might lead to another generalization—that the boiling point increases in proportion to molecular weight. Molecular weight, molecular size, number of electrons, and boiling point all tend to increase together. This molecular weight-boiling point correlation has some usefulness with molecules of similar composition and general shape, but there is no direct causative relation between molecular weight and boiling point.

EXERCISE 18-1

Gaseous phosphorus is made up of P_4 molecules with four phosphorus atoms arranged at the corners of a regular tetrahedron. With such a geometry, each phosphorus atom is bound to three other phosphorus atoms. Would you expect this gas to condense to a solid with a low, intermediate, or high melting point? After making a prediction on the basis of the valence orbital occupancy, check the melting point of phosphorus in a handbook. (*Hint:* Compare with I_2.)

EXERCISE 18-2

Natural gas used for fuel is largely CH_4. Gasoline is a mixture of molecules in the same family, with formulas ranging from about C_5H_{12} to $C_{11}H_{24}$. Explain why dry fuel gas does not freeze even in winter, while gasoline is a liquid in the middle of the summer.

18-1.2 Van der Waals Forces and Molecular Shape

A substance whose structure has a high degree of symmetry generally has a higher melting point than a closely related compound whose structure lacks this symmetry. For example, consider the two structural isomers of formula C_5H_{12}, called pentane and neopentane. Their molecular shapes differ drastically, as Figure 18-4 (next page) shows. The zig-zag shape of normal pentane allows van der Waals forces to act between the external envelope of hydrogen atoms of one molecule and those of adjacent molecules. This large surface contact results in a relatively *high boiling point*. On the other hand, this flexible, snakelike molecule does not pack readily in a regular lattice, so its crystal has a *low melting point*. Compare normal pentane with the highly compact, symmetrical neopentane. The ball-like neopentane readily packs in an orderly crystal lattice which, because of its stability, has a rather *high melting point*. Once melted, however, neopentane forms a liquid that boils at a temperature lower than does normal pentane. Neopentane has less surface contact with its neighbors and hence is more volatile; it has a relatively *low boiling point*.

Most carbon compounds condense to molecular liquids and solids. Their melting points are generally low (below about 300 °C) and many carbon compounds boil below 100 °C. The similar chemistry of the liquid and solid phases suggests that the basic geometry of the organic molecule is not changed as we go from liquid to solid. Van der Waals forces hold both liquid and solid together.

18-2 COVALENT BONDS AND NETWORK SOLIDS

As we noted in Chapter 8, solid carbon exists in two forms—the diamond and graphite structures.* Diamond is the classic example of

*A new form of carbon was reported in *Science,* **161,** 363 (July 26, 1968). It resembles graphite.

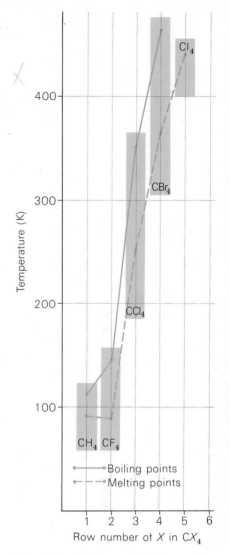

Fig. 18-3 Melting and boiling points of CX_4 molecules.

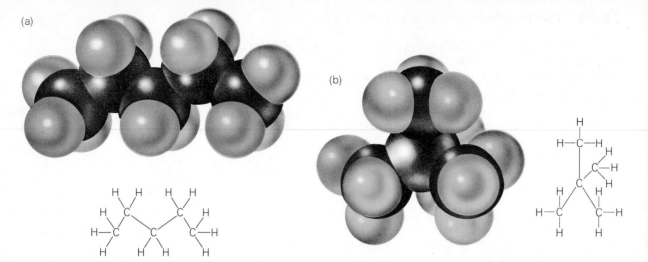

(a)

(b)

Fig. 18-4 Molecular shape influences melting and boiling points. Normal pentane (a) melts at −130 °C and boils at 36 °C; neopentane (b) melts at −20 °C and boils at 9 °C.

the **three-dimensional network solid;** graphite is typical of the **two-dimensional network solid.** Let us review their geometries.

18-2.1 The Three-Dimensional Network Solid

In the diamond each carbon atom is surrounded by four others arranged *tetrahedrally*. Since one $2s$ and three $2p$ orbitals are used to give a tetrahedral arrangement of single bonds around carbon, the bonding is sometimes described as sp^3. The very high melting point, extreme hardness, and low conductivity of a diamond can be interpreted in terms of the continuous three-dimensional structure [Figure 18-5(a)].

The compound silica (SiO_2) or quartz also has a covalent network structure. In one form silicon atoms replace carbon atoms in a diamond lattice. An oxygen atom is then placed between every pair of adjacent silicon atoms (Figure 18-6). The resulting structure is hard and has a very high melting point.

Fig. 18-5 Carbon: (a) diamond and (b) graphite.

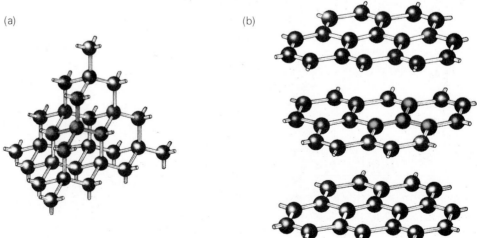

(a)

(b)

18-2.2 The Two-Dimensional Network Solid

In contrast to diamond and silica, graphite has a two-dimensional, layered structure [Figure 18-5(b)]. Each carbon is surrounded by three others *in a plane* (instead of four atoms arranged in a tetrahedron, as in diamond). The geometry suggests the sp^2 bonding notation we used for BF_3 (Section 17-2.4). Let us draw the electron dot representation for this structure. We see that each carbon is using only three electrons and orbitals. In the following structure, we are short one electron per carbon:*

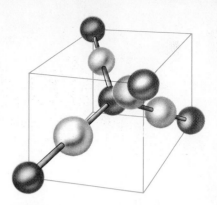

Fig. 18-6 Cubic form of silicon dioxide. One small segment of diamond-type lattice in which silicon atoms occupy the places of the carbon atoms and oxygen atoms lie between silicon atoms. (The gold spheres represent silicon atoms; the silver spheres represent oxygen atoms.)

What is to be done with the extra electron and orbital for each atom? One solution would be to use the extra electrons to form multiple bonds, as we did with C_2H_4 and N_2. Then there would be ten extra electrons (indicated below by +'s) for the ten carbons in the two rings:

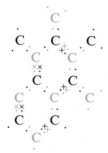

Since there is only one extra orbital and one extra electron per carbon, *only one of the three bonds per carbon can become a double bond at any one time.* A possible graphite structure is then

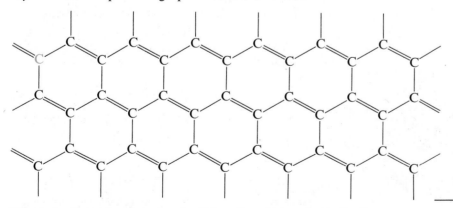

*Remember that each carbon atom should have four electrons, but in the diagram we have pictured 14 carbon atoms and 42 electrons (count them). On the average each carbon is short one electron.

By using this arrangement all carbons have filled their $2s$ and $2p$ valence levels. But this is not the only arrangement that gives carbon atoms with filled valence orbitals. There is a second arrangement:

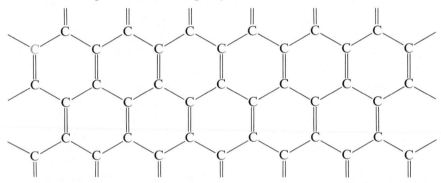

A third representation is equally valid:

Notice that the double bond can move around; *any two adjacent atoms in the sheet can be joined by a double bond*. This really means that the electrons making up the double bonds can move easily between atoms in the sheet. Such mobile electrons are described as **delocalized electrons;**[*] they are responsible for the high electrical conductivity of graphite *along the sheet*. On the other hand, there is no easy route for electrons to move between layers. Graphite is a *poor* electrical conductor in a direction *perpendicular to* the layers.

The layers themselves are bonded together by weak van der Waals forces; hence, the graphite crystal is soft and slippery. It breaks easily into layers; on the other hand, bonds between atoms in any *one* layer are strong.

Other elements forming network solids of various types with covalent bonds are shown in Figure 18-7.

18-3 THE METALLIC STATE

How do we recognize a metal? Let us review the properties of a metal and apply our expanding concept of chemical bonding.

[*]Graphite can also be described in another way. Note that the s, p_x, and p_y orbitals are used to make the planar sheets with three triangularly arranged bonds around each carbon. This is an sp^2 structure. The p_z orbitals on each carbon remain perpendicular to the graphite sheet. These p_z orbitals on adjacent carbons can overlap to make giant orbitals extending over the whole sheet. Electrons can then move easily over the sheets using these so-called "π orbitals."

Fig. 18-7 Elements forming network solids with covalent bonding.

18-3.1 Properties of a Metal

First and foremost, metals have luster; they are bright and shiny. With few exceptions (*e.g.*, gold, copper, bismuth, manganese) metals have a silvery-white color because they reflect *all* frequencies of light. This high reflectivity must have its origin in a characteristic electronic structure.

Metals have high electrical and thermal conductivity. In Section 18-2.2 we noted that the electrical conductivity of graphite is related to delocalized electrons in the carbon layers. In Chapter 8 we suggested that metals themselves might be described as positive ions immersed in a "sea" of electrons. This "sea" of electrons might account for the ability of metals to conduct electricity in any direction. Conduction of heat would also seem to be closely related to these mobile electrons.

Finally, all true metals can be drawn into wires or hammered into sheets without shattering—that is, metals are ductile and malleable; they are workable. Mobile, nonrigid electron clouds would seem to be consistent with the physical characteristics of metals.

What orbital descriptions are suggested by all these characteristics of metals?

18-3.2 Bonding in Metals

Atoms forming metals appear on the left-hand side of the periodic table (see Figure 18-8, following page). They are characterized by vacant valence orbitals and low electron ionization energies. *Vacant valence orbitals and low ionization energies, then, are the two conditions necessary for metallic bonding.* We shall see how these characteristics are essential to forming the metallic bond.

Like other bonds, the metallic bond forms because electrons are strongly attracted by two or more positive nuclei simultaneously. Our problem is to obtain some insight into the special way in which electrons in metals do this. Consider the lithium atom. Because each lithium atom has a single $2s$ electron, we would expect one single covalent bond between two lithium atoms to give Li_2.

$$Li : Li$$

Indeed, Li_2 is observed at high temperatures.

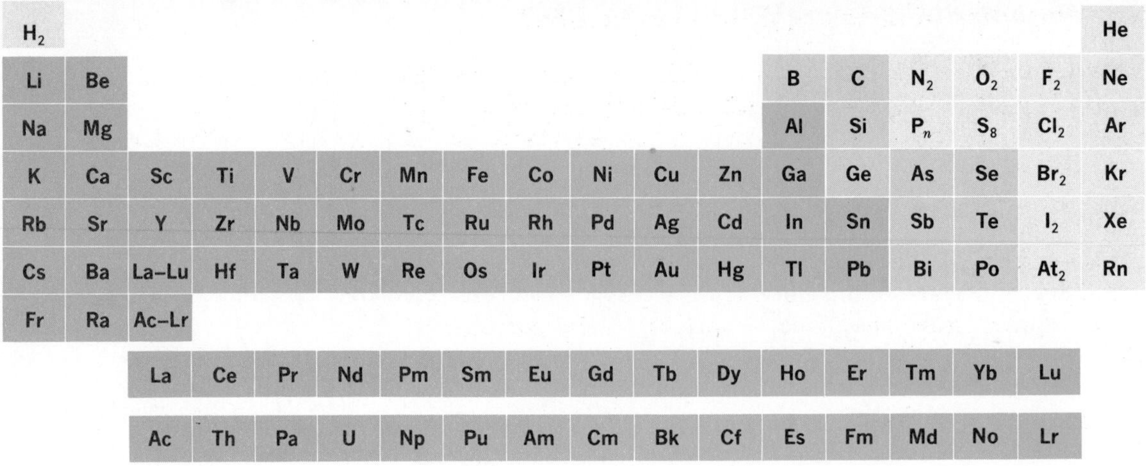

Fig. 18-8 The metallic elements.

Notice, however, that the gaseous Li_2 still has *three* unused valence orbitals in each atom. The existence of just one unused or empty orbital per carbon atom conferred a special reactivity upon the CH_2 molecule. We saw that one electron of an unused pair on carbon was promoted to the empty valence orbital, and two new covalent bonds could then form. CH_2 was a very reactive molecule. This argument suggests that Li_2 could be a reactive molecule. Three empty valence orbitals are available.

But the molecule Li_2 lacks bond-forming electrons; the valence electron for each atom is already involved in a bond between two lithium atoms; furthermore, there are no free pairs. If extra bonds *between Li_2 molecules* are to form, the valence electrons in Li_2 must do double duty. They must spend some time in the empty valence orbitals of lithium atoms from other Li_2 molecules. Simple logic suggests that *chances for this electron sharing would be best if the electrons between lithium atoms were rather weakly held.* Sharing would be achieved most easily if the atoms had a low ionization energy, which they do. Under these conditions, the electron pair between nuclei could wander toward other nuclei, all of which have empty orbitals.

Experiment suggests that this is indeed what happens. Everywhere the electron moves it finds itself between two positive nuclei with orbitals available to form a bond. Orbital geometry adjusts to permit relatively high electron density between any two atoms. (Remember that in CH_4 and C_2H_4 the orientation of orbitals was determined by the arrangement of nuclei and electrons surrounding a given atom.) The space around a central atom is a region of almost uniformly low potential energy. Each valence electron is virtually free to make its way throughout the crystal.

This valence orbital argument leads back to our earlier picture of a metal as an array of positive ions located at crystal lattice sites and immersed in a "sea" of mobile electrons. A metallic structure of this type will be formed by atoms having many vacant valence orbitals and low ionization energy for valence electrons. These are the very features which identify metals.

18-3.3 Properties of Metals and the Metallic Bond

The above idea emphasizes an important difference between metallic and covalent bonding. In covalent bonds the electrons are concentrated in certain regions of space between two atoms or are "localized." In contrast, the valence electrons in a metal are spread almost uniformly throughout the crystal or are "delocalized." The carbon atoms in diamond are held together by strongly localized covalent bonds. The diamond is very hard and rigid. Metals, on the other hand, are malleable and ductile because of the mobility of the electrons—metals can be worked. Under stress, one plane of atoms may slip over another (see Figure 18-9); but as it does so, electrons can move easily between planes to maintain bonding. If the easy movement of electrons is blocked, metals become hard and brittle. Metals can be hardened by alloying them with elements which have a strong attraction for electrons or which lack empty bonding orbitals, and thus reduce the easy mobility of metallic electrons. Often, just a trace of carbon, phosphorus, or sulfur will turn a relatively soft and workable metal into a brittle solid, much as a dam is able to control water movement over the whole stream, even though it occupies a very small fraction of the volume of the stream bed. In a sense, carbon, phosphorus, and sulfur atoms can be regarded as "dams" in the mobile electron sea.

(a)

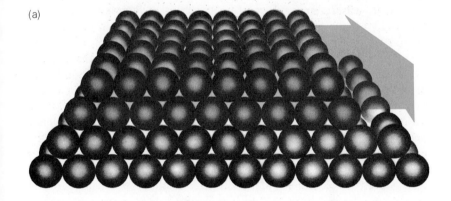

Fig. 18-9 Slippage of planes of metal atoms.

(b)

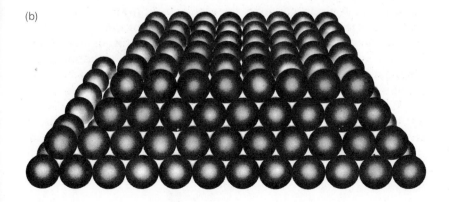

The excellent heat conductivity of metals is also due to mobile electrons. Electrons that are in regions of high temperature can acquire large amounts of kinetic energy. These electrons move through the crystal very rapidly and transfer energy to the atoms in the cooler regions. If electron movement is restricted between atoms, thermal energy can be passed stepwise from atom to atom by vibration, but the process is much slower than in pure metals.

Why do these characteristics of metals disappear as we consider elements from left to right in the periodic table? First, because as nuclear charge on the atoms increases, the ionization energy for valence electrons rises rapidly. It becomes more and more difficult for such atoms to release electrons for delocalized bonding. Furthermore, as additional orbitals are filled, empty orbitals needed to form delocalized bonds become less available. For these reasons, localized electron pair bonds (covalent bonds) between two nuclei become more attractive to electrons as we go across the periodic table. Consequently, there is less and less possibility for delocalization and metallic-bond formation.

18-3.4 Strength of the Metallic Bond

Is a metallic bond weak because electrons are mobile? We can obtain some idea of the effectiveness of this electron "sea" in binding atoms if we compare the energy necessary to vaporize 1 mole of a metallic element with the energy required to vaporize 1 mole of a covalently bonded solid element such as silicon or germanium. (Free atoms are present in the vapor in both cases.) We find that for the alkali metals the energy is only one fourth to one third that needed for 1 mole of ordinary, covalently bonded solid (85 kcal/mole for Si). This is not surprising. The ionization energy of a free alkali metal atom is small. This means that the valence electron in the free atom does not experience a strong attraction to the nucleus. Since the electron is not strongly attracted by one alkali metal nucleus, it is not strongly attracted by two or three such nuclei in the metallic crystal. Thus, the binding energy between electrons and nuclei in the alkali metal crystals is rather small, and the resulting metallic bonds are rather weak.

We might expect, however, that the metallic bond would become stronger in those elements that have a greater number of valence electrons and a greater nuclear charge. In these cases, there are both more electrons in the "sea" and a stronger attraction to the nucleus because of the increased nuclear charge. This argument is supported by the experimental heats of vaporization in Table 18-1. To discuss a particular case, let us compare the heat of vaporization of magnesium with the heat of vaporization of aluminum. The higher value for aluminum shows that the metallic bond is indeed stronger when both the number of valence electrons and the charge on the nucleus increase. Thus, the strength of the metallic bond tends to increase going from left to right along a row in the periodic table. The transition metal elements are harder and melt and boil at higher temperatures than the alkali or alkaline earth metals. This is explained by the fact that transition elements have d electrons and d orbitals that may be called upon in the process of forming bonds.

TABLE **18-1** HEATS OF VAPORIZATION OF METALS

Row of Periodic Table	Heats of Vaporization (kcal/mole)		
Second row	Li 32.2	Be 53.5	B 129
Third row	Na 23.1	Mg 31.5	Al 67.9
Fourth row	K 18.9	Ca 36.6	Sc 73
Fifth row	Rb 18.1	Sr 33.6	Y 94
Sixth row	Cs 16.3	Ba 35.7	La 96

18-3.5 The Geometry of Metals

Metals, like molecules, have a characteristic geometry. For example, the metals lithium, sodium, potassium, rubidium, and cesium all have a structure that is described as "body-centered cubic." A portion of this structure is shown in Figure 18-10. Notice that the structural unit is a simple cube with an atom at each corner and another atom inside the cube. The name **body-centered cubic arrangement** describes what we see. An atom is centered in the body of each cube. Since the actual structure of a metal is obtained by putting together thousands of cubes, we find that each atom in the structure is the same; there is no difference between central and corner atoms. *Each atom, regardless of position in the alkali metal structure, has eight neighbors.* This can be seen by focusing on the atom in the center of the cube in Figure 18-10. The body-centered cubic arrangement is typical of the alkali metals, as well as of one of our most important metals, iron. Pure iron has a body-centered cubic structure.

The metals beryllium and magnesium show a structure which can be obtained by packing balls of equal size as close together as possible in a continuing pattern. The resulting structure, known as the **hexagonal close-packed arrangement,** is shown in Figure 18-11.1. In this pattern, each atom is surrounded by 12 identical metal atoms. Six atoms are in a plane around any given atom with three atoms above the plane and three below. A close-packed arrangement is really what one should expect for metals, since atoms of identical size are being packed together. In contrast to the situation found with the localized electron-pair bonds of diamond, the electrons in the metal can adjust to accept any pattern which the atoms take. We note that in this arrangement the atoms have more valence electrons and a larger number of neighbors. The number of atoms per unit volume is slightly greater in the hexagonal close-packed arrangement than in the body-centered cubic structure. If atoms of identical mass were considered, the hexagonal close-packed arrangement would have a higher density than would the body-centered cubic form.

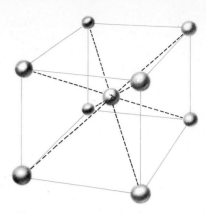

Fig. 18-10 Body-centered cubic cell. The atoms actually touch each other. The structure is "opened up" here to make it easier to see.

Fig. 18-11.1 Hexagonal close-packed structure: normal and exploded views.

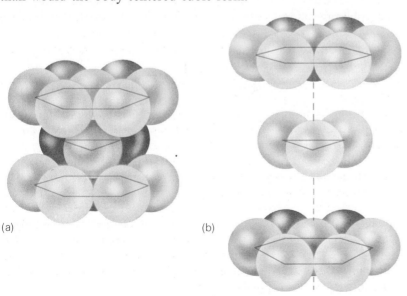

(a)   (b)

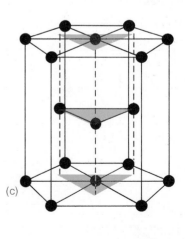

(c)

Fig. 18-11.2 Cubic close-packed structure.

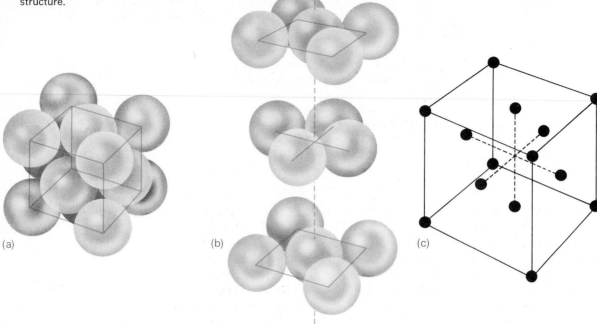

(a) (b) (c)

Aluminum displays a close-packed geometry which is very similar to that described for beryllium and magnesium. The aluminum structure is known as **cubic close-packed** and is shown in Figure 18-11.2. This structure is also known as a face-centered cubic structure because the repeating cell is a cube with an extra atom in the center of each face. As in the hexagonal close-packed structure, each atom has 12 identical neighbors. Structural differences occur only in the arrangement of atoms in the second shell of neighbor atoms. The number of atoms per unit volume is the same for both cubic and hexagonal close-packed structures. All the metals except barium of groups II (Be to Ra) and III (Al to Ac) show one of the close-packed arrangements as their room temperature form. To choose between these structures requires an analysis of a number of factors, but nearly all pure metals adopt one of these patterns or the body-centered cubic form.

18-3.6 The Band Theory of Metals

Modern-day metallurgists have another very useful way to look at the electronic structure of metals. It is sometimes described as the **band theory.** It has its origins in the simple ideas of covalent bond formation. We noted earlier that if two orbitals on two H atoms overlap, a new molecular orbital is generated which permits accumulation of negative charge between the two positive nuclei. Such a system has a lower energy than either of the two separate atoms. Figure 18-12.1 summarizes this statement. When two electrons are placed in the orbital between the atoms, the hydrogen molecule forms. This is familiar territory. Now let us branch out.

Another combination of the 1s orbitals for hydrogen would place the electrons on the outside of the two hydrogen atoms. Such an

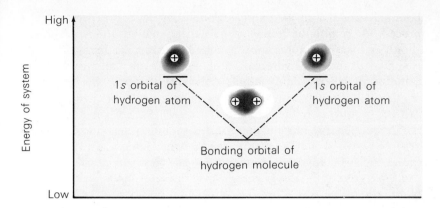

Fig. 18-12.1 Formation of a bonding orbital from the two 1s orbitals of two hydrogen atoms.

arrangement would tend to pull the nuclei apart; hence it is described as an *antibonding orbital*. It is shown in Figure 18-12.2. Because electrons are now forced away from the nuclei, the orbital is higher in energy than either of the two original orbitals. Clearly, if electrons have a free choice, they will go into the lower energy state. Hence the two electrons of the two hydrogen atoms go to the lower level and bind the two hydrogen atoms into a hydrogen molecule. The high energy level still remains, but it has no electrons in it. Hence it does not reduce the stability of the system.

We can now draw a more complete picture for the case of two hydrogen atoms forming a hydrogen molecule (Figure 18-12.3). A full

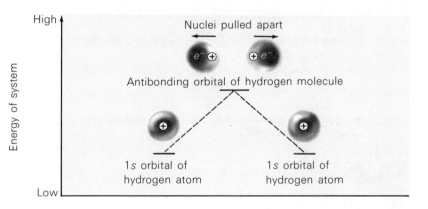

Fig. 18-12.2 Formation of an antibonding orbital from two 1s orbitals of two hydrogen atoms.

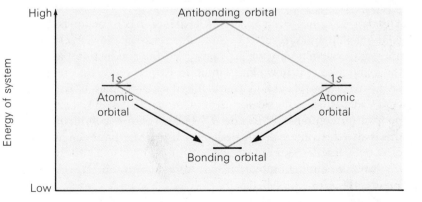

Fig. 18-12.3 Combination of two 1s orbitals on two hydrogen atoms to give one bonding and one antibonding orbital.

The BAND THEORY of METALS

bonding orbital and an empty antibonding level are present. The process for combining many orbitals from sodium atoms is similar. If only two sodium atoms are considered in space, the energy diagram is similar to that for hydrogen. Suppose, however, that we now start bringing in other sodium atoms. As many of the orbitals begin to overlap, all of the energy levels shift slightly, since only two electrons can occupy precisely the same energy level. The net effect is to split the discrete energy level of the isolated sodium atoms into a number of closely spaced energy levels termed a **band** (Figure 18-13). Because the $1s$ levels of adjacent atoms do not get close enough together to overlap significantly, the $1s$ energy level does not spread very far. The band remains narrow—the electrons remain localized. The $2s$ and $2p$ levels overlap a little more; hence the bands broaden significantly. The $3s$ levels overlap a great deal, hence the band is wide. We could predict that the $3p$ band above the $3s$ would also be wide since overlap would be extensive, and many $3p$ levels must interact strongly to push each other apart.

On the basis of the band picture we can identify metals (electrical conductors), insulators, and semiconductors.

Fig. 18-13 The formation of energy bands in metals.

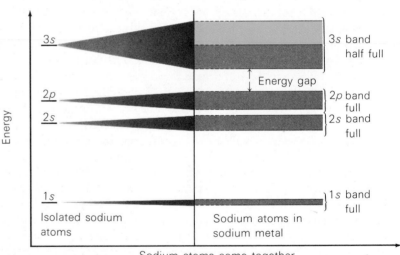

18-3.7   Metals, Insulators, and Semiconductors

Metals are characterized by having a valence or conduction band which is about half full. In such a band, electrons can flow freely to carry an electric current very well. If, however, the conduction band is full, the current can*not* flow. This situation can be compared to a person trying to walk through a room filled with people. If the room is completely filled, the person cannot move across the room. All the people are completely "localized." If the room is completely empty, this is also true. There are no people to move. Maximum net movement of people across the room can occur if it is about half full. In a metal, the valence-conduction band is half full and electrons move freely [see Figure 18-14(a)].

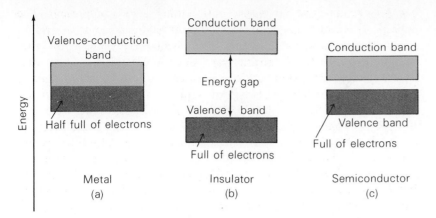

In an insulator, the valence band is full and the next empty energy band is separated by a *large energy gap* [see Figure 18-14(b)]. Conduction cannot occur unless some of the electrons in the valence band are promoted to the conduction band. (Some people move from a completely filled room to another room which was empty.) This would make both the valence band and the conduction band less than full and permit some conduction to occur. Energy needed to promote a few electrons might be provided by heating the solid to a very high temperature or by shining X rays on it. *No solid can remain as a good insulator while it is exposed to X rays*. All become conductors.

Finally in Figure 18-14(c) we see a semiconductor such as silicon. Note that the energy gap between the full valence band and the empty conduction band is small. Such a material can absorb visible light to become a conductor. When a number of electrons are promoted to the conduction band as a result of irradiation, the electrons in the semiconductor can be made to flow through a wire in an external circuit to a region where the band is empty. This is the basic principle of the silicon photocell used as a source of electrical power in space exploration. The direct conversion of sunlight to electricity by means of a silicon cell is indeed possible, but at the present time the costs are too high to provide a real answer to the world's energy crisis. The best cells available are silicon cells which convert about 14 percent of the incident light to electricity. If we assume that the efficiency can be raised to 20 percent, about 0.10 square mile (0.256 square kilometre) of cells would be required to generate one million watts. At present prices for silicon, the installed cost would be about two thousand times that of a nuclear reactor.*

18-3.8 Transistors and Other Solid State Devices

Calculators that you can put in your pocket, giant calculators of incredible power, electric watches that keep time to an accuracy of a few seconds per month, radios the size of a box of matches—all of these are possible today because of our knowledge of semiconductors.

*Ralph Roberts, *American Scientist,* **61**: 66–75 (1973).

**WILLIAM N. LIPSCOMB, Jr.
(1919–   )**

Born in Cleveland, Ohio, William Lipscomb was graduated from the University of Kentucky. His Ph.D. was granted by the California Institute of Technology in 1946. As a new Ph.D., he taught at the University of Minnesota where he rapidly rose to the rank of professor. In 1959 he went to Harvard University where he is currently the Abbott and James Lawrence Professor of Chemistry.

Lipscomb's early research used X-ray crystallography to define the structures of the formerly mysterious boron hydrides. He then developed theoretical models to explain bonding in these compounds and to tie them into the main fabric of chemistry. In more recent years, Lipscomb has turned his attention to studies on the structure and operation of enzymes and other large molecules.

Combining the best of experimental skills with remarkable insight, Lipscomb has been unusually effective in explaining and simplifying large areas of puzzling chemistry. His work clearly establishes the power of modern instrumentation in the hands of an outstanding creative scientist.

The future looks even brighter. Already a prototype television camera the size of a man's hand and weighing less than a pound has been made.* Many cars will have better fuel economy because of a small computer circuit which controls the fuel-injection system. This is the electronic age—an age which has been made possible by the application of semiconductors. Let us look more closely at the case of silicon which now is truly the backbone of the semiconductor industry.

As we noted earlier, the valence band of a very pure piece of silicon is full and the material is not an electrical conductor unless light or heat is used to promote electrons to a higher energy band. If, however, a small number of arsenic atoms are added to silicon, the arsenic atoms will replace an equal number of silicon atoms. The band structure and geometry of the silicon remain the same, but we have one extra electron for each arsenic atom. (Arsenic has five valence electrons while the silicon which it replaces has four.) The extra electrons provided by the arsenic atoms must now move up to the conduction band. Because only a few electrons are in the conduction band, the material is a conductor, but not a good one like a metal. We call it a semiconductor (literally, half of a conductor). The material described above containing a few extra electrons is called an n-type semiconductor (n for negative). Another type is also possible. If aluminum atoms (three electrons) rather than arsenic atoms (five electrons) are used to replace a few silicon atoms (four electrons), the resulting material will be short of electrons. The valence band will not be quite full and it is a weak conductor of electricity. Such a material is known as a p-type semiconductor (p for positive charge conductor).

Proper combination of n-type and p-type semiconductors has permitted the production of many very useful electronic devices which make possible most of the electronic equipment which we take for granted. Devices for changing an alternating current to a direct current, for amplifying electrical signals, and for storing information can be made which are incredibly small and effective. This entire area is a separate and fascinating area of technology. Most of the technology and research in this important subject is tied together by the band theory of solids. It is available because chemists have been able to provide the needed new materials in very pure form.

18-4 BORON—THE ELEMENT WHERE METALS AND NETWORK SOLIDS MEET

For many years after its discovery, the element boron and many of its compounds were a puzzle to chemists. The structure of the element appeared to be exceedingly complex. Furthermore, the hydrides of boron presented a challenge to the bonding rules that worked so well for carbon compounds. Why? What is unusual about boron? First, boron has four valence orbitals but only three valence electrons. *It does not have enough electrons to use all its valence orbitals in normal covalent bond formation.* In this sense it is "electron deficient" and markedly different from carbon. How do elements such as lithium and

*For an interesting and readable account of semiconductor (transistor) technology, see William C. Hittinger, *Scientific American,* **229:** 48 (August 1973).

beryllium, having even fewer electrons, handle this "problem" of "electron deficiency"? They form metallic bonds in which a single pair of electrons moves between many atoms. But boron cannot form metallic bonds with any ease because boron has only one unused valence orbital and a fairly high ionization energy for at least two of its three electrons.

Boron is an *in-between element*. It does not have enough electrons to bond like carbon, nor does it have enough empty orbitals and easily available electrons to bond like metals. What is the result of this dilemma? The answer was first provided by an X-ray structural study done by Professor J. L. Hoard and his colleagues at Cornell University in 1958.

18-4.1 The Structure of Elemental Boron

Boron, like carbon, exists in more than one form, but all these forms have some structural features in common. Structural differences are not as extreme as the differences between diamond and graphite. One form of boron is shown in Figure 18-15.1. Notice the four distinct clusters of boron atoms. Each cluster contains 12 boron atoms arranged in a regular group called an **icosahedron,** which is seen in expanded form in Figure 18-15.2. In this small cluster many of the features of a developing metallic structure appear. Some electron pairs are shared among a number of boron atoms in the cluster of 12, not between just two atoms as in the normal covalent bond, and not among an extremely large number of atoms as in a true metal. Electrons *within*

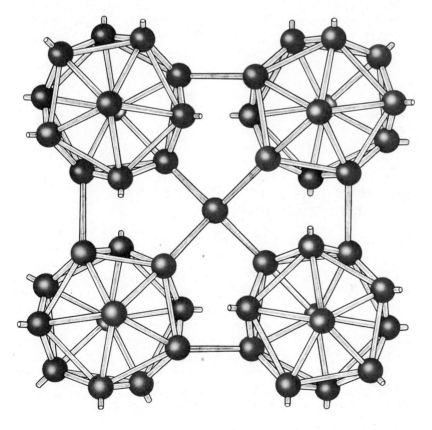

Fig. 18-15.1 Structure of elemental boron (α-tetragonal form).

Fig. 18-15.2 An icosahedral cluster of boron.

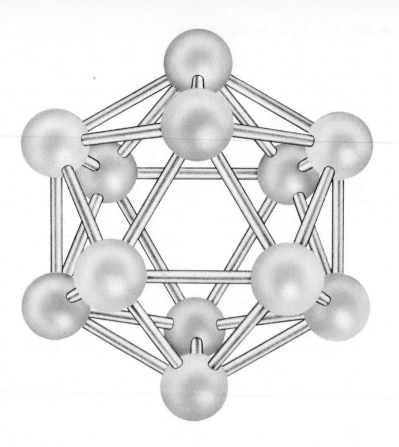

this cluster of 12 borons are delocalized to a large extent. The behavior within the cluster is strongly suggestive of many features of metallic bonding. But the boron atoms in the cluster soon run out of empty orbitals and of electrons with low ionization energies. The metallic structure cannot be continued.* At this point each boron in the icosahedron will usually form one normal covalent bond directed outward from the icosahedron. This extra bond is formed with a boron in another icosahedron or with a boron atom positioned between icosahedrons.† The net result is that all forms of elemental boron are made up of icosahedral units linked in various ways. The icosahedron—a remnant of the metallic structure—appears in all known forms of elemental boron!

Boron is neither a metal nor a normal covalent solid such as diamond. It is an in-between structure with semimetallic bonds in the icosahedral clusters and with normal covalent bonds between clusters. In retrospect this is almost what we would have expected for boron—it is neither metal nor nonmetal. It is in-between and therefore must have characteristics of both a metal and a network nonmetal.

*An icosahedral array provides an extremely efficient way to pack 12 spheres around a point. The hole in the middle is about 30 percent smaller than any other standard packing arrangement such as hexagonal close-packing, but this increase in packing efficiency for 12 is achieved at the expense of a serious loss of three-dimensional packing efficiency for the icosahedral units. Such geometry seems to be ideal for an element such as boron where a small compact cluster is important.
†In Figure 18-15.1 the boron in the center makes four regular covalent bonds to four separate icosahedrons. Each center boron must then receive a total of five electrons from the four icosahedrons around it to permit such bond formation.

18-4.2 The Boron Hydrides

We noted earlier that the compound BH_3 does *not* exist in isolatable form. Instead, a **dimer,** or molecule containing two empirical formulas of BH_3, *i.e.*, B_2H_6, is the simplest boron hydride ever isolated at room temperature. Chemists can now rationalize this formerly mystifying fact in the following way: each boron combines with three separate hydrogens to form a BH_3 unit, but when this BH_3 unit approaches the boron of another BH_3 unit, the relatively loosely held electron pair involved in one B—H bond is pulled over to share the unused orbital on the boron of the second BH_3 unit. The electrons now move in a region such that they are attracted by two boron nuclei and one hydrogen nucleus. The electrons are delocalized. (Remember how the Li:Li bonding pair was "delocalized" into a metal structure.)

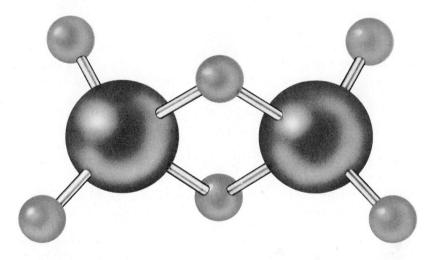

$$(1)$$

The result is a bond in which one pair of electrons links three atoms— one hydrogen and two boron atoms. It is called a **three-center bond.** As you can see in the electron dot representation above, two so-called three-center bonds fasten together the two BH_3 units. The experimentally determined structure for B_2H_6 appears in Figure 18-16.

Fig. 18-16 Structure of diborane.

Apparently, the in-between bonding characteristics of boron account for the unexpected behavior of its hydrides. Let us support this thought with the following summary:

(1) A structure in which one electron pair joins together many atoms is characteristic of metals.
(2) A structure in which one or more electron pairs link *two* atoms is characteristic of nonmetallic network solids.
(3) A structure in which one electron pair links three, four, or five atoms is characteristic of behavior intermediate between metals and nonmetallic network solids.

Case (3) is characteristic of boron. Indeed, many of the boron compounds testify to the fact that boron is more metallic than carbon and less metallic than beryllium.

Boron forms a whole family of hydrides in addition to B_2H_6. Typical formulas are B_5H_{11}, B_6H_{10}, and $B_{10}H_{14}$. Furthermore, ions such as $B_{12}H_{12}^{2-}$ have been prepared in the last few years. The compounds B_5H_{11}, B_6H_{10}, and $B_{10}H_{14}$ each have a structure in which the boron arrangement is a *fragment* of the icosahedron of elemental boron. The open edges where the fragment was broken from the icosahedron are closed by B—H—B three-center bonds. The $B_{12}H_{12}^{2-}$ ion is an icosahedron with a hydrogen covalently bonded to each boron. The ion is shaped almost like a ball. (See Figure 18-15.2 on page 450.) In retrospect, the chemistry of boron does not seem so irregular if we remember where it lies in the periodic table.

EXERCISE 18-3

By referring to the diagram of an icosahedron in Figure 18-15.2, suggest a reasonable arrangement for boron atoms in a hydride of formula B_4H_{10}.

18-5   IONIC STRUCTURES—THE IONIC BOND AND ITS CONSEQUENCES

We have not yet considered the effects that arise from charge separations. The most extreme case is represented by the formation of ionic solids. Usually, these can be considered as arrays of positive and negative ions, neatly stacked so that each positive ion has only negative-ion neighbors and each negative ion has only positive-ion neighbors. Figure 8-7 on page 181 shows such a crystal arrangement, that of sodium chloride. Why does such a solid form, and what are its properties? These are the questions we shall try to answer here.

18-5.1   The Stability of Ionic Crystals

In discussing the bonding in the gaseous LiF molecule in Section 17-3.1, the electric dipole of the molecule was explained in terms of the different ionization energies of lithium and fluorine atoms. Although the lithium fluoride molecule (LiF) holds together because the bonding electrons are near both nuclei, the energy favors an electron distribution concentrated toward the F atom. We may write $Li^+ \cdots \cdot F^-$ for gaseous LiF. When molecules of gaseous $Li^+ \cdots \cdot F^-$ approach each other the electrostatic attraction between positive Li^+ and negative F^- ions generates three-dimensional ionic clusters in which each Li^+ is surrounded by six F^- and each F^- by six Li^+. The structure is like that of NaCl in which there are no distinct molecules. Just as the atoms in metals are more stable when surrounded by other atoms in a metallic crystal, the ions in ionic solids are more stable when each has several neighboring ions of appropriate charge around it. Completely delocalized electrons are characteristic of solid metals. Solid LiF is, however, significantly different from metals. Half the atoms have high ionization energies because F atoms hold their electrons tightly. Therefore, the characteristic electron mobility of metals is not present in the ionic solids. This absence of mobile electrons implies that LiF has none of the metallic properties. Let us review the properties of ionic solids.

18-5.2 Properties of Ionic Crystals

Ionic solids, such as lithium fluoride and sodium chloride (NaCl), form regularly shaped crystals with well-defined crystal faces. Pure samples of these solids are usually transparent and colorless, but color may be caused by traces of impurities or crystal defects. Most ionic crystals have high melting points and their liquids have high boiling points. NaCl melts at 801 °C and boils at 1413 °C; LiF melts at 842 °C and boils at 1676 °C.

Molten LiF and NaCl have electrical conductivities which are lower than metallic conductivities by several factors of 10. Molten NaCl at 801 °C has a conductivity about 10^{-5} times that of copper metal at room temperature. Perhaps the electric charge does not move by the same mechanism in molten NaCl as in metallic copper. Experiments show that the charge is carried in molten NaCl by slow-moving Na^+ and Cl^- ions. Some electrical conductivity in the liquid state is a property characteristic of molten ionic substances. In contrast, molecular crystals generally melt to form molecular liquids that do not conduct electricity. Metals have higher conductivity because electrons move more rapidly and easily than Na^+ and Cl^- ions.

We have considered covalent molecules and ionic lattices. But most molecules fall between these two extremes; they are held together by bonds that are largely covalent but still have enough charge separation to affect the properties of the substance. These are the molecules we have called **polar molecules.**

Chloroform ($CHCl_3$) is an example of a polar molecule. It has four tetrahedrally oriented bonds (as in Figure 17-6.1 on page 416), three C—Cl bonds and one C—H bond. The C—Cl bonds do not have the same dipole as does the C—H bond. When the dipoles of the C—Cl and C—H bonds are added, there is a molecular dipole remaining (see Section 17-5). Such electric dipoles are important to chemists because they affect chemical properties such as solvent action. Let us see how a strongly polar solvent such as water interacts to dissolve an ionic crystal such as NaCl.

18-5.3 Solubility of Ionic Solids in Water

The dissolving of ionic solids in water is one of the most extreme and most important solvent effects that can be attributed to electric dipoles. Crystalline NaCl is quite stable, as indicated by its high melting point, yet it dissolves readily in water. To break up the stable crystal arrangement, there must be a strong interaction between water molecules and the ions that are released in the solution. This interaction can be explained in terms of the properties of the polar water molecule.

The energy is lower if an electric dipole, when brought near an ion, is oriented so that unlike charges are close together. Hence, water molecules tend to orient around ions with the positive end of the water dipole pointing inward toward a negative ion and with the negative end pointing toward a positive ion. This process is called **hydration** (refer to Section 13-1.2). Figure 18-17 shows it schematically.

Orientation of water dipoles around the ions has two effects. First, the energy is lowered because the orientation brings unlike charges near each other. This lowering of ionic energy by hydration provides the energy needed to break up the lattice. The hydration energies for the ions of NaCl are very close to the lattice energy for the solid. As a result, ΔH for the solution process for NaCl is only $+0.9$ kcal/mole. Notice that the positive sign for ΔH indicates that the energy term has a very small tendency to oppose the solution process. The hydration energy is not quite so large as lattice energy.

Why then does NaCl dissolve in water? The most important consequence must be a marked *increase in randomness* of the system when the regular NaCl lattice is broken up and the Na^+ and Cl^- ions are distributed randomly throughout the liquid phase.* *The water molecules surrounding each ion reduce the force of attraction between ions in solution and stabilize this more randomized arrangement.* There are smaller randomization decreases due to ordering of water molecules around the ions, but these are well counterbalanced by the large change in randomness associated with the breakup of the NaCl lattice.

These two effects of ion hydration—compensation for the lattice energy of the crystalline solid and stabilization of ions in a more randomized arrangement—give water distinctive properties as a solvent for ionic solids and for other electrolytes such as HCl and H_2SO_4. These two effects help explain, for example, why some salts (such as NH_4Cl)

*The randomness change, when reduced to energy terms at 25 °C, amounts to about -8.4 kcal—a term that favors solution.

Fig. 18-17 Hydration of ions, showing orientation of water dipoles.

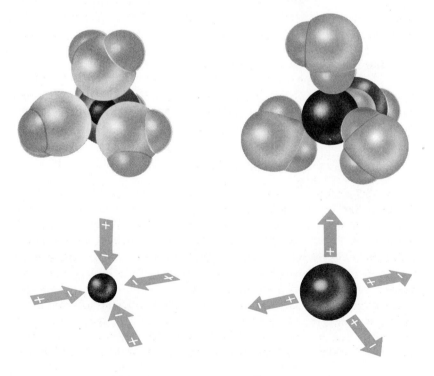

absorb heat as they dissolve in water while some (such as NaOH) release heat as they dissolve. The tendency toward maximum randomness is the dominant factor promoting solubility of all solutes in liquid solvents.

18-6 HYDROGEN BONDS

In Figure 18-3 on page 435 we saw that the boiling points of symmetrical molecules increase regularly as we move down the periodic table. Figure 18-18 shows the corresponding plot for some molecules possessing electric dipoles. Consider first the boiling points of HI, HBr, HCl, and HF. Hydrogen fluoride (HF) is far out of line, boiling at 19.9 °C instead of below −95 °C, as we would predict from an extrapolation of the other three boiling points. There is an even larger discrepancy between the boiling point of H_2O and the value we would predict from the trend suggested by the boiling points of H_2Te, H_2Se, and H_2S.

Could the extremely high boiling points of HF and H_2O be due to the fact that these are the smallest molecules of their respective series? No, this is not the explanation because there are no corresponding discrepancies in the data for the boiling points of CF_4, CCl_4, CBr_4, and CI_4. These boiling points follow a smooth trend upward from CF_4 to CI_4. In fact, smaller molecules usually have lower boiling points. There must be some other explanation for these high boiling points. There must be additional new forces between the molecules of H_2O and HF that tend to keep molecules in the liquid phase.

These forces are evident with solid compounds also. The most familiar example is solid H_2O, or ice. Ice has a structure in which the oxygen and hydrogen atoms are distributed in a regular hexagonal crystal lattice. Each O atom, like each C atom in diamond, is surrounded by four other O atoms in a tetrahedral arrangement. The H atoms are found on the lines extending between the oxygen atoms:

$$O{-}H\cdots\cdot O$$

The attractive force between O—H and O must be the bond that joins the water molecules together in the crystal lattice of ice. This bond is a **hydrogen bond.**

18-6.1 Energy of Hydrogen Bonds

The hydrogen bond is usually represented by O—H · · · · O, in which the solid line represents the original O—H bond in the parent compound, as in water (HOH) or methyl alcohol (CH_3OH), and the dotted line represents the second bond formed by hydrogen, or the bond called the hydrogen bond. It is dotted to indicate that it is much weaker than a normal covalent bond. Consideration of the boiling points in Figure 18-18, on the other hand, shows that the interaction must be much stronger than van der Waals forces. Experiments show that most hydrogen bonds release between 3 kcal/mole and 10 kcal/mole upon formation: $\Delta H = -3$ to -10 kcal/mole. The energy of this bond places it between van der Waals attractions and covalent bonds.

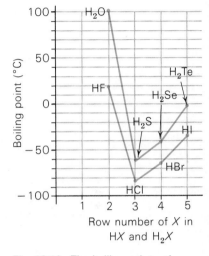

Fig. 18-18 The boiling points of some hydrides.

ENERGY of HYDROGEN BONDS

Roughly speaking, the energies are in the ratio

$$\left\{\begin{matrix}\text{van der Waals}\\\text{attractions}\end{matrix}\right\} : \left\{\begin{matrix}\text{hydrogen}\\\text{bonds}\end{matrix}\right\} : \left\{\begin{matrix}\text{covalent}\\\text{bonds}\end{matrix}\right\}$$
$$1 \quad : \quad 10 \quad : \quad 100$$

18-6.2 Where Hydrogen Bonds Are Found

Hydrogen bonds are found between only a few elements of the periodic table. The most common are those in which H connects two atoms from the group F, O, N, and, less commonly, Cl.

The hydrogen bond to fluorine is clearly evident in most of the properties of hydrogen fluoride. The high boiling point of HF, compared with boiling points of the other hydrogen halides, is one of several pieces of data indicating that HF does not exist in the liquid phase as separate HF molecules but as *aggregates of molecules*, which we describe in general terms as $(HF)_x$. Gaseous HF contains the "floppy ring" species H_6F_6 (Figure 18-19), as well as some single HF molecules and perhaps a few percent of molecules of intermediate type such as H_2F_2.

Fig. 18-19 A descriptive formula of the H_6F_6 species.

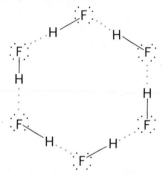

An extreme example of the fluorine-hydrogen bond is found in the hydrogen difluoride ion, HF_2^-. This ion exists in acidic solutions of fluorides,

$$H^+(aq) + F^-(aq) \rightleftharpoons HF(aq) \tag{2}$$

$$HF(aq) + F^-(aq) \rightleftharpoons HF_2^-(aq) \tag{3}$$

and in the ionic crystal lattice of salts such as KHF_2. The HF_2^- ion may be regarded as consisting of two negatively charged fluoride ions held together by a proton:

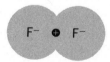

This arrangement is not typical, however, because few hydrogen bonds form with the proton equidistant from the two atoms to which it is bonded.

18-6.3 The Nature of the Hydrogen Bond

In the hydrogen bond the hydrogen atom is attached to two other atoms. Yet the bonding rules tell us that the hydrogen atom, with only the 1s orbital for bond formation, cannot form two normal covalent bonds. The second bond demands some extension of our bonding ideas.

The simplest explanation for the hydrogen bond is based upon the polar nature of F—H, O—H, and N—H bonds. In a molecule such as H_2O, the electron pair in the O—H bond is displaced toward the oxygen nucleus and away from the hydrogen nucleus. The hydrogen assumes a partial positive charge ($\delta+$) and the oxygen a corresponding negative charge ($\delta-$).* Then attraction between the positive H and the negative charge on the O of another molecule gives rise to a second weaker link to the hydrogen,

$$\overset{\delta+}{\underset{O-H}{}}\cdots\overset{\delta-}{O}$$

18-6.4 The Significance of the Hydrogen Bond

Hydrogen bonds are important in fixing properties such as solubilities, melting points, and boiling points, and in determining the form and stability of crystalline structures. They play a crucial role in biological systems. For example, water is so common in living matter that it must influence the chemical behavior of many biological molecules, most of which can also form hydrogen bonds. Water can attach itself by hydrogen bonding either by donating the proton, as in

$$\overset{H}{\underset{}{\diagup}}O-H\cdots O=C\overset{\diagup}{\underset{\diagdown}{}}$$

or by accepting the proton, as in

$$\overset{\diagdown}{\underset{\diagup}{}}N-H\cdots O\overset{\overset{\textstyle H}{\diagup}}{\underset{\diagdown H}{}}$$

Furthermore, hydrogen bonding within a single molecule is one of the chief factors in determining the structure of important biological substances such as DNA, as will be discussed in Chapter 21.

18-7 HIGHLIGHTS

Molecules in which all atoms have completed valence shells will liquefy and freeze at relatively low temperatures because of comparatively weak **van der Waals forces** acting between molecules. Van der Waals forces increase as the number of electrons in an atom increases and as the area of contact between two molecules in the system increases. The existence of strong covalent bonds between atoms in a solid gives rise to solids with very high melting temperatures, such as diamond and graphite.

Solids of metallic structure are formed by atoms having empty orbitals and electrons with low ionization energies. This model explains the geometry, high electrical and thermal conductivity, malleability, and ductility of metals.

The **band theory** of the electronic structure of metals proposes that when two metallic atoms approach each other, the energy of their overlapping orbitals spreads to form a band of closely related energies. **Metals** are characterized by a conduction band that is about half-full

*A partial charge transfer rather than a complete charge transfer is indicated by the Greek letter *delta* as $\delta+$ or $\delta-$.

of electrons. **Insulators** result when the valence band is full and the next higher band is of much higher energy. **Semiconductors** result when the valence band is full but the next higher band is not separated by much of an energy gap. Electrons can be promoted to the higher band by visible light; this is the basis of solar energy cells. Semiconduction also results when atoms containing one fewer or one more electron are added to a material having a full valence band. This permits some electron flow and is the basis of transistors and other electronic devices.

Boron is in between metallic and covalent network structures. This accounts for the fact that its chemistry has long been considered unusual.

Ionic solids have strong inter-ionic forces. **Polar solvents** such as water interact with ions to dissolve the solid. The **hydration** energy almost compensates for the lattice energy, and the solution process is driven by the tendency of the system to achieve maximum randomness.

Hydrogen bonds are able to form between two molecules if each contains an atom of F, O, N, or sometimes Cl and if there is a hydrogen atom between the two atoms. Many unexpected physical and chemical properties can be interpreted in terms of hydrogen bonds.

QUESTIONS and PROBLEMS

1 Which of the following would you expect to form liquids and solids held together by van der Waals forces? Explain why or why not.
(a) $:\ddot{F}:\ddot{F}:$ (b) $:\ddot{O}::\ddot{O}:$ (c) $:N:::N:$ (d) $\cdot\dot{C}\cdot$
(e) $\dot{B}\cdot$

2 Without looking at your textbook, draw an outline of the periodic table and indicate which elements form liquids and solids held together predominantly by van der Waals forces.

3 Explain, in terms of the relative strength of van der Waals forces, why chlorine is a gas at room temperature, bromine a liquid, and iodine a solid.

4 Methane (CH_4) is a gas at room temperature, while gasoline, a mixture of hydrocarbons typified by C_8H_{18}, is a liquid. Explain, in terms of van der Waals forces, molecular size, and number of electrons, why this is so.

5 There are two existing isomers of propyl alcohol. The first, *n*-propanol, has the molecular structure

$$\begin{array}{ccc} H & H & H \\ | & | & | \\ H-C-C-C-O-H \\ | & | & | \\ H & H & H \end{array}$$

while the second has the following molecular structure:

$$\begin{array}{ccc} H & H & H \\ | & | & | \\ H-C-C-C-H \\ | & | & | \\ H & O & H \\ & | & \\ & H & \end{array}$$

This makes *n*-propanol a rather long, slender molecule and isopropanol more round and compact.

On the basis of the relationship between van der Waals forces and molecular shape, explain why *n*-propanol's melting point is *lower than,* and boiling point *higher than,* that of isopropanol.

6 Without looking at your textbook, draw an outline of the periodic table and indicate which elements form network solids.

7 The elements carbon and silicon form oxides with similar empirical formulas, CO_2 and SiO_2. CO_2 vaporizes at -78.5 °C; SiO_2 melts at about 1700 °C, and boils at about 2200 °C. Given this large difference, propose the types of solids these are. Draw an electron dot or orbital representation of the bonding in CO_2 consistent with your answer.

8 How do you account for the following properties in terms of the structures of the solids?
(a) Both graphite and diamond are made of

carbon (C) atoms. Both are high melting, yet the diamond is very hard while graphite is a soft, greasy solid. (b) Silicon carbide, or carborundum (SiC), is a very high-melting, hard substance used as an abrasive.

9 All metals are characterized by having fewer electrons than orbitals available for bonding. Explain how this relates to the similarity of metals in electrical and heat conductivity.

10 Without looking at your textbook, draw an outline of the periodic table and indicate which elements are metals. Remembering the decreasing trend in ionization energy as one goes down a column of the periodic table, explain why the metals extend farther to the right with each succeeding row of the table.

11 Consider the successive elements sodium, magnesium, and aluminum. Considering sodium as the standard, copy the following table and fill in the blank spaces with "higher," "lower," "more," or "less" as appropriate.

	Sodium	Magnesium	Aluminum
Ionization energy	XXX		
Heat of vaporization	XXX		
Metallic character	XXX		
Hardness	XXX		

12 Explain why the alkali metals, which have the highest empty-orbital-to-valence-electron ratio, and thus are among the most "metallic" of all metals, are not useful as structural metals.

13 What kind of structure is found for metallic K? for metallic Be?

14 Using the band theory of metals and your knowledge of X rays from Chapter 16, explain the statement that "all materials become electrical conductors when irradiated with X rays."

15 How could pure germanium (no. 32) be converted into an n-type semiconductor? Explain.

16 Would you expect elemental boron to be a good conductor of heat? Explain.

17 In what way can you justify the statement that boron is in between a metallic solid and a network solid?

18 A hydride of boron can be prepared of formula B_5H_{11}. Look at Figure 18-15.2 on page 450 and suggest a possible arrangement of the five boron atoms. Number them on your drawing.

19 Describe two similarities and two differences between the bonding in a metal, such as sodium, and an ionic solid, such as sodium chloride.

20 If you were given a sample of a white solid, describe some simple experiments that you would perform to help you decide whether the solid was held together by ionic bonds, covalent bonds, or van der Waals forces.

21 Why does solid sodium conduct electricity while solid sodium chloride does not?

22 Why does sodium chloride dissolve readily in water, a polar solvent, but poorly in benzene, a non-polar solvent?

23 Identify each of the following substances as the product of van der Waals, covalent network solid, metallic, or ionic bonding. (a) He(*l*) (b) Fe(*s*) (c) WC(*s*) (d) AgCl(*s*) (e) CH_4(*l*) (f) KCl(*s*) (g) Ag(*s*) (h) Ge(*s*).

24 Which would you expect to be more soluble in water, ethane (C_2H_6) or ethyl alcohol (CH_3CH_2OH)? Explain.

The property of carbon which distinguishes it most conspicuously is its tendency to form non-ionizing links both with other carbon atoms and with atoms of different elements.

R. C. FUSON (1895–   ) and H. R. SNYDER (1924–   )

THE CHEMISTRY OF 19
CARBON COMPOUNDS

Different aspects of carbon chemistry.

WHAT IS SO SPECIAL ABOUT THE CHEMISTRY OF CARBON compounds that it merits a chapter all its own—indeed, a chemistry all its own? One answer is, of course, that carbon compounds are the basis of the chemistry of living things. Another is that there are far more carbon compounds than all of the non-carbon compounds put together. Carbon is unique in its ability to form long-chain compounds.

In this chapter we will explore methods of learning about the molecular structure of carbon compounds and will learn about the kinds of molecules that comprise hydrocarbons, alcohols, organic acids, aspirin, nylon, and other "organic" substances.

The compounds of carbon furnish one of the most intriguing aspects of chemistry. They especially interest us because they play a dominant role in the chemistry of living things, both plant and animal. Also, there are many carbon compounds useful to us as dyes, drugs, detergents, plastics, perfumes, fibers, fabrics, flavors, and fuels. The manufacturing of these compounds has given rise to a huge chemical industry requiring millions of tons of raw materials every year. Where do we find the enormous quantities of carbon and carbon compounds needed to feed this giant industry? Let us begin our study of carbon chemistry by looking at the chief sources of carbon and carbon compounds.

19-1 SOURCES OF CARBON COMPOUNDS

19-1.1 Coal

Coal, a black mineral of vegetable origin, is believed to have come from the accumulation of decaying plant material in swamps during prehistoric eras when a warm, wet climate permitted rapid growth of plants.* The cycles of decay, new growth, and decay caused successive layers of plant material to gradually build up vast deposits. The top layers of this material and of sedimentary rocks kept air from the lower material and subjected it to enormous pressures. In time the layers were compressed into hard beds composed chiefly of the carbon that was present in the original plants, and also containing appreciable amounts of oxygen, hydrogen, nitrogen, and some sulfur. Thus, coal is not pure carbon. The "hardest" coal, anthracite, contains from 85 to 95 percent carbon by weight; the "softest" coal, peat, is not really coal but one of the early stages in the geological history of coal. Peat still contains unchanged plant remains and may contain no more than 50 to 60 percent carbon.

The use of coal as a fuel is of relatively recent origin. Although some coal was used in ancient times, wood was always the preferred fuel. As late as 1760 wood was essentially the only fuel used, but by 1900 some 96 percent of the world's energy came from burning coal.

*See Isaac Asimov, "The Fascinating Story of Fossil Fuels," *National Wildlife Magazine* (August-September 1973), page 9, and W. K. Seifert, *Chemical and Engineering News* (June 25, 1973), page 13.

Today petroleum (including natural gas) is the chief fuel used. But petroleum is being used up very rapidly; we are once again turning our attention to coal. Although coal is still being formed today, we are consuming it at a rate which is fifty thousand times greater than its rate of formation. Very conservative estimates indicate that world supplies can last for no more than 500 years, even if use does not increase. We could be out of coal in 200 years.

When coal is heated to a high temperature *in the absence of air,* it decomposes; volatile products (coal gas and coal tar) distill away and a residue called **coke** remains. Coke is a valuable industrial material used chiefly in the reduction of iron ore (iron oxide) to iron for the manufacture of steel. Coke is essentially carbon that still contains the mineral substances present in all coals. About eight gallons of **coal tar** are obtained from a ton of coal. Coal tars are very complex mixtures; over 200 different carbon compounds have been isolated from them, many of which are used as industrial raw materials.

19-1.2 Petroleum and Natural Gas

Petroleum is a complex mixture that may range from a light, volatile liquid to a heavy, tarry substance. Apparently petroleum, like coal, has its origin in living matter that has undergone chemical changes over a period of time. There is now some evidence that animal matter as well as plant matter contributed to the formation of petroleum. It is found in porous rock formations called oil pools, which lie between impervious rock formations that seal off the pools. **Natural gas** is a mixture of low-molecular weight compounds of hydrogen and carbon **(hydrocarbons)** found in underground "fields" of sandstone or other porous rock.

19-1.3 Certain Plant and Animal Products

Plants and animals are themselves highly effective chemical factories; they synthesize a majority of the known carbon compounds. These include sugars, starches, plant oils and waxes, fats, gelatin, dyes, drugs, and fibers.

Because these carbon compounds have their origin in living matter, plant or animal, *the chemistry of carbon is called* **organic chemistry.** *Compounds containing carbon are called* **organic compounds.*** This term includes all compounds of carbon except CO_2, CO, and a handful of ionic substances such as sodium carbonate (Na_2CO_3) and sodium cyanide (NaCN). You may wonder how many organic substances are known. The number is actually so large it is difficult to provide a reliable estimate. Carbon compounds outnumber the compounds of all other elements with the possible exception of hydrogen (which is present in most carbon compounds). There are undoubtedly over one million different carbon compounds known. The number of *new* organic compounds synthesized in any one year (about 100,000 compounds) exceeds the total number of compounds known that contain no carbon!

*At one time it was thought that chemists could not make organic compounds. A "vital force" was believed to be essential. This was disproved when Wöhler synthesized the organic compound urea [$(H_2N)_2CO$] from the heating of the inorganic salt NH_4CNO.

19-2 MOLECULAR STRUCTURE OF CARBON COMPOUNDS

How can there be so many compounds containing this one element? The answer lies in molecular structure. In our discussion of bonding, we saw that carbon atoms have a strong tendency to form covalent bonds to other carbon atoms, resulting in long chains, branched chains, and rings of atoms. (Remember the structures of diamond and graphite.) Each different atomic arrangement gives a molecule having distinct properties. To understand why a particular substance has certain characteristic properties, its structure must be known. Thus, the determination of the molecular structure of carbon compounds is one of the central problems of organic chemistry. This problem is usually solved by applying ideas and techniques we have already considered. Let us follow the process in detail for two compounds, ethane and ethanol.

19-2.1 The Composition and Structure of Carbon Compounds

Ethane and ethanol* are two common carbon compounds. Ethane is a gas that usually makes up about 10 percent of the natural gas used for heating and cooking. Its useful chemistry is almost wholly restricted to the combustion reaction. Ethanol is a liquid that participates in a variety of useful chemical reactions. It has great value in the manufacture of chemicals, and it bears little chemical resemblance to ethane. Yet, the similarity of the two names suggests that these compounds are related. This is so. To understand how they are related and why their chemistries are nevertheless so different, we must learn about their molecular structures.

Three basic experimental steps are usually involved in determining a molecular structure. First, we determine the *empirical formula,* then the *molecular formula,* and finally the *structural formula.* Let us review the information conveyed by each of these formulas.

As you will recall, the **empirical formula** tells only *the relative number of atoms* of each element in a molecule. The empirical formula of ethane is CH_3; that of ethanol is C_2H_6O. Ways in which the empirical formula can be determined will be considered in the next section.

The **molecular formula** tells *the total number of atoms* of each element in a *molecule.* The molecular formula is derived from the empirical formula by multiplying it by a whole number. This relationship can be represented as (empirical formula)$_n$, where n is a whole number. For example, the empirical formula of ethane is CH_3. One CH_3 unit has a formula weight of 15, but ethane has a molecular weight of 30; hence, there must be *two* empirical formulas in one molecular formula. Then, the molecular formula of ethane is $(CH_3)_2$ or C_2H_6. To convert the empirical formula to a molecular formula, the molecular weight must be known.

*Ethanol is also known as ethyl alcohol.

EXERCISE 19-1

A compound of carbon and hydrogen contains two hydrogen atoms for every carbon atom. The molecular weight is found to be 84. Write the empirical formula and the molecular formula.

The **structural formula** tells *which atoms are connected* in the molecule. Consider the compound having the molecular formula $C_2H_4F_2$. There are two ways in which atoms can be connected in this molecule without violating the bonding rules developed in Chapter 17. Either two fluorine atoms can be attached to one carbon,

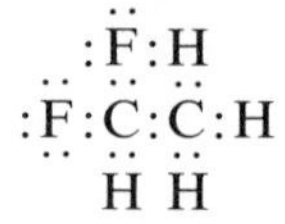

$$\ddot{:}\ddot{F}\ddot{:}H$$
$$:\ddot{F}:C:C:H$$
$$\quad\; H\; H$$

or one fluorine atom can be attached to each carbon.

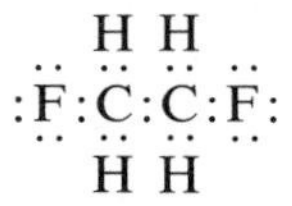

$$\quad\; H\; H$$
$$:\ddot{F}:C:C:\ddot{F}:$$
$$\quad\; H\; H$$

As you will recall from the discussion in Chapter 17 concerning $C_2H_2Cl_2$, compounds having the same molecular formula but different structural formulas are called **structural isomers.** Structural isomers differ in properties. The structural formula permits us to represent such differences, even though the two compounds have identical molecular formulas.

EXERCISE 19-2

The molecular formula of ethane is C_2H_6. How many structural formulas can be drawn for ethane without violating the bonding rules of Chapter 17?

The structural formula provides the most explicit representation for the molecule. How is the structural formula established? In Section 17-7 we listed some of the ways in which a structural formula can be determined. How can these procedures be used to determine the structural formula of ethanol? Let us check.

EXERCISE 19-3

What kind of forces would you expect to be acting between molecules of $C_2H_4F_2$? Make an estimate of the general boiling-point range that you would expect for $C_2H_4F_2$. Check your answer in Exercise 19-4.

EXERCISE 19-4

The boiling point of the compound HF_2CCH_3 is $-25\ °C$. The boiling point of FH_2CCH_2F is $10\ °C$. Make a model of each of these two molecules. Which one is most nearly like a ball? Are the differences in boiling point consistent with differences in van der Waals forces predicted on the basis of molecular symmetry? (Refer to Section 18-1.)

19-2.2 The Experimental Determination of the Molecular Formula

The compound ethanol is isolated in the laboratory as a colorless liquid that boils at the constant and reproducible temperature of $78.5\ °C$ under 1 atm pressure. It freezes at $-117.4\ °C$. The constancy of its properties during different phase changes indicates that we are dealing with a pure substance. The first step in establishing a formula for this substance is analysis. We must know the kind and number of atoms present.

Most organic compounds can be analyzed by burning the substance in pure oxygen. If the compound contains only carbon and hydrogen, only carbon dioxide and water will be produced. If the compound contains some nitrogen as well, nitrogen gas or one of the nitrogen oxides will be produced. Another way of finding out which elements are present in a compound is to allow the compound to react with hot, liquid sodium metal. If the compound contains nitrogen, sodium cyanide (NaCN) will be formed; if it contains sulfur, sodium sulfide (Na_2S) will be produced.

Once such reactions show which elements are in the compound, relative numbers of atoms of each element (the empirical formula) can be determined. For example, suppose we burn 46 g of ethanol in oxygen and obtain 88 g of CO_2 and 54 g of water. How many *moles* of carbon *atoms* and how many *moles* of hydrogen *atoms* were present in the original sample? Since all carbon was added in the ethanol, and since each mole of CO_2 contains 1 mole of carbon atoms, we see that the number of moles of carbon atoms in the ethanol is equal to the number of moles of CO_2 obtained:*

$$\text{number moles } CO_2 = \frac{\text{mass } CO_2}{\dfrac{\text{g } CO_2}{\text{mole } CO_2}}$$

$$= \frac{88\ \text{g } CO_2}{\dfrac{44\ \text{g } CO_2}{\text{mole } CO_2}} = 2.0 \text{ moles } CO_2 \qquad (1)$$

number moles $CO_2 = 2.0$ moles CO_2

number moles $CO_2 =$ number moles C atoms $= 2.0$

---

*Symbolically we can represent this by the equation

$$C_nH_yO_z + aO_2 \longrightarrow nCO_2 + \frac{y}{2}(H_2O)$$

Note that the number of carbon atoms, n, is equal to the number of moles of CO_2.

Since water contains 2 moles of hydrogen atoms per mole of water, we determine the number of moles of water and multiply the result by 2.0 to determine the number of moles of hydrogen atoms:

$$\text{number moles H}_2\text{O} = \frac{\text{mass H}_2\text{O}}{\dfrac{\text{g H}_2\text{O}}{\text{mole H}_2\text{O}}}$$

$$= \frac{54 \text{ g H}_2\text{O}}{\dfrac{18 \text{ g H}_2\text{O}}{\text{mole H}_2\text{O}}} = 3.0 \text{ moles H}_2\text{O} \qquad (2)$$

$$\text{number moles H atoms} = 3.0 \text{ moles H}_2\text{O} \times \frac{2.0 \text{ moles H}}{\text{mole H}_2\text{O}}$$

$$\text{number moles H atoms} = 6.0$$

The total sample mass accounted for so far is

$$\left(2 \text{ moles C atoms} \times \frac{12 \text{ g}}{\text{mole C atoms}}\right)$$

$$+ \left(6 \text{ moles H atoms} \times \frac{1 \text{ g}}{\text{mole H atoms}}\right) = 24 \text{ g} + 6 \text{ g} = 30 \text{ g} \quad (3)$$

The above numbers account for only 30 g of the original 46 g of sample. Since only CO_2 and H_2O were obtained as products and pure oxygen was the other reactant, the sample itself must have contained 16 g of oxygen (46 − 30). No other element can account for the difference of 16 g between mass of original sample and mass of carbon plus hydrogen in the products. Using this information, we write

$$\text{number moles oxygen atoms} = \frac{16 \text{ g O}}{\dfrac{16 \text{ g O}}{\text{mole O}}} = 1.0 \text{ mole O} \qquad (4)$$

$$\text{number moles oxygen atoms} = 1.0$$

From this information the *empirical* formula must be C_2H_6O.

This example has been much simplified by our selection of 46 g of sample. In actual practice less than 1 g of sample would be used and whole numbers of moles would not be obtained. A typical set of experimental data is given in Exercise 19-5. In most cases the sample is analyzed in a special **analytical laboratory.** Data are usually reported by chemists in this laboratory as *percentage* carbon by weight, *percentage* hydrogen by weight, and *percentage* oxygen, or other elements in the sample, by weight.

EXERCISE 19-5

Automobile antifreeze often contains a compound called ethylene glycol. Analysis of pure ethylene glycol shows that it contains only carbon, hydrogen, and oxygen. A sample of ethylene glycol with a mass of 15.5 mg is burned and the masses of CO_2 and H_2O resulting are 22.0 mg and 13.5 mg respectively.

(1) What is the empirical formula of ethylene glycol?
(2) Calculate the percentage by weight of carbon, hydrogen, and oxygen in the sample.

The molecular formula for ethanol must be a whole number multiple of the empirical formula. We can write $n \times (C_2H_6O) =$ molecular formula. What is n? Each unit of C_2H_6O has a mass of 46 g. If n is 1, the molecular weight of ethanol will be 46; if n is 2, the molecular weight of ethanol will be 92; and if n is 3, the molecular weight of ethanol will be 138. We need an experimental value for the molecular weight of ethanol!

Since ethanol can be vaporized fairly easily, a vapor-density method for molecular weight is applicable. The procedure is very much like that which you used in Experiment 5. To apply the method to a liquid such as ethanol, a temperature above the boiling point is needed. A weighed amount of liquid is placed in a gas-collecting device held at an easily regulated temperature. (A steam condenser around the device provides a convenient way of holding the temperature at 100 °C.) When the substance has vaporized completely, its pressure and volume are measured (see Experiment 5). This provides a measurement of the mass per unit volume of gaseous ethanol at a known temperature and pressure. Again, this mass is compared with the mass of the same volume of a reference gas (usually O_2) at the same temperature and pressure.

Suppose such a vapor-density measurement shows that a given volume of ethanol at 100 °C and 1 atm has a mass 1.5 times as great as the same volume of oxygen gas at 100 °C and 1 atm. Since equal volumes contain equal numbers of molecules at the same temperature and pressure (Avogadro's hypothesis), one molecule of the unknown gas must have a mass 1.5 times the mass of one molecule of oxygen gas. Therefore,

$$\text{mol wt of unknown gas} = (1.5) \times (\text{mol wt } O_2)$$
$$= 1.5 \times 32 \text{ g/mole} = 48 \text{ g/mole} \quad (5)$$

Even though this number is not very accurate, it will suffice for the purpose of deciding that the molecular formula is C_2H_6O. Clearly, formulas requiring molecular weights of 92 ($n = 2$) or 138 ($n = 3$) conflict seriously with the measured molecular weight of about 48. Only a value of $n = 1$ is consistent.

Freezing and boiling points of a solution can also be used to determine the molecular weight of a solute. Use of the mass spectrometer represents still another procedure for molecular weights. These methods will be described in subsequent courses in chemistry.

EXERCISE 19-6

Ethylene glycol, the example treated in Exercise 19-5, has an empirical formula of CH_3O. (Is this what you obtained?) A sample that has a mass of 0.49 g is vaporized completely at 200 °C and 1 atm. The volume measured under these conditions is 291 ml. The same volume, 291 ml, of oxygen gas at 200 °C and 1 atm has a mass of 0.240 g. What is the molecular formula for ethylene glycol, CH_3O, $C_2H_6O_2$, $C_3H_9O_3$, $C_4H_{12}O_4$, or some higher multiple of CH_3O?

19-2.3 The Experimental Determination of the Structural Formula—Chemical Evidence

You were told in Chapter 17 that much structural information can be obtained from an intelligent interpretation of the reactions which a compound undergoes. How can this assertion be applied to ethanol? We know that its empirical formula is C_2H_6O and its molecular formula is also C_2H_6O. It remains to discover the structural formula, the arrangement and connections of the atoms.

To begin, let us eliminate some structures we are sure are incorrect. Ethanol is not simply ethane with an oxygen atom somehow attached to a carbon atom. In ethane all four bonds of each carbon are satisfied, so there is no way in which an additional bond can form. We say that ethane is a **saturated compound.*** Nor can the oxygen atom just be attached somehow to a hydrogen atom. Each hydrogen atom in ethane has its bonding capacity already satisfied.

We have rejected a structural formula that pictures ethanol as ethane with an oxygen atom tacked onto it. By applying our bonding theory, let us start with an oxygen atom and try to build a molecule around it having two carbon atoms and six hydrogen atoms. We already know that the oxygen atom is commonly divalent, and that it makes bonds to hydrogen atoms, as in water. Let us start our molecular construction with a bond between one hydrogen atom and the oxygen atom:

$$O—H$$

The other bond the oxygen atom can make must be to a carbon atom, since if it were to another hydrogen atom we would simply have a water molecule. Therefore, we write

$$\begin{array}{c} C \\ \diagdown \\ O—H \end{array}$$

The carbon atom we have added must form three additional bonds to satisfy its tetravalent bonding capacity. If all these bonds were to hydrogen atoms, we would have the completed molecule CH_3OH and two hydrogen atoms and a carbon atom left over. Therefore, one of the bonds our first carbon atom forms must be to the other carbon atom, and the two other bonds must be to hydrogen atoms. We then have

$$\begin{array}{c} \quad\quad H \\ \quad\quad \diagup \\ C—C—H \\ \quad\quad \diagdown \\ \quad\quad O—H \end{array}$$

---

*This use of the word *saturated* shows that chemists, like other people, sometimes use the same word with two entirely different meanings. In Section 12-1 this word was used to describe a solution that contains the equilibrium concentration of a dissolved substance. In reference to organic compounds, saturated means that all bonds between carbon atoms are single bonds.

We can easily complete the structure by adding three bonds from our last carbon atom to the three hydrogen atoms we have left. The result is

$$\begin{array}{ccc} H & & H \\ | & & | \\ H-C & -C & -H \\ | & & | \\ H & & O-H \end{array}$$

We have now used all six hydrogen atoms, the two carbon atoms, and the oxygen atom required by the molecular formula of ethanol.

Since all bonding rules are satisfied, this structure is a *possible* structural formula for ethanol. Now we must decide whether this structural formula is the *only* possible one for a molecule having the molecular formula C_2H_6O. A little reflection shows it is not. Instead of beginning with one oxygen-carbon and one oxygen-hydrogen bond, why not start with two oxygen-carbon bonds?

$$\begin{array}{ccc} & O & \\ \diagup & & \diagdown \\ C & & C \end{array}$$

Since we have six hydrogen atoms at our disposal, and each carbon atom must form three more bonds, we complete the structure by writing

$$\begin{array}{ccccc} H & & O & & H \\ \diagdown & \diagup & & \diagdown & \diagup \\ & C & & & C \\ \diagup & \diagdown & & \diagup & \diagdown \\ H & & H\ H & & H \end{array}$$

If we check, we find that this structure violates no bonding rules and conforms to the empirical and molecular formula of ethanol.

Further work shows no other structural formulas for the ethanol molecule that agree with our bonding theory. While structures in conflict with current bonding theory might be considered in some situations, evidence to support them would have to be very strong. Bonding theory summarizes a large amount of experience.

According to bonding theory, the oxygen atom is either directly bonded to one carbon atom or to two carbon atoms. *Once a choice between these two possibilities is made, the structure of the rest of the molecule can be determined from the molecular formula and the bonding rules.* The two possible structures are shown in Figure 19-1 (page 470). Once again we have a choice between two structural isomers.* The existence of two compounds having the formula C_2H_6O perplexed chemists for decades. Now we recognize the crucial importance of determining the structural as well as molecular formula of a substance.

Our problem, then, is to decide whether ethanol has structure (a) or (b). How can we tell which is correct? What does the structural formula of each tell us?

In structure (b) all hydrogen atoms are the same—each is bonded to a carbon atom, which is bonded to the oxygen atom. In structure (a), however, one of the hydrogen atoms is quite different from the

*Review Section 17-6.2 if you have forgotten the meaning of structural isomers.

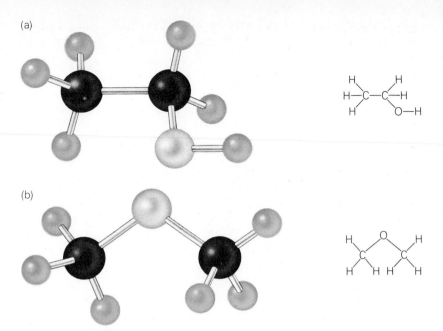

(a)

(b)

others—it is bonded to oxygen and not to carbon. Of the remaining five, two are bonded to the carbon bonded to the oxygen and three are bonded to the other carbon. Structures (a) and (b) should have very different chemistries. Which one should correspond to the chemistry of ethanol?

We can offer several kinds of evidence. Some evidence comes from the behavior of ethanol in chemical reactions and some from the determination of certain physical properties. Let us consider the reactions first.

Clean sodium metal reacts vigorously with ethanol, giving hydrogen gas and an ionic compound, sodium ethoxide, which has the empirical formula C_2H_5ONa. The reaction is quite similar to the behavior of sodium and water to give hydrogen and the ionic compound sodium hydroxide (NaOH). This suggests, but certainly does not prove, that ethanol shows some structural similarity to water. In water two hydrogen atoms are bonded to one oxygen atom, and in structure (a) one hydrogen atom is bonded to the oxygen atom. This chemical evidence supports structure (a) for ethanol.

More quantitative evidence can be obtained by using an excess of sodium and a weighed amount of ethanol and measuring the amount of hydrogen gas evolved. It is found that 46 g of ethanol (1 mole) will produce only 0.5 mole of hydrogen gas. We can therefore write a balanced chemical equation for the reaction of sodium with ethanol:

$$Na(s) + C_2H_6O(l) \longrightarrow \tfrac{1}{2}H_2(g) + C_2H_5ONa(s) \qquad (6)$$

According to equation (6), 1 mole of ethanol produces 0.5 mole of hydrogen gas. Hence, 1 mole of ethanol must contain 1 mole of hydrogen atoms that are uniquely capable of undergoing reaction with sodium. Apparently, one molecule of ethanol contains one hydrogen atom that is capable of reacting with sodium and five that are not.

Let us now consider structures (a) and (b) in the light of this information. In structure (b) all six hydrogen atoms are structurally equivalent, whereas in structure (a) there is one hydrogen atom in the molecule that is structurally unique because it is bonded to the oxygen atom. Structure (a) is therefore consistent with the experimental fact that only one hydrogen atom per molecule of ethanol will react with sodium, but structure (b) is not.

We can find further evidence that structure (a), CH_3CH_2OH, is the correct structural formula for ethanol. It is known that compounds that contain only carbon and hydrogen, such as ethane (C_2H_6), do not react readily with metallic sodium to produce hydrogen gas. In these compounds the hydrogen atoms are all bonded to carbon atoms, as in the structural formula for ethane in Section 17-6; so we can deduce that hydrogen atoms bonded to carbon atoms generally do not react with sodium to produce hydrogen gas. In structure (b), CH_3OCH_3, all hydrogen atoms are bonded to carbon atoms, so we do not expect it to react with sodium. But ethanol reacts with sodium, so it is unlikely that ethanol has structure (b). Our confidence in this reasoning is strengthened by noting that the other known structural isomer of formula C_2H_6O does *not* react with sodium at all. Its chemistry is consistent with structure (b).

Let us consider one other reaction of ethanol. If ethanol is heated with aqueous HBr, a volatile compound is formed. This compound is only slightly soluble in water and it contains bromine; by analysis and molecular weight, its molecular formula is found to be C_2H_5Br (ethyl bromide, or bromoethane). Using the bonding rules, we can see that there is only one possible structure for this compound. This result is verified by the fact that only one isomer of C_2H_5Br has ever been discovered.

Now we can ask how this chemical reaction furnishes a clue to the structure of ethanol. Structure (a) could give the structure shown in Figure 19-2 by breaking the carbon-oxygen bond. In contrast, bromoethane can be obtained from structure (b) only by a complicated rearrangement of atoms. Many years of laboratory experience show that such complicated reshufflings of atoms rarely occur. Therefore, the reaction between ethanol and HBr to form bromoethane provides more evidence that ethanol has structure (a).

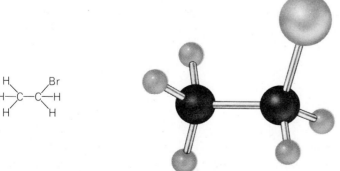

Fig. 19-2 The structural formula and model of ethyl bromide (bromoethane).

19-2.4 The Experimental Determination of the Structural Formula—Physical Evidence

The evidence cited so far has been associated with the chemistry of ethanol. Its boiling point provides a different sort of evidence, which also supports a choice of structure (a). Ethanol is a liquid with a boiling point of 78 °C. This can be compared with the boiling points of ethane (C_2H_6), which is -172 °C, and water, 100 °C. Ethanol is, then, more like water than like ethane in terms of boiling point. Once again, this can be explained better by structure (a), which, like H_2O, has oxygen linked to hydrogen. The high boiling point of water is explained in terms of an abnormally large intermolecular attraction of such an OH group to surrounding water molecules. You remember this as hydrogen bonding (see Section 18-6). If ethanol also has the OH group, as in structure (a), then it too can exert the same abnormally large attraction to neighboring ethanol molecules. Thus, structure (a) provides an explanation of the fact that the boiling point of ethanol is so high.

This possibility of forming hydrogen bonds should cause a strong attraction between water and a compound of structure (a). If there is strong attraction, then ethanol should have high solubility in water. Experiment shows that they are **miscible,** that they dissolve in all proportions. Again, the evidence tends to support structure (a).

Various spectroscopic techniques provide more direct evidence. The **infrared spectrum** of the material tentatively identified as ethanol, structure (a), can be obtained in the gas phase. It shows absorption frequencies associated with hydrogen bonded to carbon, and with hydrogen bonded to oxygen. The other structural isomer of C_2H_6O shows only the absorption frequency of hydrogen bonded to carbon.

Nuclear magnetic resonance (nmr) spectroscopy provides even clearer evidence for the structure of ethanol. As noted in Section 17-7.6, the frequency of the electromagnetic radiation needed to flip over the small electromagnet created by a spinning nucleus is determined by the environment in which the nucleus finds itself. This means that for the compound

$$\begin{array}{ccccc} & & H & H & \longleftarrow 2 \\ & & | & | & \\ 3 \longrightarrow & H-C-C-O-H & \longleftarrow 1 \\ & & | & | & \\ & & H & H & \longleftarrow 2 \end{array}$$

three different nmr frequencies corresponding to hydrogens in positions *1, 2,* and *3* should be found. The intensity of the signal is proportional to the number of hydrogen atoms in that position. For a compound of structure (b), CH_3OCH_3, only a single nmr frequency should be observed since all six hydrogens are identical. In Figure 19-3 the nmr spectra for CH_3CH_2OH and for CH_3OCH_3 are displayed. Structure (a) shows the expected three absorptions and structure (b) shows only one.

Notice that many types of evidence lead to the same conclusion, that ethanol has the structure

$$\begin{array}{ccc} H & H & \\ | & | & \\ H-C-C-O-H \\ | & | & \\ H & H & \end{array}$$

Fig. 19-3 The nmr spectra for (a) CH_3CH_2OH and (b) CH_3OCH_3.

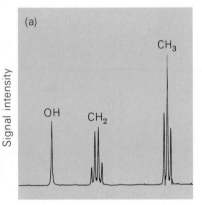

(a)

CH₃

OH

CH₂

Signal intensity

Frequency of radiation needed to flip nuclei

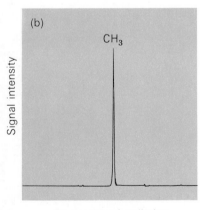

(b)

CH₃

Signal intensity

Frequency of radiation needed to flip nuclei

No fact by itself gives absolute proof of the structure, but all facts taken together establish the structure with a high degree of certainty. An X-ray diffraction or electron diffraction study would give even more detailed structural information, such as distances between nuclei in the molecule.

The second isomer with structure (b) is known as dimethyl ether.

EXERCISE 19-7

Ethylene glycol has the empirical formula CH_3O and the molecular formula $C_2H_6O_2$. Using the usual bonding rules (*e.g.*, carbon is tetravalent, oxygen is divalent, hydrogen is monovalent), draw some of the structural formulas possible for this compound.

EXERCISE 19-8

Decide which of your structures in Exercise 19-7 best fits the following properties observed for pure ethylene glycol: (a) It is a viscous (syrupy) liquid that boils at 197 °C. (b) It is miscible with water—that is, it dissolves, forming solutions, in all proportions. (c) It is miscible with ethanol. (d) It reacts with sodium metal, producing hydrogen gas. (e) A 6.2-g sample of ethylene glycol reacts with an excess of sodium metal to produce 2.4 litres of hydrogen gas at 1 atm and 25 °C. (f) The low resolution nmr signal for ethylene glycol shows two absorptions—one twice as intense as the other.

19-2.5 Structural Components—The Ethyl Group

All the reactions and the physical properties of ethanol have been explained on the basis of the behavior of the OH group in structure (a), CH_3CH_2OH. This is true of most of the reactions of ethanol—the reaction centers at the OH group or **hydroxyl group,** and the remainder of the molecule, CH_3CH_2—, remains intact. These reactions suggest that there are two parts to the ethanol molecule, the

$$
\begin{array}{c}
\ \ \ \ H\ \ H \\
\ \ \ \ |\ \ \ \ | \\
H-C-C- \\
\ \ \ \ |\ \ \ \ | \\
\ \ \ \ H\ \ H
\end{array}
$$

group, *which is unchanged during reactions,* and the —OH group, *which can change.* This concept of *the structural integrity of the hydrocarbon group* is important in organic chemistry. It focuses attention on the groups that *do* change, the so-called **functional groups.** If we understand the chemistry of a particular functional group for one compound, we can assume that its chemistry is true of other compounds containing this same functional group. Thus, compounds with the OH group are given a *family name,* **alcohols.** The rest of the molecule, the carbon skeleton, remains intact during those reactions involving only the functional group.

We mentioned earlier that when ethanol reacts with hydrogen bromide, ethyl bromide is formed. Similar treatment of ethanol with hydrogen chloride or hydrogen iodide gives us the ethyl halides:

$$CH_3CH_2OH + HBr \longrightarrow CH_3CH_2Br + H_2O \qquad (7)$$

$$CH_3CH_2OH + HCl \longrightarrow CH_3CH_2Cl + H_2O \qquad (8)$$

$$CH_3CH_2OH + HI \longrightarrow CH_3CH_2I + H_2O \qquad (9)$$

We say that the hydroxyl group has been *displaced* and that the halogen atom has been substituted for it. You can see that the group CH_3CH_2— has remained intact in all these reactions. Indeed, this group has appeared in most of our discussion so far, sometimes attached to oxygen, as in ethanol and sodium ethoxide, sometimes attached to other atoms, as in the ethyl halides. You will recall that earlier we became acquainted with ethane (C_2H_6). Looking at the structural formula of ethane, you see it is simply the CH_3CH_2— group attached to hydrogen:

$$
\begin{array}{ccc}
& H & H \\
& | & | \\
H- & C- & C-H \\
& | & | \\
& H & H
\end{array}
$$

or CH_3CH_2—H. This group, CH_3CH_2— (also written C_2H_5—), is called the **ethyl group.**

Because ethyl bromide and ethyl alcohol (ethanol) can be considered as derived from ethane (by the substitution of —Br and —OH for one of its hydrogens), we speak of these as *derivatives* of ethane, and we say that ethane is the *parent hydrocarbon* for a series of related compounds. The name "ethyl" is derived from the name of the parent hydrocarbon, ethane. In the same way the name of the **methyl group** (CH_3—) is derived from that of methane (CH_4), and the name of the **propyl group** ($CH_3CH_2CH_2$—) is derived from propane ($CH_3CH_2CH_3$).

It is important to realize that these groups are not substances that can be isolated and bottled. They are simply parts of molecules that remain intact in composition and structure during reactions. We find this way of classifying organic groups useful and convenient; but we must keep in mind that in the reactions we have described, the ethyl group is not actually formed as a distinct substance. Table 19-1 (page 485) gives more examples of group names.

19-3 SOME CHEMISTRY OF ORGANIC COMPOUNDS

19-3.1 Some Chemistry of Ethyl and Methyl Bromide

We can use ethyl and methyl bromide to illustrate one kind of organic reaction. Ethyl bromide is not particularly reactive, but it does react with bases such as NaOH or NH_3. If we mix ethyl bromide and aqueous sodium hydroxide solution and then heat the mixture for about an hour, we find that sodium bromide and ethanol are formed:

$$C_2H_5Br + OH^-(aq) \longrightarrow C_2H_5OH + Br^-(aq) \qquad (10)$$

This reaction may seem similar to the reaction between aqueous HBr and NaOH, but there are two important differences. The ethyl bromide reaction is very slow (about one hour is needed for the reaction) and the *reactants* are a covalent molecule (C_2H_5Br) and an ion (OH^-). In contrast, the reaction between HBr and NaOH in water occurs in a fraction of a second and it involves ions only:

$$H^+(aq) + OH^-(aq) \longrightarrow H_2O(l) \qquad (11)$$

Let us describe the course of the reaction of methyl bromide and OH^- in terms of a model. We shall use *methyl* bromide to simplify the description, but the reaction of ethyl bromide is of the same type. The equation for the process we shall study is

$$CH_3Br + OH^- \longrightarrow CH_3OH + Br^- \qquad (12)$$

First, let us recount a few of the experimental facts:

(1) Methyl bromide is a compound in which the chemical bonds are predominantly covalent. An aqueous solution of methyl bromide does not conduct electricity; hence, it does not form significant quantities of ions (such as CH_3^+ and Br^- ions) in aqueous solutions.
(2) The reaction takes a measurable time for completion.
(3) Experiments show that the rate of the reaction is increased by increasing the concentration of OH^- and also by raising the temperature.

These observations remind us of Chapter 10, in which we considered the factors that determine the rate of a chemical reaction. Of course, these same ideas apply here. We can obtain qualitative information about the mechanism of the reaction by applying the collision theory. A quantitative study of the effects of temperature and concentration on the rate should enable us to construct potential energy diagrams like those shown in Figure 10-11.

Figure 19-4 (page 476) shows the mechanism chemists have deduced for reaction (12). The steps of this mechanism are

(1) the approach of the hydroxide ion [Figure 19-4(a)];
(2) the formation of the atomic arrangement thought to be the activated complex [Figure 19-4(b)]; and
(3) formation of the final products from the activated complex [Figure 19-4(c)].

In the activated complex the O—C bond is beginning to form and the C—Br bond is beginning to break. The potential energy curves for the reaction are shown alongside the molecular models in Figure 19-4. The slow rate suggests that activation energy is needed. One reason why activation energy must be supplied is that in the activated complex the bond angles have been distorted from their (stable) configurations and forced into an unstable arrangement.

SOME CHEMISTRY of ETHYL
and METHYL BROMIDE

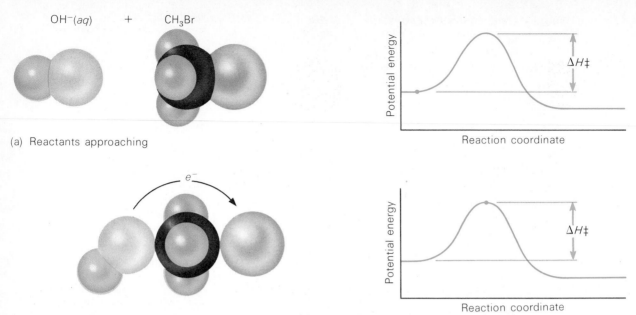

(a) Reactants approaching

$$OH^-(aq) \quad + \quad CH_3Br$$

(b) A possible form of the activated complex. Notice the unstable positions of the hydrogen atoms.

$$HOCH_3 \quad + \quad Br^-(aq)$$

(c) Products separating. Notice the new, stable positions of the hydrogen atoms.

Fig. 19-4 The mechanism and potential energy diagrams for the reaction

$$CH_3Br + OH^-(aq) \longrightarrow$$
$$CH_3OH + Br^-(aq)$$

19-3.2 Oxidation of Organic Compounds— Formation of Aldehydes

By far the majority of the million known compounds of carbon also contain hydrogen and oxygen. There are several important types of oxygen-containing organic compounds; they can be studied as an oxidation series. For example, the compound methanol (CH_3OH) is very closely related to methane, as their structural formulas show (Figures 19-5.1 and 19-5.2). Methanol can be regarded as the first step in the complete oxidation of methane to carbon dioxide and water.

Methanol (and other alcohols) react with common inorganic oxidizing agents such as potassium dichromate ($K_2Cr_2O_7$). When an acidic, aqueous solution of potassium dichromate reacts with methanol, the solution turns from bright orange to muddy green because of the production of the green chromic ion, Cr^{3+}. The solution then has a strong odor easily identified as that of formaldehyde. Its formula, CH_2O, represents the structure in Figure 19-6.1. Notice that the bond between the carbon and oxygen is a double bond (see Section 17-6), and that the C, the two H, and the O atoms lie in the same plane.

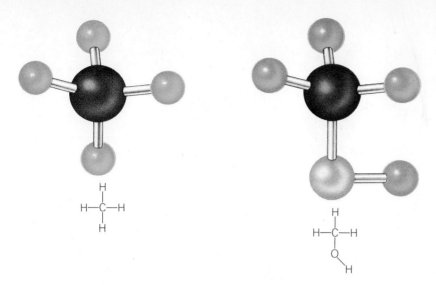

Fig. **19-5.1** (Left) The structural formula and model of methane.

Fig. **19-5.2** (Right) The structural formula and model of methanol.

The balanced net reaction for the formation of formaldehyde is

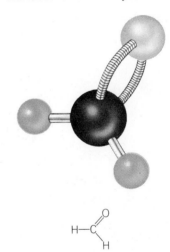

Fig. **19-6.1** The structural formula and model of formaldehyde.

$$3CH_3OH + Cr_2O_7{}^{2-}(aq) + 8H^+(aq) \longrightarrow$$
$$3CH_2O + 2Cr^{3+}(aq) + 7H_2O \quad (13)$$

Since the dichromate ion on the left side of the equation has been reduced to chromic ion, Cr^{3+}, on the right side, the conversion of methanol to formaldehyde must involve oxidation.

To show more clearly that methanol has been oxidized, let us balance this reaction by the half-reaction method. We have encountered the half-reaction involving dichromate and chromic ions before (question 18 in Chapter 15):

$$Cr_2O_7{}^{2-}(aq) + 14H^+(aq) + 6e^- \longrightarrow 2Cr^{3+}(aq) + 7H_2O \quad (14)$$

To balance the methanol-formaldehyde half-reaction, we begin with

$$CH_3OH \text{ gives } CH_2O$$

This statement does not yet show the fact that hydrogen atoms are conserved in the reaction, since there is a deficiency of two hydrogen atoms on the right. This can be remedied by adding two hydrogen ions:

$$CH_3OH \text{ gives } CH_2O + 2H^+(aq)$$

Now the equation is chemically but not electrically balanced. The addition of two electrons to the right-hand side completes the balancing procedure, and the completed half-reaction is

$$CH_3OH \longrightarrow CH_2O + 2H^+(aq) + 2e^- \quad (15)$$

This equation shows that the methanol molecule has lost electrons and has thus been oxidized. Formaldehyde is the second member in the oxidation series of methane.

OXIDATION—

FORMATION of ALDEHYDES

477

Fig. 19-6.2 The structural formula and model of acetaldehyde.

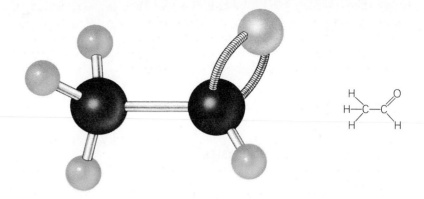

In a similar manner, ethanol can be oxidized by the dichromate ion to form a compound called acetaldehyde (CH_3CHO). The molecular structure of acetaldehyde, which is similar to that of formaldehyde, is shown in Figure 19-6.2. We see that the molecule is structurally similar to formaldehyde. The methyl group, CH_3—, replaces one of the hydrogens of formaldehyde. The balanced equation for the formation of acetaldehyde from ethanol is

$$3CH_3CH_2OH + Cr_2O_7{}^{2-}(aq) + 8H^+(aq) \longrightarrow$$
$$3CH_3CHO + 2Cr^{3+}(aq) + 7H_2O \quad (16)$$

19-3.3 Oxidation of Organic Compounds—Formation of Carboxylic Acids

Fig. 19-7.1 The structural formula and model of formic acid.

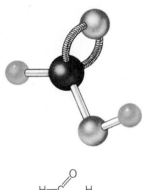

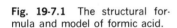

Another oxidation product can be obtained from the reaction between methanol and an acidic aqueous solution of potassium permanganate. The product has the formula HCOOH and is called formic acid. The structural formula of formic acid is shown in Figure 19-7.1. Formic acid is also related to formaldehyde structurally. If one of the hydrogen atoms of formaldehyde is replaced by an OH group, the resulting molecule is formic acid. The balanced equation for the formation of formic acid from methanol is

$$5CH_3OH + 4MnO_4{}^-(aq) + 12H^+(aq) \longrightarrow$$
$$5HCOOH + 4Mn^{2+}(aq) + 11H_2O \quad (17)$$

The half-reaction involving methanol and formic acid can be obtained by using the three steps outlined in the previous example of the methanol-formaldehyde half-reaction. Again, we begin with

$$CH_3OH \text{ gives } HCOOH$$

Chemically balanced this is

$$CH_3OH + H_2O \text{ gives } HCOOH + 4H^+(aq)$$

and with charge balanced,

$$CH_3OH + H_2O \longrightarrow HCOOH + 4H^+(aq) + 4e^- \quad (18)$$

From this completed half-reaction we see that the conversion of methanol to formic acid involves the loss of four electrons. Since the oxidation of methanol to formaldehyde was only a two-electron change, it is clear that formic acid is a more highly oxidized compound of carbon than either formaldehyde or methanol.

EXERCISE 19-9

Balance the half-reaction for the conversion of formaldehyde (CH_2O) to formic acid (HCOOH).

Just as methanol can be oxidized to formic acid, ethanol can be oxidized to acetic acid (CH_3COOH). The molecular structure of acetic acid is shown in Figure 19-7.2. The atomic grouping —COOH is called the **carboxyl group,** and acids containing this group are called **carboxylic acids.**

The balanced equation for production of acetic acid from ethanol is

$$5CH_3CH_2OH + 4MnO_4^-(aq) + 12H^+(aq) \longrightarrow$$
$$5CH_3COOH + 4Mn^{2+}(aq) + 11H_2O \quad (19)$$

Acetic acid can also be obtained by the oxidation of acetaldehyde (CH_3CHO):

$$5CH_3CHO + 2MnO_4^-(aq) + 6H^+(aq) \longrightarrow$$
$$5CH_3COOH + 2Mn^{2+}(aq) + 3H_2O \quad (20)$$

The further oxidation of acetic acid is difficult to accomplish. It does not react in solutions of $K_2Cr_2O_7$ or $KMnO_4$. Vigorous treatment, such as burning, causes its complete oxidation to carbon dioxide and water. Formic acid also can be oxidized to carbon dioxide and water by combustion with oxygen.

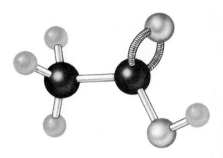

Fig. 19-7.2 The structural formula and model of acetic acid.

EXERCISE 19-10

There is a compound called propanol having the structural formula $CH_3CH_2CH_2OH$. If it is oxidized carefully, an aldehyde called propionaldehyde is obtained. Vigorous oxidation gives an acid called propionic acid. Draw structural formulas like those shown in Figures 19-6 and 19-7 for propionaldehyde and propionic acid.

EXERCISE 19-11

Balance the half-reaction involved in the oxidation of ethanol to acetic acid. Compare the number of electrons released per mole of ethanol with the number per mole of methanol in the equivalent reaction. How many electrons would be released per mole of propanol in the oxidation to propionic acid?

19-3.4 Oxidation of Organic Compounds—Formation of Ketones

The bonding rules permit us to draw two acceptable structural formulas for an alcohol containing three carbon atoms, $CH_3CH_2CH_2OH$ and $CH_3CHOHCH_3$. In the first isomer (considered in Exercises 19-10 and 19-11), the OH group is attached to the end carbon atom. In the second isomer, the OH group is attached to the second carbon atom. They are both called propanol because they are both derived from propane $(CH_3CH_2CH_3)$. They are distinguished by numbering the carbon atom to which the functional group, the OH, is attached. Thus, $CH_3CH_2CH_2OH$ is called 1-propanol because the OH is attached to the end carbon atom in the chain. The other alcohol, $CH_3CHOHCH_3$, is called 2-propanol because the OH is attached to the second carbon atom. The structures of these two alcohols are shown in Figure 19-8.

Fig. 19-8.1 (Left) The structural formula and model of 1-propanol.

Fig. 19-8.2 (Right) The structural formula and model of 2-propanol.

Fig. 19-9 The structural formula and model of acetone, the simplest ketone.

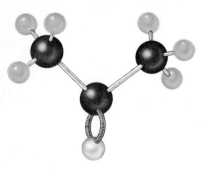

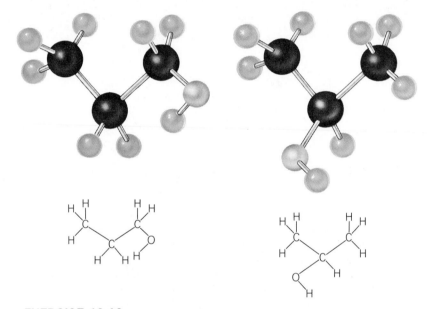

EXERCISE 19-12

We never speak of 3-propanol. Explain why.

We have already considered the oxidation of 1-propanol in Exercise 19-10. The second isomer, 2-propanol, can also be oxidized, and the product is called acetone:

$$3CH_3CHOHCH_3 + Cr_2O_7{}^{2-}(aq) + 8H^+(aq) \longrightarrow$$
$$3CH_3COCH_3 + 2Cr^{3+}(aq) + 7H_2O \quad (21)$$

Acetone is the simplest member of a class of compounds called **ketones.** They are quite similar in structure to the aldehydes, since each contains a carbon atom doubly bonded to an oxygen atom* (see Figure 19-9). They differ in that the aldehyde has a hydrogen atom attached

*The group $\diagup\kern-0.6em{}^{\diagdown}C{=}O$ is called the **carbonyl group.**

to this same carbon atom, whereas the ketone does not. (Compare Figures 19-6 and 19-9.) Since this hydrogen atom is not present, a ketone cannot be oxidized further to an acid without breaking a carbon-carbon bond. This is a difficult task to do in a controlled way.

Figure 19-10 summarizes the successive oxidation products that can be obtained from alcohols. When the hydroxyl or OH group is attached to an end carbon atom, oxidation will give an aldehyde or a carboxylic acid. When the hydroxyl group is on a carbon atom attached to other carbon atoms, oxidation will give a ketone. Huge amounts of aldehydes and ketones are used industrially in a variety of chemical processes. Furthermore, these functional groups are important in chemical syntheses of medicines, dyes, plastics, and fabrics.

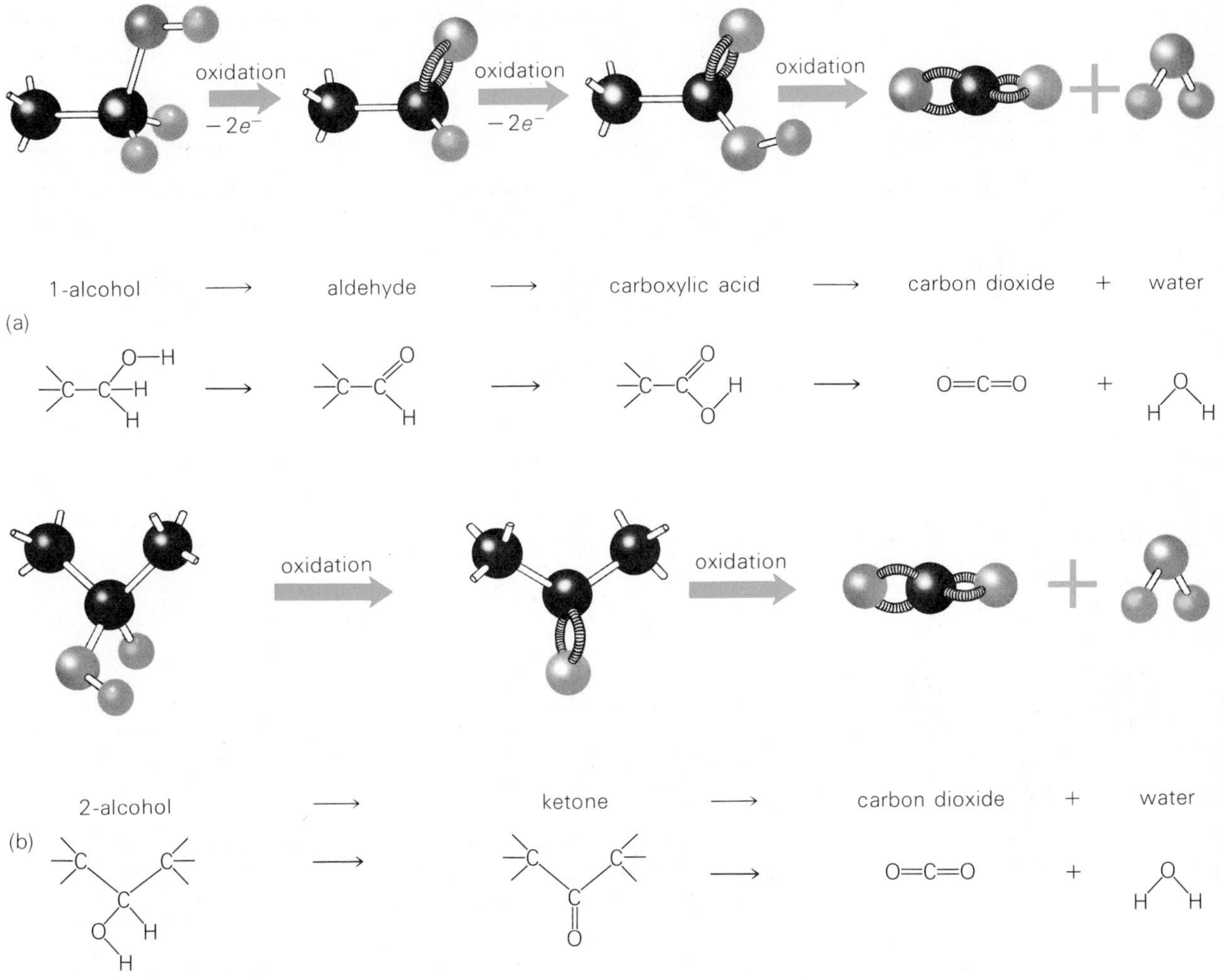

Fig. 19-10 The successive steps in the oxidation of alcohol to carbon dioxide and water.

(a)

1-alcohol ⟶ aldehyde ⟶ carboxylic acid ⟶ carbon dioxide + water

(b)

2-alcohol ⟶ ketone ⟶ carbon dioxide + water

19-3.5 The Functional Group

The reactive groups we have encountered thus far, such as —Br, —OH, —CHO, and —COOH, are called **functional groups.** They are the parts from which the molecules get their characteristic chemical behavior. For example, the ability to undergo a reaction in which the —OH group is displaced by a halogen atom, such as in the reaction of

CH_3OH and HBr or C_2H_5OH and HCl, is common to all alcohols. Characteristic of aldehydes is the ability to be oxidized to acids, as in the oxidation of formaldehyde to formic acid:

$$CH_2O + \text{source of oxygen atoms gives } HCOOH$$

These common types of behavior are shown by using the general symbol $R-$ for the part of the molecule that does not change and by writing a reaction in such a way as to focus attention on the functional group. For example,

$$RCH_2OH + HBr \longrightarrow RCH_2Br + H_2O \qquad (22)$$

$$RCH_2Br + OH^-(aq) \longrightarrow RCH_2OH + Br^-(aq) \qquad (23)$$

$$3RCHO + Cr_2O_7{}^{2-}(aq) + 8H^+(aq) \longrightarrow$$
$$3RCOOH + 2Cr^{3+}(aq) + 4H_2O \qquad (24)$$

The symbol $R-$ in these formulas represents any **alkyl group,** such as CH_3- or C_2H_5-.

19-3.6 Amines

Alcohols can be related to water by imagining that an alkyl group (such as CH_3-) has been substituted for one of the two hydrogen atoms of water. In the same way, **amines** are related to ammonia:

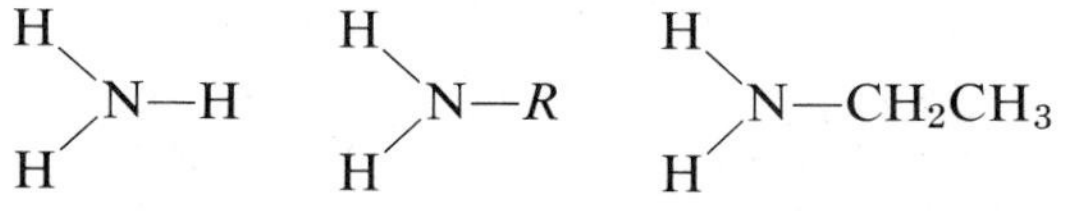

Amines can be prepared by direct reaction of ammonia with an alkyl halide, such as CH_3Br or CH_3CH_2I. Iodides react fastest, and an excess of ammonia is often used to help control formation of undesired alternate products:

$$CH_3CH_2I + 2NH_3 \longrightarrow CH_3CH_2NH_2 + NH_4I \qquad (25)$$
$$\text{ETHYL IODIDE} \qquad\qquad \text{ETHYLAMINE}$$

$$R-I + 2NH_3 \longrightarrow RNH_2 + NH_4I$$

The above equations represent a net change that occurs when an excess of ammonia reacts with an alkyl iodide. The actual reaction proceeds in two steps. The first step is analogous to the attack of the hydroxide ion on an alkyl halide (see Figure 19-4 on page 476):

$$NH_3 + RI \longrightarrow RNH_3{}^+(aq) + I^-(aq) \qquad (26)$$

The second step is a proton-transfer reaction (see Section 13-7):

$$NH_3 + RNH_3{}^+(aq) \longrightarrow RNH_2 + NH_4{}^+(aq) \qquad (27)$$

19-3.7 Acid Derivatives—Esters

We see from the equation for the oxidation of CH_2O to $HCOOH$ that oxidation of an aldehyde will give an organic acid. All these organic acids contain the functional group —COOH, the **carboxyl group.** The bonding in this group is as follows:

$$-C\underset{\displaystyle O-H}{\overset{\displaystyle O}{\Big\langle}}$$

The carboxyl group readily releases a proton, so it is an acid. Acetic acid, for example, dissolved in water gives a conducting solution; it turns blue litmus red; it is sour; and it exhibits the other properties of an acid. The reaction

$$CH_3COOH + H_2O \longrightarrow CH_3COO^-(aq) + H_3O^+(aq) \quad (28)$$

has an equilibrium constant of 1.8×10^{-5}.

In addition to this acidic behavior, an important characteristic of carboxylic acids is that the entire OH group can be replaced by other groups. The resulting compounds are called **acid derivatives.** We shall consider only two types of acid derivatives, **esters** and **amides.**

Compounds in which the —OH of an acid is transformed into —OR (such as —OCH$_3$) are called esters. They can be prepared by the direct reaction between an alcohol and the acid:

$$CH_3OH + CH_3C\underset{\displaystyle OH}{\overset{\displaystyle O}{\Big\langle}} \longrightarrow CH_3C\underset{\displaystyle O-CH_3}{\overset{\displaystyle O}{\Big\langle}} + H_2O \quad (29)$$

$$\left\{\begin{array}{l}\textbf{methyl}\\ \text{alcohol}\end{array}\right\} + \left\{\begin{array}{l}\text{acetic}\\ \textbf{acid}\end{array}\right\} \longrightarrow \left\{\begin{array}{l}\textbf{methyl}\\ \textbf{acet}\text{ate}\end{array}\right\} + \{\text{water}\}$$

The method of naming the product is indicated by the bold-faced parts of the names for the reactants and products.

EXERCISE 19-13

Write equations for the reaction of ethanol and formic acid, propanol and propionic acid, and methanol and formic acid. Name the esters produced in each case.

When equilibrium is reached in the formation of methyl acetate, appreciable concentrations of all reactants may be present. If methyl acetate alone (the product on the right) is dissolved in water, it will react with water slowly to give acetic acid and methyl alcohol until equilibrium is attained:

$$CH_3C\underset{\displaystyle O-CH_3}{\overset{\displaystyle O}{\Big\langle}} + H_2O \longrightarrow CH_3OH + CH_3C\underset{\displaystyle OH}{\overset{\displaystyle O}{\Big\langle}} \quad (30)$$

Of course, the usual equilibrium considerations apply. For example, if we add more methyl alcohol, equilibrium conditions will shift, consuming the added reagent and acetic acid to produce more methyl acetate and water, in accordance with Le Chatelier's principle. Thus, an excess of methyl alcohol causes most of the acetic acid to be converted to methyl acetate.

EXERCISE 19-14

Write the equilibrium expression relating the concentrations of reactants and products in the reaction of methyl acetate with water. Notice that the concentration of water must be included because it is not necessarily large enough to be considered constant in these nonaqueous solutions.

The reaction between methanol and acetic acid is slow, but it can be greatly accelerated if a catalyst is added. For example, adding a strong acid such as hydrochloric acid or sulfuric acid will speed up the reaction by catalysis. As mentioned in Section 11-3.3, the catalyst does not alter the equilibrium state (that is, the concentration of the reactants at equilibrium); it only permits equilibrium to be attained more rapidly.

EXERCISE 19-15

A strong acid such as hydrochloric acid or sulfuric acid will catalyze the formation of an ester from alcohol and acid. Explain why this implies that these acids will catalyze the reaction between an ester and water as well. (Refer to Section 10-2.3.)

Esters are important substances. The esters of the low-molecular weight acids and alcohols have fragrant, fruitlike odors, and are used in perfumes and artificial flavorings. Esters are useful solvents; this is the reason they are commonly found in "model airplane dope" and fingernail polish remover.

19-3.8   Acid Derivatives—Amides

A compound in which the —OH group of an acid is replaced by —NH_2 is called an **amide.** When the —OH is replaced by —NHR, the product is called a nitrogen-substituted amide or, abbreviated, an N-substituted amide. Amides can be produced from the reaction of ammonia (or an amine) with an ester:

$$CH_3C\overset{O}{\underset{O-CH_3}{\big\langle}} + NH_3 \longrightarrow CH_3C\overset{O}{\underset{NH_2}{\big\langle}} + CH_3OH \qquad (31)$$

METHYL ACETATE   ACETAMIDE

$$CH_3C\overset{O}{\underset{O-CH_3}{\big\langle}} + H_2N-CH_2CH_3 \longrightarrow CH_3C\overset{O}{\underset{\underset{H}{\overset{|}{N}}-CH_2CH_3}{\big\langle}} + CH_3OH$$

METHYL ACETATE   ETHYLAMINE   N-ETHYL ACETAMIDE (32)

Note the similarity of the two reactions. Amides are of special importance because the amide grouping

$$\begin{array}{c} O \\ \parallel \\ -C \\ \\ NH- \end{array}$$

is the basic structural element in the long-chain molecules that make up proteins and enzymes in living matter. Hydrogen bonding between two amide groups helps determine the protein structure. This will be discussed in Chapter 21.

19-4   NOMENCLATURE

The names of organic compounds have some system. Each functional group defines a family (for example, alcohols and amines), and a specific modifier is added to identify a particular member in the family (for example, *ethyl* alcohol and *ethyl* amine). As an alternate naming system, the family may be identified by a specific ending (for example, alcohol names end in *-ol*), and a particular member of the family may be indicated by an appropriate stem (ethyl alcohol would be *ethan*ol).

These naming systems are illustrated in Tables 19-1 and 19-2. Notice that we start with the name of the alkane. This is then modified systematically as we go to alcohol or amine. Notice also that acids have a less systematic name which carries over to amides and esters.

TABLE 19-1 REGULARITIES IN NAMES OF ALKANES, ALCOHOLS, AND AMINES

Number of Carbon Atoms	Alkanes	Alcohols	Amines
1	CH_4 methane	CH_3OH methyl alcohol methanol	CH_3NH_2 methylamine
2	CH_3CH_3 ethane	CH_3CH_2OH ethyl alcohol ethanol	$CH_3CH_2NH_2$ ethylamine
3	$CH_3CH_2CH_3$ propane	$CH_3CH_2CH_2OH$ propyl alcohol 1-propanol	$CH_3CH_2CH_2NH_2$ 1-propylamine
4	$CH_3CH_2CH_2CH_3$ butane	$CH_3CH_2CH_2CH_2OH$ butyl alcohol 1-butanol	$CH_3CH_2CH_2CH_2NH_2$ 1-butylamine
8	$CH_3(CH_2)_6CH_3$ octane	$CH_3(CH_2)_6CH_2OH$ octyl alcohol 1-octanol	$CH_3(CH_2)_6CH_2NH_2$ 1-octylamine

The alkane names are quite regular and systematic after we get to pentane. The prefix before the *-ane* is the Greek word indicating the number of carbon atoms in the chain. For example, we see *pent*ane with five carbons (you surely have heard the word "pentagon"), *hex*ane with six carbons (remember hexagon), heptane, octane, and so on.

TABLE **19-2** REGULARITIES IN NAMES
OF ACIDS, AMIDES, AND ESTERS

Number of Carbon Atoms	Acids	Amides	Esters—Acids with Methanol
1	HCOOH formic acid	HCONH$_2$ formamide	HCOOCH$_3$ methyl formate
2	CH$_3$COOH acetic acid	CH$_3$CONH$_2$ acetamide	CH$_3$COOCH$_3$ methyl acetate
3	CH$_3$CH$_2$COOH propionic acid	CH$_3$CH$_2$CONH$_2$ propionamide	CH$_3$CH$_2$COOCH$_3$ methyl propionate
4	CH$_3$CH$_2$CH$_2$COOH butyric acid	CH$_3$CH$_2$CH$_2$CONH$_2$ butyramide	CH$_3$CH$_2$CH$_2$COOCH$_3$ methyl butyrate
8	CH$_3$(CH$_2$)$_6$COOH octanoic acid caprylic acid	CH$_3$(CH$_2$)$_6$CONH$_2$ octanamide caprylamide	CH$_3$(CH$_2$)$_6$COOCH$_3$ methyl octanoate methyl caprylate

Compounds with more complicated shapes are described by numbering the carbon atoms. For example, the compound

$$H-\underset{\underset{\displaystyle H}{|}}{\overset{\overset{\displaystyle H}{|}}{C_1}}-\underset{\underset{\displaystyle CH_3}{|}}{\overset{\overset{\displaystyle CH_3}{|}}{C_2}}-\underset{\underset{\displaystyle H}{|}}{\overset{\overset{\displaystyle H}{|}}{C_3}}-\underset{\underset{\displaystyle CH_3}{|}}{\overset{\overset{\displaystyle H}{|}}{C_4}}-\underset{\underset{\displaystyle H}{|}}{\overset{\overset{\displaystyle H}{|}}{C_5}}-H$$

is called 2,2-dimethyl-4-methylpentane. It is also an isooctane.

19-5 HYDROCARBONS

Compounds that contain only hydrogen and carbon are called **hydrocarbons** (a contraction of hydrogen-carbon). The hydrocarbons that have only single bonds all have a similar chemistry; they are called, as a family, the **saturated hydrocarbons.** With carbon-carbon double bonds, the reactivity is much enhanced (Section 17-6); hence, hydrocarbons containing one or more double bonds are named, as a distinct family, **unsaturated hydrocarbons.** Both saturated and unsaturated hydrocarbons can occur in chain-like structures or in cyclic structures. Each of these families will be considered.

19-5.1 Saturated Hydrocarbons

Straight chain, branched chain, and cyclic hydrocarbons make up a family called the **alkanes.** Some saturated hydrocarbons with five carbon atoms are shown in Figure 19-11. Figure 19-11(a), containing no branches, is called normal pentane or *n*-pentane. Figure 19-11(b) has a single branch at the end of the chain. Such a structural type is commonly identified by the prefix *iso-*. Hence, this isomer is called isopentane. Figure 19-11(c) also contains a five-carbon molecule, but it has the distinctive feature of a cyclic carbon structure. Such a compound is identified by the prefix *cyclo-* in its name—in the case shown, cyclopentane.

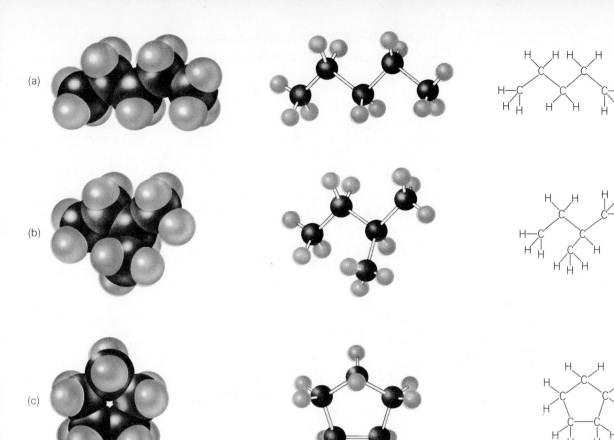

Fig. 19-11 Structural formulas and models for some five-carbon saturated hydrocarbons: (a) n-pentane, (b) isopentane, (c) cyclopentane.

EXERCISE 19-16

What are the empirical formulas of the three compounds shown in Figure 19-11? the molecular formulas? Which are structural isomers?

EXERCISE 19-17

There is one more alkane having the molecular formula C_5H_{12} called neopentane. Draw its structural formula.

The alkanes are the principal compounds present in natural gas and in petroleum. The low-molecular weight compounds are gases under normal conditions (their boiling points are shown in Table 19-3, page 488). Gasoline is a mixture of complex, branched alkanes with from 6 to 10 carbon atoms. Paraffin waxes are usually alkanes with from 20 to 35 carbon atoms.

The saturated hydrocarbons are relatively inert except at high temperatures. As a result, sodium metal can be stored under an alkane such as kerosene (8 to 14 carbon atoms) to protect it from reaction with water or oxygen. Combustion is almost the only important chemical reaction of the alkanes. That reaction alone makes the hydrocarbons one of the most important energy sources in our modern world.

TABLE 19-3 SOME PROPERTIES OF SATURATED HYDROCARBONS

Saturated Hydrocarbon	Molecular Formula	Melting Point (°C)	Boiling Point (°C)	Heat of Combustion of Gas (kcal/mole)
methane	CH_4	−182.5	−161.5	−212.8
ethane	CH_3CH_3	−183.3	−88.6	−372.8
propane	$CH_3CH_2CH_3$	−187.7	−42.1	−530.6
n-butane	$CH_3CH_2CH_2CH_3$	−138.4	−0.5	−687.7
isobutane	$CH_3-CH-CH_3$ CH_3	−159.6	−11.7	−685.7
n-hexane	C_6H_{14}	−95.3	68.7	−1,002.6
cyclohexane	C_6H_{12}	+6.6	80.7	−944.8
n-octane	C_8H_{18}	−56.8	125.7	−1,317.5
n-octadecane	$C_{18}H_{38}$	+28.2	316.1	−2,891.9

EXERCISE 19-18

Using the data given in the last column of Table 19-3, plot the heat released during combustion *per mole of carbon atoms* against the number of carbon atoms per molecule for the normal alkanes. Consider the significance of this plot in terms of the molecular structures of these compounds.

The non-reactive nature of saturated hydrocarbons is a crucial aspect of their chemistry. This inertness illustrates the fact that the chemistry of organic compounds is mainly concerned with the functional groups. The functional groups are usually so much more reactive than the carbon "skeleton" that it can be assumed that this skeleton will remain intact and unchanged in most processes.

19-5.2 Unsaturated Hydrocarbons

Unsaturated compounds are the organic compounds in which fewer than four atoms are attached to one or more of the carbon atoms. Such compounds contain double bonds. Ethylene (C_2H_4) is an unsaturated compound; and because it contains only carbon and hydrogen atoms, it is an unsaturated hydrocarbon. Propylene, the next most complicated unsaturated hydrocarbon, has the molecular formula C_3H_6. The structural formulas of ethylene and propylene are shown in Figure 19-12. Cyclic hydrocarbons also can involve double bonds. The structural formula of a cyclic unsaturated hydrocarbon is also shown in Figure 19-12.

Unsaturated hydrocarbons are quite reactive in contrast to the relatively inert saturated hydrocarbons. As we learned earlier, this reactivity is associated with the double bond. In the most characteristic reaction, called "addition," one of the bonds of the double bond opens and a new atom becomes bonded to each of the carbon atoms (see Section 17-6.1). Some of the reagents that will add to the double bond are H_2, Br_2, HCl, and H_2O. The following examples use ethylene:

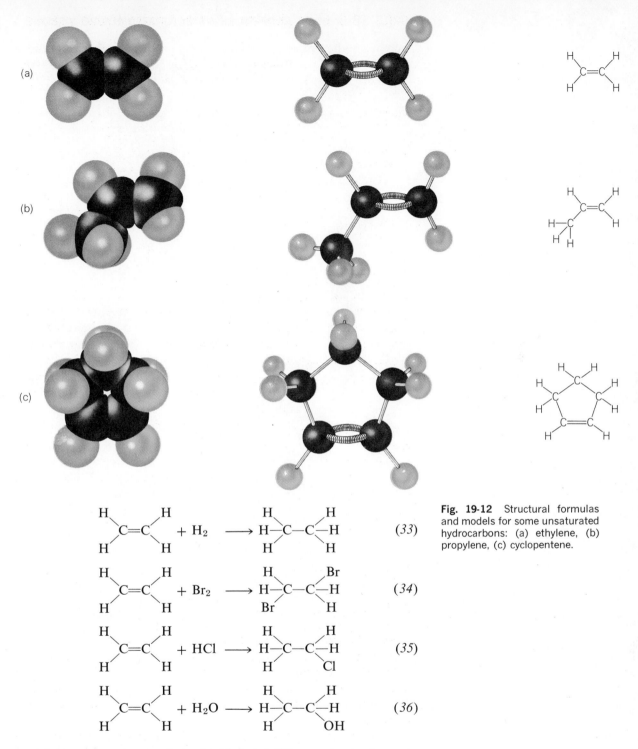

Oxidizing agents also attack the double bond. When a reaction between an unsaturated compound and the permanganate ion occurs, for example, the violet color of permanganate fades. This color change, as well as the reaction with bromine in which a change from orange to colorless occurs (bromine is orange), is used as a qualitative test for the presence of double bonds in compounds of unknown structure.

UNSATURATED HYDROCARBONS

19-5.3 Benzene—Its Structure and Representation

There is another important class of cyclic compounds that is different from the two classes just described. The simplest example is the compound benzene, a cyclic compound having six carbon atoms in the ring and the formula C_6H_6. Experiment shows that the **benzene ring** is planar with 120° angles between each pair of carbon-carbon bonds. The molecule is a regular hexagon with the following atomic arrangement:

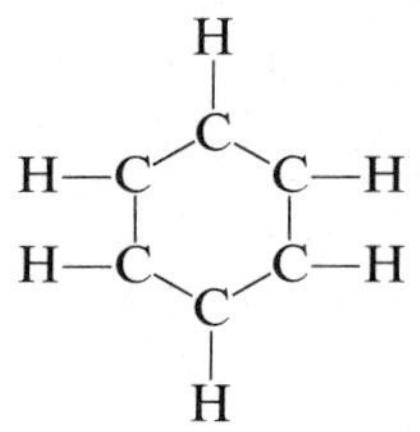

A count of electrons and atoms shows us that there must be three double bonds in a benzene ring, but a difficulty arises when we attempt to represent the bonding in the usual way. We might use either of the notations

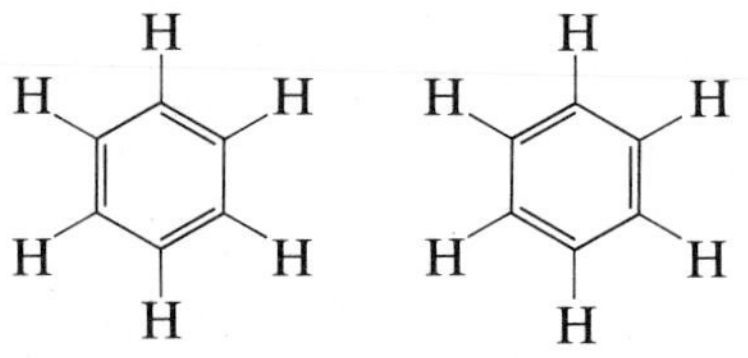

Both structures satisfy the formal valence rules for carbon, but each has a serious fault. Each structure shows three of the carbon-carbon bonds as double bonds and three as single bonds. A wealth of experimental evidence indicates that this is not the case. Any one of the six carbon-carbon bonds in benzene is the same as any other. Apparently the fourth bond of each carbon atom is shared equally with each adjacent carbon. This makes it difficult to represent the bonding in benzene by the usual diagrams. Benzene seems to be best represented as the "superposition" or "average" of the two structures. For simplicity, chemists use either structure. Expressed in a shorthand form omitting carbon and hydrogen atoms, the notation is either of the following:

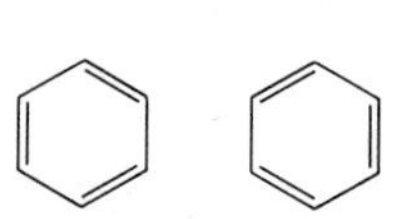

Another shorthand symbol sometimes used is

Whichever symbol is used, the chemist always remembers that the carbon-carbon bonds are actually all the same and that they have properties unlike either simple double or single bonds. The situation is very much like that which we faced with graphite, where more than one arrangement of the double bonds provided equally good representations of the structure. In the case of graphite, we said that the electrons were "delocalized," that they could wander *across the surface of the sheet* of carbon atoms. We supported this hypothesis by the fact that graphite is a good conductor of electricity along the sheets, but a poor conductor perpendicular to the sheets. Similarly, with benzene, a small fragment of the graphite lattice, electrons should move easily *around the ring*—electrical effects should be transmitted easily through the delocalized electronic cloud. (This is sometimes called the π **cloud;** it is above and below the ring surface.) Indeed, much of the chemistry of ring compounds reflects this mobility of electrons in the ring. All compounds, such as benzene, containing rings with delocalized electrons, are called **aromatic compounds.**

19-5.4 Substitution Reactions of Benzene

Benzene shows neither the typical reactivity nor the usual addition reaction of ethylene. Benzene does react with bromine (Br_2), but in a different type of reaction:

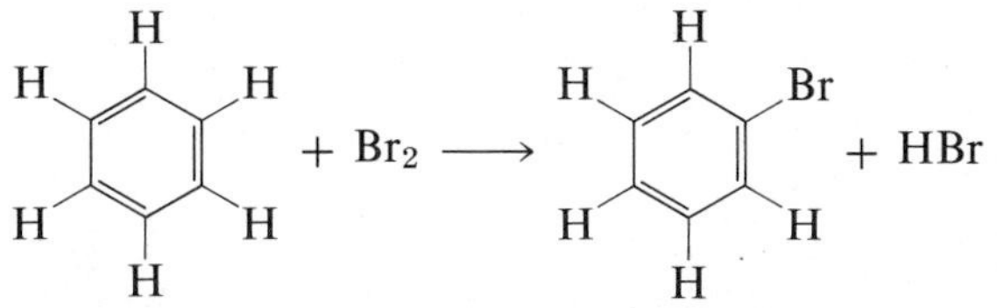

BENZENE   BROMOBENZENE

$$+ \; Br_2 \longrightarrow \qquad + \; HBr \qquad (37)$$

In this reaction, called bromination, one of the hydrogen atoms has been *replaced* by a bromine atom. Notice that the double-bond structure is not affected—this is *not* an addition reaction. Nitric acid causes a similar reaction, called nitration:

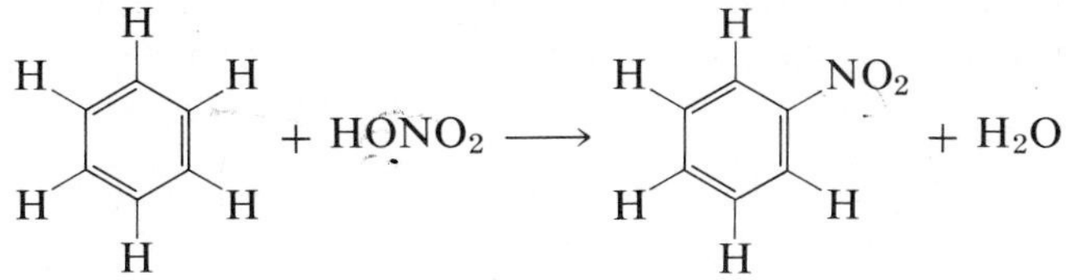

BENZENE   NITROBENZENE

$$+ \; HONO_2 \longrightarrow \qquad + \; H_2O \qquad (38)$$

Reactions of the type shown above are called **substitution reactions.** *The substitution reaction is the characteristic reaction of benzene and its derivatives.* It is the way in which a multitude of compounds are prepared by the organic chemist. By substitution one can introduce functional groups, which can then be modified in various ways.

19-5.5 Modification of Functional Groups on the Benzene Ring

One of the most important derivatives of benzene is nitrobenzene. The nitro- group is $-NO_2$. Nitrobenzene is important chiefly because it is readily converted by reduction into an aromatic amine called aniline. One procedure uses zinc as the reducing agent:

$$3Zn + \text{NITROBENZENE} + 6H^+(aq) \longrightarrow$$

$$3Zn^{2+}(aq) + 2H_2O + \text{ANILINE} \qquad (39)$$

Aniline and other aromatic amines are valuable industrial raw materials. They form an important starting point from which many of our dyestuffs, medicinals, and other valuable products are prepared. For example, you have used the indicator methyl orange in your laboratory experiments. Methyl orange is an example of an aniline-derived dye, although it is used more as an acid-base indicator than for dyeing fabrics. The structure of methyl orange is as follows:

METHYL ORANGE

The portions of the methyl orange molecule set off by the broken lines come from aromatic amines like aniline. Aniline is the starting material from which the so-called "azo dyes," such as methyl orange, are made.

Another useful aniline derivative is acetanilide, which is simply the amide formed from aniline and acetic acid:

$$\{\text{acetic acid}\} + \{\text{aniline}\} \longrightarrow \{\text{acetanilide}\} + \{\text{water}\} \qquad (40)$$

Acetanilide has been used medicinally as a pain-killing remedy.

Hydroxybenzene, or phenol, is another important derivative:

Most phenol is now made industrially from benzene, which is chlorinated as a first step:

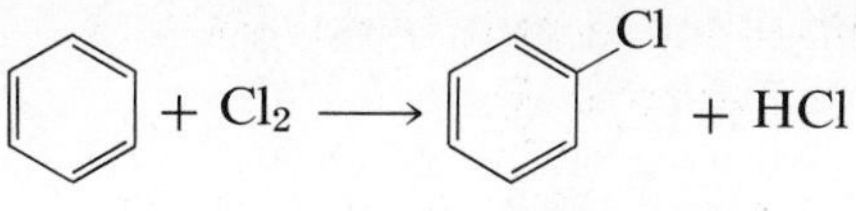

$$\text{(benzene)} + Cl_2 \longrightarrow \text{(chlorobenzene with Cl)} + HCl \qquad (41)$$

CHLOROBENZENE

The reaction of chlorobenzene with a base gives phenol:

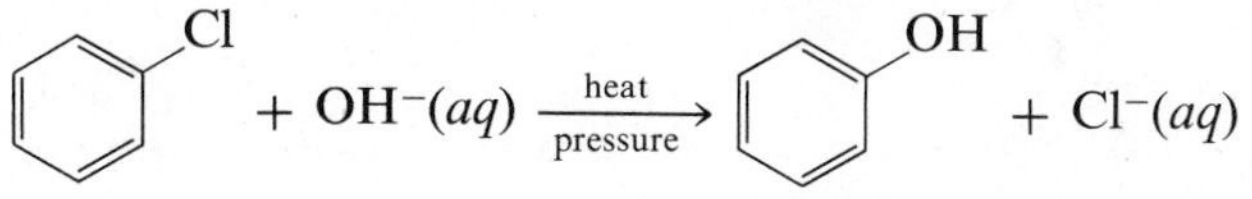

$$\text{(chlorobenzene)} + OH^-(aq) \xrightarrow[\text{pressure}]{\text{heat}} \text{(phenol with OH)} + Cl^-(aq) \qquad (42)$$

Phenol, a germicide and disinfectant, was first used by the English surgeon Joseph Lister (1827–1912) in 1867 as an antiseptic in medicine. More effective and less toxic antiseptics have since been discovered.

Perhaps the most widely known compound prepared from phenol is aspirin. If phenol, sodium hydroxide, and carbon dioxide are heated together under pressure, the sodium salt of salicylic acid is formed:

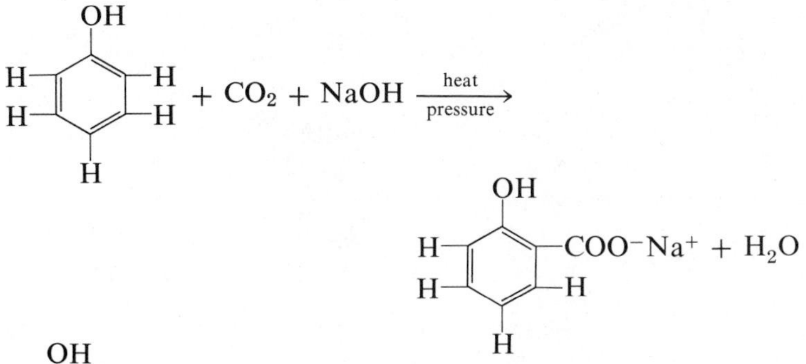

$$\text{(phenol structure)} + CO_2 + NaOH \xrightarrow[\text{pressure}]{\text{heat}}$$

$$\text{(structure with OH and COO}^-Na^+) + H_2O \qquad (43)$$

$$\text{(structure with OH and COO}^-Na^+) + H^+(aq) \longrightarrow \text{(structure with OH and COOH)} + Na^+(aq)$$

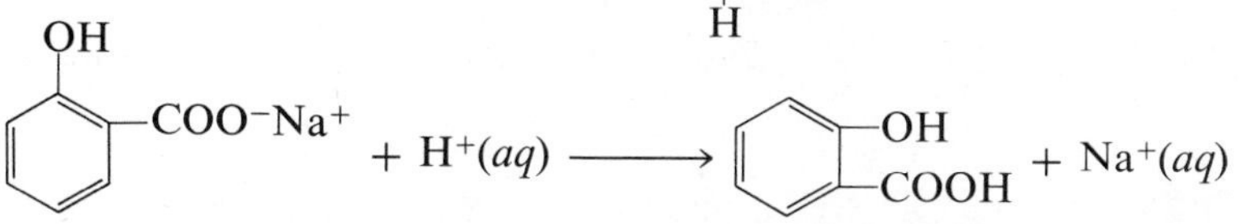

SALICYLIC ACID   (44)

Salicylic acid is quite useful. Its methyl ester has a sharp, characteristic odor and is called "oil of wintergreen." (See Table 5-5 on page 106 for the vapor pressure of methyl salicylate.) The acid itself (or the sodium salt) is a valuable drug in the treatment of arthritis. But the most widely known derivative of salicylic acid is aspirin, which has the following structure:

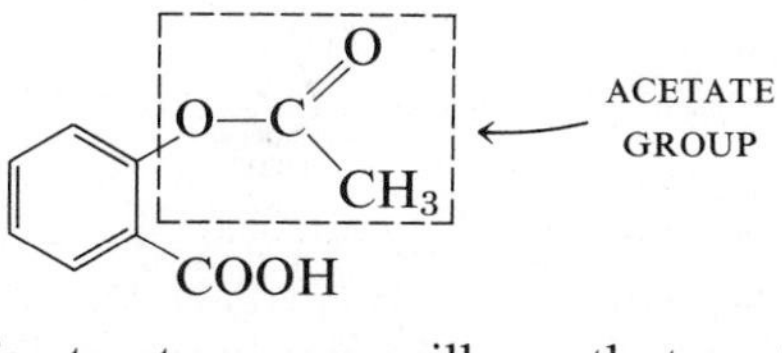

$$\text{(aspirin structure)} \longleftarrow \text{ACETATE GROUP}$$

By examining this structure, you will see that aspirin is an ester of acetic acid. Its chemical name is acetylsalicylic acid. Aspirin is the most widely used drug. Over 20 million pounds of aspirin, or about 150 five-grain tablets for every person, are manufactured each year in the United States alone!

Table 19-4 shows the structures of a few simple benzene derivatives that are important commercially. All are prepared from simpler compounds.

TABLE **19-4** STRUCTURES AND USES
OF SOME BENZENE DERIVATIVES

Structure	Name	Use
OH, OCH$_3$, C, H, O (benzene ring with aldehyde)	vanillin ("vanilla")	flavoring material
CH$_3$CH$_2$O, N, H, C, O, CH$_3$ (benzene ring)	phenacetin	pain-reliever (in headache remedies)
OH, OH (benzene ring)	hydroquinone	photographic developer
NH$_2$, C, O, OCH$_2$CH$_2$N, C$_2$H$_5$, C$_2$H$_5$ (benzene ring)	procaine ("Novocain")	local anaesthetic
CH=CH$_2$ (benzene ring)	styrene	monomer for preparation of polystyrene plastics

19-6 POLYMERS

Table 19-3 on page 488 shows that the melting points of the normal alkanes tend to increase as the number of carbon atoms in the chain increases. Ethane (C_2H_6) is a gas under normal conditions; octane (C_8H_{18}) is a liquid; octadecane ($C_{18}H_{38}$) is a solid. We noted in Chapter 18 that van der Waals forces increase as the area of molecular surface in contact and the size of the molecules increase. We see that desired physical properties in a solid can be obtained by controlling the length of the chain. Functional groups attached to the chain provide additional variability, including chemical reactivity. In fact, by adjusting the chain length and the percentage of high-molecular weight compounds, chemists have produced a multitude of organic solid substances called **plastics.** These have been tailored for a wide variety of uses, giving rise to an enormous chemical industry.

The key to this chemical treasure chest is the process by which extended chains of atoms are formed. Inevitably, it is necessary to begin with relatively small chemical molecules and with carbon chains of only a few atoms. These small units, called **monomers,** must be bonded together, time after time, until the desired range of molecular weight is reached. Often the desired properties are obtained only with giant molecules, each containing hundreds or even thousands of monomers. These giant molecules are called **polymers,** and the process by which they are formed is called **polymerization.**

19-6.1 Types of Polymerization

Polymerization involves the chemical combination of a number of identical or similar molecules to form a complex molecule of high molecular weight. The small units may be combined by **addition polymerization** or **condensation polymerization.**

Addition polymers are formed by the reaction of the monomeric units without the elimination of atoms. The monomer is usually an unsaturated organic compound such as ethylene ($H_2C{=}CH_2$), which in the presence of a suitable catalyst will undergo an addition reaction to form a long chain molecule such as polyethylene. A general equation for the first stage of such a process is

$$\text{(45)}$$

The same addition process continues, and the final product is the very familiar polymer polyethylene:

where n is a very large number.

When one or more of the hydrogens are replaced by groups such as fluorine (F), chlorine (Cl), methyl (CH_3), or methyl ester ($COOCH_3$), polymers such as Teflon, Saran, Lucite, and Plexiglas result. It is thus possible to create molecules with custom-built properties for various uses as plastics or fibers.

Condensation polymers are produced by reactions in which some simple molecule (such as water) is eliminated between functional groups (such as alcoholic OH or acidic COOH groups). In order to form long chain molecules, two or more functional groups must be present in each of the reacting units. For example, when ethylene glycol ($HOCH_2CH_2OH$) reacts with *para*phthalic acid,

$$HOOC-\!\!\!\bigcirc\!\!\!-COOH$$

a **polyester** of high molecular weight called Dacron is produced. The diagram below shows the first stages of this process:

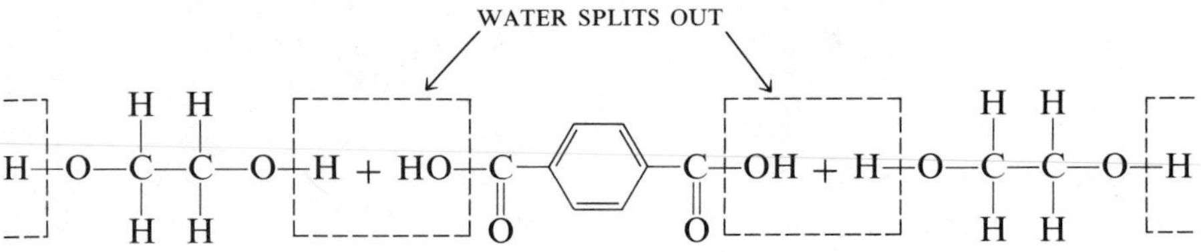

WATER SPLITS OUT

$$H-O-\overset{H}{\underset{H}{C}}-\overset{H}{\underset{H}{C}}-O-H \ + \ HO-\overset{O}{\underset{}{C}}-\langle\bigcirc\rangle-\overset{O}{\underset{}{C}}-OH \ + \ H-O-\overset{H}{\underset{H}{C}}-\overset{H}{\underset{H}{C}}-O-H$$

19-6.2   Nylon, a Polymeric Amide

Nylon, a material widely used in plastics and fabrics, consists of molecules of extremely high molecular weight made from adipic acid,

$$HOOC-CH_2-CH_2-CH_2-CH_2-COOH$$
ADIPIC ACID

and 1,6-diaminohexane,

$$H_2N-CH_2-CH_2-CH_2-CH_2-CH_2-CH_2-NH_2$$
1,6-DIAMINOHEXANE

These monomeric molecules can react repeatedly by removal of water. Amide linkages are formed at both ends:

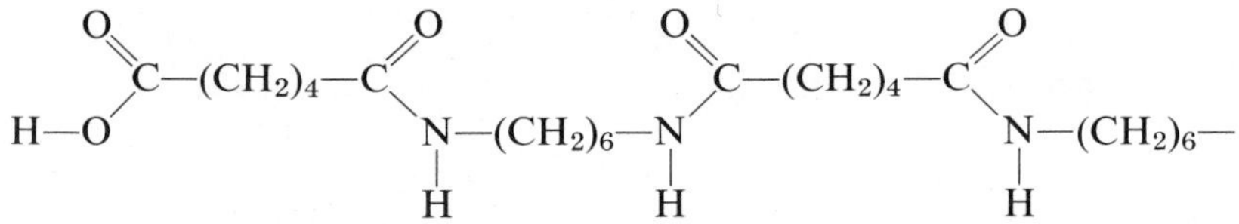

$$H-O-\overset{O}{\underset{}{C}}-(CH_2)_4-\overset{O}{\underset{}{C}}-\underset{H}{N}-(CH_2)_6-\underset{H}{N}-\overset{O}{\underset{}{C}}-(CH_2)_4-\overset{O}{\underset{}{C}}-\underset{H}{N}-(CH_2)_6-$$

Other polyamides can be made from different acids and other amines, giving a variety of properties suited to a variety of uses. Nylon is rather similar to natural silk in its structure.

19-6.3   Protein, Another Polymeric Amide

A most important class of polyamides is **proteins,** the essential structures of all living matter. They are necessary to the human diet as a source of the "monomeric" units, the amino acids, from which living protein materials are made.

Proteins are polyamides formed by the polymerization, through amide linkages, of α-amino acids. Three of the 25 to 30 important natural α-amino acids are shown in Figure 19-13. Each acid has an amine group, $-NH_2$, attached to the α-carbon, the carbon atom immediately adjacent to the carboxylic acid group.

The protein molecule may involve hundreds of such amino acid molecules connected through the amide linkages. A portion of this chain might be represented as in Figure 19-14.

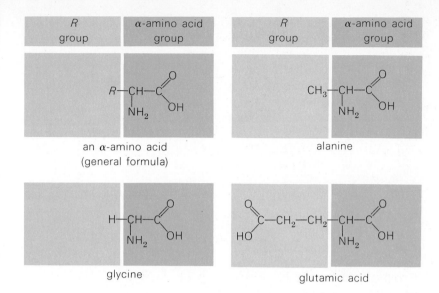

Fig. 19-13 Molecular structures of α-amino acids.

an α-amino acid (general formula)

alanine

glycine

glutamic acid

An amide is decomposed by aqueous acids to an acid and the ammonium salt of an amine:

$$CH_3C\underset{NHCH_3}{\overset{O}{\diagup}} + H_3O^+(aq) \longrightarrow CH_3C\underset{OH}{\overset{O}{\diagup}} + CH_3NH_3^+(aq) \qquad (46)$$

N-METHYL ACETAMIDE

ACETIC ACID

METHYL AMMONIUM ION

In this same type of reaction, a protein can be broken down into its constituent amino acids. In this way most of what we call the "natural" amino acids have been discovered. Studies have been made of proteins from many sources—egg yolk, milk, animal tissues, plant seeds, gelatin, and so on—to learn of what amino acids they are composed. In this

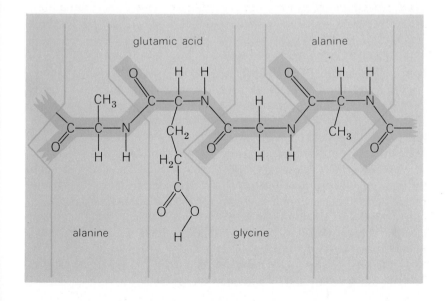

Fig. 19-14 The structure of protein showing the amide chain.

glutamic acid

alanine

alanine

glycine

PROTEIN, ANOTHER

POLYMERIC AMIDE

way about 30 of the natural amino acids have been identified. When you consider how many different ways up to 30 amino acids can be combined in long chains of 100 or more amino acid units, you will see why there are so many known proteins, and why different living species of plants and animals can have in their tissues a great many different proteins.

One of the very active areas of modern research involves an identification of the order in which different amino acids have been combined to build proteins. If hydrolysis can be carefully controlled, fragments containing two to five amino acid units can be liberated. By cutting these chains in different ways, it is possible to obtain fragments with common units which can be matched up with one another to obtain the overall sequence. The determination of amino acid sequences in proteins is a difficult and very important area of science.

Enzymes, the biological catalysts, are also proteins. Each enzyme, of course, has its own particular structure, determined by the order and spatial arrangement of the amino acids from which it is formed. Perhaps the most marvelous part of the chemistry of living organisms is their ability to synthesize just the right protein structures from the myriad of structures possible and to reproduce structures like themselves. This topic is considered in Chapter 21.

EXERCISE 19-19

Take the letters *A, B, C,* and see how many different three-unit combinations you can make; for example, *ABC, BAC, AAC, CBC.* This will convince you that a chain made of hundreds of groups with up to 30 different kinds of units in each group can have an almost unlimited number of combinations.

19-7 HIGHLIGHTS

We are using up natural supplies of carbon compounds (oil, gas, and coal) at a very rapid rate. Long-range planning is critical if the future is to be protected.

The **structural formula** for a compound is a summary of a great deal of explicit information about a compound. From the structural formula we can deduce the **empirical formula,** the **molecular formula,** and many chemical and physical properties of the molecule. The structural formula is obtained from many laboratory observations.

Hydrocarbons are compounds containing carbon and hydrogen. Straight chain, **saturated hydrocarbons** have only single bonds in the molecule and each carbon atom is bonded to four atoms such as carbon and hydrogen. **Unsaturated hydrocarbons** contain double bonds. Cyclic hydrocarbons have the carbon atoms arranged in a ring. They may be saturated or unsaturated.

One or more hydrogen atoms on a hydrocarbon framework can be replaced with a **functional group.** A functional group is a reactive unit such as $-OH$, $-NH_2$, $-\overset{O}{\underset{}{\overset{\|}{C}}}-$, $-\overset{O}{\underset{}{\overset{\|}{C}}}-OH$. Much of the chemistry of organic compounds can be discussed in terms of the functional groups. Common and important hydrocarbon radicals or units are methyl ($-CH_3$), ethyl ($-C_2H_5$), propyl ($-C_3H_7$), butyl ($-C_4H_9$), and phenyl ($-C_6H_5$). New compounds can be made by appropriate reactions carried out on functional groups. For example, oxidation of an alcohol ($R-OH$, where R is the hydrocarbon radical) gives an **aldehyde**

($R-\underset{\underset{H}{|}}{C}=O$) or a **ketone** ($R-\overset{O}{\overset{\|}{C}}-R'$). Further oxidation of an aldehyde

gives a **carboxylic acid** ($R-\overset{O}{\overset{\|}{C}}-OH$). Each of these units has its own interesting chemistry, which gives rise to the many thousands of organic compounds in the world around us.

QUESTIONS and PROBLEMS

1 How does "oil" differ in composition from coal?

2 Several formulas are listed below. Which of these would you class as an empirical formula, which as a molecular formula, and which as a structural formula? (a) CH_3 (b) $C_2H_4O_2$ (c) CH_3-O-CH_3 (d) C_4H_{10} (e) C_nH_{2n+2}.

3 What information is needed to convert an empirical formula to a molecular formula? Suggest one way in which such information might be obtained.

4 A compound of *molecular formula* $C_4H_{10}O$ reacts with sodium to liberate $\frac{1}{2}$ mole of hydrogen. (a) Write a structural formula which would be consistent with this information. (b) Write the structural formula for an isomer which would also be consistent with the data given. (c) Write the structural formula for a compound of this molecular formula which would *not* react with sodium.

5 Draw all of the structural formulas for the compounds of molecular formula $C_2H_3Cl_3$. Repeat for $C_3H_4Cl_4$. Do these answers help you to understand the large number of organic molecules?

6 What angle would you expect to be formed by the C, O, and H nuclei in an alcohol molecule? Explain.

7 Draw structural formulas of all compounds having the formula C_6H_{12} *which contain* a three-membered ring.

8 When 0.601 g of a sample having an empirical formula CH_2O was vaporized at 200 °C and 1 atm pressure, the volume occupied was 388 ml. This same volume was occupied by 0.301 g of ethane under the same conditions. What is the molecular formula of CH_2O? One mole of the sample, when allowed to react with zinc metal, liberated (rather slowly) 0.5 mole of hydrogen gas. Write the structural formula. (*Answer:* The molecular formula is $C_2H_4O_2$.)

9 A compound was found to contain 24 g of carbon, 4 g of hydrogen, and 32 g of oxygen. The molecular weight of the compound is 60. Which one of the following formulas would be consistent with this information?

(a) C_2H_5OH (b) $CH_3\overset{O}{\underset{H}{\overset{\diagup}{C}\diagdown}}$ (c) CH_3OCH_3

(d) COH (e) $H_3C\overset{O}{\underset{OH}{\overset{\diagup}{C}\diagdown}}$

10 A 100-mg sample of a compound containing only C, H, and O was found by analysis to give 149 mg CO_2 and 45.5 mg H_2O when burned completely. Calculate the empirical formula.

11 A compound is found to have the empirical formula C_2H_4O. The measured molecular weight is 44. The nuclear magnetic resonance spectrum (low resolution) shows *two* distinct peaks. One covers three times as much area as the second. Which one of the structures at the top of the following page would be indicated by these data?

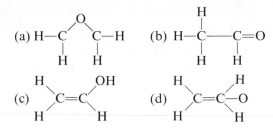

(a) H—C—C—H
(b) H—C—C=O
(c) C=C
(d) C=C—O

12 How many separate peaks would you expect to see in the nmr (low resolution) spectrum of methyl alcohol? Explain.

13 A compound has the following composition: C = 24.26 percent; H = 4.08 percent; Cl = 71.65 percent. It was found that 140.2 millilitres of the vapor at 100 °C and 740 mm pressure had a mass of 0.4416 g. What is the molecular formula of the compound?

14 How much methyl amine can be made from 75 grams of methyl iodide and all of the NH_3 needed? Assume 100 percent yield.

15 Write balanced equations to represent the conversion of the compound $H_3CCH_2CH_2OH$ to $H_3CCH_2C\overset{O}{\underset{H}{\diagdown}}$. To what class of compounds does the product belong?

16 What is the major commercial use of the hydrocarbons?

17 One mole of an organic compound reacts with 1 mole of oxygen to give an acid, $R-C\overset{O}{\underset{OH}{\diagup}}$. To what class of compound did the original material belong? Write the balanced equation for the process.

18 Give simple structural formulas of an alcohol, an aldehyde, and an acid, each derived from methane, from ethane, from butane, and from octane.

19 Ethyl acetate is made from acetic acid and ethyl alcohol. Write the structural formula of ethyl acetate.

20 How can an ester be converted back to the acid and alcohol from which it was formed? Write the equation.

21 When a worker bee stings, it emits a substance of molecular formula $C_7H_{14}O_2$. This substance attracts other bees to the site and causes them to sting too! The compound is a sweet smelling ester. When it is treated with sodium hydroxide, sodium acetate and 2-methyl-butanol-1 are formed. What is the structure of the attractant?

22 A liquid is known to be either an aldehyde or a ketone. What simple test based on oxidation processes could be used to tell which it is? Explain.

23 A 10-gram sample of ethyl acetate is treated with ammonia. Write the equation for the major reaction which is expected. How much of the amide is formed? What is the name of the amide which is formed?

24 An ester is formed by the reaction between an acid, $RCOOH$, and an alcohol, $R'OH$, to form an ester, $RCOOR'$, and water. The reaction is carried out in an inert solvent. (a) Write the equilibrium relation among the concentrations, including the concentration of the product water. (b) Calculate the equilibrium concentration of the ester if $K = 10$ and the concentrations at *equilibrium* of the other constituents are

$$[RCOOH] = 0.1\ M$$
$$[R'OH] = 0.1\ M$$
$$[H_2O] = 1.0\ M$$

(c) Repeat the calculation of part (b) if the equilibrium concentrations are

$$[RCOOH] = 0.3\ M$$
$$[R'OH] = 0.3\ M$$
$$[H_2O] = 1.0\ M$$

25 How many different compounds of formula $C_2H_2Cl_2$ can be formed? Write structural formulas, and name the compounds.

26 Cyclohexene, ⬡, formula C_6H_{10}, and benzene, ⬡, C_6H_6, are each treated with bromine. The reaction of C_6H_6 is very slow unless $FeBr_3$ is present as a catalyst. Write equations for each process.

27 There are three isomers of dichlorobenzene (empirical formula C_3H_2Cl). Draw the structural formulas of the isomers.

28 What product would be expected if the product from the reaction of benzene and bromine (question 26) were treated with sodium hydroxide? Write the equation.

29 Consider the compound phenol,

OH

(a) Predict the angle formed by the nuclei of C, O, and H. Explain your choice in terms of the valence-shell electron-pair repulsion theory. (b) Predict qualitatively the boiling point of phenol. (The boiling point of benzene is 80 °C.) Explain your answer. (c) Write an equation for the reaction of phenol as a proton donor in water. (d) In a 1.0 M aqueous solution of phenol, $[H^+] = 1.1 \times 10^{-5}$ mole/litre. Calculate K_A.

30 You have referred to each of the following terms in your daily life. Indicate by a chemical formula what the *repeating unit* characteristic of each polymer is. (a) polyethylene (b) polyester (c) nylon.

31 The following raw materials are available in the laboratory:

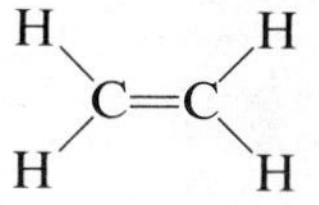

H_2O HBr   NaOH

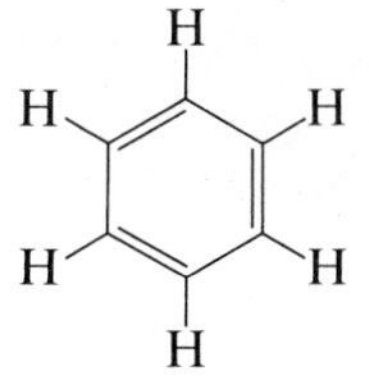

Br_2 $FeBr_3$ H_2SO_4 CO_2

Select the appropriate starting materials and write equations to show the synthesis of each of the compounds indicated below. (You can use products from syntheses in early parts of the question as raw materials for syntheses in later parts of the question.)

(a) C_2H_5Br

(b) C_2H_5OH

(c)

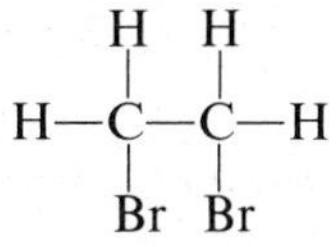

(d)

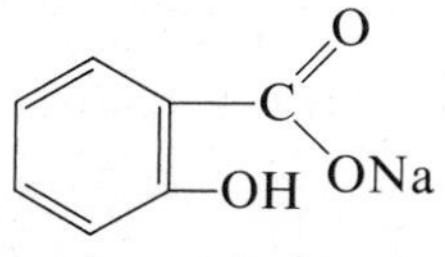

(e) ethylsalicylate

The best and safest way of doing scientific work seems to be, first to enquire diligently
into the properties of things, and of establishing these properties by experiment, and then
to proceed slowly to theories for the explanation of them.

SIR ISAAC NEWTON (1642–1727)

THE TRANSITION ELEMENTS: 20
THE FOURTH ROW OF THE PERIODIC TABLE

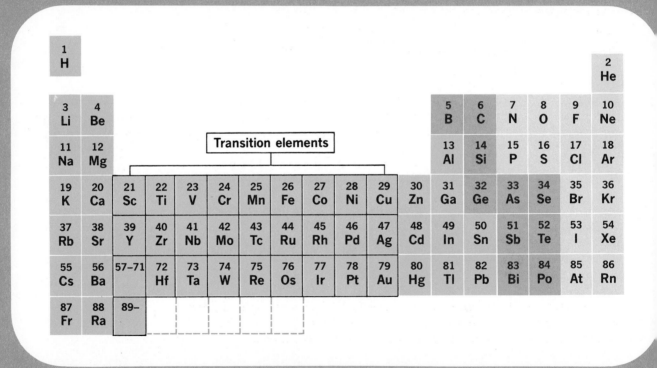

IN CHAPTER 16 WE NOTED BRIEFLY THAT THE TRANSITION elements—the ones which cause the second and third rows of the periodic table to be separated into two parts—correspond to the filling of the *d* orbitals with electrons. Since these elements are among the most well-known, useful, and interesting of all, they deserve more attention than we have given them.

All of these elements are metals, and most of them have many common uses. Because they have several oxidation states, some of their ions were met frequently when we studied oxidation-reduction reactions. Surely you'll never forget chromium and manganese? Many of the ions are colored, and a change of color with change in oxidation state is often used in the laboratory as visible evidence that a reaction has taken place. Let's see what other personality traits these elements have!

In Chapter 8 we found that elements change from metals to nonmetals as we go across the periodic table. In Chapter 16 we found that a large family of metals appears in the fourth horizontal row of the table as the 3*d* electron levels fill up. Similar groups appear in the fifth and sixth rows. These horizontal groups, containing the metals arising from the filling of the 3*d*, 4*d*, and 5*d* levels, are called the **transition elements.** They are a most interesting collection of elements and are worth some of our time.

20-1 IDENTIFICATION AND ELECTRONIC STRUCTURE OF TRANSITION ELEMENTS

There is some disagreement among chemists as to just which elements should be called transition elements. For our purposes, it will be convenient to include all the elements in the columns of the periodic table headed by scandium through copper.

Across the first row of the transition region, we have the elements scandium (Sc), titanium (Ti), vanadium (V), chromium (Cr), manganese (Mn), iron (Fe), cobalt (Co), nickel (Ni), and copper (Cu). On the left, we have the scandium column, which also includes yttrium (Y), lanthanum (La), and actinium (Ac). For reasons that we shall mention later, the elements that follow lanthanum (no. 58 to no. 71) are not considered transition elements but are placed in a separate group, the **lanthanides.** This is also true of the elements following actinium (no. 90 to no. 103), the **actinides.**

On the right, the transition elements end with the copper column. Besides copper, this column includes silver (Ag) and gold (Au). The periodic table will be a useful guide as our discussion proceeds.

20-1.1 Electron Configuration

Now that we know where the transition elements are in the periodic table, we must ask two questions:

(1) Why do we consider these elements together?
(2) What is special about their properties?

These questions are closely related because they both depend upon the electron configurations of the atoms. What, then, is their electronic configuration?

We saw in Chapter 16 that as an atom is built up from its nucleus and electrons, each added electron goes into the lowest energy level which is not already fully occupied. With this principle as a guide, let us consider the electron configurations of the first row of transition elements from scandium to copper.

Looking at the periodic table, we see that calcium (no. 20) comes just before scandium. The 20 electrons in a calcium atom are distributed as in the following diagram:

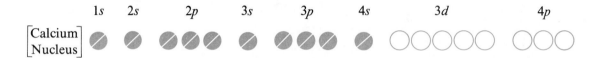

In element number 21, we must accommodate one more electron. After our experience with the second and third rows, we might predict that the twenty-first electron would go into the $4p$ orbital. More careful inspection shows, however, that there is a set of five $3d$ orbitals *between* the $4s$ and $4p$ orbitals. The twenty-first electron goes into a $3d$ orbital, the level of next higher energy. (See Figure 20-1, which is actually Figure 16-16 reproduced here for convenient reference.)

Five $3d$ orbitals are available; all are more or less of the same energy in an isolated atom in space. Putting a pair of electrons in each of these five orbitals means that a total of ten electrons can be accommodated before it is necessary to go to a higher energy level. Not only scandium but the nine following elements can be built up similarly by placing additional electrons in $3d$ orbitals. Not until we come to gallium (no. 31) do we proceed to another set of orbitals.

EXERCISE 20-1

Using Figure 20-1, decide which orbital will be used after the five $4d$ orbitals have been filled. To what element does this correspond?

With the help of Figure 20-1, or with an atomic orbital chart, you should now be able to work out the electron configurations of most of the transition elements. You will not be able to deduce all of them exactly because there are some exceptions resulting from special stabilities caused by a set of orbitals being filled or half-filled. The fourth-row transition elements have the set of electron configurations shown in Table 20-1. Notice that chromium (no. 24) and copper (no. 29) provide interruptions to the continuous buildup. In the case of chromium, the whole atom has lower energy if one of the $4s$ electrons moves into the $3d$ set to give a half-filled set of $3d$ orbitals and a half-filled $4s$ orbital. In the case of copper, the atom has lower energy if the $3d$ set is completely filled by ten electrons and the $4s$ orbital is half-filled, instead of the $3d$ orbitals having nine electrons and the $4s$ orbital two.

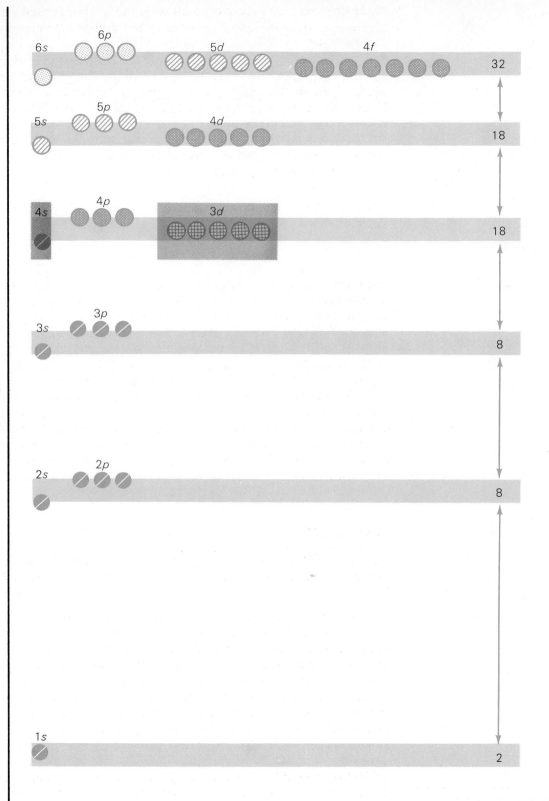

Fig. 20-1 The energy-level scheme of a many-electron atom.

EXERCISE 20-2

Make an electron configuration table like Table 20-1 for the fifth-row transition elements—yttrium (no. 39) through silver (no. 47). In elements 41 through 45, one of the 5s electrons moves over to a 4d orbital. In element 46, two electrons do this.

TABLE 20-1 THE ELECTRON CONFIGURATIONS OF THE FOURTH-ROW TRANSITION ELEMENTS

Element	Symbol	Atomic Number	Electron Configuration	
Scandium	Sc	21	$1s^2 \quad 2s^2 \quad 2p^6 \quad 3s^2 \quad 3p^{6*}$	$3d^1 \; 4s^2$
Titanium	Ti	22		$3d^2 \; 4s^2$
Vanadium	V	23		$3d^3 \; 4s^2$
Chromium	Cr	24		$3d^5 \; 4s^1$
Manganese	Mn	25		$3d^5 \; 4s^2$
Iron	Fe	26		$3d^6 \; 4s^2$
Cobalt	Co	27		$3d^7 \; 4s^2$
Nickel	Ni	28		$3d^8 \; 4s^2$
Copper	Cu	29		$3d^{10}4s^1$

*Each fourth-row transition element has these levels filled.

In the sixth-row transition elements—lanthanum (no. 57) through gold (no. 79)—there is a further complication. There are seven $4f$ orbitals which are very close in energy to the $5d$ orbitals. Putting electrons into these $4f$ orbitals means there will be fourteen additional elements in this row. These fourteen elements are almost identical in many chemical properties. These closely related elements (from no. 58 to no. 71), in which the $4f$ orbitals are filling up, are called the **inner transition elements.** Sometimes the term **lanthanides** or the older term **rare earth elements** is used. The elements following actinium, in which the $5f$ orbitals are being filled, are also inner transition elements. Sometimes this group is called the **actinides.**

20-1.2 General Properties

What properties do we actually find for the transition elements? What kinds of compounds do they form? How can the properties be interpreted in terms of the electron populations of the atoms?

Looking at a sample of each transition element in the fourth row, we see that they are all metallic. When clean, they are shiny and lustrous solids. They are good conductors of electricity and also of heat. Some—copper, silver, and gold, for example—are outstanding in these respects.

We find a tremendous range of chemical reactivity. Some of the transition elements are extremely unreactive. For example, gold and platinum can be exposed to air or water for long periods without any change. Others, such as iron, can be polished so they are brightly metallic for a while; but on exposure to air and water they slowly corrode. Still others such as scandium and lanthanum are very reactive.*

It is difficult to generalize about the chemical reactivities of a group of elements because reactivities depend upon two factors:

(1) the relative stability of the specific compounds formed, compared with the reactants used up and
(2) the rate at which the reaction occurs.

What about compounds of the transition elements? Suppose we go into the chemical stockroom and see what kinds of compounds are on the shelf for a particular element, say chromium. First, we might find a bottle of green powder labeled Cr_2O_3, chromic or chromium(III) oxide. Next to it there probably would be a bottle of a reddish powder, CrO_3, chromium(VI) oxide. On an amply stocked chemical shelf, we might also find, in a sealed and evacuated container, some black powder marked CrO, chromous or chromium(II) oxide. There would probably also be some other simple compounds such as $CrCl_3$, chromic or chromium(III) chloride, a flaky, violet solid, and perhaps in another sealed tube, some $Cr(CH_3CO_2)_2$, red chromium(II) acetate. Elsewhere in the stockroom we would find K_2CrO_4, potassium chromate, a bright yellow powder, probably next to a bottle of orange $K_2Cr_2O_7$, potassium dichromate. We would soon come to the conclusion that the compounds of chromium, at least the common ones, correspond to oxidation numbers of $2+$ [CrO and $Cr(CH_3CO_2)_2$], $3+$ (Cr_2O_3 and $CrCl_3$), and $6+$ (CrO_3, K_2CrO_4, and $K_2Cr_2O_7$).

EXERCISE 20-3

What is the oxidation number of chromium in each of the following: $Cr_2O_7{}^{2-}$, $CrO_4{}^{2-}$, $Cr(OH)_3$, and CrO_2Cl_2?

Along with these simple compounds, we might also find some more complex substances. For example, we might find next to $CrCl_3$ vials of several brightly colored solids labeled $CrCl_3 \cdot 6NH_3$ (yellow), $CrCl_3 \cdot 5NH_3$ (purple-red), $CrCl_3 \cdot 4NH_3$ (green or violet), and $CrCl_3 \cdot 3NH_3$ (violet). The dot in these formulas simply indicates that a certain number of moles of NH_3 is bound to 1 mole of $CrCl_3$. Thus, the oxidation number of chromium is $3+$ in these compounds. Looking further, we might find other complex compounds such as $Na_3Cr(CN)_6$ (bright yellow) and $KCr(SO_4)_2 \cdot 12H_2O$ (violet). In all these the chromium has a $3+$ oxidation number. As a result of our stockroom search, we would form three conclusions:

(1) Chromium forms both simple (Cr_2O_3) and complex ($CrCl_3 \cdot 6NH_3$) compounds.
(2) Chromium forms a number of stable solids, most of them colored.
(3) Chromium may have different oxidation numbers, including $2+$, $3+$, and $6+$.

*The inner transition elements lanthanum and cerium will burn if exposed to air in a finely divided state. They are found in the "flints" of some cigarette lighters.

Similar conclusions would have resulted from a study of most of the other transition elements.

Is there any regularity to the kind of compounds the fourth-row transition elements form? Table 20-2 shows what has been found.

TABLE 20-2 TYPICAL OXIDATION NUMBERS FOUND FOR FOURTH-ROW TRANSITION ELEMENTS

Symbol	Representative Compounds					Common Oxidation Numbers*					Number of Valence 3d and 4s Electrons
Sc		Sc_2O_3					**3+**				3
Ti	TiO	Ti_2O_3	TiO_2			2+	**3+**	**4+**			4
V	VO	V_2O_3	VO_2	V_2O_5		2+	**3+**	4+	5+		5
Cr	CrO	Cr_2O_3		CrO_3		2+	**3+**		6+		6
Mn	MnO	Mn_2O_3	MnO_2	K_2MnO_4	$KMnO_4$	**2+**	3+	4+	6+	7+	7
Fe	FeO	Fe_2O_3				**2+**	**3+**				8
Co	CoO	Co_2O_3				**2+**	3+				9
Ni	NiO	(Ni_2O_3)	NiO_2			**2+**	(3+)	4+			10
Cu	Cu_2O CuO					1+	**2+**				11

* The most common oxidation numbers are in bold type. Parentheses indicate uncertainty.

EXERCISE 20-4

Look through a handbook of chemistry and find one other compound for each oxidation number given for the elements in Table 20-2.

We can make the following generalizations from this table:

(1) For most of the transition elements, *several* oxidation numbers are possible.
(2) When several oxidation numbers are found for the same element, they often differ from each other by increases of one unit. For example, in the case of vanadium the common oxidation numbers form a continuous series from $2+$ to $3+$ to $4+$ to $5+$. In contrast, the halogens differ from each other by increments of two units in a series, such as Cl^-, ClO^-, ClO_2^-, ClO_3^-, ClO_4^-.
(3) The *maximum* oxidation state observed for the elements first increases and then decreases as we go across the row of the transition elements. We have $3+$ for scandium, $4+$ for titanium, $5+$ for vanadium, $6+$ for chromium, and $7+$ for manganese. The $7+$ represents the highest value observed for this transition row. After manganese, the maximum value diminishes as we continue toward the end of the transition row.

What explanation can we give for these observations? Why does the combining capacity vary from one transition element to another in such a way that the above pattern of oxidation numbers develops?

Many factors must be considered in answering these questions. The combining capacity of an atom depends in part upon how many electrons the atom uses for bonding to other atoms. The unique feature of the transition elements is that they have several electrons in the outermost d and s orbitals, and the ionization energies of all of these electrons are relatively low. It is therefore possible for an element like vanadium to form a series of compounds in which from two to five of its electrons are either lost to or shared with other elements. Consider, for example, the oxides VO and V_2O_3, which contain the V^{2+} and the V^{3+} ions, respectively. Although more energy is needed to form V^{3+} than V^{2+}, the V^{3+} has, because of its higher charge, a greater attraction for the O^{2-} ion than does V^{2+}. This extra attraction in V_2O_3 compensates for the energy needed to form the V^{3+} ion, and both oxides (as well as VO_2 and V_2O_5) are stable compounds. Notice, moreover, that the maximum oxidation number of the transition elements never exceeds the total number of s and d valence electrons. The higher oxidation states become increasingly more difficult to form as we proceed along a row, because the ionization energies of the d and s electrons increase with the atomic number.

20-2 COMPLEX IONS

The remaining general point to be made about the transition elements is that they form a great variety of complex ions in which other molecules or ions are bonded to the central transition-element ion to form more complex units. These are called **complex ions.** Consider the series already mentioned: $CrCl_3 \cdot 6NH_3$, $CrCl_3 \cdot 5NH_3$, $CrCl_3 \cdot 4NH_3$, and $CrCl_3 \cdot 3NH_3$. How can we account for the existence of such a series? To answer this question we must consider some of the observed facts about complex compounds. For example, if we dissolve 1 mole of each in water and add a solution of silver nitrate in an attempt to precipitate the chloride as AgCl,

$$Ag^+ + Cl^- \rightleftharpoons AgCl(s) \qquad (1)$$

we find that sometimes much of the chloride cannot be precipitated. The observed results are:

Compound	Moles of Cl^- Precipitated	Moles of Cl^- Not Precipitated
$CrCl_3 \cdot 6NH_3$	3 of 3	0
$CrCl_3 \cdot 5NH_3$	2 of 3	1 of 3
$CrCl_3 \cdot 4NH_3$	1 of 3	2 of 3
$CrCl_3 \cdot 3NH_3$	0	3 of 3

Evidently, there are two ways in which chlorine is bound in these compounds, one which allows the Cl^- to be precipitated by Ag^+ and another which does not. In $CrCl_3 \cdot 6NH_3$, all the chloride can be precipitated; in $CrCl_3 \cdot 3NH_3$, none can be precipitated. Other data also indicate different types of bonding. For example, $CrCl_3 \cdot 6NH_3$ forms a highly conductive solution. On the other hand, $CrCl_3 \cdot 3NH_3$ solution conducts very poorly. The explanation of this behavior was provided in the early 1900's by Alfred Werner (1866–1919), who suggested that complex compounds of Cr^{3+} can be accounted for by assuming that each chromium is bonded to six neighbors. In

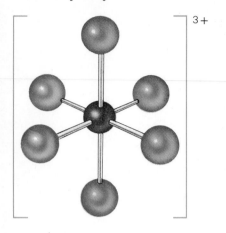

Fig. 20-2 A structural model of the cation $[Cr(NH_3)_6]^{3+}$ in $CrCl_3 \cdot 6NH_3$.

$3+$

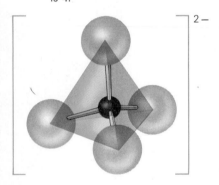

Fig. 20-3.1 The cobalt complex, $[CoCl_4]^{2-}$, is tetrahedral and colors its solutions blue. The coordination number of the cobalt in it is 4.

$2-$

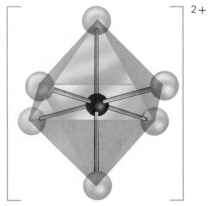

Fig. 20-3.2 The cobalt complex, $[Co(H_2O)_6]^{2+}$, is octahedral and colors its solutions red. The coordination number of the cobalt in it is 6.

$2+$

$CrCl_3 \cdot 6NH_3$, the cation consists of a central Cr^{3+} surrounded by six NH_3 molecules at the corners of an octahedron; the three chlorine atoms exist as anions, Cl^-. In $CrCl_3 \cdot 5NH_3$, the cation consists of the central chromium surrounded by the five NH_3 and one of the chlorines; the other two chlorines are anions. In $CrCl_3 \cdot 4NH_3$, the chromium is bound to four NH_3 and two Cl, leaving one chloride anion. In $CrCl_3 \cdot 3NH_3$, all three Cl atoms and all three NH_3 molecules are bonded to the central chromium. The formulas can be written $[Cr(NH_3)_6]Cl_3$, $[Cr(NH_3)_5Cl]Cl_2$, $[Cr(NH_3)_4Cl_2]Cl$, and $[Cr(NH_3)_3Cl_3]$, respectively.

20-2.1 Geometry of Complex Ions

The way in which atoms or molecules are arranged in space around a central atom has a great influence on the properties of the substance. What kinds of arrangements are found in complex ions? What shapes do these complex ions show? Can we find any regularity in the transition elements that will enable us to predict what complex ions will form?

First, let us introduce a concept useful in giving spatial descriptions: *the **coordination number** is the number of near neighbors (ions or molecules) that an atom has.* For example, in the complex ion $CrCl_3 \cdot 6NH_3$, structural studies show that each Cr^{3+} *ion* is surrounded by six NH_3 *molecules* arranged at the corners of a regular octahedron, as shown in Figure 20-2. The electron pair on each NH_3 points in toward the Cr^{3+} ion. We say that chromium has a coordination number of 6 in $CrCl_3 \cdot 6NH_3$.

Some of you have probably seen humidity indicators which have a piece of colored cloth or paper as the moisture-sensitive unit. When the humidity is low, the color of the cloth or paper is blue; when the humidity is high, the color is pink or red. Many different, ingenious, and even humorous devices, purportedly to forecast the weather, have been developed to utilize commercially this change in color. The colored material absorbed by the paper or cloth is cobalt(II) chloride solution ($CoCl_2$). Some dissolved NaCl may also be present in it. The blue color is attributed to a complex ion of cobalt, presumably the well-known blue ion $[CoCl_4]^{2-}$. In this ion four chloride ions are arranged tetrahedrally around a central cobalt(II) cation, Co^{2+} (see Figure 20-3.1). The coordination number of cobalt in this complex is 4. The pink color is due to $[Co(H_2O)_6]^{2+}$, in which six water molecules surround the central Co^{2+} ion. The negative ends of the water molecules (electron pairs) point inward (Figure 20-3.2). The Co^{2+} ion has a coordination number of 6 in this species. The basis for the color change is found in the nature of the complex ions in the solution:

$$\underbrace{[CoCl_4]^{2-}}_{\substack{\text{tetrahedral} \\ \text{blue} \\ \text{coordination} \\ \text{number} = 4}} + 6H_2O \rightleftharpoons \underbrace{[Co(H_2O)_6]^{2+}}_{\substack{\text{octahedral} \\ \text{pink} \\ \text{coordination} \\ \text{number} = 6}} + 4Cl^- \qquad (2)$$

It should be clear to us from Le Chatelier's principle that when water evaporates into the room because of low relative humidity, the equilibrium will shift to give the blue chloro-complex. On the other hand, if water is picked up from very moist air, the equilibrium shifts to give the pink water complex. Cobalt(II) shows a coordination number of 4 for chloride and 6 for water under the conditions used in the humidity indicator. This same $CoCl_2$ solution is sometimes used as an invisible ink since the pink color cannot be seen in dilute solution, but a color develops if the paper is dried.

EXERCISE 20-5

What is the coordination number of a metal atom in a body-centered cubic structure? (See Chapter 18.) in a cubic close-packed structure? in a hexagonal close-packed structure? Why are the last two quite similar in properties?

EXERCISE 20-6

The mineral cryolite ($AlF_3 \cdot 3NaF$) contains a complex ion. Draw a structural formula for the complex ion. What is the coordination number of aluminum in the complex ion? What is the charge on the complex ion? What other ions are present in cryolite?

Water and NH_3 show rather striking similarities in their ability to coordinate around a metal cation. We have already mentioned $[Cr(NH_3)_6]^{3+}$ and $[Co(H_2O)_6]^{2+}$. As you might expect, we also see $[Cr(NH_3)_5H_2O]^{3+}$. One of the ammonia molecules in $[Cr(NH_3)_6]^{3+}$ has been replaced by a water molecule. Additional replacements of this type give $[Cr(NH_3)_4(H_2O)_2]^{3+}$, and so on.

Not only water molecules but many anions such as chloride ions can replace ammonia molecules. For example, the purple compound with formula $CrCl_3 \cdot 5NH_3$ found on the shelf in our hunt through the stockroom has a structure in which one of the three chloride ions of $CrCl_3$ is attached to the chromium. One of the six NH_3 molecules of yellow $CrCl_3 \cdot 6NH_3$ is replaced. Notice that this complex ion would have a charge of only $2+$, $[Cr(NH_3)_5Cl]^{2+}$, since one charge on Cr^{3+} is neutralized by a Cl^-.

In the compound $CrCl_3 \cdot 4NH_3$, two species of distinctly different color were reported, one violet and the other green. Can we justify this observation? The octahedral models shown in Figure 20-4 suggest that two distinct structures should be possible. As we see, the two chlorine atoms may occupy octahedral positions which are next to each other on the *same* side of the metal atom (Figure 20-4.1) or on *opposite* sides of the metal atom (Figure 20-4.2). The structure in which the two similar groups are located on the same side of the metal atom is called the *cis*-isomer and is violet; the other is called the *trans*-isomer and is green (see Section 17-6.2).

The complex ion $[Fe(C_2O_4)_3]^{3-}$ is formed when rust stains are bleached out of cloth with oxalic acid solution. The complex contains a transition element showing a coordination number of 6, even though

Fig. 20-4.1 The violet-hued *cis*-isomer of $[Cr(NH_3)_4Cl_2]^+$.

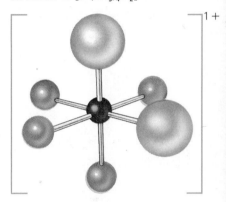

Fig. 20-4.2 The green-hued *trans*-isomer of $[Cr(NH_3)_4Cl_2]^+$.

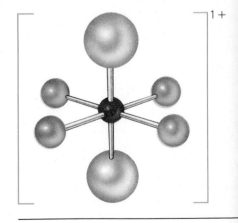

GEOMETRY of COMPLEX IONS

Fig. 20-5 A structural model of $[Fe(C_2O_4)_3]^{3-}$.

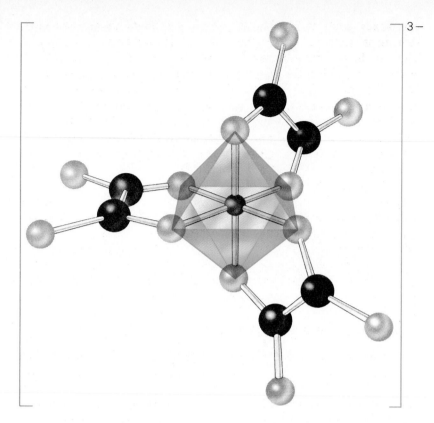

there are only three $[C_2O_4]^{2-}$ groups around each iron ion. Figure 20-5 shows the arrangement. Each $[C_2O_4]^{2-}$, the oxalate group, uses two of its oxygen atoms to bond with the central iron atom. The number of near neighbors, *as viewed from the iron atom,* is six oxygen atoms at the corners of an octahedron. Picturesquely, a *group* such as oxalate, *which can furnish simultaneously two atoms for coordination,* is said to be **bidentate,** which literally means "double-toothed."

In addition to these tetrahedral and octahedral complexes, there are two other types commonly found—the square planar and the linear. In a **square planar complex,** the central atom has four near neighbors at the corners of a square. The coordination number is 4, the same number as in the tetrahedral complexes. An example of a square planar complex is the complex nickel cyanide anion, $[Ni(CN)_4]^{2-}$.

In a **linear complex,** the coordination number is 2, corresponding to one group on each side of the central atom. An example is the silver-ammonia complex, which generally forms when a very slightly soluble silver salt such as silver chloride dissolves in aqueous ammonia (see Figure 20-6). Another example of a linear complex is $[Ag(CN)_2]^-$, which is formed during the leaching of silver ores with NaCN solution.

Fig. 20-6 A linear complex, $[Ag(NH_3)_2]^+$.

20-2.2 Bonding in Complex Ions

What holds the atoms of a complex ion together? There are two possibilities. In some complexes, such as $[AlF_6]^{3-}$, the major contribution to the bonding comes from the attraction between a positive ion (Al^{3+}) and a negative ion (F^-). The bonding is ionic. In other complexes, such as $[Fe(CN)_6]^{3-}$, there is thought to be substantial sharing of electrons between the central atom and the attached groups. The bonding is mainly covalent. When there is such sharing, an electron or an electron pair from the attached group spends part of its time in an orbital furnished by the central atom. In either type, as emphasized in Chapter 17, *both* atoms attract the electron.

For transition elements there are usually empty d orbitals to accommodate electrons from attached groups, but any vacant orbital, low enough in energy to be populated, can be used to form the coordinate covalent bond of a complex.

The geometry of a complex ion often can be correlated with the orbitals of the central atom that are used in the bonding process. For example, we have already seen in Section 17-4.8 that an sp bonding situation is associated with a linear arrangement. $[Ag(NH_3)_2]^+$ is a good example. We associated sp^3 bonding with tetrahedral geometry, as seen in $Ni(CO)_4$. When d orbitals are involved, other geometries are found. For example, dsp^2 has square planar geometry; d^2sp^3, octahedral geometry.

20-2.3 Significance of Complex Ions

In addition to their occurrence in solid compounds, complex ions such as those we have mentioned are important for three other reasons:

(1) They may determine what species are present in aqueous solutions.
(2) Some of them are very important in biological processes.
(3) Some of them are very important catalysts.

As an example of the role of a complex in determining the species in solution, consider the case of a solution made by dissolving some potassium chrome alum $[KCr(SO_4)_2 \cdot 12H_2O]$ in water. The aqueous solution is distinctly acidic. Apparently the chromic ion, $[Cr(H_2O)_6]^{3+}$, in water solution can act as a weak acid, dissociating to give a proton (or hydronium ion). Schematically, the dissociation can be represented as the transfer of a proton from one water molecule in the $[Cr(H_2O)_6]^{3+}$ complex to a neighboring H_2O to form a hydronium ion, H_3O^+. Note that removal of a proton from an H_2O bound to a Cr^{3+} leaves an OH^- group at that position. The reaction is reversible and comes to equilibrium:

$$[Cr(H_2O)_6]^{3+} + H_2O \rightleftharpoons [Cr(H_2O)_5OH]^{2+} + H_3O^+ \qquad (3)$$

We see that $[Cr(H_2O)_6]^{3+}$ acts as a proton-donor—that is, as an acid. The complex determines the pH of the solution.

20-2.4 Amphoteric Complexes

Another reason chemists find the above complex-ion picture of aqueous solutions useful is that it is easily extended to explain other facts. Chromium hydroxide $[Cr(OH)_3]$ dissolves very little in water, but is quite soluble in both acid and excessively strong base. Presumably it can react with either. How can this behavior be explained in terms of the complex-ion model?

JOHN C. BAILAR, Jr.
(1904–   )

John Bailar was born in Golden, Colorado, where his father was a professor of chemistry at the Colorado School of Mines. After receiving his B.A. and M.A. degrees from the University of Colorado, Bailar went to the University of Michigan where he received the Ph.D. in 1928. He then joined the faculty of the University of Illinois where he has remained as one of the most respected and distinguished members of an outstanding department.

Bailar has been widely recognized for his research in the area of metal coordination compounds, for his outstanding abilities as a teacher, and for his scientific leadership. His work on the relationship between structure and chemical reactivity of metal coordination compounds laid the foundation for much of the current work on homogeneous catalysis and for modern studies on the role of metals in biological chemistry.

Honored by his students for his excellence as a teacher, recipient of national and international prizes for accomplishments in research, and of national prizes for excellence in teaching, Bailar has always retained his warm and genuine interest in people.

AMPHOTERIC COMPLEXES

First, consider the equilibrium represented by equation (3). If NaOH is added to the solution, the OH^- ion combines with the H_3O^+ ion to form H_2O. This removes one of the species on the right side of the equation (H_3O^+), so formation of the other species, $[Cr(H_2O)_5OH]^{2+}$, is favored. In other words, as OH^- is added to $[Cr(H_2O)_6]^{3+}$, the reaction which is favored is that which will pull a proton from $[Cr(H_2O)_6]^{3+}$. What will happen when enough NaOH has been added to remove *three* protons from each $[Cr(H_2O)_6]^{3+}$? Loss of three protons leaves the neutral species $Cr(H_2O)_3(OH)_3$, or $Cr(OH)_3 \cdot 3H_2O$. Because this neutral species has no charges to repel other molecules of its own kind, it clusters and precipitates. But as more NaOH is added to this solid phase, one more proton can be removed to produce $[Cr(H_2O)_2(OH)_4]^-$, and the $Cr(OH)_3 \cdot 3H_2O$ dissolves. [In principle, more protons could be removed, perhaps eventually to form $[Cr(OH)_6]^{3-}$, but there is as yet no evidence for this.]

The following equations summarize the steps believed to occur when NaOH is slowly added to a solution of $[Cr(H_2O)_6]^{3+}$. Step (3c) corresponds to formation of solid hydrated chromium hydroxide; step (3d) corresponds to its dissolving in excess NaOH.

$$[Cr(H_2O)_6]^{3+} + OH^- \rightleftharpoons [Cr(H_2O)_5OH]^{2+} + H_2O \qquad (3a)$$

$$[Cr(H_2O)_5OH]^{2+} + OH^- \rightleftharpoons [Cr(H_2O)_4(OH)_2]^+ + H_2O \qquad (3b)$$

$$[Cr(H_2O)_4(OH)_2]^+ + OH^- \rightleftharpoons [Cr(H_2O)_3(OH)_3](s) + H_2O \qquad (3c)$$

$$[Cr(H_2O)_3(OH)_3](s) + OH^- \rightleftharpoons [Cr(H_2O)_2(OH)_4]^- + H_2O \qquad (3d)$$

When an acid is added to a solution, as in equation (3d), the above set of reactions is progressively reversed: precipitation of chromium hydroxide, $Cr(OH)_3$, is first observed; and this then dissolves to give $[Cr(H_2O)_6]^{3+}$.

20-2.5 Complexes Found in Nature

Complex ions have important roles in certain physiological processes of plant and animal growth. Two such complexes are **hemin**—a part of **hemoglobin,** the red pigment in the red cells of the blood—and **chlorophyll**—the green pigment in plants. Hemoglobin contains iron (Fe, no. 26), so it belongs in a discussion of complex compounds of the transition elements. Chlorophyll, however, is a complex compound of magnesium (Mg, no. 12), which is not a transition element. We shall discuss chlorophyll here both because it has some features in common with hemoglobin and because considering it here will help us avoid the misconception that only transition elements form complexes.

As extracted from plants, chlorophyll is actually made up of two closely related compounds, chlorophyll A and chlorophyll B. These differ slightly in molecular structure and can be separated because they have different tendencies to be adsorbed on a finely divided solid, such as powdered sugar.

EXERCISE 20-7

If you wish to prepare some chlorophyll, grind up some fresh leaves and extract with alcohol. The alcohol dissolves the chlorophyll, as the solution color shows.

To show the complexity of this biologically important material, the structural formula of chlorophyll A is shown in Figure 20-7(a). The formula need not be memorized. Note simply that it is a large organic molecule with a magnesium atom in the center. Around the magnesium atom are four near-neighbor nitrogen atoms, each of which is part of a five-membered ring.

EXERCISE 20-8

If a typical plant leaf yields 40.0 mg of chlorophyll A, how many milligrams of this will be magnesium? The molecular weight of chlorophyll A is 893.

Figure 20-7(b) shows the structure of hemin. It appears next to the model of chlorophyll A to emphasize their astonishing similarity. The portions within the unshaded areas identify the differences. Except for the central metal atom, the differences are all on the periphery of these cumbersome molecules. We cannot help wondering how nature managed to standardize this molecular skeleton for molecules with such different functions.

The most important function of hemoglobin in the blood is to carry oxygen from the lungs to the tissue cells. This is done through a weak complex between the iron atom in the complex and an oxygen molecule. The O_2 is readily released to the cells from the bright red weak complex (color of arterial blood). When the O_2 is stripped from the iron, the complex becomes purplish red, the color of blood in the veins.

Fig. 20-7 The structure of (a) chlorophyll and (b) hemin.

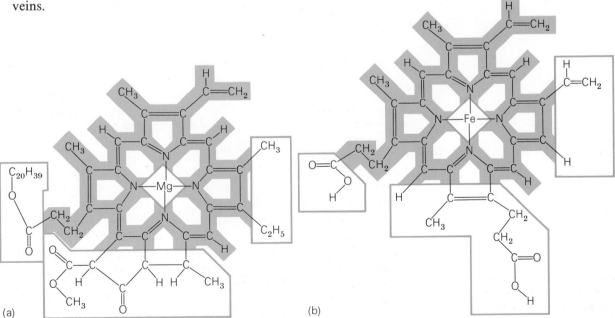

(a)

(b)

Groups in addition to oxygen molecules can be bound to the iron atom of hemoglobin. Specifically, carbon monoxide molecules can be so attached and, in fact, CO is more firmly bound to hemoglobin than is O_2. This is one detail of the carbon monoxide poisoning mechanism. If we breathe a mixture of CO and O_2 molecules, the CO molecules are preferentially picked up by the red blood cells. Since the sites normally used to carry O_2 molecules are thus filled by the CO molecules, the tissue cells starve for lack of O_2. If caught in time, carbon monoxide poisoning can be treated by raising the ratio of O_2 to CO in the lungs (in other words, by administering fresh air or oxygen). Both reactions,

$$O_2(g) + \text{hemoglobin} \rightleftharpoons \text{complex}_1 \qquad (4)$$

$$CO(g) + \text{hemoglobin} \rightleftharpoons \text{complex}_2 \qquad (5)$$

have tendencies to go to the right. If the concentration of O_2 is much higher than that of CO, O_2 will be used in complex formation instead of CO. Another remedial measure is to inject methylene blue directly into the bloodstream. CO bonds more strongly to methylene blue than to hemin. Equilibrium conditions then favor the transfer of CO to the methylene blue, thus freeing hemoglobin for its normal oxygen-transport function.

Another biologically significant material, cobalmin—the coenzyme of vitamin B_{12}—has been identified as a cobalt complex. Indeed, many catalysts, both industrial and biological, are known to function as a result of complex formation. Chemists are now very excited about complexes of cobalt and other metals which contain a *nitrogen molecule* in one coordination position. The interest in these complexes partially stems from the fact that they may help us understand how a colony of bacteria on the root of a clover plant in a field at 20 °C can take nitrogen from the air (partial pressure = 0.8 atm) and convert it to protein. To do this in a laboratory or factory would require temperatures of 450 °C to 500 °C and pressures of hundreds of atmospheres. We hope to learn from the bacteria; their chemistry is better than ours for this particular process.

20-3 SPECIFIC PROPERTIES OF FOURTH-ROW TRANSITION ELEMENTS

The preceding discussion of the transition elements has been quite general. In Table 20-3 their specific properties are summarized.

EXERCISE 20-9

Refer to Chapter 15. Can you show from the E^0 values that all of the elements listed in Table 20-3 except one should dissolve in 1 M HCl? What is the exception?

TABLE **20-3** SOME PROPERTIES OF FOURTH-ROW TRANSITION ELEMENTS

Description	Sc	Ti	V	Cr	Mn	Fe	Co	Ni	Cu
Atomic number	21	22	23	24	25	26	27	28	29
Atomic wt	45.0	47.9	51.0	52.0	54.9	55.9	58.9	58.7	63.5
Abundance* (% by wt)	0.005	0.44	0.015	0.020	0.10	5.0	0.0023	0.008	0.0007
Melting point (°C)	1400	1812	1730	1900	1244	1535	1493	1455	1083
Boiling point (°C)	3900	3130†	3530†	2480†	2087	2800	3520	2800	2582
Density (g/cm³)	2.4	4.5	6.0	7.1	7.2	7.9	8.9	8.9	8.9
First ionization energy (kcal/mole)	151.3	157.5	155.5	155.9	171.4	182.1	181.3	176.1	178.1
2+ ion radius ($\times 10^{-10}$ metre)	—	0.90	0.88	0.84	0.80	0.76	0.74	0.72	0.72
3+ ion radius ($\times 10^{-10}$ metre)	0.81	0.76	0.74	0.69	0.66	0.64	0.63	0.62	—
E^0 $M(aq)^{2+} + 2e^- \longrightarrow M(s)$ (volt)	−2.1‡	−1.6	−1.2	−0.90	−1.18	−0.44	−0.28	−0.25	+0.34

* In the Earth's crust.
† Estimated.
‡ $M(aq)^{3+} + 3e^- \longrightarrow M(s)$.

EXERCISE 20-10

Plot the size of (a) the 2+ ions and (b) the 3+ ions as a function of atomic number for the fourth-row elements.

20-4 SOME CHEMISTRY OF CHROMIUM— A TYPICAL TRANSITION METAL

Most of us are familiar with chromium as the shiny bright metal on household appliances and auto parts. We recognize chromium as an inert metal which is not attacked by the oxygen in the air. Yet the E^0 value for the half reaction

$$\text{Cr}(s) \longrightarrow \text{Cr}^{2+}(aq) + 2e^- \qquad (6)$$

is +0.90 volt. This high positive value suggests that chromium should corrode in air or water more readily than does zinc ($E^0 = +0.76$ volt). (Review Chapter 15 if necessary.) We find, in fact, that bulk chromium which has been obtained by the reduction of Cr^{2+} or Cr^{3+} salts is easily oxidized by air; it tarnishes fairly easily. Why then is "chrome plate" so inert? The answer recalls our earlier explanation of the inert character of aluminum and magnesium. In the case of chromium, as in

SOME CHEMISTRY
of CHROMIUM

the case of aluminum, an impervious, closely adhering oxide coat is believed to form over the metal surface and to protect the active chromium metal below. Acids, such as HCl, that dissolve the oxide coating attack chromium readily as do reagents, such as Cl_2, which can convert the oxide layer to an oxychloride and remove it. Even abrasion which removes the coat will make the chromium reactive again.

Why is the chromium of "chrome plate" protected by an oxide coat while most bulk chromium metal is not? The answer to this question demands an examination of the plating process. In commercial plating, a thin coating of chromium is deposited over a thin nickel or copper plate on steel. The chromium plate is applied by making the object the negative electrode (the cathode) in an electrolysis cell containing chromic acid (H_2CrO_4) and sulfuric acid (H_2SO_4) in a mass ratio of about 100 to 1. Coatings obtained from the strongly oxidizing H_2CrO_4 solution seem to be protected by an oxide layer. One might then guess that passivity (inert character) of chromium could be induced by dipping the metal in strong oxidizing agents such as nitric acid, chromic acid, or hydrogen peroxide. This is indeed the case. Passivity is also achieved by making the metal the positive electrode (the anode) in a suitable alkaline electrolysis cell.

20-4.1 Chromium in Alloys

Chromium is a relatively heavy metal which alloys well with many other transition elements. For example, Nichrome and chromel are alloys of nickel and chromium which are widely used as resistance wires in electrical fixtures. Chromium is also a very important component in stainless steel (14–18 percent Cr plus small percentages of Ni) and in high chrome tool steels. In conjunction with nickel, vanadium, or tungsten, chromium makes steel of great hardness and toughness— steels suitable for making bank vaults. Without chromium, industry would be severely handicapped.

20-4.2 Production of Chromium

The major ore of chromium is the mineral chromite [$Fe(CrO_2)_2$]. The known world production of chromite in 1970 was about six million metric tons with major world supplies coming from the Soviet Union, South Africa, Turkey, Rhodesia, and the Philippines. The U.S. is not a primary producer of metallurgical grade chromite.

Chromite may be converted to chromate by fusing the ore in sodium hydroxide or carbonate under an oxygen stream:

$$2Fe(CrO_2)_2(s) + 4Na_2CO_3(s) + 3\,O_2(g) \longrightarrow$$
$$4Na_2CrO_4(s) + 2FeCO_3(s) + 2CO_2(g) \quad (7)$$

The water-soluble chromate can be extracted and purified. Acidification of the yellow chromate solution gives the orange dichromate. The appropriate equation is

$$2CrO_4^{2-}(aq) + 2H^+(aq) \longrightarrow Cr_2O_7^{2-}(aq) + H_2O \qquad (8)$$

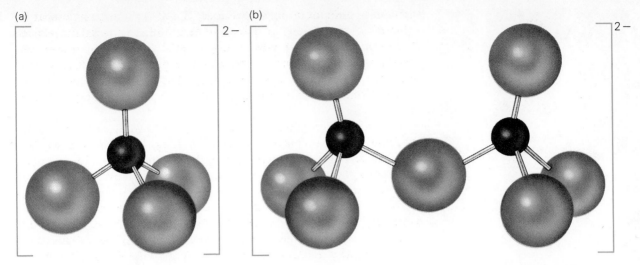

(a)   (b)

Fig. 20-8 Structural models of (a) chromate, $[CrO_4]^{2-}$, and (b) dichromate, $[Cr_2O_7]^{2-}$, ions.

The structural relationship between chromate and dichromate is shown in Figure 20-8. Sodium dichromate, added to concentrated sulfuric acid, gives a deep red syrup from which red crystals of CrO_3 separate:

$$Na_2Cr_2O_7(s) + H_2SO_4 \longrightarrow H_2Cr_2O_7 \longrightarrow$$
$$\underbrace{2CrO_3(s) + H_2O}_{\text{REMOVED BY } H_2SO_4} \qquad (9)$$

These crystals may be dissolved in dilute sulfuric acid to give the chromate plating solution.

Chromite may also be reduced with carbon in a high temperature electric furnace to give the alloy ferrochrome.

$$Fe(CrO_2)_2(s) + 4C(s) \longrightarrow \underbrace{Fe(s) + 2Cr(s)}_{\text{FERROCHROME}} + 4CO(g) \qquad (10)$$

This can be added to steels and other metals where a chrome alloy is desired. An interesting preparation of chromium can be achieved by the reduction of Cr_2O_3 with aluminum metal. The reaction is quite spectacular.

EXERCISE 20-11

Write the equation for the reduction of Cr_2O_3 by Al. If it takes 399 kcal/mole to decompose Al_2O_3 into the elements and 270 kcal/mole to decompose Cr_2O_3, what will be the net heat liberated in the reaction you have just written?

20-4.3   Chemistry of Chromium

Chromium exhibits those properties most characteristic of a transition element. It has several oxidation states, $2+$, $3+$, and $6+$. Its compounds are usually colored and its ions are always colored in water solution. The chromium(II) salts are blue in water; the chromium(III)

salts are green; potassium chromate (K_2CrO_4) is yellow; and potassium dichromate ($K_2Cr_2O_7$) is orange. The chromium(II) salts are such strong *reducing* agents that they will liberate hydrogen from water solution:

$$2Cr^{2+}(aq) + 2HOH \longrightarrow H_2(g) + 2Cr^{3+}(aq) + 2\,OH^-(aq) \quad (11)$$

This reaction is usually rather slow, but it is strongly catalyzed by the presence of platinum metal. On the other hand, the chromium(VI) salts are very strong oxidizing agents:

$$[Cr_2O_7]^{2-}(aq) + 14H^+(aq) + 6e^- \longrightarrow 2Cr^{3+}(aq) + 7H_2O$$
$$E^0 = 1.33 \text{ volts} \quad (12)$$

and are used extensively for this purpose in all branches of chemistry. For example, iron can be determined quantitatively in a solution through titration of Fe^{2+} with standard potassium dichromate ($K_2Cr_2O_7$) solution.

Chromium can form an extremely large number of complex ions. The yellow $[Cr(NH_3)_6]^{3+}$ and the red $[Cr(NH_3)_5H_2O]^{3+}$ ions are two members of a very large family of brightly colored complexes. Chromium frequently shows up in pigments such as chrome-yellow and chrome-green. The very name chromium indicates the frequent incidence of color in chromium compounds.

Like many transition elements, chromium is frequently used in the preparation of catalysts. Its ability to pass through a variety of oxidation states is probably responsible for its effectiveness as a catalyst for many reactions.

One other characteristic of the transition elements is found in the low basic strength of the hydroxides. In general, transition-element hydroxides are insoluble and are very weak bases when compared to hydroxides of such elements as potassium and calcium. You will recall from Section 20-2.4 that chromium(III) hydroxide even has weakly acidic properties.

As chromium demonstrates, the transition elements are a colorful, interesting, and useful group.

20-5   SOME CHEMISTRY OF IRON—OUR MOST WIDELY USED TRANSITION METAL

No discussion of metals is complete without some mention of iron, the element which gives its name to the so-called Iron Age. Since 1947 annual world steel production has increased a little over four-fold. Much of our iron is obtained commercially from naturally occurring deposits of an iron oxide, usually Fe_2O_3 or Fe_3O_4.

20-5.1   Steel

Examination of the formulas Fe_2O_3 and Fe_3O_4 shows that oxygen must be removed from the iron by the process of reduction. Commercial reduction is carried out on a tremendous scale in a blast furnace which is a tall, circular, high-temperature chemical reactor. Raw materials—iron ore, limestone, and the reducing agent coke—are fed into the top and oxygen is blown in at the bottom. The limestone ($CaCO_3$) reacts with the sand (SiO_2) in the ore to give calcium silicate ($CaSiO_3$) slag, which floats on top of the iron and can be removed. The coke serves a double function. It burns in oxygen to produce heat and CO, thus generating the high temperatures needed in the furnace. The carbon monoxide formed reduces the iron oxide to metallic iron. The overall equation is

$$3CO(g) + Fe_2O_3(s) \longrightarrow 2Fe(s) + 3CO_2(g) \qquad (13)$$

As the molten metal trickles down over the white hot coke, it absorbs an excess of carbon which forms a much lower melting alloy. This is drained from the bottom as an impure, high-carbon pig iron. The product is brittle and of little direct value until it is converted to steel.

The conversion of pig iron into steel can be described as a relatively simple chemical process, but it is a complicated technological process. In simple terms, the excess carbon may be burned out in an oxygen or air blast (Bessemer process) or it may be oxidized by iron oxides which are added as rusty scrap iron or fresh ore:

$$FeO(s) + Fe_3C(s) \longrightarrow 4Fe(s) + CO(g) \qquad (14)$$

Undesirable impurities accumulate in the glasslike molten slag which can be removed. Special steels are made by adding alloying metals (*i.e.*, chromium, vanadium, manganese) to the molten mass. Most steel is a heterogeneous mixture, the exact nature of which is dependent upon its content of carbon and other components. A low-carbon steel consists of crystals of pure iron (which have a body-centered cubic arrangement) and a material known as pearlite. Pearlite is an intimate mixture composed of very tiny flakelike crystals of iron and iron carbide (Fe_3C). Pearlite gets its name from its pearly appearance. Higher carbon steels have clearly visible crystals of pearlite and iron carbide (Fe_3C) known as cementite. Iron carbide is hard and tough; hence high-carbon steels are hard and tough.

In steel-making, sulfur and phosphorus must be removed. This is usually done through adding lime or other basic material which combines with the phosphorus oxides and remaining sulfur oxides to give slag.

20-5.2 The Rusting of Iron

The rusting of iron and its consequences are so well known that it does not need to be described visually. What is the chemistry of corrosion? Let us review the known facts about this process.

First, H_2O and O_2 are *both* necessary; $H^+(aq)$ speeds up the reaction; some metals, such as zinc, hinder corrosion, while other metals, such as copper, speed it up. It is also known that strains in the metal (like those produced when a car fender is pressed out during manufacture) accelerate corrosion.

How can these observations be interpreted? The most widely accepted mechanism involves many steps. First, the iron acts as an anode to *give up* two electrons and form Fe^{2+}. Second, the electrons are picked up by H^+ to give reactive H atoms. Third, the reactive H atoms combine with the required O_2 to form OH or H_2O. Fourth, the OH or O_2 oxidizes the Fe^{2+} to hydrated $Fe(OH)_3 \cdot xH_2O$, or rust.

Various strategies for fighting corrosion interfere with key steps in the above corrosion process. For example, applying a coat of paint completely excludes O_2 and H_2O. Another scheme is to attach the iron by a conducting wire to a more readily corroded metal such as Zn or Mg. Under these circumstances the Zn or Mg instead of the iron loses electrons and corrodes.

Corrosion is a fascinating problem of great economic importance. Many treatises have been written on it, yet we still find that about one person in every four in the steel industry works to replace iron lost by corrosion. The Iron Age would be history now were it not for the steel industry.

20-6 HIGHLIGHTS

The groups of elements formed by the filling of the *d* electron levels occupy a position in the middle of the periodic table. These elements, known as the **transition elements,** include atomic numbers 21 to 29, 39 to 47, and 72 to 79. The elements in which the *f* levels are filling are known as the **inner transition elements.** These include atomic numbers 58 to 71 and 90 to 103. The similarities among the transition elements in any one row of the periodic table are fairly strong, and they are very strong among the inner transition elements.

Transition elements have metallic characteristics, relatively high density, many oxidation states, colored ions and compounds, hydroxides which are weak bases, and metal ions with the ability to form **complex ions.** Many of the transition elements and their compounds have marked activity as catalysts for reactions of organic compounds.

Some of our most useful metals (*e.g.,* copper, chromium, and iron) are transition elements.

QUESTIONS and PROBLEMS

1 Bohr identified four groups of elements based on electronic structure. One of these was the noble gases in which the *s* and *p* levels were filled. Can you identify and describe the electronic configuration of the remaining three groups? One element in the second group is silicon; one element in the third group is iron; and one element in the fourth group is dysprosium (Dy).

2 Write out the electronic structure (*i.e.,* $1s^2$ $2s^2 2p^6$ $3s^2$, etc.) for each of the following metals: (a) titanium (b) cobalt (c) iron (d) nickel (e) molybdenum (f) tungsten.

3 A useful rule of thumb for predicting color of metal ions is that "an ion with *more than 8 but less than 18* electrons in its outer shell will be colored in water solution." (a) What general group of metal ions is defined by this description? (b) Which of the following metal *ions* should be colored in water solution: Sc^{3+}, Ti^{4+}, Ti^{3+}, Cr^{3+}, Ni^{2+}?

4 Metals are familiar to you. Suppose you were to classify all of the known elements of the universe into two piles—one we call metals, and one nonmetals. (a) What operational criteria (see Section 13-3, page 309, for an illustration of operational criteria) would you use to do the sorting? (b) What conceptual criteria would you use to define metals? (See Chapter 18 on the nature of the metallic bond.) (c) In terms of these criteria, place *iron* in one pile or the other; justify your choice on both operational and conceptual grounds. (d) What elements lie on the borderline between metals and nonmetals? Indicate this by a line on the periodic table. (e) Identify at least two pure elements which are used to make semiconductors. Where do they lie in the periodic table? (See Chapter 18.)

5 Ferrous ion, iron(II), forms a complex with six cyanide ions, CN^-; the octahedral complex is called ferrocyanide. Ferric ion, iron(III), forms a complex with six cyanide ions; the octahedral complex is called ferricyanide. Write the structural formulas for the ferrocyanide and ferricyanide complex ions.

6 If $CoCl_2$ is mixed with a solution containing excess NH_3 and some NH_4Cl, and then air is bubbled through the solution, the following reaction takes place:

$$2CoCl_2 + 10NH_3 + 2NH_4Cl + \tfrac{1}{2}O_2 \longrightarrow$$
$$2CoCl_3 \cdot 6NH_3 + H_2O$$

(a) Draw a structural formula to represent the yellow compound $CoCl_3 \cdot 6NH_3$. (b) Another product which may be produced in the same reaction is a purple material of formula $CoCl_3 \cdot 5NH_3$. Draw a structural formula to represent this compound. (c) Two compounds of formula $CoCl_3 \cdot 4NH_3$ can also be isolated from this reaction. Suggest possible structural formulas for these compounds and ways in which you might tell them apart.

7 Refer to question 6. What are common oxidation numbers for cobalt?

8 Why does NH_3 readily form complexes while NH_4^+ does not? Consider bonding possibilities in the two cases.

9 Chromium(III) oxide (Cr_2O_3) is used as a green pigment and is often made by the reaction between $Na_2Cr_2O_7(s)$ and $NH_4Cl(s)$ to give $Cr_2O_3(s)$, $NaCl(s)$, $N_2(g)$, and $H_2O(g)$. Write a balanced equation and calculate how much pigment can be made from 1.0×10^2 kg of sodium dichromate.

10 Note that the nickel atom in $Ni(CO)_4$ has not lost any of its electrons. Electronically it is still a nickel atom. What orbitals are available to bind four CO molecules to Ni to get $Ni(CO)_4$? Can you suggest a geometry for $Ni(CO)_4$?

11 Name at least two complex ions that are of great biological significance. Describe their functions.

12 If manganous chloride is heated in a fluorine gas stream, a red-purple solid of formula MnF_3 is formed. When this solid is dissolved in water, a solution of MnF_2 (very light pink) and a black precipitate of MnO_2 form. (a) What is the oxidation number of manganese in each compound? (b) Write a balanced equation for this *disproportionation* process. (c) If the MnF_3 is dissolved in a fairly concentrated solution of KHF_2, a deep red solution forms from which one can obtain a solid, K_3MnF_6. Write the equation for the process. Is manganese oxidized in this process?

13 Nickel carbonyl $[Ni(CO)_4]$ boils at 43 °C and uses the sp^3 orbitals of Ni for bonding. Give reasons to justify the following: (a) It forms a molecular solid. (b) The molecule is tetrahedral. (c) Bonding to other molecules is of the van der Waals type. (d) The liquid is a nonconductor of electricity. (e) It is not soluble in water.

14 Write balanced equations to show the dissolving of $Cu(OH)_2(s)$ when $NH_3(aq)$ is added and the reprecipitation caused by the addition of an acid. [Cu^{2+} forms a complex $[Cu(NH_3)_4]^{2+}$ ion.]

15 Copper is one of the very few metals found free in nature. For example, large pieces of pure copper were found free near Lake Superior in upper Michigan. Can you relate this fact to the fact that historically the Bronze Age came before the Iron Age?

16 Plot the first ionization energies of the transition elements from Sc to Cu. Do you notice any trend? How do they compare with ionization energies for potassium, fluorine, and argon? Does this have an influence on your classification of the transition elements as metals? Explain.

17 Look at the line in Table 20-3 labeled "Abundance, % by Weight." Comment upon the long-term effect of our practice of dumping old cars in deserts, in the ocean, and other places. What metals are present in the car?

18 A blue solution of Cr^{2+} is relatively stable if air is kept away from it. If, however, a piece of platinum is dropped into the solution, the following reaction takes place:

$$2[Cr(H_2O)_6]^{2+} \xrightarrow{\text{Pt}} H_2(g) + 2[Cr(H_2O)_5OH]^{2+}$$

What is the function of the platinum?

19 What general chemical process is needed to prepare any metal from its ore? What is a common reagent used to prepare the metal? Write a representative equation.

20 What is steel? How does it differ from "pig iron"?

SOME ASPECTS 21
OF BIOCHEMISTRY

Biochemistry determines the mechanism of both animal and plant life.

THE CHEMISTRY OF LIVING THINGS IS OF SPECIAL INTEREST TO us because, of course, we *are* living things. Is the chemistry of life processes unique, or can we apply our knowledge of the chemistry of nonliving things to the chemistry of life?

In Chapter 19 we were introduced to the great number and complexity of organic compounds and also to some of the techniques which enable chemists to study them. The compounds which make up living things are among the most complex known, but the discovery of the structure of DNA and the synthesis of both a virus and an enzyme from nonliving materials confirm our belief that investigation of biochemical reactions is within our ability—and control of undesirable reactions, such as those causing disease, perhaps not too far off.

One and a half centuries ago the chemistry of living organisms was regarded as something quite distinct from the chemistry of rocks, minerals, and other nonliving things. Indeed, people were inclined to believe that living things were imbued with some mysterious "vital force" that was beyond their power to define and understand. But as time went on, it became apparent that the mystery in the chemistry of living things was due to ignorance. As understanding of chemical principles increased, the mystery began to disappear. Compounds that were obtained only from plants and animals were produced in the laboratory from ordinary inorganic substances. By the middle of the nineteenth century the superstitious belief in a "vital force" had disappeared; most chemists now believe that it is possible to understand the chemistry of living organisms.

This point of view received dramatic support in the fall of 1967 when L. A. Kornberg and M. Goulian of Stanford University reported the laboratory synthesis of a biologically active virus from nonliving compounds called **nucleotides** (see Section 21-3). The synthetic virus of Drs. Kornberg and Goulian could attack and destroy bacterial cells just like the natural living virus.* Their work suggests that biological chemistry is not fundamentally different from other chemistry.

We still, however, describe a large area of chemical study by the term **biochemistry.** This is not because biochemistry is fundamentally different from chemistry in general. It is because a chemist working effectively in a *particular* area of science must devote special (but not exclusive) attention to what is known about that field of knowledge. Biochemists are concerned fundamentally with the chemical processes that go on in living organisms, but they must use information from all branches of chemistry to answer the questions they ask. Some of these questions are:

(1) What kinds of molecules make up living systems?
(2) What structures do biologically significant materials have?
(3) How is biologically significant information passed from parents to offspring?

*These experiments raise a fascinating philosophical question. Have Drs. Kornberg and Goulian synthesized life in a test tube? Certainly the synthesized virus, produced from nonliving compounds by the action of a biological catalyst (an enzyme) and a template-pattern molecule, has all the characteristics of a natural virus, which is usually defined as a living body. The identity of natural and synthetic viruses was established by R. Sinsheimer of the California Institute of Technology in 1967. (See Section 21-3.)

21-1 MOLECULAR COMPOSITION OF LIVING SYSTEMS

The chemical system of even the smallest plant or animal is extremely complex. This system has a multitude of compounds, many of polymeric nature, existing in hundreds of interlocking equilibrium reactions whose rates are influenced by a number of specific catalysts. We shall not try to study such a complex system. Instead, we shall focus on some parts of it that serve as examples of material that has been well studied and which illustrate the applicability of chemical principles. *All our knowledge of biochemistry has come through use of the same basic ideas and the same experimental methods you have learned in this course.* Specifically, we shall consider in this chapter four classes of compounds that have great importance in biochemistry. **Sugars, fats,** and **proteins** occur in most animals and plants, while **cellulose** is more common in plants.

21-1.1 Sugars

SIMPLE SUGARS

The word *sugar* brings to mind the sweet, white, crystalline grains found on any dinner table. The chemist calls this substance **sucrose** and knows it as just one of many "sugars" which are classed together because they have a related composition and undergo similar reactions. Sugars are part of the larger family of **carbohydrates,** a name given because many such compounds have the empirical formula CH_2O, or hydrate of carbon, $C \cdot H_2O$.

EXERCISE 21-1

Glucose, a sugar that is simpler than sucrose, has a molecular weight of 180 and the empirical formula CH_2O. What is its molecular formula?

The structure of the **glucose** molecule was deduced by a series of steps similar to those described in Chapter 19 for ethanol. Glucose was found to contain one aldehyde group

$$\left(-C\begin{smallmatrix} O \\ \\ H \end{smallmatrix} \right)$$

and five hydroxyl groups (—OH). These functional groups exhibit their typical chemistry. The aldehyde part can be oxidized to an acid group. The reaction is like equation (*20*) for aldehyde oxidation in Section 19-3.3. If a mild oxidizing agent (such as the hypobromite ion in bromine water) is used, the aldehyde group can be oxidized without oxidizing the hydroxyl groups.

EXERCISE 21-2

Write the equation for the oxidation of

MARSHALL W. NIRENBERG
(1927–   )

A native of New York City, Marshall W. Nirenberg received the Ph.D. in biochemistry from the University of Michigan in 1957. He is now affiliated with the National Institutes of Health, Bethesda, Maryland.

Nirenberg's research has centered on the chemical mechanism by which information carried in the DNA molecule is transferred and used in the synthesis of proteins. He devised a series of experiments to identify the combinations of nucleotides which determine the specific amino acids used in the formation of protein. Previous work by others had suggested that a three-nucleotide "code" exists for each amino acid. Nirenberg was able to "break the code"—to identify the sequence which carries information for each of the twenty amino acids. For his work, Marshall Nirenberg was one of the recipients of the 1968 Nobel Prize in Medicine or Physiology.

If all the oxygen-containing groups are reduced, *n*-hexane,

$$
\begin{array}{cccccc}
H & H & H & H & H & H \\
| & | & | & | & | & | \\
H-C- & C- & C- & C- & C- & C-H \\
| & | & | & | & | & | \\
H & H & H & H & H & H
\end{array}
$$

results. This test helps establish that the glucose molecule has a chain structure. One representation of the structural formula of glucose ($C_6H_{12}O_6$) is

$$
\begin{array}{c}
H \diagdown \ \diagup O \\
C \\
| \\
CHOH \\
| \\
CHOH \\
| \\
CHOH \\
| \\
CHOH \\
| \\
CH_2OH
\end{array}
$$

The sugar **fructose** also occurs naturally and also has the molecular formula $C_6H_{12}O_6$. It is an isomer of glucose with the carbon of the $C{=}O$ group at the second position in the carbon chain instead of at the end. This makes fructose a ketone (see Section 19-3.4).

EXERCISE 21-3

Draw a structural formula for the fructose molecule. (Remember that fructose is an isomer of glucose.) Explain why fructose cannot be oxidized to a six-carbon acid.

Another aspect of the structure of glucose and fructose is that they, like other simple sugars, can exist as a straight chain in equilibrium with a cyclic structure. In solutions the cyclic structure prevails. Equation (*1*) shows both forms of glucose:

$$(1)$$

The ring form can be written in a simpler way, showing the hydrogen atoms attached to carbon atoms by lines only and omitting the symbols for the ring carbons:

The sugar structure will be important in our discussion of DNA in Section 21-3.

EXERCISE 21-4

At equilibrium in a 0.1 M solution of glucose in water, only 1 percent of the glucose is in the straight chain form. What is K for the cyclization of glucose (the formation of a cyclic structure)?

The two sugars we have discussed are **monosaccharides**—they have a single, simple sugar unit in each molecule. The sugar on your table is a **disaccharide**—it has two units. Each molecule of sucrose contains one molecule of glucose and one of fructose hooked together (losing a molecule of water in the joining reaction). Fructose has a slightly different ring structure because the $>C=O$ group is not on the end carbon. The formation of sucrose is shown in equation (2):

$$+ H_2O \quad (2)$$

PROPERTIES OF SUGARS

Sugars occur in many plants. The major commercial sources are sugar cane (a large, specialized grass which stores sucrose in the stem) and sugar beet (as much as 15 percent of the root is sucrose). In addition, fruits, some vegetables, and honey contain sugars.

Sugars are fairly soluble in water; about 5 moles dissolve per litre (solubility varies somewhat with the sugar). High solubility in water is readily explained because sugars have many functional groups that can form hydrogen bonds. From your study of hydrogen bonding in Section 18-6, you will recall that from 3 to 10 kcal of energy are released for each hydrogen bond formed. This energy can then be used as part of the energy needed to disrupt the structure of the crystal.

Aldehyde sugars are easily oxidized, as in the oxidation reaction that involves cupric hydroxide:

$$R-\overset{\displaystyle O}{\underset{\displaystyle H}{C}} + 2Cu(OH)_2 \longrightarrow R-\overset{\displaystyle O}{\underset{\displaystyle OH}{C}} + Cu_2O(s) + 2H_2O \qquad (3)$$

The reaction is more complicated than shown. The $Cu(OH)_2$ is not very soluble in the basic solution used, so tartaric acid is added to form a complex ion. The $Cu_2O(s)$ is a red solid which precipitates from solution because Cu^+ does not form such a complex ion. The reaction is characteristic and is used as a qualitative test for simple aldehydes and aldehyde sugars.

An important metabolic reaction of disaccharides is the reverse of sucrose formation—the **hydrolysis** of sucrose to give glucose and fructose. Water in the presence of $H^+(aq)$ reacts with sucrose to give glucose and fructose. The term hydrolysis means "reaction with water."

21-1.2 Cellulose and Starch

Cellulose is an important part of woody plants, occurring in cell walls and making up part of the structural material of stems and trunks. Cotton and flax are almost pure cellulose. Chemically cellulose is a **polysaccharide**—a *polymer* made by successive reaction of many glucose molecules giving a high molecular weight ($\sim$600,000) structure. This polymer is not basically different from the polymers that were discussed in Section 19-6:

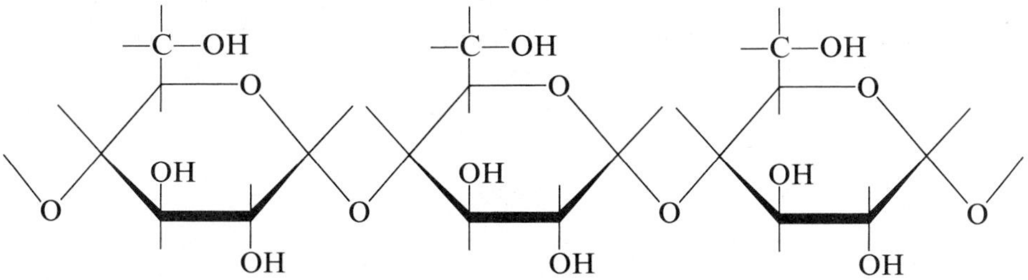

Starch is a mixture of glucose polymers, some of which are water-soluble. This soluble portion consists of comparatively short chains (molecular weight $\sim$4,000). The portion of low solubility consists of much longer chains with frequent branching.

EXERCISE 21-5

The monomer unit in starch and cellulose has the empirical formula $C_6H_{10}O_5$. These units are about 5.0×10^{-10} metre long. Approximately how many units occur and how long are the molecules of cellulose and soluble starch?

21-1.3 Fats

Fats, as well as animal and plant oils, are esters. Actually they are triple esters of glycerol (1,2,3-propanetriol or $C_3H_8O_3$):

$$\underset{\substack{| \\ O \\ | \\ H}}{H}-\underset{\substack{| \\ O \\ | \\ H}}{\overset{\substack{H \\ |}}{C}}-\underset{\substack{| \\ O \\ | \\ H}}{\overset{\substack{H \\ |}}{C}}-\underset{\substack{| \\ }}{\overset{\substack{H \\ |}}{C}}-H$$

When carboxylic acids, similar to those you studied in Section 19-3.3, react with glycerol OH groups, a fat is formed. In natural fats the acids usually have 12 to 20 carbon atoms, C_{16} or C_{18} acids being most common.

EXERCISE 21-6

Write the formula for glycerol tributyrate, and then write the formula of the fat made from glycerol and one molecule each of stearic ($C_{17}H_{35}COOH$), palmitic ($C_{15}H_{31}COOH$), and myristic ($C_{13}H_{27}COOH$) acids. How many isomers are possible for the last fat? How many would be possible if all possible combinations of the three acids were used? Compare your answer with that for Exercise 19-19.

Common fats (*e.g.*, butter, tallow) and oils (*e.g.*, olive, palm, and peanut) are mixed esters: each molecule has either (most often) three, (sometimes) two, or (rarely) one kind of acid combined with a single glycerol. There are so many combinations in a given sample that fats and oils do not have sharp melting or boiling points. Melting and boiling occur over a range of temperatures instead.

An important reaction of fats is the reverse of ester formation. They hydrolyze, or react with water, just as disaccharides do. Usually hydrolysis is carried out in aqueous $Ca(OH)_2$, NaOH, or KOH solution. The metal salts of natural carboxylic acids, such as sodium stearate, are called **soaps.** The products of hydrolysis are, then, soap (*e.g.*, sodium stearate) and glycerol. Because soap is formed, the alkaline hydrolysis is called **saponification:**

$$\begin{array}{c}
\text{A FAT}
\end{array} + 3Na^+(aq) + 3OH^-(aq) \longrightarrow \text{GLYCEROL} + \text{SODIUM STEARATE} + \text{SODIUM MYRISTATE} \qquad (4)$$

Fats make up as much as half the diet of many people. Fats are a good source of energy because when they are completely "burned" in the body, they supply twice as much energy per gram as do proteins and carbohydrates. As many people know, this is often a mixed blessing, particularly when weight is a problem.

21-2 MOLECULAR STRUCTURES IN BIOCHEMISTRY

Some of the most exciting recent advances in biochemistry have come from recognition of the importance of the structural arrangement of molecular parts. You saw in Chapter 19 that the chemistry of a C_2H_6O compound depends upon structure. Thus, an ether (CH_3—O—CH_3) behaves quite differently from an isomeric alcohol (CH_3CH_2OH). You also learned how interactions between molecules can influence the properties of water (Section 18-6), and how attractions between ions and water can arrange the water molecules in preferred positions around an ion (Figure 18-17). Structure influences the observed properties of systems. Both covalent bonds and intermolecular interactions are involved in fixing the structure of biochemical substances. We shall consider a few examples.

21-2.1 Proteins

In Section 19-6.3 the composition of proteins was given. They are large, amide-linked polymers of amino acids. However, the long chain formula (Figure 19-14) does not represent all that is known about the structure of proteins. It properly shows the covalent structure but does not indicate the relative positions of the atoms in space.

The use of X-ray diffraction (Section 17-7.2) and the principles that describe hydrogen bonding (Section 18-6) have led to the recognition of a coiled form of the chain in natural proteins. This model is consistent with other tests also and has received general acceptance. It is shown in Figure 21-1. This form has a great deal of regularity—it is not at all a random shape. Order must have some energy factor sustaining it; in the protein molecule, this energy is provided by the hydrogen bonds. These are represented in Figure 21-1 by dotted lines, just as they were in Section 18-6. When the hydrogen bonds are broken (by heating or putting the protein in alcohol), the order disappears and the coiled form loses its shape. Often this damage cannot be repaired and the coil is permanently deformed. Cooking an egg destroys the coiled form of the proteins it contains. A few moments of thought concerning the profound differences of an egg before and after cooking will suggest the very great importance of molecular structure in biochemistry.

Proteins come in all types and shapes. Current intensive research on a protein called "interferon" promises possible cell defense against infection by viruses.*

21-2.2 Enzymes

Nearly all biochemical reactions proceed at ordinary temperatures and pressures. Most biochemical reactions (especially those in the human body) take place at about 37 °C (98 °F) and proceed at a rate adequate for the role they play. People live, grow, and reproduce under very mild conditions. Most reactions would not proceed at a measurable rate at this temperature outside living organisms. Glucose, starches,

*See M. R. Hilleman and A. A. Tytell, "The Induction of Interferon," *Scientific American*, **225**, 26 (July 1971).

Fig. 21-1 The coiled form of a protein molecule.

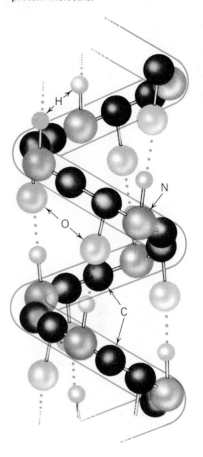

and fats are very stable compounds and can remain in contact with oxygen without apparent change. This is so, even though their oxidation to carbon dioxide and water releases large amounts of energy. To make these reactions proceed, nature uses catalysts to provide new paths with lower activation energies. Measurable reaction rates are then achieved.

Biological catalysts are called **enzymes.** Nearly every step in the breakdown of a complex molecule to a series of smaller ones is catalyzed by a specific enzyme within living cells. For instance, when acetaldehyde is reduced to ethanol in yeast cells, the reaction takes place in the presence of a specific enzyme called alcohol dehydrogenase:

$$CH_3-C{\overset{O}{\underset{H}{}}} + 2H^+ + 2e^- \xrightarrow[\text{dehydrogenase}]{\text{alcohol}} CH_3-CH_2{\overset{OH}{}} \tag{5}$$

The electrons are furnished by undefined reducing agents in the cell. You can see that the hydrogenation of acetaldehyde is the reverse of the dehydrogenation of ethanol. The enzyme is named for the latter reaction, but of course it catalyzes the reaction in either direction. Conditions at equilibrium are not affected by the enzyme, but the rate at which the reacting substances reach the equilibrium state is affected by the enzyme (as with any catalyst).

The synthesis of enzymes remained an impossible problem until early in 1969. At that time Drs. Robert B. Merrifield and Bernd Gutte of Rockefeller University and Drs. Robert G. Denkewalter and Ralph F. Hirschmann of the Merck, Sharp & Dohme Research Laboratories reported the synthesis of ribonuclease, an enzyme which helps to break down ribonucleic acid (RNA). (See Section 21-3.6.)

REACTION MECHANISM

Enzymes are protein molecules. Although all enzymes are proteins, not all proteins can act as enzymes. The protein molecules of enzymes are very large, with molecular weights of the order of 100,000. In comparison, the substance upon which the enzyme acts (called a **substrate**) is made up of small molecules. Thus, the reaction involves a small substrate molecule which has become attached to the surface of a large protein molecule, where the reaction occurs. [Refer to equations (5), (9), and (10).] The products of the reaction then dissociate from the enzyme surface; a new substrate molecule is attached to the enzyme and the reaction is repeated. We can write the following sequence:

$$\text{enzyme} + \text{substrate} \longrightarrow \text{enzyme-substrate complex} \tag{6}$$

$$\text{enzyme-substrate complex} \longrightarrow \text{enzyme} + \text{reaction products} \tag{7}$$

Adding these equations and canceling gives

$$\text{substrate} \longrightarrow \text{reaction products} \tag{8}$$

Despite the large size of an enzyme molecule, there is reason to believe that there is only one or a few places on its surface at which reaction can occur. These are usually referred to as **active centers.** The evidence supporting this view comes from many kinds of observations. One such observation is that enzyme reactions can often be stopped or slowed down by adding only a small amount of a "false" substrate. A false substrate is a molecule so similar to the real substrate that it can attach itself to the active center, but sufficiently different that no reaction (and consequently no release) can occur. Thus, the active center is "blocked" by the false substrate.

SPECIFICITY OF ENZYMES

Most enzymes are quite specific for a given substrate. For example, the enzyme urease that catalyzes the reaction

$$O{=}C\begin{array}{l} \diagup NH_2 \\ \diagdown NH_2 \end{array} + H_2O \xrightleftharpoons{\text{urease}} CO_2 + 2NH_3 \qquad (9)$$

UREA

is specific for urea. If we use urease to try to catalyze the reaction of a very similar molecule, N-methyl urea, no catalysis is observed:

$$O{=}C\begin{array}{l} \diagup NHCH_3 \\ \diagdown NH_2 \end{array} + H_2O \xrightleftharpoons{\text{urease}} \text{no reaction occurs} \qquad (10)$$

N-METHYL UREA

This suggests that on the surface of the enzyme there is a special arrangement of atoms (belonging to the amino acids of which the protein is constructed) that is just right for attachment of the urea molecule but upon which the methyl urea will not "fit."

Specificity is not always perfect. Sometimes an enzyme will work with any member of a *class* of compounds. For example, some esterases (enzymes that catalyze the reaction of esters with water) will work with numerous esters of similar, but different, structures. Usually, in cases of this kind, one of the members of the substrate class will react faster than the others, so the rates will vary from one substrate to another.

A PRACTICAL APPLICATION OF ENZYME INHIBITION BY A FALSE SUBSTRATE

It is now believed that many of our useful drugs exert their beneficial action by the inhibition of enzyme activity in bacteria. Bacteria such as *staphylococcus* require for their growth the simple organic compound *para*-aminobenzoic acid; they can grow and multiply in the human body because sufficient amounts of this compound occur in blood and the tissues. The control of many diseases caused by these (and other) bacteria was one of the first triumphs of **chemotherapy,*** and the first

---

*Chemotherapy is the control and treatment of disease by synthetic drugs. Most of these are organic compounds, often of remarkably simple structure. Sulfanilamide is one example of an organic compound synthesized by chemists for the treatment of bacterial infections.

compound found to be an effective drug of this type was sulfanilamide:

$$NH_2 \qquad\qquad NH_2$$

para-AMINOBENZOIC ACID   SULFANILAMIDE

It seems reasonable that an enzyme which uses *para*-aminobenzoic acid as a substrate might be "deceived" by sulfanilamide—the two compounds are very similar in size and shape and in many chemical properties. To explain the success of sulfanilamide, it is proposed that the amide can form an enzyme-substrate complex that uses up the active centers normally occupied by the natural substrate.

Usually fairly high concentrations of such a drug are needed for effective control of an infection because the inhibitor (the false substrate) should occupy as many active centers as possible, and also because the natural substrate will probably have a greater affinity for the enzyme. Thus, a high concentration of the false substrate must be used so that the false substrate-enzyme complex will predominate. The bacteria, deprived of a normal metabolic process, cannot grow and multiply. Now the body's defense mechanisms can take over and destroy them.

21-3 THE "NUCLEIC ACIDS," DNA AND RNA, NATURE'S MESSENGERS

So far we have discussed the *composition* of living systems, molecular changes in living systems, and certain *structural features* associated with living systems. But we have not considered one of the most characteristic and still mysterious properties of a living body—its ability to reproduce an organism which is like itself, yet different enough to be a new individual.

An egg cell from a female and a sperm cell from a male meet and immediately growth begins. The "nonliving" chemicals surrounding the now fertilized egg are *organized* and a new *living body* begins to grow. The living body which grows may be a mouse, an elephant, a red-headed human male, or a dark-haired human female. How are the "directions" for the synthesis of an elephant or a mouse or a boy or a girl carried in the egg and sperm cells? Where is the biological pattern which seems to provide a means of organizing nonliving raw materials into a living body? This is a profound and exciting question.

Real progress has been made toward answering it during the last 20 years, progress such as the already mentioned dramatic synthesis of a virus from nucleotides by Drs. Kornberg and Goulian. Let us see if we can use the ideas we have learned to understand what happened in this challenging synthesis of a "living" virus. First we must learn something about the structure of the **"nucleic acids"—DNA** (deoxyribonucleic acid) and **RNA** (ribonucleic acid).

21-3.1 DNA—Its Early History and Significance

DNA is the active biological component which transmits the hereditary characteristics of living organisms. The existence of DNA has been known for a century. It was first isolated in rather impure form as a gelatinous material in 1869 by the German biochemists F. Hoppe-Seyler and F. Miescher.* The name *nucleic acid* is from the name *nuclein,* the substance they first used. DNA's role as a carrier of genetic information was suggested in 1884, but it was not until 1943 that Oswald Avery and his co-workers at Rockefeller Institute provided sound evidence to resolve questions in a confused field. For years biologists have used the term "gene" in describing hereditary processes. At the present time genes have been identified as segments of a very long DNA molecule. DNA is also the living component of a virus. A virus is known to be an active DNA thread covered with a nonactive protective sheath, usually of protein.

The study of DNA was approached like that of any other interesting organic chemical; that is, its structural formula had to be determined. The same principles used to study simpler molecules were used to determine its structure, but the DNA "molecule," because of its tremendous polymeric size, was much more complex and difficult to determine. Many scientists struggled to obtain the structure; a major breakthrough was made in 1953 when J. D. Watson, Maurice Wilkins, and Francis Crick established with reasonable certainty the now accepted structure of DNA. Their work was recognized by a Nobel Prize in 1962.

21-3.2 The Structure of DNA—Nucleotides

The most important structural feature of DNA is that it consists of two very long thin polymeric chains twisted about each other in the form of a regular **double helix** (see Figure 21-2). These chains are made up of nucleotide units fastened together. The nucleotide units themselves are not unduly complex; in fact, four different nucleotide units appear to provide the basis for transmitting all necessary hereditary information. A nucleotide unit includes a phosphoric acid molecule to which a sugar molecule, deoxyribose, is linked by loss of water:

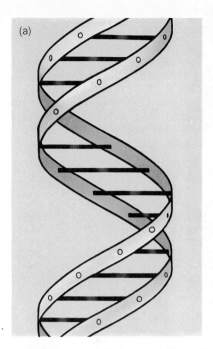

(a)

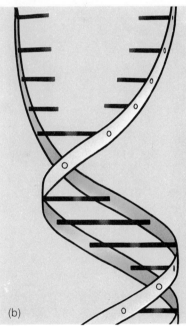

(b)

Fig. 21-2 The double helix of DNA: (a) coiled, (b) partially uncoiled.

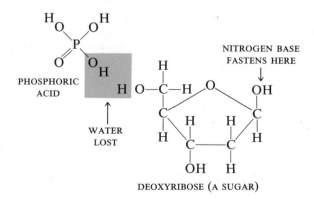

PHOSPHORIC ACID

WATER LOST

NITROGEN BASE FASTENS HERE

DEOXYRIBOSE (A SUGAR)

*See E. A. Mirsky, "The Discovery of DNA," *Scientific American,* **218,** 78 (June 1968).

Fig. 21-3 The formation of a nucleotide of DNA. The complete unit represents one nucleotide.

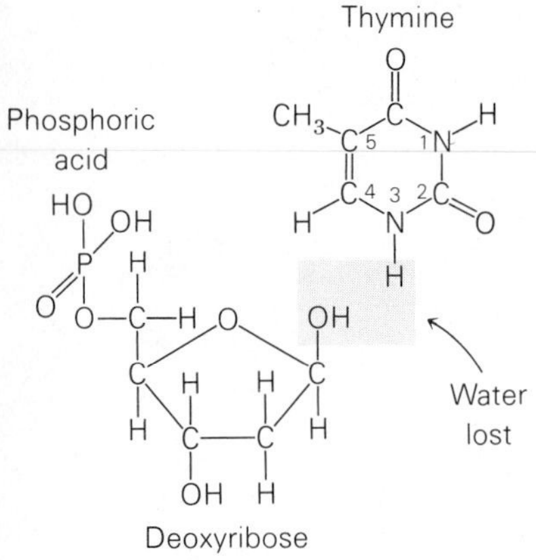

To the resulting structure one of four nitrogen bases is linked also by loss of water. The base thymine can serve as an illustration (see Figure 21-3). Four different nucleotides are found in DNA. Notice in Figure 21-4 that different nucleotides differ only in the identity of the base linked to the deoxyribose phosphate structure. The phosphate and sugar molecules in each nucleotide are *identical* to those found in every other nucleotide of DNA. The bases attached to these groups differentiate the four distinct nucleotides.

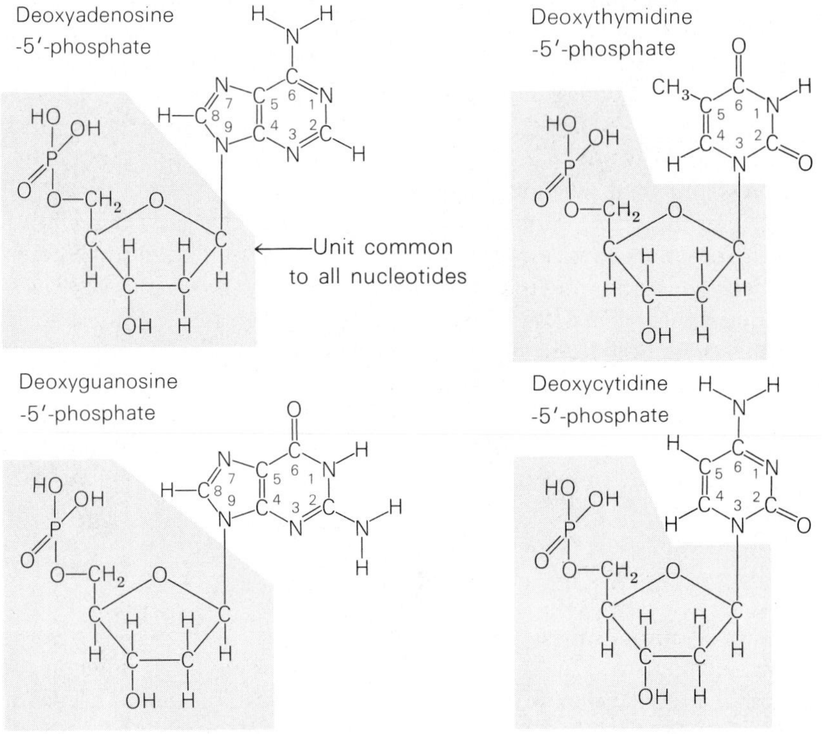

Fig. 21-4 The four nucleotide building blocks of DNA.

21-3.3 The Single Helix

Nucleotides can also link together under the influence of a catalyst by losing one water molecule. A polymeric unit results (see Figure 21-5). The resulting polymeric chain, made by removing a water molecule from between nucleotide units, is shown in Figure 21-5. Notice that each chain is composed of a *backbone* consisting of sugar molecules linked together by phosphate groups in a very regular fashion. The backbone of the chain is seen as the shaded portion of Figure 21-6. Attached to each sugar molecule is *one* of the nitrogen-containing bases—adenine, cytosine, guanine, or thymine. The method of fastening these bases to the chain is seen in Figure 21-6. Thymine (abbreviated T) and cytosine (C) are *single, six-membered ring structures containing two nitrogens per ring.* They are of a chemical family called **pyrimidines.** Adenine (A) and guanine (G) are *double ring structures, each having one five- and one six-membered ring, and each ring containing two nitrogen atoms.* These larger bases are of a family called **purines.**

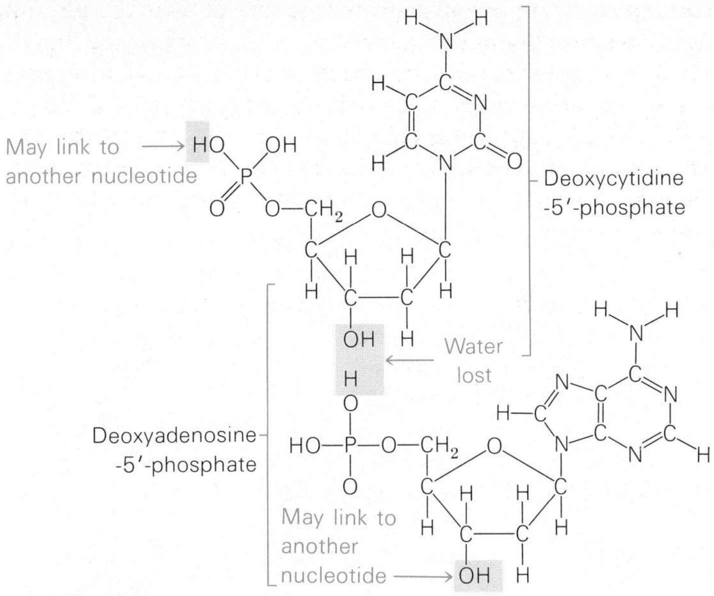

Fig. 21-5 Linkage of nucleotide units in a DNA chain.

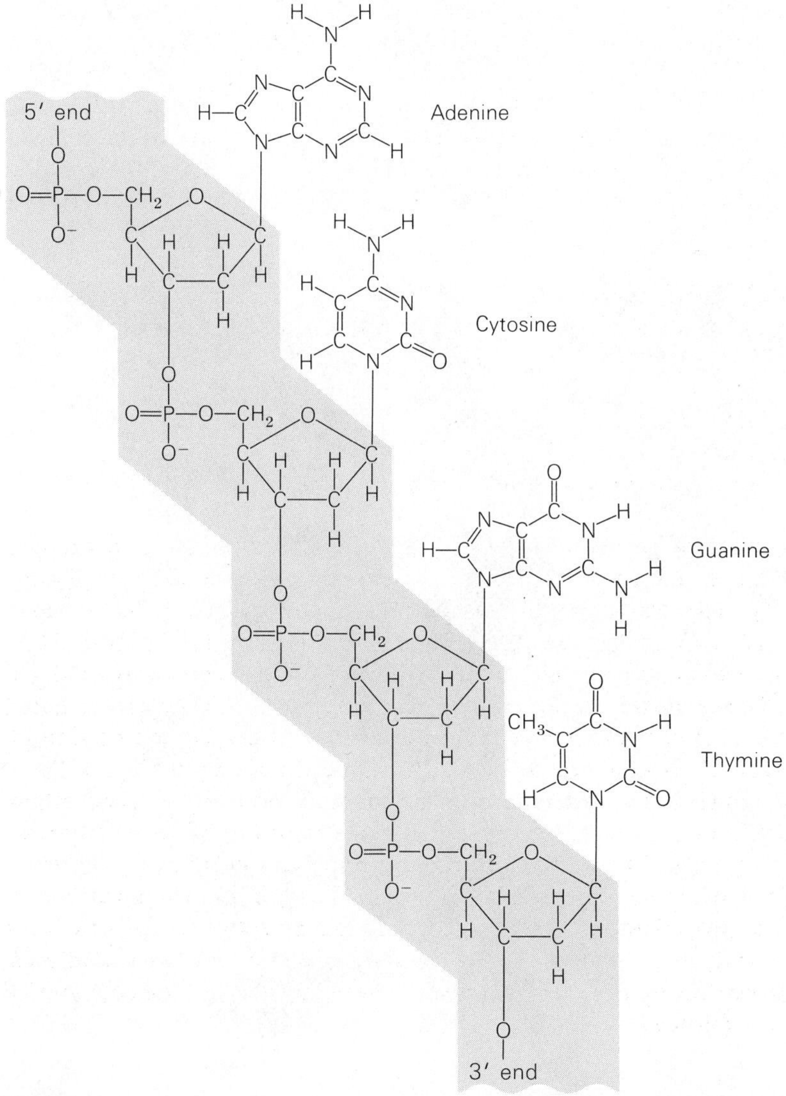

May link to → another nucleotide

—Deoxycytidine-5′-phosphate

Water lost

Deoxyadenosine-5′-phosphate

May link to another nucleotide →

Fig. 21-6 A section of the DNA chain.

5′ end

Adenine

Cytosine

Guanine

Thymine

3′ end

These four base molecules identify the four nucleotides used as starting materials for DNA synthesis. These long polymeric chains formed by linking nucleotides assume a helical form with different nucleotides making up the chain (*i.e.*, different bases attached to the backbone). The order in which nucleotides are linked provides the means of communicating hereditary information. Or, *the hereditary information is transmitted by the order in which the bases are attached to the backbone of deoxyribose-phosphate.* The purine and pyrimidine bases are flat, relatively water-insoluble molecules which tend to stack above each other perpendicular to the direction of the helical axis of the backbone (see Figure 21-7). The order of the purine and pyrimidine bases along the backbone chain varies greatly from one DNA molecule to another. Each carries a definite message.

21-3.4 The Double Helix—Template Action

Two such chains joined by hydrogen bonds between base pairs give a double helix. The convincing experimental data for this structure is from X-ray diffraction studies. A recent electron micrograph (see Figure 21-8) provides a visual image which appears to be in agreement. Because of the physical sizes of the bases, adenine (A) is always bonded to thymine (T) and cytosine (C) to guanine (G) (see Figure 21-9). These pairing rules restrict the possible sequence of bases on two intertwined chains. If we have a sequence of ATGTC on one chain, the complementary chain must be TACAG. The two polynucleotide chains must

Fig. 21-7 (Left) A space-filling model of DNA.

Fig. 21-8 (Right) An electron micrograph of a short section of a DNA molecule. This electron micrograph is consistent with the established model. Note double helix in picture. Courtesy J. Griffith, California Institute of Technology.

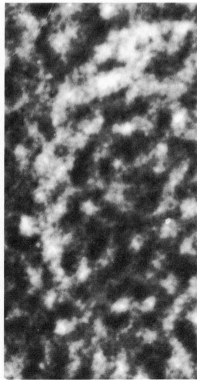

be similar but running in reverse order; one is a **template** or mold for the synthesis of the other.

Genetic information is carried by the sequence of the four bases A, G, C, and T. Perhaps you will worry that having only four nitrogen bases on the DNA molecule will limit the amount of information carried, but such fears are groundless. The number of possible arrangements is 4^n, where n is the number of nucleotide units (*i.e.*, number of separate base units) in a molecule of DNA. Since each molecule is very long, many arrangements are possible. DNA molecules have an average molecular weight in excess of 10^6. That means there are at least 1,500 nucleotide units in the chain; hence, *the possible number of different molecules of DNA is $4^{1,500}$, more than the number of different molecules of DNA that have existed in all of the chromosomes present since the origin of life.* The **genetic "code"** is the sequence of bases on the backbone chain. Hereditary information is passed on in this way.

The next question of significance is: how does this order within the DNA molecule pass on biological information? The current view of this process is that the hydrogen bonds holding the DNA chains together are weak enough to break under certain conditions, permitting the chains to uncoil [see Figure 21-2(b)]. Each helix can then serve as a template for combining and organizing smaller nucleotide units into the complementary helix for that chain. One chain determines the order of new chains made from it. The nucleotide units are the raw material.

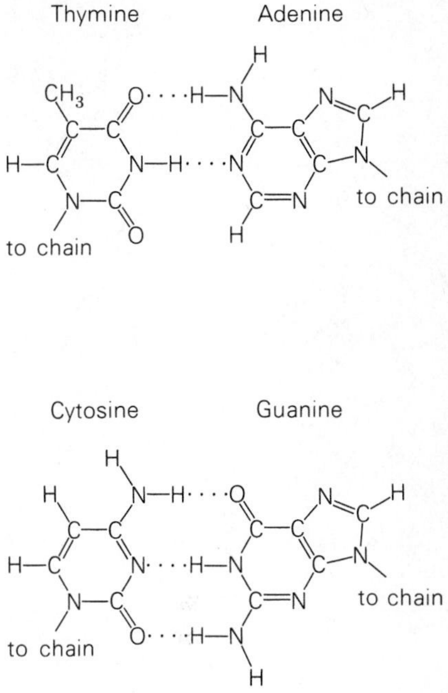

21-3.5 The Synthesis of a Virus

We are now in a position to understand the experiments of Kornberg and Goulian described at the beginning of this chapter. These chemists took from the shelf the four essential, nonliving nucleotides (Figure 21-4). They then added DNA polymerase, a *catalyst* which *accelerates* the linking of nucleotide units by removing water. They then added some natural DNA to serve as a template. The result was a strand consisting of about 6,000 nucleotide units, the *mirror image* of the strand in the original helix. Then, using the mirror-image molecule as a template, the process was repeated to produce a precise but *synthetic* duplicate of the natural DNA molecule. The result was a virus which could attack bacteria and kill them as effectively as the natural DNA (see Figure 21-10, page 540).

Using the procedure described above, it was possible to assemble a DNA molecule from nonliving nucleotides using a natural DNA molecule as a pattern. While this accomplishment is a major one, it represents only the first step in the long process of unraveling the mysteries surrounding genetic information transfer. Making one DNA molecule like another is a much easier job than directing the synthesis of a complete mouse or a complete elephant from foodstuffs and water. We return to the realm of mystery. How does the DNA direct the synthesis of a creature 3 cm tall rather than one 5 metres tall? Honestly we do not know; but some interesting facts and theories have been assembled. The key to the more complex operation seems to be the compound called **ribonucleic acid** or **RNA**.

Fig. 21-9 Hydrogen bonding to link bases of two helical DNA chains.

21-3.6 RNA

RNA is a very close relative of DNA, but it differs from DNA in two important ways. First, the sugar in the chain is ribose,

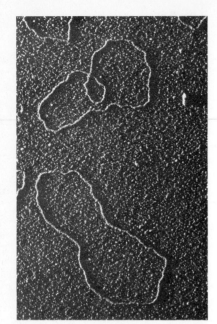

not deoxyribose,

(*deoxy-* means "oxygen removed"). Second, the thymine on the chain,

is replaced by uracil,

Most RNA does *not* exist as double-helical strands, but rather as non-hydrogen-bonded, single *polyribonucleotide* strands.

What is the function of RNA and how does it work? According to molecular biologists, the process can be *described* in simple terms: DNA directs the synthesis of RNA which in turn directs the synthesis of all proteins produced by the cell.* (For example, the human body is 64 percent water, 15 percent protein, 15 percent fat, 5 percent inorganic materials, and 1 percent carbohydrate.) Protein structures are the key to life since much of the fat and carbohydrate represent a reserve energy supply. People are proteins. There are as many as 100,000 different kinds of protein in a single human body, but only 20 amino acids are used in building these proteins. Modern ideas on the way in which RNA functions to direct protein synthesis can best be discussed in your biology course where more information on biological structures will be available.

*Recent results indicate that in certain cancer-producing viruses, genetic information flows "in reverse" from RNA to DNA. See H. M. Temin, *Scientific American,* **226,** 25 (January 1972).

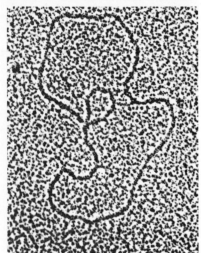

Fig. 21-10 Natural DNA (top) and synthetic DNA (bottom).

The field of molecular biology is a complex one which is closely related to the fields of medicine, chemistry, and general biology. Work is being developed rapidly.

The ideas about template structure developed in an analysis of the operation of DNA and RNA have been used successfully against certain forms of cancer. By putting a fluorine in the 5 position on uracil,

5-FLUORO-URACIL

the molecule is changed just enough to block the use of uracil in cancer growth and destroy enzyme catalysts.

The modern approach to disease is closely related to structural biochemistry. Many more examples could be cited.

21-4 HIGHLIGHTS

Living organisms are complex chemical factories employing and synthesizing the same types of molecules studied in Chapter 19. Biologically significant molecules are frequently large polymeric units made by joining simpler units. **Starches, cellulose, fats,** and **proteins** are typical of these large molecules.

The material of which genes are made, **DNA,** is the material by which hereditary information is passed from generation to generation. DNA has a "backbone" of alternating sugar and phosphate units to which is attached at each sugar unit one of four nitrogen bases— thymine, cytosine, adenine, and guanine. The hereditary information is transmitted by the order in which bases are attached to the backbone of the DNA molecule. This is known as the **genetic code.** A material called **RNA** appears to be important in transforming the information on the DNA strand into chains of proteins and into complex biological units.

We still have a long way to go in answering the questions concerning heredity and life, but progress is being made. Perhaps we will someday understand the chemistry of life itself.

Certainly the facts as we know them require the asking of the most basic questions.

WILLIAM D. RUCKELSHAUS **(Administrator of Environmental
Protection Agency, 1969–1973)**

THE NITROGEN FAMILY: 22
FRIEND OR FOE?

After many thousands of years, a clean, deep lake becomes a swamp through the natural process of eutrophication.

BUMPER STICKERS ASK, "IS DILUTION THE SOLUTION TO pollution?" Household cleaning products advertise themselves to be phosphate-free and biodegradable. Some automobiles chastely declare, "This is a propane-powered vehicle which produces no smog." The news media proclaim, "First stage smog alert," which means that all athletic activity is stopped at schools in the affected area. We are all familiar with pollution of our planet and most of us are concerned, since it is the only planet we have.

What is to be done about the pollution situation is of concern to citizens, chemists, and legislators. As in most chemical processes, the more that is known about the reactions which cause pollution, the more intelligently and perhaps even successfully the problems can be attacked. Since nitrogen, phosphorus, and arsenic frequently play the part of villain in the pollution drama, we will have a look at their role.

On August 4, 1970, the prestigious *New York Times* published an editorial entitled, "Deadly Detergents." The implication to the reader was clear: phosphates are deadly chemicals which have no real place in human life. Newspapers carry reports on the concentration of nitrogen oxides in the air whenever the subject of air pollution arises. Arsenic has long been known as a deadly poison and has been the stealthy weapon used in more than one murder. All of this is bad news. What do the elements nitrogen, phosphorus, and arsenic have in common? A quick glance at the periodic table shows that all three are members of Group Five, the nitrogen family. The reports seem to suggest that this is not a very friendly part of the periodic table. Perhaps we should probe more deeply—are the elements in the nitrogen family friend or foe?

22-1 PHOSPHORUS AND THE ENVIRONMENT

In Chapter 21 we learned that phosphates link to ribose or deoxyribose to make the backbone structures for DNA and RNA. All of the basic information for heredity as well as for protein synthesis—for life itself—is contained in giant molecules which are rich in both phosphorus and nitrogen. Phosphates and nitrogen compounds are *essential* for all forms of life. Why then are these otherwise friendly elements cast in their present role as villains?

22-1.1 Phosphorus Pollution and Eutrophication

The answer to this question is based on the role of phosphates in promoting deterioration of lakes and streams through excessive plant growth. This is the process called **eutrophication.** It is a natural process, characteristic of every body of water. Here is the normal pattern: a clear, clean body of water formed from melting snow picks up a few plants, including algae and bacteria. Soon fish and insects appear, followed by more algae, bigger aquatic plants, and bigger fish. As time goes on, organic materials from dead plants and animals begin to accumulate in the bottom of the water. Plant remains and soil are washed in by streams. Bigger plants grow. As thousands of years pass, the deposit on the bottom gets thicker; the lake becomes more and more shallow. The temperature of the water increases, and its dissolved oxygen content decreases. Ultimately, the plant life changes character and plants begin to grow up out of the water and into the air. After many thousands of years the original clean, deep lake has become a swamp. The lake has undergone the process of eutrophication. This process existed long before detergents or even people existed. We have not been able to stop eutrophication, but we have been able to speed it up. Therein lies the problem.

As any farmer, gardener, or student of biology knows, phosphorus and nitrogen represent two of the three most important fertilizer elements used. The reason for their importance is clear from a casual review of Chapter 21. If appropriate compounds of nitrogen and phosphorus are provided in large amounts, and *if other conditions are favorable* (*e.g.*, lots of water, CO_2, Ca^{2+}, Mg^{2+}, and so on), plant growth is luxuriant. This is true whether one is dealing with a crop of corn in Iowa or a "crop" of algae in a Wisconsin lake. In our present scale of values the corn crop is good and the algae crop is bad. People, looking superficially at the problem of the lake, correlate algae and fertilizer materials and condemn phosphorus and nitrogen in general. The term "deadly phosphates" appears. A simplistic solution for a complex problem is suggested. The chances are that we will suffer while we grope for sound information. This is not to belittle the seriousness of the problem. Good estimates indicate that the shallow western basin of Lake Erie has aged an equivalent of 15,000 years over the last half century. Sewage, garbage, and all manner of debris are accumulating in the bottom of the lake while great mats of decaying, smelly algae accumulate on the water surface. What are these mats of algae and why do they appear?

Algae are plants which live suspended in water. They can make a body of water become green like a thick pea soup or even blood-red in color. The colors of Green Bay in Lake Michigan and of the Red

Fig. 22-1 Masses of algae along a lake shore.

Sea in the Middle East arise from the algae suspended in the water. Algae in great masses are among the most obnoxious plants in our lakes and streams. They have come to be the symbol of polluted water. Our feelings toward great masses of algae are well founded. As heavy mats of algae grow and then die, the dead cells either settle slowly to the bottom or are blown onto the shore in great stinking masses. Bacteria attacking the dead cells use up large quantities of dissolved oxygen. Fish and desirable aquatic plants begin to suffer and die from toxins and from lack of oxygen. Soon the lake is in a mess. Everyone agrees that the results of excessive algal growth are very bad. The problem deserves our best efforts. The disagreement arises over what should be done about the problem.

22-1.2 Detergents and Eutrophication

In the minds of many people the problem is simple. Just take phosphates out of our modern detergents and the problem will go away. Unfortunately the problem of pollution control goes beyond detergents and soaps.

"Algal blooms" are almost as old as recorded history. In the Bible, Exodus 7:19–21, an apparent algal bloom in the Nile River is described in some detail. It was interpreted as a divine warning of impending catastrophe. We read, "and all the water . . . changed to blood. The fish . . . died, and the river smelt so foul that the Egyptians found it impossible to drink its water." In 77 A.D., Pliny the Elder noted that "waters in a lake near Babylon are red for eleven days in the summer." Red tides still plague our beaches.

While ancient blooms were occasional problems, the introduction of modern sewage systems changed an occasional problem to a modern nightmare. The change occurred long before detergents were introduced in the late nineteen forties. The appearance of serious pollution problems and algal blooms correlates well with the practice of dumping untreated sewage into rivers and streams. A report in the transactions of the Wisconsin Academy of Science for 1889,* some fifty years before the widespread use of detergents, describes problems in the lakes of Madison, Wisconsin, which sound like today's problems at their worst. Even Lake Erie suffered a very serious algal bloom in 1928, some twenty years before detergents appeared. Today certain areas have outlawed detergents containing phosphates. The data accumulated so far do not indicate a spectacular increase in water quality in many areas; a recent report,† however, has indicated that a particularly obnoxious blue-green alga did not appear in Lake Onondoga in New York after Syracuse, N.Y. limited detergent phosphate to 8.7 percent. Green algae were present, however. On the other hand, some European countries such as Sweden and Britain feel that control of phosphates in detergents is not a profitable approach to the eutrophication problem.

These statements bring into sharp focus a statement made in an editorial in *Science* in 1970 written by Philip H. Abelson. Dr. Abelson

*W. Trelease, "The *Working* of the Madison Lakes," Wisconsin Academy of Science, Arts, and Letters, 7:121–129 (1889).

†C. B. Murphy, *Science*, **182,** 379 (October 26, 1973).

wrote, "Elimination of phosphates from detergents would not solve the eutrophication problem. There are too many other sources of these chemicals in municipal, industrial, and agricultural wastes. The treatment of municipal wastes is of particular importance in minimizing eutrophication. If these were managed properly, phosphates arising from human wastes and detergents would be simultaneously eliminated. Effective treatment would attenuate the flow of organic matter into lakes."*

22-1.3   Limiting Factors in Plant Growth

Do the facts support Dr. Abelson's position? Let us review the information available. It is well known to biologists that algae *growing in water* need at least 19 other elements for effective growth. These, in order of quantities needed, are carbon, nitrogen, potassium, magnesium, phosphorus, sulfur, sodium, silicon, calcium, iron, vanadium, boron, molybdenum, manganese, zinc, cadmium, copper, cobalt, and chlorine. All are not needed in equal quantities; large quantities of carbon are needed and only traces of cobalt. Still if *any element* is not present in *quantities demanded by the growing plant,* growth will be inhibited. This substance will become the *limiting element* in plant growth. An average algae plant uses 106 atoms of carbon to every 16 atoms of nitrogen and one of phosphorus. If a lake contained a carbon to nitrogen to phosphorus ratio of 106 to 16 to 0.1, the addition of phosphate would have spectacular effects on algal growth if other elements (including C and N) were present in adequate absolute amounts. If, however, the C:N:P ratio were 106 to 16 to 16, addition of phosphates would not alter the growth rate. Another element or elements would be the limiting factor.

The suggestion that phosphate be controlled is a reasonable one, since CO_2 is available in the air and in most lakes as a result of the decomposition of organic matter of all types by bacteria. Nitrogen supply is difficult to control since some of the most obnoxious blue-green algae can obtain nitrogen supplies from nitrogen in the air. In average lake water, most of the other elements are usually present in adequate amounts as a result of the dissolving of soil materials. It then seems logical to control algal growth by controlling phosphorus supply. Most reasonable people can agree that if phosphorus supply were reduced *well below the limiting level,* algal growth would be checked. The vigorous debate surrounding water clean-up centers on the effectiveness of various methods for controlling phosphorus levels. A sizable body of information suggests that removal of phosphates from detergents will still give water with a phosphate content which is well above the level needed to support vigorous algal growth. This is the point made by Dr. Abelson. A little arithmetic will help establish his point.

Let us start with people. Physiologists tell us that each person consumes and excretes about 1.4 pounds of phosphorus per year. With about 203 million people in the U.S.† this amounts to about 284 million

---

*P. H. Abelson, "Excessive Emotion about Detergents," *Science,* **169,** 1033 (September 11, 1970). Copyright 1970 by the American Association for the Advancement of Science.

†1970 Census of U.S.

pounds of phosphorus in sewage which result directly from the life processes of human beings. Production figures for phosphorus show that about 500 million pounds of phosphorus went into detergents of all kinds in 1970. Municipal sewage must therefore contain about 780 million pounds of phosphorus per year. Our arithmetic now shows that about 64 percent of known sewage phosphorus came from detergents and 36 percent from people.* Unfortunately this total sewage phosphate is estimated to contribute only about half of the total phosphate going into our rivers and streams each year. The remainder is from agricultural and industrial runoff—from fields, feed lots, and factories. Thus, about 32 percent of the phosphorus in streams and lakes is from detergents. Most authorities agree pretty well up to here.†

At this point people disagree sharply on two issues. These are

(1) Will removal of the detergent phosphate remove enough phosphorus to have a significant effect on lake eutrophication?
(2) What will be the environmental effect of substitutes used in place of modern-day detergents?

We have virtually no information on question (2). Experience has shown that reagents which appear to be perfectly safe and harmless when used in small amounts can become monsters when usage increases, and many substitutes are not without their problems even now. (This, in fact, was the history of phosphate usage.)

On the matter of question (1), a number of authorities have provided impressive calculations which indicate that removal of detergent phosphates will still leave phosphate levels which are much too high for the control of algae in rivers and lakes. Other people dispute this answer. In actual fact, the answer seems to depend on the lake or stream being considered. The problem is a complex one. We are sure of one thing—simplistic solutions to complex problems may turn out to be harmful because they direct our attention to trivial aspects of the situation. Most people agree that real progress on the question of clean water will be made if we concentrate on the construction of complete sewage treatment facilities which can remove up to 95 percent of the phosphorus as well as nitrogen and organic materials from the water. The technology to return water of extremely high quality to streams is at hand and can be operated now at reasonable economic costs.‡ Use of such technology plus farming and industrial practices which minimize runoff into streams will go a long way

---

*The authors are grateful to Dr. A. D. F. Toy for much of the information here. A monograph by Dr. Toy on "Phosphorus in Everyday Living" is available from the American Chemical Society, Washington, D.C.

†An independent estimate suggests that 30 to 40 percent of the phosphorus going into streams and lakes comes from detergents. [R. D. Grundy, *Environ. Sci. Technol.*, **5**, 1184 (1971).]

‡Such a plant is in operation at Lake Tahoe in California. Costs of amortization and operation were estimated at less than $1.50 per month per person. The plant has been described in both technical and popular reports. Information is available from R. L. Culp, South Tahoe Public Utility District, P.O. Box AU, South Lake Tahoe, California 95705. It is interesting to note, however, that in a deep lake with slow water turnover, the 5 percent phosphorus which remains after treatment can ultimately be a very serious problem. For this reason, the "pure" water from the treatment plant is never returned to Lake Tahoe, but is pumped out of the valley.

Fig. 22-2 Waste-treatment plant at Lake Tahoe.

toward cleaning up our streams and lakes. One should remember, however, that the treatment of water consumes energy. Work must be done to separate the components of a mixture. Reversal of the "randomness driving force" requires work. Since the generation of energy from fossil or nuclear fuels produces pollutants such as SO_2 in the air and radioactive nuclei in water, even this solution is not perfect. More research for a workable long-term solution is *desperately* needed; chemists, biologists, and engineers now and in the future can contribute to this research.

In 1972 the U.S. Congress passed the Federal Water Pollution Control Act Amendments of 1972, Public Law 92-500, which asserts the desire of the Congress to work toward clean water in the U.S. Unfortunately the bill does not provide sound provisions for research to give long-range solutions. An interesting discussion of the testimony and of the arguments pro and con on this law is available.* Wise legislation and the commitment of federal resources to permit the application of better and better technology to water treatment can guarantee us an improvement in water quality. Emotional attacks on phosphorus can only confuse the issue and impede progress. To those who know, phosphorus is a friend to all forms of life. Sometimes it is too helpful to some organisms and causes problems for us, but without some of it, we would be lost.

22-2 NITROGEN AND THE ENVIRONMENT

Nitrogen compounds appear as gases, liquids, and water-soluble solids. For this reason nitrogen is frequently mentioned in discussions of both air and water quality.

22-2.1 Nitrogen and Water Quality

Nitrogen, like phosphorus, is an essential element for plant growth. The nitrogen supply, like the phosphorus supply, frequently limits the

*See David E. Gushee, "Clean Water," *Chem. Tech.* (June 1973), page 334. (Published by the American Chemical Society, 1155 16th Street N.W., Washington, D.C. 22036.)

growth of algae in streams and lakes. Addition of nitrogen in the form of sewage or discharges from farm and industry promotes eutrophication. Of this there can be no question. On the other hand, control of the total nitrogen supply is not a realistic procedure for controlling algae growth. This is so since some species of algae can "fix" nitrogen from the air. Because of this unusual ability, such algae have an unlimited supply of nitrogen as long as air is available. We can do little to deny them nitrogen. Instead popular attention has been focused on denying them phosphorus. Complete sewage and waste processing is the only realistic long-term answer.* Even this answer will fail if the population in an area grows without restraint.†

22-2.2 Nitrogen and Air Quality

In any discussion of air quality standards, the allowable nitrogen oxide level is usually given. Why? Why is nitrogen oxide important in air quality control? To understand this question, let us review several very important processes which we have considered earlier.

Oxygen and nitrogen in the air can react in accordance with the equation:

$$\text{energy} + N_2 + O_2 \rightleftharpoons 2NO \qquad (1)$$

Applying Le Chatelier's principle to this process, we find that N_2 and O_2 should combine at high temperatures to give NO. We further note that as the temperature falls, NO should decompose to N_2 and O_2. The overall forward reaction occurs naturally as a result of lightning flashes in thunderstorms. The NO is converted to NO_2 by oxygen and the NO_2 is washed out of the air as *very dilute* nitric and nitrous acids:

$$2NO_2 + H_2O \longrightarrow HNO_3 + HNO_2 \qquad (2)$$

Plants benefit; they get nitrate and nitrite fertilizer in a very usable form.

In an automobile cylinder, temperatures can also go up to very high values as a result of the combustion of fuel.‡ Both N_2 and O_2 are present in the air used to burn the fuel. Hence the two gases

---

*The goal of the Clean Water Act of 1972 is zero discharge of pollutants into streams by 1985.

†Lake Michigan poses a special problem. Because of the intensive agriculture, the large number of people around its shores, and the very slow circulation of its water, even 5 percent of the phosphorus from domestic sewage plus all of the phosphorus from agricultural runoff will give a long-term problem. Research is urgently needed if Lake Michigan is to be preserved.

‡As we predicted from Le Chatelier's principle and the equation

$$\text{energy} + N_2 + O_2 \rightleftharpoons 2NO$$

yields of NO go up as combustion temperatures rise. Temperatures in the cylinder are higher if the entering air and fuel have been preheated. Such preheating is done by compressing the gases in the cylinder. Higher compression ratios give higher combustion temperatures, higher engine efficiency, and, unfortunately, more NO.

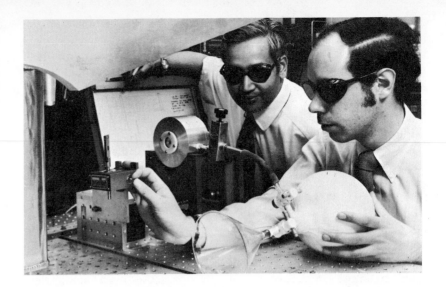

Fig. 22-3 Laser-light absorption technique used to measure the amount of NO in an air sample. The air sample in the round flask (right) enters the cylindrical absorption cell (center) where it contacts an infrared laser beam. The quantity of NO is plotted on the recorder at the left.

combine to give very small, but still significant quantities of NO. The mixture is then cooled rapidly as it is discharged from the cylinders into the atmosphere. At the low temperatures of the atmosphere, NO is unstable but the decomposition process to N_2 and O_2 is *very slow*. The final result is a gradual buildup of NO in the atmospheres of cities where large numbers of automobiles clog the streets and freeways and air circulation is poor.

What happens to the NO as it accumulates in the air? To answer this question let us first study NO contained in a tank. If the tank valve is opened, the colorless NO is rapidly converted to brown NO_2 as the NO mixes with the air. The equation for the process is

$$2NO + O_2 \longrightarrow 2NO_2 \tag{3}$$

Kinetic studies show that the rate of this process is given by the expression

$$\text{rate of oxidation of NO} = k[NO]^2[O_2] \tag{4}$$

The rate equation suggests that the actual mechanism involves a collision between *two* NO molecules and one O_2 molecule. Such an event occurs frequently when the concentration of NO in the air is high, as, for example, when a stream of NO escapes into the air. On the other hand, if NO molecules are very few and far between, as in urban air where the concentration of NO may be 0.5 parts per million, the probability that two NO molecules will collide simultaneously with an oxygen molecule is *very* low; so low in fact, that the rate of conversion of NO to NO_2 by direct reaction with oxygen is too slow to be important. In pure air, in the dark, the NO would remain as a highly dilute and probably relatively harmless pollutant. Trouble starts when the sun shines on polluted air containing chemicals such as NO, CO, and unburned gasoline from automobile exhaust. Under these conditions the very dilute NO is converted to NO_2 at a fairly rapid rate. The process is a complex one and many different types of reaction can bring about this oxidation; one series of steps to illustrate the process is shown on page 552. As NO oxidation proceeds, the air contains a mixture of NO and NO_2 which is usually referred to as NO_x (x lies somewhere between 1 and 2). Since only a very small amount of NO_x is formed by any one car, no problem can develop unless the number of cars per square mile is high and air circulation is low. Under these conditions even the very small amounts of NO_x generated by each car can develop into a problem.*

Why is NO_x bad? The question of direct damage to humans resulting from commonly observable levels of NO_x in the atmosphere is still being debated. High concentrations of NO_x are known to be toxic, but we do not know the effects of NO_x itself in very low concentrations. There are, however, *indirect* bad effects of NO_x which are established with some certainty. NO_x is listed as a major cause of "photochemical smog," which is responsible for a reduction in visibility, crop damage, cracking of rubber, and the production of eye and lung irritations. The role of NO_x in smog production is a complicated one. The most obnoxious gas in the NO_x mixture seems to be the NO_2.

It is quite generally agreed that the process of photochemical smog production is initiated when NO_2 is acted on by sunlight to give NO and atomic oxygen:

$$NO_2 + \text{sunlight (or } h\nu) \longrightarrow NO + O \qquad (5)$$

This atomic oxygen is very reactive and can act on many different materials in the atmosphere to give strongly oxidizing species. For example, most of the atomic oxygen reacts with readily available molecular oxygen to give ozone:

$$O + O_2 + M \longrightarrow O_3 + M \qquad (6)$$

*Again we see the problems of unlimited population growth.

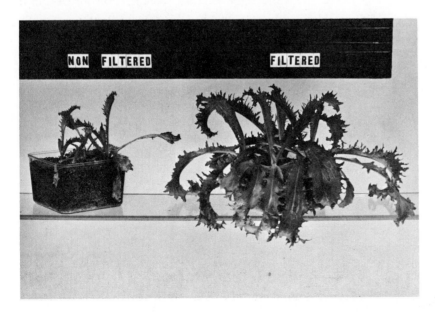

Fig. 22-4 The effect of air pollution on endive plants. (Left) Plant injured by air pollution. (Right) Healthy plant.

In this equation, M is a third body which will carry away excess kinetic energy and permit the O and O_2 to combine. Without M the resulting O_3 would have so much vibrational energy that it would fly apart.

The ozone produced in this process is also extremely reactive. For example, it can oxidize NO_2 to give an unusually powerful oxidizing species of formula NO_3:

$$O_3 + NO_2 \longrightarrow NO_3 + O_2 \qquad (7)$$

Ozone itself is also decomposed by sunlight to give oxygen and a super-reactive oxygen atom (an oxygen atom with electrons in higher energy levels):

$$O_3 + \text{sunlight} \longrightarrow O_2 + O^* \text{ (super-reactive, excited atom)} \qquad (8)$$

This very reactive oxygen atom can react with H_2O to initiate a chain process for oxidizing dilute NO to NO_2. One set of equations suggested for the conversion begins as follows:

$$O^* + H_2O \longrightarrow 2HO \cdot \qquad (9)$$

The resulting $HO \cdot$ has one unpaired electron and is called a **free radical;** it is very reactive and can oxidize CO to CO_2 and H.

$$HO \cdot + CO \longrightarrow H + CO_2 \qquad (10)$$

Then the H reacts:

$$H + O_2 + M \longrightarrow HO_2 + M \qquad (11)$$

$$HO_2 + NO \longrightarrow NO_2 + HO \cdot \qquad (12)$$

The resulting $HO \cdot$ can again combine with CO to continue the conversion of NO to NO_2 in a chain reaction. Note that this process also generates other reactive species such as HO_2 which can attack organic molecules in the air directly. So far we have found that the photochemical decomposition of NO_2 can give rise to O, O_3, O^*, HO_2, NO_3, and HO. All of these can attack normally inert gasoline hydrocarbons in the air. As an example, consider their reactions with propylene,

$$\underset{\displaystyle H}{\overset{\displaystyle H \quad H \quad H}{H-C=C-C-H}} :$$

$$O + H_2C-CH-CH_3 \longrightarrow HO \cdot + CH_2=CH-\dot{C}H_2 \qquad (13)$$

Note that two very reactive *free radicals* are formed. With the other oxidants, reactive products are also generated:

$$O_3 + H_2C=CH-CH_3 \longrightarrow \underset{\displaystyle O-O-O}{CH_3-CH-CH_2} \qquad (14)$$

AN OZONIDE

$$HO_2 + H_2C=CH-CH_3 \longrightarrow HO_2CH_2-\overset{\cdot}{C}H-CH_3 \qquad (15)$$

FREE RADICAL

$$NO_3 + H_2C=CH-CH_3 \longrightarrow HONO_2 + H_2C=CH-\overset{\cdot}{C}H_2 \quad (16)$$

FREE RADICAL

All of these products are reactive and can be converted to unpleasant materials. One of the most obnoxious and unpleasant materials in smog is a substance called peroxyacetylnitrate or (PAN). It has the formula

$$R-\overset{\overset{\displaystyle O}{\|}}{C}OO-N\overset{\nearrow O}{\underset{\searrow O}{}}$$

It is made by reactions which begin with the last member on our list of reactive oxidizers, the HO· radical. The HO· radical will attack even saturated hydrocarbons in a complex process to give a peroxy radical:

$$n\text{HO·} + RH \longrightarrow R-\overset{\overset{\displaystyle O}{\|}}{\underset{O_2^{\cdot}}{C}} + \text{other products} \qquad (17)$$

PEROXY RADICAL

$$R-\overset{\overset{\displaystyle O}{\|}}{\underset{O_2^{\cdot}}{C}} + NO_2 \longrightarrow R-\overset{\overset{\displaystyle O}{\|}}{C}OO-N\overset{\nearrow O}{\underset{\searrow O}{}} \qquad (18)$$

PEROXY RADICAL   (PAN) = TROUBLE

As you can see, the actual process to generate photochemical smog is a complex one. It is even more complex than our analysis shows. Much is still not understood. It does appear, however, that a major part of the process starts when sunlight shines on polluted air containing NO and

Fig. 22-5 Pinto bean plants exposed to 5 ppm (PAN) for 10 minutes. The plant on the left was in the light during exposure; the plant on the right was in the dark.

NO_2. The NO_2 breaks up to give NO and a very reactive oxygen atom. This oxygen atom goes on to generate more powerful oxidizing agents such as ozone which then attack hydrocarbons to produce *very* obnoxious chemicals. When such materials accumulate in stagnant air, life can become very unpleasant. This is photochemical smog in a nutshell.

Fig. 22-6 In this smog chamber, high intensity lamps simulate sunlight. The importance of gasoline composition and vehicle emissions in photochemical smog formation can be evaluated.

What can be done about it? One obvious answer would be to eliminate the automobile, but to Americans this is like suggesting suicide as a cure for a toothache. Even going back to the horse would create its own special pollution problem. Congress wrestled with the question and came up with the Clean Air Act of 1970, but this act does not solve the problem. It only demands that it be solved. No real provision for developing the new technology needed to meet the standards has been made. The result has been constant controversy between the Environmental Protection Agency, charged with enforcing the act, and various industrial and political groups who have had to deal with the problems of putting the new standards into effect. A summary of some of the problems is given in a review* by Dr. Noel de Nevers who has seen the controversy from both sides. Newspapers throughout the country are carrying accounts of the arguments as they develop. Without a tremendous technical development it is doubtful that the standards of the Clean Air Act of 1970 can be met. Legislation properly indicates our desire for a change, but the technical problems are still formidable.

Some people have suggested drastic changes in automobile design as a solution to the problem.† Others hold that such changes will not do the job. Instead, recirculating systems and exhaust catalysts have been used to speed up the decomposition of NO to N_2 and O_2. Unfortunately, the technical problems remain unsolved.

*See Noel de Nevers, "Enforcing the Clean Air Act of 1970," *Scientific American,* **228,** 14 (June 1973).

†See (a) David E. Cole, "The Wankel Engine," *Scientific American,* **227,** 14 (August 1972); (b) G. Walker, "The Stirling Engine," *Scientific American,* **229,** 80 (August 1973).

22-3 ARSENIC AND THE ENVIRONMENT

While nitrogen and phosphorus are clearly important in life processes, arsenic is not. It is generally toxic to life and most of its use has been based on this fact. It has been widely used in agricultural sprays and was a vital component in one of the first medicinals used to fight venereal disease.

Today its use is declining. Alternative sprays have been developed and penicillin and other antibiotics have largely replaced arsenicals in medicine. Some arsenic is used as a doping material for transistors (see Chapter 18), but the total usage in this application is small. Arsenic, because of its toxicity, is being replaced.

A large effort today centers on removing arsenic from foodstuffs and consumer products. Because phosphorus and arsenic are in the same part of the periodic table, arsenic appears as a contaminant in both commercial phosphorus and the phosphoric acid which is made from it. Arsenic must be removed from the phosphoric acid and phosphates. The procedure adopted is a simple application of principles which we have already considered. Gaseous hydrogen sulfide is bubbled through phosphoric acid. Arsenic sulfides precipitate and are filtered off. Excess hydrogen sulfide can then be removed from the acid by blowing a stream of air through the liquid. What one does with the arsenic sulfide which is filtered off is now a problem! Problems might even arise if it is buried.

Arsenic sulfides are colored compounds and some have been used as pigments in paints. This is no longer allowed. All in all, one would have to say that even though nitrogen and phosphorus should be classed as friends when controlled, arsenic is still a foe which has to be watched carefully. In some cases it can help, but its potential for damage is great.

22-4 HIGHLIGHTS

Phosphorus and nitrogen are both essential to life and both promote the growth of plants and animals. Excessive growth of algae (plants) in rivers and lakes causes serious problems. Water treatment processes are available which will return water of high quality to streams from sewage plants. Fairly good technology to minimize water pollution is available. The questions in its use are economic, environmental, and philosophical. Even better technology is urgently needed.

The oxides of nitrogen are important in air quality control because they play a key role in the development of photochemical smog. Smog is a complex mixture of very irritating chemicals which results from the action of atomic oxygen on other materials present in the air. The atomic oxygen is generated by the action of sunlight on NO_2. The technical problems in the control of air quality are still very formidable; legislation has established our desire for clean air, but no one yet knows just how to reach our goal. Still, it is very important that we try. We all hope that continuing research will point the way.

22-5 EPILOGUE

Today our attention is being focused on energy problems, preservation of our environment, food supplies, and shortages of key materials. The problems are all real and serious, but there is every reason for optimism. To the best of our present knowledge, the chemical principles used today apply throughout the solar system. Our past experience tells us that if the chemical and physical laws governing a problem are understood, the problem can be conquered. Chemistry can help us solve our problems, if we will use what we know.

APPENDICES

A DESCRIPTION OF A BURNING CANDLE

A photograph of a burning candle is shown[1]* in Figure A1-1. The candle is cylindrical in shape[2] and has a diameter[3] of about $1\frac{1}{2}$ cm. The length of the candle was initially about 8 cm[4] and it changed slowly[5] during observation, decreasing about 1 cm per hour[6]. The candle is made of a translucent[7], white[8] solid[9] which has a slight odor[10] and no taste[11]. It is soft enough to be scratched with the fingernail[12]. There is a wick[13] which extends from the top to the bottom[14] of the candle along its central axis[15] and which protrudes above the top of the candle about 1 cm[16]. The wick is made of three strands of string braided together[17].

The candle is lighted by holding a source of flame close to the wick for a few seconds. The source of the flame can then be removed and the flame will sustain itself at the wick[18]. The burning candle makes no sound[19]. While burning, the body of the candle remains cool to the touch[20] except near the top. Within about 1 cm from the top the candle is warm (but not hot)[21] and sufficiently soft to mold easily[22].

The flame flickers in response to air currents[23] and tends to become quite smoky while flickering[24]. In the absence of air currents, the flame is of the form shown in Figure A1-1, although it exhibits some movement at all times[25]. The flame begins about $\frac{1}{4}$ cm above the top of the candle[26] and at its base the flame has a blue tint[27]. Immediately around the wick in a region about $\frac{1}{2}$ cm wide and extending about 1 cm above the top of the wick[28], the flame is dark[29]. This dark region is roughly conical in shape[30]. Around this zone and extending about 1 cm above the dark zone is a region which emits yellow light[31], which is bright but not blinding[32]. The flame has rather sharply defined sides[33] but a ragged top[34].

The wick is white where it emerges from the candle[35]; from the base of the flame to the end of the wick, it is black, appearing burnt[36], except for the last 0.1 cm, where it glows red[37]. The wick curls over about $\frac{1}{2}$ cm from its end[38]. As the candle becomes shorter, the wick becomes shorter too, so as to extend roughly a constant length above the top of the candle[39].

Heat is emitted by the flame[40], enough so that it becomes uncomfortable in 10 or 20 seconds if a finger is held $\frac{1}{2}$ cm to the side of the flame[41] or 6 to 8 cm above the flame[42].

The top of a quietly burning candle becomes wet with a colorless liquid[43] and becomes bowl-shaped[44]. If the flame is blown, one side of this bowl-shaped top may liquefy, and the liquid trapped in the bowl may drain down the side of the candle[45]. As it runs down, the colorless liquid cools[46], becomes translucent[47], and gradually solidifies from the outside[48] and attaches itself to the side of the candle[49]. When there is no draft, the candle can burn for hours without such drippings[50]. Under these conditions, a stable pool of clear liquid remains in the bowl-shaped top of the candle[51]. The liquid rises slightly around the wick[52], wetting the base of the wick as high as the base of the flame[53].

*The numbers refer to distinct observations made by the observer. Note the careful differentiation between observation and interpretation.

Fig. A1-1 A burning candle.

Several aspects of this description deserve specific mention. Compare your own description with this one in each of the following characteristics:

(1) The description is comprehensive in *qualitative* terms. Did *you* mention appearance? smell? taste? feel? sound? (*Note:* **A chemist quickly becomes reluctant to taste or smell an unknown chemical. A chemical should be considered poisonous unless it is *known* not to be!**)

(2) Wherever possible, the description is stated *quantitatively*. This means the question "How much?" is answered, the quantity is specified. The remark that the flame emits yellow light is made more meaningful by the "how much" expression "bright but not blinding." Any statement to the effect that heat is emitted might lead a cautious investigator who is lighting a candle for the first time to stand in a concrete blockhouse 100 metres away. A few words telling "how much" heat would save this precaution.

(3) The description does not make assumptions regarding the relative importance of observations. Thus the observation that a burning candle does not emit sound deserves to be mentioned just as much as the observation that it does emit light.

(4) The description does not confuse observation and interpretation. To say that the top of the burning candle is wet with a colorless liquid is to make an observation. To suggest a possible composition for this liquid is to offer an interpretation.

DETERMINING THE RATIO OF CHARGE TO MASS FOR AN ELECTRON

One of the key steps in obtaining the mass of an electron is determining the ratio of charge to mass for the particle—that is, e/m. Most experimental procedures used are based upon the behavior of the electron in electric and magnetic fields. Let us begin this study by considering the behavior of electrons as they move in the space between the poles of a magnet. Here is the experiment.

Rapidly moving electrons are generated in the cathode ray tube shown in Figure A2-1. A narrow beam of electrons can be obtained in the tube by using the metal plate Z with a small slit in it. When this narrow beam hits the glass plate coated with zinc sulfide that is at the end of the tube, a glowing line appears. If the tube is now placed between the pole faces of a very large electromagnet, the electron beam will be moving in a magnetic field. The strength of the field is determined by the amount of current flowing through the electromagnet. Under the influence of the magnetic field created by the electromagnet, the electron beam bends into a circular path of radius r. The circular path is parallel to the two pole faces (see Figure A2-1). Because the beam is bent, it will now hit the zinc-sulfide coated glass plate at a higher point. By measuring the distance which the beam has moved upward on the screen and by applying a little geometry, it is possible to calculate the radius r of the circle in which the electrons moved between the poles of the magnet.

What is the force acting on an electron in the beam? The force acting on an electron moving within and perpendicular to a magnetic field is dependent upon the electron's velocity and charge and upon the strength of the perpendicular magnetic field. The equation for this force is

$$\left\{ \begin{array}{l} \text{force acting on electron} \\ \text{moving in magnetic field} \end{array} \right\}$$

$$= \left\{ \begin{array}{c} \text{velocity of} \\ \text{electron} \end{array} \right\} \times \left\{ \begin{array}{c} \text{charge on} \\ \text{electron} \end{array} \right\} \times \left\{ \begin{array}{c} \text{strength of} \\ \text{magnetic field} \end{array} \right\}$$

Fig. A2-1 An electron beam passing through a magnetic field.

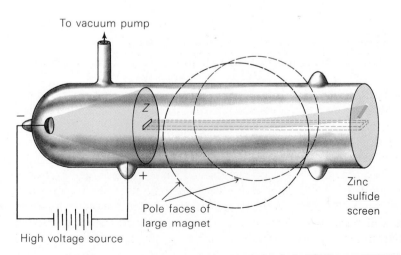

To vacuum pump

Zinc sulfide screen

Pole faces of large magnet

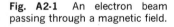

High voltage source

or

$$\text{force}_1 = v \times e \times B \qquad (1)$$

where v = the velocity of the electron, e = the charge on the electron, and B = the strength of the magnetic field.

The force required to make an electron move in a circular path of a certain radius is dependent upon the mass of the electron and the square of the velocity of the electron. The equation for this force is

$$\left\{ \begin{matrix} \text{force required} \\ \text{to make electron} \\ \text{move in a} \\ \text{circular path} \end{matrix} \right\} = \dfrac{\left\{ \begin{matrix} \text{mass of} \\ \text{electron} \end{matrix} \right\} \times \left\{ \begin{matrix} \text{velocity of} \\ \text{electron} \end{matrix} \right\}^2}{\left\{ \begin{matrix} \text{radius of} \\ \text{circular path} \end{matrix} \right\}}$$

or

$$\text{force}_2 = \dfrac{m \times v^2}{r} \qquad (2)$$

where m = the mass of the electron, v = the velocity of the electron, and r = the radius of the circular path described by the electron.

If the electron is actually to follow a circular path, then force$_1$ must be equal to force$_2$, or

$$v \times e \times B = \dfrac{m \times v^2}{r} \qquad (3)$$

Solving this equation for e/m, we have

$$\dfrac{e}{m} = \dfrac{v}{r \times B} \qquad (3a)$$

or

$$\dfrac{\text{charge}}{\text{mass}} = \dfrac{\text{velocity of electron}}{\text{strength of magnetic field} \times \text{radius of circular path}}$$

The radius of the circular path, r, can be calculated from the geometry of the tube and the upward shift of the line on the screen as the magnetic field is applied. The strength of the magnetic field, B, can be determined from the construction of the electromagnet and from the current flowing through its coils.

The quantity e/m can now be calculated if the velocity of the electron is known. This quantity has been determined in several ways. One way is by using both an electrostatic and a magnetic field. As you will recall from Section 6-3, the force of attraction between an electron and a proton, which are separated by distance d, measured in centimetres, is given by the expression

$$\left\{\begin{matrix}\text{force of attraction}\\\text{between electron}\\\text{and proton}\end{matrix}\right\} = \frac{\text{charge on electron} \times \text{charge on proton}}{(\text{distance between electron and proton})^2}$$

$$\text{force} = \frac{e_1 \times e_2}{d^2} \tag{4}$$

where e_1 = charge on the electron, e_2 = charge on the proton, and d = distance between them.

If an electron is placed between two plates, one negatively and the other positively charged, the quantity e_2/d^2 is replaced by a quantity called the **electrostatic field strength.** The electrostatic field strength is determined by the charge on the plates and by the distance between them. If we use the symbol Q to represent the electrostatic field strength, the earlier equation for force on the electron becomes

$$\left\{\begin{matrix}\text{electrostatic force}\\\text{on electron}\end{matrix}\right\} = e \times Q \tag{5}$$

where Q = electrostatic field strength.

If a beam of electrons is now generated in the cathode ray tube and passed between the two charged plates, P_1 and P_2, the electrostatic field acting between the plates makes the beam bend (Figure A2-2).

If a tube is now made with plates P_1 and P_2 on the top and bottom of the tube, respectively, and with magnetic-pole faces on each side of the tube (see Figure A2-3), the moving electron can be subjected to both electrostatic and electromagnetic forces at the same time. If the electrostatic force tending to bend the beam downward is just balanced by the magnetic force tending to bend the beam upward,

Fig. A2-2 An electron beam passing through an electrostatic field.

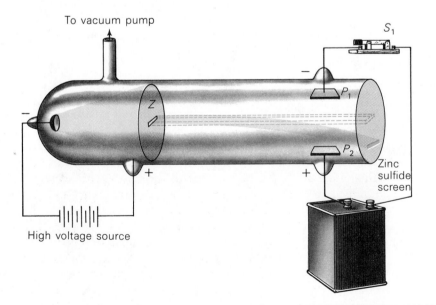

To vacuum pump

S_1

P_1

Z

P_2

Zinc sulfide screen

High voltage source

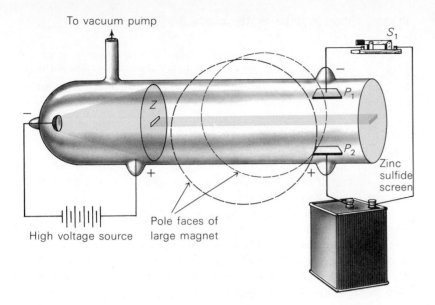

To vacuum pump

S_1

P_1

Z

P_2

Zinc
sulfide
screen

High voltage source

Pole faces of
large magnet

Fig. A2-3 An electron beam passing through magnetic and electrostatic fields.

the electrons will pass through both fields without deflection. Under these conditions

$$\begin{Bmatrix} \text{force acting on electron} \\ \text{moving in magnetic field} \end{Bmatrix} = \begin{Bmatrix} \text{electrostatic force} \\ \text{on electron} \end{Bmatrix}$$

or

$$v \times \mathscr{e} \times B = \mathscr{e} \times Q \qquad (6)$$

$$v = \frac{Q}{B} \qquad (6a)$$

$$\begin{Bmatrix} \text{velocity} \\ \text{of electron} \end{Bmatrix} = \frac{\text{electrostatic field strength}}{\text{magnetic field strength}}$$

If this value for v is now put into our earlier expression for e/m, (*3a*), the following is obtained:

$$\frac{e}{m} = \frac{v}{r \times B} = \frac{Q}{B \times r \times B} = \frac{Q}{r \times B^2} \qquad (3b)$$

All quantities on the right can be measured directly. Q is the electrostatic field strength and can be determined for the tube in Figure A2-3 by reading the voltmeter attached to the plates; B is the magnetic field strength and is caused by the current flowing in the coils of the electromagnet; r is the radius of the circle described by the path of the electron in the magnetic field and can be obtained from the shift in the bright line appearing on the zinc sulfide screen when the magnet is turned on. The quantity e/m can thus be obtained.

RATIO of CHARGE to

MASS for an ELECTRON

THE OPERATION OF THE MASS SPECTROMETER

In Appendix 2 a procedure was described for determining the ratio of charge to mass for the electron. This is written as *e/m*. The value obtained can be coupled with experiments giving the charge on the electron to yield a precise determination of the mass of the electron. The same procedure can be modified slightly to determine the mass of positive ions. The instrument used to carry out this procedure is known as a **mass spectrometer.** It permits the measurement of the masses of individual atomic or molecular ions.

One type of mass spectrometer is shown in Figure A3-1. Positive ions are generated from atoms in the tube by bombardment with an electron beam. The rapidly moving electrons of the beam knock electrons from the atoms in the tube. The positive ions produced are accelerated to a known velocity by attraction for the highly charged negative electrode, which has a slit in it. This rapidly moving beam of positive ions, emerging from the slit in the negative electrode, is made into a narrower beam by passage through a slit in another charged metal disk. This thin beam then passes through a uniform magnetic field.

Figure A3-1 shows neon gas entering at the bottom. The gas passes through the electron beam; some atoms collide with the electrons of the beam to form neon ions. Both Ne^+ and Ne^{2+} ions are formed and they are accelerated by passing through the slits in the negative electrodes.

Fig. A3-1 A mass spectrometer.

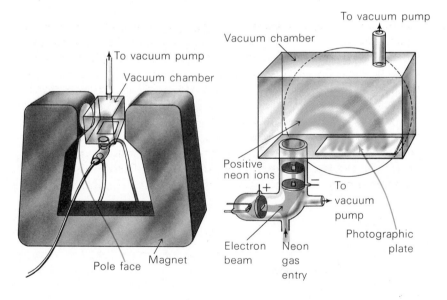

After the beam of positive ions is formed, it enters the magnetic field, where the charged ions move in a circular path. The circular path has a large radius if the *mass* of the particle is high and a small radius if the *charge* is high. Each positive ion follows a distinctive circular path fixed by its mass and charge. After traveling half a circle (an arc of 180°), the ions hit a photographic plate. The impact of ions on the plate causes a chemical reaction which darkens the plate, just as exposure to light darkens the plate. The plate, then, will have a dark spot for each ion at a position fixed by the ratio of charge to mass for each ion. The record is called a **mass spectrum.**

Ions can be detected by methods other than the use of the photographic plate. After being sorted according to mass and charge, the ions can be "counted" by a charge-measuring device. The advantage of such a detector is that the result can be presented continuously on a paper chart, thus eliminating a cumbersome photographic process. The mass spectrum obtained in this way consists of peaks on a chart.

Closer examination of the mass spectrum for neon (see Figure A3-2) shows in more detail how the data are interpreted. The record consists of two widely separated groups of three peaks each. The three peaks corresponding to ions moving in a circle with large radii are caused by neon ions with a single positive charge. The other set of three peaks corresponding to ions moving in circles of smaller radii are caused by ions carrying two positive charges. For each ionic charge there are three slightly separated peaks. This second group of peaks is not visible in Figure A3-2. These peaks indicate that neon has three different isotopes. The relative abundance of each isotope can be determined by measuring the relative heights of the peaks caused by each ion beam.

The mass of the ion causing a given spot can be calculated from the following equation:

$$m = \frac{n \times e \times r^2 \times B^2}{2V}$$

where n = an integer indicating number of charges on the ion, e = the electron charge, r = the radius of the circular path of the ions (a value which is obtained from the position of the line on the plate), B = the strength of the magnetic field causing the ions to move in a circular path, and V = the voltage between positive and negative electrodes, which accelerates ions.

Atomic weights are today determined by the mass spectrometer. It is possible to determine the precise mass of all isotopes making up an element. It is also possible to determine the percent of each isotope present in a normal sample of the element. (See Figure A3-2.) These numbers permit calculation of the atomic weight of that element.

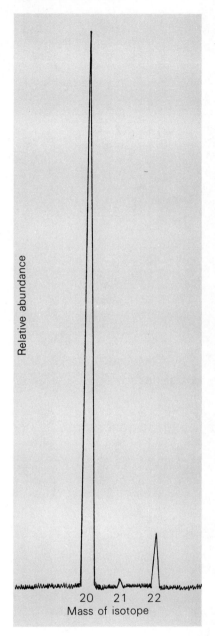

Fig. A3-2 A mass spectrometer tracing for a sample of neon gas containing 90.5% $^{20}Ne^+$, 0.3% $^{21}Ne^+$, and 9.2% $^{22}Ne^+$.

Relative abundance

20   21   22
Mass of isotope

MOSELEY'S EXPERIMENT: THE RELATIONSHIP BETWEEN ATOMIC NUMBER AND THE FREQUENCY OF LINES IN X-RAY SPECTRA

If a beam of cathode rays (a stream of electrons) is allowed to impinge upon a piece of metal in a vacuum tube, X rays or light of very short wavelength is produced (see Chapter 16). The metal hit by the electrons is called the target. A device of this type which generates X rays is known as an X-ray tube (see Figure A4-1). In 1913, H. G. J. Moseley

Fig. A4-1 A schematic drawing of an X-ray tube.

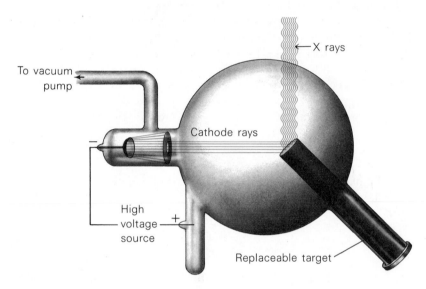

studied the nature of the X radiation given off when X-ray tubes were made which contained different elements as the target. For example, he measured the frequency (see Chapter 16) of the X radiation when elemental cobalt was the target. The same measurements were made using nickel, copper, zinc, and so on, as targets. He then found that a plot of the square root of the frequency against the atomic number of the target gave a straight line (see Figure A4-2). This result was

Fig. A4-2 The relationship of X-ray spectra to atomic number.

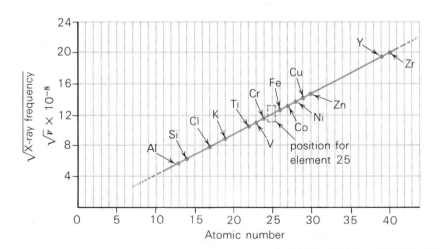

of great significance since it clearly identified the atomic number mentioned by Bohr and Rutherford as a fundamental characteristic of the atom. The relationship also was important in showing the atomic numbers for undiscovered elements. For example, if in the graph of Figure A4-2 the element of atomic number 25 were still undiscovered, a blank space would appear in the Moseley plot at this atomic number. If chemists knew the atomic number of a missing element, guesses as to its properties could be made and procedures for its separation could be devised. Furthermore, the expected characteristic X-ray line (predicted by the plot) would provide an easy and certain method for identifying the new element when it was found.

It was also possible to derive the Moseley relationship using Planck's equation $E = h\nu$ (see Section 16-2.1) and the Bohr model of the atom as well as the quantum-theory model of the atom (see Section 16-2 and Section 16-3). This derivation will be delayed until your college course in chemistry.

NAMES, FORMULAS, AND CHARGES
OF SOME COMMON IONS

POSITIVE IONS (CATIONS)

Name	Symbol	Name	Symbol
Aluminum	Al^{3+}	Lead	Pb^{2+}
Ammonium	NH_4^+	Lithium	Li^+
Barium	Ba^{2+}	Magnesium	Mg^{2+}
Calcium	Ca^{2+}	Manganese(II), manganous	Mn^{2+}
Chromium(II), chromous	Cr^{2+}	Mercury(I),* mercurous	Hg_2^{2+}
Chromium(III), chromic	Cr^{3+}	Mercury(II), mercuric	Hg^{2+}
Cobalt	Co^{2+}	Potassium	K^+
Copper(I),* cuprous	Cu^+	Silver	Ag^+
Copper(II), cupric	Cu^{2+}	Sodium	Na^+
Hydrogen, hydronium	H^+, H_3O^+	Tin(II),* stannous	Sn^{2+}
Iron(II),* ferrous	Fe^{2+}	Tin(IV), stannic	Sn^{4+}
Iron(III), ferric	Fe^{3+}	Zinc	Zn^{2+}

NEGATIVE IONS (ANIONS)

Name	Symbol	Name	Symbol
Acetate	CH_3COO^-	Hydrogen oxalate ion, bioxalate	$HC_2O_4^-$
Bromide	Br^-		
Carbonate	CO_3^{2-}	Oxide	O^{2-}
Hydrogen carbonate ion, bicarbonate	HCO_3^-	Perchlorate	ClO_4^-
		Permanganate	MnO_4^-
Chlorate	ClO_3^-	Phosphate	PO_4^{3-}
Chloride	Cl^-	Monohydrogen phosphate	HPO_4^{2-}
Chlorite	ClO_2^-	Dihydrogen phosphate	$H_2PO_4^-$
Chromate	CrO_4^{2-}	Sulfate	SO_4^{2-}
Dichromate	$Cr_2O_7^{2-}$	Hydrogen sulfate ion, bisulfate	HSO_4^-
Fluoride	F^-		
Hydroxide	OH^-	Sulfide	S^{2-}
Hypochlorite	ClO^-	Hydrogen sulfide ion, bisulfide	HS^-
Iodide	I^-		
Nitrate	NO_3^-	Sulfite	SO_3^{2-}
Nitrite	NO_2^-	Hydrogen sulfite ion, bisulfite	HSO_3^-
Oxalate	$C_2O_4^{2-}$		

* Aqueous solutions are readily oxidized by air.

NOTE: In ionic compounds the relative number of positive and negative ions is such that the sum of their electric charges is zero.

RELATIVE STRENGTHS OF ACIDS IN AQUEOUS SOLUTION AT ROOM TEMPERATURE

The equation for the ionization is

$$HB(aq) \rightleftharpoons H^+(aq) + B^-(aq)$$

Since all ions and molecules in water solution are aquated, the (aq) is assumed in the notation. We then write for K_A

$$K_A = \frac{[H^+][B^-]}{[HB]}$$

Acid	Strength	Reaction	K_A
Perchloric acid	very strong	$HClO_4 \longrightarrow H^+ + ClO_4^-$	very large
Hydriodic acid		$HI \longrightarrow H^+ + I^-$	very large
Hydrobromic acid		$HBr \longrightarrow H^+ + Br^-$	very large
Hydrochloric acid		$HCl \longrightarrow H^+ + Cl^-$	very large
Nitric acid		$HNO_3 \longrightarrow H^+ + NO_3^-$	very large
Sulfuric acid	very strong	$H_2SO_4 \longrightarrow H^+ + HSO_4^-$	very large
Oxalic acid		$HOOCCOOH \longrightarrow H^+ + HOOCCOO^-$	5.4×10^{-2}
Sulfurous acid ($SO_2 + H_2O$)		$H_2SO_3 \longrightarrow H^+ + HSO_3^-$	1.7×10^{-2}
Hydrogen sulfate ion	strong	$HSO_4^- \longrightarrow H^+ + SO_4^{2-}$	1.3×10^{-2}
Phosphoric acid		$H_3PO_4 \longrightarrow H^+ + H_2PO_4^-$	7.1×10^{-3}
Ferric ion		$Fe(H_2O)_6^{3+} \longrightarrow H^+ + Fe(H_2O)_5(OH)^{2+}$	6.0×10^{-3}
Hydrogen telluride		$H_2Te \longrightarrow H^+ + HTe^-$	2.3×10^{-3}
Hydrofluoric acid	weak	$HF \longrightarrow H^+ + F^-$	6.7×10^{-4}
Nitrous acid		$HNO_2 \longrightarrow H^+ + NO_2^-$	5.1×10^{-4}
Hydrogen selenide		$H_2Se \longrightarrow H^+ + HSe^-$	1.7×10^{-4}
Chromic ion		$Cr(H_2O)_6^{3+} \longrightarrow H^+ + Cr(H_2O)_5(OH)^{2+}$	1.5×10^{-4}
Benzoic acid		$C_6H_5COOH \longrightarrow H^+ + C_6H_5COO^-$	6.6×10^{-5}
Hydrogen oxalate ion		$HOOCCOO^- \longrightarrow H^+ + OOCCOO^{2-}$	5.4×10^{-5}
Acetic acid	weak	$CH_3COOH \longrightarrow H^+ + CH_3COO^-$	1.8×10^{-5}
Aluminum ion		$Al(H_2O)_6^{3+} \longrightarrow H^+ + Al(H_2O)_5(OH)^{2+}$	1.4×10^{-5}
Carbonic acid ($CO_2 + H_2O$)		$H_2CO_3 \longrightarrow H^+ + HCO_3^-$	4.4×10^{-7}
Hydrogen sulfide		$H_2S \longrightarrow H^+ + HS^-$	1.0×10^{-7}
Dihydrogen phosphate ion		$H_2PO_4^- \longrightarrow H^+ + HPO_4^{2-}$	6.3×10^{-8}
Hydrogen sulfite ion		$HSO_3^- \longrightarrow H^+ + SO_3^{2-}$	6.2×10^{-8}
Ammonium ion	weak	$NH_4^+ \longrightarrow H^+ + NH_3$	5.7×10^{-10}
Hydrogen carbonate ion		$HCO_3^- \longrightarrow H^+ + CO_3^{2-}$	4.7×10^{-11}
Hydrogen telluride ion		$HTe^- \longrightarrow H^+ + Te^{2-}$	1.0×10^{-11}
Hydrogen peroxide	very weak	$H_2O_2 \longrightarrow H^+ + HO_2^-$	2.4×10^{-12}
Monohydrogen phosphate ion		$HPO_4^{2-} \longrightarrow H^+ + PO_4^{3-}$	4.4×10^{-13}
Hydrogen sulfide ion		$HS^- \longrightarrow H^+ + S^{2-}$	1.2×10^{-15}
Water		$H_2O \longrightarrow H^+ + OH^-$	1.8×10^{-16}*
Hydroxide ion		$OH^- \longrightarrow H^+ + O^{2-}$	$< 10^{-36}$
Ammonia	very weak	$NH_3 \longrightarrow H^+ + NH_2^-$	very small

*The acid equilibrium constant, K_A, for water equals $\frac{K_w}{H_2O} = \frac{1.00 \times 10^{-14}}{55.6}$.

STANDARD REDUCTION POTENTIALS FOR HALF-REACTIONS: IONIC CONCENTRATIONS = 1 MOLAR IN WATER, TEMPERATURE = 25 °C

All ions are in water.

Strength As Oxidizing Agent	Half-Reaction	E^0 (volts)	Strength As Reducing Agent
very strong oxidizing agents	$F_2(g) + 2e^- \longrightarrow 2F^-$	$+2.87$	very weak reducing agents
	$H_2O_2 + 2H^+ + 2e^- \longrightarrow 2H_2O$	$+1.77$	
	$MnO_4^- + 8H^+ + 5e^- \longrightarrow Mn^{2+} + 4H_2O$	$+1.52$	
	$Au^{3+} + 3e^- \longrightarrow Au(s)$	$+1.50$	
	$Cl_2(g) + 2e^- \longrightarrow 2Cl^-$	$+1.36$	
	$Cr_2O_7^{2-} + 14H^+ + 6e^- \longrightarrow 2Cr^{3+} + 7H_2O$	$+1.33$	increasing strength as reducing agent
	$MnO_2(s) + 4H^+ + 2e^- \longrightarrow Mn^{2+} + 2H_2O$	$+1.28$	
	$\frac{1}{2}O_2(g) + 2H^+ + 2e^- \longrightarrow H_2O$	$+1.23$	
	$Br_2(l) + 2e^- \longrightarrow 2Br^-$	$+1.06$	
	$AuCl_4^- + 3e^- \longrightarrow Au(s) + 4Cl^-$	$+1.00$	
	$NO_3^- + 4H^+ + 3e^- \longrightarrow NO(g) + 2H_2O$	$+0.96$	
	$\frac{1}{2}O_2(g) + 2H^+ (10^{-7} M) + 2e^- \longrightarrow H_2O$	$+0.82$	
	$Ag^+ + e^- \longrightarrow Ag(s)$	$+0.80$	
	$\frac{1}{2}Hg_2^{2+} + e^- \longrightarrow Hg(l)$	$+0.79$	
	$Hg^{2+} + 2e^- \longrightarrow Hg(l)$	$+0.78$	
	$NO_3^- + 2H^+ + e^- \longrightarrow NO_2(g) + H_2O$	$+0.78$	
	$Fe^{3+} + e^- \longrightarrow Fe^{2+}$	$+0.77$	
	$O_2(g) + 2H^+ + 2e^- \longrightarrow H_2O_2$	$+0.68$	
	$I_2(s) + 2e^- \longrightarrow 2I^-$	$+0.53$	
	$Cu^+ + e^- \longrightarrow Cu(s)$	$+0.52$	
	$Cu^{2+} + 2e^- \longrightarrow Cu(s)$	$+0.34$	
increasing strength as oxidizing agent	$SO_4^{2-} + 4H^+ + 2e^- \longrightarrow SO_2(g) + 2H_2O$	$+0.17$	
	$Cu^{2+} + e^- \longrightarrow Cu^+$	$+0.15$	
	$Sn^{4+} + 2e^- \longrightarrow Sn^{2+}$	$+0.15$	
	$S + 2H^+ + 2e^- \longrightarrow H_2S(g)$	$+0.14$	
	$2H^+ + 2e^- \longrightarrow H_2(g)$	0.00	
	$Pb^{2+} + 2e^- \longrightarrow Pb(s)$	-0.13	
	$Sn^{2+} + 2e^- \longrightarrow Sn(s)$	-0.14	
	$Ni^{2+} + 2e^- \longrightarrow Ni(s)$	-0.25	
	$Co^{2+} + 2e^- \longrightarrow Co(s)$	-0.28	
	$Se + 2H^+ + 2e^- \longrightarrow H_2Se(g)$	-0.40	
	$Cr^{3+} + e^- \longrightarrow Cr^{2+}$	-0.41	
weak oxidizing agents	$2H^+ (10^{-7} M) + 2e^- \longrightarrow H_2(g)$	-0.41	
	$Fe^{2+} + 2e^- \longrightarrow Fe(s)$	-0.44	
	$Ag_2S + 2e^- \longrightarrow 2Ag(s) + S^{2-}$	-0.69	
	$Te + 2H^+ + 2e^- \longrightarrow H_2Te(g)$	-0.72	
	$Cr^{3+} + 3e^- \longrightarrow Cr(s)$	-0.74	
	$Zn^{2+} + 2e^- \longrightarrow Zn(s)$	-0.76	
	$2H_2O + 2e^- \longrightarrow 2OH^- + H_2(g)$	-0.83	
	$Mn^{2+} + 2e^- \longrightarrow Mn(s)$	-1.18	
	$Al^{3+} + 3e^- \longrightarrow Al(s)$	-1.66	
	$Mg^{2+} + 2e^- \longrightarrow Mg(s)$	-2.37	
	$Na^+ + e^- \longrightarrow Na(s)$	-2.71	
	$Ca^{2+} + 2e^- \longrightarrow Ca(s)$	-2.87	
	$Sr^{2+} + 2e^- \longrightarrow Sr(s)$	-2.89	
	$Ba^{2+} + 2e^- \longrightarrow Ba(s)$	-2.90	
	$Cs^+ + e^- \longrightarrow Cs(s)$	-2.92	very strong reducing agents
very weak oxidizing agents	$K^+ + e^- \longrightarrow K(s)$	-2.92	
	$Rb^+ + e^- \longrightarrow Rb(s)$	-2.92	
	$Li^+ + e^- \longrightarrow Li(s)$	-3.00	

BALANCING HALF-REACTIONS

When potassium chlorate solution ($KClO_3$) is added to hydrochloric acid, chlorine gas is evolved. Although we can find the half-reaction $Cl_2(g) + 2e^- \longrightarrow 2Cl^-$ in Appendix 7 we find no equation involving ClO_3^-. We can guess that ClO_3^- accepts electrons and releases chlorine. Let us write a partial half-reaction in which we indicate an unknown number of electrons and in which we conserve only chlorine atoms:

$$ClO_3^- + xe^- \longrightarrow \tfrac{1}{2}Cl_2(g) + \text{other products} \qquad (1)$$

From experience we know that in acid solution, the oxygen in such oxidizing agents as MnO_4^- and $Cr_2O_7^{2-}$ combines with H^+ to give water. Let us incorporate our knowledge by showing $6H^+$ among the reactants and $3H_2O$ among the products:

$$ClO_3^- + 6H^+ + xe^- \longrightarrow \tfrac{1}{2}Cl_2(g) + 3H_2O \qquad (2)$$

Finally, we have to remember that charge is conserved. Since the products are neutral molecules, x must be 5 if the total charge among the reactants is to be zero. Our desired half-reaction is

$$ClO_3^- + 6H^+ + 5e^- \longrightarrow \tfrac{1}{2}Cl_2(g) + 3H_2O \qquad (3)$$

This balanced half-reaction can now be combined with the half-reaction for chloride oxidation to produce a balanced equation representing the reaction between HCl and $KClO_3$. To show 1 mole of chlorine produced, equation (3) becomes

$$2ClO_3^- + 12H^+ + 10e^- \longrightarrow Cl_2 + 6H_2O \qquad (4)$$

Combining this equation with the proper equation for chloride oxidation gives

$$(5 \times 2)Cl^- \longrightarrow 5Cl_2 + (5 \times 2)e^- \qquad (5)$$

$$\underline{2ClO_3^- + 12H^+ + 10e^- \longrightarrow Cl_2 + 6H_2O \qquad (4)}$$

$$10Cl^- + 2ClO_3^- + 12H^+ \longrightarrow 6Cl_2 + 6H_2O \qquad (6)$$

Notice that both numbers of atoms and the numbers of charges now balance.

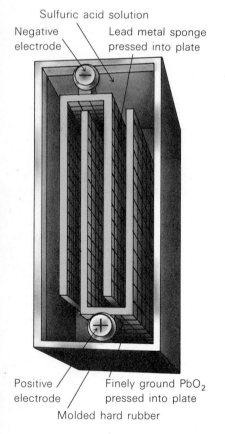

Fig. A9-1 One cell of a lead storage battery. Batteries of this general type are used to start automobiles.

Sulfuric acid solution

Negative electrode

Lead metal sponge pressed into plate

Positive electrode

Finely ground PbO_2 pressed into plate

Molded hard rubber

APPENDIX 9

ELECTRIC CARS, ANYONE?

The automobile is a wonderful convenience, but too much of a good thing can cause trouble. Internal combustion engines produce a very small amount of obnoxious fumes (NO, NO_2, and unburned carbon compounds). If we have a few cars and rapidly circulating air, there are no problems. If we have lots of rapidly circulating cars and stagnant air, the problems of air pollution become extreme. Many of America's biggest cities have done the experiment and have the data. All they lack now is the solution to the problem. Some people, uninhibited by facts, have been quick to come up with easy solutions. The hard problems still remain. Electric cars have been suggested. These would store their energy in electrochemical cells. What are the prospects? As background for this question, let us look at several commercial cells or batteries which are now used to store energy.

A9-1   The Automobile Storage Battery

The little "power-packed" black box which dutifully starts your car on the coldest morning is a collection of six lead-lead dioxide electrochemical cells connected in series. Each of the six cells has a potential of about 2 volts. All six working together in series become the 12-volt battery which we so often depend upon. The chemistry in each 2-volt "cell" is not too different in principle from that which we discussed in Chapter 15. The fundamental half-reactions are

Negative electrode
$$Pb(s) + SO_4^{2-} \longrightarrow PbSO_4(s) + 2e^-$$
$$E^0 = +0.35 \text{ volt} \quad (1)$$

Positive electrode
$$2e^- + PbO_2(s) + 4H^+ + SO_4^{2-} \longrightarrow PbSO_4(s) + 2H_2O$$
$$E^0 = +1.68 \text{ volts} \quad (2)$$

Overall
$$Pb(s) + PbO_2(s) + 2H_2SO_4 \longrightarrow 2PbSO_4(s) + 2H_2O$$
$$E^0 = +2.03 \text{ volts} \quad (3)$$

Although concentrations are far from 1 M, differences cancel and the observed value is close to the theoretical one.

The cell is constructed as shown in Figure A9-1. Because both the major reactants (Pb and PbO_2) and the major product ($PbSO_4$) are insoluble solids, they can be mounted in frames or "plates." When sulfuric acid bathes these plates, the overall reaction can occur.

The equation tells us a lot about battery care and operation. A battery which is discharged has converted its sulfuric acid to water. Such a battery may freeze in cold weather and break its case. On the other hand, a fully charged battery contains a concentrated solution of sulfuric acid which freezes with great difficulty.

The extent of charge in a battery can be determined by measuring the density of the liquid in the cells. A fully charged battery has lead and lead dioxide on plates which are bathed in sulfuric acid. A discharged battery has lead sulfate on both plates and water in the cell. Because the density of very concentrated H_2SO_4 is about 1.8 g/ml while that of water is 1.0 g/ml, we can estimate the charge on the battery from the density of the liquid in the cell.

The cell works best if the lead sulfate forms as very small crystals which can be reconverted to porous lead and lead dioxide *on the plates*. If a discharged battery is allowed to stand, the lead sulfate crystals get larger and may fall off during charge to "short out" the cells (*i.e.*, establish electrical contact between them). "Dry charge batteries" are shipped without liquid. The sulfuric acid is added just before use. Hopefully no deterioration of the plates has started up to that time.

Why can we not use lead storage batteries to drive our cars as well as to start them? The amount of energy available per pound is too low to provide a reasonable source of energy. (Estimates place this at about 16 watt-hours per pound.) The lead storage battery does not hold the answer.

A9-2 Other Kinds of Batteries— Where Do We Go From Here?

Many books could be written about battery systems and their problems. Our treatment is brief. The power for a battery must ultimately come from the power line during the night. Since we have only a few hours late at night when excess generating capacity is available, acceptable car batteries would have to be recharged rapidly. Thus, a high recharge rate is essential. Furthermore, the battery must discharge, or release its energy, efficiently with little heat loss.

For purposes of argument, let us assume that such an efficient and effective battery can be produced. If all cars became electric (90,000,000 in the United States) and driving remained as at present (about 6,000 miles per car per year), it is estimated that we would need about 1.5×10^{12} kilowatt-hours per year to keep the cars moving. This is an amount of electricity equal to the present generating capacity of the entire U.S. Unless effective methods are developed to clean up the pollutants such as SO_2 or radioactive liquids (nuclear) produced in power-generating stations, electric cars would have pollution problems too. They would change only the site of the contamination. Still, it might be easier to clean up gases or liquids from a few stationary power plants than from 90 million cars scattered around the country. Logistics favor the electric car.

Two of the most attractive electric car battery prospects under test today use the reaction between elemental sulfur and an alkali metal. In one case, the reaction between elemental lithium and sulfur is employed:

$$2Li + xS \longrightarrow Li_2S_x \qquad (4)$$

where x varies from 3 to 5 or higher. The energy density is great—more than 150 watt-hours per pound, but the battery has some problems. It must be operated at 380 °C and the materials used in its construction (lithium) run the material cost up to about $2.40 per kilowatt-hour.

Another cheaper prospect uses the reaction between sodium metal and sulfur. The product is a sodium polysulfide, Na_2S_x, where x is

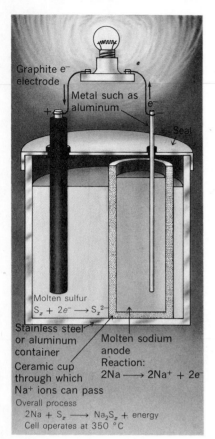

Fig. A9-2 Diagram of a sodium-sulfur "battery."

Graphite e⁻ electrode

Metal such as aluminum

Seal

Stainless steel or aluminum container

Ceramic cup through which Na⁺ ions can pass

Molten sulfur
$S_x + 2e^- \longrightarrow S_x^{2-}$

Molten sodium anode

Reaction:
$2Na \longrightarrow 2Na^+ + 2e^-$

Overall process
$2Na + S_x \longrightarrow Na_2S_x + energy$
Cell operates at 350 °C

above 3. While the cost of this battery now runs at about 23¢ per kilowatt-hour for materials, its energy density is significantly lower than the lithium-sulfur unit—about 100 watt-hours per pound. It also operates at a high temperature (350 °C). Both batteries, however, are very efficient and have a high charge rate. Both still have many unresolved technical design problems which currently limit their use. Still, real progress is being made in battery technology.

A block diagram of one type of sodium-sulfur cell is shown in Figure A9-2. The anode or negative electrode is molten sodium which gives up electrons to the external circuit. The sodium ions produced can pass through the ceramic [β-alumina (Al_2O_3)] membrane or cup which holds the molten sodium. The set-up is similar in many ways to the porous cup cell which we considered earlier. The solid cup will allow sodium *ions* to pass through at high temperature, but will hold back sodium metal, molten sulfur, and sodium polysulfides. The electrons go through the external circuit to a graphite cathode and the ions through the cup.* At the graphite electrode sulfur picks up electrons to give negative polysulfide ions. These are neutralized by the sodium ions which came through the ceramic cup.

The chief disadvantage of this battery for cars is the high temperature of operation. The battery is inoperative at room temperature, so a cold start is impossible. An auxiliary heating system or a design which keeps the battery molten all of the time would be needed. Both consume energy. There is no problem during operation since internal power loss in the battery will keep it hot—even too hot.

The facts now available indicate that electric cars would not be impossible, but a tremendous support system of charging outlets, new power plants, heaters, and other equipment would be needed. This assumes also that technical problems with the ceramic barrier and other things can all be met. Answers to automobile pollution are not available yet.

*Strips of felt covered with graphite help to increase the conductivity of the sulfur mass.

Acknowledgments

COVER AND TITLE PAGE Drs. Cagnet, Françon, and Mallick, Laboratoire d'Optique, Faculté des Sciences de Paris, France.

CHAPTER ONE Page 2 Swiss National Tourist Office. Page 5 (top) Stephen W. Mulvey. Page 5 (bottom) DPI/Maxwell Coplan. Pages 6, 8 Adapted from a cartoon by Louis Nitka. Page 9 (left) Larry Mulvehill. Page 9 (right) The Department of the Interior, National Park Service, Photo by John M. Kauffmann. Page 17 (top) General Mills. Page 17 (bottom) Zimble from Monkmeyer.

CHAPTER TWO Page 20 C. L. Martonyi, Photographic Services, The University of Michigan. Pages 22–23 Jerrold J. Stefl.

CHAPTER THREE Page 42 Basil King Photo. Page 49 From the CHEM Study film *Molecular Motions*. Page 51 National Bureau of Standards.

CHAPTER FOUR Page 72 Charles E. Miller. Page 76 C. L. Martonyi, Photographic Services, The University of Michigan.

CHAPTER FIVE Page 96 DPI/Kenneth Hill. Page 115 Corning Glass Works.

CHAPTER SIX Page 120 "Ascending and Descending" and "Waterfall," M. C. Escher, Escher Association.

CHAPTER SEVEN Page 144 Brookhaven National Laboratory. Page 163 U. S. Atomic Energy Commission.

CHAPTER EIGHT Page 168 Sovfoto. Pages 178–179 Neil Bartlett.

CHAPTER NINE Page 200 NASA. Page 219 G. Herzberg.

CHAPTER TEN Page 222 United Press International. Page 230 Henry Eyring.

CHAPTER ELEVEN Page 246 DPI/Pearl Korn. Pages 249, 251–252, 256 C. L. Martonyi, Photographic Services, The University of Michigan. Page 257 Alburtus, Yale News Bureau. Page 269 (left) Aspen Corporation. Page 269 (right) Oregon State Highway Department. Page 271 C. L. Martonyi, Photographic Services, The University of Michigan.

CHAPTER TWELVE Page 276 Stockpile, New York City. Page 277 DPI/Robert W. Young.

CHAPTER THIRTEEN Page 296 Jerrold J. Stefl. Pages 302, 314 C. L. Martonyi, Photographic Services, The University of Michigan.

CHAPTER FOURTEEN Page 328 Rapho Guillumette Pictures (by Bruce Roberts).

CHAPTER FIFTEEN Page 340 C. L. Martonyi, Photographic Services, The University of Michigan.

CHAPTER SIXTEEN Pages 364, 366, 374 C. L. Martonyi, Photographic Services, The University of Michigan. Pages 383–384 Don T. Cromer, University of California, Los Alamos Scientific Laboratory, and W. T. Lippincott, Editor, *Journal of Chemical Education.* Reproduced from *J. Chem. Ed.,* **45,** 626 (1968). Page 396 Luis W. Alvarez.

CHAPTER SEVENTEEN Page 400 Jerrold J. Stefl. Page 415 The California Institute of Technology. Page 416 C. L. Martonyi, Photographic Services, The University of Michigan. Page 428 D. C. Hodgkin.

CHAPTER EIGHTEEN Page 432 Rapho Guillumette Pictures (by Bruce Roberts). Page 448 W. N. Lipscomb (Photo by Lotte Meitner—Graf, London).

CHAPTER NINETEEN Page 460 (left) DPI/J. H. Atkinson. Page 460 (right) Dr. E. R. Degginger. Page 495 Fabian Bachrach.

CHAPTER TWENTY Page 513 J. C. Bailar. Page 520 E. O. Fischer.

CHAPTER TWENTY-ONE Page 524 Rapho Guillumette Pictures (by Marc & Evelyne Bernheim). Page 526 M. W. Nirenberg. Page 538 (left) M. H. C. Wilkins. Page 538 (right) J. Griffith, The California Institute of Technology. Page 540 (top) H. Fernandez-Moran. Page 540 (bottom) United Press International and L. A. Kornberg.

CHAPTER TWENTY-TWO Page 542 DPI/Lida Moser. Pages 544, 548 EPA-DOCUMER-ICA—Belinda Rain. Page 550 Bell Labs. Pages 551, 553 Environmental Protection Agency. Page 554 Gulf Research & Development Company.

APPENDIX ONE Page 558 Jerrold J. Stefl.

ACKNOWLEDGMENTS

INDEX

of N—H bond in ammonia, 415
of O—H bond in water, 415
and solvent action, 453
Disaccharide, 528
Discharge tube, 153
Dissolving:
  of NaCl in water, 453–454
  of sugar in water, 277
Distance, effect of, on electrical
    attraction, 127–128
Dissociation:
  of electrolytes, 299
  of water, 299
Distillation, 113
Divalent atoms, 408, 424
DNA, 534–539
  definition, 534
  electron micrograph of, 538
  history, 535–536
  model, 535
  natural and synthetic, 539
  structure, 535
  template action, 539
Döbereiner, J. W., 196
Double arrow, use of, 252
Double bond, 424–426
Double helix, 539
  see also DNA
Doyle, Sir Arthur Conan, 4–5
Dyes, azo, 492

E

e/m, 157, 560
$E = mc^2$, 216
E^0, 349–351
  definition, 350
  and equilibrium, 355–356
  of hydrogen half-cell, 350
  predicting reactions from, 352–353
  table, 350
Einstein, Albert:
  relationship of mass to energy, 216,
    220
  special theory of relativity, 216
Elastic collisions, 12
Electric automobiles, 572–574
Electric charges:
  detection of, 126–127
  of electron, 155–157
  and Faraday's experiment, 129
  interaction of like, 127
  interaction of unlike, 127
  negative, 134–135
  net, 135
  neutral, 135
  in nuclear reactions, 162
  positive, 134–135
  production of, 127
Electric current, 126
Electric dipole, 414; *see also* Dipole
Electric discharge tube, 153
Electric field:
  in electromagnetic radiation,
    369–370, 398
  in oil drop experiment, 155–156
Electric force:
  effect of distance on, 127–128
  in electrometer, 126–127
  in oil drop experiment, 155–156
Electrical conductivity; *see*
    Conductivity, electrical
Electrical nature of matter, 125–128
Electrical phenomena, 125–126
Electrical properties of condensed
    phases, 128–134
Electrochemical cell, 340–362
  and electrolysis, 357

examples, common, 341
half-reactions in, 341–344
operation of, 344–345
terminology of, 344–345
voltages of, 351–352
Electrode:
  defined, 135, 344
  in electrochemical cell, 344–345
  negative, 136
  positive, 136
  processes, 135–137
Electrolysis, 357–360
  of copper chloride, 136
  model for, 135–137
  of water, 67, 210
Electrolytes:
  in aqueous solutions, 282
  dissociation of, 298
  strong, 298
  weak, 298
Electrolytic cell, 357
Electrolytic solutions, 129–131, 283
Electromagnetic radiation, 369–370,
    398
  and energy, 373–374
Electromagnetic spectrum, 370–372
Electromagnetic waves, 369
Electrometer, 128
Electron:
  affinity, 405
  affinity of fluorine atom, 405
  arrangements;
    of first 20 elements, 176
    stable, 173
  and attracting power of ions,
    345–351
  charge on, 155–157, 167
  charge/mass ratio, 156
  competition for, 335–336, 338, 347
  configuration;
    alkaline earth metals, 184
    of elements; *see individual*
     elements
    and periodic table, 385
    orbital chart of, 416–417
    transition metals, 390, 503–506
  definition, 134
  delocalized, 438
  diffraction, 428
  energy of, 169
  extranuclear, 147, 151
  flow, 357
  kinetic energy, 170
  location, 382
  mass of, 146, 157
  measurement of a mole of, 138–139
  and metallic properties, 441–442
  naming of, 135
  in nuclear reactions, 162
  promotion of, 410
  "sea" of, 198, 439–440
  "seeing," 153–155
  spin, 385
  trajectory, 382
  transition, 385
  valence, 395
  van der Waals forces and, 434–435
  volt, 170
  wave nature of, 148, 380
Electron dot notation, 405, 430
Electron micrograph of DNA, 538
Electronic structure and periodic table,
    385
Electrostatic field strength, 562
Elements:
  definition, 50
  discovery of, 50
  names, 53–54, 121

symbols, 53–54, 121
Empirical formula:
  compared to molecular formula, 463
  definition, 181
Empty orbital, 412
Endive plants, damage done by air
    pollution, 551
Endothermic reaction, 68, 205, 220,
    238, 255
Energy:
  absorption of, 202
  activation, 235
  binding, 218
  changes;
    and chemical reactions, 65–67
    in manufacture of water gas, 203
    in phase changes, 67, 101–102
    on warming, 214
  conservation of, 209–212
  content; *see* Enthalpy
  of covalent bonds, 455
  crisis, 447
  of electric car battery, 573
  electrical, 350
  and electromagnetic radiation,
    373–374
  and equilibrium, 268–270, 272
  of fats, 530
  gap, and semiconductor, 547
  of hydration, 301
  of hydrogen bond, 455–456
  and hydrogen spectrum, 373–379
  in ion formation, 151–152
  ionization; *see* Ionization energy
  kinetic; *see* Kinetic energy
  law of conservation of, 67, 68, 212
  of lead storage battery, 573
  levels;
    and atomic number, 397
    of bookcase analogy, 376–377
    of hydrogen atom, 378, 384,
     393–394
    and ionization energies, 392–397
    of many-electron atom, 386
    and the periodic table, 392–397
  liberation of, 202
  of motion; *see* Kinetic energy
  of position; *see* Potential energy
  potential; *see* Potential energy
  quantitative relationships, 202–203
  and reaction rates, 234–242
  of rotation, 213
  and solubility, 279–281
  stored in a molecule, 212–214
  stored in a nucleus, 215–219
  of sugars, 529
  and sunlight, 447
  thermal, 84
  threshold, 234
  of translation, 213
  of van der Waals forces, 455
  of vibration, 213
Energy diagram, for sodium, 446
Enthalpy:
  defined, 204
  and entropy, 272
  molar, 214
  molecular, 213
  tendency toward minimum, 272, 279,
    293

of Saturn rocket, 71
  shortage of, 540
Fuel-injection system, 448
Functional groups:
  definition, 473, 481
  examples, 482
Fundamental property, 128
Furnace, blast, 521
Fusion, molar heat of:
  definition, 110
  pure substances, 110
Fusion, nuclear, 217–219

G

Gallium:
  electron configuration, 390
  halides of, 390
  oxides of, 390
Garbage collector analogy, 121–123, 145
Gas:
  bulb, 76
  combining volumes of, 28–29, 43–46
  distance between particles of, 73–74
  effect of temperature change on, 75–76
  elements found as, 101
  ideal, 89
  ideal gas constant, 89
  ideal gas law, 89
    calculations, examples, 89–91
    and kinetic theory, 91
  inert, 8, 177
  kinetic theory of, 81–87
  liquid-gas phase change, 103
  liquid-vapor equilibrium, 103–105
  measuring pressure of, 77–78
  model for, 10
  molar volume of, 34–37, 73
  molecular structures of, 401–431
  natural gas, 462
  noble, 8, 177–179
  nonideal, 97–100
  pressure, 11, 77
  pressure-volume data for, 27
  properties of, 28–29
  relative masses of, 31–32, 40
  solubility in a liquid, 280–281
  standard state for, 350
Gasoline:
  combustion of, 71
  composition of, 487
  and pollution, 554
Geiger, H., 147, 158, 161
General gas equation, 87–88
  development of, 88–89
  values of R in, 89
Generalization, 7
  melting points, 9
  reliability of, 7
Genetic code, 539, 541
Geometry; see also individual elements and compounds:
  of complex ions, 510
  determination of, 427–430
  of fluorine compounds, 421–423
  of metals, 443–444
  molecular, 416–421; see also Molecular geometry
  of molecular collisions, 231, 235
  of water, 417–418
Germer, L. H., 380
Gillespie, R. J., 416
Glucose, 526
Glutamic acid, 497
Glycerol, 530
Glyceryl tributyrate, 530

Glycine, 497
Gold:
  components of atom, 146
  mass of one mole, 69
Gold-copper alloy, 113
Goulian, M., 525, 539
Graphing, value of, 26
Graphite, 192–193
  compared with diamond, 458–459
  delocalized electrons in, 438
  double bonds in, 437
  electrical conductivity, 193, 438
  properties of, 192–193
  structure of, 436–437
Green Bay, discoloration of, 544–545
Grocery store analogy, 244
Grundy, R. D., 547
Guanine, 539
Gushee, David E., 548
Gutte, Bernd, 532

H

h (Planck's constant), 374
H and ΔH, 204, 220
$\Delta H\ddagger$, 238
[H^+]; see also Hydrogen ion:
  in acidic solution, 313
  in basic solution, 313
  in neutral solution, 302
Haber, Fritz, 262
Haber process, 260–262
Half-cell, 346
  Ag$^+$-Ag, 348
  H$^+$-H$_2$, 348
  potential; see Half-cell, voltage and E^0
  reaction; see Half-reactions
  selection of standard, 347–348
  standard, 347
  voltage, 347
    against copper reference cell, 347–348
    against nickel reference cell, 348
    effect of concentration on, 348–349
    and Le Chatelier's principle, 349
    standard half-cell potentials, 349–351
    use of half-cell potentials, 351–355
  zinc, 350
Half-life, 164, 243, 573
Half-reactions, 341, 350
  in automobile batteries, 572
  balancing, 357
  combined to form an overall reaction, 344
  and concentration, 352
  definition, 343
  in an electrochemical cell, 341–344
  and electron flow, 343
  multiplying, 356
  and production of new chemical species, 344
  standard reduction potentials of, 350
  use of in balancing oxidation-reduction equations, 356–357, 361
Halides:
  of hydrogen, 186–187
  metal, solubility of, 187
  solubility of, 285–287
  variety, 187
Halogens:
  boiling points, 185, 434
  chemistry of, 185–186
  and covalent bond, 185
  covalent radii, 188

melting points, 185, 434
  oxidation numbers, 508
  properties of, 185
  reactions with hydrogen, 186
  reactions with sodium, 185
  summary of, 188–189
  van der Waals radii, 188
Hardness of metals and alloys, 441
Heat, definition, 201
Heat changes and chemical reactions; see Enthalpy and Energy
Heat conductivity:
  of metals, 442
  of transition elements, 506
Heat content, 203–204, 220; see also Enthalpy and Energy
Heat of combustion, 65–66
  n-butane, 488
  cyclohexane, 488
  of ethane, 488
  n-hexane, 488
  of hydrogen, 66
  isobutane, 488
  of magnesium, 65
  of methane, 488
  molar, 65–66
  n-octadecane, 488
  n-octane, 488
  propane, 488
Heat of formation, 208; see also Heat of reaction
Heat of fusion, 110
Heat of melting; see Fusion, molar heat of
Heat of reaction, 204, 237–238
  additivity of, 204–206
    law of, 206, 212
  between elements, 207
  measurement of, 206
  predicting, 206–209
Heat of reaction to form:
  ammonia, 207
  carbon dioxide, 207
  carbon monoxide, 207
  CO and H$_2$, 202
  ethane, 207
  fluorine molecules, F$_2$, 406, 427
  hydrogen atoms, 401
  hydrogen iodide, 207
  nitric oxide, 207
  nitrogen atoms, 427
  nitrogen dioxide, 207
  propane, 207
  sulfur dioxide, 207
  sulfuric acid, 207
  water, 207
  water vapor, 207
Heat of solution, 279
  of chlorine in water, 281
  of iodine in alcohol, 279
  of iodine in benzene, 280
  of iodine in carbon tetrachloride, 279
  of nitrous oxide in water, 281
  of oxygen in water, 281
Heat of vaporization, 101–103
  of aluminum, 442
  of barium, 183, 442
  of beryllium, 183, 442
  of boron, 442
  of calcium, 183, 442
  of cesium, 442
  of chlorine, 103

Nitrogen oxide:
  in air, 549–551, 555
    measurement of, 550
  and automobiles, 549–551
  decomposition in falling
    temperature, 549–550
  and smog, 551
Nitrogen trichloride, 71
  decomposition of, 71
Nitrogen trifluoride:
  electron dot formula, 409
  geometry of, 419–420
  naming, 55
Nitrous acid, K_A of, 316
Nitrous oxide:
  heat of solution in water, 281
  solubility in water, 281
nmr spectroscopy, 430
nmr spectrum:
  dimethyl ether, 472
  ethanol, 472
Nobel prize, 97, 257, 396, 415, 428,
    495, 520, 526, 535
Nobelium, 156
Noble gases, 177–179, 198
  chemical reactivity of, 178–179
  compounds of, 178–179
  electron arrangements, 173–174
  ionization energies of, 174
  melting and boiling points, compared
    to halogens, 434
  properties of, 178
Nomenclature; see Names
Novocain, 494
n-pentane:
  properties, 435
  structure, 487
nu, ν, frequency of light, 368
Nuclear age, 415
Nuclear chemistry, 161–165
Nuclear energy, relationship to
    chemical energy, 215
Nuclear fission, 215
Nuclear fusion, 217–219
Nuclear reactions:
  electric charges in, 162
  effect of temperature on, 243
  rate of, 242–243
Nuclear reactor, 215
  cost of, 447
Nuclear magnetic resonance, 430, 472
Nucleic acids, 534–541
Nuclein, 535
Nucleon, 215, 218
Nucleotides, 525, 535–538
Nucleus:
  binding energy per nucleon of, 218
  charge of, 152
  components of, 147, 165
  decay processes of, 161–165
    rate of, 164
  diameter of, 148
  energy stored in, 215–219
  nuclear model of atom, 147–148
  properties of, 161
  "seeing," 158–161
  size of, 148
  stability of, 164–165
  structure of, 365
Number; see Atomic number
Nyholm, R., 416
Nylon, 496

O

Observation:
  accuracy of, and conclusions, 13–14
  and belief in atoms, 123

characteristics of, 5
  and conclusion, 121
  power of, 4–6
n-Octadecane, properties of, 488
Octahedral complex, 511
Octanamide, 486
Octane, 485
n-Octane, properties of, 488
Octanoic acid, 486
1-Octanol, 485
"Octaves, Law of," 196
Octyl alcohol, 485
1-Octylamine, 485
OH group:
  behavior with ethyl group, 473
  bonding in, 408
Oil drop experiment, Millikan's,
    155–156
Oil film, color of, 366
Oil of wintergreen, 493
Onondaga, Lake, decrease of algae in,
    545
Onsager, Lars, 257
Operational definition, 309, 325
Orbital representation of chemical
    bonding, 404–405, 430
Orbitals:
  arrangement of electrons in, 416–417
  computer plots of;
    1s, 2s, 3s, 383, 445
    2p, 384
  contrasted with an orbit, 381
  d, 384
  empty, 412
  formation of a bonding orbital, 445
  hybrid, 417
  of hydrogen, 445
  introduction of protons into, 417–418
  notation of, 421
  p, 383–384
  s, 383
  shapes, 383
  of sodium, 446
  in transition elements, 504
Organic chemistry, 462
Organic compounds, 462
  nomenclature of, 485–486
  oxidation of, 476–481
Oscillating force fields, 368, 398
Overall reaction, 344
Oxalate ion, 224
Oxidation:
  of acetaldehyde, 478
  of alcohol, 476–478, 481
  of ammonia, 208
  of copper, 333–334, 343
  definition, 329, 332, 338
  of ethanol, 478
  of formaldehyde, 478–479
  of hydrogen bromide, 227–228
  of iron, 521–522
  of magnesium, 329, 338
  of methanol, 476–478
  of organic compounds, 476–481
  and oxidation number, 330–335
  of propanol, 479–480
  of sugars, 526–527
  of sulfur, 330–331
  of sulfur dioxide, 331
  of zinc, 329, 334
Oxidation numbers, 330–335
  of chromium, 507, 519
  of elements, 332
  maximum, 509
  of monatomic ions, 332
  net change in, 333–334, 337
  and oxidation, 331
  and reduction, 331

rules for assigning, 332
  of transition elements, 508
  use in balancing oxidation-reduction
    equations, 337–338
  of vanadium, 509
Oxidation-reduction reactions, 329–335,
    338
  balancing by half-reactions 356–357,
    361
  balancing by oxidation numbers,
    337–338
  in a beaker, 333–335
  and electrochemical cells, 341–345
  standard state in, 350
Oxide ion:
  proton interaction with, 418
  schematic representation, 418
Oxides:
  of chromium, 507
  of second-row elements, 193
Oxidizing agent, definition, 330
Oxygen:
  boiling point, 100
  bonding capacity of, 407–409
  combining volume, 45
  conservation of oxygen atoms, 337
  electron arrangement, 176
  electron configuration, 387, 408
  fluorine compounds, 409
  formed in laboratory, 93
  heat of solution in water, 281
  intake by humans, 71
  ionization energy, 199
    first, 171
  isotopes, composition of, 149–150
  molar volume, 38, 77, 100
  molecular vibrations, 399
  molecular weight, 32–33
  oxidation numbers of, in compounds,
    332
  properties of, 192
  reaction with nitrogen in air, 549, 555
  solubility in water, 281
  and water vapor formation, 69
Oyster shells, calcium carbonate in, 291

P

p electron, 384
p orbitals, 384, 504
p-type semiconductors, 448
Packing, crystal:
  body-centered cubic, 443
  hexagonal close-packed structure,
    443
Paints, arsenic sulfide in, 555
Palladium, 242
Palmitic acid, 530
Para-aminobenzoic acid, 533
Paraffin:
  burning of, 59–60
  composition of, 487
Paraphthalic acid, 495
Partial pressure:
  explained, 82–84
  and vapor pressure, 105–107
Particle model for light, 380
Particles:
  alpha, 159–161
  fundamental, 146
Pauli Exclusion Principle, 385

Wilkins, M. H. F., 535
Wintergreen, oil of, 493
Wood, reaction rate of burning, 226
Woodward, Robert B., 495
Work, 152, 209, 271, 350

X

Xenon:
  boiling point, 434
  compounds of, 178–179
  electron arrangement of, 174
  ionization energy, 178
  melting point, 434
  properties of, 178
Xenon hexafluoroplatinate, 178
X rays:
  crystallography, 426, 448
  diffraction of, 428
    to determine distance between
      atoms, 184
  frequency and wavelength of,
    372–373
  and insulators, 447
  spectra of, and atomic number, 566
  wavelength of, 371–372
Xylene, 10

Y

Yttrium:
  heat of vaporization, 442
  X-ray spectrum of, 566

Z

Zinc:
  in corrosion prevention, 521
  electron configuration, 390
  oxidation of, 334
  X-ray spectrum of, 566
Zirconium, X-ray spectrum of, 566

IA								
1 1.0080 **H** Hydrogen								

| **3** 6.941 **Li** Lithium | **IIA** **4** 9.012 **Be** Beryllium | | | | | | | |

KEY

Atomic Number ⟶ | **26** 55.85 ⟵ Atomic Weight

Symbol of Element ⟶ | **Fe**

Iron ⟵ Name of Element

| **11** 22.990 **Na** Sodium | **12** 24.30 **Mg** Magnesium |

19 39.098 **K** Potassium	**20** 40.08 **Ca** Calcium	**21** 44.96 **Sc** Scandium	**22** 47.90 **Ti** Titanium	**23** 50.94 **V** Vanadium	**24** 52.00 **Cr** Chromium	**25** 54.94 **Mn** Manganese	**26** 55.85 **Fe** Iron	**27** 58.93 **Co** Cobalt
37 85.47 **Rb** Rubidium	**38** 87.62 **Sr** Strontium	**39** 88.91 **Y** Yttrium	**40** 91.22 **Zr** Zirconium	**41** 92.91 **Nb** Niobium	**42** 95.94 **Mo** Molybdenum	**43** (97)■ **Tc** Technetium	**44** 101.1 **Ru** Ruthenium	**45** 102.91 **Rh** Rhodium
55 132.90 **Cs** Cesium	**56** 137.34 **Ba** Barium	**57–71** ✳ below	**72** 178.49 **Hf** Hafnium	**73** 180.95 **Ta** Tantalum	**74** 183.85 **W** Tungsten	**75** 186.2 **Re** Rhenium	**76** 190.2 **Os** Osmium	**77** 192.2 **Ir** Iridium
87 (223)■ **Fr** Francium	**88** (226)■ **Ra** Radium	**89–103** ✳ below	**104** (261)■	**105** (262)■				

✳ LANTHANIDE SERIES	**57** 138.91 **La** Lanthanum	**58** 140.12 **Ce** Cerium	**59** 140.92 **Pr** Praseodymium	**60** 144.24 **Nd** Neodymium	**61** (145)■ **Pm** Promethium	**62** 150.35 **Sm** Samarium	**63** 152.0 **Eu** Europium
✳ ACTINIDE SERIES	**89** (227)■ **Ac** Actinium	**90** 232.04 **Th** Thorium	**91** (231)■ **Pa** Protactinium	**92** 238.03 **U** Uranium	**93** (237)■ **Np** Neptunium	**94** (244)■ **Pu** Plutonium	**95** (243)■ **Am** Americium